Data Mining Techniques

Data Mining Techniques

Fourth Edition

Arun K Pujari

Advisor and Professor Emeritus, Department of Computer Science & Engineering
Mahindra University, Hyderabad
Formerly, School of Computer and Information Sciences
University of Hyderabad, Hyderabad

Universities Press

DATA MINING TECHNIQUES, FOURTH EDITION

UNIVERSITIES PRESS (INDIA) PRIVATE LIMITED

Registered Office
3-6-747/1/A & 3-6-754/1, Himayatnagar, Hyderabad 500 029, Telangana, India
info@universitiespress.com; www.universitiespress.com

Distributed by
Orient Blackswan Private Limited

Registered Office
3-6-752 Himayatnagar, Hyderabad 500 029, Telangana, India

Other Offices
Bengaluru / Chennai / Guwahati / Hyderabad / Kolkata /
Mumbai / New Delhi / Noida / Patna

First published 2001; 10th reprint 2008
Second edition 2010
Reprinted 2011, 2012, 2013
Third edition 2013
Reprinted 2015
Fourth Edition 2016
Reprinted 2019, 2020, 2023, 2024

ISBN 978 93 86235 05 3

Cover and book design

Typeset in Life BT 10/12 *by*
Orient BlackSwan

Printed at
B.B. Press, Tronica City Ghaziabad (UP) 201102

Published by
Universities Press (India) Private Limited
3-6-747/1/A & 3-6-754/1, Himayatnagar, Hyderabad 500 029, Telangana, India

To
my mother

Late Smt. Tilottama Devi

— *A very fragile and delicate lady who was the pillar of strength for her children and her husband*

Contents at a Glance

List of Contents

FOREWORD

Vast amounts of operational data are routinely collected and stored away in the archives of many organisations. To take a simple example, the railway reservation system has been operational for over a decade and a vast amount of data is generated each day on train bookings. Much of this data is probably archived for audit purposes. This archived operational data can be effectively used for tactical strategic management of the railways. For instance, by analyzing the reservation data it would be possible to find out traffic patterns in various sectors and use it to add or remove bogies in certain trains, to decide on the mix of various classes of accommodation, etc. This, however, was not feasible until recently due to limitations in both hardware and software. In the last five years there has been a tremendous improvement in hardware—512 MB of main memory, 40 GB disk and CPU clock of 1.6 GHZ is now available on a PC. Thus, computer programs which sift massive amounts of operational data, recognise patterns and provide hints to formulate hypotheses for tactical and strategic decision-making can now be executed in a reasonable time. This has opened up a fertile area of research to formulate appropriate algorithms for mining archival data to formulate and test hypotheses. An array of ideas from computer science, statistics and management science are being applied in this area. This subject is currently an active research area.

I am extremely happy that Professor Arun K. Pujari has written this book on Data Mining Techniques. It is a timely addition to the existing computer science literature and will be a boon to students. Professor Pujari has been an active researcher in this area. He has also introduced a course on Data Mining at the University of Hyderabad and has been teaching it. His rich experience in teaching and research is evident in the selection of topics and their treatment in this book. The book starts with a brief introduction followed by a detailed chapter on data warehousing. It has chapters which discuss a large number of diverse algorithms using association rules, clustering techniques, decision tree techniques, neutral networks, genetics, rough sets, and support vector machines. A novel aspect of this book is its discussion of the emerging area of web mining of textual data. A large number of references are cited and the treatment is lucid and up to date. I recommend this book to students who want to explore this important subject.

V. Rajaraman
Honarary Professor
Super Computer Education & Research Center
Indian Institue of Science, Bangalore

2001

PROLOGUE

In this Information Age, the data generated by the day-to-day operations constitute one of the powerful assets of an enterprise. Most enterprises generate unlimited amounts of data from their On-Line Transaction Processing (OLTP) systems, Point-of-Service (POS) systems, financial ATMs and the Web. The challenge faced by these enterprises with regard to the massive data-rich but information-poor collection is to extract valuable *information* to be available at a particular time, place and in the form needed to support the decision-making process.

Scientific organisations also generate large volumes of data. Artificial satellites are streaming in volumes of remote sensing data every minute. Worldwide activities on the genome and related projects are resulting in massive technical material. These are only two examples of modern technology resulting in valuable data of a highly specialised nature. The challenge is to analyze the data to arrive at meaningful conclusions.

Techniques like clustering, decision tree, and NN are known in pattern recognition, statistics and other disciplines and several algorithms have been devised. However, these algorithms are not suitable for the purpose of mining and hence new algorithms had to be proposed in recent years for this purpose.

This book deals with those algorithms that are specially designed for data mining. It begins with an introduction to the basic concepts of data mining and gradually brings the reader to the frontiers of research on this topic. It discusses all the major and current techniques of data mining. Specific mining problems such as web mining, text mining, temporal mining and spatial mining will be of great interest to researchers who are already familiar with the basic mining techniques.

Professor Pujari, a distinguished Professor of Computer Science in our University, with over 10 years of teaching and research experience in our University, has striven hard to put together this valuable monograph. I am sure that besides students in Computer Science, those in Mathematical Science and Management Studies will find it immensely useful. I wish this publication every success.

P. Rama Rao
Vice-Chancellor
University of Hyderabad

2001

Preface to the 4th Edition

Data mining techniques have matured considerably from the time this book was first written. Since then, I have included newer developments in the subsequent editions of the book. The effort was in some measure prompted by feedback from readers, for which I am very grateful. As a result, over the last two editions newer content such as FP-Tree Growth algorithm, Eclat and dEclat algorithms, a completely revised and expanded discussion on data warehousing, and chapters on genetic algorithms and rough set theory have been included in the book. Continuing in the same vein, this edition includes a chapter on ROC curves, an understanding of which is of considerable importance to data mining and to the making of business decisions. I hope readers will find the enhanced coverage useful. I welcome any feedback that will help me improve the book further and motivate me to take it to its next edition.

A K Pujari
August 2016

PREFACE TO THE FIRST EDITION

Data mining and data warehousing are increasingly becoming popular among IT professionals, academics and pupils. In the last few years, almost in every meeting which has anything to do with databases, neural networks, genetic algorithms, E-commerce, or artificial intelligence has had a theme or session on data mining and warehousing. Researchers from different disciplines are gradually being attracted to work in this new frontier of research. Business enterprises, small-, medium- or large-scale, are considering the deployment of a warehouse as a major progressive step and as a matter of pride. Business intelligence, customer relation management (CRM) and E-commerce all hinge on data mining and warehousing. Universities and other training institutions, keeping pace with technological development, are also beginning to introduce this subject in their curricula. These two terms are now justly becoming household terms.

During 1997–98, many of the universities in US and Europe were introducing this as a course at the graduate level. To keep abreast of this development, I started an optional course on data mining and warehousing during the winter semester of 1997–98 at the University of Hyderabad. Since then, this course has become increasingly popular. I had to depend on the collection of research papers as the course material, and my own compilation of these results became the reading material for the course. Recently, many other universities have decided to introduce this as an optional course for the degree as well as postgraduate level. This development and the self-compiled lecture notes prompted me to venture into writing this book.

My aim is to present all the major techniques of data mining and warehousing in a comprehensible manner so that it can serve not only as a textbook but also as a handbook for any researcher. Efforts have been made to include the most recent algorithms (till the latter half of 2000). I have tried to include all the major techniques of data mining here. Some of the recent techniques like Support Vector Machines, Rough Set Theory, etc., are also introduced as tools of data mining. I feel that it will be useful for many researchers and students of computer science, management science and mathematical sciences. The present text is envisaged as a textbook as well as a research handbook in the areas of data mining and data warehousing. Since I am trying to address heterogenous categories of readers, there is some unevenness in the presentation styles of the chapters. Chapters 2, 3, 4, 5 and 6 are presented in a textbook style for the benefit of any graduate-level student. In Chapter 7, my intention is to apprise the reader about the basic (introductory level) concepts of NN, GA, Rough Sets and SVM and to show that these techniques are also important for data mining. The content of this chapter, though self-explanatory, is not very elaborate like other chapters. Readers who are interested in learning the algorithmic details of these techniques may have to refer to other books/articles addressing the specific technique. Chapter 8 and Chapter 9 are meant for advanced-level readers. In future, I intend prepare materials elaborating the details of the contents of Chapters 7, 8 and 9.

Readers are requested to send their comments and suggestions on the text without hesitation.

Arun K Pujari
akpcs@uohyd.ernet.in
February 2001

ACKNOWLEDGEMENTS

Writing a textbook is not an easy task. If this book has taken shape, it is primarily because of persons around me who motivated, encouraged and helped me to ensure that this project reached the stage of completion. I am indebted to a number of individuals in academic as well as in social circles who have contributed in different, but important ways in the preparation of this book. I take this opportunity to express my gratitude to all those who have helped and encouraged me to prepare this book.

I am also indebted to Professor Gautam Das who introduced me to some of the newer areas of data mining. My thanks go to Professor Malaya Dutta, Dr Dhruba Bhattacharya, and Dr Rajiv K Das of Tezpur University for going through the first draft of the book and pointing out errors.

This book grew out of the lecture notes for the course on Data Mining and Data Warehousing introduced by me in the Department of Computer & Information Sciences, University of Hyderabad. Thanks are also due to the three batches (1997–98, 1998–99 and 1999–2000) of 100+ students who have opted for this course and patiently sat through it. They have provided their most helpful assistance in the improvement of the text material. Special thanks are due to Suresh Reddy, Rajesh, Priyambada, Atul, Karthik, Sivaramakrishna and many other students who have pointed out errors in the text. In addition, I am indebted to a large number of masters and doctoral students who helped me in implementing new ideas and applications in this area. This contributed significantly to my understanding of the subject. I am thankful to Adilakshmi, Shailaja, Vijaya Kumari and Dhananjay Naidu for helping me in proofreading, formatting, diagrams, etc., during the preparation of this manuscript. While preparing the text, I gave talks at seminars on some of the chapters at different institutions. I am grateful to IIM/Calcutta, IDRBT/Hyderabad, ADRIN/Hyderabad, and Tezpur University for this.

I acknowledge gratefully the authors of innumerable research papers who have promptly mailed me copies of their research articles at my request and also to the authors for making their papers downloadable. I owe my gratitude to the University of Hyderabad for granting me sabbatical leave to prepare the book. I am grateful to Vice-Chancellor Professor P Rama Rao for the prologue to this book and for his words of encouragement. Many organisations have extended their facilities to me during the preparation of the book. These are the University of Hyderabad, the University of Memphis, and Griffith University.

Writing a book involves a major commitment of time and energy and a commensurate loss of availability of that time and energy for any other purpose. All my doctoral students – Sreenivasa Rao, Vijaya Kumari, Durga Bhavani, Adilaxmi and Jayasree – had to bear with me for not being able to attend to their dissertation work. The love, patience, understanding, and encouragement of my wife Sheila and our son Pinak are greatly appreciated. Sheila had to play many roles during this period—taking dictation, formatting, and editing the manuscript. I often found myself in the difficult situation of having to answer Pinak's query regarding the progress of the book during his weekend visits from the hostel. The early influences of my parents and my teachers are also reflected in the presentation style.

Finally, I am grateful to Universities Press for agreeing to publish this book. Mr Madhu Reddy's personal interest in the book has helped me to complete the manuscript on time. My special thanks to Ms Chandini Rao for patiently going through the material repeatedly for corrections. I am also very grateful to Professor V Rajaraman for agreeing to comment on the manuscript and for writing the Foreword.

Arun K Pujari
Hyderabad
February 2001

1 INTRODUCTION

1.1 INTRODUCTION

The advent of computing technology has significantly influenced our lives and two major impacts of this are business data processing and scientific computing. During the initial years of the development of computer techniques for business, computer professionals were concerned with designing files to store the data so that information could be efficiently retrieved. There were restrictions on storage size for storing data and on the speed of accessing the data. Needless to say, the activity was restricted to a very few, highly qualified professionals. Then came an era when the task was simplified by a DBMS. The responsibility of intricate tasks, such as declarative aspects of the programs were passed on to the database administrator, and the user could pose his query in simpler languages such as query languages. Thus, almost any business – small, medium or large scale – began using computers for day-to-day activities.

The scenario on the hardware side was also encouraging. Storage and machine cost were drastically reduced so that almost any business house could afford a standard machine. Thus, due to widespread computerisation and also due to affordable storage facilities, there is now an enormous wealth of information embedded in huge databases belonging to different enterprises. Every organisation is now accumulating a large volume of daily transaction data and storing them as archival files. As a result, masses and masses of data – megabytes, gigabytes, terabytes – are piling up in the electronic vaults of companies, governments and research institutions.

Business is inherently competitive and in this competitive world of business one is constantly on the lookout for ways to beat the competition. A question that naturally arose is whether the enormous data that is generated and stored as archives can be used for improving the efficiency of business performance.

In the domain of scientific computing, the major problem is to infer some valuable information from the observed data. The use of computing technology has helped researchers to collect very large volumes of data. The development of other scientific disciplines helped the community to collect such large volumes of data effortlessly. Some typical examples are remote-sensing data, as satellites are streaming in an enormous amount of such data every day. In the area of health science, the repository of protein data and genome data are an invaluable source of scientific experiments. On the other side, we are drowning in oceans of text data and data of other media that are generated from the Web.

What use are all these data? Up to the early 1990s, the answer was 'not much'. No one was really interested in utilizing the data accumulated during the process of daily activities. Once transaction processing is over, these data were dumped into archival files.

Such collections of data, whether their origin is business enterprise or scientific experiment, have recently spurred a tremendous interest in the areas of knowledge discovery and data mining. Statisticians and data miners now have faster analysis tools that can help sift and analyse the stockpiles of data, turning up valuable and often surprising information. As a result, a new discipline in computer science, data mining, gradually evolved. Data mining is the exploration and analysis of large data sets to discover meaningful patterns and rules. The key idea is to find effective ways to combine the computer's power to process data with the human eye's ability to detect patterns. The techniques of data mining are designed for, and work best with, large data sets.

The evolution of data mining began when business data was first stored in computers and technologies were generated to allow users to navigate through the data in real time. Data mining takes this evolutionary process beyond retrospective data access and navigation, to prospective and proactive information delivery. This evolution is due to the support of three technologies that are sufficiently mature: massive data collection, high performance computing and data mining algorithms. The core components of the data mining technologies have been under development for decades, and today the maturity of these techniques coupled with the high performance relational database engines and broad data integration efforts have made these techniques practically applicable.

Data mining is a component of a wider process called knowledge discovery from databases. It involves scientists from a wide range of disciplines, including mathematicians, computer scientists and statisticians, as well as those working in fields such as machine learning, artificial intelligence, information retrieval and pattern recognition. Before a data set can be mined, it first has to be cleaned. This removes errors, ensures consistency and takes missing values into account. Data mining may use quite simple statistical techniques or it may use highly sophisticated data analysis. What is new for data miners is the employment of these techniques on vast quantities of data.

Business enterprises are beginning to realise that information about customers and their buying patterns are the most valuable. Competitiveness increasingly depends on the quality of decision making and learning to make quality decision from past transactions and decisions. The large databases maintained (generated during the routine operations) by retailers, telecom service providers and credit card companies contain very valuable information related to customers. These enterprises could benefit immensely in the areas of marketing, advertising and sales, if interesting and previously unknown customer buying and calling patterns can be discovered from the large volumes of data. Several factors have contributed to bring data mining to the forefront. To identify a few of these factors:

- The untapped value in large databases
- The concept of data warehousing
- The dramatic drop in the cost/performance ratio of hardware systems

The most important of the these is the development of data warehousing technology. Let us take a few minutes to review the layered architecture of the modern database management systems and the modern applications of these DBMSs. The different layers can be viewed as follows:

1. **External Interface** This layer deals with the concepts of data definition language, data manipulation language and host language interfaces.
2. **Language Processing** Query processing, algebraic optimisation and plan creation are the components of this layer.
3. **Code Generation** The procedural part is handled in this layer in the form of index structures and the implementation of algebraic operations.
4. **Transaction Management** The important aspects of modern DBMS are concurrency control, logging and recovery.
5. **Storage Management** This layer is concerned with memory and buffer management, secondary storage and device management.

A major change in the above approach is data integration. Integration of data from multiple sources is the key term in modern database applications. Modern applications of database technology demand an integrated access to multiple databases. Typical applications where data integration is relevant arise from the merging of different companies, accessing healthcare data from different institutions, and data access through Web-browsing. Recent developments of e-commerce also demand data integration. Data integration can be carried out in two modes, virtual or materialised. The virtual modes of data integration adopt a search engine to collect data from multiple sources, or a mediated mode to decompose the queries to each of the sources and present the result in a uniform manner. The materialised mode of data integration can be either through a universal DBMS or a data warehouse. In a universal DBMS, data are integrated by physically migrating data from different sources to a new database in OO-DBMS or OR-DBMS. The data warehouse collects data from different sources for OLAP and data mining applications. Among all these modes of integrations, data warehousing is considered the most efficient for decision support applications. This is particularly relevant in the contexts of Data Mining and OnLine Analytical Processing (OLAP).

As the terms "Data Mining" and "Data Warehousing" are becoming popular, the last few years have witnessed the emergence of extremely innovative and elegant techniques for data mining and warehousing. Most of these results are presented at different international fora. However, more and more researchers from other areas are interested in knowing about the subject. The present work aims at providing in one place the most recent and important techniques of data mining and warehousing.

1.2 Data Mining as a Subject

Data mining will be of interest to three major streams:

- Statistics
- Computer science
- Business management

The course structure and the major thrust of subtopics may differ, based on which of the above groups is the target audience. Thus, there can be three different areas of activities:

- Theory
- Algorithm and implementations
- Applications

The first approach broadly deals with the underlying theoretical concepts of data mining techniques. One attempts to develop a theoretical foundation to extract information from data. The theoretical background of the decision tree, clustering, fuzzy sets, and other statistical techniques, fall into this category of study. A student from mathematics or statistics may find this approach very interesting.

Just developing the theoretical foundation for data mining and data warehousing will not suffice. One has to also develop the appropriate algorithms to handle large databases. For example, the theory of the decision tree has been known to statistians for quite some time, and it is widely used by the Machine Learning community. But in order to make the decision tree construction process suitable for data mining, it is necessary to design new algorithms that can handle large databases which are stored in secondary memory. Moreover, one needs to work out the details of integrating the algorithm with a repository of data, either through a DBMS or through a data warehouse. These aspects are more relevant to computer scientists.

The third one is to identify new areas of data mining application for effective business processes. Much of the data mining community comes from an academic background and has focused on algorithms buried deep in the bowels of technology. But algorithms are not what business users care about. Over the past few years the technology of data mining has moved from the research lab to Fortune 500 companies, requiring a significant change in focus. Companies spend millions of dollars to build data warehouses to store their data and data mining applications must take advantage of this. Solving a business problem is much more valuable to a user than solving a statistical modelling problem. This means that a cross-selling specific application is more valuable than a general modelling tool that can create cross-selling models. Different case studies are to be analysed in detail in this approach to training. A management science student will find such an approach useful.

Thus, we attempt to establish here that the techniques of data mining and data warehousing have grown to such an extent that they can be considered as a full-fledged subject and a part of the training in statistics, computer science and business management.

This book is envisaged to cater to the needs of these three communities. Of course, computer science is given more emphasis in the text. In the following section, we provide a navigation chart for each of these disciplines.

1.3 Guide to this Book

This section presents a guide to reading this book. The layout of the remainder of the book and the contents of the individual chapters are reviewed briefly. This book is divided into eleven chapters. Chapter 2 presents the basic concepts, architecture and different components of data warehousing techniques. It also demonstrates the relevance of data mining in the context of data warehousing. Chapter 3 introduces the fundamentals of data mining. Different definitions and techniques of data mining are discussed in this chapter. Chapter 4 deals with the techniques of discovering Association Rules. It discusses in details all the major algorithms of finding frequent sets for a large database. Chapter 5 provides a detailed survey of clustering techniques for data mining. It may be noted that clustering also happens to be a topic for study in pattern recognition and statistics. This book, however, concentrates on this technique solely with regard to data mining applications. Readers interested in the general theory of clustering technique may refer to other books for reference. Chapter 6 deals with the Decision Tree techniques of data mining. It begins with the basic concepts of decision trees and proceeds to survey the techniques to build decision trees for data mining applications. The goal of this chapter is to provide a synthesised exposition on decision trees. Chapter 7 is devoted to rough set theory, a relatively new artificial intelligence technique used in classification, being increasingly applied to derive rules, provide reasoning and discover relationships in qualitative, incomplete and imprecise data. Chapter 8 discusses genetic algorithms, a class of computational

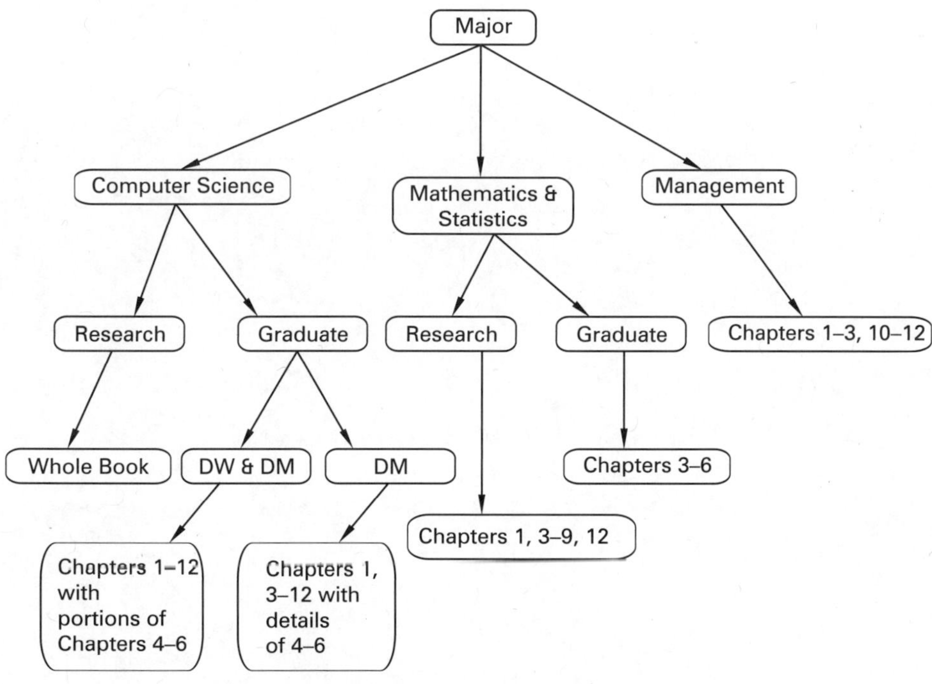

Decision-tree-like structure

models that mimic natural evolution to solve complex optimisation problems, which has been found to be an effective tool in data mining. Chapter 9 discusses some of the other data mining techniques like neural networks and support vector machines and provides pointers to their possible use in data mining. Chapter 10 deals with receiver operating characteristic (ROC) curve, which is being increasingly used in the recent years for displaying in a single graph the performance of classifiers for all possible costs of misclassification. The Web is a very important source of massive amounts of data. Mining of data in the Web is as important as mining data in a DBMS or in a warehouse. Chapter 11 discusses the techniques of Web mining. Finally, Chapter 12 deals with mining of temporal and spatial data.

A decision-tree–like structure is given on the previous page for readers to select appropriate chapters according to their interests. For instance, if a reader is a graduate student with CS major and is doing a course on data warehousing and mining, then he could read Chapters 1 through 12, ignoring the details of Chapters 4, 5 and 6.

2

Data Warehousing

2.1 Introduction

2.1.1 Data Access Crisis

Data is one of the critical resources of information age. Today, information technology is an inseparable part of organisations, be they large or small. Organisation typically create billions of bytes of data on various aspects of their businesses—products, operations, clients and other stakeholders. These are generated by a number of application systems using databases for transacting businesses at various levels. However, in spite of the availability of powerful computing systems and communication networks that span the globe, very often decision makers are unable to easily access critical information existing within their organisations. For most part the required data is locked up in the myriad of computer systems, is poorly integrated and inconsistent across systems, making it exceedingly difficult to extract *information*. This situation has appropriately been described as *data in jail*. Data access crisis does exist. To illustrate, let us take the example of the online booking service for train tickets in India. IRCTC is the nodal agency responsible for the booking service. To book a railway ticket one can go directly to the railway booking counter, fill-up the prescribed form by giving details regarding the journey along with some personal details, or, alternatively, one can log on to the IRCTC web site, feed the same information online and buy an e-ticket. One could even ask an agent to do this process on one's behalf. In all these cases, the traveller provides many details that are collected by the system effortlessly. Imagine the amount of data the IRCTC online booking system must be collecting every day! But this data is either archived or put to legacy systems after the journey is completed. The efficiency of the IRCTC booking system is measured by how accurately, quickly and efficiently travellers are able to book their journey, make secure payment and obtain an authentic ticket. Once the ticket is used (by actually travelling or modifying/cancelling the ticket), details such as the name of the passenger, age, telephone number, originating point, destination, journey date, etc., are of no use to the system. The data is thereafter archived in an expensive mainframe or in tapes. As a result, any further analysis on the data, though possible theoretically, is never achieved in real time at reasonable cost. A decision maker in the Indian Railways who wants, for instance, to do a route planning or assess the need for adding more coaches on a specific train or introduce a new train along a route based on the data captured by the booking system, has no easy access to it. The lead time required to develop a strategic reporting application based on the captured data often turns out to be longer than what is affordable by the decision maker. This situation is true of many cases of transactional data storage. Only a small fraction of the data that is captured, processed and stored by an enterprise is actually available to decision makers in a usable format.

The realisation that the critical data required for decision making is poorly integrated and difficult to access spurred the development of tools for consolidating data for better decision support systems. In the past few years, a set of significant concepts and tools have evolved for providing access to the information existing within the enterprise itself to key people at all levels within an organisation. Such information is critical for organisations to survive and prosper in an increasingly competitive environment. The term used for this new technology is '**data**

warehousing'. A data warehouse leverages data, an organisation's most critical and valuable asset, for managing knowledge and enabling decision making.

Before we begin our discussion on data warehouse technology, let us look at the aspects typical to transaction processing systems, also called operational systems.

2.1.2 Operational vs. Analytical Applications

Most business processes involve a series of events whose nature and frequency may differ. Examples of some such events are: a product is manufactured; one account is credited while another is debited; a seat is reserved; an order is booked; an invoice is generated; a payment is posted. The operational applications for such processes are designed to be highly efficient—they optimise the execution of a large number of atomic transactions with near fault-tolerant availability of data. We call such systems 'Online Transaction Processing' systems (OLTPs). They support the running activities of an organisation. The inventory system, sales processing system, billing system, tax returns filing system, etc., are examples of transaction processing systems of a typical business enterprise. In such a system, the data is being constantly changed or updated and represents the current information at a given point of time (snapshot). This data is highly volatile—it can change any moment. For instance, at a given time the data may show a pending order, the current balance of an account, or the number of items currently out-of-stock.

In our example of the IRCTC booking system, the system can show the names of trains running between two cities on a specific day and the availability of accommodation on a specific train on a specified date. This information is not static and is likely to change in a matter of minutes, or sometimes less. Since the system has been optimised to carry out the booking of tickets efficiently (without error, in real-time), it does not have the ability to provide analytical information like the overall usage of a train or the total revenue earned by it in a month or any other similar information that a decision-maker might want. Such analyses are enabled by analytical applications which call for fast, interactive access to a wider range of information than available in OLTP systems.

Primarily, operational applications differ from analytical applications in the type of questions that the respective systems are capable of addressing. For instance, operational application queries are of the 'What' or 'Who' type, whereas those of the analytical applications are of the 'Why', and 'What if' type. Secondly, an analytical application database differs from the operational in respect of the wider spectrum of data contained in it and the *many-data* relationships maintained amongst the data, offering a *multidimensional* view for dealing with complex queries. Operational applications facilitate insights into data through fast, interactive access to a wide range of business information unlike transaction processing, where the focus is on efficient execution of a particular business transaction. Analytical applications are thus able to provide insight into business patterns overlooked by operational applications that deal with just routine business.

A data warehouse application is an instance of analytical application, as we shall soon see. It will be useful to have a quick look at the behaviour of data in operational and analytical environments (Table 2.1) before we proceed.

Table 2.1 Operational data vs. analytical data

Application	Operational	Analytical
Content changes	Real-time	Daily to monthly
Structural changes	Infrequent	Slowly changing
Detail level	Transaction	Summary level
User interface	Static, Application dependent	Dynamic, Business-dependent
Response time	Real-time	Real-time
Age of data	Current	Historical
Access path	Deterministic	Non-deterministic

Data warehouse technology supports business intelligence (provision of analytical information), whereas traditional transaction processing systems optimise the handling of operational data.

Having identified data warehouse as a solution to data access crisis and for its suitability in analytical applications, let us study the motivation for data warehouse in another perspective.

2.1.3 INTEGRATED ACCESS TO MULTIPLE DATA SOURCES

Today's communication and computer networks provide us the facility to access a wide variety of databases. These may be the company directories, airlines schedules, product catalogues, weather reports, patients' reports or any other such source of structured data. Different departments of an organisation design their operational databases taking into account their local requirements and the resources available to them at the local level. At the level of the top management though, it is highly desirable to integrate these autonomous, heterogeneous and distributed multiple databases. It is possible that the answer to a particular business query is contained within a single database. In that case it is simple to get the query answered. But more often than not, the data is distributed over multiple databases. Data integration becomes a necessity then, and this involves combining data from multiple and heterogeneous sources. The objective of such integration would be to provide the decision maker access to an integrated data source, which gives the illusion of a single homogenous database designed for the specific need at hand.

Data integration can be effected in two modes: *on-demand* and *in-advance*. The *on-demand* method of integration is also called the *lazy model* or *query-driven* or *virtual* system. In this mode the integration process for a given query goes through the following steps: (i) find the relevant information sources; (ii) generate a subquery for each source; (iii) integrate the results obtained and; (iv) return the results to the application. In *in-advance* mode, also known as the *eager model* or the *analysis-driven* or *materialised* systems, the relevant information is extracted from multiple sources in advance, and is filtered, consolidated and stored in a (*separate*) database. Queries can then be put to this new database (data warehouse) *directly.* In a virtual system, in contrast, the data remains in the local sources, and it is the queries that get ported to operate on the sources. The aspect of integration occurs during query processing.

A data warehouse is essentially a separate repository of analytical data gathered in a materialised system by the integration of operational data, which is made accessible to all levels of managers in an enterprise for decision making.

2.1.4 Data warehouse — Definition

From the foregoing discussion we notice that data warehousing is the technology that provides integrated and summarised information extracted from multiple, heterogeneous operational system in a separate repository for the benefit of decision making process. A data warehouse is thus essentially a decision-support environment which leverages data stored in different sources by organising it and delivering it to decision-makers across the enterprise regardless of their platform or their technical skill level. A large number of organisations have found data warehouse systems to be valuable tools to survive in a competitive and fast evolving world.

Data warehouse was formally defined by Inmon, and this definition is accepted as the standard definition.

> A data warehouse is a subject-oriented, integrated, time-variant, non-volatile collection of data in support of management's decision making process.
>
> W. H. Inmon, 1993

Let us look at the terms used in this definition to gain an understanding of the concept of a data warehouse.

Subject-oriented

The data warehouse approach encompasses the subject as a whole, covering all the individual applications concerning an organisation. The data warehouse is oriented around the major subjects of an enterprise, e.g., customer, vendor, product and productivity. The focus is on data modelling and database design of the subjects exclusively—the model excludes data that is not useful for decision support systems (DSS) processing but pertains to a specific application. In contrast, operational applications which are designed around processes and functions, e.g., loans, savings, bank card, financial trusts, etc., are concerned with both database design and process design.

Integrated

Closely related to subject-orientation is the aspect of integration. The data contained within the boundaries of the warehouse, derived from disparate sources (i.e., underlying operational systems which may store data in different ways), is integrated in a singular, globally acceptable fashion. Data warehouse systems prove to be most successful when data from multiple source applications are combined in such a way that data inconsistencies and conflicts of all sorts are effectively addressed. This process, known by the term *data scrubbing*, essentially enables a DSS analyst to focus on using the data in the warehouse without having to wonder about its credibility or consistency. The integration of data is manifested in many ways—consistent naming conventions, consistent measurement of variables, consistent encoding of structures, consistent physical definition of attributes and so on.

Time-variant

The data in a data warehouse is time dependent, i.e., it has an associated temporal attribute. Every key structure in the data warehouse contains an element of time, either implicitly or explicitly.

The time horizon represented for a data warehouse is much longer than that of the operational environment because analysts need large amounts of data over longer periods of time to discover trends. This is in contrast to operational systems, which move historical data to archives to optimise their performance. A data warehouse's focus on 'change over time' is what is meant by the term 'time-variant'. The data in a data warehouse is accurate as *of some moment in time*, whereas in the operational environment the data is accurate as *of the moment of access*.

NON-VOLATILE

The data warehouse is non-volatile. In other words, it contains only *read-only* data. The data warehouse data is a long series of snapshots and cannot be updated once it is correctly recorded, while updates (insertions, deletions and changes) are done regularly in the operational environment. This means that once the data is loaded into the warehouse from an application-oriented environment (and/or external sources), it does not change and is there merely for accessing. Therefore, there is no need to be cautious about *update anomaly*, of concern in operational application systems. Nor does data warehousing require complex technologies for supporting backup and recovery. Data 'updating' in the warehousing environment consists of *refreshing* or periodic mass *loading* of data from the operational environment.

The data in the data warehouse does not change (since no writing happens) while it is being accessed. The new data from operational systems are loaded (in other words, data is refreshed) only at specific time intervals. This makes the data in data warehouse non-volatile and read-only.

2.1.5 DATA WAREHOUSE VS. DATABASE

Data warehouses, as we have seen, have become very important for business enterprises in the information age. These are much more elaborate than mere databases and it is possible to find connections in data not readily found in discrete databases. Though a data warehouse is a special kind of database (analytical database used as the base for decision support system), there are a number of fundamental differences which distinguish a data warehouse from a database. For one, it contains read-only, historical and aggregated data that cannot be modified. We discuss next the aspects of a data warehouse that make it different from a database.

SUBJECT-ORIENTATION

Data in a database is generally application-oriented. For instance, consider an application like Pay-roll. All data relevant to pay-roll application are stored in the database associated this application. For another application, say, Recruitment and Promotion, a different set of data is stored in its database. In contrast, the data in a data warehouse is categorised on the basis of a subject. In the present case, the subject being employees, all data relevant to the subject is stored, encompassing all applications related to employees. Data in a database is within a domain, though occasionally multiple domains are not uncommon. In data warehouse, the data from multiple domains are handled simultaneously. This allows a data warehouse user a holistic view of the organisation rather than restricted application-specific views.

DIMENSIONALITY

Dimensionality is a concept that shows that data is connected in various ways; it is an inherent property of the data residing in a warehouse. A decision maker is interested in analysing data on different, independent aspects or *dimensions*. The queries put to a data warehouses are typically ad hoc in nature, and to accommodate these, a data warehouse has to support multidimensional data analysis. Data analysts exploit the many-dimensional aspect of data for arriving at the kind of analyses not possible with the limited view afforded by operational databases. We shall study the concept of dimensionality in detail later. Database systems do not exhibit multidimensionality characteristics.

TIMESPAN

Generally, operational data deals with short time frames, such as 'the business today' and concerns specific data facts. Decision support data, such as that needed for strategic reports, trend detection, etc., deal with longer time frames. Many company managers are interested in transactions that occurred over a certain time period. For example, instead of dealing with the purchase of one customer, managers are often more interested in the buying patterns of a group of customers. This can be obtained only if one looks at the data in a warehouse, integrated over a period of time.

GRANULARITY

Granularity is another feature that distinguishes databases from data warehouses. The decision support system's data should be shown at different levels of aggregation (i.e., summarised at various levels), depending on the requirements of the query. Managers within an organisation are likely to need information summarised to various degrees or at various levels of refinements/coarseness for satisfying their particular need. Operational databases on the other hand, contain information about specific transactions that occur at a given time. Granularity refers to the level of detail of the data stored in a data warehouse. For example, we might have a time dimension which could be at the level of granularity of the year, the month, the quarter, the period, the week, the day, the hour, the minute, or the second. Granularity is therefore the lowest level of the depth of data. (Data at the transaction level is usually referred to as atomic-level data). Summarised data can be lightly as in hourly or daily summaries, or highly summarised, such as yearly data.

EXACTNESS

While operational systems demand procedural exactness, analytical system should offer users the ability to create ad hoc queries when they are unable to define the information they need. In this context, we identify two aspects of data storage—*location* and *content*. The content can be *weakly-specified* or *exactly-specified*, the location can be *deterministic* or *non-deterministic*. The easiest of the data access process happens when we have a strongly-specified, deterministic data query. In the well-known query and browse method, the *query* is an access method where the location is deterministic but the content is weakly-specified, while *browse* is an access method where the location is non-deterministic but the content is strongly specified. Data warehousing tackles the toughest of the two situations—weak specification (of content) and non-determinism (of location)—by supporting *weakly-specified, non-deterministic* access. That is, a data warehouse facilitates both querying and browsing.

2.1.6 Advantages and Disadvantages of a Data Warehouse

There are several advantages of maintaining a data warehouse. It is a single point contact for all decision makers in an enterprise for accessing data for their particular needs. Due to cleaning and summarisation of data that takes place prior to loading, the data in the warehouse has a better quality than the heterogenous data of the original sources. The *materialised* integration helps in quick response time to queries. And since the data is only read-only, there is no loss of historical data during accessing. Also, with OLTP being in a separate storage, data warehouse activities do not hamper transaction processing.

As to the disadvantages of a data warehouse as a central repository, one is that the data in the warehouse is not up-to-date. This is so as the data is loaded from the operational systems only periodically and does not reflect real-time information. Besides, a separate repository to store all the subjects of an enterprise-wide businesses process, which the data warehouse is, calls for an allocation of a very large storage space. Any wrong planning of the warehouse design will have serious repurcussion on the organisation's ability to leverage on the data stored therein.

2.2 Data Warehouse Architecture

Many conceptual architectures have been proposed for a data warehouse. We shall learn about these in this section. But first, let us try to understand some of the terminology associated with different data stages.

Operational data is the data collected and available in the transaction processing system. It resides in the (source) databases. Before loading into the warehouse, the data from many different sources, including transaction database systems and applications, are processed for consistency. The detailed transaction-level data that have been cleaned and confirmed for consistency is called *reconciled data*. It serves as the 'base' data for all warehouse activities. The data that has been aggregated, selected, and/or formatted for end-user and decision support system application from the reconciled data are called *derived data*.

Three-level Architecture

The data for decision support in a data warehouse is derived in two phases: (i) the reconciliation of operational data belonging to different sources; (ii) the derivation of decision support data from the reconciled data. Based on this, a three-level-architecture for a data warehouse is generally considered. The classical three-level architecture of a data warehouse is represented in Figure 2.1. Tier 1 is essentially the warehouse server, tier 2 the OLAP engine for analytical processing, and tier 3 the client, containing reporting tools, visualisation tools, data mining tools, etc. In addition to these, the warehouse environment has also the backend ETL processes

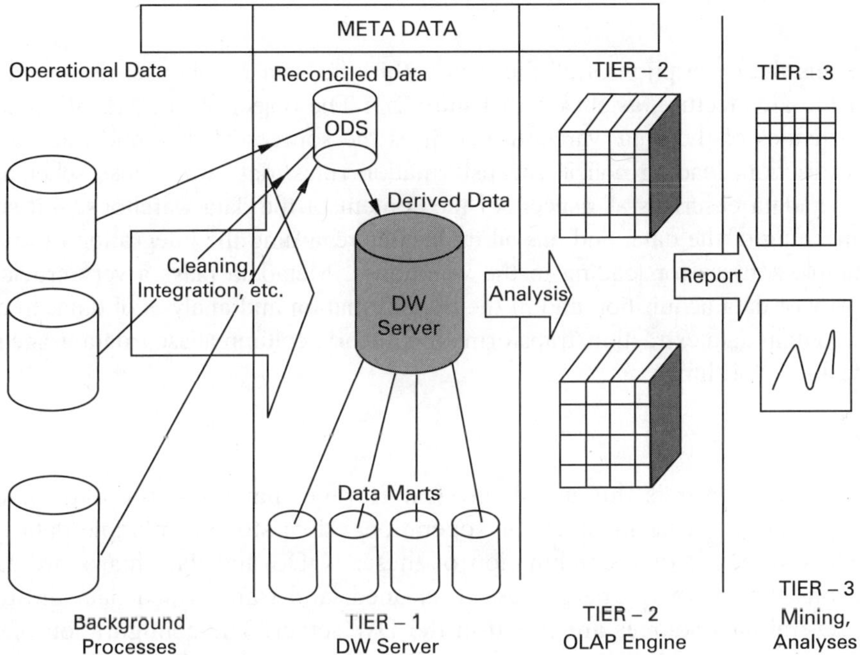

Figure 2.1 Blocks of the three-tier architecture of a data warehouse

concerned with the extraction of data from operational systems and external sources. We will learn about the ETL process in detail later on in the chapter (Section 2.23). The constituents of the data warehouse architecture depicted in Figure 2.1 are touched upon first.

To facilitate business analysis and query processing, data from the operational systems needs to loaded regularly into the warehouse. The process of extracting data from source systems and loading it in the warehouse is a very crucial component of data warehouse design. This *background process*, called the ETL (extract, transform and load) process, is responsible for the extraction of data from several sources, its cleansing, customisation, reformatting, integration, and insertion into the data warehouse. Building the ETL process is one of the biggest tasks in the building of a warehouse. It is a complex and time-consuming task, and most of the data warehouse project's implementation efforts, costs, and resources are expended in this activity. The ETL tools manage this function and perform the following tasks.

1. Extraction of data from different data sources
2. Transportation of data to the data *staging area*, where it is transformed and cleansed
3. Loading of data in the data warehouse

The above processes typically include schema transformations (e.g., pivot, normalise), cleansing activities (e.g., duplicate detection, check for integrity constraint violations), filters (e.g., based on some regular expression), sorters, groupers, flow operations (e.g., router, merge), function application (e.g., built-in function, script written in a declarative programming language, call to an external library) and so on.

Metadata

Metadata contains the description of all the data within the data warehouse; it encompasses all three levels of the architecture, as shown in Figure 2.1. The objective of metadata is to keep a record of all activities of the data warehouse such as the sources of data and their structures, frequency of extraction, loading policies, transformation rules, data warehouse schema, etc. In other words, metadata describes all aspects of the content of the data warehouse—it stores the location and meaning of the data, and has all the details regarding the integration of operational data from multiple sources for loading in the warehouse. Metadata plays a very crucial role in ensuring integrity of data acquisition and in the transformation and analysis of data. In addition, metadata may contain data extraction/transformation history, column aliases, data usage statistics and data modelling algorithms.

DW Server

The data warehouse server is the actual physical storage that holds the data of the data warehouse. It can be in the form of ODSs (operational data stores), multiple data marts or centralised data warehouse or a combination of these. (ODS and data marts are explained in the subsections that follow.) The processed, cleaned, and transformed data through ETL process from several data sources are stored in the DW server. The configuration of the DW server is critical to an organisation's decision support system. It is important that the data warehouse design and the data warehouse software installed in the server are optimised to run as a unit for efficient online analytical processing (OLAP) or multidimensional analysis, and for discovering previously unknown data characteristics, relationships, dependencies, or trends (data mining).

Operational Data Store (ODS)

The transformation of transaction data into integrated, consistent input for decision support applications by the data warehouse consumes a certain amount of time—the result is non-volatile, aggregated information. Many operational decisions, however, require up-to-date yet integrated and *subject-oriented data* in or near real-time (i.e., tactical analysis of short term volatile data), as in studying the effectiveness of an ongoing promotion campaign for a product. Since real-time access is not possible for the integrated, consistent and aggregated warehouse data, the concept of operational data stores (ODS) was introduced for providing such decision support that required data integration from multiple sources in real time. The basic difference between an ODS and a the warehouse is that the data in an ODS is volatile, whereas the data in data warehouse is non-volatile. Further, the recency of data in a ODS can get as close to a few seconds, unlike the historical data residing in the warehouse. In order to do that, ODS facilitates easy and quick access to up-to-date information on transformed and integrated operational data, with smaller volumes of data representing the current data from the data warehouse. Basically, ODS is designed around a specific set of data created to serve topic-specific requirements.

Whether it is necessary to introduce ODS in addition to a data warehouse requires careful consideration. A typical requirement of an ODS is CRM (customer relationship management) operations that involve extracting of relevant stored operational data and doing a quick profiling. Customer profiling, risk analysis for credit scoring, and campaign management are some typical applications that require ODS.

DATA MART

A data mart can be viewed as smaller data warehouse or a subset of a data warehouse customised for a particular aspect of business. If we think of the data warehouse as covering all aspects of an enterprise's business, then a data mart is a subset built specifically for a department. Data marts may contain overlapping data. A store's sales-data-mart, for example, might also contain some data from the inventory or payroll marts. We shall learn more about *data marting* in Section 2.22.

OLAP ENGINE

The data warehouse is huge repository of homogenous, integrated data (millions of records occupying several gigabytes), but to exploit it we need tools to query it and extract the relevant information. The OLAP (OnLine Analytical Processing) tools facilitate this. The term 'online' implies that even though huge quantities of data are involved, the system must respond fast enough to queries to allow an interactive exploration of data. OLAP tools are designed for information analysis (extracting relevant knowledge) and for efficient navigation through the all the data stored in the warehouse. They enable users to manually explore and analyse the summarised multidimensional data for finding answers to ad hoc queries in real time.

The term OLAP was first introduced by E F Codd in 1993, but N Pendse's description of it as FASMI (*fast analysis of shared multidimensional information*) describes it more aptly. According to this description, an OLAP tool must provide for *fast* query answering without frustrating the end-user's reasoning; offer *analysis* tools, implement security and concurrent mechanisms to *share* business *information* from a *multidimensional* point of view. Multidimensionality of data is a feature that allows the user to analyse the subject of interest from many points of view or dimensions. This aspect will be dealt with in more detail in section 2.3.

DATA MINING

OLAP requires the user to know what information he or she is seeking for and only gives an analysis of the past facts—it does not analyse data for hidden meaning or provide insights into future events. For business enterprises, however, a knowledge of statistical patterns and trends (prediction of future events) is critical to their survival in a competitive environment. Enabling *data mining,* a tool for the exploration and analysis of large quantities of data in order to discover meaningful patterns and rules, is the final goal of a data warehouse system. The field of data mining is an area of study in itself, and the later chapters of this book are devoted entirely to it.

VIRTUAL DATA WAREHOUSE

A very special case of a data warehouse that adopts a single-level architecture is a *virtual data warehouse*. There is no actual warehouse in this concept, only a 'simulated view' of one, wherein the user is provided access to operational data from wherever it is resident with the help of a middleware-like level that builds connections to the different data sources. In this sense, the operational data source is the only physical data source. Each piece of data is stored once and only once, and the middleware-like level operates as an interface between users and the operational databases. This kind of architecture allows for a rather quick deployment of a data warehouse with reduced costs, as there is no separate investment in building a warehouse. However, each query will require planning for activities such as data source identification, data transformation, and so on to be carried out. Because of this, for the end user the access time is fairly unpredictable. This architecture comes in handy as an initial step to convince all stake holders of the importance of data warehousing before committing major investment to the development of one.

2.3 Dimensional Modelling

The multidimensional data model, distinguished by a *fact/dimension* structure, is well suited to interactive analysis of large amounts of data for decision making. *Facts* represent the subjects of analysis and *dimensions* show the different points of view from which facts can be analysed. As pointed out earlier, OLAP tools exploit this multidimensional structure of data for fast query processing. The multidimensional data model permits friendly, easy-to-understand and intuitive visualisation of data for the non-expert end-user.

Let us look again at our example of the online railway ticket booking system. Decision makers may be interested in examining the total revenue generated through the sale of railway tickets by each train, or by trains of different types such as express, superfast or as operated by different divisions such as SE Railways, Central Railways, etc. The analysis may also be required on a daily, weekly, monthly, quarterly or even yearly basis. Further, the decision maker may be interested in studying sales patterns varying with age group, income group or districts the travellers belong to. It may also be required to analyse the profitability of a train, a sector or a route, in addition to the analysis of the sales proceeds. The subject that we wish to analyse here is the performance in terms of revenue, profit or number of travellers, which are *facts*. Since the analysis is to be carried out for different trains, different time schedules, different demographic parameters such as the age of the traveller, these represent *dimensions*. In the present case, the dimensions are trains, train timings, age, income, etc. Moreover, it is possible to analyse sales at different levels of granularity, such as daily, monthly or yearly; a similar analysis can be carried out for individual trains or for different types of trains. It can thus be seen that dimensions have associated *hierarchies*. For example, the 'location' dimension of a consumer product may be aggregated city-wise, state-wise or nation-wise, in which case *city* → *state* → *nation* show the hierarchy of the location dimension. Also associated with facts are summarisation or *aggregation functions*, which are essentially numerical formulae for computing a particular aggregation. For example, the total sales, average age, or total profit are calculated using different arithmetic functions.

The four important aspects of multidimensional data are thus *facts* and *summary measures*, *dimensions* and *dimension hierarchy*. The representation of multidimensional data comprising the above features is often referred to as a data cube.

FACTS

Facts represent the subjects on which a data warehouse is built which can be examined and analysed for deriving business intelligence. For example, if we are interested to build a data warehouse for the subject 'students in a university', facts would contain all subjects the decision-makers are interested in, such as the number of students admitted, graduated or dropped. In a sense, facts represent the interesting pattern or event in an enterprise that must be analysed in order to understand its behaviour. Further, facts contain measures representing attributes of the subject of analysis, e.g., the quantity of goods sold. Facts without contexts are however not meaningful, e.g., 'twenty units sold' does not tell what products were sold or when they were sold or whom they were sold by. This information is provided by dimensions, which are attributes of facts qualifying them. Thus, facts are implicitly defined by a combination of dimension values, and there are summary measures associated with facts.

DIMENSIONS

Dimensions, as stated above, are a category of information used to describe the context of facts. They are qualifiers that make the measures of the fact meaningful because they answer the *what, when,* and *where* aspects of a query. In a retail store, for example, the name of the product sold, and the date/time it was sold, provide the context for the 'twenty units sold'. Time, Region, Product, etc., are thus dimensions of the Sales fact. The attributes of dimensions either form a hierarchy, or are descriptive. For example, one possible hierarchy of the Time dimension could be *year* → *quarter* → *month* → *day*, while another could be *year* → *month* → *day*. Product id, customer name, sales date, etc., are examples of descriptive dimension attributes. An important goal of multidimensional modelling is to use dimensions for providing as much context as possible for a fact.

Dimensions are also used for selecting and aggregating data at the desired level of detail. They can be described as an abstract concept for grouping data sharing common semantics within the domain being modelled. As an illustration, we have in Table 2.2 *month, product, salesman,* and *city* as dimensions, while *sales-count, sales-sum* are facts.

Table 2.2

month	product	salesman	city	sales-count	sales-sum
January	Toy	Jagdish	Pune	5	200
March	TV	Piyush	Pune	40	100
March	Music Syst	Jagdish	Pune	20	100
March	TV	Jagdish	Mumbai	10	100
April	TV	Piyush	Pune	8	100
April	Toy	Piyush	Mumbai	5	100

Dimensions are organised in multiple levels and levels in a dimension are represented as entity types. Every instance of a level is called *member*. A *member* is a specific attribute (or a group of attributes) taking its values on a well defined domain. *Time* can be a broad dimension whose members are *day, month, year* … . Individual months such as January and February are the values of the *month* dimension. For dimension *location,* we have *city* as a member. The instances of member *city* are Pune, Mumbai, etc. *Property attributes* of a dimension is used to describe the members which contain one or several *key attributes* and may also have other *descriptive attributes*. For example, for *city* as a member, its attribute can be *state,* which is the name of the state the *city* belongs to. Please note that *state* is also a member at a different level of the same dimension. *city* can also have other attributes like *population, area* or *type* of city.

The multidimensional data model composed of logical cubes (described in detail next) with measures, dimensions, hierarchies, levels and attributes, serves well to represent real-world business entities, enabling intuitive analysis for decision making. This is because analysts know which business measures they are interested in examining, which dimensions and attributes make the data meaningful, and how the dimensions of their business are organised into levels and hierarchies.

DATA CUBES

A data cube is essentially the multidimensional representation of data, wherein data are partitioned into different cells based on the values of their dimension attributes. Let $D = \{1,2, ..., d\}$ denote a set of dimensions. A d-dimensional data cube can be represented by a d-dimensional array A of size $n_1 \times n_2 \times \ldots \times n_d$, where $n_j > 2$, the number of members of dimension j. For convenience, their each element is called a cell. Each cell contains the aggregate value (obtained by applying an aggregate function) of a measure attribute. A data cuboid is formed by constituting cells created from the same set of dimension attributes. Each data cuboid represents a unique view of the underlying data. A collection of data cuboids, which are based on different combinations of dimension attributes, forms a data cube.

Although the term 'cube' implies three dimensions, a data cube can theoretically have any number of dimensions. A collection of related cubes comprises a multidimensional database in a data warehouse.

For example, consider a 4-dimensional data cube maintained by an insurance company, whose dimensions are *customer_age, year, state* and *insurance_type*, and one of its measures is *sales*. This implies that the data warehouse is designed to analyse *sales* (*facts*) for different variations of *age, time, location* and *types* of insurance. Further, assume that the domain of *customer_age* is between 1 and 100, that of *year* is 1990–1999, of *state* is the states and union-territories of India, and of *insurance_type* is {home; auto; health}. The data cube contains $100 \times 10 \times 7 \times 3$ cells, and each cell contains the total sales for the corresponding combination of *customer_age, year, state* and *insurance_type*. Such a data cube provides the aggregate sales figures for all states and for each year from 1990 to 1999.

Consider another example of a automobile manufacturer, say, Maruti Suzuki, examining its sales data for its different products. The data considered here has three dimensions, *year, model* and *colour*. The data is given in a tabular form in Table 2.3.

We can view this as a data cube as shown in the Figure 2.2.

Table 2.3 Base data

Model	Colour	Year	Sales
Maruti 800	White	2010	134
Alto	Red	2010	76
Swift DZire	Silver	2010	87
SX4	Red	2010	124
AStar	White	2010	37
Alto	black	2010	34
Maruti 800	Silver	2011	213
Alto	Red	2011	72
Swift DZire	White	2011	154
SX4	Silver	2011	39
AStar	Black	2011	23
Alto	White	2011	26

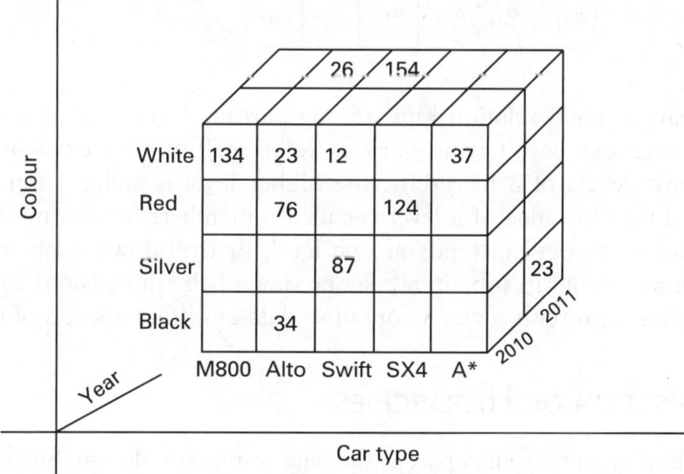

Figure 2.2

A Note on Notation

In this book we use the term *data cube* in two different (more or less similar) senses. If we add one set of extra cells to the data cube shown in Figure 2.2 to get another similar structure (Figure 2.3), the additional cells can be used to contain the aggregated measures at different levels. In most data warehousing literature, this modified structure is referred to as a *cube,* which contains, in addition to the base data, summarisations at all possible levels. We often refer to this process of computing the *cube* as *cubing procedure*. Each individual summarisation is referred to as *cuboid* and the set of all cuboids (*full cube*) forms a lattice structure. Thus, in the modified sense of the cube, the base data is also a cuboid, which is called the *base cuboid*. We will dwell on this aspect in detail later in Section 2.9.

Dimension Hierarchy

A dimension can be visualised as a containment-like structure composed of numerous levels, each representing a level of detail required by decision makers for their analysis.

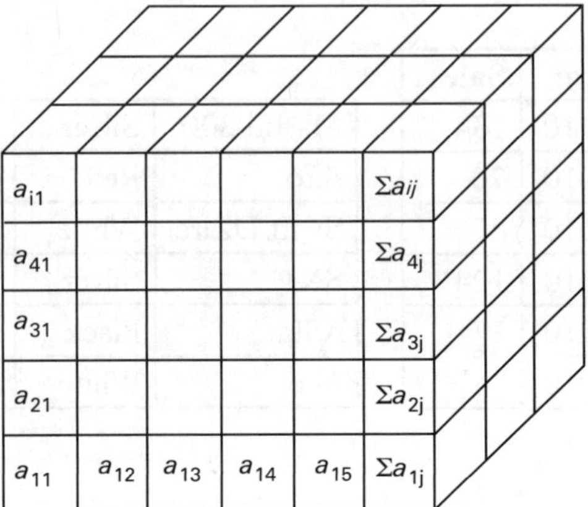

Figure 2.3

Hierarchy defines parent–child relationships among various levels within a single dimension Hierarchies of occurrences result from various relationships that exist in the real world. Given two consecutive levels of a hierarchy, the higher level is called parent, and the lower level is called child. Every instance of a level is called a member. In viewing data, analysts use dimension hierarchies to recognise trends at one level, or drill down (obtain a more detailed view of the dimension) or roll up (obtain a coarser view of the dimension) to discover further trends. A *hierarchy* thus represents a way to organise data at different levels of aggregation.

2.4 Categorisation of Hierarchies

Hierarchical dimensions are an essential part of the data warehouse design. Since hierarchies allow users to study facts at different levels of detail, it is therefore essential to have good hierarchical structures for ensuring correct and efficient calculation of aggregation functions. Consistency in the structure of hierarchies reduces the occurrence of logical errors.

The hierarchies of dimensions can be of different types. Most data warehouse models require dimension hierarchies to form balanced trees and each node (except the root) to have precisely one parent. Dimension hierarchies can also be seen as being either simple or multiple hierarchies. We will explore the various types of hierarchies next.

Simple hierarchies are those hierarchies where the relationship between the members can be represented as a tree. These hierarchies use only one criterion for analysis. Simple hierarchies can be further categorised into symmetric, asymmetric, and generalised hierarchies.

A *symmetric hierarchy* has at the schema level only one path for any leaf node, and all levels are mandatory. At the instance level the members form a tree, where all the branches have the same length. All parent members must have at least one child member and a child member cannot belong to more than one parent member (see Figure 2.4).

An *asymmetric hierarchy* has only one path at the schema level, but some lower levels of the hierarchy are not mandatory. For example, a university is composed of several schools, some of which have departments while some do not. As a consequence, at the instance level the members represent a non-balanced tree. In other words, the branches of the tree have different lengths since some parent members do not have associated child members (see Figure 2.5).

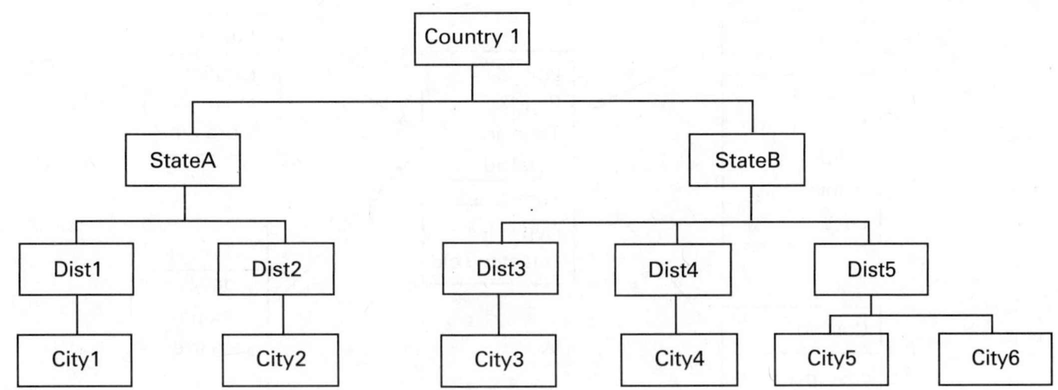

Figure 2.4 Symmetric hierarchy at the instance level

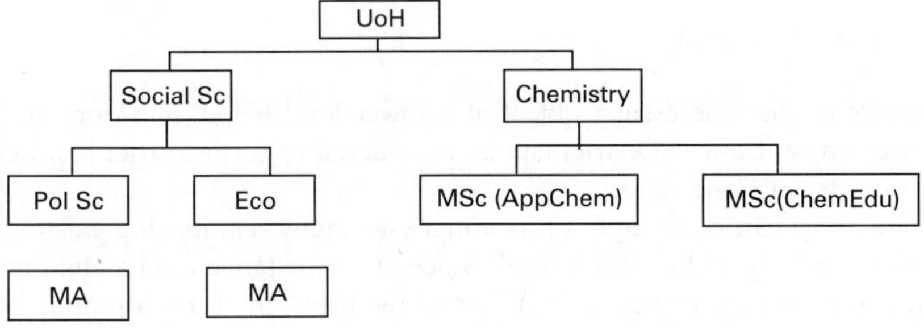

Figure 2.5 Asymmetric hierarchy

Consider a situation where the *customer* can be a *company* or a *person*, each with an individual hierarchy. The hierarchy for the subtype *Company* could consist of the following levels: *company type – sector – branch – area,* while the hierarchy for the *Person* subtype could consists of the levels *profession name – category – branch – area*. Notice that both subtypes include common levels for *branch* and *area*. While both hierarchies can be represented independently by repeating the common levels, the complexity of the schema reduces if shared levels are characterised by the same granularity of aggregation. This is termed *generalised hierarchy*. At the schema level a *generalised hierarchy* can contain multiple exclusive paths sharing some levels. All these paths represent one hierarchy. At the instance level each member of the hierarchy can belong to only one of the paths.

Generalised hierarchies include a special case referred to as *non-covering hierarchy.* This is a special case comes with the additional restrictions that at the schema level (i) the root and the leaves are the same for all paths and, (ii) only one (or several) intermediate level(s) can be skipped without including additional levels. An example of this kind of hierarchy is illustrated in the following situation. A university has several schools of study and some schools have several teaching departments. The schools which do not have any department offer their programmes of study at the schools level, whereas a school having different departments offer the programmes of study at the department level. Hence, *university — school — departments – programmes* is an example of non-covering hierarchy.

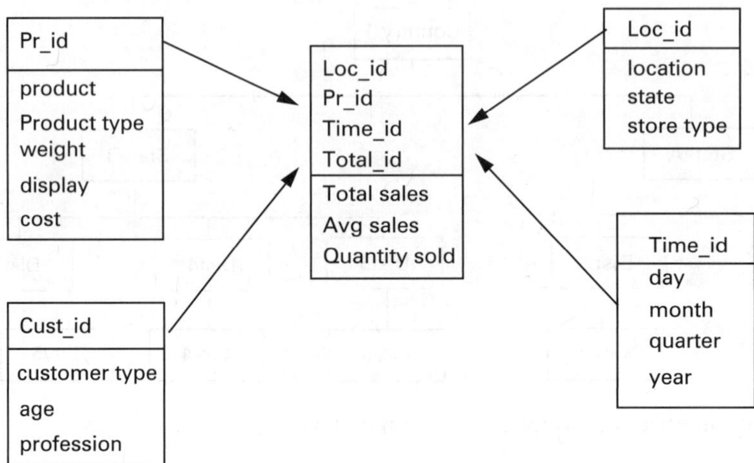

Figure 2.6 Generalised hierarchy

A *strict hierarchy* is one where each object at a lower level belongs to only one value at a higher level. For example, State – District can be considered to form a strict hierarchy because each district belongs to only one state.

A *non-strict hierarchy* can be thought of as a many-to-many relationship existing between a higher level of the hierarchy and its lower level. Since at the instance level a child member may have more than one parent member, the members of the hierarchy form a graph. An employee may be working for more than one section, a programme can be offered by more than one department, or a professor can be a teaching in two or more departments. These are examples of symmetric non-strict hierarchies.

Multiple alternative hierarchies represent the situation where at the schema level there are several non-exclusive simple hierarchies sharing some levels. At the instance level, such hierarchies form a graph (may contain a cycle), since a child member can be associated with more than one parent member belonging to different levels. In such hierarchies, it is not semantically correct to simultaneously traverse the different composing hierarchies. The user must choose one of the alternative hierarchies for analysis. An example is the tTime dimension including two hierarchies corresponding to different calendar subdivisions: *day–month–quarter–year* and *day–week–year*. As can be seen, it is meaningless to combine both hierarchies.

Completeness in hierarchies means that all members belong to one higher-class object which consists of those members only. For instance, the Month–Date hierarchy would be considered complete if there were data instances for all dates, for all months. In other situations, it may not be possible to capture all of the possible values. If a classification hierarchy is incomplete, incorrect summaries may result.

2.5 AGGREGATE FUNCTION

In the multidimensional model, *facts* are described in terms of *summary measures*. For example, in the *Students* data warehouse, the *total* number of students admitted or the *average* age of the students graduated or the *percentage* of students detained, etc., are subjects of interest. Likewise, the total number of items sold or total sale proceeds ina business would be the measures of interest to an analyser. These are also called aggregate values, summarised by aggregate functions. An aggregate function normally takes in multiple numeric values and returns one aggregate value. The need for aggregation arises as one moves up in the hierarchy of one or more dimensions.

The summarisability of facts is reflected in the aggregate function chosen. Normally, aggregate values are numeric and the aggregate function tries to combine these values as one moves up or down a dimension's hierarchy. For example, in order to determine the total weekly sales, the daily sales values for the days of the week are added up. To determine the average age of all students, the average age of male and female students are computed. The aggregate function takes multiple summarised values as input and outputs an aggregated numeric value. Given the total number of travellers in individual trains for each day of the month, aggregate functions can give the total number of travellers on different types of train for every month. Here, facts along the *time* hierarchy are aggregated by moving from *daily* to *monthly* level, and by moving up in the *train-type* dimension from individual trains to different types of trains, e.g., express-train, superfast-trains, etc.

Aggregate functions are categorised as distributive, algebraic, and holistic functions depending on how an aggregate on a partition is computed from aggregates on its sub-partitions.

This categorisation can also be looked at from the point of view how the finer grain aggregates are reused to compute the coarser grain aggregates. We shall see that this idea of reusing subaggregates to compute aggregate is not applicable for all types of aggregate functions.

DISTRIBUTIVE FUNCTION

An aggregate function F is *distributive* if there is a function G such that $F(S) = G(\{F(S_i) \mid i = 1, \ldots n\})$ for a data set S and partitioning $\{S_1; \ldots ; S_n\}$ of S. By partitioning, we mean $S = \cup S_i$ and $S_i \cap S_j = \varnothing$ for all pairs of S_i, S_j.

For example, if S is set of all students, then the set of male students S_1 and female students S_2 form a partition of S. Since COUNT(S) = SUM(COUNT(S_1), COUNT(S_2)), COUNT is a distributive aggregate function. Similarly, other instances of such functions are Sum and Max. However, one can see that AVG is not a distributive aggregate function.

It is important to note that S can be partitioned in multiple ways and the same F and G apply to all possible partitions.

Consider Table 2.4, which gives the total sales by product type by cities.

Suppose we compute the subaggregate as total sales by *cities*. If we consider $S = \{t_1, \ldots, t_9\}$, then S can be partitioned by cities as $S_1 = \{t_1, t_2, t_3\}$, $S_2=\{t_4, t_5\}$, and $S_3=\{t_6, t_7, t_8, t_9\}$. We see that $F(S) = SUM(F(S_1), F(S_2), F(S_3))$, where F is *total sales*. You can check that this method is applicable to all possible partitions. Hence coarser level aggregate can be computed directly from subaggregates without referring to the source data.

Table 2.4

	Cities	Product type	Total sales (in thousands)
t_1	Hyderabad	Jeans	10
t_2	Hyderabad	Jackets	11
t_3	Hyderabad	Shirts	12
t_4	Delhi	Jeans	5
t_5	Delhi	Jackets	6
t_6	Kolkata	Jeans	7
t_7	Kolkata	Jackets	8
t_8	Kolkata	Shirts	9
t_9	Kolkata	Formals	3

ALGEBRAIC FUNCTION

An aggregate function F is *algebraic* if it can be computed by a function H with several arguments, each of which is obtained by applying a distributive aggregate function. AVG, VAR, Standard-DEVIATION, and MAXN and MINN are all algebraic functions. AVG is algebraic, for example, since AVG(S) = SUM(S)/COUNT(S), and both SUM and COUNT are distributive. All distributive aggregations are algebraic. The distributive aggregations used for computing algebraic functions F are called *auxiliary aggregates*.

Algebraic aggregate functions are more general than distributive functions. Hence, we can define algebraic function in the same line as algebraic function as follows.

A measure F is algebraic if there are functions G and H such that $F(S)=G(H(S_1), \ldots, H(S_n))$, where functions H return k values and k is a constant for all S_i.

Continuing with the same example, let us assume that we study the average selling price by product types by cities. The aggregate function AVG cannot be computed directly from subaggregates. But it is also not necessary to refer to the base level data if we have two auxillary aggregates namely total price and COUNT.

Table 2.5

	Cities	Product type	TOT Total selling price (in thousands)	COUNT
t_1	Hyderabad	Jeans	10	3
t_2	Hyderabad	Jackets	11	2
t_3	Hyderabad	Shirts	12	4
t_4	Delhi	Jeans	5	3
t_5	Delhi	Jackets	6	5
t_6	Kolkata	Jeans	7	2
t_7	Kolkata	Jackets	8	7
t_8	Kolkata	Shirts	9	3
t_9	Kolkata	Formals	3	5

Thus the auxillary aggregate H returns two values, (TOT, COUNT), for each S_i. AVG(S) can be computed once we know $H(S_i)$=(TOT(S_i) COUNT (S_i)), i=1,2,3.

Holistic Function

An aggregate measure F is holistic if it is neither distributive not algebraic. In other words, an aggregate function is holistic if no such functions G and H exist for all possible partitions of S. RANK, MODE an MEDIAN are examples of holistic functions.

In the above example, MEDIAN (S_1)=11, MEDIAN (S_2)=7.5 whereas MEDIAN (S) =8. This aggregate function cannot be computed from subaggregates of partitions, and it is necessary to use the base level source data for computation of aggregates at every level of granularity.

The RANK function returns the position of an item within a partition when items are ordered in the partition according to the given ranking criteria. The RANK of an item is expressed as an ordinal number and all items with the same value of the ranking criteria are designated the same number. If there are t items at rank r, the first next item is assigned a rank $r+t$. You can check that RANK is a holistic aggregate function.

Partially Algebraic

An aggregate function that is not algebraic (or distributive) but exhibits the property of being algebraic (or distributive) when restricted to some subset of dimensions is called partially algebraic (or partially distributive). Since algebraic aggregate measure is more general than distributive aggregate measure, it suffices to discuss only the case of algebraic measure. A partially algebraic measure is a measure that satisfies the definition for some partitions of S, whereas an algebraic measure satisfies for all possible partitions of S. We give below the formal definition of partially algebraic function.

A measure F is called partially algebraic if there are functions G and H such that $F(S)=G(H(S_1), H(S_2), ..., H(S_n))$ for some partition of S. The function H returns k values and k is constant regardless of the partitions of S.

Consider the user log of any academic library. When a user borrows or returns a book, the log records the userid, name of the book, subject area of the book, and date of issue. Suppose we want to know the total number of users by month. This operation amounts to counting the number of distinct userids for every month. Thus, we partition on the set of transaction by userid. But if we partition the data on distinct subject area, counting the transaction will not be proper. Discovering whether a holistic measure is also partially algebraic is not a trivial problem.

Duplicate Sensitive

An aggregate function G is *duplicate insensitive* if the result of G computed over a bag of values is the same as the result of G computed over a core set of the bag. Otherwise, G is *duplicate sensitive*. MAX and MIN are duplicate-insensitive measures.

Self Maintainable

An aggregate function is *self-maintainable* if a new value of the function can be computed solely from the old values of the aggregate function and the changes to the source data. COUNT and SUM are self-maintainable with respect to insertions and deletions. MAX and MIN are self-maintainable with respect to insertions, but not self-maintainable with respect to deletions. AVG is not self-maintainable in itself, but it can be computed by SUM and COUNT that are themselves self-maintainable with respect to insertions and deletions.

For an aggregate function to be self-maintainable, a necessary condition is that the function must be distributive. In fact, all distributive aggregate functions are self-maintainable with respect to insertions. However, not all distributive aggregate function are self-maintainable with respect to deletion. For example, MIN and MAX are not self-maintainable with respect to deletion.

Types of Additivity

Additive measure is a very popular and widely used measure. *Fully additive* facts can be meaningfully added across all dimensions. For example, Quantity Ordered in the Order Item entity can be added across dates, products or customers to get the total sales volumes for a particular day, product or customer. *Semi-additive* facts can be meaningfully added across some dimensions but not others (usually time). For example, Quantity On Hand from the Stock Level entities can be added across products and warehouses (to get the total quantity on hand for a particular product or warehouse) but not across time, as this would lead to double counting of stock. Quantity On Hand can be averaged over time (to get average daily inventory levels), but not added. *Non-additive* facts cannot be meaningfully added across any dimension. For example, Unit Price from the Order Item entity cannot be added across any dimension. Unit Price cannot even be sensibly averaged over time, because to calculate the average selling price of a product you need to take into account the quantity sold.

Wherever possible, additive facts should be used to prevent errors in queries. This means converting semi and non-additive facts to additive facts. For example, Unit Price (a non-additive fact) can be converted to an additive fact by multiplying it by Quantity Ordered to form Extended Price (the total price for an individual order item). Note that this transformation does not result in loss of information in the process of transformation.

2.6 Summarisability

From the above discussions it becomes clear that correct summarisation of facts depends on the right choice of hierarchy and aggregate functions. S*ummarisability* in multidimensional model refers to the correct computation of aggregate values at a coarser level from the aggregate values at a finer level of detail. Typically, data is aggregated along multiple hierarchies, summarising data along multiple dimensions. For example, a summary may show the total sales in the year 2010 at all branch locations in Jharkhand. In this case, sales is aggregated along the time dimension and location dimension. If summarisability condition is violated, then the correct result will not be derived by the data analysis tools, resulting in an erroneous decision.

For illustration, let us consider that SB College is affiliated to Kolhapur University and that it offers BA progammes. The college has a social science department and some language departments. Let us assume that the number of students enrolled in each department is as given Table 2.6.

Table 2.6

Department	**Students enrolled**
English	256
Marathi	256
Economics	64
History	63
Geography	61
Political Science	32
Home Science	45
Sociology	29
All (college)	256

For the BA programme, students are required to take 2 to 3 optional subjects and a language subject. It will be incorrect to say that the total number of students enrolled in the college is the sum total of the students enrolled in each department. The same student might have taken, say, Economics, Political Science and a language, say English, which will be reflected in the enrolment of three different departments, whereas this data pertains to just one student. This is a case of *incorrect summarisation*. Let us assume a slightly modified example (Table 2.7), where the fact measure is the minimum age of students in a group. One can see that this can be summarised correctly.

Take another instance where the BA programme in the dimension hierarchy (at the instance level) is categorised into First-Year-BA, Second-Year-BA and Third-Year-BA and the fact-measure is the total number of students appearing for the university examinations. If we add up this fact year-wise, we should get the total number of students enrolled for the BA programme in the college. But this may not be strictly true as there may be some students who have backlog from previous years, who are not in the enrolled list. These students do not appear in any of the three groups.

Table 2.7 $d_{l1}, d_{l2}, ..., d_{l8}$ are instances of m_1 which is a descendant of M_u. age_{l1} is the associated measure of d_{li}.

Department	**Notation**	**Min_Age**	
English	d_{l1}	25	age_{l1}
Marathi	d_{l2}	25	age_{l2}
Economics	d_{l3}	24	age_{l3}
History	d_{l4}	23	age_{l4}
Geography	d_{l5}	21	age_{l5}
Political Science	d_{l6}	22	age_{l6}
Home Science	d_{l7}	25	age_{l7}
Sociology	d_{l8}	29	age_{l8}
All (college)		23	

Let us try to understand these concepts more formally. Assume that in a dimension hierarchy, a member m_u appears at a higher (coarser) level than a member m_l. In other words, m_l is a descendant of m_u in the schema level of the hierarchy. Let us also assume that at the instance level, an instance of m_u, say $d_{u,}$, has an associated fact called f_u. The descendant d_u at the level corresponding m_l are, say, d_{l1}, d_{l2}, ..., $d_{lk,}$, with associated facts f_{l1}, f_{l2}, ..., f_{lk}. Let us assume that we aggregate these facts at level m_l to get a fact at m_u. The aggregate function in this dimension hierarchy is summarisable if the aggregation of f_{l1}, f_{l2}, ..., f_{lk} results in f_u. For the example in Table 2.8, this condition fails to hold.

Table 2.8 (Same as Table 2.4 but with illustrated d_{ij} and f_{ij})

Department		**Students enrolled**	
English	d_{l1}	256	f_{l1}
Marathi	d_{l2}	256	f_{l2}
Economics	d_{l3}	64	f_{l3}
History	d_{l4}	63	f_{l4}
Geography	d_{l5}	61	f_{l5}
Political Science	d_{l6}	32	f_{l6}
Home Science	d_{l7}	45	f_{l7}
Sociology	d_{l8}	29	f_{l8}
All (college)		256	

A member m_u of a dimension is summarisable from a set of members $\{m_{l1}, \ldots, m_{lk}\}$ of the same dimension if, for every fact and every distributive aggregate function, the facts associated with m_u can be computed from the facts associated with $\{m_{l1}, \ldots, m_{lk}\}$. The summarisability condition for Table 2.7 holds for a specific aggregate function, but not for all distributive aggregate functions.

The concept of summarisability is the core of multidimensional modelling. There are three necessary conditions for summarisability, namely *disjointness, completeness* and *type compatibility*, which every dimension hierarchy must fulfil.

Disjointness

The *disjointness* condition states that the members $\{m_{l1}, \ldots, m_{lk}\}$ must form mutually disjoint subsets over individuals/objects. In the above example, the BA students enrolled in different departments do not form a disjoint set of data groups over departments. An inaccurate summarisation can result if summaries from different paths of the same hierarchy are merged. Specifically, data cannot be merged among members that have overlapping data instances.

For example, it is incorrect to merge total sales from an area code with the total sales in a city that the area code served. This is because data instances would be rolled up into both categories, and measures would be added twice if the summaries are merged. Table 2.6 represents another example that violates disjointness.

COMPLETENESS

Completeness in hierarchies means that all members of $\{m_{l1}, \ldots, m_{lk}\}$ belong to one higher-class object m_u, which consists of those members only. Given that disjointness is satisfied, it is necessary to test whether the categorisation of individuals/objects into groups is 'complete'. The term *complete* in this context has two parts. The first is that all the elements of the clusters exist. That is, the union of all clusters constitutes the entire set of the individuals/objects. For example, in the case of students assigned to departments, we need to know that all the students are accounted for in the cluster of categories. The second condition is that each individual/ object is assigned to some category. If, for example, some student is not assigned to any department, this test is being violated.

TYPE COMPATIBILITY

Type compatibility becomes relevant when summarisation is undertaken. Summarisation is performed quite differently with respect to temporal dimensions (such as months or years) as opposed to non-temporal dimensions (such as sex, race, or spatial regions). In order to understand summarisability property, the concept of *summary attribute type* is introduced here. For temporal dimensions, summary attributes can be classified into three types: *flow* (or *rate*), *stock* (or *level*) and *value-per-unit*. *Flow* refers to time periods and is recorded at the end of a time interval. *Stocks,* on the other hand, though related to time, are measured and recorded at particular points in time. Examples of *flow* are daily attendance, annual income and weekly wages, while examples of *stock* are number of students, number of examinees, etc. Examples of *value-per-unit* are item price, cost per unit manufactured, exchange rate, etc. *Value-per-units,* though determined for a fixed time, are not similar to *stocks* because their units are different. For instance, the unit of price per car is INR/car, while the unit of an inventory of cars is either cars or say Indian rupee (INR), based on whether the count is of cars or of the value of cars.

The distinction between *flow* and *stock* is made on *what* is recorded, not on *when* it is recorded. *Flows* record the cumulative effect over a period, while *stocks* record the state at specific points in time. While temporal summarisability of *flows* is semantically meaningful, temporal summarisability of *stocks* and *values-per-unit* depends on the aggregate function such as SUM, AVG, MAX, etc. For instance, monthly income can be summed to annual income, but it makes no sense to sum monthly inventories of cars (at the end of each month) into years.

Thus, by compatibility we understand that the summarisation is compatible in respect of three aspects, namely (i) whether the summarisation is temporal or non-temporal, (ii) whether the aggregate function is distributive, algebraic or holistic, and (iii) whether the type is flow, stock or value-per-unit.

2.7 FACT—DIMENSION RELATIONSHIP

Summarisability has been looked at so far in the context of dimension hierarchy and aggregate functions. But it has been observed recently that summarisability problem arises not only in the context of dimensional modelling but also in facts modelling. The scope of multi-dimensional modelling includes summarisability for fact–dimension relationship as well. We will study next the fact–dimension relationship.

Regular Fact—Dimension Relationship

A fact measure may have zero or multiple dimensions associated with it. If the fact's measures are assigned to a uniquely identified combination of dimension instances, the multiplicity at the dimension end will be exactly one. This is the regular fact–dimension relationship.

Dimension instances may typically occur in zero or more fact instances. It is desirable to know that dimension instances occur in at least one or at most one fact instance to ensure that the fact is associated with exactly one instance of that dimension. Thus, it is necessary to specify the minimum and maximum number of instances associated with a dimension, and it is desirable that the multiplicities at the dimension's end of the association specify a minimum and maximum multiplicity of 1.

Incomplete Fact—Dimension Relationship

Fact–dimension relationship is said to be *complete* if for every fact instance there exists a dimension instance which is related to that fact instance; otherwise, the association is *incomplete*. This situation represents a summarisability violation since there is a granularity mismatch in the instances of the fact. Consider the following example. Jotsna and Annapurna buy some products from a supermarket in January, and Gul goes shopping in April to the same supermarket. All of them use their membership cards to get discounts on purchases and the sales are recorded directly along with their personal information in the store's Customer Data database. However the sales of goods to customers without cards are also recorded in the Sales Data without recording any personal information (anonymous). When the sales are analysed by Customer Data (see Table 2.9b), some entries recorded in the Sales Data (Table 2.9a) are seen missing; these correspond to anonymous customers. This is an instance of inconsistent totals resulting from incomplete fact–dimension relationship.

Table 2.9 Inconsistencies in sales for customer-time-wise and time-wise records

Table 2.9a Sales data

Date	Sales
January 2011	25
April 2011	15
Total	40

Table 2.9b Customer data

Date	Customer	Sales
January 2011	Annapurna	10
January 2011	Jotsna	05
October 2011	Gul	15
Total		30

Non-strict Fact—Dimension Relationship

Relationship between fact and dimension is said to be *strict* if for every instance of the fact *f* there exists at most one instance of the dimension *d* which is related to that fact instance; otherwise, it is called *non-strict*. Non-strict fact–dimension relationships indicate summarisability problems because for each measure in a fact instance, there could be several instances of the same dimension that are associated with that measure, thus causing a granularity mismatch.

The Double Counting Problem

In Table 2.10, the association between the *Sales* fact and the *Sales-person* is non-strict because more than one salesperson (Satya and Uma) were involved in the same sale. This situation requires special care to be taken while recording data to avoid the *double counting problem*, i.e., of measuring the fact more once when the data is analysed, thereby producing erroneous results. The sale made on 31 January 2011 should be correctly counted just once, but more likely than not it does not happen. Situations of non-strict fact–dimension relationships occur in a plethora of real-world situations such as the relationships between bank customers and accounts, between insured drivers and policy holders, or between patients and diagnoses.

Table 2.10a Date-wise sales

Date	Sales–Person	Sales
31 January 2011	Satya, Uma	10
30 October 2011	Satya	05
30 October 2011	Uma	05

Table 2.10b Sales-person-wise sales

Date	Sales-Person	Sales
31 January, 2011	Satya	10
31 January, 2011	Uma	10
30 October, 2011	Satya	05
30 October, 2011	Uma	05

Facts of Fact

Sometimes, one fact type called primary fact type, can be characterised by several other fact types called secondary fact types. Consider the example of a surgery. It is characterised by primary fact attributes such as cost, duration and other details. Post operation, some other medicines are prescribed which has attributes such as the number of times they should be taken per day, or the number of days they should be taken for, as specified by the prescription. It is not adequate to include these facts in the primary type. One solution is to have a secondary fact type, which holds a reference to the primary fact type. This, in this case, can be achieved by specifying two different fact types, *prescription* and *operation*, and installing in *prescription* a reference to *operation*. It should also be noted that *prescription* has a normal reference to the root, the *medicine* dimension. There is an instance of *prescription* for each kind of medicine in a prescription. For the secondary fact type, all the dimensions of the primary type can be also used as its dimensions. For example, *cost* and *duration* can be analysed using *time* and *surgeon* dimensions, and *number days* can be analysed using not only *medicine* dimension but also *time* and *surgeon* dimensions.

2.8 OLAP OPERATIONS

Once the data warehouse is modelled as multidimensional data, it is necessary to explore the different analytical tools with which to perform the complex task of analysing the data. Several data analysis tools are made use of during OLAP (OnLine Analytical Processing). There are a number of OLAP operations that facilitate interactive querying and analysis. In this section, we will look at the set of well-defined and standard OLAP operations.

ROLL UP

The roll-up operation collapses the dimension hierarchy along one dimension(s) so as to present the data at a coarser level of granularity. The input parameters for the roll-up operation are the multidimensional data and the dimension on which the aggregation is being rolled up. Consider the multidimensional data of Table 2.11. ('Ind' and 'org' respectively represents purchases made by individuals and organisations under the Customer category.)

Each product is categorised by product type {home-appliances, entertainment, computer}. Thus the dimension hierarchy here is *product* → *product_type* → *ALL*. The roll-up operation on product dimension results in a new multidimensional data (Table 2.12). Note that though we have three entries for *year*= 2009, *Location*= "Pune" and *Customer* = "Ind" when we roll-up in the hierarchy of *product* dimension, all these three records correspond to same *product_type* (though to different *products*). The total sales for these three records are aggregated in the process of roll-up.

Table 2.11

Year	Location	Product	Customer	Total sales
2008	Mumbai	Oven	Ind	32
2008	Mumbai	Juicer	Org	34
2008	Mumbai	TV	Org	12
2008	Mumbai	Music Syst	Ind	11
2009	Pune	Computer	Org	43
2009	Pune	Music Syst	Ind	21
2009	Pune	TV	Ind	14
2009	Pune	Play_st	Ind	10
2010	Chennai	Oven	Org	09
2010	Chennai	Music Syst	Ind	02
2010	Chennai	Computer	Org	13
2010	Chennai	TV	Ind	24
2011	Hyderabad	Music Syst	Ind	22
2011	Hyderabad	Computer	Ind	15
2011	Hyderabad	Oven	Org	03
2011	Hyderabad	TV	Ind	07

Drill Down

The drill-down function allows users to obtain a more detailed view of a given dimension. This is the inverse of the roll-up operation. By drill-down on product dimension, we get Table 2.11 from Table 2.12.

Table 2.12

Year	Location	Product_type	Customer	Total sales
2008	Mumbai	home_appliances	Ind	32
2008	Mumbai	home_appliances	Org	34
2008	Mumbai	entertainment	Org	12
2008	Mumbai	entertainment	Ind	11
2009	Pune	computer	Org	43
2009	Pune	entertainment	Ind	45
2010	Chennai	home_appliances	Org	09
2010	Chennai	computer	Org	13
2010	Chennai	entertainment	Ind	26
2011	Hyderabad	entertainment	Ind	29
2011	Hyderabad	computer	Ind	15
2011	Hyderabad	home_applicances	Org	03

Please note that it is necessary to carry out appropriate aggregation while using roll-up or drill-down. Let us assume that the same multidimensional data has different sets of measures for the fact *sales* (Table 2.13).

Table 2.13

Year	Location	Product	Customer	Average sales	Sold_quantity
2008	Mumbai	Oven	Ind	12	03
2008	Mumbai	Juicer	Org	14	04
2008	Mumbai	TV	Org	12	01
2008	Mumbai	Music Syst	Ind	11	10
2009	Pune	Computer	Org	13	07
2009	Pune	Music Syst	Ind	21	04
2009	Pune	TV	Ind	14	05
2009	Pune	Play_st	Ind	10	03
2010	Chennai	Oven	Org	09	02
2010	Chennai	Music_Syst	Ind	02	09
2010	Chennai	Computer	Org	13	05
2010	Chennai	TV	Ind	24	03
2011	Hydeabad	Music_syst.	Ind	22	07
2011	Hyderabad	Computer	Ind	15	04
2011	Hyderabad	Oven	Org	03	05
2011	Hyderabad	TV	Ind	07	03

Though in the earlier example we could sum up the *total-sales* of the three records while rolling-up, we cannot do so in the present case because the measure is *average sales*. We will need to compute the resulting average with the help of other measures. Also note that *total sales* and *sold_ quantity* are distributive functions, whereas *average sales* is an algebraic function. It is important to pay attention to the properties of aggregate functions while performing roll-up or drill-down operations. Table 2.14 is the result of roll-up when the measure is *average sales.*

Table 2.14

Year	Location	Product_type	Customer	Average sales	Sold_quantity
2008	Mumbai	home_appliances	Ind	12	03
2008	Mumbai	home_appliances	Org	14	04
2008	Mumbai	entertainment	Org	12	01
2008	Mumbai	entertainment	Ind	11	10
2009	Pune	computer	Org	13	07
2009	Pune	entertainment	Ind	15.3	12
2010	Chennai	home_appliances	Org	09	02
2010	Chennai	computer	Org	13	05
2010	Chennai	entertainment	Ind	7.5	12
2011	Hyderabad	entertainment	Ind	17.5	10
2011	Hyderabad	computer	Ind	15	04
2011	Hyderabad	home_appliances	Org	03	05

DRILL ACROSS

Drill across is an OLAP operation that analyses the cells of two data cubes having same set of dimensions by moving data from one cube to the other at the respective cells. Quite often, different data cubes in a business model are found closely related, and analysts want to jump from one to another. They are usually interested in generating several reports showing different sets of data organised from the same point of view so that they are easily comparable. For instance, it could be interesting to analyse evolution of sales along *Time* and *Product*, and compare it with production in the same period of time for the same product. Probably, that information will be stored in different cubes, and users will need to drill across multidimensional schemas.

Drill-across obtains data cells from a data cube (origin cube) which are linked to a particular data cell of the input data cube (destination cube) by holding a conformity predicate in order to build the resulting data cube. *Drill across* operation between two multidimensional data cubes is defined if the data cubes have the same or equal dimension attributes. In drilling across, the *n*-dimensional space remains exactly the same, only the cells placed on it change. For example, consider a cube of Stocks data. One could drill-across from this data cube to another with exactly the same amount of cells but, instead of containing sales instances alone, it could contain sales and stock information. Drill across changes the subject of analysis of the data cube by means of a one-to-one relationship existing in the data.

SLICE

The role of slice operation is to extract a slice of the original cube corresponding to a single value of a given dimension. The slice operation selects one dimension and the values of this dimension are returned to another data sub-cube. This operation is used for decreasing the multidimensional data by one dimension. If the input data is of n dimensions, then the slicing operation will result in a data cube of $n-1$ dimensions. No aggregation is required with this operation.

Consider the multidimensional data given in Table 2.14. Slice it on *location* = "Hyderabad" and we get the result given in Table 2.15.

Table 2.15

Year	Location	Product_type	Customer	Average sales	Sold_quantity
2011	Hyderabad	entertainment	Ind	17.5	10
2011	Hyderabad	computer	Ind	15	04
2011	Hyderabad	home_appliances	Org	03	05

DICE

The dice operation is a somewhat similar to slice in the sense that it is also a type of selection. But unlike slice operation where one dimension and one value are used for selection, in dice operation two or more dimensions and two or more values are used for selection.

A dice operation on the data given Table 2.14 for location= ("Hyderabad" OR "Chennai") AND product_type = ("Computer" OR "Home_appliances") results in Table 2.16.

Table 2.16

Year	Location	Product_type	Customer	Average sales	Sold_quantity
2010	Chennai	home_appliances	Org	09	02
2010	Chennai	computer	Org	13	05
2011	Hyderabad	computer	Ind	15	04
2011	Hyderabad	home_appliances	Org	03	05

PIVOT

Pivot is a simple but effective operation that allows OLAP users to visualise cube values in different ways by changing the orientations of dimensions in the cube.

RANGE QUERY AND RANGE-SUM QUERY

A *range query* in a data cube applies a given aggregation operation over selected cells when the selection is specified as contiguous ranges in the domains of some of the attributes.

Consider, for illustration, the data given in Table 2.12. If we are interested in the total sales for the period, say from 2008 to 2010, denoted by [2008, 2010], then the range query will return the measure value by aggregating in all records for this range. The result in this case is a single numeric value obtained by adding all the sales for the years 2008, 2009 and 2010, i.e., 225. The same range query for the Table 2.13 will require computing of the average value for the range specified (here, simply adding the average sales will not be correct). Since the range in the range query is given in terms of contiguous values, it is essential that it be given only on dimensions which are numeric (or at least ordered). Thus, a range query for *location* dimension is not meaningful.

A *range-sum query* in a d-dimensional data cube is employed to find the *sum* of the values in cells that fall within a specified range. It is different from the range query in the sense that it is applied only to additive aggregation functions.

In addition to the straightforward OLAP queries discussed above, there are several other complex OLAP queries like *iceberg* queries, *top-k* queries and *skyline* queries. We will discuss this after we have understood the concept of lattice of cuboids.

2.9 Lattice of Cuboids

Please recall the note in Section 2.3 regarding the notations used for the term 'data cube'. Henceforth we shall refer to the term 'cube' for the base multidimensional data, together with all the levels of summarisation.

In an n-dimensional data cube, a cell $a = (a_1; a_2; \ldots ; a_n; c)$ (where c is a measure) is called an m-dimensional cell (i.e., a cell in an m-dimensional cuboid) if and only if there are exactly m $(m \leq n)$ values among $(a_1; a_2; \ldots; a_n)$ which are not marked as 'ALL' (sometimes, * is used to depict ALL). It is called a base cell (i.e., a cell in a base cuboid) if $m = n$; otherwise, it is an aggregate cell. The term ALL for any dimension stands for the coarsest-level aggregation in that dimension.

Consider the multidimensional data of Table 2.17, which is a modification of Table 2.13, with 4 dimensions—time, location, product, and customer. Let us assume very simple, two-level hierarchies for these dimensions. For *Time* the hierarchy is *year* → *quarter*; for *Location* it is *state* → *city*; for *Product* the hierarchy is *home appliance, entertainment, computer*; and for *Customers* it is *individual* or *organisation*.

Cuboids

When the multidimensional data cube, often referred to as *cuboid*, is rolled up along different dimensions, different cuboids result. The data in Table 2.15 represents a cuboid at the finest level of granularity. Let us call this *base cuboid,* consisting of 16×4×4×2 = 2048 cells in 4 dimensions—16 Quarters, 4 Cities, 4 Products and 2 Customer-types—as C_0. We denote C_0 by <*Quarter, City, Product, Customer-type*>. Each cell is referred to by the corresponding instantiations of four dimensions, namely *Quarter, City, Product* and *Customer-type*. For example, the cell *C*(*Q2'09, Pune, TV, Individual*) corresponds to the total number of TVs sold to *individuals* by the *Pune* branch during the *second quarter* of the year 2009. The content of this cell is 0. In Table 2.17, only the cells that have nonzero facts are listed.

Table 2.17 Cuboid C_0

Quarter	Location	Product	Customer	Total sales
Q1'08	Mumbai	Oven	Ind	32
Q2'08	Mumbai	Oven	Org	34
Q3'08	Mumbai	TV	Org	12
Q4'08	Mumbai	Music Syst	Ind	11
Q1'09	Pune	Computer	Org	43
Q2'09	Pune	Music Syst	Ind	21
Q3'09	Pune	TV	Ind	14
Q4'09	Pune	Music Syst	Ind	10
Q1'10	Chennai	Oven	Org	09
Q2'10	Chennai	Music Syst	Ind	02
Q3'10	Chennai	Computer	Org	13
Q4'10	Chennai	TV	Ind	24
Q1'11	Hyderabad	Music Syst	Ind	22
Q2'11	Hyderabad	Computer	Ind	15
Q3'11	Hyderabad	Oven	Org	03
Q4'11	Hyderabad	TV	Ind	07

By roll-up of data along any dimension, we get another cuboid. For example, Table 2.18 is the result of roll-up operation on C_0 along *Time* dimension, aggregating the 4 quarters of the year. It corresponds to cuboid C_1 denoted by <*Year, City, Product, Customer-type*>, which has 4×4×4×2 = 128 cells. Cuboid C_2 (Table 2.19) represents another cuboid obtained from the base cuboid C_0 by aggregating along dimension *Location* (city to state). It has 16×3×4×2 = 384 cells.

When we aggregate cuboid C_1 along *Location* dimension, we get cuboid C_{12}, as given in Table 2.20. Please note that since total sales is an additive aggregation function, we are able to add the values as we roll-up.

Table 2.21 represents cuboid C_{123} obtained by aggregating C_{12} along Product dimension. The cuboid is obtained by aggregating on *Customer* dimension, represented as <*Year, State, Product-class, ALL*>. Note that when we reach the top level of the dimension hierarchy, '*ALL*' is used to represent all entries. Alternatively, * is also used in place of *ALL*.

Similarly, we get Table 2.22 as the cuboid <*All, All, Product-class, All*> by repeated aggregation.

When we complete all aggregations in all dimensions, we get a cuboid consisting of a single cell. This is called the *apex cuboid*, denoted by <*All, All, All, All*> (Table 2.23).

Let us now study the same concepts more formally for a general situation.

A *cuboid* represents a unique view of data at a given level of granularity. Each cuboid can be computed from another one by the process of aggregation along a dimension. We can define a *partial order* between cuboids, $C_j < C_i$, if C_j can be computed using only the results of C_i by roll-up operations. In this case, we say C_j is dependent on C_i. The relation < induces a partial order on the set of all cuboids. Thus, the set of all cuboids forms a *lattice* called the *lattice of cuboids*.

Table 2.18 Cuboid C_1

Year	Location	Product	Customer	Total sales
2008	Mumbai	Oven	Ind	32
	Mumbai	Oven	Org	34
	Mumbai	TV	Org	12
	Mumbai	Music Syst	Ind	11
2009	Pune	Computer	Org	43
	Pune	Music Syst	Ind	21
	Pune	TV	Ind	14
	Pune	Music Syst	Ind	10
2010	Chennai	Oven	Org	09
	Chennai	Music Syst	Ind	02
	Chennai	Computer	Org	13
	Chennai	TV	Ind	24
2011	Hyderabad	Music Syst	Ind	22
	Hyderabad	Computer	Ind	15
	Hyderabad	Oven	Org	03
	Hyderabad	TV	Ind	07

Table 2.19 Cuboid C_2

Quarter	Location	Product	Customer	Total sales
Q1'08	Maha	Oven	Ind	32
Q2'08	Maha	Oven	Org	34
Q3'08	Maha	TV	Org	12
Q4'08	Maha	Music Syst	Ind	11
Q1'09	Maha	Computer	Org	43
Q2'09	Maha	Music Syst	Ind	21
Q3'09	Maha	TV	Ind	14
Q4'09	Maha	Music Syst	Ind	10
Q1'10	TN	Oven	Org	09
Q2'10	TN	Music Syst	Ind	02
Q3'10	TN	Computer	Org	13
Q4'10	TN	TV	Ind	24
Q1'11	AP	Music Syst	Ind	22
Q2'11	AP	Computer	Ind	15
Q3'11	AP	Oven	Org	03
Q4'11	AP	TV	Ind	07

Table 2.20 Cuboid C_{12}

Year	Location	Product-class	Customer	Total sales
2008	Maha	Home	Ind	32
	Maha	Home	Org	34
	Maha	Ent	Org	12
	Maha	Ent	Ind	11
2009	Maha	Computer	Org	43
	Maha	Ent	Ind	45
2010	TN	Home	Org	09
	TN	Ent	Ind	26
	TN	Computer	Org	13
2011	AP	Ent	Ind	29
	AP	Computer	Ind	15
	AP	Home	Org	03

Table 2.21 Cuboid C_{123}

Year	Location	Product-class	All customers	Total sales
2008	Maha	Home	ALL	68
	Maha	Ent	ALL	23
2009	Maha	Computer	ALL	43
	Maha	Ent	ALL	45
2010	TN	Home	ALL	09
	TN	Ent	ALL	26
	TN	Computer	ALL	13
2011	AP	Ent	ALL	29
	AP	Computer	ALL	15
	AP	Home	ALL	03

Table 2.22

Year	All locations	Product-class	Customer	Total sales
ALL	ALL	Home	ALL	68+09+03 = 80
ALL	ALL	Ent	ALL	23+45+26+29= 123
ALL	ALL	Computer	ALL	43+13+15 = 71

Table 2.23 Apex cuboid

All Years	All locations	All products	All customers	Total sales
ALL	ALL	ALL	ALL	80 + 123+71 = 274

Every cuboid is dependent on the *base* cuboid. In data warehouse literature, the term *CUBE* represents the collection of all cuboids, or in other words, the whole lattice. In this lattice, the cuboid corresponding to the finest level of granularity is called the *base cuboid,* and the cuboid corresponding to the coarsest level of granularity is called the *apex cuboid*. Every other cuboid lies between the *apex* and *base* cuboids. An edge in the lattice represents a *parent/child relationship* between two cuboids. For example, *<All, State, Product, Customer-type>* is the child of *<All, All, product, customer-type>*.

Having learnt about cuboids, it now becomes convenient to use a notation introduced for OLAP operations. Please note that most of OLAP operators take a cuboid as input and outputs a cuboid. We use the following notations for slice and dice.

dice **Location = 'Maha'** OR **'AP'** AND **Product-class = 'Home'** OR **'Ent'** **C123**

and

slice **Location = 'Maha'** **C123**

We see that using roll-up and drill-down operations, one can navigate the cuboids in the lattice. Thus, any OLAP query (which is a combination of OLAP operations) can be viewed as (or even rewritten as) an equivalent query consisting of two phases: the first phase is a set of roll-up or drill-down operation to reach the appropriate cuboid, and the second phase involves other operations such as slice dice, etc., for extracting the summarised data. The efficiency of a query process lies in minimising the processing time to carry out these two steps. Cubing process aims at pre-computing the cuboids of the lattice so that the first phase is avoided during query processing as the appropriate cuboid is readily available.

There are different alternatives of pre-computation of cuboids to handle OLAP queries. The following are three major alternatives for such materialisation of cuboids.

Full Materialisation

This means that we physically materialise the whole data cube, that is, every cuboid of the lattice of cuboids. This approach gives the best query response time. But, precomputing and storing the full cube is not a feasible alternative for large data cubes, as the space consumed in the process is quite large.

No Materialisation

In this case we are going to the raw data (that is, only base cuboid is available) and computing every cell on request. Though this approach is very space-efficient, the processing time for responding to queries is very high.

Partial Materialisation

This approach suggests that we materialise only part of the data cube. In a data cube, the values of many cells are computable from those of the other cells in the data cube. The more cells we materialise, the better the query performance is. For large data cubes however, we may be able to materialise only a small fraction of the cells of the data cube due to space and other constraints. It is thus important that we pick the right cells to materialise. There are two different approaches employed in this category. We either choose a subset of cuboids from the lattice that are completely materialised, or alternatively, we materialise all cuboids of the lattice but select only the relevant cells in each cuboid for pre-computation.

We will discuss the different algorithms and approaches for full and partial materialisation in sections 2.13 and 2.21 respectively.

Having understood the concept of lattice of cuboids, we now look at the complex OLAP queries, namely, iceberg query, skyline query, top- K query and nearest neighbour query.

Iceberg Query

In many cases, a substantial amount of the cube's space is taken up by a large number of cells with very low measure values. It is useful to materialise only those cells in the cuboid whose measure value is above some minimum threshold. This is called *iceberg constraint*. The *iceberg query* performs an aggregate function over a specified dimension list and then eliminates aggregate values below some specified threshold. The cells that cannot pass the threshold are likely to be too trivial to warrant further analysis. These cells do not satisfy the iceberg constraint.

Skyline Query

Given a set of multidimensional tuples p_1, p_2,.., p_N, the skyline operator returns all tuples p_i such that p_i is not dominated by another tuple p_j. The term 'domination' is dependent on the aggregate function. Using the MIN condition, a tuple p_i dominates another point p_j if and only if the values of p_i on any dimension is not larger than the corresponding values of p_j. Informally, this implies that p_i is preferable to p_j according to any preference (scoring) function that is monotone on all dimensions. We call a function to be monotone on a dimension d if its value increase monotonically for monotonic increase (or decrease) of the values of d.

Nearest Neighbour Query

One of the commonest multidimensional queries is the *nearest neighbour* query, which seeks elements that are 'close' to a provided target. For example, given a set of users, we might seek users whose profiles are similar to the current user. The query then finds the *k nearest neighbours* (kNN), that is, *k* neighbours that are as close as possible to the target.

Top-k Query

In aggregation queries (discussed earlier), aggregates are computed over groups with respect to some grouping attributes. Decision making procedures naturally involve comparing and ranking aggregates (or assigning preferences to aggregates). Among the large number of groups, only the ones with certain significance are of interest to decision makers in many cases. To support such applications, ranking (top-k) aggregate queries rank the groups by their aggregate values and return the top k groups with the highest aggregates. A top-k query returns *k* data points satisfying some optimality criterion on dimensional attributes which are specified by the users.

For example, a shoes company may have a sales database with *number of items* as a measure attribute and {color, year, type} as three-dimensional attributes. The user may wish to find the top 3 sales made since 2010 by the *number of items*.

It is not trivial to evaluate top-k queries in multidimensional settings. A straightforward method to evaluate a top-k OLAP query is to compute the aggreate value for each dimension and then select the highest aggregation. However, it will be an extremely slow process as the number of possible cubes in an OLAP may be very large. There are several approaches that have been proposed in the literature to solve this problem.

2.10 OLAP Server

An OLAP server is a data manipulation engine specifically designed for supporting and performing OLAP operations on multidimensional data. It provides a user-friendly platform to users to perform OLAP queries on the data warehouse data. There two fundamentally different structures of OLAP servers in existence: relational OLAP (ROLAP) and multidimensional OLAP (MOLAP), based on the two basic storage structures for data in the warehouse. In ROLAP, multidimensional data is stored in a relational database, whereas in MOLAP, a large multidimensional array is used to store data. ROLAP and MOLAP are covered in detail in the following sections.

There are arguments in favour of both ROLAP as well as MOLAP. Since ROALP makes use of relational database technology, it integrates easily with the existing OLTP systems and exploits matured technologies for security, data privacy, storage efficiency, indexing, etc. MOLAP, on the other hand, is held in favour because multidimensionality is natural to the data in the warehouse as it provides for higher efficiency in storage and retrieval. The use of hybrid OLAP (HOLAP), employing MOLAP for storing dense regions of the cube and a ROLAP approach for the rest is not uncommon either.

2.11 ROLAP

The ROLAP approach is based on the premise that data need not be stored multidimensionally in order to be viewed multidimensionally, and that it is possible to exploit the well-proven relational database technology to handle multidimensionality of data. Relational OLAP (ROLAP) systems use relational database technology for storing data and specialised index structures such as bit-mapped indices to achieve good query performance. To implement the same, typically, the cube is mapped to a set of base tables (fact table and dimension tables) in the relational DBMS, and OLAP queries are formulated using a sequence of SQL queries.

Let us first understand some of the useful concepts before studying the various ROLAP schemes.

Dimension Tables

A dimension table is a relational table that stores a dimension, its members, instances, and hierarchy and property attributes. The primary key of a dimension table uniquely identifies each row of the dimension table. Typically, a dimension table is wide, which means that it has more number of columns than rows. This is natural as the dimension table captures the dimensional hierarchy and property attributes by its columns. Instances of dimensions form rows of the dimension table. Since the entries in the dimension table are seldom used for calculation, the attributes of the table can be in textual format. Further, the property attributes and hierarchical attributes in a dimension table need not be directly related. Dimension tables are denormalised tables, and as a practice, surrogate keys are used as the primary key. The surrogate keys are a system-generated sequence of numbers which do not have any semantics associated with the application data. This is an advantage because any change taking place in OLTP does not affect the dimension table. The metadata keeps track of the mapping between the surrogate key and the primary key of the operational system.

Let us consider the product dimension of Table 2.13. The corresponding dimension table may look like the one given Table 2.24. Note how the hierarchy information and the attribute information are recorded in one table. The table is not in normal form. The attribute, *product_type*, is at a higher level of the dimension hierarchy. The attributes *weight*, *display*, *cost*, etc., are property attributes of the dimension. The table has *product_id* as the surrogate key.

In a similar manner, the dimension table for the dimension *location* is shown in Table 2.25.

Table 2.24 Dimension table for product dimension

Product_id	**Product**	**Product_type**	**weight**	**display**	**cost**
Pr01	Oven	Home appliances	07	-	5
Pr02	TV	Entertainment	10	LED	49
Pr03	Music Syst	Entertainment	05	-	35
Pr04	Computer	Computer	10	LED	65
Pr05	Play_st	Entertainment	07	HD	57

Table 2.25 Dimension table for location dimension

Loc_id	**Location**	**State**	**Store_type**
Loc01	Mumbai	Maha	wholesale
Loc02	Pune	Maha	retail
Loc3	Chennai	TN	wholesale
Loc04	Hyderabad	AP	showroom
Loc05	Allahabad	Gujrat	retail

Facts Tables

Facts tables are relational tables containing summary values. A row in the fact table corresponds to a cell in the cuboid (or even the cube) that the schema represents. A row in the fact table contains a combination of dimension values for each dimension. Thus, a row in the fact table relates to a combination of rows from all dimension tables. The primary key of the fact table is the concatenation of the primary keys of all the dimension tables. Typically, a fact table is not wide, but deep. It contains fewer attributes and a large number of rows. Apart from the concatenation of primary keys, a fact table contains facts or measures. The primary key of each dimension table is a foreign key in the fact table.

Take the same instance of Table 2.13. The fact table is given in Table 2.26.

Table 2.26 Fact table

Loc_id	Pr_id	Cust_id	Time_id	Total Sales	Avg Sales	Quantity_sold
Loc01	Pr01	Cust01	Time01	32	12	03
Loc01	Pr01	Cust02	Time02	34	14	04
Loc01	Pr02	Cust02	Time03	12	12	01
Loc01	Pr03	Cust01	Time04	11	11	10
Loc02	Pr04	Cust02	Time05	43	13	07
Loc02	Pr03	Cust01	Time06	21	21	04
Loc02	Pr02	Cust01	Time07	14	14	05
Loc02	Pr03	Cust01	Time08	10	10	03
Loc03	Pr01	Cust02	Time09	09	09	02
Loc03	Pr03	Cust01	Time10	02	02	09
Loc03	Pr04	Cust02	Time11	13	13	05
Loc03	Pr02	Cust01	Time12	24	24	03
Loc04	Pr03	Cust01	Time13	22	22	07
Loc04	Pr04	Cust01	Time14	15	15	04
Loc04	Pr01	Cust02	Time15	03	03	05
Loc04	Pr02	Cust01	Time16	07	07	03

Factless Facts

In some cases, fact tables may contain no numerical facts at all. For example, the fact table recording the incidence of crimes may contain records of when and where a crime took place, the type of offenses committed, and people who committed it. However, there are no measures involved—the important information contained therein is simply that a crime has taken place. Such a table is called a factless fact table. Other examples of factless fact tables are records of traffic accidents, student enrollment, and disease statistics. The only relevant aggregation operation for such types of events is COUNT, which can be used to analyse the frequency of events over time.

Three types of relational schemas are employed in ROLAP: *star schema, snowflake schema* and *galaxy schema*.

Star Schema

The star schema consists of a central table called the *fact table,* surrounded by a number of *dimension tables* laid out in a star formation (Figure 2.7). The fact table forms the 'centre' of the star, while dimension tables form the 'points' of the star. Dimensions are often highly denormalised tables consisting of one or more embedded hierarchies.

The star schema has several advantages over other schemas like the snowflake schema that we will be discussing next. A star schema has the least number of tables and hence the overhead

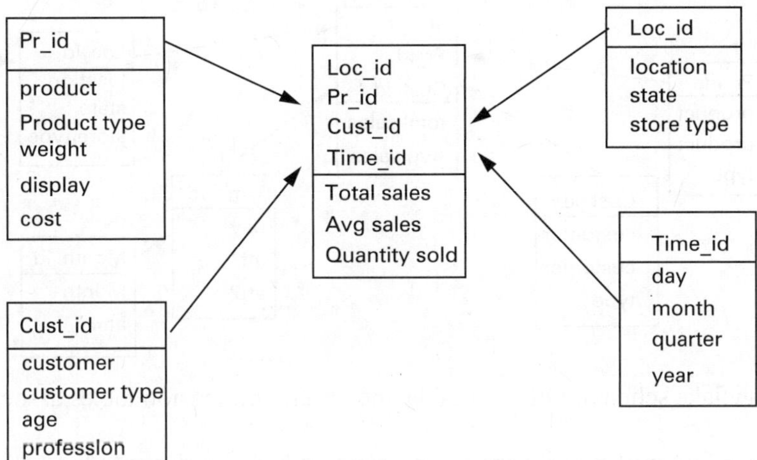

Figure 2.7 Star schema: One fact table and several dimension tables associated with it

on join operation is less. This makes it easier to formulate queries. A typical OLAP query easily maps to the star schema. The star schema can serve as a generic logical schema for all data warehouses. It is a symmetric structure not biased towards facilitating any particular query, which allows a designer to add new dimension tables with least disruption to the user's view of data.

Snowflake Schema

A snowflake schema is a star schema with fully normalised dimensions – it is so named because its shape is similar to a snowflake. Unlike the regular structure of the star schema, the 'arms' of the snowflake can grow to arbitrary lengths in each direction. A snowflake schema can be produced from a star schema by normalising each dimension table.

One step of normalising the dimension product (Table 2.24) results in following decomposition of schemas:

Product_id	Product	weight	display	cost

Product_id	Product	Product_type

Thus we have one dimension table describing individual *products,* referring to another dimension table containing the *product-type* (the next level in dimension hierarchy).

The process of decomposing dimension tables by normalisation to bring out explicitly the hierarchical structure of a dimension is termed *snowflaking*. Although snowflaking adds complexity to the data model, it supports complex queries and saves space but at the cost of increased query response time. It has been seen from studies that the performance of the snowflake schema depends upon the DBMS and OLAP tools used.

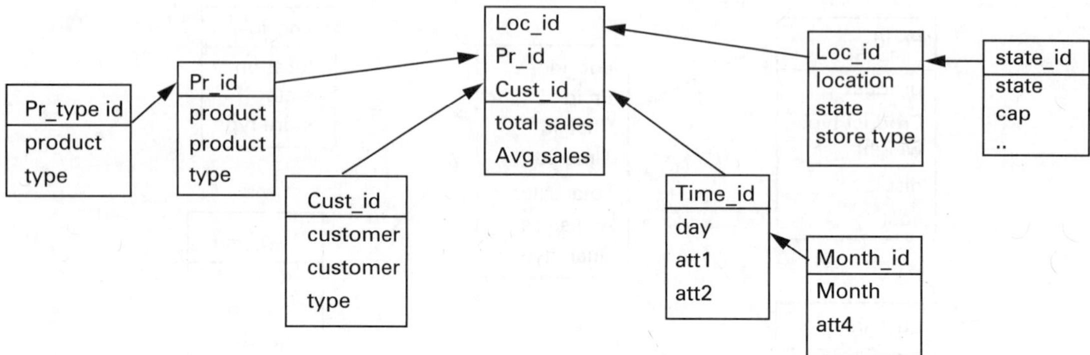

Figure 2.8 Snowflake schema: One fact table and several dimension tables associated with it

A star schema might suffer performance problems when the denormalised dimension table becomes very large. On the other hand, when after normalisation if the outer dimension tables are small in size, there are no significant join costs because the dimension tables can be permanently stored in a memory buffer. Some queries will not access data from the outer-level dimension tables. These queries execute effectively against the star schema containing smaller dimension tables. Therefore, under some circumstances, a snowflake schema is more efficient than a star schema.

Galaxy Schema

Sometime, it is necessary to have more than one fact table, and these fact tables may have some dimensions in common. Such a schema is called fact constellation or *constellation schema* or *galaxy schema*.

Let us consider a modification of the above example. In addition to sales data, we are interested also to store the data related to the manufacturing of these products. Thus we have two fact tables: one for *sales* and the other for *production*. Both the fact tables have *product* as a common dimension and *time* is a mandatory dimension for all fact tables. But *customer* dimension is specific to sales data, whereas it is not relevant to production data. This is an example of *galaxy schema*. It has more than one fact tables and the fact table share some common dimensions.

Starflake Schema

A star schema is a dimensional model with fully denormalised hierarchies, while a snowflake schema is a dimensional model with fully normalised hierarchies. However as in many design problems, the best solution is often a balance between the two extremes. A *starflake* schema represents a compromise between a star schema and a snowflake schema. It is a star schema selectively normalised (or 'snowflaked') to remove overlap between dimensions.

Overlap between dimensions is undesirable as it increases complexity of load processes and can lead to inconsistent query results if hierarchies become inconsistent. A starflake schema is a star schema in which shared hierarchical segments are separated out into *subdimension* tables. These represent the 'highest common factors' between dimensions.

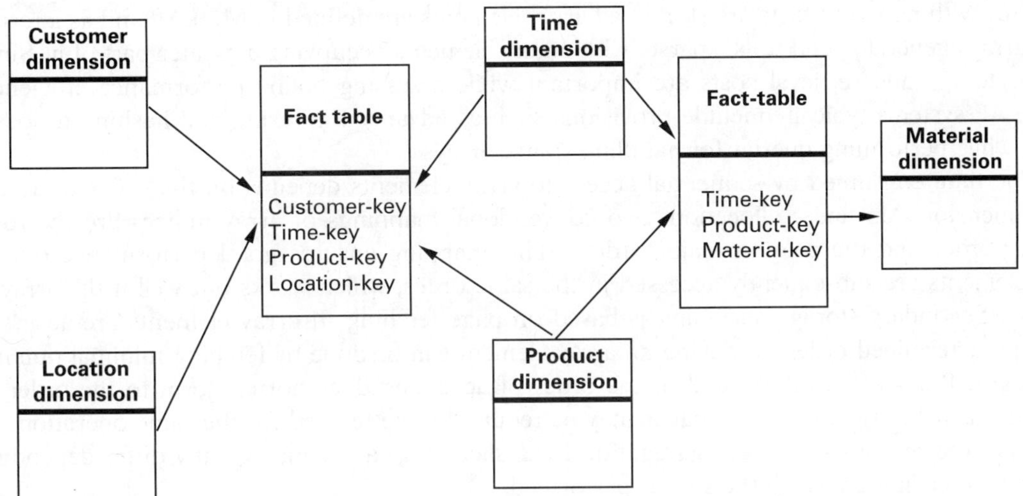

Figure 2.9 Galaxy schema: Two facts tables sharing some common dimensions

The above schemas of ROLAP represent different trade-offs between complexity and redundancy. For instance, the star schema is the simplest structure as it contains the least number of tables. However it also has the highest level of data redundancy, as the dimension tables all violate third normal form (3NF). This schema maximises understanding and simplifies queries to pairwise joins between tables. The snowflake schema is structurally the most complex and has more than five times as many tables as the star schema, requiring several multi-table joins to satisfy queries. The starflake schema has a slightly more complex structure than the star schema. However while it has redundancy within each table (the dimension tables and subdimension tables all violate 3NF), the redundancy between dimensions is eliminated, thereby reducing the possibility of inconsistency between them.

Please note that all these structures are semantically equivalent. They all contain the same data and support the same set of queries. It is only that in some structures the query processing is more complex than the others or the space requirement is more than the others.

2.12 MOLAP

MOLAP (multidimensional OLAP) stores data on disks in specialised multidimensional array structures. OLAP is performed on it relying on the random access capability of the arrays. Array elements are determined by dimension instances, and the fact data or measure value associated with each cell is usually stored in the corresponding array element. The data in Table 2.26 is stored as as a 3-dimensional array, where each array element contains triplet of values corresponding to *total-sales, avg-sales* and *quantity-sold*. An array element is referred to by the corresponding values of its four dimensions.

In MOLAP, the multidimensional array is usually stored in a linear allocation according to nested traversal of the axes in some predetermined order. But unlike ROLAP, where only records with non-zero facts are stored, all array elements are defined in MOLAP and as a result, the arrays generally tend to be sparse, with empty elements occupying a greater part of it. Since both storage and retrieval costs are important while assessing online performance efficiency, MOLAP systems typically include provisions such as advanced indexing and hashing to locate data while performing queries for handling sparse arrays.

The time consumed by sequential access to array elements depends on the order of access of dimensions. In linear allocation, two conventional mappings of array indices are the row-major order and the column-major orders. This mapping ensures good performance only if the elements are subsequently accessed in the same order, which works out well if the array is dense. Secondary storage accessing is based on page fetching. If array elements are accessed in a predetermined order, retrieving an array element can be done by fetching minimal number of pages. But, on the other hand, if the order of accessing does not conform to the order of storage, a very large number of pages may be required to be fetched for the same operation. As a result, the response time for aggregation for a slice of an array may greatly differ depending on the dimension on which the slice is performed.

For illustration, consider the following case. Let us assume a three-dimensional array of size 8×8×8 (Figure 2.10a). Let us assume that a single disk page can hold 8 array elements. The array elements are linearly ordered contiguously along the x axis. If we want to perform a slice operation to get a slice of the x–z plane, we have to fetch a maximum of 8 pages. On the other hand, if we perform a slice to get a two-dimensional array on the y–z plane, we will need 64 page fetching and similarly, a slicing along the x–y plane will require at most 8 page fetching. One can see that when the access order is favourable to the predetermined order of dimension used for storage, we need minimal number of page fetching for the slice operation.

Thus, retrieval performance depends on the ordering of dimensions along which the array elements are allocated in the secondary storage. This phenomenon is termed as *dimensional dependency* in OLAP. This is not a desirable feature for a data warehouse. To get over this difficulty, *chunking* of the cuboids is proposed.

CHUNKING

Chunking is a way of dividing an n-dimensional array into smaller hypercube-shaped subarrays called *chunks* and storing each chunk in a page in the secondary storage. Chunking is employed in order to moderate dimensional dependency, but care must be taken in making use the process of the same for achieving this objective. Chunks are also called *tiles*.

DEFINITION

A *chunk* of an n-dimensional array A is an n-dimensional hypercube-shaped subarray of A, the logical size of which is within a single disk page, with the elements of the chunk occupying contiguous disk spaces.

A chunk is defined by the index of values along each dimension. An OLAP query retrieves either the entire array or a subarray, in which case for all the arrays that overlap the chunks, query results are retrieved. If we divide the cube of Fig. 2.10b into 64 chunks of size 2×2×2, we get access to 16 disk pages for slicing along any of the dimension pairs. Figure 2.10a corresponds to chunk size 1×8.

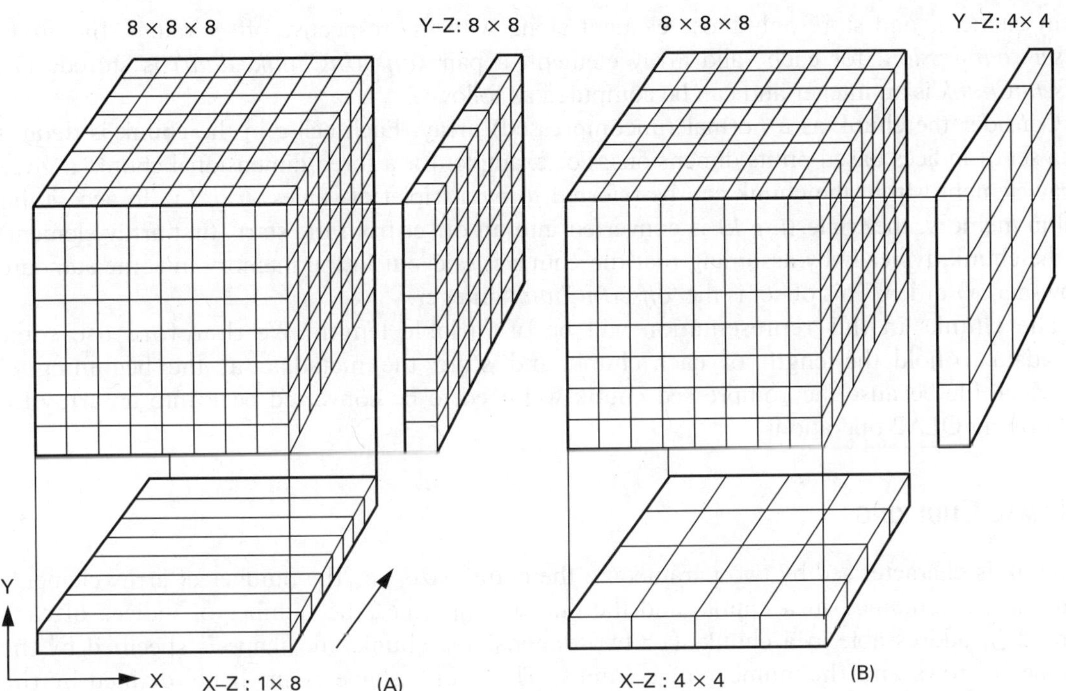

Figure 2.10a Chunk size 8×1×1

Figure 2.10b Chunk size 4×4×4

Thus, rather than map the array elements directly onto consecutive linear storage in the secondary memory, it is the chunks that are mapped onto storage and, within each chunk, the array elements are laid out by some conventional technique such as row-major or column-major.

There are many techniques proposed for allocating chunks to disk storage. These include, besides the conventional row-major or column-major schemes, mapping functions of space filling curves or the B^+-tree kind of indexing. Space-filling curve mappings such as Z-ordering, Morton sequence, Hilbert, or Gray-coded curve, order the chunks in such a way that the spatial locality is preserved as much as possible within the linearised disk abstraction. The property of preserving spatial locality does not take advantage of the disk characteristics—access along each dimension has (nearly) identical cost. The elements contained in each chunk can be stored either in row-major order or column-major order, or in general, any linear allocation scheme.

One of the major disadvantages of MOLAP is that in the multidimensional array, a large number of unimportant cells (cells having measure value zero) are stored. The array is, in general, therefore very sparse. The way to overcome this disadvantage is to compress the array. We will now look at how to compress arrays after it has undergone the process of chunking.

A chunk is said to be *dense* if it has more than 40% valid (non-zero valued) array elements. A chunk which is not dense is a *sparse* chunk, with most of the space in it devoted to invalid cells. Storing such an array without compression is wasteful. *Chunk-offset compression is* one of the techniques to compress sparse chunks. The main idea behind this scheme is to identify the valid array elements and store only those element along with the respective offset values. In *chunk-offset compression*, for each valid array element, a pair (*offsetInChunk, data*) is stored. The *offsetlnChunk* is an integer and can be computed as follows.

Consider the chunk as a normal (uncompressed) array. Each cell *c* in the chunk is defined by a set of indices based on its dimensions. For example, for a three-dimensional chunk, a given array element within the chunk can be referred to by a triplet of values, (*i, j, k*). To access this cell in memory, the triple *(i, j, k)* is converted into an offset from the start (first array element) of the chunk, typically by assuming that the chunk is laid out in the memory in some standard (row-major) order. This offset is the '*offsetInChunk*' integer.

The chunks in this representation will be of variable length. We therefore use some metadata to hold the length of each chunk and store the metadata at the beginning of the data file because the compressed chunk will need to be converted back into an array for performing OLAP operations.

Optimal Chunking

A chunk is characterised by two parameters: the chunk size, i.e., the number of array elements that can be contained in a chunk, and the chunk shape, i.e., the number of indices of each dimension addressable in a chunk. For two-dimensional chunks the shape is specified by the number of rows and the number of columns. The chunk shape is implicitly defined by the chunk size. Recalling from the definition of a chunk, we know that the chunk size is limited by the size of a page in the disk. Large chunk sizes may cause unnecessary data to be read for queries with a small result set, while small chunk sizes may necessitate many more *fetch* operations to retrieve all the relevant chunks required for satisfying a query with a bigger result set. Thus, chunk shape becomes an important parameter for measuring the performance of OLAP operations. The expected number of chunks retrieved by queries also becomes an important metric of performance; this in turn is dependent on the appropriate choice of chunk shape and chunk size.

2.13 Cube Computation

Conceptually, a *full cube* includes all the possible multidimensional groupings and is an invaluable tool for generating fast query response. Cube computation provides users with a convenient way to discover insights from data by computing aggregate measures over all possible groups. This involves the pre-computing of all cuboids of the lattice from the base cuboid. A complex OLAP query, which is essentially a combination of basic operations such as slice, dice, roll-up and drill-down, can be processed more efficiently (faster) if the appropriate cuboid is *a priori* computed. One possible approach to cube computing is to pre-compute all the cuboids and look up the materialised cuboids in response to a query. The other extreme would be to compute on the fly the cuboid that is best suited to answer the query. The middle path would be to pre-compute a subset of cuboids and compute on the fly any other cuboid that may be necessary.

As mentioned earlier, these three approaches are called *full materialisation, no materialisation* or *partial materialisation*, respectively. In the case of partial materialisation, the issue is to select an appropriate subset of the matter of cuboids for materialisation. The aspect of reducing the total workload of aggregation for reducing the overhead on space and time, is a matter of prime concern to cube computation. Called cubing techniques, many studies have been devoted to designing efficient techniques for the same. Several commercial database software include computation of the cube, called CUBE operation, as one of the appended facilities on the offer.

In cube computation, sets of tuples are taken in as input and computed with or without some auxiliary data structure to materialise the aggregated results for cells in all cuboids. A straightforward representation of the cube is to enumerate all cells. This results in a size usually much larger than that of input dataset, since a table with n-dimensions results in 2^n cuboids. The main challenge is to compute the cuboids with limited space and time.

In the following sections we will learn about some of the novel techniques of cube computation. We will start with MultiWay (also termed as ArrayCube) algorithm that computes a cube when the data is stored as a multidimensional array. Next, we will learn about BUC, yet another interesting approach to cube computation. While MultiWay computes the cuboid by moving from the base cuboid to the apex cuboid (called top-down approach), BUC works in a bottom-up manner by computing first a cuboid of coarser granularity and then moving to the finer granularity. StarCubing is another technique which involves a combination of bottom-up as well as top-down approaches.

We start with the generic categorisation of these algorithms. There are two approaches of reducing the cube size—*lossless* and *lossy*. In lossless approach the size of the cube is reduced without losing any information content, while in lossy approach, the cube size is reduced by eliminating some unimportant information.

The lossless approaches can be further classified into four categories. The first is one where neither the input nor the output is compressed. In this category, we discuss two techniques, *MultiWay* and *BUC,* which scan the dataset on disk and generate all cells one by one without compressing either the base table or the resulting cube. In the second category, *StarCubing* (its earlier version being H-cubing), a compressed structure of input dataset in a specialised structure called Star-tree or H-tree is used. The dataset is compressed by prefix sharing, to be kept in memory. However, the resulting cube is not compressed and StarCubing generates cells of all cuboids, one by one. The third category of approach scans the input dataset which is not compressed to generate a compressed cube. *Dwarf,* the most influential method in this category, compresses *full cube* in a tree-like data structure in memory by utilising prefix-sharing and suffix coalescing. Some algorithms in this category condense the cube size by coalescing cells with identical aggregation values. Other popular techniques under this category are *Quotient Cube* and *Coalesced Cube*. The fourth category of techniques uses special structures to compress the input data, resulting in a compressed cube. In this category, *range-cubing* generates a compressed data cube which is both semantic-and format-preserving. It also uses compressed input base table for computation.

In all these four categories, whenever compression is used it is used in a lossless fashion without losing any content of the input and output data.

The lossy approach includes computations called *Iceberg Cube* and *Skyline Cube*. In lossy technique the resulting cube is compressed by ignoring some unimportant portion of the information. In real-life applications, it is observed that many of the cuboids are sparse. In other words, many of the cells of a cuboid do not contain any relevant information. For example, we may not have any sales for some months of a year. Thus, though there are 12 cells in a cuboid for each year, every city, and for every product, many of these cells may not have any data. In that case, it is appropriate to store only those cells that contains non-zero data, or more generally, meaningful data in some sense or the other. Thus, whether it is full materialisation or partial, whenever we materialise a cuboid, we only compute those cells of the cuboid that have relevant data. The definition of relevance may vary for different techniques. We define below two such concepts.

ICEBERG CUBE

A cube containing only cells that satisfy an aggregate constraint called *iceberg constraint* is called an *iceberg cube*. It is called iceberg because by materialising only a fraction of the cells in a data cube, the result is seen as being the tip of the iceberg, where the iceberg is the potential full cube including all the cells. The *iceberg-cubing* problem is to compute all group-by partitions for every combination of the grouping attributes that satisfy an aggregate selection condition. In other words, choose tuples that have an aggregate exceeding some minimum support. The minimum threshold is called the minimum support threshold, or minimum support (*minsup*, for short).

SKYCUBE

A skyline operator on a cuboid identifies cells which are not dominated by any other cell in the cuboid. A cube containing all cells satisfying the *skyline condition* is termed as *Skycube*.

EXAMPLE

Consider the base data or the base cuboid of Table 2.27.

Table 2.27

Transaction	A	B	C	M
t_1	0	1	1	50
t_2	1	1	1	100
t_3	2	3	1	60
t_4	4	5	1	70
t_5	6	5	2	80
t_6	8	3	2	40

The full cube contains the following tuples (Table 2.28). The iceberg cube with min sup = 80 is given in Table 2.29. The skycube is given in Table 2.30. Domination means higher numeric value.

In the following section, we will discuss some of the important cubing algorithms.

Table 2.28 Full cube

	A	B	C	M
t_{35}	ALL	ALL	ALL	400
t_{29}	0	ALL	ALL	50
t_{30}	1	ALL	ALL	100
t_{31}	2	ALL	ALL	60
t_{32}	4	ALL	ALL	70
t_{33}	6	ALL	ALL	80
t_{26}	ALL	1	ALL	150
t_{27}	ALL	3	ALL	100
t_{28}	ALL	5	ALL	150
t_5	6	5	2	80
t_6	8	3	2	40
t_{24}	ALL	ALL	1	280
t_{25}	ALL	ALL	2	120
t_{18}	0	1	ALL	50
t_{19}	1	1	ALL	100
t_{20}	2	3	ALL	60
t_{21}	4	5	ALL	70
t_{22}	6	5	ALL	80
t_{23}	8	3	ALL	40
t_{13}	0	ALL	1	50
t_{14}	1	ALL	1	100
t_{15}	2	ALL	1	60
t_{16}	4	ALL	1	70
t_{17}	6	ALL	1	80
t_{12}	8	ALL	2	40
t_7	ALL	1	1	150
t_8	ALL	3	1	60
t_9	ALL	5	1	70
t_{10}	ALL	5	2	80
t_{11}	ALL	3	2	40
t_1	0	1	1	50
t_2	1	1	1	100
t_3	2	3	1	60
t_4	4	5	1	70

2.14 Multiway Simultaneous Aggregation (ArrayCube)

Let us assume that the multidimensional array is represented as a chunked array (not necessarily compressed). This method is also known by the name ArrayCube [Harinarayan, 96]. The main idea of the algorithm is given below. For notational convenience, let us use the notation $D_1D_2D_3 \ldots D_k(j)$ to denote chunks j of cuboid $D_1D_2D_3 \ldots D_k$.

We fetch one chunk of the base cuboid at a time and after computing the aggregation of data in the current chunk, this chunk is written back and the next chunk is fetched. When the data in the current chunk is aggregated in all dimensions, the aggregated values are used to update the chunks of the intermediate cuboids. Hence it becomes necessary to make available those chunks of intermediate cuboids which require updating due to the aggregation of the current chunk. This implies that whenever a chunk of the base cuboid is read, we determine the set of relevant chunks of intermediate cuboids. These chunks may already be available or may need to be fetched. Note that the current chunk is not the only chunk that is required for aggregation of

Table 2.29 Iceberg cube

	A	B	C	M
t_{35}	ALL	ALL	ALL	400
t_{30}	1	ALL	ALL	100
t_{35}	6	ALL	ALL	80
t_{26}	ALL	1	ALL	150
t_{27}	ALL	3	ALL	100
t_{28}	ALL	5	ALL	150
t_{24}	ALL	ALL	1	280
t_{25}	ALL	ALL	2	120
t_{22}	6	5	ALL	80
t_{14}	1	ALL	1	100
t_{17}	6	ALL	2	80
t_7	ALL	1	1	150
t_{10}	ALL	5	2	80
t_2	1	1	1	100
t_5	6	5	2	80

Table 2.30 Skycube

	A	B	C	M
t_{35}	ALL	ALL	ALL	400
	8	ALL	ALL	40
t_{28}	ALL	5	ALL	150
t_{25}	ALL	ALL	2	120
t_{22}	6	5	ALL	80
t_{23}	8	3	ALL	40
t_{12}	8	ALL	2	40
t_{10}	ALL	5	2	80
t_5	6	5	2	80
t_6	8	3	2	40

any chunk of the intermediate cuboid. We may need many chunks to be read for the complete computation of a chunk of an intermediate cuboid. Once fetched, the chunk of any intermediate cuboid remains in the main working memory until it is fully computed. It is written back only after all its cells are fully aggregated. Thus, MultiWay works on repeated execution of the following generic steps.

- Read a chunk of the base cuboid (chunks are read in a specific order)
- Determine the set of relevant chunks of the intermediate cuboids.
- Determine if any relevant chunk is not fetched earlier, and then fetch this chunk.
- Aggregate the values in each dimension of the current chunk.
- Update the aggregate of relevant chunks.
- If any chunk is now completely aggregated, write the chunk back to the disk.

Consider a 3-dimensional base multidimensional array stored as 8 chunks (Figure 2.11). Its dimensions are in the order, *X*, *Y* and *Z*. In Figure 2.11, the chunks are numbered according to the reading order. Let us assume that we use the base cuboid *XYZ* to simultaneously compute the cuboids, *XY*, *XZ*, and *YZ*. First we read chunk 1 of *XYZ*, i.e., *XYZ*(1) (a 3-dimensional chunk). When we aggregate the cells of this chunk along the *X* dimension, we get values that

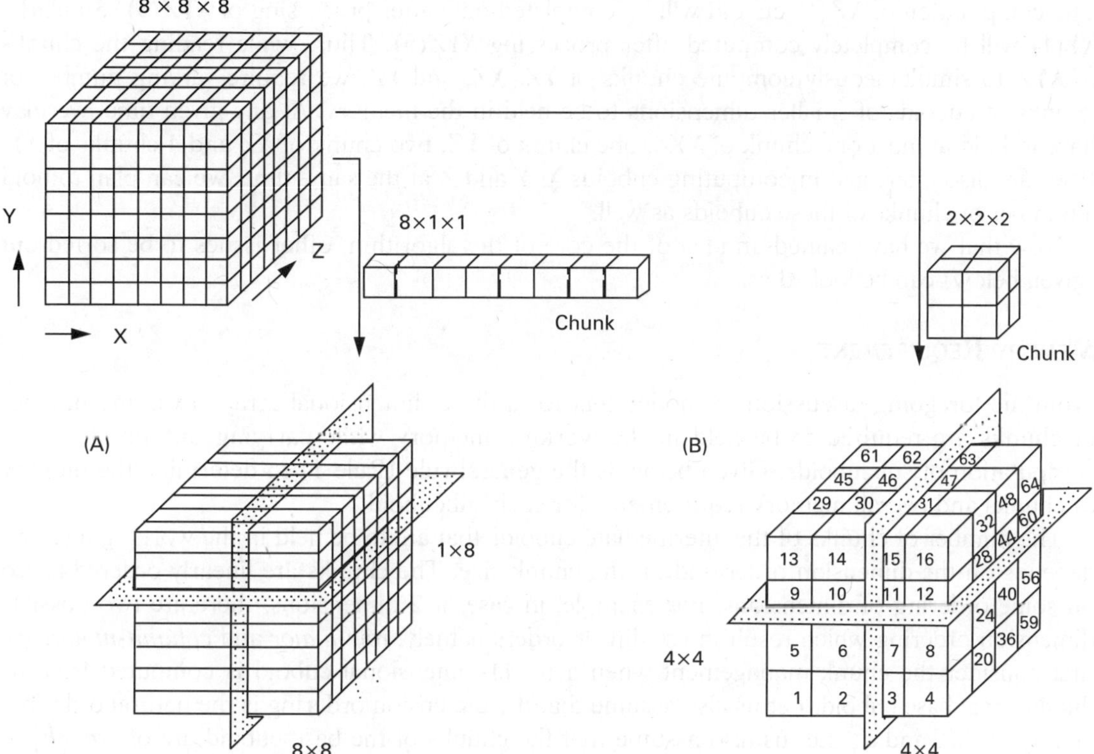

Figure 2.11

are relevant to the cells of the *YZ* cuboid. The relevant cells are in *YZ*(1). We simultaneously aggregate in all three dimensions, *X*, *Y* and *Z*, individually, and update these values in the corresponding 3-dimensional chunks, *YZ*(1), *XZ*(1) and *XY*(1).

Note that the computation of *YZ*(1) is not yet complete at this stage because *YZ*(1) can be completely computed by aggregating chunks *XYZ*(1) and *XYZ*(2).

XYZ(1) is written back (the necessary aggregation having been completed) and *XYZ*(2) is read into the memory. Meanwhile, *YZ*(1), *XZ*(1) and *XY*(1) cuboids are retained in the working memory. We aggregate *XYZ*(2) in a similar manner in all the three dimensions; these aggregated values are relevant to cells in chunks *YZ*(1), *XZ*(2), and *XY*(2). Thus, at this stage chunks which are available in the working memory are *XYZ*(2) *YZ*(1), *XZ*(1), *XZ*(2), *XY*(1) and *XY*(2). After aggregating, we write back *XYZ*(2) and also chunk *YZ*(1). We read *XYZ*(3) into memory. While aggregating *XYZ*(3), we need chunks *YZ*(2), *XZ*(1) and *XY*(3) to be available. Hence, we have the following chunks in the working memory.

- *XYZ*(3) of *XYZ* cuboid
- *YZ*(2) of *YZ* cuboid
- *XZ*(1), and *XZ*(2) of *XZ* cuboid
- *XY*(1), *XY*(2) and *XY*(3) of *XY* cuboid

The computation of $XZ(1)$ cuboid will be completed only after processing of $XYZ(3)$. Similarly, $XY(1)$ will be completely computed after processing $XYZ(5)$. Thus, while reading the chunks of *XYZ* to simultaneously compute chunks of *YZ*, *XZ*, and *YZ*, we require varying number of chunks of cuboids of smaller dimensions to be held in the memory. At any given time, we may have to hold at most one chunk of *XYZ*, one chunk of *YZ*, two chunk of *XZ* and 4 chunks of *XY*. If we are also interested in computing cuboids *X*, *Y* and *Z* at the same time, we can plan to hold a number of chunks of these cuboids as well.

Now that we have gained an idea of the core of the algorithm, other issues to be sorted out (given below) can be looked at.

Memory Requirement

From the foregoing discussion we notice that for a three-dimensional array, a varying number of chunks are required to be held in the working memory while carrying out simultaneous computation of subcuboids. Given below is the general rule (Rule 1) to determine the number of chunks and overall memory requirements for each subcuboid.

The number of chunks of the intermediate cuboids that are to be held in the working memory depends on the dimension order and on the chunk size. The chunks are linearly ordered based on some ordering of dimensions. For example, in case of 2 dimensions, there are two possible dimension ordering which result in two linear orders namely, *row-major* and *column-major*. We first consider the chunk management when a $(n–1)$-dimensional cuboid is computed from n-dimensional base cuboid. Let us also assume that the dimension ordering is the natural ordering, i.e., d_1, d_2, ..., and d_n. Let us also assume that the chunks of the base cuboid are of size $ch_1 \times ch_2 \times ... \times ch_n$. The chunks of any intermediate cuboid are assumed to be projections of chunks of base cuboids on the respective dimensions. Assume that the $(n–1)$-dimensional cuboid that is to be computed from the base cuboid has dimensions d_{j1}, d_{j2}, ..., $d_{j(n-1)}$. These dimensions are also ordered in the same order as the dimensions of the base cuboid. Assume that $d_{j1}d_{j2} \ldots d_{j(n-1)}$ and $d_1d_2, \ldots d_n$ have have p common prefix, (first p common dimensions). In the above example, the based cuboid XYZ and the intermediate cuboid XZ has one prefix, common whereas the intermediate cuboid YZ has no common prefix with XYZ.

Rule 1

While computing intermediate cuboid d_{j1}, d_{j2}, ..., $d_{j(n-1)}$ from the base cuboid $d_1d_2 \ldots d_n$, where there are p common prefixes, the maximum number of chunks required to be maintained in memory is given by

$$\frac{(|d_1| \times |d_2| \times \ldots \times |d_p|) \times ch_{j(p+1)} \times ch_{j(p+2)} \times \ldots \times chj(n-1)}{ch_{j1} \times ch_{j2} \times \ldots \times ch_{j(n-1)}}$$

where $|d_1|$ is the domain size of dimension d_j.

For example, assume that the base cuboid *XYZ* is of 4×4×4 size, and two-dimensional cuboids have chunks of size 2×2. To compute cuboid *XZ* from the array *XYZ* requires, by the above rule, at most $(d_x \times ch_z)/(ch_x \times ch_z) = 2$ chunks to be held in the working memory at any given time.

The next issue is to determine whether the set of cuboids of smaller dimensions are to be computed simultaneously from a given cuboid, i.e., should we calculate all the cuboids from the base cuboid, or should we work out a precedence relation such that we calculate some set of subcuboids from the base cuboid and then use these to compute another set of subcuboids and so on. The most naive approach would be to compute all of the aggregates from the initial array. But the main constraint in doing so would be the total requirement of memory for holding all the relevant chunks of all subcuboids. If there is no restriction of memory availability, we can very well calculate all cuboids simultaneously. Otherwise, we may have to schedule the cuboids in some precedence order for aggregation. In order to determine the minimum memory requirement to compute all cuboids simultaneously, we embed a tree on the lattice of cuboids. We view the lattice as a graph, and each edge with a numeric weight indicates the memory requirement (using the above rule) for computing a subcuboid from a given cuboid connected by an edge in the lattice. For this weighted graph, we compute the minimum weight spanning tree and call it the MMST (minimum memory spanning tree).

Minimum Memory Spanning Tree (MMST)

A minimum memory spanning tree is a spanning tree of the lattice of cuboids with its root as base cuboid (d_1, ..., d_n) and with associated order of dimensions (d_{j1}, ..., d_{jn}) such that the total memory requirement is minimum.

MMST has $n + 1$ levels, with the root as the base cuboid at level n. Any node N at level i below the level n can be computed from nodes one level above and whose dimensions contain the dimensions of node N. There can be more than one node from which node N can be computed, but MMST selects the node that requires minimum memory according to Rule 1. The prefix of the parent node contained in node N has the minimum length. So, the MMST for a given dimension order is minimum in terms of the total memory requirement for that dimension order. If node N contains the minimum prefix for several upper level nodes, we use the size of those nodes to break the tie and choose the node with the minimum size as the parent of node N.

Dimension Order

Due to dimensional dependency, the appropriate choice of the access sequence of the chunks is very important. The sequence in which the chunks are read depends on the ordering of the dimension. One can see that the same lattice yields two different MMST, each one corresponding to a different dimension order, and as a result the minimum memory requirement drastically varies. For illustration, consider a four-dimensional array *ABCD*, which has 10×10×10×10 chunks, with the dimension sizes of *A*, *B*, *C*, and *D* being 10, 100, 1000, and 10000, respectively. The MMST for (*D*, *B*, *C*, *A*) and for (*A*, *B*, *C*, *D*) are not only different, their memory requirement are drastically different as well. If we order the dimensions as *DBCA*, we would require approximately 4 GB of memory, whereas for the order *ABCD* we require only 4 MB (Figure 2.12a and 2.12b).

A natural question that comes to mind is whether there is some optimal ordering among the possible ones. It is observed that if we arrange the dimensions in the increasing order of their size, we get a minimum memory requirement.

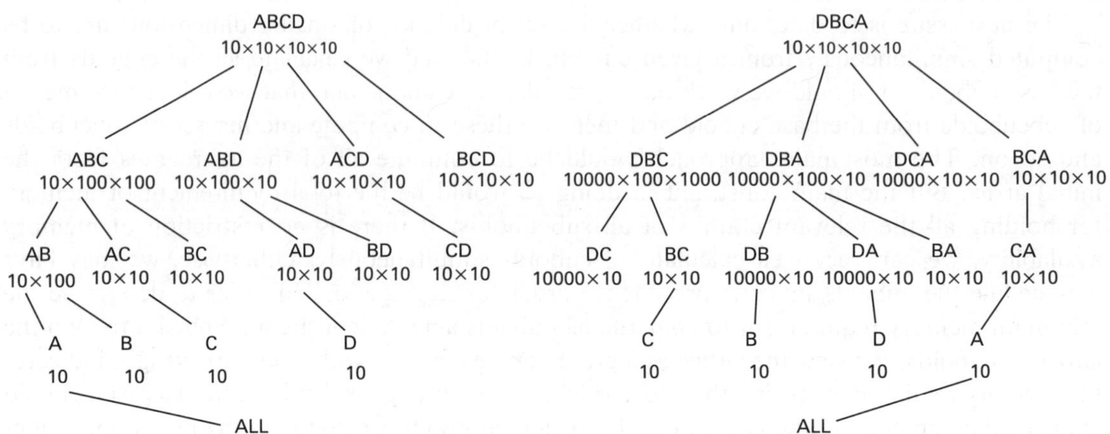

Figure 2.12 (a) MMST with dimension order *ABCD* (b) MMST with dimension ordering *DBCA* (Source: Harinarayan et. al, 1996)

Let us now describe the MultiWay algorithm step by step.

Step 1. Order the dimensions in increasing order of dimension size.

Step 2. Compute MMST to determine the total memory requirement.

Step 3.

a. **Single pass:** If the total memory required for entire computation is less than the available memory, compute all subcuboids from the base cuboid by maintaining appropriate number of chunks for all subcuboids.

b. **Multiple pass:** Else, MMST sequence can be followed level-by-level for a multiple-pass method.

MultiWay algorithm is one of the first major cubing algorithms to be formulated. It is also know by the name ArrayCube. Subsequent algorithms that were formulated later do not rely so heavily on array structure. These were designed mostly for the ROLAP environment.

At this stage, it is necessary to learn a little more about the spanning trees of the lattice of cuboids. We can see that the lattice can be viewed as a graph, where each individual cuboid is a node, and there is an edge connecting two nodes if one cuboid is obtained from the other through a single roll-up (or drill-down) step. Two kinds of spanning trees exist, namely, top-down and bottom-up trees. In top-down tree, the base cuboid is the root and the apex cuboid appears as a leaf-node. In bottom-up spanning tree, the apex cuboid is the root node and the base cuboid appears as one of the leaf-nodes.

2.15 BUC - Bottom-Up Cubing Algorithm

BUC, or Bottom-Up Cube computation, works in an order reverse to the MultiWay algorithm in that the order in which the cuboids are generated is in a bottom-up fashion as opposed to the top-down approach of the MultiWay technique of computing cuboids. Figure 2.13 shows the sequence in which the cuboids are computed, and the numbers indicate the order in which BUC generates cuboids. An advantage of using bottom-up computation is that when the aggregation function is anti monotone, the algorithm efficiently computes the iceberg cube.

Assume that P is the base cuboid with dimension set $S = \{D_1, D_2, ..., D_n\}$, and any cuboid is referred to by a subset of the dimensions. Let us denote S_i as $D_i D_{i+1}...D_n$.

```
INITIALISATION
        S0 = D1D2 ... Dn
        P = base tuple set
        Curr-cuboid = ALL
BUC(P, S, curr-cuboid)

Procedure BUC

BUC(P, S, curr_cuboid)
    aggregate P
    write a tuple to cuboid curr_cuboid
        If curr_cuboid = ALL then curr-cuboid ← ∅
    do while S ≠∅
        for each i; such that Di ∈ S
        S ← S \ {Di}
        curr_cuboid ← curr_cuboid ∪{Di}
        let C = cardinality[Di];
        partition P on distinct values of Di as Pi1, Pi2, ..., PiC;
          do for each partition Pij
            BUC(Pij, Si+1, curr_cuboid)
          end do
        curr_cuboid ← curr_cuboid \ { Di }
        S ← S ∪{ Di }
      end for
```

To illustrate the working of BUC, consider the following example (Table 2.31).

The algorithm first computes the aggregate of all tuples to get the apex cuboid and writes a tuple as given in Table 2.32.

In the next step, the data is partitioned on one dimension, say dimension A. The domain of dimension A is $\{a_1, a_2, a_3, a_4\}$, and we get four partitions of the data as $\{t_1, t_2, t_3\}$, $\{t_4, t_5, t_6, t_7\}$, $\{t_8, t_{10}\}$, and $\{t_9, t_{11}, t_{12}\}$, for values $a_1 = 0$, $a_2 = 1$, $a_3 = 2$ and $a_4 = 3$, respectively. BUC takes each of these four partitions one by one for recursion. When it takes the first partition, it aggregates the summary value and writes a tuple to cuboid A as given in Table 2.33.

In the next level of recursion, BUC takes, say, dimension B, with the domain B being $\{b_1, b_2, b_3\}$. At this stage the partition $\{t_1, t_2, t_3\}$ is partitioned further on dimension B to get three subpartitions as $\{t_1\}$, $\{t_2\}$ and $\{t_3\}$ for three distinct values, b_1, b_2, and b_3 of B. It aggregates and writes a tuple for each of the partitions, (a_1, b_1), (a_1, b_2), (a_1, b_3), for the AB cuboid. We get the following table (Table 2.34) as part of the AB cuboid. Note that AB cuboid is not fully computed yet; it will be completed when recursion backtracks and completes all the four partitions.

Table 2.31 Base cuboid

Transaction	A	B	C	D	M
t_1	0	4	0	4	10
t_2	0	3	1	8	20
t_3	0	2	1	4	10
t_4	1	4	0	8	20
t_5	1	2	1	8	30
t_6	1	3	0	8	20
t_7	1	1	0	4	40
t_8	2	4	1	8	50
t_9	3	1	0	8	10
t_{10}	2	3	1	4	40
t_{11}	3	4	0	4	30
t_{12}	3	3	1	4	10

Table 2.32 Apex cuboid

A	B	C	D	M
ALL	ALL	ALL	ALL	290

Table 2.33 Cuboid *A*

A	B	C	D	M
0	ALL	ALL	ALL	40

Table 2.34

A	B	C	D	M
0	4	ALL	ALL	10
0	3	ALL	ALL	20
0	2	ALL	ALL	10

The algorithm recurses on the $(a_1; b_1)$ partition to get partitions for different and distinct values of the next dimension in order, say *C*. For each partition, it writes *a* tuple in *ABC* cuboid. Then BUC takes $(a_1; b_1; c_1)$, to get $(a_1; b_1; c_1; d_1)$, and a tuple is written for the *ABCD* cuboids. At this stage, it returns to recurse again on the $(a_1; b_1; c_1; d_2)$ partition. Once all the distinct values of dimension *D* are covered during recursion, BUC recurses on the $(a_1; b_1; c_2)$ partition. When all values of the domain of *C* are completed, it returns to partition $(a_1; b_2)$ and so on.

During recursion, if the algorithm encounters a partition with single tuple, then the recursion becomes trivial and can be skipped. Thus, if at any stage $|P| = 1$, an optimising step can stop the recursion and the tuples can be directly written to all cuboids to be generated from this stage.

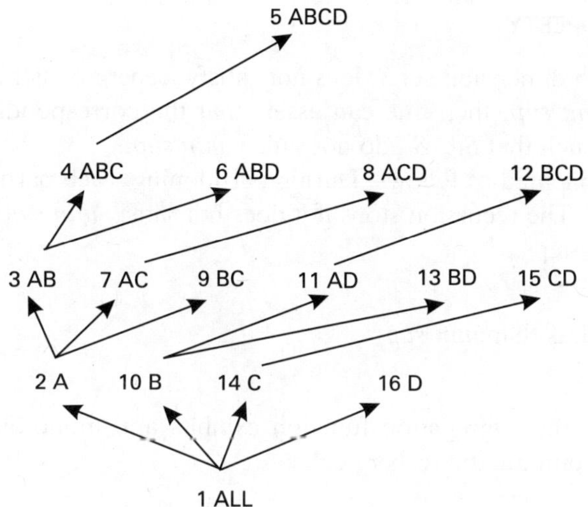

Figure 2.13 BUC processing tree (numbers indicate the order of deriving the cuboids)

In the example above, since we get a single tuple for partition (a_1; b_1), we know that even if the algorithm recurses on C and D, there will not be any change in the partitions. Hence, as a result we get trivially the following partitions (Table 2.35). Figure 2.13 shows the order in which nodes of the lattice are generated.

Table 2.35

A	B	C	D	M
0	4	0	ALL	10
0	3	1	ALL	20
0	2	1	ALL	10
0	4	0	4	10
0	3	1	8	20
0	2	1	4	10

Dimension Ordering

The performance of BUC is sensitive to the ordering of the dimensions. The goal of BUC is to prune as early as possible, i.e., find partitions that have only one tuple. For the best performance, the most discriminating dimensions should be used first. As in the case of MultiWay algorithm, ordering the dimensions in the increasing order of cardinality is a good heuristic.

Iceberg-cube With BUC

BUC's bottom-up approach comes handy for iceberg computation if the measure exhibits anti-monotone property. Details can be found in [Beyer et al , 1996] and [Fang et al, 1998].

Anti-Monotone Property

If a cell in a cuboid with dimension set S does not satisfy iceberg constraint, i.e., its aggregated measure is less than *min sup*, then one can assert that the corresponding cells in the cuboid with dimension set S', such that $S \subseteq S'$, do not satisfy *min sup*.

In BUC this is implemented as follows. During partitioning, each partition's measure value is compared with *min sup*. The recursion stops if it does not satisfy *min sup*. The line 'aggregate *P*' is replaced by following steps.

"aggregate *P*;

if aggregate value is less than *min sup*

return end if"

Please note that unless the aggregation function exhibits anti-monotone property, the above steps cannot correctly compute the Iceberg cube.

2.16 Condensed Cube

The concept of condensed cube by Wang et al is based on two key ideas namely, *base single tuple* compression and *projected single tuple* compression, which come from the observation that a number of partitions (cells) contain only one tuple in the base table. It is easy to notice that there are a large number of partitions that contain only one base tuple.

Given a set of dimension attributes, $SD \subseteq \{D_1, D_2, \ldots, D_n\}$, if r is the only tuple in a partition when the base dataset is partitioned on SD, we say tuple r is a *base single tuple* on SD, and SD is called the *single dimensions* of r.

Let us consider one example (Table 2.27). Consider $SD = \{B\}$. When the base relation (base cuboid) is partition on $\{B\}$, we get three partitions, $\{t_1, t_2\}$, $\{t_3, t_6\}$ and $\{t_4, t_5\}$, for the three distinct values in the domain of B. None of these partitions contains a single tuple. On the other hand, if we partition on $SD = \{B, C\}$, we get $\{t_1, t_2\}$, $\{t_3\}$, $\{t_4\}$, $\{t_5\}$ and $\{t_6\}$. $\{t_3\}$, $\{t_4\}$, $\{t_5\}$ and $\{t_6\}$ are called single base tuples with respect to dimension set $\{B, C\}$. Please note that if a tuple r is a base single tuple on SD, then r is also a single tuple on any superset of SD. Hence, $\{t_3\}$ is also a base single tuple with respect to the dimension set $\{A, B, C\}$. To represent the fact that a tuple can be a base single tuple on different set of dimensions, we associate with each base single tuple a set of *SD*s, called *SDSET*, rather than a single *SD*. It is easy to see that if r is a *base single tuple* (BST) on dimension sets *SDSET*, then cube tuples generated from r in all cuboids on $SD_i \in SDSET$ have the same aggregation value. Thus the cube can be efficiently stored, without loss of any information, by avoiding repetition of single tuples for all cuboids in *SDSET* and storing it only once. This is possible if we append the tuples with an additional field indicating the respective *SDSET*. It is not hard to expand the condense cube to get the full cube. For the base cuboid given in Table 2.27, the condensed cube is depicted in Table 2.36.

The BUC algorithm can be trivially modified so that it yields the condensed cube instead of the full cube. The main idea of such modification is to check whether a partition is the single tuple, and then write the tuple along with its *SDSET*.

Table 2.36 Condensed cube

	A	B	C	M	SDSET
	ALL	ALL	ALL	400	
	ALL	3	ALL	100	B
	ALL	5	ALL	150	B
	ALL	ALL	1	280	C
	ALL	ALL	2	120	C
	ALL	1	1	150	BC, B
BSt_1	0	1	1	50	ABC, AC, AB, A
BSt_2	1	1	1	100	ABC, AC, AB, A
BSt_3	2	3	1	60	ABC, BC, AC, AB, A
BSt_4	4	5	1	70	ABC, BC, AC, AB, A
BSt_5	6	5	2	80	ABC, BC, AC, AB, A
BSt_6	8	3	2	40	ABC, BC, AC, AB, A

2.17 COALESCING

Suffix redundancy occurs when a set of tuples contributes exactly the same aggregates to different partitions. The operation that eliminates suffix redundancies is called coalescing. The resulting cube is called a *coalesced cube* and we refer to its tuples as *coalesced tuples*.

The concept of coalescing is yet another novel process for condensing the full cube. In this category, there are several proposals of condensation such as Coalesced Cube, Quotient Cube and Dwarf. We will learn here the basic concepts of coalescing.

It is the elimination of suffix redundancies that dramatically condense the exponential growth of high dimensional full cubes, without any loss in precision. Consider the base data as given in Table 2.36. The coalescing process results in the following table (Table 2.37). The cube has 30 tuples, whereas the coalesced cube has 10 tuples. The redundancy of the cube is eliminated by storing the coalesced areas just once. For example, the aggregate 100 appears in total of five tuples, (ALL, 3, ALL), (1, ALL, ALL), (1, 1, ALL), (1, ALL, 1), and (1, 1, 1) in the cube and it is coalesced in just one tuple. For the running example (Table 2.27), the coalesced cube is the following (Table 2.37).

2.18 DWARF

Dwarf [Sismanis, 2002] is a highly compressed directed acyclic graph structure for computing, storing, and querying data cubes. It identifies and eliminates prefix and suffix redundancies and introduces dramatic gains on storage and computational requirements of data cubes. The suffix and prefix redundancies are automatically detected *a priori*, prior to its computation, which results in substantial computational savings.

Table 2.37 Coalesced cube

Coalesced tuples	M
(ALL, ALL, ALL)	400
(ALL, ALL, 1)	280
(ALL, 1, ALL), (ALL, 5, ALL), (ALL, 1, 1)	150
(ALL, ALL, 2)	120
(ALL, 3, ALL), (1, ALL, ALL), (1, 1, ALL), (1, ALL, 1), (1, 1, 1)	100
(6, ALL, ALL), (6, 5, ALL), (6, ALL, 2), (ALL, 5, 2), (6, 5, 2)	80
(4, ALL, ALL), (4, 5, ALL), (4, ALL, 1), (ALL, 5, 1), (4, 5, 1)	70
(2, ALL, ALL), (2, 3, ALL), (2, ALL, 1), (ALL, 3, 1), (2, 3, 1)	60
(0, ALL, ALL), (0, 1, ALL), (0, ALL, 1), (0, 1, 1)	50
(8, ALL, ALL), (8, 3, ALL), (8, ALL, 2), (ALL, 3, 2), (8, 3, 2)	40

The Dwarf structure provides an index mechanism inherent to it.

The height of the Dwarf is equal to the number of dimensions, each of which is mapped onto one of the levels (Figure 2.14). The root node contains cells of the form [*key, pointer*], one for each distinct value of the first dimension. The pointer of each cell points to a node in immediate lower level containing distinct values of the next dimension. Each non-leaf node has a special ALL cell, shown in gray to the right of the node, correspond to all values of the node and holding a pointer.

The Dwarf data structure has the following properties.

- ❖ The Dwarf is a directed acyclic graph with one root node and has exactly n levels, where n is the number of dimensions with one level for each dimension. A node contains several cells.
- ❖ Cells of a *leaf node* (node at the nth level) are of the form [*key, aggregateValue*].
- ❖ Cells of *non-leaf nodes* are of the form [*key, pointer*]. A cell C in a non-leaf node of level i points to a node at level $i+1$, which it dominates. The dominated node then has the node of C as its parent node.
- ❖ Each node also contains a special cell, which corresponds to ALL as its key. This cell contains either a pointer to a non-leaf node or to the aggregate value of a leaf node.
- ❖ Cells belonging to nodes at level i of the structure contain keys that are values of the cube's ith dimension. No two cells within the same node contain the same key value.
- ❖ Each cell C_i at the ith level corresponds to the sequence S_i of i keys found in a path from the root to the cell's key. All partitions having S_i as their prefix will correspond to cells that are descendents of C_i in the Dwarf. Thus, prefix redundancy is avoided as we store the common prefix only once.

❖ When two or more nodes (either leaf or non-leaf) generate identical nodes and cells to the structure, their storage is coalesced, and only one copy of them is stored. In such a case, the coalesced node will be reachable through more than one paths from the root, all of which will share a common suffix. If a node *N* is coalesced, then any node *X* which is a descendant of *N* is also a coalesced node.

We illustrate the structure Dwarf with an example.

Figure 2.14 gives the Dwarf structure for the base data given in Table 2.27. Since there are three dimensions, there are three levels in this Dwarf structure. The dimensions are assumed to be in some order—the first level is dimension *A*, the second level is *B* and the last (leaf) level corresponds to *C*. The construction requires just a single sequential scan over the sorted fact table. For the first tuple of the fact table, the corresponding nodes and cells are created on all the levels of the Dwarf structure. As the scan continues, tuples with prefixes common with the last tuple get read. We create the necessary cells to accommodate new key values as we progress through the fact table. At each step of the algorithm, the common prefix *P* of the current and the previous tuple is computed. We read the first tuple as (0, 1, 1, 50). A cell is created at the root node for the first dimension (dimension *A*) and its pointer to a node in the second level which points to a leaf node. The cell in the leaf node has also the aggregate value. Since there is no tuple starting with value 0 for dimension *A*, we look for the tuple with the next value of *A*, which is the tuple (1, 1, 1, 100). In other words, any tuple having common prefix with the most recent tuple is processed next. For this purpose, the Dwarf algorithm first sorts the tuples based on the given dimension order so that the tuples having maximum common prefixes appear consecutively. In the present example, since there is no other tuple sharing prefix with the first tuple, we take the next tuple. Hence, the node at level 2 and level 3, which are just created, are

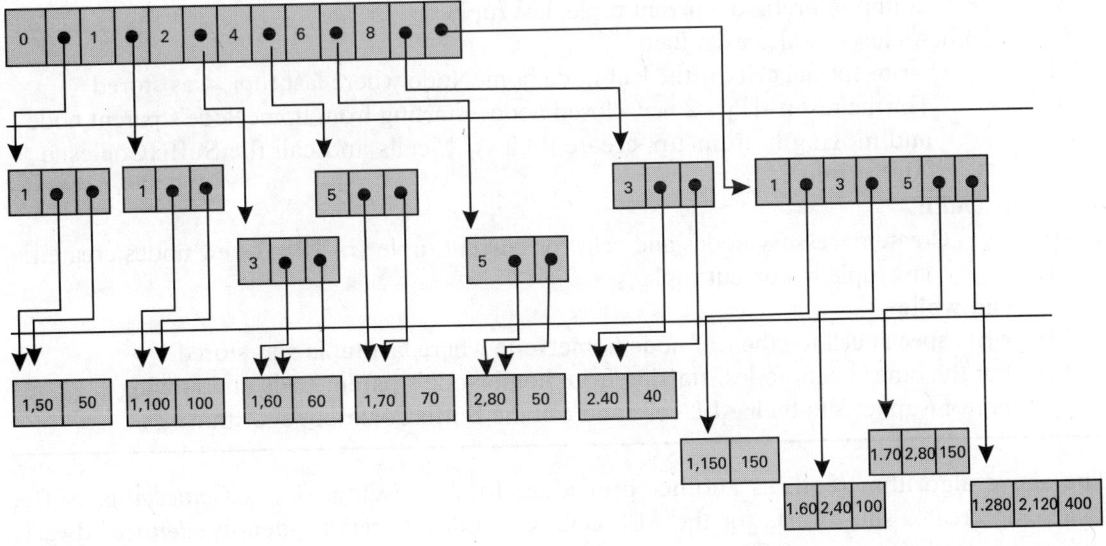

Figure 2.14 Dwarf structure

now declared closed by appending ALL cells to these nodes. These nodes will be processed for suffix coalescing subsequently. Thus, the ALL cell of level 2 node points to the same leaf cell as (0, 1, 1, 50), (0, ALL, 1, 50) and (0, ALL, ALL, 50); they all have same suffix and are shown only once by coalescing this suffix. When a leaf node is closed, the ALL cell is produced by aggregating the contents (aggregate values) of the other cells in the node. When a non-leaf node is closed, the ALL cell is created and the coalescing procedure is initiated for this cell.

At level 1, we create the root node having 7 cells, 6 for each of the 6 elements of the domain of dimension *A*, and one special cell representing ALL.

We now define some terms which are used in the description of the algorithms. The *dwarf of a node N* is defined to be the node itself and all the dwarfs of the nodes are dominated by the cells of *N*. The dwarf of a node *X* that is dominated by some cell of *N* is called a *sub-dwarf of N*. Since the leaf node cells dominate no other nodes, the dwarf of a leaf node is the node itself. The number of cells in the node N_j, in which a cell C_i dominates, is called *the branching factor of* C_i. A sequence of *i* keys, followed in any path from the root to a node *N* at level $i+1$ of the Dwarf structure is called the leading prefix of *N*. A leading prefix of *N*, which contains no coordinate with ALL, is called the primary leading prefix of *N*. The content of a cell C_i, belonging to a node *N*, is either the aggregate values of C_i if *N* is a leaf node, or the sub-dwarf of C_i if *N* is a non-leaf node.

CreateDwarfCube Algorithm

Input: P sorted fact table, *n*. number of dimensions

```
create all nodes and cells for the first tuple
last tuple = first tuple of base table
while more unprocessed tuples exist do
   current tuple = extract next tuple from sorted fact table
   P = common prefix of current tuple, last tuple
   if new closed nodes exist then
         write special cell for the leaf node homeNode where last tuple was stored
         For the rest n–|Pj|–2 new closed nodes, starting from homeNode's parent node
         and moving bottom-up, create their ALL cells and call the SuffixCoalesce
         Algorithm
   end if
      Create necessary nodes and cells for current tuple {n–|P|–1 new nodes created}
      last tuple = current tuple
end while
write special cell for the leaf node homeNode where last tuple was stored
For the other open nodes, starting from homeNode's parent node and moving
bottom-up, create their ALL cells and call the SuffixCoalesce Algorithm
```

The above algorithm requires another procedure for coalescing, *Suffix Coalescing.* Suffix coalescing creates sub-dwarfs for the ALL cell of a node. It tries to identify *identical* dwarfs and coalesces their storage. Two or more dwarfs are *identical* if they are constructed by the same subset of the tuples. The SuffixCoalesce algorithm is presented below.

SuffixCoalesce Algorithm

```
Input: inputDwarfs = set of Dwarfs
    if only one dwarf in inputDwarfs then
        return dwarf in inputDwarfs {coalescing happens here}
    end if
    while unprocessed cells exist in the top nodes of inputDwarfs do
    find unprocessed key Key_min with minimum value in the top nodes of inputDwarfs
    toMerge = set of cells of top nodes of inputDwarfs having keys with values equal to
      Key_min
       if already in the last level of structure then
       write cell [Key_min calculateAggregate(toMerge.aggregateValues)]
       else
       write cell [Key_min SuffixCoalesce(toMerge.sub-dwarfs)]
       end if
    end while
    create the ALL cell for this node either by aggregation or by calling SuffixCoalesce
    return position in disk where resulting dwarf starts
```

There have been several modification made to Dwarf in the recent years, resulting in many variants of the same.

2.19 Other Cubing Techniques

StarCubing

The StarCubing algorithm explores both top-down and bottom-up models for the computation of the iceberg cube. Like the MultiWay algorithm, it employs top-down tree but has an underneath layer that uses the information of the bottom-up model to explore the concept of shared dimension. If we examine the top-down spanning tree of a lattice, we see that an intermediate node has some dimension common with a leaf node in its subtree. Interestingly, this common dimension appears as a part in every node in the subtree. The maximal set of dimensions shared by all nodes in a subtree is called *shared dimension*. StarCubing is hinged on the fact that the shared dimension can be computed in advance, which helps in pruning certain cells in the computation of the iceberg cube. In the top-down spanning tree, every node stores a pair of cuboids, one as the upper bound for the cuboids appearing in the subtree with the node as the root, and the other as the lower bound cuboid. Since, due to the property of the lattice that the lower bound itself is a node in the subtree, this cuboid is removed at the subtree level to avoid duplication. However, in order to accomplish this, a separate data structure called *star tree* is to be maintained.

Quotient Cube

Quotient cube is the summary structure arrived at by carefully partitioning the cells into classes such that cells in a class have the same aggregate measures and, in addition, satisfy some desired properties. Also, whereas a user drills down from a cell to another in the cube lattice, in a *quotient cube*, the drilling down happens from one class to another. Quotient cube makes use of a compact data structure called QC-tree, to represent information compactly as a tree by prefix sharing. *Closed cube* is a variation of the quotient cube, which only stores the upper bounds of a quotient cube, thereby saving considerable amount of storage.

PipeSort

This is one of first cubing algorithms to have been formulated. It searches the space of possible sort orders for the best set of sorts that convert the CUBE lattice into a processing tree. This processing tree is similar to MMST described earlier. The search attempts to minimise the number of sorts while at the same time seeks to compute a cuboid from its smallest parent. Except when sorting, PipeSort uses at most $d + 1$ memory cells for each of the simultaneous aggregates, where d is the number of dimensions. When computing sparse cubes, many of the intermediate results that are sorted cannot fit into the memory and so, external sort will be used.

PipeHash

PipeHash [Sarawagi, 94] computes a group-by from its smallest parent in the lattice. The cuboid size estimates are assumed to be proportional to the product of the cardinalities of the dimensions. Using this as the weight, a minimum cost spanning tree is constructed to determine the set of simultaneously computed cuboids. PipeHash uses a hash table for every simultaneously computed cuboids. If all of the hash tables cannot fit in the memory, PipeHash partitions the data on some attribute and processes each partition independently.

2.20 Skycube

Skyline queries have gained popularity for multi-criteria analysis of large-scale datasets they support. However, skyline queries are also known to return too many results for high-dimensional data. To address this problem, Skycube was introduced to efficiently precompute the skyline tuples for all possible partitions of a given dataset. We give below an example of a Skycube. Considering the base cuboid of Table 2.38, the Skycube is given Table 2.39.

The complexity of computing skycube is known to be NP-hard. In particular, skyline or skycube computation depends heavily on CPU-intensive, row-wise comparisons to check the dominance relationships between rows, called dominance tests. But, under certain conditions, skyline cells exhibit monotonic property. We outline in brief the basic concepts of an algorithm for skycube computing.

Table 2.38

	A	B	C	D
t_1	7	1	8	4
t_2	5	7	1	2
t_3	4	4	2	1
t_4	1	6	3	3
t_5	2	5	4	6
t_6	3	2	5	8
t_7	5	3	2	6
t_8	4	5	7	2
t_9	6	4	5	7
t_{10}	6	6	2	6

Table 2.39

Cuboid	Skyline
ABCD	$t_1, t_2, t_3, t_4, t_5, t_6, t_7$
ABC	$t_1, t_2, t_3, t_4, t_5, t_6, t_7$
ABD	$t_1, t_3, t_4, t_5, t_6, t_7$
ACD	t_2, t_3, t_4, t_7
BCD	t_1, t_2, t_3, t_6, t_7
AB	t_1, t_4, t_5, t_6
AC	t_2, t_3, t_4
AD	t_3, t_4
BD	t_1, t_3
CD	t_2, t_3
A	t_4
B	t_1
C	t_2
D	t_3

Bottom-Up Skycube Algorithm (BUS)

This algorithm serially computes cuboids by using the principle of *sharing result* in a bottom-up manner. That is, BUS exploits skyline monotonicity to bypass dominance tests for skylines on cuboid C1 when computing a skyline on cuboid C2. It is seen that any skyline cell in C1 is derived from a skyline cell of C2 if C2 $\subseteq$ C1. The limitation of this approach is that, by sharing only the results, the dominance tests of non-skyline points cannot be reused. Specifically, if a point p is a non-skyline point on C1, BUS needs to perform dominance tests for p on C2 without reusing dominance tests on C1. In addition, BUS requires repeated access to an entire dataset in computing each cuboid, thereby incurring additional overhead.

2.21 View Selection - Partial Materialisation

Though materialised views provide great benefit for OLAP query processing, the selection of a set of views relative to the different levels of aggregation to be materialised in the DW must be carried out carefully, considering the compromise between query performance with view maintenance restrictions.

Workload: A workload or a query workload is a given set of queries, $q = \{q_1, q_2, \dots, q_p\}$. Each query q_i has an associated non-negative weight $f(q_i)$ which describes the query frequency. The set of materialised views is dependent on the query workload.

View selection: Given a base cuboid and a query workload, the objective is to select an appropriate set of materialised views (cuboids) to improve query performance. The process of selecting a set of materialised views is known as view selection.

View maintenance: Whenever a base cuboid is changed, the materialised views built on it have to be updated in order to compute the up-to-date query results. The process of updating a materialised view is known as view maintenance.

The problem of view selection can be formulated as follows. For a lattice of cuboids (or CUBE) C and a query workload $q = \{q_1, q_2, \ldots, q_p\}$ defined over C, the problem is to select an appropriate set of materialised views, $M = \{V_1, V_2, \ldots, V_m\}$, such that the query workload is answered with the lowest cost under a limited amount of resources, e.g., storage space and/or view maintenance cost.

Cost model: The cost model is an important issue for the view selection process. The main objective in view selection problem is the minimisation of the weighted query processing cost, defined by the formula:

$$QP_{\text{cost}} = \sum_{q_i} f(q_i) \times \text{cost\_}p\,(q_i, M)$$

,

where cost_$p(q_i, M)$ is the processing cost of query q_i for materialisation M.

Because materialised views have to be kept up-to-date, the view maintenance cost has to be considered. Let us assume that for any materialised cuboid (view), we know the update-frequency $f(V_i)$. This cost is weighted by the update frequency indicating the frequency of updating materialised views. The view maintenance cost is computed as follows:

$$VM\_\text{cost} = \sum_{V_i} f(V_i) \times \text{cost\_maint}(V_i, M)$$

,

where cost_maint(V_i, M) is the maintenance cost of view V_i for materialisation M.

There can be varieties of cost models, the simplest model being the linear cost model.

Linear Cost Model

One way of deciding on the set of cuboids to be materialised is based on a cost model, in which we associate a cost for processing each query. Then the problem of partial materialisation can be viewed as an optimisation problem for minimising the average cost to answer a query subject to the constraint that at most k cuboids of the lattice can be materialised. The decision problem is to select a set of cuboids for materialisation for meeting the above objective.

Let us assume that a query can be answered by a cuboid C, which may or may not be in the set of materialised cuboids. We choose the nearest (and least-cost) materialised cuboid C', from which C can be derived. The cost of answering the query is a function of the size of C'. The simplest cost model, *Linear Cost model*, assumes that this cost is equal to the number of tuples of C', while the actual query may ask for single cells, or a small numbers of cells rather than a complete cuboid. For the sake of uniformity, it is assumed that the cost is proportional to the number of rows that must be aggregated to compute the value in the cell, in which case the behaviour of a single cell and the full view queries are essentially the same.

Under this assumption, the partial materialisation problem can be solved by a greedy algorithm, which is described below.

Suppose we are given a lattice of cuboids with space costs associated with each cuboid. Let *cost*(*C*) be the cost of cuboid *C*. In linear cost model, *cost*(*C*) is equal to number of tuples in *C*. Suppose also that there is a limit *k* on the number of cuboids to be materialised.

Suppose that at any stage of the algorithm a set *S* of cuboids is materialised. *S* certainly includes the base cuboid. Benefit of C_v with respect to *S*, called *benefit*(C_v, *S*), is defined as the reduction in the overall cost if the cuboid C_v is added to the set of materialised set *S*. This quantity can be computed as follows.

We first compute a quantity B_w for each $C_w < C_v$.

Let C_u be the least-cost cuboid in *S* such that $C_u < C_w$. Since the base cuboid is in *S*, there must be at least one such C_u in *S*. If cost(C_v) < cost (C_u), then $B_w = C_v - C_u$; otherwise, B_w = 0. Define *benefit*(*Cv, S*) = $\Sigma_{w \leq v} B_w$.

In simpler terms, we compute the *benefit*(C_v, *S*) by considering how it can improve the cost of evaluating other cuboids, including itself. For each C_w that C_v covers, we compare the cost of evaluating C_w using C_v and using whatever cuboid from *S* offering the cheapest way of evaluating C_w. The difference represents part of the benefit of selecting C_v as a materialised cuboid. The total benefit is the sum over all C_w.

Greedy Algorithm

Initialise *S* = {C_0, the base cuboid}
for *i*=*1* to *k* do begin
    select that cuboid C_v not in *S* such that *benefit*(C_v, *S*) is maximum.
$S \leftarrow S \cup \{C_v\}$
end

EXAMPLE

Let us consider a three-dimensional data with dimensions *A*, *B* and *C*. The base cuboid is *ABC,* and the number of tuples of each cuboid in the lattice is given by Table 2.40.

Table 2. 40

Cuboids	**No. of tuples**
ABC	100
AB	50
AC	30
BC	75
A	20
B	35
C	10
All	1

At the first instance, the base cuboid is chosen. Suppose that we have to choose 3 more cuboids to be materialised, i.e., *k* =4. At the intial stage when *S* contains only the base cuboid, the cost associated with each other cuboid is the same as the cost of the nearest materialised cuboid, that is, *S*. Hence, each cuboid has an associated cost of 100.

In the next stage, we calculate the benefit of each of the cuboids. For instance, the benefit of the cuboid *AB* can be calculated as follows. If we materialise *AB*, in addition to the base cuboid, cuboids *AB, A, B* and ALL (the apex cuboid) can be derived from *AB* and each cuboid has a cost advantage of (100–50). Thus the benefit is 200 (see Table 2.41 to see how this is arrived at). We calculate similarly for each of the cuboid, to find that cuboid *AC* corresponds to maximum benefit. So, *AC* is chosen to be materialised.

In the next stage, the benefit for *AB* is calculated in a similar manner. Four cuboids, *AB, A, B* and ALL, can be derived from *AB*. The benefit of *AB* (and *B* too), is (100–50) as *AB* (and *B*) would otherwise be derived from *ABC*. The benefit for *A* is 0 as *A* is derived from *AC* with cost 30 (less than the cost of *AB*). Thus the total benefit of materialising *AB* at this stage is 100. We can calculate the benefit for all other cuboids. This is shown in third column of Table 2.41. We see that cuboid AB gives the maximum benefit and is chose for materialisation.

In the third stage, the benefit for cuboid *C* is maximum, and hence cuboid *C* is materialised.

There are many other cost models proposed in literature, where besides space cost other costs such as view maintenance cost and query frequency are taken into account. Query frequency is an interesting concept in the sense that in a specified time period, the number of times a cuboid is accessed gives a weighting factor for materialising it.

The number of cuboids in the lattice is an exponential function of the number of dimensions, and hence greedy algorithm is not a very effective algorithm. In order to obtain better solutions for a bigger number of views and better view maintenance and query processing costs, genetic algorithms have been proposed.

Table 2.41

	First step	**Second step**	**Third step**
AB	(100–50)×4 = 200	50+50+0+0 = 100	
AC	(100–30)×4 = 280		
BC	(100–75)×4 = 100	25+25+0+0= 50	25
A	(100–20)×2 = 160	0	20
B	(100–35)×2 = 130	65+0 = 65	15
C	(100–10)×2 = 180	(30–10) ×2 = 80	40
all	(100–1)×1 = 99	(30–1) = 29	29

2.22 Data Marting

We have discussed data marts in an earlier section. Data marting is concerned with the policy and design issues of data marts. Depending on the manner in which we couple data marts in the design of a data warehouse, we can have two competing architectures for data warehousing, each advocated by one of the two luminaries in the field: Ralph Kimball for the data mart bus architecture and Bill Inmon for the enterprise data warehouse. But before discussing these two aspects, let us first understand the concept of an independent data mart.

Independent Data Marts

Independent data marts in an enterprise are data marts for each department, designed, managed and maintained independently. Just as companies have legacy operational systems, they also have legacy-independent *data marts*. These marts are independent of other data stores and meet localised needs—they do not provide '*a single version of the truth*' for the entire organisation. They typically have inconsistent data definitions and use different dimensions and measures, i.e., they are non-conformed, which makes it difficult to analyse data across such marts.

Data Mart Bus Architecture (DBA) - Kimbal Approach

Kimbal's approach to data marting professes that the development of the data warehouse begins with the stage of identification of the business requirements for a specific business process, such as orders, deliveries, customer calls, or billing. The first mart is built for a single business process using dimensions and measures. Thereafter, additional marts are developed using these conformed dimensions. Atomic and summarised data are maintained in the marts, which are organised in star schemas to provide a dimensional view of the data.

Stated otherwise, the *Data Warehouse Bus Architecture* is composed of '*a master suite of conformed dimensions*' and *standardised definition of facts* in an enterprise. Business process data marts throughout the enterprise can plug into this bus to receive dimensions and relevant fact tables. The bus thus supports various processes and the associated data marts that measure the key aspects of these processes. The logical union of these data marts is said to be the data warehouse. All the data marts could be located in either one server, or, they could be distributed on many servers across an enterprise. In a sense the data warehouse is a virtual entity, being the sum total of all data marts.

Conformed dimensions

An important design consideration in a bus architecture is that different data marts should use the dimension tables available in the master suite in such a way that they mean and treat any dimension in a similar manner. Dimension tables are said to be non-conformed if the attributes are labelled differently or contain different values. For example, if a customer or product dimension is deployed in a non-conformed manner, then either the separate data marts cannot be used together or, worse, attempts to use them together will produce invalid results. Conformed dimensions are not necessarily identical dimensions, but they are conformed at several levels of abstractions.

At the most basic level, dimensions which are conformed mean the same thing with every possible fact table to which they are joined. For example, *time* dimension connected to *sales* facts is identical to *time* dimension connected to *inventory* facts. In fact, the conformed dimension may be the same physical table within the database. However, it is possible that the dimensions are duplicated synchronously in each data mart. In either case, the date dimensions in both data marts will have the same number of rows, same key values, same attribute labels, same attribute definitions, and same attribute values. That is , there is consistent data content, data interpretation, and user presentation.

At a higher level, two conformed dimensions could be at different rolled-up levels of granularity. The roll-up dimension becomes necessary because fact tables represents aggregated facts associated with aggregated dimensions. However, attributes that are common to both the detailed and rolled-up dimension tables should be labelled, defined, and valued identically in both tables. For example, in a case study on agricultural product, we can have a *time* dimension with *week* as the finest level for weather, whereas the *time* dimension for export may be *yearly*. These two dimensions, though not identical, enable one to be derived from the other by roll-up process. These are also therefore conformed dimensions.

CONFORMED FACTS

Facts should also be defined consistently between different star schemas to avoid inconsistent results from queries. This means that the definition of things like 'revenue' are consistent throughout the warehouse. This also means that calculation of the fact (if required) is always the same and units of measure for each fact is consistent as well. For example, we can define *Profit* = *Revenue – fixed cost – variable cost,* which should be consistent throughout the warehouse.

Note that conformed dimensions should be built once the data is in the staging area. The responsibility for each conformed dimension is vested in a group which may be called the dimension authority. The dimension authority has the responsibility for defining, maintaining, and publishing a particular dimension or its subsets to all the data mart clients who need it. It takes the responsibility for staging the gold-standard dimension data. This may involve sourcing from multiple operational systems to publish a complete, high-quality dimension table.

The process of building data marts with conformed facts and dimensions can be visualised as follows. It may be noted that data marts, which are essentially collections of related facts, need not have to be exclusive. The first step in the methodology comprises naming of all data marts that can be possibly built. The next step is to list all conceivable dimensions for each data mart. At this point an ad-hoc matrix to capture the multidimensional requirements is built. Rows represent the data marts while columns represent dimensions. A given intersection is marked where a dimension exists for a data mart. This matrix is also used to show the associations among data marts if we look at which dimensions they share. The third step uses the following step method to design each fact table once a data mart is chosen.

a. First, declare the grain of detail. This may be declared by the design team at the beginning itself despite the facility that it can be reconsidered during the process. Normally, it would be determined by primary dimensions.
b. Next, choose the dimensions for a particular fact table that should be tested against the grain selected. This is a creative step since one needs to look for the pieces (i.e.

levels and descriptors) of the dimension in different models and through different documents, which is a time-consuming task. At this point, it is ideal to choose a large number of descriptors to populate the dimensions.

c. Finally, as the last step, add as many measures as possible within the context of the declared grain.

Enterprise Data Warehouse Architecture (EDW) - Inmon Approach

The EDW architecture aims to provide an extensive enterprise-level analysis of data. The architecture for the same is developed in an iterative manner, subject-area by subject-area. The data is transferred from OLTP systems into a centralised data warehouse. The data can be made accessible at a detailed atomic level or at summary level depending on the granularity and drill-up/down facilities provided at the centralised place. The data marts are treated as subsets of the data warehouse, and each data mart is built for an individual department/unit of the enterprise from the centralised warehouse and optimised for the analysis needs of that particular department. Data is loaded from the transactional system to the staging area, and once it is validated and consolidated, ensuring the desired level accuracy, it is transferred to the centralised data warehouse. Once the data warehouse aggregation-summarisation process is complete, the data mart refresh cycle will extract data from the data warehouse.

Such data marts are called dependent data marts. Dependent data marts source data from the warehouse. They may be developed for a department, functional area, or special purposes (e.g., data mining) and may have normalised, denormalised, or summarised/atomic dimensional data structures based on user needs. Most users query the dependent marts for their needs.

The advocates of the bus architecture strongly believe that it provides an enterprise-wide solution. If the various marts are developed over time in a planned manner with conformed dimensions, the end result is an enterprise data warehouse. In contrast, rather than starting with a single mart and growing, the Inmon approach (both in terms of architecture and methodology) is more enterprise-wide oriented at the outset. An enterprise data warehouse is the potential result of evolution in the Kimball model, whereas it is the initial target of the Inmon approach.

Federated Architecture (FED)

The federated architecture deviates from the existing decision support structures such as operational systems, data marts, and warehouses. It does not strive to integrate the existing complex decision support environment into a single integrated solution, often due to political and implementation challenges faced by the organisation, possibly as a result of acquisitions, mergers and reorganisation. Here the data is either logically or physically integrated using shared keys, global metadata, distributed queries, enterprise information integration (EII), or other methods. This architecture is advocated as a practical 'realistic' solution for firms that have a pre-existing, complex decision support environment and do not want to rebuild or plan to rebuild at a later date.

2.23 ETL

The extraction–transformation–loading (ETL) processes are responsible for the operations in the background of the data warehouse architecture. The data warehouse back-stage activities extract data from various sources, clean them for logical or syntactical inconsistencies, transform them into the format of the data warehouse, and eventually, load these data into the warehouse. The main functionalities of ETL are the following.

- Identification of relevant information at the source side
- Extraction of this information
- Customisation, cleaning and integration of the information coming from multiple sources into a common format
- Cleaning and transforming of the data set on the basis of database and business rules
- Propagation of the data to the data warehouse and/or data marts

In an ETL process, first the data are extracted from the data sources such as OLTP or legacy systems (files under any format), web pages, various kinds of documents (e.g., spreadsheets and text documents), or even data coming in a streaming fashion. Initially, while first populating the data warehouse, the whole data from these sources go through the ETL process but subsequently, only the data that are different from the previous execution of an ETL process (newly inserted, updated, and deleted information) are extracted from the sources. The data are then parked at an intermediate repository called data staging area (DSA), where their transformation, homogenisation and cleansing take place. The most frequently used transformations include filters and checks to ensure that the data propagated to the warehouse respects business rules and integrity constraints as well as schema transformations that ensure that the data fits the target data warehouse schema. Finally, the data is loaded to the central data warehouse or data marts. In a traditional data warehouse setting, the ETL process periodically refreshed the data warehouse during idle or low-load periods of its operation (e.g., every night) and had a specific time-window to complete these tasks.

Extraction

The first step in ETL is data extraction, responsible for extracting data from various source systems. Each data source has its distinct set of characteristics such as different database management systems, different operating systems and different communications protocols that need to be managed in order to effectively extract data. The process of extraction takes place in two phases: *initial extraction*, and *changed data extraction*.

The very first population of a data that enters the warehouse is referred to as the *initial load*. During initial loading, data is extracted exhaustively from the sources and delivered to the data warehouse. This *initial extraction* process takes place only once after building the data warehouse to populate it with a huge amount of data from various source systems.

The source data changes over time, however, and hence after the data warehouse is initially populated, the ETL process subsequently refreshes the data warehouse by extracting only the current data from the data sources. At this stage, no complete refreshing of the facts and dimension tables (full loading) is necessary. The incremental extraction that is taking place is called *changed data capture* (CDC), where, the ETL process refreshes the data warehouse with the modified and added data in the source systems since the last extraction. However, this process is periodic, in accordance with the refresh cycle and business needs. There are several interesting methods of implementing CDC. We list some of these techniques next.

Audit columns

In most cases the source database has a provision for (or is appended with) an extra column called the *audit column*. This column records the date and time at which the record is added or modified. During the extraction process, one can identify the portion of data that has changed since the last update by accessing the audit column.

Timed extracts

In timed extracts, all records with the time of creation or modification of data fields equal to the system time are selected from the source database. Timestamps can be applied to records in order to note the time when a record has been inserted or updated. However, it is not possible to capture record deletion with timestamps because the timestamps get deleted with the record.

Full diff compare

A *full diff compare* keeps a full snapshot of the old database and compares it record by record against the current database to find the changes that have taken place.

Triggers

A trigger is a piece of code (mostly, user-written) that automatically executes when a predefined set of events occur. Such events include any type of change in data. When change data arrives, a trigger will fire, sending the changed data to the cache area. The cache is polled to capture the change. The usage of *triggers,* however, impacs the performance of operational systems. OLTP systems typically handle very large volumes of data and having to process triggers will be a burden on them.

Log sniffing

Database log *sniffing* is yet another method of CDC implementation. The idea is to exploit transaction logs maintained by the data sources, normally for the purpose of backup and recovery. Log-based CDC involves scanning database logs and deducing from them any changes made to the data. This is the least invasive approach as it does not intervene with the data sources. Some OLTP systems do not have the provision for producing a log, and most systems create logs in their own format. Log *sniffing* technique is implemented by appropriate parsing of log files of the OLTP sources. All modifications of committed transactions are detected and they can be *replayed* at the warehouse. However, log files can become large in a short space of time, and so they are either moved to an off-line storage or purged to keep the file size to a minimum.

Data Staging Area

Data staging area (DSA) is a transit storage for data in the ETL process. Data is brought here after the extraction phase for transformations/cleansing. The dimensions are decided at this stage. Finished dimensions are copied from DSA to relevant marts. Two major activities are carried out here – data cleaning and data transformation. We will briefly outline the transformation activities below and take up the data cleaning part in the next section.

Data transformation

The objective of the transformation step of ETL is to take the extracted data as input and produce, through a set of transformation steps, accurate data which is clean, correct, complete, consistent and unambiguous. This process includes data derivation, transformation and integration. All transformation rules and the resulting schemas are stored in the metadata repository. The integration and transformation tasks involve a wide variety of functions, such as normalising, denormalising, reformatting, recalculating, summarising and merging of data from multiple sources, modifying key structures, adding of the element of time, identifying default values, supplying decision commands to choose between multiple sources, and so forth. Data transformation (mainly schema transformation) is a subject of study in itself.

2.24 Data Cleaning

Data cleaning, also called *data cleansing* or *scrubbing*, deals with the detection and removal of errors and inconsistencies from data in order to improve the quality of data. All data cleaning is typically performed in DSA before loading the transformed data into the warehouse. A large number of tools of varying functionality are available to support these tasks, but often, a significant portion of the cleaning and transformation work has to be done manually or by low-level programs that are difficult to write and maintain.

A data cleaning approach should satisfy several requirements. First of all, it should detect and remove all major errors and inconsistencies both in individual data sources and those generated when integrating multiple sources. The approach should be supported by tools to limit manual inspection and programming effort and be extensible to easily cover additional sources. Furthermore, data cleaning should not be performed in isolation but should be carried out together with schema-related data transformations based on comprehensive metadata.

The very first step of any data cleaning process is to identify occurrences of dirty data. Such identification will not only help in the cleaning step, but also be useful in the transformation step as a whole. Different cases of occurrences of dirty data are categorised based on whether the data source is single or multiple, and whether these occur at the schema level or at the instance level.

SINGLE SOURCE CASES

When identifying the occurrence of dirty data at a single source, the data cleaning issues may arise at an individual field, individual record, set of records of the same type (a table) or at the overall source level (multiple tables). The field or attribute-level dirty data may arise if the available data in a particular field is not within the domain of the field. For example, if the date field shows 32.32.2043, then the value is outside the specified domain. At the record level, it is desirable that fields within a record should observe the attribute dependencies. Hence, bad data creeps into the system if attribute dependency is violated. For example, if a business rule says that every semester the long theory paper is for 100 marks and practical paper is for 80 marks, then the condition is violated for a record if it contains entries semester = 3, credit = 4, course-type= "theory", marks = 80. Bad data occurs in multiple records of the same type if the uniqueness condition is violated by records. For example, in a table same entities may be described in two different records, but some attribute that is required to be unique for every entity has non-unique values. When we have multiple tables (relations), data quality problem arises when referential integrity is deviated. For example, in sales table a reference to product *home_appliances* is made but in product table there is no product named *home_appliances*.

Though these are standard situations when bad quality data may arise and gets detected at the schema level, there are other situations that cannot be captured at schema level but may appear at the instance level. There may be a missing value at the individual field. For example, attribute *PIN* = 999999. Further, there may be misspelling or phonetic errors of *city*="Hydabad" or *state* = "Hariana". There may also be different abbreviated values used in different records in a table such as *course* = "DW" or *course* = "DWh". Sometimes, extra values are embedded in operational systems. For example, entries like *city* ="Delhi-36"embeds additional values to the field. The situation of misfielded value occurs when the data source contains data of one attribute in place of another. For example, *city* = "Haryana". Haryana is not a city but a state. There may be cases of violated attribute dependencies at the instance level when the values of multiple attributes do not conform to the same entities. For example, *city*="Hyderabad", *PIN*=100016. There are situation of dirty data arising due to word transpositions, such as name1= "P. Indira", name2="Indira Puri".

MULTIPLE SOURCE PROBLEM

The problems present in single sources are aggravated when multiple sources need to be integrated. Each source may contain dirty data, and the data in the sources represented differently may overlap or contradict. This is because the sources are typically developed, deployed and maintained independently.

The main problems of schema design differences are in naming and structural conflicts. These differences are to be handled at the schema integration step. Naming conflicts arise when the same name is used for different objects (homonyms), or different names are used for the same object (synonyms). Structural conflicts refer to different representations of the same object in different sources—different component structure, different data types, different integrity constraints, etc. It becomes necessary to apply a schema integration step at this stage.

In addition to schema-level conflicts, many conflicts appear at the instance level. For instance, there may be the same attribute names and data types, but different value representations (e.g., marital status) or different interpretation of the values (e.g., measurement units such as Dollar vs. INR) across sources. Different sources may be providing information at different aggregation levels too (e.g., *sales per product vs. sales per product group*) or be refering to different ranges of time (e.g. *current sales* as of yesterday for source 1 vs. as of last week for source 2).

Data Cleaning Approaches

Several phases of data cleaning have been proposed by experts.

Data analysis

In order to detect which kinds of errors and inconsistencies are to be removed, a detailed data analysis is to be carried out. In addition to manual inspection of the data or data samples, analysis programs should be used to detect data quality problems. For example, in order to detect misspelt value of a field, a common practice is to sort the values alphabetically so that most often misspelt entries appear close to correctly spelt entries. A major problem for cleaning data from multiple sources is the identification of overlapping data, in particular matching records referring to the same real-world entity (e.g., customer). This problem is also referred to as the object identity problem, duplicate elimination or the *merge/purge problem*. *Data profiling* focuses on the instance analysis of individual attributes. It derives information such as the data type, length, value range, discrete values and their frequency, variance, uniqueness, occurrence of null values, typical string pattern (e.g., for phone numbers), etc., providing an exact view of the various quality aspects of the attribute.

Schema transformation and integration

Schema integration

Given a set of independently developed schemas, the construction of a global view involves addressing the problem of integrating independently developed ontologies into a single ontology. Since the schemas are independently developed, they often have different structure and terminology. Thus, a first step in integrating the schemas is to identify and characterise these interschema relationships. This is a process of schema matching. Once they are identified, the matching elements can be unified under a coherent, integrated schema or view. During this integration, or sometimes as a separate step, programs or queries are created that permit translation of data from the original schemas into the integrated representation.

Schema translation and matching

Sometime, a schema translation is used to map sources to a common data model. When we are dealing with multiple-source data cleaning, it becomes necessary to transform and integrate schemas to a common schema. For instance, if one source describes *customer* by *name* (as a whole) and the other source identifies by *last_name* and *first_name*, then it becomes difficult to integrate the data and hence we need schema transformation. These steps should be specified by a declarative query and mapping language as far as possible, to enable automatic generation of the transformation code. In addition, it should be possible to invoke user-written cleaning code and special purpose tools. This is a well-studied problem and an active research area.

Workflow and Mapping Rules

Depending on the number of data sources, their degree of heterogeneity and the 'dirtiness' of data, a large number of data transformation and cleaning steps may have to be executed. For data warehousing, the control and data flow for these transformation and cleaning steps should be specified within a ETL workflow that defines the ETL process.

Verification

The correctness and effectiveness of a transformation workflow and the transformation definitions should be tested and evaluated, e.g., on a sample or copy of the source data, to improve the definitions if necessary. Multiple iterations of the analysis, design and verification steps may be needed since some of the errors only become apparent after applying some transformations.

Backflow of Cleaned Data

After errors (single-source) are removed, the cleaned data should also replace the dirty data in the original sources also in order to give legacy applications the improved data and to avoid redoing the cleaning work in future data extractions. For data warehousing, the cleaned data is available from the data staging area.

Schema Mapping

Queries will be used for representing the mapping between the source and the target data, thus, allowing DBMS to play an expanded role as a data transformation engine as well as a data store. This approach enables a complete interaction between the mapping metadata and the warehousing tool. In addition, it addresses the efficiency of a query-based data warehousing ETL tool without suggesting any graphical models. It describes a query generator for reusable and more efficient data warehouse processing.

Mapping expression of an attribute is the information needed to recognise how a target attribute is created from the sources attributes. For example:

- *Break-down/concatenation*: The value of a field is established by breaking down the value of a source and by concatenating it with another value.
- *Conditional mapping*: sometimes the value of a target attribute depends on the value of another attribute, e.g., if $X = 1$ then $Y = A$ else $Y = B$.
- *Schema mapping*: For database schema mapping, the mapping expression is needed to define the correspondence between the matched elements.

LOADING

Loading data on to the target multidimensional structure is the final ETL step. In this step, extracted and transformed data is written into the dimensional structures actually accessed by the end users and application systems. This step includes the loading of both dimension tables and fact tables. Data loading starts after the data sets are ready in the DSA. The key consideration in the loading process is to achieve speed of loading. During loading one has to be careful about logging and indexing.

A typical dilemma faced by developers concerns the choice between bulk loading data through a DBMS-specific utility and the inserting of data as a sequence of rows. Clear performance reasons strongly suggest the former solution, due to the overheads of the parsing of the insert statements, the maintenance of logs and rollback-segments (or, the risks of their deactivation in the case of failures). Another performance issue is to do with the existence of indexes, materialised views, or both, defined over the warehouse relations. Every update to these relations automatically incurs the overhead of maintaining the indexes and the materialised views.

MODELLING OF ETL

The ETL developer community typically expresses an ETL task procedurally as a data-flow graph consisting of sources, operators and targets in a very procedural, bottom-up

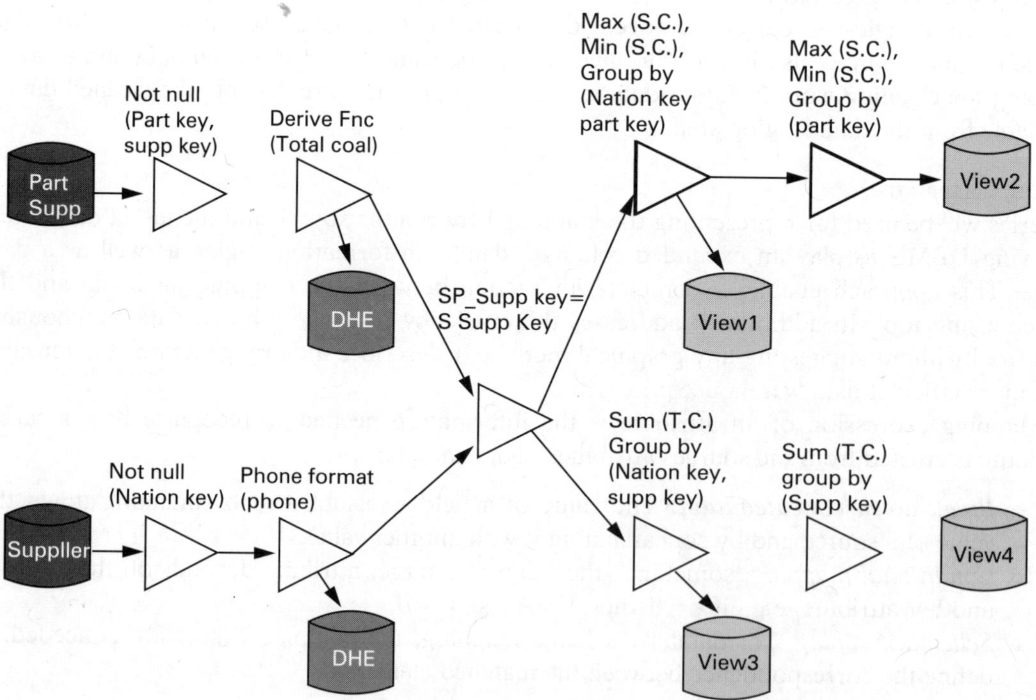

Figure 2.15 Typical example of ETL workflow

manner. During an ETL run, data is extracted from the sources, flows through a number of intermediate nodes in a streaming manner, and reaches the resulting tables or files as its final form. Some ETL operations can be naturally mapped to relational algebra expressions (such as join). However, others may be procedural (such as unique id generation) or beyond the range of relational algebra (such as the pivot operation). The workflow is an abstract design at the logical level, which has to be implemented physically, i.e., to be mapped to a combination of executable programs/scripts that perform the ETL workflow. The full layout of an ETL workflow, involving activities and recordsets can be modelled as a directed acyclic graph, with the ETL activities and recordsets (either relations or files) constituting the graph nodes. According to their placement into one of the three ETL phases, the recordsets can be classified as source, intermediate (including any logging, staging or temporary data store), and target. The relationships among the nodes constitute the graph edges. Each node has input and output schemata, which can be empty as well. A source recordset has an empty input schema. A typical ETL workflow is given in Figure 2.15, where data from different operational sources go through different stages to be loaded to the data warehouse.

ETL WORKFLOW

The ideal execution of ETL workflows suggests pipelining the flow of tuples all the way from the source to the target data stores. Typically, this cannot happen due to the blocking nature of many ETL activities (e.g., sorters), and to the structural nature of the flow (e.g, activities with multiple input/output schemata). An appropriate scheduling policy is required for orchestrating the smooth flow of data towards the target data stores. In that sense, activity scheduling during the ETL workflow execution results in efficient prioritisation of active activities at any time point with the goal of minimising the overall execution time without any data losses.

2.25 ELT vs. ETL

ELT stands for Extract, Load and Transform and hence it is different from ETL in that the transformation is carried out after loading. Of the two, which is preferable is one of the major debate in the industry today. In ELT, data is 'extracted' from the data sources (line of business applications) into the 'Staging Database' using a data - tool via whatever data connectivity is available, whilst in the staging area, integrity and business rules checks are applied, and relevant corrections are made. The source data is then loaded into the warehouse. In effect, this provides a validated and cleaned offline copy of the source data in the data warehouse. Once in the warehouse, transformations are performed to re-shape (transformation stage) the data into its target output format. The extract and load process can be isolated from the transformation process. There are a number of benefits of doing so. Isolating the load process from the transformation process removes the inherent dependency between these stages. In addition to including the data necessary for the transformations, the extract and load process can include elements of data that may be required in the future. Note that in transformation we lose the original cleaned data and only transformed data is available. Indeed, in ELT the load process could take the entire source and load it into the warehouse. This approach also helps to ensure that only cleaned and checked data is loaded into the warehouse for transformation. Isolating the transformations from the load process helps to encourage a more staged approach to the warehouse design and implementation. Tools are available that inherently implement the ELT process. However, their availability is limited since this is a more recent approach to warehouse process design.

In implementing ELT as a warehouse build process, the inherent tools provided with the database engine can be used. Alternatively, the ELT process could be run on the same hardware as the database engine underpinning the data warehouse, using the existing hardware. By using the functionality provided by the database engine, the existing investments in database skills are re-used to develop the warehouse. No new skills need be learned and the full weight of the experience in developing the engine's technology is utilised, further reducing the cost and risk in the development process.

ELT is an emergent approach to data warehouse design and development. Whilst it has proven itself many times over through implementations throughout the world, it does require a change in mentality and design approach against traditional methods. One of the major weaknesses of ELT is that it suffers from a limited availability of tools.

2.26 Cloud Data Warehousing

Traditional warehouses present a strictly centralised and offline approach in terms of data location and processing. Views are usually calculated on a daily or weekly basis after the operational data have been transferred from various locations. Furthermore, the need to keep large volumes of historical data online and ensure their availability and provide fast access even under heavy workload dictates a continuous investment in hardware, electrical power and software maintenance. To mitigate this, some workers in the field have proposed a distributed warehousing system, but with the warehouse and its aggregation, update and querying functionality remaining centralised. Recently, efforts are on to distribute the data warehouse itself by applying techniques from the field of peer-to-peer (P2P) computing, but with no a priori consideration for group-by queries.

In recent years, two alternative architectures have emerged to support such *big data* analytics: *data warehouse appliances and MapReduce engines*. A data warehouse appliance is an integrated set of storage hardware, operating system and DBMS software, specifically *pre-installed* and *pre-optimised* for data warehousing. Appliances can also push part of the query processing into specialised hardware, thereby speeding up the analytic query-processing significantly. The motivation for the MapReduce paradigm originally comes from the need to have a scalable infrastructure for index generation and analytics over query logs and web data. More recently, however, such engines are being extended to support a more general class of parallel data execution tasks, thereby to traditional data warehousing.

Cloud computing is the latest trend in distributed computing. Cloud providers offer clients a reliable service for outsourcing their computing, storage and networking at small, incremental costs, made available over the Net for managing complex tasks such as data storage, system administration or application deployment. The advantage is that the user of the cloud service will not be required to make any heavy investment in infrastructure for their application and storage needs; instead the 'cloud' manages it for them at a nominal fee. The service is available on demand, is reliable and offers users easy access to virtually infinite computing, storage and networking resources. Because of the enhanced resources available, users can utilise these new capabilities for performing analysis across all data in an organisation.

It may be noted that all data-intensive applications are not equally amenable to cloud computing. For instance, it is more suitable for OLAP than OLTP primarily because of two cloud characteristics: *elasticity and security*. OLTP, even though dealing with databases of average sizes, require more stringent data protection and quick response time guarantees than OLAP applications dealing with historical databases of very large sizes. A shared-nothing cluster supports elasticity very well and is the architecture generally deployed by cloud providers. This is the best solution for providing high-scalability provided careful data partitioning is done. Since data warehouses are very large and mostly read-only, it is possible to do data partitioning and carry out parallel query processing in an effective manner.

Two major cloud computing design patterns are *utility clouds* and *data clouds*. Data clouds aggregate massive amounts of data while utility clouds focus on offering infrastructure, platforms, and software as services to users. *Data clouds* divide processing tasks into smaller units distributed over servers across the cluster, ensuring that the computing and storage capabilities are co-located, allowing highly scaled computation to takes place across all of the data in the cloud. Data clouds thus focus on enabling massively parallel computation, speedy access to data and shared analysis algorithms, while and are concerned with enabling multiple users to share the same application (multitenancy) while making it appear as if they are running on separate physical machines (virtualisation).

Further Reading

In this chapter we have discussed some new concepts and techniques of datawarehousing. The information provided in this chapter is mostly compilation of results from several recent publications listed at the end of this chapter. Readers who are interested in detailed study of the techniques are directed to the original research publications. Malinowski et al discusses categorisation of hierarchies in detail. Shoshani [Lenz & Shoshani'97; Shoshani'97] studies different aspects of summarisation for warehousing. PIPESORT method was proposed by Agarwal et al. Condensed cube was proposed by Wang et al in 2002 and the authors have proposed several new algorithms to compute condensed cube. BUC algorithm was proposed by Bayer and Ramakrishnan in 1999 and there have been several developments in it in recent years. Harinarayan et al has proposed MultiWay algorithm, and subsequently, several aspects of accesing the chunks have been discussed in many subsequent papers. View selection is yet another recent topic and researchers have begun using genetic algorithms for view selection.

Exercises

1. A data warehouse is said to contain a 'time-varying' collection of data because
   a. Its contents vary automatically with time.
   b. Its life-span is very limited.

c. It contains historical data.
d. Its content has explicit time-stamp.

2 The content of a data warehouse is said to be 'non-volatile', because
a. It remains the same even after the system crashes.
b. Its life-span is very long.
c. It is a read-only data
d. It disappears when the system is switched off

3. A data warehouse is said to contain a 'subject-oriented' collection of data because
a. Its contents have a common theme.
b. It is built for a specific application.
c. It cannot support multiple subjects.
d. It is a generalisation of 'object-oriented'.

4. A data warehouse is an 'integrated' collection of data because
a. It is a collection of data of different types.
b. It is a collection of data derived from multiple sources.
c. It is a relational database.
d. It contains summarisedata.

5. A data warehouse is built on historical data and is not guaranteed to be up-to-date information. True or False?

6. A data warehouse is built as a separate repository of data, different from the operational data of an enterprise because
a. It is necessary to keep the operational data free of any warehouse operations.
b. A data warehouse cannot afford to allow corrupted data within it.
c. A data warehouse contains summarised data whereas the operational database contains transactional data.

7. In order to populate the data warehouse, which of the following set of operations are appropriate?
a. Refresh and load.
b. Create and edit.
c. Insert and delete.
d. Query and update.

8. Dimension data within a warehouse exhibits one of the following properties:
a. It comprises the minor part of the warehouse
b. The aggregated information is actually dimension data
c. It contains historical data
d. Dimension data is the information that is used to analyse the elemental transaction.

9. The 'Slice' operation deals with
a. Selecting all but one dimension of the data cube.
b. Merging of cells along one dimension.
c. Merging cells of all but one dimension.
d. Selecting the cells of any one dimension of the data cube.

10. Institutional finance for the rural sector consists essentially of loans extended by financial institutions for rural development. The financial institutions are Scheduled Commercial Banks, Regional Rural Bank, Cooperatives, Large-size Adivasis Multipurpose Banks. A data warehouse is built to study the institutional finance of the rural sector. We are interested in finding out the year-wise details of loan disbursements and outstanding loans. It is to study the loan disbursement of the bank—group-wise, purpose-wise and region-wise. The country is categorised into different regions namely, North, North-East, East, Central, West and South. Each region consists of a set of states.

    A. Given the information of total loans disbursed (in Rs.) during the period 1991–95 and 1996–2000 for each of the states, if we want to get the total loan disbursement for the period 1991–95 for each region, then which of the following is the correct sequence of operations ?
        a. A slice followed by dice
        b. A dice followed by slice
        c. A slice followed by roll-up
        d. A slice followed by drill-down
        e. None of these

    B. Given the information of the total loans disbursed during the period 1991–95 and 1996–2000 for each of the states, if we want to arrive at the total loan disbursement year-wise and region-wise, then which of the following is the correct sequence of operations ?
        a. A roll-up followed by dice
        b. A drill-down followed by slice
        c. A slice followed by roll-up
        d. A roll-up followed by drill-down
        e. None of these

    C. Given the information of the total loans disbursed during the period 1991–95 and 1996–2000 for each of the states, if we want to arrive at the total loan disbursement for the period 1991–95, for two states say, Maharashtra and Bihar, then which of the following is the correct sequence of operations ?
        a. A slice only
        b. A dice followed by slice
        c. A dice only
        d. A drill-down followed by slice
        e. None of these

    D. Given the information of the total loans disbursed during the period 1991–95 and 1996–2000 for each bank group-wise, (there are three bank groups, namely the SBI and its associates, nationalised banks and cooperative banks), if we want to arrive at the total loan disbursement for the period 1991–95 and 1996–2000 for all the banks taken together, which of the following operations is appropriate?
        a. A slice
        b. Roll-up

c. Drill-down
d. Dice
e. No single operation suffices

E. If we want to design a star schema, the content of the Fact Table would be
   a. The details of all banks and corresponding loans disbursed
   b. Details of the loan amounts disbursed
   c. Details of banks—groups, regions, years
   d. None of these

F. If we want to design a star schema for this, there are several dimensions. Identify the ones which are not dimensions.
   a. Bank-groups
   b. Purpose
   c. Year
   d. Region
   e. Loan amount

G. If we want to design a star schema for this, the content of the join-keys will be
   a. Bank-id, Region-id, Loan-id
   b. Bank-id, loan-id, region-id, year-id, purpose-id
   c. Loan-id
   d. None of these

H. If we want to design a data warehouse, the attributes of a bank such as its manager, interest rates, and address are stored in
   a. Fact tables
   b. Dimension tables
   c. Metadata

11. The 'Dice' operation is concerned with
   a. multiple runs of slice.
   b. slice on more than one dimension.
   c. selecting certain cells of more than one dimension.
   d. two consecutive slice operations in two different dimensions

12. A 'virtual warehouse' is essentially
   a. A traditional relational database providing a multidimensional view through a middleware and it is different from the enterprise's operational database
   b. It is the operational database but provides warehouse facilities through a middleware.
   c. It is the materialised view of the operational and transactional database.

13. 'Roll-up' is an OLAP operation which
   a. switches from the details to the aggregate level within a classification hierarchy.
   b. switches from the details to the aggregate level along many dimensions.
   c. switches from the aggregate to the detail level within a classification hierarchy
   d. switches from the details to the aggregate levels across many classification hierarchies.

14. A 'drill-down ' operation is concerned with
    a. Which merges cells of two dimensions
    b. Which merges cells of any one dimension based on the characteristics of the dimension
    c. Which splits cells of two dimensions
    d. Which splits cells of any one dimension based on the characteristics of the dimension
15. A 'drill-through' is an OLAP operation that is derived from drill-down in the following sense
    a. Drill-through navigates along many dimensions whereas drill-down navigates only in one dimension
    b. Drill-through moves both upward and downward, whereas drill-down moves only downward.
    c. Drill-through is a bi-directional approach, whereas drill-down is a uni-directional approach
16. A data mart
    a. is the analysis unit of the overall architecture of a warehouse.
    b. is a stand-alone of a data warehouse, by itself, of a department of the enterprise.
    c. is an essential component, in the sense that every data warehouse necessarily has several data marts.
17. ROLAP is
    a. an OLAP engine for (i) multidimensional models and (ii) SQL based OLAP operations. OLAP engine for (i) relational model and (ii) SQL-based OLAP operations.
    b. ROLAP is an OLAP engine for (i) multidimensional models and (ii) SQL queries, but does not support 'slice' and 'dice' operations.
    c. ROLAP is a set of relational operations equivalent to OLAP operations.
18. What is 'MOLAP'?
    a. An OLAP engine for (i) relational models and (ii) multidimensional OLAP operations.
    b. An OLAP engine for (i) multidimensional models and (ii) SQL-based OLAP operations.
    c. An OLAP engine for (i) multidimensional models and (ii) supports multidimensional OLAP operations.
    d. An ROLAP with a supporting multidimensional model.
19. Which of the following statements are false? MOLAP is preferred to ROLAP
    a. when relational tables are not suitable for warehouse modelling.
    b. because multidimensional arrays provide efficiency in storage and operations.
    c. because the current technology of a relational system does not provide full-fledged OLAP operations.
    d. because indexing and hashing techniques are easy to implement for MOLAP.
20. The weather data is stored for different locations in a warehouse. The weather data consists of 'temperature', 'pressure', 'humidity' and 'wind velocity'. The location is defined in terms of 'latitude', 'longitude', 'altitude' and 'time'. Assume that nation() is a function that returns the name of the country for a given latitude and longitude. Assume that this information is stored in a data warehouse as a data cube.

A. If we want to extract the average temperature and maximum pressure for all locations for every week, which of the following is the appropriate sequence operations on the multidimensional model?
   a. Compute the average temperature and the highest value of pressure for each week, slice along time to get the values week-wise.
   b. The average temperature and maximum pressure are precomputed while constructing the warehouse. It is required to carry out only a slice operation on 'time'.
   c. The average temperature and maximum pressure are precomputed while constructing the warehouse. It is required to carry out only a roll-up operation on 'time'.
   d. The average temperature and maximum pressure are to be computed as in (a.) and to carry out slice and drill-down operation on 'time'.
   e. None of these.

B. Assume that this information is stored in a data warehouse as a data cube, along with the average temperature and maximum pressure for all dimensions. Which of the following is the appropriate sequence operations to get the average temperature year-wise?
   a. Slice on time.
   b. Slice on temperature
   c. Roll-up on time
   d. Roll-up on temperature.
   e. None of these

C. We want to build a warehouse using the above information with the numeric measures such as average temperature, maximum pressure, maximum and minimum humidity, and average wind velocity. In a constellation (galaxy), schema, which of the following tables store the above information?
   a. Fact table
   b. Summary table
   c. Dimension table

21. Consider the following table. Compute the lattice of cuboid and specify the number of tuples at each node.

A	B	C	D	Measure
1	1	1	3	10
1	1	2	5	12
1	2	1	4	14
1	2	2	5	16
1	3	1	2	18
2	1	2	3	13
2	2	1	4	19

2	2	2	3	15
2	3	1	3	17
2	3	2	5	20

22. Use the above tuple 8 to show the working of roll-up and drill-down operations.
23. In MultiWay algorithm, it is assumed that chunks are accessed linearly. How does the accessing pattern of chunks affect the efficiency of the algorithm.
24. Consider a datawarehouse represented as chunked multidimensional array of five dimensions A, B, C, D and E with sizes 100, 16, 8, 64 and 100, respectively. The sizes of the chunk in a different dimensions are as follows: A-2, B-2, C-2, D-1, E-1. If the dimension ordering is (A, B, C, D, E) then calculate the maximum number of chunks that are to be held in memory at any given time for computing the cuboids ACDE or ABCE.
25. Calculate the same quantities as above when the dimension ordering is (C, D, E, A, B).
26. What do you think is the best dimension ordering?
27. Construct the MMST for the above situation.
28. Consider the following base cuboid in the form of a table.

A	B	C	D
1	1	1	10
1	1	2	12
1	2	1	14
1	2	2	16
1	3	1	18
2	1	2	13
2	2	1	19
2	2	2	15
2	3	1	17
2	3	2	20

   a. Compute the CUBE by BUC algorithm.
   b. Use Condense Cube algorithm for identifying the BSTs and SD-set for the above table.
   c. Identify the tuples that are going to be in Skyline cube of the above cube.
   d. Suppose the iceberg constraint is to allow tuples with summary value greater than 35, write the Iceberge cube.
29. Consider the following base cuboid and compute the quantities asked for in questions (a – d) above.

A	B	C	M
1	male	a	310
1	male	b	112
1	female	a	34

1	female	b	416
1	female	a	123
2	male	b	145
2	female	a	219
2	female	b	215
2	female	a	117
2	female	b	210
1	female	b	310
1	female	a	112
2	male	b	110
2	female	b	416
2	female	b	145
1	female	a	77
2	male	b	135

BIBLIOGRAPHY

Abadi D. J., Madden S. R., and Hachem N. Column-stores vs. row-stores: how different are they really. *SIGMOD '08*, 2008.

Agarwal S., Agrawal R., Deshpande P. M. , Gupta A., Naughton J. F., Ramakrishnan R., and Sarawagi S. On the computation of multidimensional aggregates. In *Proc. of the 22nd VLDB Conf.*, pages 506–521, 1996.

Agrawal R., Gupta A., and Sarawagi, S. Modeling multidimensional databases. In *Proceedings of 13th International Conference on Data Engineering,* pp. 232-243, Birmingham, U.K, 1997.

Beyer K. and Ramakrishnan R. Bottom-up computation of sparse and iceberg cubes. *SIGMOD*, pp. 359–370, Philadelphia, PA, USA, 1999.

Börzsönyi S, Kossmann D., and Stocker K. The skyline operator. *ICDE '01, IEEE Computer Society*, pp. 421–430, 2001.

Chaudhuri S. and Dayal U. An overview of data warehousing and olap technology. *SIGMOD Record,* 26(1):65–74, 1997.

Donjerkovic D. and Ramakrishnan R. Probabilistic optimization of top n queries. *VLDB'99*, pp. 411–422, 1999.

Fang M., Shivakumar N., Garcia-Molina H., Motwani R, and Ullman J. D. Computing iceberg queries efficiently. *VLDB'98*, pp. 299–310, 1998.

Feng Y., Agrawal D., El Abbadi A., and Ahmed Metwally. Range CUBE: efficient cube computation by exploiting data correlation. In *Proceedings of the 20th International Conference on Data Engineering (ICDE'04)*, 2004.

Goil S., and Choudhary A. Sparse data storage of multi-dimensional data for OLAP and data mining. *Technical Report CPDC-TR-9801-005*, Northwestern University, 1998.

Golfarelli M. and Rizzi S. A methodological framework for data warehouse design. *First International Workshop on Data Warehousing and OLAP (DOLAP), ACM*, Nov 1998.

Golfarelli M., Maio D., and S. Rizzi. Conceptual Design of Data Warehouses from E/R Schemas. *International Conference on Systems Science, IEEE, Ene.*, Hawaii, 1998.

Gyssens M., and Lakshmanan L. A foundation for multidimensional databases. *International Conference on Very Large Data Bases(VLDB)*, pp. 25–29, Athens, Greece, August, 1997.

Han J., Pei J., Dong G., and Wang K. Efficient computation of iceberg cubes with complex measures. In *Proceedings of ACM Int'l Conf. Management of Data (SIGMOD '01)*, 2001.

Harinarayan V., Rajaraman A., and Ullman J. Implementing data cubes efficiently. In *SIGMOD*, pp. 205–216, Montreal, Canada, June 1996.

Ho C., Agrawal R., Megiddo N., and Srikant R. Range queries in OLAP data cubes. In *Proceedings of the 1997 ACM SIGMOD Conference*, pp. 73–88, 1997.

Horner J. and Song I. Y. A taxonomy of inaccurate summaries and their management in OLAP systems. *ER2005, LNCS 3716, Springer-Verlag*, pp. 433-448, 2005.

Hurtado C.A., and Mendelzon Alberto O. Reasoning about summarizability in heterogeneous multidimensional hierarchies. In *Proceedings of the 8th International Conference on Database Theory*, pp. 375-389, Jan.2001.

Inmon W.H. *Building the Data Warehouse,* 3rd edition. Wiley, New York, 2002.

Indyk P., Motwani R., Raghavan P., and S. Vempala. Locality-preserving hashing in multidimensional spaces. In *STOC '97, ACM*, pp. 618–625, New York, NY, USA, 1997.

Jagadish H., Lakshmanan L., and Srivastava D. What can hierarchies do for data warehouses? In *Proceedings of the 25th International Conference on Very Large Data Bases,* Morgan Kaufmann, 1999.

Karayannidis N., and Sellis T. K. SISYPHUS: The implementation of a chunk-based storage manager for OLAP data cubes. *Data Knowl. Eng.* 45(2):155-180, 2003.

Kemper A. and Neumann T. HyPer: A hybrid OLTP & OLAP main memory database system based on virtual memory snapshots. *ICDE 2011: 195-206,* 2011.

Korn F., and Muthukrishnan S. Influence sets based on reverse nearest neighbor queries. In *Proceedings of the 2000 ACM SIGMOD international conference on Management of data, SIGMOD '00, ACM*, pp. 201–212, New York, USA, 2000.

Lee M., and Hammer J. Speeding up materialized view selection in datawarehouses using a randomized algorithm. *Int. J. Cooperative Inform. Syst. 10*, pp. 327–353, 2001.

Lenz H. J, and Shoshani A. Summarizability in OLAP and statistical data bases. In *SSDBM*, pp. 132-143, 1997.

Li, X., Han J., and Gonzalez H. High-dimensional OLAP: A minimal cubing approach. In *VLDB*, pp. 528–539, 2004.

Liang, W., Hui Wang, and Orlowska M. E. Range queries in dynamic OLAP data cubes. *Data & Knowledge Engineering,* 34:21-38, 2000.

Malinowski, E. and Zimanyi E. Hierarchies in a multidimensional model: From conceptual modeling to logical representation. *Accepted for publication in Data & Knowledge Engineering,* 2005.

Malinowski E., and Zimanyi E. A conceptual solution for representing time in data warehouse dimensions. In *Proc. of the 3rd Asia-Pacific Conf. on Conceptual Modelling,* pp. 45-54, 2006.

March S. T., and Hevner A. R. Integrated decision support system: A data warehouse perspective. *Decision Support Systems,* 43:1031– 1043, 2007.

Mazon J.N., Lechtenborger J., and Trujillo J. Solving summarizability problem in fct-dimension relationships for multidimensional model. *DOLAP'08,* Napa Valley, California, USA, October 30, 2008.

Miller, R.J., Haas, L.M., and Hernandez M.A. Schema mapping as query discovery. In *Proceedings of the 26th VLDB Conference*, Cairo, 2000.

Nilakanta S., Scheibe K., and Rai A., Dimensional issues in agricultural data warehouse design, *Computers and Electronics in Agriculture*. 60:263-278, 2008.

Rozeva A. Dimensional hierarchy- Implementation in data warehouse logical scheme design. In *CompSysTech07*, 2007.

Sarawagi S., Agrawal R., and Gupta A. On computing the data cube. *Technical Report RJ10026, IBM Almaden Research Center*, San Jose, CA, 1996.

Sarawagi S. and Stonebraker M. Efficient organization of large multidimensional arrays. In *Proc. of ICDE*, pp.328-336, 1994.

Shoshani. A., OLAP and statistical databases: Similarities and differences. In *Proceedings of PODS'97*, pp. 183–196, May 1997.

Shukla A., Deshpande P., and Naughton J. Materialized view selection of multidimensional datasets. In *Proceeding of the 24th VLDB Conference*, pp. 488–499, 1998.

Shanmugasundaram J., Fayyad U. M., and Bradley P. S. Compressed data cubes for OLAP aggregate query approximation on continuous dimensions. In *KDD'99*, 1999.

Sismanis Y., Deligiannakis A., Roussopoulos N., and Kotidis Y. Dwarf: Shrinking the PetaCube. In *SIGMOD*, pp. 464–475, Madison, Wisconsin, 2002.

Song I. Y., Rowen B., Medsker, C., and Ewen, E. An analysis of many-to-many relationships between fact and dimension tables in dimensional modeling. *DMDW'01,* 2001.

Tsirogiannis D., Harizopoulos S., Sha M. A., Wiener J.L., and Goetz Greafe. Query processing techniques for solid state drives. *SIGMOD '09*, 2009.

Tsois A., Karayiannidis N., and T. Sellis. MAC: Conceptual data modeling for OLAP. *DMDW'01*, 2001.

Wang W., Lu H., Feng J., and J. X. Yu. Condensed cube: An effective approach to reducing data cube size. In *ICDE'02*, 2002.

Xin, D, Han, J. Cheng, H. and X. Li. Answering top-k queries with multi-dimensional selections: The ranking cube approach. In *VLDB*, pp. 463–475, 2006.

Yiu, M. L. and Mamoulis N., Efficient processing of top-k dominating queries on multi-dimensional data. In *VLDB'07*, pp. 483–494, 2007.

Yuan. Y. *Efficient computation of Skyline queries*. PhD thesis, University of New South Wales, Australia, 2007.

Yuan, Y. Lin, X. Liu, Q., Wang, W., J. Xu Yu, and Q. Zhang. Efficient computation of the Skyline cube. In *31st International Conference on Very Large Data Bases* (*VLDB*), pp. 241-252, Trondheim, Norway, 2005.

Zhao, Y., Prasad, M., Deshpande, P., and J. F. Naughton. An array-based algorithm for simultaneous multidimensional aggregates. In *Proc. of SSDBM*, pp.218-227, 1994.

Zhang C. and Yang, J. Genetic algorithm for materialized view selection in data warehouse environments. *DaWaK 1999. LNCS, Springer,* 1676:116–125, Heidelberg, 1999.

3

Data Mining

3.1 Introduction

We have seen in the earlier chapter that when an enterprise has made substantial investments in capturing, cleaning, storing and managing data for decision support and has built a data warehouse, it is in a position to generate a range of reporting applications through *ad hoc* query capabilities, visualization and drill-down functionalities via OLAP tools. Data mining complements all of these. It also adds value to existing investments by enabling people who understand the warehousing environment (and others) to exploit data assets and gain deeper insights into key aspects of business performance. For example, a marketing department might have well-established models for modelling customer profiles. Data mining helps the marketing analyst to break free of established customer models and construct detailed customer profiles reflecting actual behaviour in different situations. In a marketing situation, such profiles can be used as a basis for enabling promotion costs to be cut and response ratios to be increased. The net impact of an effective data mining project can be very high.

In this chapter, we shall introduce the concept of data mining. In a sense, we build up arguments to motivate the reader to undertake a detailed study of data mining techniques. We shall present a number of definitions of data mining and discuss the important features of the subject. We shall also identify the major techniques of data mining and discuss possible areas of data mining applications. Data mining is a component of data warehousing, but it can also be a stand-alone process for data analysis, even in the absence of a data warehouse.

In Section 3.2, we shall explain the basic concept of data mining. Different definitions of data mining are given in Section 3.3. We also discuss different aspects of these definitions. Though popularly DM and KDD are often used interchangeably, there are some differences between them. This is highlighted in Section 3.4. The DM process can be coupled with a DBMS in tightly-coupled mode or loosely-coupled mode. The advantages and disadvantages of these modes are discussed in Section 3.5. Section 3.6 is concerned with the relationship of DM with other disciplines in Computer Science. Section 3.7 briefly outlines several data mining techniques. Some of these techniques are elaborated in subsequent chapters. It may be noted that database research is no longer confined only to data repository stored in a DBMS. Unstructured data such as text data, time series data or spatial data have already been identified as different fields of research. In Section 3.8, we shall discuss the data mining problems for these types of data. In Section 3.9, we shall identify the current trends which have influenced the development of DM techniques. Section 3.10 discusses the issues and trends of DM. There are many possible areas where DM methodology can be applied. In Section 3.10, we identify the sources of voluminous data and hence the possible domains of applications of DM. Section 3.12 illustrates some typical applications of DM.

3.2 WHAT IS DATA MINING?

Data mining is the non-trivial process of identifying valid, novel, potentially useful, and ultimately understandable patterns in data. With the widespread use of databases and the explosive growth in their sizes, organizations are faced with the problem of information overload. The problem of effectively utilizing these massive volumes of data is becoming a major problem for all enterprises. Traditionally, we have used data for querying a reliable database repository via some well-circumscribed application or canned report-generating utility. While this mode of interaction is satisfactory for a large class of applications, many other applications demand exploratory data analyses. We have seen that in a data warehouse, the OLAP engine provides an adequate interface for querying summarised and aggregate information across different dimension-hierarchies. Though such methods are relevant for decision support systems, they lack the exploratory characteristics of querying.

The OLAP engine for a data warehouse (and query languages for DBMS) supports the query-triggered use of data, in the sense that the analysis is based on a query posed by a human analyst. On the other hand, data mining techniques support automatic exploration of data. Data mining attempts to source out patterns and trends in the data and infers rules from these patterns. With these rules the user will be able to support, review and examine decisions in some related business or scientific area. This opens up the possibility of a new way of interacting with databases and data warehouses. Consider, for example, a banking application where the manager wants to know whether there is a specific pattern followed by defaulters. It is hard to formulate an SQL query for such information. It is generally accepted that if we know the query precisely we can turn to query language to formulate it. But if we have some vague idea and we do not know the precise query, then we can resort to data mining techniques.

The evolution of data mining began when business data was first stored in computers, and technologies were generated to allow users to navigate through the data in real time. Data mining takes this evolutionary process beyond retrospective data access and navigation to prospective and proactive information delivery. This evolution is due to the support of three technologies that are sufficiently mature: massive data collection, high performance computing and data mining algorithms.

We shall study some definitions of the term data mining in the following section.

3.3 Data Mining: Definitions

Data mining, the extraction of the hidden predictive information from large databases, is a powerful new technology with great potential to analyse important information in the data warehouse. Data mining scours databases for hidden patterns, finding predictive information that experts may miss, as it goes beyond their expectations. When implemented on a high performance client/server or parallel processing computers, data mining tools can analyse massive databases to deliver answers to questions such as which clients are most likely to respond to the next promotional mailing. There is an increasing desire to use this new technology in the new application domain, and a growing perception that these large passive databases can be made into useful actionable information.

Definitions

The term 'data mining' refers to the finding of relevant and useful information from databases. Data mining and knowledge discovery in the databases is a new interdisciplinary field, merging ideas from statistics, machine learning, databases and parallel computing. Researchers have defined the term 'data mining' in many ways. We discuss a few of these definitions below.

1. *Data mining or knowledge discovery in databases, as it is also known, is the non-trivial extraction of implicit, previously unknown and potentially useful information from the data. This encompasses a number of technical approaches, such as clustering, data summarization, classification, finding dependency networks, analysing changes, and detecting anomalies.*

Though the terms data mining and KDD are used above synonymously, there are debates on the difference and similarity between data mining and knowledge discovery. In the present book, we shall be using these two terms synonymously. However, we shall also study the aspects in which these two terms are said to be different.

Data retrieval, in its usual sense in database literature, attempts to retrieve data that is stored explicitly in the database and presents it to the user in a way that the user can understand. It does not attempt to extract implicit information. One may argue that if we store 'date of birth' as a field in the database and extract 'age' from it, the information received from the database is not explicitly available. But all of us would agree that the information is not 'non-trivial'. On the other hand, if one attempts to find out the average age of the employees in a particular company, it can be visualised as a sort of non-trivial extraction of implicit information. Then, can we say that extracting the average age of the employees of a department from the employees database (which stores the date of birth of every employee) is a data-mining task? The task is surely a 'non-trivial extraction of implicit information'. It is indeed a type of data mining task, but at a very low level. A higher level task would, for example, be to find correlations between the average age and average income of individuals in an enterprise.

2. *Data mining is the search for the relationships and global patterns that exist in large databases but are hidden among vast amounts of data, such as the relationship between patient data and their medical diagnosis. This relationship represents valuable knowledge about the database, and the objects in the database, if the database is a faithful mirror of the real world registered by the database.*

Consider the employee database and let us assume that we have some tools to determine some relationships between fields, say the relationship between age and lunch-patterns. Assume, for example, that we find that most of employees in their thirties like to eat pizzas, burgers or Chinese food during their lunch break. Employees in their forties prefer to carry a home-cooked lunch. And employees in their fifties take fruits and salads during lunch. If our tool finds this pattern from the database which records the lunch activities of all employees for the last few months, then we can term our tool a data mining tool. The daily lunch activity of all employees collected over a reasonable period of time makes the database very vast. Just by examining the database, it is impossible to notice any relationship between age and lunch patterns.

3. *Data mining refers to using a variety of techniques to identify nuggets of information or decision-making knowledge in the database and extracting these in such a way that they can be put to use in areas such as decision support, prediction, forecasting and estimation. The data is often voluminous, but it has low value and no direct use can be made of it. It is the hidden information in the data that is useful.*

Data mining is a process of finding value from volume. In any enterprise, the amount of transactional data generated during its day-to-day operations is massive. Although these transactions record every instance of any activity, it is of little use in decision making. Data mining attempts to extract smaller pieces of valuable information from this massive database.

4. *Discovering relations that connect variables in a database is the subject of data mining. The data mining system self-learns from the previous history of the investigated system, formulating and testing hypothesis about rules which systems obey. When concise and valuable knowledge about the system of interest is discovered, it can and should be interpreted into some decision support system, which helps the manager to make wise and informed business decision.*

Data mining is essentially a system that learns from existing data. One can think of two disciplines which address such problems—Statistics and Machine Learning. Statistics provide sufficient tools for data analysis and machine learning deals with different learning methodologies. While statistical methods are theory-rich–data-poor, data mining is the data-rich–theory-poor approach. On the other hand, machine learning deals with the whole gamut of learning theory, while most often data mining is restricted to areas of learning with partially specified data.

5. *Data mining is the process of discovering meaningful, new correlation patterns and trends by sifting through large amounts of data stored in repositories, using pattern recognition techniques as well as statistical and mathematical techniques.*

One important aspect of data mining is that it scans through a large volume of data to discover patterns and correlations between attributes. Thus, though there are techniques like clustering, decision trees, etc., in different disciplines, these are not readily applicable to data mining as they are not designed to handle large amounts of data. Thus, in order to apply statistical and mathematical tools, we have to modify these techniques to be able efficiently sift through large amounts of data stored in the secondary memory.

3.4 KDD vs. Data Mining

Knowledge Discovery in Database (KDD) was formalised in 1989, with reference to the general concept of being broad and high level in the pursuit of seeking knowledge from data. The term *data mining* was then coined; this high-level application technique is used to present and analyse data for decision-makers.

Data mining is only one of the many steps involved in knowledge discovery in databases. The various steps in the knowledge discovery process include data selection, data cleaning and preprocessing, data transformation and reduction, data mining algorithm selection and finally post-processing and the interpretation of the discovered knowledge. The KDD process tends to be highly iterative and interactive. Data mining analysis tends to work up from the data and the best techniques are developed with an orientation towards large volumes of data, making use of as much data as possible to arrive at reliable conclusions and decisions. The analysis process starts with a set of data, and uses a methodology to develop an optimal representation of the structure of data, during which knowledge is acquired. Once knowledge is acquired, this can be extended to large sets of data on the assumption that the large data set has a structure similar to the simple data set.

Fayyad et al distinguish between KDD and data mining by giving the following definitions.

Knowledge Discovery in Databases is the process of identifying a valid, potentially useful and ultimately understandable structure in data. This process involves selecting or sampling data from a data warehouse, cleaning or preprocessing it, transforming or reducing it (if needed), applying a data mining component to produce a structure, and then evaluating the derived structure.

Data Mining is a step in the KDD process concerned with the algorithmic means by which patterns or structures are enumerated from the data under acceptable computational efficiency limitations.

Thus, the structures that are the outcome of the data mining process must meet certain conditions so that these can be considered as knowledge. These conditions are: *validity, understandability, utility, novelty* and *interestingness*.

Stages of KDD

The stages of KDD, starting with the raw data and finishing with the extracted knowledge, are given below.

Selection

This stage is concerned with selecting or segmenting the data that are relevant to some criteria. For example, for credit card customer profiling, we extract the type of transactions for each type of customer and we may not be interested in details of the shop where the transaction took place.

Preprocessing

Preprocessing is the data cleaning stage where unnecessary information is removed. For example, it is unnecessary to note the sex of a patient when studying pregnancy! When the data is drawn from several sources, it is possible that the same information is represented in different sources in different formats. This stage reconfigures the data to ensure a consistent format, as there is a possibility of inconsistent formats.

Transformation

The data is not merely transferred across, but transformed in order to be suitable for the task of data mining. In this stage, the data is made usable and navigable.

Data Mining

This stage is concerned with the extraction of patterns from the data.

Interpretation and Evaluation

The patterns obtained in the data mining stage are converted into knowledge, which in turn, is used to support decision-making.

DATA VISUALIZATION

Data visualization makes it possible for the analyst to gain a deeper, more intuitive understanding of the data and as such can work well alongside data mining. Data mining allows the analyst to focus on certain patterns and trends and explore them in-depth using visualization. On its own, data visualization can be overwhelmed by the volume of data in a database but, in conjunction with data mining, can help with exploration.

Data visualization helps users to examine large volumes of data and detect the patterns visually. Visual displays of data such as maps, charts and other graphical representations allow data to be presented compactly to the users. A single graphical screen can encode as much information as a far larger number of text screens. For example, if a user wants to find out whether the production problems at a plant are correlated to the location of the plant, the problem locations can be encoded in a special colour, say red, on a map. The user can then discover locations in which the problems have occurred. He may then form a hypothesis about why problems have occurred in those locations, and may verify the hypothesis against the database.

3.5 DBMS VS. DM

We have seen that DBMS supports query languages which are useful for query-triggered data exploration, whereas data mining supports automatic data exploration. If we know exactly what information we are seeking, a DBMS query would suffice; whereas if we only vaguely know the possible correlations or patterns, then data mining techniques are useful. One of the tasks of data mining is hypothesis testing, wherein we formulate a hypothesis and test it by sifting through the database. This task can be handled by a DBMS query. Thus, in these senses, DBMS supports some primitive data mining tasks.

From the architectural perspective, let us look the way a data mining system makes use of an existing database.

There are three different ways in which data mining systems use a relational DBMS: they may not use it at all, be *loosely coupled* or be *tightly coupled*.

A majority of data mining systems do not use any DBMS and have their own memory and storage management. They treat the database simply as a data repository from which data is expected to be downloaded into their own memory structures, before the data mining algorithm starts. The advantage of such an approach is that one can optimise the memory management specific to the data mining algorithm. On the contrary, these systems ignore the field-proven technologies of DBMS, such as recovery, concurrency, etc.

The second approach is to have a *loosely-coupled* DBMS. In this case, the DBMS is used only for storage and retrieval of data. For instance, one can use a loosely-coupled SQL to fetch data records as required by the mining algorithm. The front-end of the application is implemented in a host programming language, with embedded SQL statements. The applications use an SQL select statement to retrieve the set of records of interest from the database. A loop in the application program copies records in the result set one by one from the database address space to the application address space, where computation is performed. This loosely-coupled approach does not use the querying capability provided by the DBMS.

In the *tightly-coupled* approach, the portions of the application programs are selectively pushed to the database system to perform the necessary computation. Data are stored in the database and all processing is done at the database end. It is different from bringing the data from the database to the data mining area. On the other hand, the data mining application goes where the data naturally reside. This avoids performance degradation and takes full advantage of database technology. The performance of this approach depends on the way to optimise the data mining process while mapping it to a query. There are two suggested approaches. We can leave the optimization task to a built-in query optimiser of the DBMS or we can use an external optimiser.

3.6 Other Related Areas

Data mining research has drawn on a number of other fields such as machine learning and statistics. We review the relations of data mining with some of the important areas.

Statistics

As we mentioned earlier, statistics is a theory-rich approach to data analysis. Statistics, with its solid theoretical foundation, generates results that can be overwhelming and difficult to interpret. These require user guidance as to where and how to analyse the data. Notwithstanding these, statistics is one of the foundational principles on which data mining technology is built. Statistical analysis systems are used by analysts to detect unusual patterns and explain patterns using statistical models, such as linear models. Statistics has an important role to play and data mining will not replace such analyses, but rather statistics can act upon more directed analyses based on the results of data mining.

Machine Learning

Machine learning is the automation of a learning process and learning is tantamount to the construction of rules based on observations. This is a broad field which includes not only learning from examples, but also reinforcement learning, learning with a teacher, etc. A learning algorithm takes the data set and its accompanying information as the input and returns a statement, e.g., a concept representing the results of learning as output.

Inductive learning, where the system infers knowledge by observing its environment, has two main strategies: Supervised Learning and Unsupervised Learning. The model produced by inductive learning methods can be used to predict the outcome of future situations; in other words, not only for states encountered but rather for unseen states that could occur. There can be many possible models from a given set of examples. In such situations, the principle of Occam's Razor is appropriate. It states that if there are multiple explanations for a particular phenomena, it makes sense to choose the simplest because it is more likely to capture the nature of the phenomenon.

Supervised Learning

Supervised learning means learning from examples, where a training set is given which acts as examples for the classes. The system finds a description of each class. Once the description (and hence a classification rule) has been formulated, it is used to predict the class of previously unseen objects. This is similar to discriminant analysis which occurs in statistics.

Unsupervised Learning

Unsupervised learning is learning from observation and discovery. In this mode of learning, there is no training set or prior knowledge of the classes. The system analyses the given set of data to observe similarities emerging out of the subsets of the data. The outcome is a set of class descriptions, one for each class, discovered in the environment. This is similar to cluster analysis in statistics.

Data mining and the part of machine learning dealing with learning from examples overlap in the algorithms used and the problems addressed. Data mining is concerned with finding understandable knowledge, while machine learning is concerned with improving the performance of an intelligent system or agent for problem-solving tasks. When integrating machine learning techniques into database systems, some of the databases require more efficient learning algorithms because realistic databases are normally very large and noisy.

Mathematical Programming

The relationship between mathematical programming and data mining was not so obvious until the pioneering work by O L Mangasarian. Most of the major data mining tasks can be equivalently formulated as problems in mathematical programming for which efficient algorithms are available. It provides a new insight into the problems the data mining. One of the major active research topics in this field is the *Support Vector Machines* approach for classification. We shall discuss this approach briefly in the following section.

3.7 DM Techniques

Researchers identify two fundamental goals of data mining: prediction and description. *Prediction* makes use of existing variables in the database to predict unknown or future values of interest, and *description* focuses on finding patterns describing the data and the subsequent presentation for user interpretation. The relative emphasis of both prediction and description differ with respect to the underlying application and technique. There are several data mining techniques fulfilling these objectives. Some of these are associations, classifications, sequential patterns and clustering. The basic premise of an association is to find all associations, such that the presence of one set of items in a transaction implies the other items. Classification develops profiles of different groups. Sequential patterns identify sequential patterns subject to a user-specified minimum constraint. Clustering segments a database into subsets or clusters.

Another approach to the study of DM techniques is to classify the techniques as

- User-guided or verification-driven data mining, and
- Discovery-driven or automatic discovery of rules

Most of the techniques of data mining have elements of both models.

Verification Model

In this process of data mining, the user makes a hypothesis and tests the hypothesis on the data to verify its validity. The emphasis is on the user who is responsible for formulating the hypothesis and issuing the query on the data to affirm or negate the hypothesis.

In a supermarket, for example, with a limited budget for a mailing campaign to launch a new product, it is important to identify the section of the population most likely to buy the new product. The user formulates a hypothesis to identify potential customers and their common characteristics. Historical data about transactions and demographic information can then be queried to reveal comparable purchases and the characteristics shared by those purchasers. The whole operation can be repeated by successive refinements of hypotheses until the required limit is reached. The user may come up with a new hypothesis or refine the existing one and verify it against the database.

Discovery Model

The discovery model differs in its emphasis, in that it is the system that automatically discovers important information hidden in the data. The data is sifted in search of frequently occurring patterns, trends and generalizations about the data without intervention or guidance from the user.

The manner in which the rules are discovered depends on the class of the data mining application.

An example of such a model is a supermarket database, which is mined to discover the particular groups of customers to be targeted by a mailing campaign. The data is searched with no hypothesis in mind other than for the system to group the customers according to the common characteristics found.

The typical discovery driven tasks are

- Discovery of association rules
- Discovery of classification rules
- Clustering
- Discovery of frequent episodes
- Deviation detection

These tasks are of an exploratory nature and cannot be directly handed over to currently available database technology. We shall concentrate on these tasks now.

Discovery of Association Rules

An association rule is an expression of the form $X \Rightarrow Y$, where X and Y are the sets of items. The intuitive meaning of such a rule is that the transaction of the database which contains X tends to contain Y. Given a database, the goal is to discover all the rules that have the support and confidence greater than or equal to the minimum support and confidence, respectively.

Let $L=\{l_1,l_2,\ldots,l_m\}$ be a set of literals called items. Let D, the database, be a set of transactions, where each transaction T is a set of items. T supports an item x, if x is in T. T is said to support a subset of items X, if T supports each item x in X. $X \Rightarrow Y$ holds with *confidence* c, if c% of the transactions in D that support X also support Y. The rule $X \Rightarrow Y$ has *support* s in the transaction set D if s% of the transactions in D support $X \cup Y$. *Support* means how often X and Y occur together as a percentage of the total transactions. *Confidence* measures how much a particular item is dependent on another.

Thus, the association with a very high support and confidence is a pattern that occurs often in the database that should be obvious to the end user. Patterns with extremely low support and confidence should be regarded as of no significance. Only patterns with a combination of intermediate values of confidence and support provide the user with interesting and previously unknown information. We shall study the techniques to discover association rules in Chapter 4.

Clustering

Clustering is a method of grouping data so that the data in each group share similar trends and patterns. Clustering constitutes a major class of data mining algorithms. The algorithm attempts to automatically partition the data space into a set of regions or clusters, to which the examples in the table are assigned, either deterministically or probability-wise. The goal of the process is to identify all sets of similar examples in the data, in some optimal fashion.

Clustering according to similarity is a concept which appears in many disciplines. If a measure of similarity is available, then there are a number of techniques for forming clusters. Another approach is to build set functions that measure some particular property of groups. This latter approach achieves what is known as optimal partitioning.

The objectives of clustering are:

- to uncover natural groupings
- to initiate hypothesis about the data
- to find consistent and valid organization of the data.

A retailer may want to know where similarities exist in his customer base, so that he can create and understand different groups. He can use the existing database of the different customers or, more specifically, different transactions collected over a period of time. The clustering methods will help him in identifying different categories of customers. During the discovery process, the differences between data sets can be discovered in order to separate them into different groups, and similarity between data sets can be used to group similar data together. In Chapter 5, we shall discuss in detail about using the clustering algorithm for data mining tasks.

Discovery of Classification Rules

Classification involves finding rules that partition the data into disjoint groups. The input for the classification is the training data set, whose class labels are already known. Classification analyses the training data set and constructs a model based on the class label, and aims to assign a class label to the future unlabelled records. Since the class field is known, this type of classification is known as supervised learning. A set of classification rules are generated by such a classification process, which can be used to classify future data and develop a better understanding of each class in the database. We can term this as *supervised learning* too.

There are several classification discovery models. They are: decision trees, neural networks, genetic algorithms and statistical models like linear/geometric discriminants. The applications include the credit card analysis, banking, medical applications and the like. Consider the following example.

The domestic flights in our country were at one time only operated by Indian Airlines. Recently, many other private airlines began their operations for domestic travel. Some of the customers of Indian Airlines started flying with these private airlines and, as a result, Indian Airlines lost these customers. Let us assume that Indian Airlines wants to understand why some customers remain loyal while others leave. Ultimately, the airline wants to predict which customers it is most likely to lose to its competitors. Their aim to build a model based on the historical data of loyal customers versus customers who have left. This becomes a classification problem. It is a supervised learning task as the historical data becomes the training set which is used to train the model. The decision tree is the most popular classification technique. In Chapter 6, we shall discuss different methods of decision tree construction.

Frequent Episodes

Frequent episodes are the sequence of events that occur frequently, close to each other and are extracted from the time sequences. How close it has to be to consider it as frequent is domain dependent. This is given by the user as the input, and the output are the prediction rules for the time sequences.

Given a set R of event types, an event is a pair (A, t) where $A \in R$ is an event type and t is an integer, we can calculate the occurrence time of the event. An event sequence s of R is a triple (Ts, Tc, S), where $Ts < Tc$ are integers. Ts is the starting time and Tc is the ending time.

$S = \{(A_1, t_1), (A_2, t_2), (A_n, t_n)\}$ is the ordered sequence of events, such that $A_i \in R$ and $Ts \le t_i \le Tc$ for all $i = 1, 2\ldots n{-}1$.

These episodes can be of three types. The serial episodes which occur in sequence. The parallel episodes in which there are no constraints on the order of the event types A and B given. And the non-serial and non-parallel episodes which occur in a sequence if the occurrences of A and B precede an occurrence of C, and there is no constraint on the relative order of A and B given.

The applications include telecommunications, and share market analysis, and these are mainly used for temporal data.

Deviation Detection

Deviation detection is the identification of outlying points in a particular data set, and explain whether they are due to noise or other impurities being present in the data or due to trivial reasons. It is usually applied with database segmentation, and is the source of true discovery, since the outliers express deviation from some previously known expectation and norm. By calculating the values of measures of current data and comparing them with previous data as well as with the normative data, the deviations can be obtained. They can be applied in forecasting, fraud detection, customer retention, etc.

Neural Networks

Neural networks are a new paradigm in computing, which involves developing mathematical structures with the ability to learn. The methods are the result of academic attempts to model the nervous system learning. Neural networks have the remarkable ability to derive meaning from complicated or imprecise data and can be used to extract patterns and detect trends that are too complex to be noticed by either humans or other computer techniques. Neural networks have broad applicability to real world business problems and have already been successfully applied in many industries. Since neural networks are best at identifying patterns or trends in data, they are well suited for prediction or forecasting needs.

Neural networks use a set of processing elements (or nodes) analogous to neurons in the brain. These processing elements are interconnected in a network that can then identify patterns in data once it is exposed to the data, i.e., the network learns from experience just as people do. This distinguishes neural networks from traditional computing programs that simply follow instructions in a fixed sequential order.

Neural networks have been used successfully for classification but suffer somewhat in that the resulting network is viewed as a black box and no explanation of the results is given. This lack of explanation inhibits confidence, acceptance and application of results. Another problem is that neural networks suffer from long learning times, which become worse as the volume of data grows.

Genetic Algorithms

Genetic algorithms are a relatively new computing paradigm, inspired by Darwin's theory of evolution. A population of individuals, each representing a possible solution to a problem, is initially created at random. Then pairs of individuals combine (crossover) to produce offspring for the next generation. A mutation process is also used to randomly modify the genetic structure of some members of each new generation. The algorithm runs to generate solutions for successive generations. The probability of an individual reproducing is proportional to the goodness of the solution it represents. Hence, the quality of the solutions in successive generations improves. The process is terminated when an acceptable or optimum solution is found, or after some fixed time limit. Genetic algorithms are appropriate for problems which require optimization, with respect to some computable criterion.

This paradigm can also be applied to data mining problems. Here, the quantity to be minimised is often the number of classification errors in a training set. However, the mining of large data sets by genetic algorithms has only recently become practical due to the availability of affordable, high-speed computers. But there is hardly any special genetic algorithm designed to suit data mining problems.

Rough Set Techniques

The rough set theory has recently become popular in the field of data mining. The theory, introduced by Pawlak in the early 1980s, provides a formal framework for the automated transformation of data into knowledge. The rough set theory, though mathematically simple, has displayed its fruitfulness in a variety of data mining areas. A rough set is a pair of approximations—lower approximation and upper approximation sets. The lower approximation is also said to be positive cases and the upper approximation is said to be possible cases. Using these approximations, the rough set theory develops tools to discover rules from the given databases. A wide range of applications utilise the ideas of the theory. Medical data analysis, aircraft pilot performance evaluation, image processing and voice recognition are a few examples. Almost inevitably, the database used for data mining will contain imperfections, such as noise, unknown values or errors due to inaccurate measuring equipment. The rough set theory is handy for dealing with these types of problems, as it is a tool for handling vagueness and uncertainty inherent to decision situations. An important result from the theory is that it simplifies the search for dominating attributes leading to specific properties, or just rules pending in the data.

Support Vector Machines

Support Vector Machines (SVM) is based on statistical learning theory and is increasingly becoming useful in data mining. The main idea is to non-linearly map the data set into a high-dimensional feature space and use a linear discriminator to classify the data. Its success has been demonstrated in the areas of regression, classification and decision-tree construction. Unlike other classification techniques, which attempt to minimise the error of classification, SVMs incorporate structured risk minimization which minimises an upper bound on the generalised error. Consider a simple case when two sets A and B are linearly separable. The idea is to determine from an infinite number of planes correctly separating A and B, the one which will have the smallest generalization error. SVMs select the plane which maximises the margin separating the two classes. The margin is defined as the distance between the separating hyperplane to the nearest point of A, plus the distance from the hyperplane to the nearest point in B.

3.8 Other Mining Problems

We observed that a data mining system can either be a portion of a data warehousing system or a stand-alone system. Data for data mining need not always be enterprise-related data residing on a relational database. Data sources are very diverse and appear in varied form. It can be textual data, image data, CAD data, map data, ECG data or the much talked about genome data. Some data are structured and some unstructured. Data mining remains an important tool, irrespective of the forms or sources of data. We shall study the DM problems for different types of data.

Sequence Mining

Sequence mining is concerned with mining sequence data. It may be noted that in the discovery of association rules, we are interested in finding associations between items irrespective of their order of occurrence. For example, we may be interested in the association between the purchase of a particular brand of soft drink and the occurrence of stomach upset. But it is more relevant to identify whether there is some pattern in the stomach upset which occurs after the purchase of the soft drink. Then one is inclined to infer that the soft drink causes a stomach upset. On the other hand, if it is more likely that the purchase of the soft drink follows the occurrence of the stomach upset, then it is probable that the soft drink provides some sort of relief to the user. Thus, the discovery of temporal sequences of events concerns causal relationships among the events in a sequence. Another application of this domain concerns drug misuse. Drug misuse can occur unwittingly, when a patient is prescribed two or more interacting drugs within a given time period of each other. Drugs that interact undesirably are recorded along with the time frame as a pattern that can be located within the patient records. The rules that describe such instances of drug misuse are then successfully inducted based on medical records.

Another related area which falls into the larger domain of temporal data mining is *trend discovery*. One characteristic of sequence-pattern discovery in comparison with trend discovery is the lack of shapes, since the causal impact of a series of events cannot be shaped.

Web Mining

With the huge amount of information available online, the World Wide Web is a fertile area for data mining research. Web mining research is at the crossroads of research from several research communities, such as database, information retrieval, and within AI, especially the subareas of machine learning and natural language processing. Web mining is the use of data mining techniques to automatically discover and extract information from web documents and services. This area of research is so huge today partly due to the interests of various research communities, the tremendous growth of information sources available on the web and the recent interest in e-commerce. This phenomenon often creates confusion when we ask what constitutes web mining. Web mining can be broken down into following subtasks:

1. Resource finding: retrieving documents intended for the Web.
2. Information selection and preprocessing: automatically selecting and preprocessing specific information from resources retrieved from the Web.

3. Generalization: to automatically discover general patterns at individual Web sites as well as across multiple sites.
4. Analysis: validation and/or interpretation of the mined patterns.

TEXT MINING

The term text mining or KDT (Knowledge Discovery in Text) was first proposed by Feldman and Dagan in 1996. They suggest that text documents be structured by means of information extraction, text categorization, or applying NLP techniques as a preprocessing step before performing any kind of KDTs. Currently the term text mining is used to cover many applications such as text categorization, exploratory data analysis, text clustering, finding patterns in text databases, finding sequential patterns in texts, IE (Information Extraction), empirical computational linguistic tasks and association discovery.

SPATIAL DATA MINING

Spatial data mining is the branch of data mining that deals with spatial (location) data. The immense explosion in geographically-referenced data occasioned by developments in IT, digital mapping, remote sensing, and the global diffusion of GIS, places demands on developing data-driven inductive approaches to spatial analysis and modelling. Spatial data mining is regarded as a special type of data mining that seeks to perform similar generic functions as conventional data mining tools, but modified to take into account the special features of spatial information.

For example, we may wish to discover some association among patterns of residential colonies and topographical features. A typical spatial association may look like: 'The residential land pockets are dense in a plain region and rocky areas are thinly populated"; or, "The economically affluent citizens reside in hilly, secluded areas whereas the middle income group residents prefer having their houses near the market".

3.9 ISSUES AND CHALLENGES IN DM

Data mining systems depend on databases to supply the raw input and this raises problems, such as that databases tend to be dynamic, incomplete, noisy and large. Other problems arise as a result of the inadequacy and irrelevance of the information stored. The difficulties in data mining can be categorised as
Limited information

- Noise or missing data
- User interaction and prior knowledge
- Uncertainty
- Size, updates and irrelevant fields

Limited information A database is often designed for purposes other than that of data mining and, sometimes, some attributes which are essential for knowledge discovery of the application domain are not present in the data. Thus, it may be very difficult to discover significant knowledge about a given domain.

Noise and missing data Attributes that rely on subjective or measurement judgments can give rise to errors, such that some examples may be misclassified. Missing data can be treated in a number of ways—simply disregarding missing values, omitting corresponding records, inferring missing values from known values, and treating missing data as a special value to be included additionally in the attribute domain. The data should be cleaned so that it is free of errors and missing data.

User interaction and prior knowledge An analyst is usually not a KDD expert, but simply a person making use of the data by means of the available KDD techniques. Since the KDD process is by definition interactive and iterative, it is challenging to provide a high performance, rapid-response environment that also assists the users in the proper selection and matching of the appropriate techniques to achieve their goals. There needs to be more human–computer interaction and less emphasis on total automation, which supports both the novice and expert users. The use of domain knowledge is important in all steps of the KDD process. It would be convenient to design a KDD tool which is both interactive and iterative.

Uncertainty This refers to the severity of error and the degree of noise in the data. Data precision is an important consideration in a discovery system.

Size, updates and irrelevant fields Databases tend to be large and dynamic, in that their contents keep changing as information is added, modified or removed. The problem with this, from the perspective of data mining, is how to ensure that the rules are up-to-date and consistent with the most current information.

3.10 DM Application Areas

The discipline of data mining is driven in part by new applications which require new capabilities that are not currently being supplied by today's technology. These new applications can be naturally divided into three broad categories [Grossman, 1999].

A. Business and E-commerce Data

This is a major source category of data for data mining applications. Back-office, front-office, and network applications produce large amounts of data about business processes. Using this data for effective decision making remains a fundamental challenge.

Business Transactions

Modern business processes are consolidating with millions of customers and billions of their transactions. Business enterprises require necessary information for their effective functioning in today's competitive world. For example, they would like know: "Is this transaction fraudulent?";

"Which customer is likely to migrate?", and "What product is this customer most likely to buy next?".

ELECTRONIC COMMERCE

Not only does electronic commerce produce large data sets in which the analysis of marketing patterns and risk patterns is critical but, it is also important to do this in near-real time, in order to meet the demands of online transactions.

B. SCIENTIFIC, ENGINEERING AND HEALTH CARE DATA

Scientific data and metadata tend to be more complex in structure than business data. In addition, scientists and engineers are making increasing use of simulation and systems with application domain knowledge.

GENOMIC DATA

Genomic sequencing and mapping efforts have produced a number of databases which are accessible on the web. In addition, there are also a wide variety of other online databases. Finding relationships between these data sources is another fundamental challenge for data mining.

SENSOR DATA

Remote sensing data is another source of voluminous data. Remote sensing satellites and a variety of other sensors produce large amounts of geo-referenced data. A fundamental challenge is to understand the relationships, including causal relationships, amongst this data.

SIMULATION DATA

Simulation is now accepted as an important mode of science, supplementing theory and experiment. Today, not only do experiments produce huge data sets, but so do simulations. Data mining and, more generally, data intensive computing is proving to be a critical link between theory, simulation, and experiment.

HEALTHCARE DATA

Hospitals, healthcare organisations, insurance companies and the concerned government agencies accumulate large collections of data about patients and health care-related details. Understanding relationships in this data is critical for a wide variety of problems—ranging from determining what procedures and clinical protocols are most effective, to how best to deliver health care to the maximum number of people.

WEB DATA

The data on the Web is growing not only in volume but also in complexity. Web data now includes not only text, audio and video material, but also streaming data and numerical data.

MULTIMEDIA DOCUMENTS

Today's technology for retrieving multimedia items on the Web is far from satisfactory. On the other hand, an increasingly large number of matters are on the Web and the number of users is also growing explosively. It is becoming harder to extract meaningful information from the archives of multimedia data as the volume grows.

DATA WEB

Today, the Web is primarily oriented toward documents and their multimedia extensions. HTML has proved itself to be a simple, yet powerful, language for supporting this. Tomorrow, the potential exists for the Web to prove equally important for working with data. Extensible Markup Language (XML) is an emerging language for working with data in networked environments. As this infrastructure grows, data mining is expected to be a critical enabling technology for the emerging data web.

3.11 DM APPLICATIONS—CASE STUDIES

There is a wide range of well-established business applications for data mining. These include customer attrition, profiling, promotion forecasting, product cross-selling, fraud detection, targeted marketing, propensity analysis, credit scoring, risk analysis, etc. We shall now discuss a few mock case-studies and areas of DM applications.

HOUSING LOAN PREPAYMENT PREDICTION

A home-finance loan actually has an average life-span of only 7 to 10 years, due to prepayment. Prepayment means that the loan is paid off early, rather than at the end of, say, 25 years. People prepay loans when they refinance or when they sell their home. The financial return that a home-finance institution derives from a loan depends on its life-span. Therefore, it is necessary for the financial institutions to be able to predict the life-spans of their loans. Rule discovery techniques can be used to accurately predict the aggregate number of loan prepayments in a given quarter (or, in a year), as a function of prevailing interest rates, borrower characteristics and account data. This information can be used to fine-tune loan parameters such as interest rates, points, and fees, in order to maximise profits.

MORTGAGE LOAN DELINQUENCY PREDICTION

Loan defaults usually entail expenses and losses for the banks and other lending institutions. Data mining techniques can be used to predict whether or not a loan would go delinquent within the succeeding 12 months, based on historical data, on account information, borrower demographics and economic indicators. The rules can be used to estimate and fine-tune loan loss reserves and to gain some business insight into the characteristics and circumstances of delinquent loans. This will also help in deciding the funds that should be kept aside to handle bad loans.

Crime Detection

Crime detection is another area one might immediately associate with data mining. Let us consider a specific case: to find patterns in 'bogus official' burglaries.

A typical example of this kind of crime is when someone turns up at the door pretending to be from the water board, electricity board, telephone department or gas company. Whilst they distract the householder, their partners will search the premises and steal cash and items of value. Victims of this sort of crime tend to be the elderly. These cases have no obvious leads, and data mining techniques may help in providing some unexpected connections to known perpetrators.

In order to apply data mining techniques, let us assume that each case is filed electronically, and contains descriptive information about the thieves. It also contains a description of their *modus operandi*. We can use any of the clustering techniques to examine a situation where a group of similar physical descriptions coincide with a group of similar *modus operandi*. If there is a good match here, and the perpetrators are known for one or more of the offences, then each of the unsolved cases could have well been committed by the same people.

By matching unsolved cases with known perpetrators, it would be possible to clear up old cases and determine patterns of behaviour. Alternatively, if the criminal is unknown but a large cluster of cases seem to point to the same offenders, then these frequent offenders can be subjected to careful examination.

Store-level Fruits Purchasing Prediction

A super market chain called 'FruitWorld' sells fruits of different types and it purchases these fruits from the wholesale suppliers on a day-to-day basis. The problem is to analyse fruit-buying patterns, using large volumes of data captured at the 'basket' level. Because fruits have a short shelf-life, it is important that accurate store-level purchasing predictions should be made to ensure optimum freshness and availability. The situation is inherently complicated by the 'domino' effect. For example, when one variety of mangoes is sold out, then sales are transferred to another variety. With the help of data mining techniques, a thorough understanding of purchasing trends enables a better availability of fruits and greater customer satisfaction.

Other application Areas

Risk Analysis

Given a set of current customers and an assessment of their risk-worthiness, develop descriptions for various classes. Use these descriptions to classify a new customer into one of the risk categories.

Targeted Marketing

Given a database of potential customers and how they have responded to a solicitation, develop a model of customers most likely to respond positively, and use the model for more focussed new customer solicitation. Other applications are to identify buying patterns from customers; to find associations among customer demographic characteristics, and to predict the response to mailing campaigns.

Customer Retention
Given a database of past customers and their behaviour prior to attrition, develop a model of customers most likely to leave. Use the model for determining the best course of action for these customers.

Portfolio Management
Given a particular financial asset, predict the return on investment to determine the inclusion of the asset in a folio or not.

Brand Loyalty
Given a customer and the product he/she uses, predict whether the customer will switch brands.

Banking
The application areas in banking are:

- detecting patterns of fraudulent credit card use
- identifying 'loyal' customers
- predicting customers likely to change their credit card affiliation
- determine credit card spending by customer groups
- finding hidden correlations between different financial indicators
- identifying stock trading rules from historical market data

3.12 Conclusions

Successful applications of data mining are increasingly appearing in diverse applications. These are driven mainly by a glut in databases that have grown to surpass raw human processing ability. Some success stories in data mining applications in industries are reported by Brachman et al [Brachman, 1996], and in scientific analysis by Fayyad et al [Fayyad, 1996]. Driving the growth of this field are strong forces that are a product of the data overload phenomenon. In recent years, government agencies and industrial enterprises are using the Web as the medium of publication. As a result, a very large collection of documents, images and other forms of data in structured, semistructured and unstructured forms are available on the Web. Demands are being posed by the Web-user community to provide data mining solutions to explore the massive repository of hyperlink data. On the other side, the database community have evolved themselves to address database-related solutions, not only for data in a DBMS but also for data in the form of time-series, sequence, temporal and spatial data. These developments will not only ensure the emergence of a new engineering discipline, but will also provide a real-world test platform for any theoretical research that results from such studies.

One, of course, cannot ignore the fact that the fundamental problems of data analysis are still as difficult as they were in the past. In the following chapters, we shall elaborate upon some of the major data mining techniques.

Current Trends Affecting DM

Five external trends are identified by Grossman [Grossman, 1999], which promise to have a fundamental impact on data mining. We shall briefly discuss these trends.

Data Trends

Perhaps the most fundamental external trend is the explosion of digital data over the past two decades. The amount of data has probably grown between 6 and 10 orders of magnitude. Much of this data is now available on the Web or accessible through networks. In order to avoid dumping such data in archive files without any practical use, techniques such as data mining must be developed, which can automate this data, and extract meaningful knowledge.

Hardware Trends

Data mining requires numerically and statistically intensive computations on large data sets. The increasing memory and processing speed of workstations enables the mining of data sets using current algorithms and techniques that were too large to be mined just a few years ago.

Network Trends

With the next generation internet connectivity, it becomes possible to correlate distributed datasets using current algorithms and techniques. In addition, new protocols, algorithms, and languages can facilitate distributed data mining using current and next generation networks.

Scientific Computing Trends

Data mining and knowledge discovery play an important role in linking theory, experiment and simulation, especially for those cases in which the experiment or simulation results in large datasets.

Business Trends

Today's businesses must be more profitable, react quicker, and offer higher quality services than ever before, and do it all using fewer people and at a lower cost. With these types of expectations and constraints, data mining becomes a fundamental technology in enabling businesses to predict opportunities and risks generated by their customers and their customers' transactions more accurately.

FURTHER READING

The detailed bibliography for most of the major techniques are given at the end of each chapter. This chapter deals with the general concept of data mining.

The Bayesian Network approach to data mining is introduced in [Heckerman, 1997]. P-. Shapiro and Frawley give some definition of data mining. Grossman et al [Grossman, 1999] and Virmani [Virmani, 1998] identify the trends in data mining. The special issue in *Communication ACM* in 1996 [Fayyad, 1996] provides an interesting reading of the general subject of data mining and its applications. Nestorov outlines the different types of integrating RDBMS with data mining. IBM group also have investigated the possible integration of data mining with DB2.

EXERCISES

1. What is data mining?
2. How is data mining different from KDD?
3. Discuss the role of data mining in data warehousing.
4. Discuss different data mining tasks.
5. Give a brief account of data mining techniques.
6. What is spatial data mining?
7. What is sequence mining?
8. What is Web mining?
9. What is text mining?
10. Give some examples where temporal mining is relevant.
11. Discuss the applications of data mining in the banking industry.
12. Discuss the applications of data mining in customer relationship management.
13. What is clustering of data? Distinguish supervised and unsupervised classifications.
14. What do you understand by deviation detection? Is it similar to association rule discovery? Justify.
15. Write an essay on 'Data Mining: Concepts, Issues and Trends".
16. "Text mining is different from conventional data mining." Comment.
17. What are the different application areas of data mining?
18. How can you link data mining with a DBMS.
19. How is data mining relevant to scientific data?
20. How is data mining relevant for Web-based computing?
21. Discuss the usefulness of data mining in e-commerce.
22. Can we do data mining on the data generated by the Web? Justify.
23. What are different ways of interfacing a data mining system with database systems?
24. Discuss the possibilities of formulating data mining tasks using SQL-92.
25. Discuss the application of data mining in science data.

26. How is sequence mining different from mining of data in DBMS?
27. What are 'nuggets' of information? Why are they important?

BIBLIOGRAPHY

Agarwal S., Agarwal R., Deshpande P.M., and Gupta A. On the computation of multidimensional aggregates. *VLDB*, 1998.

Agrawal R., Gupta A., and Sarawagi S. Modelling multidimensional databases. *ICDE*, 1997.

Anahory S., and Murray D. *Data Warehousing in the Real World: A practical guide for building decision support systems*. Addison Wesley Longman, 1997.

Barbara D. (ed.) Special Issue on Mining of Large Datasets. *IEEE Data Engineering Bulletin*, 21 (1), 1998

Brachman R., Khabaza T., Kloesgen W., Shapiro G.P., and Simoudis E. Industrial applications of data mining and knowledge discovery. *Communication of ACM*, 1996.

Fayyad U.M., Piatetsky-Shapiro G., Smyth P., Uthurusamy R. (Eds.). *Advances in Knowledge Discovery and Data Mining*. Menlo Park, CA: AAAI Press / The MIT Press, 1996

Fayyad U.M., Uthurusamy R. (eds.) Special issue on data mining. *Communication of ACM*, 1996.

Grossman R., Kasif S., Moore R., Rocke D. and Ullmann J. *Data Mining Research Opportunities and Challenges, A Report*. www. ncdm.uic.edu/M3D-final-report.htm., Jan 1999.

Heckerman D. Bayesian networks for data mining. *Data Mining and Knowledge Discovery*, 1997.

Imielinski T., Virmani A. Association Rules ... and What's Next? — Towards Second Generation Data Mining Systems. In *Proceedings of the 2nd East-European ADBIS Conference.*, pp. 6–25, 1998.

Mannila H. Methods and Problems in Data Mining. In *Proceedings of the 6th International Conference on Database Theory,* Springer LNCS 1186, 1997.

Nestorov S., and Tsur S. Integrating data mining with relational DBMS: A tightly coupled Approach. www-db.stanford.edu/people/evitmov.html, 1998.

Piatetsky-Shapiro G., and Frawley W. (eds.) *Knowledge Discovery in Databases*. MIT Press, Cambridge, MA, 1991.

Sarawagi S., *et al* Integrating Association Rule Mining with Relational Database Systems. Alternatives and Implications. In *Proceedings of the ACM SIGMOD International Conference on Management of Data, pp.* 343–354,1998.

Virmani A. *Second Generation Data Mining: Concepts and Implementation*. Ph.D. Thesis, Rutgers University, April 1998.

4

ASSOCIATION RULES

4.1 INTRODUCTION

Among the areas of data mining, the problem of deriving associations from data has received a great deal of attention. The problem was formulated by Agrawal et al in 1993 and is often referred to as the *market–basket problem*. In this problem, we are given a set of items and a large collection of transactions, which are subsets *(baskets)* of these items. The task is to find relationships between the various items within these baskets.

There are numerous applications of data mining which fit into this framework. The classic example, from which the problem gets its name, is the supermarket. In this context, the problem is to analyse customers' buying habits by finding associations between the different items that customers place in their shopping baskets. The discovery of such association rules can help the retailer develop marketing strategies, by gaining insight into matters like "which items are most frequently purchased by customers". It also helps in inventory management, sale promotion strategies, etc.

It is widely accepted (except for some recent developments) that the discovery of association rules is solely dependent on the discovery of frequent sets. Thus, a majority of the algorithms are concerned with efficiently determining the set of frequent itemsets in a given set of the transaction database. The problem is essentially to compute the frequency of occurrences of each itemset in the database. Since the total number of itemsets is exponential in terms of the number of items, it is not possible to count the frequencies of these sets by reading the database in just one pass. The number of counters are too many to be maintained in a single pass. As a result, using multiple passes to generate all the frequent itemsets is unavoidable. Thus, different algorithms for the discovery of association rules aim at reducing the number of passes by generating candidate sets, which are likely to be frequent sets. In other words, these algorithms attempt to eliminate, as early as possible, those sets which can be estimated to be infrequent. The algorithms differ from one another in the method of handling the candidate sets and the method of reducing the number of database passes. However, one of the recent algorithms attempts to discover frequent sets without having to generate candidate sets.

There are other related problems in this context. One can ask whether it is possible to find association rules incrementally. The algorithms for discovering frequent sets are not directly suitable when the underlying database is incremented intermittently. The idea is to avoid computing the frequent sets afresh for the incremented set of data. The concept of border sets becomes very important in this context. The set of border sets can be determined without any extra effort. And if no border set is affected by a database update, then it is shown that the set of frequent sets can be found without having to search through the whole database.

In real-life applications, frequent sets are very large in number and, as a result, the number of association rules are also too large to be useful. It then becomes meaningful to generate only those association rules in which the user is interested. The user can specify the constraint to indicate which combinations of items are the subject of his interest. The discovery of frequent itemsets with item constraints is one such important related problem, which is discussed in this chapter.

In this chapter, we shall study the important methods of discovering association rules in a large database. The main aim of this chapter is to introduce different data mining tasks related to association rule discovery and to study different approaches to discover such rules. In Section 4.1, we shall introduce the basic concepts of frequent sets, border sets, etc., and in Section 4.4, the most popular algorithm for the discovery of frequent sets, the Apriori Algorithm, is discussed. Section 4.5 outlines the Partition Algorithm and in Section 4.6, we present the Pincer-Search Algorithm. The Dynamic Itemset Counting Algorithm is given in the next section. The most recent one, the FP-Tree Growth Algorithm is discussed in Section 4.8 followed by the Eclat Algorithm. In the subsequent sections, we shall study other related problems such as incremental computation of frequent sets and frequent sets with item constraints.

4.2 What is an Association Rule?

In this section, the basic definitions and concepts of the association rule are introduced.

Let $A = \{l_1, l_2, \ldots l_m\}$ be a set of items. Let T, the transaction database, be a set of transactions, where each transaction t is a set of items. Thus, t is a subset of A.

Definition 4.1 Support

A transaction t is said to support an item l_i if l_i is present in t. t is said to support a subset of items $X \subseteq A$, if t supports each item l in X. An itemset $X \subseteq A$ has a support s in T, denoted by $s(X)_T$, if s% of transactions in T support X.

Support can also be defined as a fractional support, which means the proportion of transactions supporting X in T. It can also be defined in terms of absolute number of transactions supporting X in T. In the present text, unless otherwise specified, we assume the support to be %-support. We shall often drop the subscript T in the expression $s(X)_T$, when T is obviously implied. For absolute support, we refer it to as *support count*.

Example 4.1

Let us consider the following set of transactions in a bookshop.

We shall look at a set of only 6 transactions of purchases of books. In the first transaction, purchases are made of books on Compiler Construction, Databases, Theory of Computation, Computer Graphics and Neural Networks; we shall denote these subjects by CC, D, TC, CG and ANN, respectively. Thus, we describe the 6 transactions as follows;

t_1 := { ANN, CC, TC, CG}

t_2 := {CC, D, CG}

t_3 := {ANN, CC, TC, CG}

t_4 := {ANN, CC, D, CG}

t_5 := {ANN, CC, D, TC, CG}

t_6 := {CC, D, TC}.

A := {ANN, CC, D, TC, CG} and $T := \{t_1, t_2, t_3, t_4, t_5, t_6\}$.

We can see that t_2 supports the items CC, D and CG. The item D is supported by 4 out of 6 transactions in T. Thus, the support of D is 66.6%.

Definition 4.2 Association Rule

For a given transaction database T, an association rule is an expression of the form $X \Rightarrow Y$, where X and Y are subsets of A and $X \Rightarrow Y$ holds with *confidence* τ, if τ % of transactions in D that support X also support Y. The rule $X \Rightarrow Y$ has *support* σ in the transaction set T if σ % of transactions in T support $X \cup Y$.

The intuitive meaning of such a rule is that a transaction of the database which contains X tends to contain Y. Given a set of transactions, T, the problem of mining association rules is to discover all rules that have support and confidence greater than or equal to the user-specified minimum support and minimum confidence, respectively.

There are two important basic measures for association rules, *support* and *confidence*. Since the database is large and users are concerned only about frequently appearing items, usually, thresholds of support and confidence are pre-defined by them. Confidence is a measure of the strength of the association rules. Suppose the confidence of the association rule $X \Rightarrow Y$ is 70%; it means that 70% of the transactions that contain X also contain Y. In order to identify the set of association rules having reasonable support and confidence, there are two user-specified thresholds. The two thresholds are called *minimal support*, σ, and *minimal confidence*, τ, respectively. Thus, we say that $X \Rightarrow Y$ is an association rule with confidence τ' if $\tau' \geq \tau\%$ of transactions in T that support X also support Y. The association rule $X \Rightarrow Y$ has support σ' in the transaction if $\sigma' \geq \sigma$ percentage of transactions in T support $X \cup Y$.

EXAMPLE 4.1 (CONTD.)
Consider the example of the bookshop. Assume that σ = 50% and τ = 60%. Clearly, ANN $\Rightarrow$ CC holds. The confidence of this rule is, in fact, 100%, because all transactions that support ANN also support CC. On the other hand, CC $\Rightarrow$ ANN also holds but its confidence is 66%.

There is a famous myth in data mining that involves an apocryphal discovery that the sales of beer and diapers are correlated. Although it probably never happened, we will use *diapers* and *beer* as examples in our discussion. Association (and sequencing) tools discover rules like

When people buy diapers they also buy beer 50% of the time.

Each rule has a *left-hand side* (buy diapers) and a *right-hand side* (buy beer). The left-hand side is also called the antecedent and the right-hand side the consequent. In general, both the left-hand side and the right-hand side can contain multiple items, but for simplicity we will use single items for now.

As we have defined above, an association rule has two measures, *confidence* and *support*. To see what these terms mean and how they are computed, consider the following example of beer and diapers.

Let T consist of 500,000 transactions; 20,000 transactions of these contain diapers; 30,000 transactions contain beer; 10,000 transactions contain both diapers and beer.

Support (or prevalence) measures how often beer and diapers occur together as a percentage of the total transactions, 2% in this case (10,000/500,000). Confidence (or predictability) measures how much a particular item is dependent on another. Since 20,000 transactions contain diapers and 10,000 also contain beer, when people buy diapers, they also buy beer 50% of the time.

The *inverse* rule has a confidence of 33.333% (computed as 10,000/30,000) and would be stated as

When people buy beer they also buy diapers 1/3 of the time.

Note that these two rules have the same support. Support does not depend on the direction (or implication) of the rule; it is only dependent on the set of items in the rule. For this reason, association tools also identify frequently occurring itemsets, whether or not any rules are being generated.

In the absence of any knowledge about what else was bought, we can also make the following assertions:

People buy diapers 4% of the time.
People buy beer 6% of the time.

These numbers (4% and 6%) are called the *expected confidence* of buying diapers or beer, respectively.

Observe that our transaction database is a very simplistic one, in the sense that we assume that an item is either present or absent in a transaction. For instance, in the above example, we do not distinguish between t_1 and t_3 even when t_1 may involve 2 books of Neural Networks, 3 books of Compiler Construction, 1 book of Theory of Computation and 5 books of Computer Graphics; and t_3 may have one book of each of these subjects. Theoretically, it is possible to translate any of the real-life transaction databases to this model. But it will be a cumbersome process. The first part of our study deals only with a binary database, that is, transaction records with only the presence or absence of an item. After understanding the basic concepts and techniques of this simple model, we shall study different generalisations of this mode.

4.3 Methods to Discover Association Rules

Association rule mining is finding out association rules that satisfy the predefined minimum support and confidence from a given database. The problem is usually decomposed into two subproblems. One is to find those itemsets whose occurrence exceeds a predefined threshold in the database; those itemsets are called *frequent* or *large itemsets*. The second problem is to generate association rules from those large itemsets with the constraints of minimal confidence.

The discovery of association rules is the most well-studied problem in data mining. There are many interesting algorithms proposed recently and we shall discuss some of the important ones. One of the key features of all algorithms is that each of these methods assume that the underlying database size is enormous and they require multiple passes over the database. For disk-resident databases, this requires reading the database completely for each pass, resulting in a large number of disk-reads. In these algorithms, the effort spent in performing just the I/O may be considerable for large databases. For example, a 1 GB database will require 125,000 block reads for a single pass (for a block size of 8 KB). If the algorithm requires 10 passes, this results in a 1,250,000-block read. Assuming an average read time of 12 ms per page, the time spent in just performing the I/O is 1,250,000 × 12 ms = 4 hours.

Apart from poor response times, this problem places a huge burden on the I/O system. Usually, the data is collected by an online transaction processing system running hundreds or thousands of transactions per second. Running this algorithm under such workloads will adversely affect the transaction response time, and may even disrupt the daily database server.

Over a network such as LAN, it will create network congestion problems and lead to poor resource utilisation. Thus, the desirable features of any efficient algorithm are: (a) to reduce the I/O operations, and (b) at the same time be efficient in computing.

PROBLEM DECOMPOSITION

The problem of mining association rules can be decomposed into two subproblems:

- Find all sets of items *(itemsets)* whose support is greater than the user-specified minimum support, σ. Such itemsets are called *frequent* itemsets.
- Use the frequent itemsets to generate the desired rules. The general idea is that if, say *ABCD* and *AB* are frequent itemsets, then we can determine if the rule $AB \Rightarrow CD$ holds by checking the following inequality

$$\frac{s(\{A,B,C,D\})}{s(\{A,B\})} \geq \tau$$

where $s(X)$ is the support of X in T.

Much research has been focussed on the first subproblem, as the database is accessed in this part of the computation, and several algorithms have been proposed.

Let us first define some important concepts.

DEFINITION 4.3 FREQUENT SET

Let T be the transaction database and σ be the user-specified minimum support. An itemset $X \subseteq A$ is said to be a *frequent itemset* in T with respect to σ if

$$s(X)_T \geq \sigma$$

In Example 4.1, if we assume σ = 50%, then {ANN, CC, TC} is a frequent set as it is supported by at least 3 out of 6 transactions. You can see that any subset of this set is also a frequent set. On the other hand, {ANN, CC, D} is not a frequent itemset and hence, no set which properly contains this set is a frequent set.

You can also see that the set of frequent sets for a given T, with respect to a given σ, exhibits some interesting properties.

- **Downward Closure Property** Any subset of a frequent set is a frequent set.
- **Upward Closure Property** Any superset of an infrequent set is an infrequent set.

Discovering all frequent itemsets and their supports is a non-trivial problem if the cardinality of A, the set of items and the database T are large. For example, if $|A| = m$, the number of possible distinct itemsets is 2^m. The problem is to identify which of these are frequent in the given set of transactions. One way to achieve this is to set up 2^m counters, one for each distinct itemset and count the support for every itemset by scanning the database once. However, for many applications m can be more than 1,000; clearly, this approach is impractical. It should be noted that a large number of itemsets would have minimum support. Hence, it is not necessary to test the support for every itemset. Even if it is practically feasible, testing the support for every possible itemset results in considerable wasted effort. On the other hand, we have just one counter and make a database pass to count the support for each database. This is not practical either, as we may have to carry out a very large number of I/O operations on the database.

To reduce the combinatorial search space, all algorithms exploit the two properties outlined above. All existing algorithms for discovering frequent sets are variants of this approach.

DEFINITION 4.4 MAXIMAL FREQUENT SET

A frequent set is a *maximal frequent* set if it is a frequent set and no superset of this is a frequent set.

DEFINITION 4.5 BORDER SET

An itemset is a *border set* if it is not a frequent set, but all its proper subsets are frequent sets.

One can see that if X is an infrequent itemset[1], then it must have a subset (not necessarily a proper subset) that is a border set. It is easy to derive a proof for this. Since X is not frequent, it is possible that it is a border set. In that case, the proof is complete. Let us assume that X is not a border set too. Hence, there exists at least one proper subset of cardinality $|X| - 1$ that is not frequent, say X'. If X' is a border set, then the proof is complete. Let us, hence, assume that X' is not a border set. We recursively construct $X, X', X'', \ldots$, and so on, having the common property that neither of these is a frequent set nor a border set and this construction process terminates when we get a set which is a border. This construction process must terminate in a finite number of steps as we are decreasing the size of the sets by 1 in every step. In a most peculiar case, we may end up with a singleton itemset (the empty itemset is always considered to be a frequent set).

Note that if we know the set of all maximal frequent sets of a given T with respect to a σ, then we can find the set of all frequent sets without any extra scan of the database. Thus, the set of all maximal frequent sets can act as a compact representation of the set of all frequent sets. However, if we require the frequent sets together with their respective support values in T, then we have to make one more database pass to derive the support values when the set of all maximal frequent sets is known.

We shall often refer to the lattice of subsets of A throughout this chapter. For example, if $A = \{a, b, c, d, e\}$, then the lattice is given the following figure (Figure 4.1). In this lattice, the set of maximal frequent sets acts as a boundary between the set of all frequent sets and the set of all infrequent sets. It is thus easy to characterize the class of frequent sets and the class of infrequent sets in terms of the boundary sets between these two classes. Note that some maximal frequent sets are proper subsets of some border sets. But there can also be a maximal frequent set which is not a proper subset of any border set. Similarly, it is possible that a proper subset of a border set, of cardinality one less than the border set, is not necessarily always maximal.

---

[1] I use this expression to mean an itemset which is not frequent.

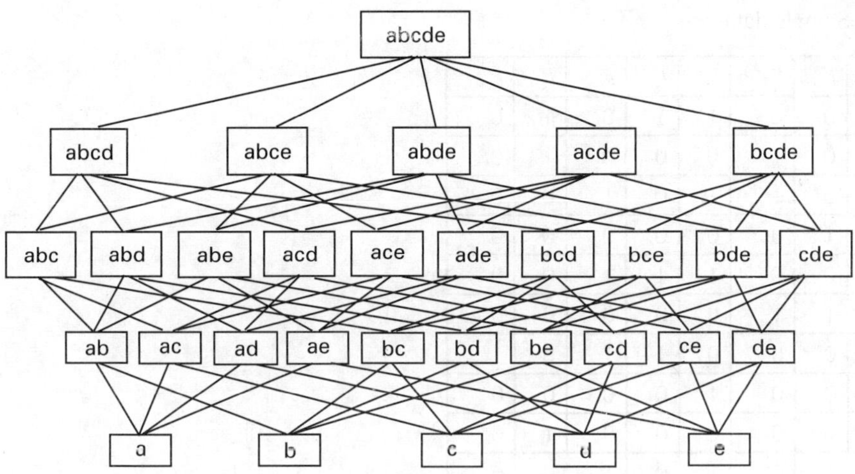

Figure 4.1 Lattice of subsets

Thus, we cannot establish a definite relationship between the set of maximal frequent sets and the set of border sets. However, the set of all border sets and the set of the maximal frequent sets, which are not proper subsets of any of the border sets, jointly provide a better representation of the set of frequent sets.

Example 4.2

Study the transaction database given in Table 4.1. We shall use this database for illustration throughout this chapter.

$A = \{l_1, l_2, l_3, l_4, l_5, l_6, l_7, l_8, l_9\}$. Assume $\sigma = 20\%$. Since T contains 15 records, it means that an itemset that is supported by at least three transactions is a frequent set.

The number of transactions supporting some of the itemsets are given in Table 4.2. Please note that we are using the index i for the item l_i. We shall use this notational convention henceforth. So {1} is not a frequent set with respect to σ, but {3} is a frequent set.

It is easy to check that {5, 6, 7} is a border set; {5, 6} is a maximal frequent set; {2, 4} is also a maximal frequent set. But there is no border set having {2,4} as a proper subset. Thus, {2, 4} and {5, 6, 7} jointly represent the set of all frequent sets of T with respect to σ. This is so because we can generate all the frequent sets from these two itemsets. If we know the set of all maximal frequent sets, we can generate all the frequent sets. Alternatively, if we know the set of border sets and the set of those maximal frequent sets which are not subsets of any border set, then also we can generate all the frequent sets.

4.4 Apriori Algorithm

This algorithm is also called *level-wise algorithm*. It was proposed by Agrawal and Srikant in 1994. It is the most popular algorithm to find all the frequent sets. It makes use of the

Table 4.1 Sample database

I_1	I_2	I_3	I_4	I_5	I_6	I_7	I_8	I_9
1	0	0	0	1	1	0	1	0
0	1	0	1	0	0	0	1	0
0	0	0	1	1	0	1	0	0
0	1	1	0	0	0	0	0	0
0	0	0	0	1	1	1	0	0
0	1	1	1	0	0	0	0	0
0	1	0	0	0	1	1	0	1
0	0	0	0	1	0	0	0	0
0	0	0	0	0	0	0	1	0
0	0	1	0	1	0	1	0	0
0	0	1	0	1	0	1	0	0
0	0	0	0	1	1	0	1	0
0	1	0	1	0	1	1	0	0
1	0	1	0	1	0	1	0	0
0	1	1	0	0	0	0	0	1

downward closure property. As the name suggests, the algorithm is a bottom-up search, moving upward level-wise in the lattice. However, the nicety of the method is that before reading the database at every level, it graciously prunes many of the sets which are unlikely to be frequent sets.

The first pass of the algorithm simply counts item occurrences to determine the frequent itemsets. A subsequent pass, say pass k, consists of two phases. First, the frequent itemsets L_{k-1} found in the $(k-1)^{th}$ pass are used to generate the candidate itemsets C_k, using the apriori candidate generation procedure described below. Next, the database is scanned and the support of candidates in C_k is counted. For fast counting, we need to efficiently determine the candidates in C_k contained in a given transaction t. The set of candidate itemsets is subjected to a pruning process to ensure that all the subsets of the candidate sets are already known to be frequent itemsets. The candidate generation process and the pruning process are the most important parts of this algorithm. We shall describe these two processes separately below.

CANDIDATE GENERATION

Given L_{k-1}, the set of all frequent $(k-1)$-itemsets, we want to generate a superset of the set of all frequent k-itemsets. The intuition behind the apriori candidate-generation procedure is that if an itemset X has minimum support, so do all subsets of X. Let us assume that the set of

Table 4.2 Frequent Count for Some Itemsets

X	Support count
{1}	2
{2}	6
{3}	6
{4}	4
{5}	8
{6}	5
{7}	7
{8}	4
{9}	2
{5,6}	3
{5,7}	5
{6,7}	3
{5,6,7}	1

frequent 3-itemsets are {1, 2, 3}, {1, 2, 5}, {1, 3, 5}, {2, 3, 5}, {2, 3, 4}. Then, the 4-itemsets that are generated as candidate itemsets are the supersets of these 3 itemsets and in addition, all the 3-itemset subsets of any candidate 4-itemset (so generated) must be already known to be in L_3. The first part and part of the second part is handled by the apriori candidate-generation method. The following pruning algorithm prunes some candidate sets which do not meet the second criterion.

The candidate-generation method is described below.

---

gen_candidate_itemsets *with the given* L_{k-1} *as follows:*
$C_k = \varnothing$
for all itemsets $l_1 \in L_{k-1}$ ***do***
for all itemsets $l_2 \in L_{k-1}$ ***do***
if $l_1[1] = l_2[1] \wedge l_1[2] = l_2[2] \wedge \ldots \wedge l_1[k-1] < l_2[k-1]$
then $c = l_1[1], l_1[2] \ldots l_1[k-1], l_2[k-1]$
$C_k = C_k \cup \{c\}$

Using this algorithm: C_4: = { {1, 2, 3, 5}, {2, 3, 4, 5}} is obtained from L_3 := {{1, 2, 3}, {1, 2, 5}, {1, 3, 5}, {2, 3, 5}, {2, 3, 4}}. {1, 2, 3, 5} is generated from {1, 2, 3} and {1, 2, 5}. Similarly, {2, 3, 4, 5} is generated from {2, 3, 4} and {2, 3, 5}. No other pair of 3-itemsets satisfy the condition

$$l_1[1] = l_2[1] \wedge l_1[2] = l_2[2] \wedge \ldots \wedge l_1[k-1] < l_2[k-1].$$

PRUNING

The pruning step eliminates the extensions of (k–1)-itemsets which are not found to be frequent from being considered for counting support. For example, from C_4, the itemset {2, 3, 4, 5} is pruned, since all its 3-subsets are not in L_3 (clearly, {2, 4, 5} is not in L). The pruning algorithm is described below.

---

prune (C_k)
for all $c \in C_k$
for all (k–1)-subsets d of c **do**
    if $d \notin L_{k-1}$
    then $Ck = Ck \setminus \{c\}$

The apriori frequent itemset discovery algorithm uses these two functions (candidate generation and pruning) at every iteration. It moves upward in the lattice, from level 1 till level k, where no candidate set remains after pruning.

Apriori Algorithm

Initialize: k := 1, C_1 = all the 1-itemsets;
read the database to count the support of C_1 to determine L_1.
L_1 := {frequent 1-itemsets};
k := 2; // *k represents the pass number//*
while ($L_{k-1} \neq \varnothing$) **do**
begin
  C_k := ***gen_candidate_itemsets*** *with the given* L_{k-1}
  prune (C_k)
  for all transactions $t \in T$ **do**
  increment the count of all candidates in C_k that are contained in t;
  L_k := All candidates in C_k with minimum support ;
  $k := k + 1$;
end
Answer := $\cup_k L_k$;

APRIORI ALGORITHM BY EXAMPLE

We illustrate the working of the algorithm with Example 4.2 discussed above.

k:= 1

Read the database to count the support of 1-itemsets (Table 4.3). The frequent 1-itemsets and their support counts are given below.

L_1 := { {2} → 6. {3} → 6, {4} → 4, {5} → 8, {6} → 5, {7} → 7, {8} → 4 }

k:= 2

In the *candidate generation* step, we get

C_2: = {{2,3}, {2,4}, {2, 5}, {2,6}, {2, 7}, {2, 8}, {3, 4}, {3, 5}, {3, 6}, {3, 7}, {3,8}, {4, 5}, {4, 6}, {4,7}, {4, 8},{5, 6}, {5, 7}, {5, 8}, {6,7}, {6, 8}, {7, 8}}

The *pruning* step does not change C_2.

Read the database to count the support of elements in C_2 to get

L_2 := { {2, 3} → 3, {2,4} → 3, {3, 5} → 3, {3, 7} → 3, {5, 6} → 3, {5, 7} → 5, {6, 7} → 3 }

Table 4.3

{1}	2
{2}	6
{3}	6
{4}	4
{5}	8
{6}	5
{7}	7
{8}	7
{9}	2

***k*:=3**

In the *candidate generation* step,

using {2,3} and {2, 4} , we get {2, 3, 4}
using {3, 5} and {3, 7}, we get {3, 5, 7} and
similarly from {5, 6} and {5, 7}, we get {5, 6, 7}

C_3 := {{2, 3, 4}, {3, 5, 7} , {5, 6, 7}}

The *pruning* step prunes {2, 3, 4} as not all subsets of size 2, i.e., {2, 3}, {2, 4}, {3, 4} are present in L_2. The other two itemsets are retained.

Thus the pruned C_3 is {{3, 5, 7}, {5, 6, 7}}.

Read the database to count the support of the itemsets in C_3 to get

L_3 := {{3, 5, 7} → 3}

***k*:= 4**

Since L_3 contains only one element, C_4 is empty and hence the algorithm stops, *returning* the set of frequent sets along with their respective support values as

$$L := L_1 \cup L_2 \cup L_3$$

Remark

The AIS algorithm was the first published algorithm developed to generate all frequent itemsets in a transaction database (Agarwal, Imielinski et al 1993). This technique is limited to only one item in the consequent. The AIS algorithm makes multiple passes over the entire database. During each pass it scans all the transactions. Frequent itemsets of each pass are extended to generate candidate itemsets in a slightly different manner. It uses an estimation tool and a pruning technique. One can see that the Apriori algorithm is an improvement of AIS.

4.5 Partition Algorithm

The partition algorithm is based on the observation that the frequent sets are normally very few in number compared to the set of all itemsets. As a result, if we partition the set of transactions to smaller segments such that each segment can be accommodated in the main memory then we can compute the set of frequent sets of each of these partitions. It is assumed that these sets (set of local frequent sets) contain a reasonably small number of itemsets. Hence, we can read the whole database (the unsegmented one) once, to count the support of the set of all local frequent sets.

The partition algorithm uses two scans of the database to discover all frequent sets. In one scan it generates a set of all potentially frequent itemsets. This set is a superset of all frequent itemsets, i.e., it may contain false positives; but no false negatives are reported. During the second scan, counters for each of these itemsets are set up and their actual support is measured

The algorithm executes in two phases. In the first phase, the partition algorithm logically divides the database into a number of non-overlapping partitions. The partitions are considered one at a time and all frequent itemsets for that partition are generated. Thus, if there are n partitions, Phase I of the algorithm takes n iterations. At the end of Phase I, these frequent itemsets are merged to generate a set of all potential frequent itemsets. In this step, the local frequent itemsets of same length from all n partitions are combined to generate the global candidate itemsets. In Phase II, the actual support for these itemsets are generated and the frequent itemsets are identified. The algorithm reads the entire database once during Phase I and once during Phase II. The partition sizes are chosen such that each partition can be accommodated in the main memory, so that the partitions are read only once in each phase.

A partition P of the databases refers to any subset of the transactions contained in the database. Any two partitions are non-overlapping. We define *local support* for an itemset as the fraction of the transaction containing that particular itemset in a partition. We define a local frequent itemset as an itemset whose local support in a partition is at least the user-defined minimum support. A local frequent itemset may or may not be frequent in the context of the entire database.

Partition Algorithm

```
P = partition_database(T); n = Number of partitions
// Phase I
    for i = 1 to n do begin
        read_in_partition(T_i in P)
        L^i = generate all frequent itemsets of T_i using apriori method in main memory.
    end
// Merge Phase
    for (k = 2; L_k^i ≠ ∅, i = 1, 2, ..., n; k++) do begin
        C_G^k = ∪_{i=1}^{n} L_i^k
    end
// Phase II
    for i = 1 to n do begin
        read_in_partition(T_i in P)
        for all candidates c ∈ C^G compute s(c)_Ti
    end
```

$L^G = \{c \in C^G \mid s(c)_{Ti} \geq \sigma\}$
Answer = L^G

The partition algorithm is based on the premise that the size of the global candidate set is considerably smaller than the set of all possible itemsets. The intuition behind this is that the size of the global candidate set is bounded by n times the size of the largest of the set of locally frequent sets. For sufficiently large partition sizes, the number of local frequent itemsets is likely to be comparable to the number of frequent itemsets generated for the entire database. If the data characteristics are uniform across partitions, then large numbers of itemsets generated for individual partitions may be common.

EXAMPLE 4.3

Let us take the same database T given in Example 4.2 and the same σ. Let us partition T, for the sake of illustration, into three partitions T_1, T_2, and T_3, each containing 5 transactions. The first partition T_1 contains transactions 1 to 5, T_2 contains transactions 6 to 10 and, T_3 contains transactions 11 to 15. We fix the local support as equal to the given support, that is 20%. Thus, $\sigma_1 = \sigma_2 = \sigma_3 = \sigma = 20\%$. Any itemset that appears in just one of the transactions in any partition is a local frequent set in that partition.

The local frequent sets of the T_1 partition are the itemsets X, such that $s(X)_{T1} \geq \sigma_1$.

L^1 := { {1}, {2}, {3}, {4}, {5}, {6}, {7}, {8}, {1, 5}, {1, 6}, {1, 8}, {2, 3}, {2, 4}, {2, 8}, {4, 5}, {4, 7}, {4, 8}, {5, 6}, {5, 8}, {5, 7}, {6, 7}, {6, 8}, {1,6, 8}, {1,5,6}, {1,5,8}, {2,4,8}, {4,5,7}, {5,6,8}, {5,6,7}, {1,5,6,8} }

Similarly,

L^2 := { {2}, {3}, {4}, {5}, {6}, {7}, {8}, {9}, {2,3}, {2,4}, {2,6}, {2,7}, {2,9}, {3,4}, {3, 5}, {3, 7}, {5, 7}, {6,7}, {6,9}, {7,9}, {2,3,4}, {2,6,7}, {2,6,9}, {2,7,9}, {3, 5, 7}, {2,6,7,9} }

L^3 := { {1}, {2}, {3}, {4}, {5}, {6}, {7}, {8}, {9}, {1,3}, {1,5}, {1,7}, {2,3}, {2,4}, {2,6}, {2,7}, {2,9}, {3,5}, {3,7}, {3,9},{4,6}, {4,7}, {5,6}, {5,7}, {5,8}, {6,7}, {6,8}, {1,3,5}, {1,3,7}, {1,5,7}, {2,3,9}, {2,4,6}, {2,4,7}, {3,5,7}, {4,6,7}, {5,6,8}, {1, 3, 5, 7}, {2, 4, 6, 7} }

In Phase II, the candidate set is

$C := L^1 \cup L^2 \cup L^3$

C := { {1}, {2}, {3}, {4}, {5}, {6}, {7}, {8}, {9}, {1,3}, {1, 5}, {1, 6}, {1,7}, {1, 8}, {2,3}, {2, 4}, {2,6}, {2,7}, {2, 8}, {2,9},{3,4}, {3,5}, {3,7}, {3,9}, {4, 5}, {4,6}, {4,7}, {4, 8}, {5, 6},{5,7}, {5, 8}, {5, 7}, {6, 7}, {6, 8}, {6,9}, {7,9},{1,3,5}, {1,3,7}, {1,5,6}, {1,5,7}, {1,5,8}, {1,6,8}, {2,3,4}, {2,3,9}, {2,4,6}, {2,4,7}, {2,4,8}, {2,6,7}, {2,6,9}, {2,7,9}, {3,5,7}, {4,5,7}, {4,6,7}, {5,6,8}, {5,6,7}, {1,5,6,8}, {2,6,7,9}, {1, 3, 5, 7}, {2, 4, 6, 7} }

Read the database once to compute the global support of the sets in C and obtain the final set of frequent sets.

REMARKS

It is worthwhile discussing certain aspects of local support vs. global support. We saw, in the previous example, that the local support is the same as global support. This implies that if an itemset is not frequent in any of the segments, it is not frequent in the whole database either.

4.6 PINCER-SEARCH ALGORITHM

One can see that the Apriori algorithm operates in a bottom-up, breadth-first search method. The computation starts from the smallest set of frequent itemsets and moves upward till it reaches the largest frequent itemset. The number of database passes is equal to the largest size of the frequent itemset. When any one of the frequent itemsets becomes longer, the algorithm has to go through many iterations and, as a result, the performance decreases.

A natural way to overcome this difficulty is to somehow incorporate a bi-directional search, which takes advantages of both the bottom-up as well as the top-down processes. The pincer-search algorithm is based on this principle. It attempts to find the frequent itemsets in a bottom-up manner but, at the same time, it maintains a list of maximal frequent itemsets. While making a database pass, it also counts the support of these candidate maximal frequent itemsets to see if any one of these is actually frequent. In that event, it can conclude that all the subsets of these frequent sets are going to be frequent and, hence, they are not verified for the support count in the next pass. If we are lucky, we may discover a very large maximal frequent itemset very early in the algorithm. If this set subsumes all the candidate sets of level k, then we need not proceed further and thus we save many database passes. Clearly, the pincer-search has an advantage over Apriori algorithm when the largest frequent itemset is long.

In this algorithm, in each pass, in addition to counting the supports of the candidate in the bottom-up direction, it also counts the supports of the itemsets of some itemsets using a top-down approach. These are called the *Maximal Frequent Candidate Set* (MFCS). This process helps prune the candidate sets very early on in the algorithm. If we find a maximal frequent set in this process, it is recorded in the MFCS.

Consider a pass k, during which itemsets of size k are to be classified. If some itemset that is an element of the MFCS, say X, of cardinality greater than k is found to be frequent in this pass, then all its subsets must be frequent. Therefore, all of its subsets of cardinality k can be pruned from the set of candidate sets considered in the bottom-up direction in the pass. They, and their supersets, will never be candidates throughout the rest of the execution, potentially improving the performance.

Similarly, when a new infrequent itemset is found in the bottom-up direction, the algorithm will use it to update the MFCS. The subsets of the MFCS should not contain this in frequent itemsets.

The MFCS initially contains a single element, the itemset of cardinality n containing all the elements of the database. If some m 1-itemsets are infrequent after the first pass (after reading the database once), the MFCS will have one element of cardinality $n–m$. Removing the m infrequent items from the initial element of the MFCS generates this itemset. In this case, the top-down search goes down m levels in one pass. Unlike the search in the bottom-up direction which goes in one pass, the top-down search can go down many levels in one pass. This is because we may discover a maximal frequent set very early in the algorithm.

Pincer-Search Method

```
L_0 := ∅; k := 1; C_1 := {{i} | i ∈I}; S_0 = ∅;
MFCS := {{1,2, ..., n}}; MFS := ∅;
do until C_k = ∅ and S_{k-1} = ∅
        read database and count supports for C_k and MFCS;
        MFS := MFS ∪{frequent itemsets in MFCS};
        S_k := {infrequent itemsets in C_k};
        call MFCS-gen algorithm if S_k ≠ ∅;
        call MFS-pruning procedure;
        generate candidates C_{k+1} from C_k; (similar to Apriori's generate and prune)
        if any frequent itemset in C_k is removed in MFS-pruning procedure
            call the recovery procedure to recover candidates to C_{k+1};
        call MFCS prune procedure to prune candidates in C_{k+1};
        k := k+1;
return MFS
MFCS-gen
for all itemsets s ∈ S_k
    for all itemsets m ∈ MFCS
     if s is a subset of m
     MFCS := MFCS\{m};
     for all items e ∈ itemset s
       if m\{e} is not a subset of any itemset in MFCS
            MFCS := MFCS ∪{m\{e}};
  return MFCS
Recovery
for all itemsets l ∈ C_k
    for all itemsets m ∈ MFS
     if the first k–1 items in l are also in m
          /* suppose m.item_j = l.item_{k-1} */
          for i from j+1 to |m|
          C_{k+1} := C_{k+1} ∪ {{l.item_1, l.item_2, ..., l.item_k, m.item_i}}
MFS-Prune
    for all itemsets c in C_k
    if c is a subset of any itemset is the current MFS
    delete c from C_k;
MFCS-Prune
    for all itemsets c in C_{k+1}
    if c is not a subset of any itemset in the current MFCS
    delete c from C_{k+1};
```

EXAMPLE 4.4

We shall use Example 4.2 to illustrate the working of the example.

STEP 1: $L_0 := \varnothing$; $k := 1$;

$C_1 := \{\{1\}, \{2\}, \{3\}, \{4\}, \{5\}, \{6\}, \{7\}, \{8\}, \{9\}\}$

MFCS := {1, 2, 3, 4, 5, 6, 7, 8, 9}

MFS := ∅;

PASS ONE: Database is read to count the support as follows

$\{1\} \to 2$, $\{2\} \to 6$, $\{3\} \to 6$, $\{4\} \to 4$, $\{5\} \to 8$, $\{6\} \to 5$, $\{7\} \to 7$, $\{8\} \to 4$, $\{9\} \to 2$

$\{1, 2, 3, 4, 5, 6, 7, 8, 9\} \to 0$.

So MFCS := {1, 2, 3, 4, 5, 6, 7, 8, 9} and MFS := ∅;

$L_1 := \{\{2\}, \{3\}, \{4\}, \{5\}, \{6\}, \{7\}, \{8\}\}$

$S_1 := \{\{1\}, \{9\}\}$

At this stage we call the MFCS-gen to update MFCS.

For {1} in S_1 and for {1, 2, 3, 4, 5, 6, 7, 8, 9} in MFCS, we get the new element in MFCS as {2, 3, 4, 5, 6, 7, 8, 9}.

For {9} in S_1 and for {2, 3, 4, 5, 6, 7, 8, 9} in MFCS, we get the new element in MFCS as {2, 3, 4, 5, 6, 7, 8}.

We generate the candidate itemsets
$C_2 := \{ \{2,3\}, \{2,4\}, \{2,5\}, \{2,6\}, \{2,7\}, \{2,8\}, \{3,4\}, \{3,5\}, \{3,6\}, \{3,7\}, \{3,8\}, \{4,5\}, \{4,6\}, \{4,7\}, \{4,8\}, \{5,6\}, \{5,7\}, \{5,8\}, \{6,7\}, \{6,8\}, \{7,8\}\}$

PASS TWO: read the database to count the support of elements in C_2 and MFCS as given below:

$\{2,3\} \to 3$, $\{2,4\} \to 3$, $\{2,5\} \to 0$, $\{2,6\} \to 2$, $\{2,7\} \to 2$, $\{2,8\} \to 1$, $\{3,4\} \to 1$, $\{3,5\} \to 3$, $\{3,6\} \to 0$, $\{3,7\} \to 3$, $\{3,8\} \to 0$, $\{4,5\} \to 1$, $\{4,6\} \to 1$, $\{4,7\} \to 2$, $\{4,8\} \to 1$, $\{5,6\} \to 3$, $\{5,7\} \to 5$, $\{5,8\} \to 2$, $\{6,7\} \to 3$, $\{6,8\} \to 2$, $\{7,8\} \to 0$

$\{2, 3, 4, 5, 6, 7, 8\} \to 0$.

MFS:= ∅;

$L_2 := \{ \{2,3\}, \{2,4\}, \{3,5\}, \{3,7\}, \{5,6\}, \{5,7\}, \{6,7\} \}$
$S_2 := \{ \{2,5\}, \{2,6\}, \{2, 7\} \{2,8\}, \{3,4\}, \{3,6\}, \{3,8\}, \{4,5\}, \{4,6\}, \{4,7\}, \{4,8\}, \{5,8\}, \{6,8\}, \{7,8\}\}$

For {2, 5} in S_2 and for {2, 3, 4, 5, 6, 7, 8} in MFCS, we get the new elements in MFCS as {3, 4, 5, 6, 7, 8} and {2, 3, 4, 6, 7, 8}.

For {2,6} in S_2 and for {3, 4, 5, 6, 7, 8} in MFCS, since {2,6} is not contained in this element of MFCS and hence, no action.

For {2, 3, 4, 6, 7, 8} we get two new elements in MFCS in place of {2, 3, 4, 6, 7, 8} as {3, 4, 6, 7, 8} and {2, 3, 4, 7, 8}. Since {3, 4, 6, 7, 8} is already contained in an element of MFCS, it is excluded from MFCS.

So at this stage MFCS := {{ 3, 4, 5, 6, 7, 8}, {2, 3, 4, 7, 8}}.

For {2,7} in S_2, we get

MFCS := {{3, 4, 5, 6, 7, 8}, {2, 3, 4, 8}}.

For {2,8} in S_2, we get

MFCS := {{3, 4, 5, 6, 7, 8}, {2, 3, 4}}.

For {3,4} in S_2, we get

MFCS := {{3, 5, 6, 7, 8}, {4, 5, 6, 7, 8}, {2, 3}, {2, 4}}.

For {3,6} in S_2, we get

MFCS := {{3, 5, 7, 8}, {4, 5, 6, 7, 8}, {2, 3}, {2, 4}}.

For {3,8} in S_2, we get

MFCS := {{3, 5, 7}, {4, 5, 6, 7, 8}, {2, 3},{2, 4}}.

For {4,5} in S_2, we get

MFCS := {{3, 5, 7}, {5, 6, 7, 8}, {4, 6, 7, 8}, {2, 3}, {2, 4}}.

For {4,6} in S_2, we get

MFCS := {{3, 5, 7}, {5, 6, 7, 8}, {4, 7, 8}, {2,3}, {2, 4}}.

For {4,7} in S_2, we get

MFCS := {{3, 5, 7}, {5, 6, 7, 8}, {4, 8}, {2, 3}, {2, 4}}.

For {4,8} in S_2, we get

MFCS := {{3, 5, 7}, {5, 6, 7, 8}, {2, 3}, {2, 4}}.

For {5,8} in S_2, we get

MFCS := {{3, 5, 7}, {6, 7, 8}, {5, 6, 7}, {2,3}, {2, 4}}.

For {6,8} in S_2, we get

MFCS := {{7, 8}, {3, 5, 7}, {5, 6, 7}, {2,3}, {2, 4}}.

For {7,8} in S_2, we get

MFCS := {{8}, {3, 5, 7}, {5, 6, 7}, {2,3}, {2, 4}}.

We generate the candidate sets as

C_3 := {{2, 3, 4}, {3, 5, 7}, {5, 6, 7}}

In the pruning stage, the itemsets {2, 3, 4} are pruned from C_3 and hence,

C_3 := {{3, 5, 7}, {5, 6, 7}}

At this stage, we make one more pass of the database to count the supports of {{3, 5, 7}, {5, 6, 7}}.

EXAMPLE 4.5

The above example illustrates the algorithm. However, you can see that it takes the same number of passes as the Apriori algorithm. The following example illustrates (Table 4.4) the advantages of the pincer-search algorithm.

Table 4.4

i_1	i_2	i_3	i_4	i_5	i_6	i_7	i_8	i_9
1	0	0	0	1	1	0	1	0
0	1	0	1	0	0	0	1	0
0	0	0	1	1	0	1	0	0
0	0	1	0	0	0	0	0	0
0	0	0	0	1	1	1	0	0
0	1	1	1	0	0	0	0	0
0	1	0	0	0	1	1	0	1
0	0	0	0	1	0	0	0	0
0	0	0	0	0	0	0	1	0
0	0	1	1	1	0	1	0	0
0	0	1	1	1	0	1	0	0
0	0	0	0	1	1	0	1	0
0	1	1	1	0	1	1	0	0
1	0	1	1	1	0	1	0	0
0	1	1	0	0	0	0	0	1

During the first pass, the supports counted are

$\{1\}\to 2$, $\{2\}\to 5$, $\{3\}\to 7$, $\{4\}\to 7$, $\{5\}\to 8$, $\{6\}\to 5$, $\{7\}\to 7$, $\{8\}\to 4$, $\{9\}\to 2$

$\{1, 2, 3, 4, 5, 6, 7, 8, 9\}\to 0$.

We update MFCS as {2, 3, 4, 5, 6, 7, 8}.

In the second pass, we count the supports as
$\{23\} \to 3$, $\{24\} \to 3$, $\{25\} \to 0$, $\{26\} \to 2$, $\{27\} \to 2$, $\{28\} \to 1$, $\{34\} \to 5$, $\{35\}\to 3$,
$\{36\} \to 1$, $\{37\} \to 4$, $\{38\} \to 0$, $\{45\} \to 4$, $\{46\} \to 1$, $\{47\} \to 5$,
$\{48\} \to 1$, $\{56\} \to 3$, $\{57\} \to 5$, $\{58\} \to 2$, $\{67\} \to 3$, $\{68\} \to 2$, $\{78\} \to 0$.

At this stage, we update the MFCS to obtain

$$\text{MFCS} := \{\{2, 3, 4\}, \{3, 4, 5, 7\}, \{5, 6, 7\}, \{8\}\}$$

$$\text{and } C_3 := \{\{2, 3, 4\}, \{3, 4, 5\}, \{3, 5, 7\}, \{4, 5, 7\}, \{5, 6, 7\}\}.$$

We then make a database pass to read the frequency of these itemsets. The algorithm stops at this point. It can be noted that the A priori algorithm would have made 4 passes while the pincer-search makes only 3 passes.

4.7 Dynamic Itemset Counting Algorithm

This algorithm was proposed by Bin et al in 1997. The rationale behind DIC is that it works like a train running over the data, with stops at intervals M between transactions. When the train reaches the end of the transaction file, it has made one pass over the data, and it starts all over again from the beginning for the next pass. The passengers on the train are itemsets. When an itemset is on the train, we count its occurrence in the transactions that are read. When an a priori algorithm is considered in this metaphor, all itemsets get on at the start of a pass and get off at the end. The 1-itemsets take the first pass, the 2-itemsets take the second pass, and so on. In DIC, there is the added flexibility of allowing itemsets to get on at any stop as long as they get off at the same stop the next time the train goes around. Therefore, the itemset has seen all the transactions in the file.

Consider for example, if we are mining 40,000 transactions and $M = 10{,}000$, we will count all the 1-itemsets in the first 40,000 transactions we read. However, we will begin counting 2-itemsets after the first 10,000 transactions have been read. We will begin counting 3-itemsets after 20,000 transactions. For now, let us assume that there are no 4-itemsets that we need to count. Once we get to the end of the file, we will stop counting the 1-itemsets and go back to the start of the file to count the 2- and 3-itemsets. After the first 10,000 transactions we will finish counting the 2-itemsets and after 20,000 transaction, we will finish counting the 3-itemsets. In total, we have made 1.5 passes over the data instead of the 3 passes a level-wise algorithm would make.

Initially, we identify certain 'stops' in the database. It is assumed that we read the records sequentially as we do in other algorithms, but pause to carry out certain computations at the 'stop' points. For notational convenience, we assign numbers to each stop sequentially.

We then define four different structures:

- Dashed Box
- Dashed Circle
- Solid Box
- Solid Circle

Each of these structures maintains a list of itemsets. Itemsets in the 'dashed' category of structures have a counter and the stop number. The counter is to keep track of the support value of the corresponding itemset. The stop number is to keep track whether an itemset has completed one full pass over a database.

The itemsets in the 'solid' category structures are not subjected to any counting. The itemset in the solid box is the confirmed set of frequent sets. The itemsets in the solid circle are the confirmed set of infrequent sets.

The algorithm counts the support values of the itemsets in the dashed structure as it moves along from one stop point to another.

During the execution of the algorithm, at any stop point, the following events take place:

- Certain itemsets in the dashed circle move into the dashed box. These are the itemsets whose support-counts reach σ value during this iteration (reading records between two consecutive stops).
- Certain itemsets enter afresh into the system and get into the dashed circle. These are essentially the supersets of the itemsets that move from the dashed circle to the dashed box.
- The itemsets that have completed one full pass move from the dashed structure to the solid structure. That is, if the itemset is in a dashed circle while completing a full pass, it moves to the solid circle. If it is in the dashed box, then it moves into the solid box after completing a full pass.

We shall formally describe the DIC algorithm now.

DIC Algorithm

Initially,

Solid box contains the empty itemset;

Solid circle is empty;

Dashed box is empty;

Dashed circle contains all 1-itemsets with the respective stop-number as 0;

Current stop-number := 0;

do until the dashed circle is empty

read the database till the next stop point and increase the counters of the itemsets in the dashed box and in the dashed circle as we go along, record by record, to reach the next stop.

increase the current-stop-number by 1;
for each itemset in the dashed circle

    if count of the itemset is greater than σ
    then move the itemset to the dashed box
        generate a new itemset to be put into the dashed circle
        with counter value = 0 and stop number = current stop number.
    else
        if its stop number is equal to the current stop number
        then move this itemset to solid circle.

for each itemset in the dashed box
    if its stop-number is equal to the current stop number
    then move this itemset to the solid box
end
return the itemsets in solidbox

EXAMPLE 4.6

The example in Table 4.5 illustrates the working of the DIC algorithm (see Figure 4.2).

Step 1. The empty itemset is in the solid box.

All the 1-itemsets are in the dashed circles.

The sets {1}, {2}, {3}, {4}, {5}, {6}, {7}, {8}, and {9} are in the dashed circle.

All other itemsets are free, i.e., not in any of the 4 types of boxes.

Step 2. First read 5 transactions (transactions t_1–t_5).

For each transaction, increment the counts of the respective counters of the itemsets in the dashed box or dashed circle.

The counts of the itemsets in the dashed circles are given below.

{1} = 1, {2} = 1, {3} = 1, {4} = 2, {5} = 3, {6} = 2, {7} = 2, {8} = 2, and {9} = 0.

Thus, itemset {5} is put in a dashed box and removed from the dashed circle.

Step 3. Read the next 5 transactions (transactions t_6–t_{10}).

The updated counts of the itemsets in the dashed box and in the dashed circle are

{1} = 1, {2} = 3, {3} = 3, {4} = 3, {5} = 5, {6} = 3, {7} = 4, {8} = 3, and {9} = 1.

The itemsets {2}, {3}, {4}, {5}, {6}, {7}, and {8} are now put in dashed box and are removed from the dashed circle.

The additional itemsets which are put in the dashed circle are

{2, 3}, {2, 4}, {2, 5 }, {2, 6}, {2, 7}, {2, 8}, {3, 4}, {3, 5}, {3, 6}, {3, 7}, {3, 8}, {4, 5}, {4, 6}, {4, 7}, {4, 8}, {5, 6}, {5, 7}, {5, 8}, {6, 7}, {6, 8}, {7, 8}.

We include a counter for each of these itemsets at this stage.

Step 4: Read the next 5 transactions (transactions t_{11}–t_{15}). The updated count of each of the counters are

{1} = 2, {2} = 5, {3} = 6, {4} = 4, {5} = 8, {6} = 5, {7} = 7, {8} = 4, and {9} = 2. {2, 3} = 1, {2, 4} = 1, {2, 5}= 0, {2, 6} = 1, {2, 7}= 1, {2, 8} = 0, {3, 4} = 0, {3, 5} = 2, {3, 6} = 0, {3, 7}= 2, {3, 8} = 0, {4, 5}= 0, {4, 6}= 1, {4, 7}= 1, {4, 8}= 0, {5, 6}= 1, {5, 7}= 2, {5, 8}= 1, {6, 7}= 1, {6, 8}= 1, {7, 8} = 0.

The 1-itemsets have completed their traversal of the whole set of transactions and hence, {2}, {3}, {4}, {5}, {6}, {7}, and {8} are put in the solid box and are removed from the dashed box. The itemset {1} and {9} are removed from the dashed circle and is put in the solid circle. The counters for these sets are now dropped.

Step 5: Read the first 5 transactions(t_1–t_5) and update the count of the itemsets in the dashed box and the dashed circle. The updated counts are

{2, 3} = 1, {2, 4} = 2, {2, 5}= 0, {2, 6} = 1, {2, 7}= 1, {2, 8} = 1, {3, 4} = 0, {3, 5} = 2, {3, 6} = 0, {3, 7}= 2, {3, 8} = 0, {4, 5}= 1, {4, 6}= 1,

{4, 7}= 2, {4, 8}= 1, {5, 6}= 3, {5, 7}= 4, {5, 8}= 2, {6, 7}= 2, {6, 8}= 2, {7, 8} = 0.

At this stage, {5, 6} and {5, 7} are moved from the dashed circle to the dashed box, as their count exceeds the required support.

Step 6: Read the transactions t_6–t_{10}. The updated counts are

{2, 3} = 2, {2, 4} = 3, {2, 5}= 0, {2, 6} = 2, {2, 7}= 2, {2, 8} = 1, {3, 4} = 1, {3, 5} = 3, {3, 6} = 0, {3, 7}= 3, {3, 8} = 0, {4, 5}= 0, {4, 6}= 1,

{4, 7}= 2, {4, 8}= 1, {5, 6}= 3, {5, 7}= 5, {5, 8}= 2, {6, 7}= 3, {6, 8}= 2, {7, 8} = 0.

Clearly, the itemsets {2, 4}, {3, 5}, {3, 7} and {6, 7} are moved to the solid box from the dashed circle; and {5, 6} and {5, 7} are moved from the dashed box to the solid box. The remaining itemsets (listed below) in the dashed circle are moved to the solid circle.

{2, 3}, {2, 5}, {2, 6}, {2, 7}, {2, 8}, {3, 4}, {3, 5}, {3, 6}, {3, 7}, {3, 8}, {4, 5}, {4, 6}, {4, 7}, {4, 8}, {5, 8}, {6, 8}, {7, 8}.

The counters for these sets are dropped. The itemset {5, 6, 7} is now put in the dashed circle and a counter for this is introduced.

Table 4.5

A1	A2	A3	A4	A5	A6	A7	A8	A9
1	0	0	0	1	1	0	1	0
0	1	0	1	0	0	0	1	0
0	0	0	1	1	0	1	0	0
0	0	1	0	0	0	0	0	0
0	0	0	0	1	1	1	0	0
0	1	1	1	0	0	0	0	0
0	1	0	0	0	1	1	0	1
0	0	0	0	1	0	0	0	0
0	0	0	0	0	0	0	1	0
0	0	1	0	1	0	1	0	0
0	0	1	0	1	0	1	0	0
0	0	0	0	1	1	0	1	0
0	1	0	1	0	1	1	0	0
1	0	1	0	1	0	1	0	0
0	1	1	0	0	0	0	0	1

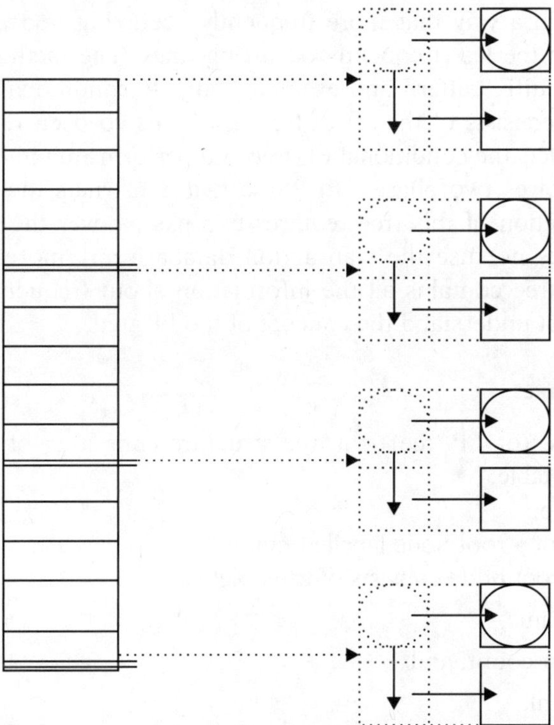

Figure 4.2 A pictorial depiction of the working of DIC. The horizontzal arrow indicates movement of the itemset after completion of database pass. The vertical arrow indicates movement of the itemset after reaching the frequency threshold. The dashed arrow indicates the new itemset entering the system at a stop-point.

Step 7. We need to scan the transactions t_{10}–t_{15} and the transactions t_1–t_5 to count the support of {5, 6, 7}. Thus, the algorithm requires only 2.75 database passes instead of 3 passes as in the level-wise method.

4.8 FP-TREE GROWTH ALGORITHM

Most of the above algorithms suffer from the following two shortcomings:

1. It is costly to handle large numbers of candidate sets. For instance, if there are 10^4 frequent 1-itemsets, then approximately, 10^7 candidate 2-itemsets are generated. Moreover, if there is a frequent set of size 100, then roughly 10^{30} candidate sets are generated in this process.
2. It is tedious to repeatedly scan the database and check a large set of candidates by pattern matching.

Keeping this in mind, a new class of algorithms have recently been proposed which avoids the generation of large numbers of candidate sets. We describe one such method, called the FP-Tree Growth algorithm. It is proposed by Han et al. The main idea of the algorithm is to maintain a Frequent Pattern Tree (FP-Tree) of the database. It is an extended prefix-tree structure, storing crucial and quantitative information about frequent sets. The tree nodes are frequent items and are arranged in a such a way that more frequently occurring nodes will have better chances of sharing nodes than the less frequently occurring ones. The method starts from frequent 1-itemsets as an initial suffix pattern and examines only its conditional pattern base (a subset of the database), which consists of the set of frequent items co-occurring with the suffix pattern. The algorithm constructs the conditional FP-tree and performs mining on this tree.

The algorithm involves two phases. In Phase I, it constructs the FP-tree with respect to a given σ. The construction of this tree requires two passes over the whole database. In Phase II, the algorithm does not use the transaction database any more, but it uses the FP-tree. Interestingly, the FP-tree contains all the information about frequent itemsets with respect to the given σ. Let us first understand the concept of the FP-tree.

DEFINITION 4.6 FP-TREE

A *frequent pattern tree* (or FP-tree) is a tree structure consisting of an item-prefix-tree and a frequent-item-header table.

- ❖ Item-prefix-tree:
  - It consists of a root node labelled null
  - Each non-root node consists of three fields:
    - ➤ Item name,
    - ➤ support count, and
    - ➤ node link.
- ❖ Frequent-item-header-table: it consists of two fields:
  - Item name
  - Head of node link which points to the first node in the FP-Tree carrying the item name.

It may be noted that the FP-tree is dependent on the support threshold σ. For different values of σ, the trees are different. There is another typical feature of the FP-tree; it depends on the ordering of the items. The ordering that is followed in the original paper is the decreasing order of the support counts. However, different ordering may offer different advantages. Thus, the header table is arranged in this order of the frequent items. Let us study the construction of an FP-tree from a transaction database.

We make one scan of the database T and compute L_1, the set of frequent 1-itemsets. For convenience, let us call this the set of frequent items. In other words, we refer to L_1 as a set of items rather than a class of singleton sets. Then we sort the items in L_1 in the decreasing order of frequency counts. From this stage onwards, the algorithm ignores all the non-frequent items from the transaction and views any transaction as a list of frequent items in the decreasing order of frequency. Without any ambiguity, we can refer to the transaction t as such a list. The first element of the list corresponding to any given transaction is the most frequent item among the items supported by t. For a list t, we denote *head_t* as its first element and *body_t* as the remaining part of the list (the portion of the list t after removal of *head_t*). Thus, t is [*head_t* | *body_t*]. The FP-tree construction grows the tree recursively using these concepts.

FP-Tree/Growth Algorithm for Association Rule Mining

```
Procedure : FP Growth (T, s)
Define and clear F-list: F[];
 do for each transaction t_i in T
    do for each item l_j in t_i
          F[l_j]++;
    end
 end
Sort F[]
Define and clear the root of FP-Tree: root ;
 do for each transaction t_i in T
    make t_i ordered according to F ;
    call insert_tree(t_i, root);
 end
do for each item l_j
call Growth(root, l_j, s)
end
```

FP-Tree Construction Algorithm

```
Procedure: insert-tree(t, node)
 do while t is not empty
    if node has a child node with label head_t
      then increment the link count between node and head_t by 1
      else create a new child node of node with label head_t with link count 1
  call insert-tree (body_t, head_t)
end do
```

EXAMPLE 4.7

Let us consider the database given in Example 4.5 (Table 4.4). The frequent items are 2, 3, 4, 5, 6, 7 and 8. If we sort them in the order of their frequency, then they appear in the order 5, 3, 4, 7, 2, 6, and 8. If the transactions are written in terms of only frequent items, then the transactions are

5, 6, 8
4, 2, 8
5, 4, 7
3
5, 7, 6
3, 4, 2
7, 2, 6
5
8
5, 3, 4, 7
5, 3, 4, 7
5, 6, 8
3, 4, 7, 2, 6
5, 3, 4, 7
3, 2.

The scan of the first transaction leads to the construction of the first branch of the tree (Figure 4.3). Notice that the branch is not ordered in the same way as the transaction appears in the database. The items are ordered according to the decreasing order of frequency of the frequent items. The complete table is given in Figure 4.4.

It is now easy to read the frequent itemsets from the FP-tree. The algorithm starts from the leaf node in a bottom-up approach. Thus, after processing item 6, it processes item 7. Let us consider, for instance, the frequent item {6}. There are four paths to 6 from the root; these are {5 7 6}, {5 6}, {4, 7, 2, 6}, and {7, 2, 6}. All these paths have labels of 1. A label of a path is the smallest of the link counts of its links. Thus, each of these combinations appear just once. The paths {5, 7, 6}, {5, 6}, {4, 7, 2, 6} and {7, 2, 6} from the root to the nodes with label 6 are called the prefix subpaths of 6. The prefix subpath of a node a are the paths from the root to the nodes labelled a and the count of links along a path are adjusted by adjusting the frequency count of every link in such a path, so that they are the same as the count of the link incident on a along the path. This is called a transformed prefix path. The transformed prefix paths of a node a form a truncated database of patterns which co-occur with a. This is called a conditional pattern base. Once the conditional pattern base is derived from the FP-tree, one can compute all the frequent patterns associated with it in the conditional pattern base. By creating a small conditional FP-tree for a, the process is recursively carried out starting from the leaf nodes.

The conditional pattern base for {6} is following.

For the prefix subpath {5, 7, 6}, we get {5, 6} $\rightarrow$ 1, {7, 6} $\rightarrow$ 1, {5, 7, 6} $\rightarrow$ 1.

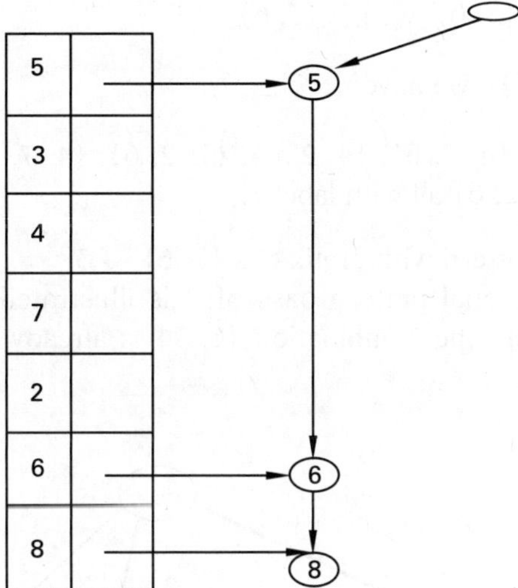

Figure 4.3 Illustration of insert (*t*, root) operation.

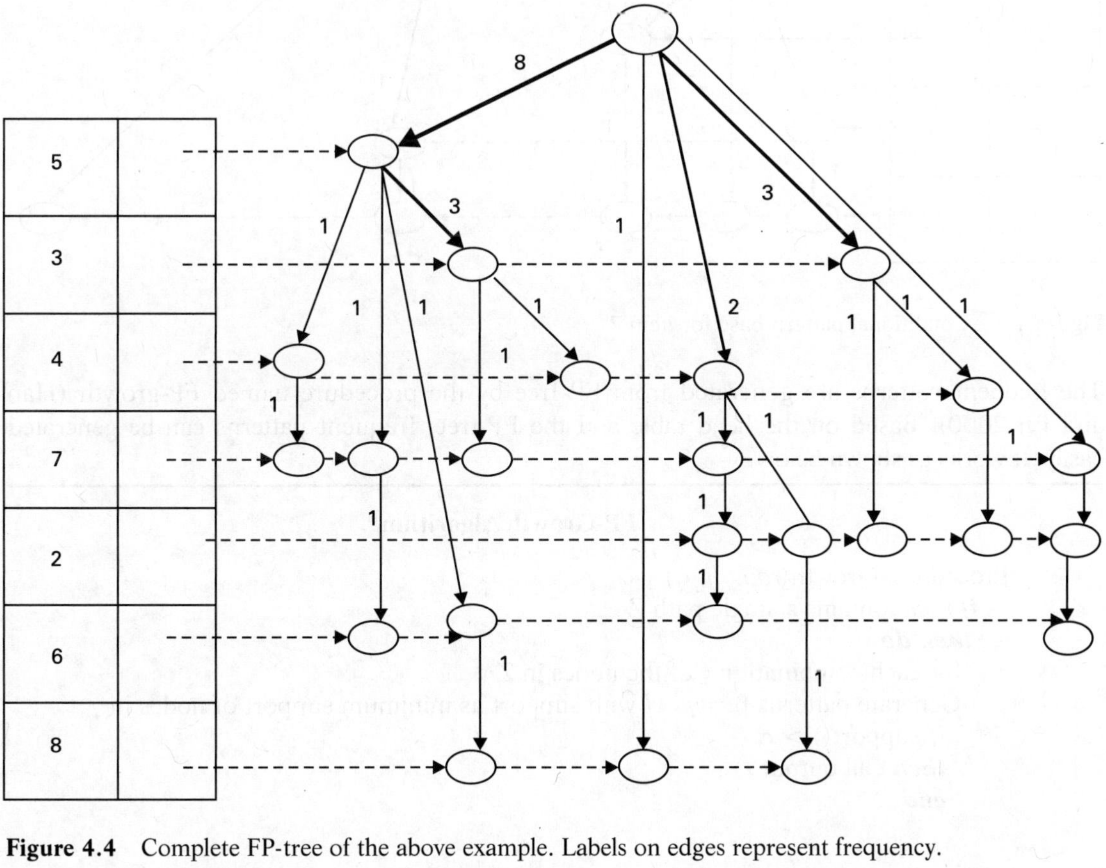

Figure 4.4 Complete FP-tree of the above example. Labels on edges represent frequency.

For the prefix subpath {5, 6}, we get {5, 6} → 1.

For the path {4, 7, 2, 6}, we have

{4, 6}, {7, 6}, {2, 6}, {4, 7, 6}, {4, 2, 6}, {7, 2, 6}, {4, 7, 2, 6} and for the path {7, 2, 6}, {7, 6}, {2, 6}, {7, 2, 6} all with label 1.

Thus the only frequent pattern with prefix 6 is {7, 6} → 3.

In Figure 4.5, the conditional pattern base of 7 is illustrated. Please note that since the processing now is bottom-up, the combination {6, 7} is already considered when the item 6 was considered.

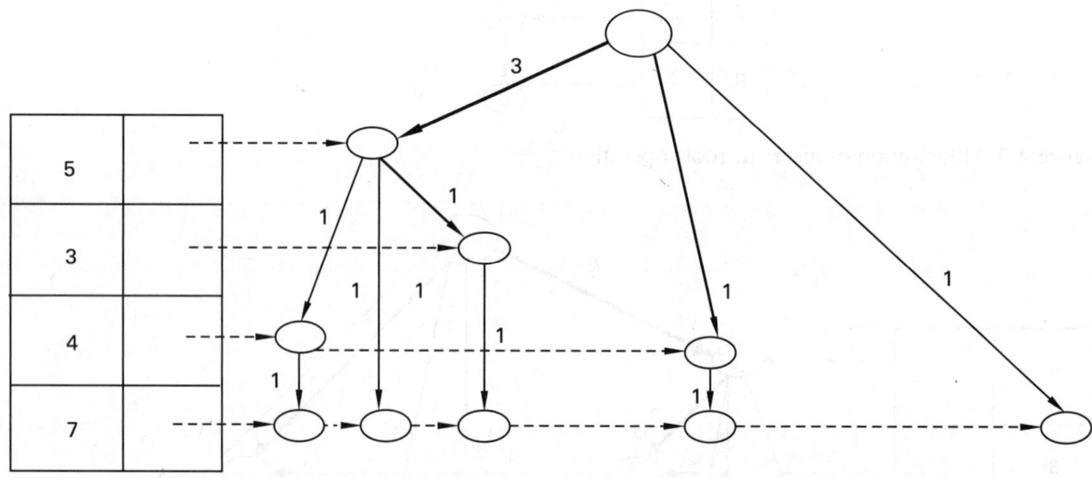

Figure 4.5 Conditional pattern base for item 7

The frequent patterns are generated from FP-Tree by the procedure named FP-growth (Han and Pei 2000). Based on the head table and the FP-tree, frequent patterns can be generated easily. It works as shown below.

FP-Growth Algorithm

Procedure: Growth(*root, lj,* σ)
  if *root* contains a single path Z
  then do
    for each combination γ of the nodes in Z
    Generate patterns $\beta = \gamma \cup l$ with support as minimum support of nodes in γ
      if support() > σ
      then call output () ;
      end

```
        end
      end
    do for each descendant bi of root
    Generate pattern β = bi ∪ l with support as support(b_i)
        if support(β) > σ
        then call output (β) ;
        end
    Construct β's conditional database;
    Construct β's conditional FP-tree Tree_β ;
        if Tree_β not empty then Call Growth(root of Tree_β, β, σ);
      end
    end
```

The efficiency of FP-tree algorithm accounts for three reasons. First, the FP-tree is a compressed representation of the original database because only frequent items are used to construct the tree, other irrelevant information are pruned. Also by ordering the items according to their supports the overlapping parts appear only once with different support count. Secondly this algorithm only scans the database twice. The frequent patterns are generated by the FP-growth procedure, constructing the conditional FP-tree which contain patterns with specified suffix patterns, frequent patterns can be easily generated as shown in above the example. Also the computation cost decreased dramatically. Thirdly, the FP-tree uses a divide and conquer method that considerably reduced the size of the subsequent conditional FP-tree, longer frequent patterns are generated by adding a suffix to the shorter frequent patterns. In [Han et al 2000] [Han and Pei 2000] there are examples to illustrate all the detail of this mining process.

Every algorithm has his limitations, for FP-tree it is difficult to be used in an interactive mining system. During the interactive mining process, users may change the threshold of support according to the rules. However, for FP-tree the changing of support may lead to repetition of the whole mining process. Another limitation is that FP-tree is that it is not suitable for incremental mining. Since as time goes on databases keep changing, new datasets may be inserted into the database, those insertions may also lead to a repetition of the whole process if we employ FP-tree algorithm.

Let us consider one more example.

There are five transactions as {*facdgimp, abcflmo, bfhjo, bcksp, afcelpmn*}. Let us assume $\sigma = 3$. After computing the support count and eliminating the infrequent items, the sorted transactions are {*fcamp, fcabm, fb, cbp, fcamp*}. The algorithm represents this as a pre-fix tree. Each path on the tree represents a set of transactions that share the same prefix. The conditional transaction for each items read from the bottom-up process will be the following. This is another way of viewing the FP-tree.

Transaction 1	*p : f c a m;*	*m : f c a;*	*a : f c;*	*c : f;*
Transaction 2	*m : f c a b;*	*b : f c a;*	*a: f c;*	*c : f*
Transaction 3	*b : f*			

Transaction 4	*p : c b;*	*b : c*		
Transaction 5	*p : f c a m;*	*m : f c a;*	*a: f c;*	*c : f*

The conditional database will be the following.

p : { *fcam /fcam /cb* }

m : { *fca /fca /fcab* }

b : { *fca /f /c /* }

a : { *fc /fc /fc* }

c : { *f /f /f* }

The conditional FP-trees are the following

{(*c*:3)} | *p* ; { (*f*:3, *c*:3, *a*:3)} |*m* ; {}|*b*, {(*f*:3, *c*:3)}|*a* ; { (*f*:3)}|*c* .

Although *FP-growth* has become popular, it faces several resource challenge. The compact representation does not reduce the potential combinatorial number of candidate patterns.

Let us identify some shortcomings of this algorithm. For huge databases the corresponding FP-tree is also huge and cannot fit in main memory.

4.9 ECLAT AND dECLAT

Eclat was introduced by Zaki (2000) using the power of a vertical database layout and intersection-based counting mechanism along with a depth-first search strategy and a bottom-up search for finding frequent patterns from a database. It is based on the prefix-based equivalence relation. The prefix-based equivalence relation is depicted by the symbol θ_k, which means that two itemsets are in the same equivalence class if they share a common k-length prefix. For calculating the 1-length frequent patterns, Eclat assumes that the vertical tid-list database is given and for each item it simply reads its corresponding tid-list from the disk into memory, incrementing the item's support for each entry. For calculating the 2-length frequent pattern items, it uses a support-dependent pre-processing step to gather the counts, and as this information is invariant, it has to be computed only once and that "... the cost can be amortised over the number of times the data is mined....". Eclat attempts to to improve the support counting step by indexing the database in such a way that it allows fast support computations. The basic idea is that the support of a candidate itemset can be computed by intersecting the tid list of suitably chosen subsets.

Let us take a simple example for illustration for understanding the underlying concept of the algorithm.

	l_1	l_2	l_3	l_4	l_5
t_1	1	1	1	0	0
t_2	0	0	1	1	0
t_3	0	0	0	0	1
t_4	0	1	0	1	0
t_5	1	0	1	1	1
t_6	0	0	0	0	1
t_7	1	1	0	1	1
t_8	1	0	1	1	1
t_9	0	0	0	0	1
t_{10}	0	1	1	0	0
t_{11}	0	1	0	1	0
t_{12}	0	0	1	1	1
t_{13}	1	1	1	0	1
t_{14}	0	0	0	0	1
t_{15}	1	1	0	1	1

We scan the database once and create the vertical database which identifies for each item the list of transactions that support the item.

We count the support of 1-itemsets to determine frequent 1-itemsets. Let us assume $\sigma = 5$. So, all 1-itemsets are frequent.

All 2-itemsets with l_1 are $l_1\ l_2,\ l_1\ l_3,\ l_1\ l_4,$ *and* $l_1\ l_5$. The transactions that support $l_1\ l_2$ are common to the set of transactions supporting l_1 and transactions supporting l_2. Thus from our above tid-list, we can obtain the transactions supporting $l_1\ l_2$ by intersecting the first two rows. Thus the support for 2-itemsets can be obtained from the tid-list.

Item	Tid-list
l_1	$t_1, t_5, t_7, t_{13}, t_{15}$
l_2	$t_1, t_4, t_7, t_{10}, t_{11}, t_{13}, t_{15}$
l_3	$t_1, t_2, t_5, t_8, t_{10}, t_{12}, t_{13}$
l_4	$t_2, t_4, t_5, t_7, t_8, t_{11}, t_{12}, t_{15}$
l_5	$t_3, t_5, t_6, t_7, t_8, t_9, t_{12}, t_{14}, t_{15}$

$l_1\ l_2$ - tids are t_1, t_7, t_{15}
$l_1\ l_3$ - tids are t_1, t_5, t_8, t_{13}
$l_1\ l_4$ - tids are t_5, t_7, t_8, t_{15}
$l_1\ l_5$ - tids are t_5, t_7, t_8, t_{15}

Since none of these has support value 5, these are all infrequent itemsets and hence no superset of l1 can be a frequent itemset. We proceed in the same way for

2-itemsets with I2 to find no 2-itemset as frequent. This is also true for 2-itemsets with I3. Now the 2-itemset with I4 is only I4 I5 which has support value 5 and is hence a frequent set. We proceed for 3-itemsets and the algorithm terminates.

We look at another simple example. The vertical database is directly given here item-wise. As per our earlier convention, we write here just indices (the indices here are of the transactions for vertical database whereas the indices are for items in our earlier discussion).

Item	Tid-list
l_1	1 3 4 5
l_2	1 2 3 4 5 6
l_3	2 4 5 6
l_4	1 3 5 6
l_5	1 2 3 4 5 6

Algorithm Eclat

Procedure: IntersectTIDsets(T, σ)
Input: T is available as vertical database
Output: list of frequent itemsets.
Initialize : P = { < l_j , t (l_j) > for all 1-itemsets in T}
for each itemset X with < X, t(X) > in P *do*
$P_X \leftarrow \varnothing$
for each <Y, t(Y)> in P such that Y is lexicographically greater than X *do*
$N_{XY} = X \cup Y$
$t(N_{XY}) = t(X) \cap t(Y)$
if support of $N_{XY} \geq \sigma$
then $P_x \leftarrow P_x \leftarrow \{<N_{XY}, t(N_{XY})>\}$
end
end
IntersectTIDsets(P_X, σ)
end

Source: Zaki 2009

It is noteworthy in the above algorithm that Eclat does not fully exploit the monotonicity property, but generates a candidate itemset based on only two of its subsets; the number of candidate itemsets that are generated is much larger as compared to the breadth-first approaches. Eclat essentially generates candidate itemsets using only the join step of Apriori but the pruning condition is missing. In comparison to Apriori, Eclat counts the supports of all itemsets much more efficiently using the intersection of tid-lists. In comparison to the Partition algorithm, the memory usage is much lower as at any depth d, Eclat needs only the tid-lists of at most all k-itemsets with same $(k-1)$-prefix, with $k \leq d$, whereas Partition needs to store in the main memory all the tid-lists along with the frequencies of all the itemsets in the kth level.

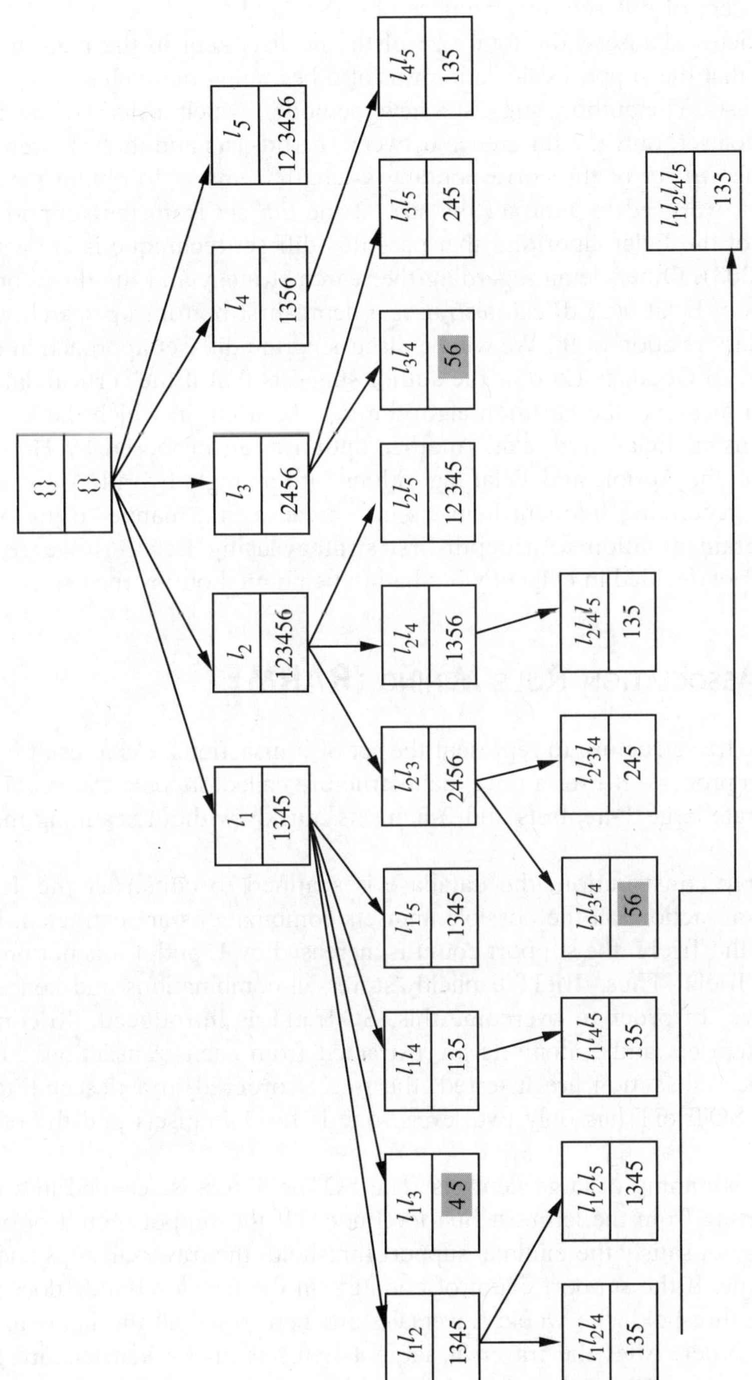

Figure 4.6 The tree search for Eclat. Shaded boxes are discarded as the support is below the threshold.

Recently, the concept of diff-sets was proposed by Zaki and Gouda in 2003. It is observed that in case of the dense datasets, the total size of the tid-lists kept in the main memory was becoming huge and that the support calculation was also becoming quite challenging due to the huge size of the tid-lists. The authors suggest a new method in which instead of storing the tid-list of the k-length itemset, only the difference between the tid-lists and its k–1-prefix is stored. This is known as the *diff-set* of the corresponding k-length itemset. To obtain the support of this k-length itemset, we need to subtract the size of the *diff-set* from the support of its k–1 prefix. The version of the Eclat algorithm that uses this diff-set technique is known as *dEclat* (Zaki and Gouda 2003). Other detail regarding the search strategy and the direction of search remains the same as in Eclat, i.e., dEclat also uses a depth-first bottom-up search with prefix-based equivalence class relation of θ_1. We will be discussing the diff-set approach in details in a forthcoming chapter. In Goethals (2003), the author suggests that if the vertical database does not fit into the main memory, the Partition algorithm can be used, in which the local frequent patterns are found using Eclat or dEclat. Another optimisation proposed by Hipp, Guntzer et al (2000) combine the Apriori and Eclat algorithms into a single hybrid. More specifically, the algorithm starts generating frequent itemsets in a breadth-first manner using Apriori and switches after a certain iteration to a depth-first strategy using Eclat. However, the exact switching point was not decided intelligently but had to be pointed out by the user.

4.10 Rapid Association Rule Mining (RARM)

RARM also uses the tree structure to represent the set of transactions. As a result it avoids the candidate generation process. It uses a novel data structure called *Support Ordered Trie Itemset* (SOTrieIT) to generate large 1-itemsets and 2-itemsets quickly without scanning the database for the second time.

First, as in FP-tree construction, the database is scanned to construct the Trie itemset (TrieIT). For each transaction, all the possible itemsets combinations are extracted. If the item is already present in the TrieIT, the support count is increased by 1, and if it is not present, then it is inserted to the TrieIT. Thus, TrieIT explicitly stores all combinations and hence demands higher memory space. In order to overcome this, SOTrieIT is introduced. To construct the SOTrieIT, only 1-itemsets and 2-itemsets are extracted from each transaction. After all the itemsets of the same transaction are inserted, the tree is ordered in a descending order of support count. The SOTrieIT has only two levels: one is for 1-itemsets and the other for 2-itemsets.

The second stage is mining of large itemsets. The SOTrieIT tree is scanned in a depth-first search approach starting from the leftmost first level node. If the support count of one item in the second level does not satisfy the minimal support threshold, the traversal stops and moves to another first level node. If the support count of one item in the first level node does not satisfy the minimal support threshold, the whole traversal stops here since all the items in SOTrieIT are in a descending order. After the traversal, large 1-itemsets and 2-itemsets are generated; the Apriori algorithm is used to further discover other large itemsets. Since generating large 2-itemsets is the costliest process during mining, experiments, Das et al (2001) have shown that the efficiency of generating large 1-itemsets and 2-itemsets in the SOTrieIT algorithm improves the performance dramatically. SOTrieIT is much faster than FP-tree but it also faces the same problem as FP-tree. The difference between FP-tree and TrieIT is that TrieIT only increases the support count of the leaf node items while FP-tree increases all the support counts along the path of the itemsets.

4.11 Discussion on Different Algorithms

We observe that all the algorithms have two important and common steps: (i) candidate generation, and (ii) I/O operation. The initial candidate set generation, especially for the frequent 2-itemsets, is the key issue to improve the performance of frequent set discovery algorithms. Another performance measure is the amount of data that has to be scanned during the discovery of the frequent itemset. The level-wise algorithm requires one pass over the database of all transactions for each iteration. The partition algorithm attempts to reduce the I/O operations by considering smaller segments of the database. The pincer-search algorithm attempts to reduce the number of candidate sets by considering Maximal Frequent Sets (MFS). But in order to get the frequency count of each frequent set, it requires one additional pass. DIC is based on a very novel idea, but in one sense it is similar in principle to the partition algorithm. The recent development of the FP-tree algorithm avoids the candidate generation steps.

There are different variations of all the algorithms that have been studied to improve the performance of mining association rules.

A hash-based technique is used to reduce the size of the candidate k-itemsets. Another variation is to reduce the number of transactions to be scanned at higher values of k. Since a transaction that does not contain any frequent k-itemset cannot contain any frequent $(k+1)$-itemset, these types of transactions can be marked during the kth scanning and are not considered in the subsequent scanning. We have observed that the other major variation is to reduce the number of database passes.

Note that as k increases, not only is there a smaller number of frequent k-itemsets, but there also are fewer transactions containing any frequent k-itemsets. Reducing the number of transactions to be scanned and trimming the number of items in each transaction can improve the efficiency of the algorithms. A modification of the level-wise algorithm, Apriori-TID attempts to handle this issue. In this algorithm, reading the complete database after the first iteration is avoided. During the first pass, the transaction id's and candidate frequent k-itemsets present in each transaction are generated in each iteration. This is used to determine the frequent sets of size $k+1$ present in each transaction during the next iteration.

Another factor that seriously affects the performance of an algorithm is the distribution of transactions over the whole database. If the data is distributed fairly uniformly throughout, then by choosing the stop points in DIC reasonably close, one can improve the performance substantially. To take care of randomness in the distribution, Toivonen proposes a sampling algorithm, where random samples of the database are taken and frequent sets with smaller support are computed for each sample. The sample size is so chosen that the sampled database can be accommodated in the main memory. Though it is an effective way of computing frequent sets, it pays the additional penalty of having to count more itemsets due to the reduced threshold.

The bi-directional search used by the pincer-search has an advantage over the bottom-up search only when there are some very large frequent itemsets. In that event, the bottom-up search may take a large number of passes, whereas the pincer-search may detect a maximal frequent set very early and hence may reduce the number of passes.

Recently Shenoy et al proposed an efficient algorithm – Vertical Itemset Partitioning for Efficient Rule Extraction – VIPER, which is based on vertical mining. The database can be represented either by a set of tuples, each tuple listing the presence or absence of items; or it can be represented as a list of items, each item indicating the tuples in which it is present. The latter representation is called the vertical representation, as its basic structure is a column. VIPER stores data in compressed bit-vector called 'snakes' and provides manipulations with this structure.

The next few years will witness some very innovative algorithms to improve performance. In the following sections, we shall study other problems related to the discovery of association rules.

4.12 Incremental Algorithm

In the previous sections we have studied different algorithms for the discovery of frequent sets and for mining of association rules. We have analysed the possibilities of reducing the I/O operations and segmenting the database into smaller fragments to increase efficiency. But one common assumption in all these approaches is that the database itself does not change. In practice, no transaction database is static. It is possible that more transactions are added intermittently to the database. Such updates to the transaction database could potentially invalidate the existing set of association rules. It is possible that the updates may also introduce more new association rules. The problem is to update the association rules when the database is updated. As we discussed earlier, the crucial step of finding association rules is to discover the set of frequent itemsets. In the present context, the problem boils down to updating the set of frequent itemsets. One simple method will be to compute afresh the set of frequent itemsets for the whole database. But in this case, all efforts have been expended in computing the frequent sets before the update is wasted. Moreover, if we can somehow make intelligent use of the earlier computation, we may be able to reduce the I/O operations in computing the updated set of frequent itemsets.

Let us assume that T_{old} is the existing database for which the set of frequent itemsets L_{old} is already computed. The respective support values of the frequent sets in L_{old} are also known. Let us assume that another set of transactions, T_{new} is now added to the database to get $T_{whole} = T_{old} \cup T_{new}$. The problem of incremental computation of frequent sets is to determine the set of all frequent sets L_{whole} of T_{whole}.

Let us assume that L_{new} is the set of all frequent sets of T_{new}. It is assumed that L_{new} is initially unknown. Then the following observations are obvious:

1. An itemset will be in L_{whole} if it is an element of both L_{new} and L_{old}.
2. Any itemset which is neither in L_{new} nor in L_{old} cannot be in L_{whole}.

Thus, if we simply start finding L_{new}, we can use condition 1 given above to determine L_{whole}, we are going to make some passes over T_{new}. Hence, we make use of these passes to compute the support of itemsets of L_{old} in T_{new}. That is, $s(X)_{Tnew}$ for X in L_{old}. But unless we read T_{old}, we may not be able find those frequent itemsets, if any, which are frequent in T_{new} as well as in T_{whole}, but infrequent in T_{old}.

Keeping the above observations in mind, let us design an incremental method. If we find $s(X)_{Tnew}$ for all X in L_{old} (in other words, if we count the supports of frequent sets of old database with respect to the increment part of the database), and if we identify those sets which reach the σ level of support, then we can partially characterise L_{whole}. This can be achieved by just one pass over T_{new} only (supports of all the frequent itemsets can be counted in one pass). It is a partial characterisation because this process takes into account the following cases:

a. The itemsets of L_{old} that are frequent in T_{new} (hence, in T_{whole}) can be determined.
b. The itemsets that belong to L_{old} but are not in L_{new} are automatically eliminated.
c. The itemsets that are neither in L_{new} nor in L_{old} are not considered.

But those itemsets that are not in L_{old} but are frequent sets in T_{whole} are not taken into account in the above step.

One way of achieving a complete characterisation is to find L_{new} first and compute the supports of the itemsets in $L_{new} \setminus L_{old}$ by making one pass over T_{old}. This requires exactly one pass over the main database T_{old} and many passes over T_{new}.

This process has another disadvantage in that the database pass may not turn out to be fruitful, in the sense that there may not be any new frequent set generated by this process. In that case the database pass is unnecessary. Then the question is whether we can know in advance if any database pass is required at all or not. In other words, whether there exists a frequent set of T_{whole} which is not in L_{old}. If there is no such frequent sets, then we do not need the additional database pass.

In order to estimate this, we require a new concept called the *Promoted Border Set.*

Let X be an itemset which is not frequent in T_{old}, but is frequent in T_{new} as well as in T_{whole}. All the subsets of X are frequent in T_{whole}. Since X is not frequent in L_{old}, it has a subset that is a border set in T_{old}. This border set becomes a frequent set after update. We call such a set a *promoted border.*

DEFINITION 4.7 PROMOTED BORDER

An itemset that was a border set before update and becomes a frequent set after update, is called a *promoted border* itemset.

The existence of a promoted border is an indication that we may have to read the old transaction database once again. The incremental algorithm to discover frequent sets critically depends on this observation. It is clear from the above discussion that $L_{whole} \cap (L_{new} \setminus L_{old}) \neq \emptyset$ if and only if there exists a promoted border itemset. The correctness of this statement can be derived from the argument given in the foregoing paragraph.

However, there are few more issues to be sorted out for implementation. How do we find border sets of T_{old}? How do we determine a promoted border?

Interestingly, finding border sets is not difficult. A simple modification to the level-wise algorithm will generate the set of border itemsets along with the set of frequent sets. The idea is that while reading the database to count supports of the candidate itemsets, those itemsets having support less than σ are the border itemsets. We give below the modified algorithm with the additional step to compute border sets.

Modified *Apriori* Algorithm to Generate Border Sets and Frequent Sets

Initialize: $k := 1$, C_1 = all the 1-itemsets;
read the database to count the support of C_1 to determine L_1.
$L_1 :=$ {frequent 1-itemsets};
$k := 2$; // *k represents the pass number//*
while $(L_{k-1} \neq \varnothing)$ *do*
begin
  $C_k :=$ ***gen_candidate_item sets with the given*** L_{k-1}
  prune C_k
  for all transactions $t \in T$ ***do***
  increment the count of all candidates in C_k that are contained in t ;
  $L_k := \{c \in C_k \mid s(c)_T \geq \sigma\}$;
  $B_k := \{c \in C_k \mid s(c)_T < \sigma\}$;
  $k := k + 1$;
end
  $L := \cup_k L_k$;
  $B := \cup_k B_k$;

Example 4.2 (contd.)
If we use the above modification of the level-wise algorithm in Example 4.2, we get the following itemsets as the border set.

$\{1\} \to 2$, $\{9\} \to 2$, $\{2,5\} \to 0$, $\{2,6\} \to 2$, $\{2,7\} \to 2$, $\{2,8\} \to 1$,
$\{3,4\} \to 1$, $\{3,6\} \to 0$, $\{3,8\} \to 0$, $\{4,5\} \to 1$, $\{4,6\} \to 1$,
$\{4,7\} \to 2$, $\{4,8\} \to 1$, $\{5,8\} \to 2$, $\{6,8\} \to 2$, $\{5,6,7\} \to 1$.

Thus, no additional effort is needed to generate the border itemsets.

An incremental method called the *border algorithm* makes use of the concept of promoted border to avoid a fruitless pass.

4.13 Border Algorithm

The border algorithm maintains support counters for all frequent sets and all border sets. Thus, when we get a promoted border (more precisely, when a border set is promoted to a frequent set), an additional pass over the database is made. If there is no promoted border, then the algorithm does not require even a single pass over the whole database.

The algorithm works as follows. Initially, the L_{old} and B_{old} are known along with their respective support counts. The algorithm starts by counting the supports of the itemsets of L_{old}

$\cup B_{old}$ in T_{new}. This requires one pass over the increment portion of the database. During this phase, the algorithm collects two categories of itemsets: F and B.

Set F contains the itemset of L_{old} which becomes a frequent set in T_{whole}. We should take care of the threshold count while counting the support. For example, consider that $\sigma = 5\%$, $|T_{old}| = 1000$. Clearly, any itemset that is supported by 50 or more transactions in T_{old} is its frequent set. Let $|T_{new}| = 400$ and hence, $|T_{whole}| = 1400$. The itemset X is frequent in T_{whole}, if it is supported by 70 or more transactions. Thus, while determining frequent sets in T_{old}, our threshold of absolute count is 50, whereas the same in T_{whole} is 70.

Set B contains all the border sets whose support count reach the level σ and hence, are promoted border sets. If there is no promoted border, then F contains all the frequent sets of T_{whole}. But if there is at least one border set that becomes a promoted border, then the algorithm generates candidate sets which are supersets of the promoted border sets. It makes one pass over the database to count the support of these candidate sets.

Thus, the algorithm makes one pass over the increment database, and at most one pass over the whole database. We give below the formal description of the border algorithm.

Border Algorithm

read T_{new} and increment the support count of X for all $X \in L_{old} \cup B_{old}$

$F := \{X \mid X \in L_{old} \text{ and } s(X)_{Twhole} \geq \sigma\}$
$B := \{X \mid X \in B_{old} \text{ and } s(X)_{Twhole} \geq \sigma\}$
Let m be the size of the largest element in B.
Candidate-generation
for all itemsets $l_1 \in B_{k-1} \cup C_{k-1}$ ***do begin***
for all itemsets $l_2 \in B_{k-1} \cup F_{k-1} \cup C_{k-1}$ ***do begin***
  if $l_1[1] = l_2[1] \wedge l_1[2] = l_2[2] \wedge \ldots \wedge l_1[k-1] < l_2[k-1]$ ***then***
  $c = l_1[1], l_1[2] \ldots l_1[k-1], l_2[k-1]$
  $C_k = C_k \cup \{c\}$
end do
end do

Prune C_k: for all k
all subsets of $k-1$ size should be present in $B_{k-1} \cup F_{k-1} \cup C_{k-1}$
$k := k+1$
Candidate $C := \cup C_k$
read T_{whole} and count the support values of each itemset in C.
new_frequent_sets := $\{X \mid X \in C \text{ and } s(X)_{Twhole} \geq \sigma\}$
L_{whole} := $F \cup$ new_frequent_sets
$B_{whole} := (B_{old} \setminus B) \cup \{X \in C \text{ and } s(X)_{Twhole} < \sigma \text{ and all its subsets are in } L_{whole}\}$

We illustrate the working of the algorithm using the table (Table 4.1) given in Example 4.2.

EXAMPLE 4.8

Let Table 4.1 be T_{old} and add the following 5 transactions (Table 4.6) to the database. We know L_{old} and B_{old} with their respective support values.

STEP 1: Read T_{new} to count supports of itemsets in L_{old} and of B_{old} and collect the itemsets which reach the σ level with respect to T_{whole} in F and B, respectively. We indicate below the itemsets that are in F and B, along with the old support and incremented support.

F:= {{2} → 6+2, {3} → 6+4, {5} → 8+4, {6} → 5+4, {7} → 7+4, {8}→4+2, {2,3} → 3+1, {3,5} → 3+4, {3,7} → 3+4, {5,6} → 3+4, {5,7} → 5+4, {6,7} → 3+4, {3,5,7} → 3+4}

B:= {{1}→2+2, {3,6}→0+4, {5,6,7}→1+4}

Thus, we see that we have 3 promoted border sets.

Table 4.6 T_{new}

1	0	1	0	1	1	1	0	0
0	0	1	0	1	1	1	0	0
0	1	1	0	1	1	1	0	0
1	1	0	0	0	0	0	1	0
0	0	1	0	1	1	1	1	0

Candidate Generation We generate the candidate sets in a level-wise fashion.

Since {1} is now frequent, we need to check the supports of itemsets {1,2}, {1,3}, {1,5}, {1,6}, {1,7}, {1,8}. Note that since {4} ceases to be a frequent set after the update, we do not generate {1,4}.

For the next level of candidate-set generation, we take the all the candidate 2-itemsets generated so far and the promoted border 2-itemset, that is {1,2}. {1,3}, {1,5}, {1,6}, {1,7}, {1,8}, and {3,6} on one side. On the other side we take all the 2-itemsets in F too, that is, {2,3}, {3,5}, {3,7}, {5,6}, {5,7}, {6,7}, {1,2}. {1,3}, {1,5}, {1,6}, {1,7}, {1,8}, and {3,6}.

The candidate sets that we generate are {1,2,3}, {1,2,5}, {1,2,6}, {1,2,7}, {1,2,8}, {1,3,5}, {1,3,6}, {1,3,7}, {1,3,8}, {1,5,6}, {1,5,7}, {1,5,8}, {1,6,7}, {1,6,8}, {1,7,8}, {2,3,5}, {3,5,6}, {3,6,7}.

Similarly, the candidate 4-itemsets are {1,3,5,7} and {3,5,6,7}.

We make a single database pass.

The border algorithm was proposed by Ronen Feldman in the year 1997. Thomas et al concurrently developed a similar approach for incremental discovery. Their algorithm is slightly different from the border algorithm. But both these algorithms use the same principle of determining the promoted border itemset and deciding whether a full scan is required or not. Hence, both these algorithms maintain the set of border sets along with the set of frequent sets.

One major difference in this algorithm is that it first computes L_{new}. The algorithm is described below.

Update Algorithm

compute L_{new};
for each itemset $X \in L_{old} \cup B_{old}$ ***do***
  count support of X in T_{new};
$L_{whole} := \emptyset$;
for each $X \in L_{old}$ ***do***
  if support of X in T_{whole} exceeds σ
  then $L_{whole} := L_{whole} \cup \{X\}$
for each itemset $Y \in L_{new}$ *do*
  if $Y \notin L_{old} \wedge Y \in B_{old}$ and this support of Y in T_{whole} exceeds σ
  then $L_{whole} := L_{whole} \cup \{Y\}$;
if $L_{old} \neq L_{whole}$
then compute the border set of T_{whole}
else $B_{whole} = B_{old}$
if $L_{old} \cup B_{old} \neq L_{whole} \cup B_{whole}$
then $S = L_{whole}$
repeat
  compute $S = S \cup$ border set of S
until S does not grow
count frequency of S to determine L_{whole}
generate the border set B_{whole}

4.14 GENERALISED ASSOCIATION RULE

In the most general form, an association rule is of the form $C_1 \Rightarrow C_2$, where C_1, C_2 are conjunctions of conditions and each condition is either $l_i = v$; or $l_i \in$ [*low*, *upper*] for each item l_i in A, where v, *low* and *upper* are some values in the domain of l_i. In this framework, the association rule that we have studied so far becomes a special case where $C = [l_i =$ 'yes']. Databases in the real world usually have numeric values such as age and balance of account. Thus, it is important to find association rules for numeric and categorical attributes.

Another feature of association rule generators is an *item hierarchy*. In our example, we were using generic terms: diapers and beer. Let us assume that stores sell specific items: 6d beer in a 31b box, 24 oz diapers product ID 32225, etc. Normally, rules that are somewhat more general, like the rules we have been using as examples, are frequently what is expected. But in some cases, one might be interested in rules that deal in specific items or we might be interested in rules that differentiate between, say, beers sold in boxes vs. beer sold in bulk. A product hierarchy can be used to structure a hierarchy of items that permits grouping at different levels.

Note also that in an association rule time does not play a part. Contrast this with a sequencing rule in which time is important, and that might read: *When people buy diapers, they also buy beer 2 to 4 months later, 18% of the time*. We shall discuss this problem in Chapter 10.

Association rules, and the support-confidence framework used to mine them, are well-suited to the market–basket problem. Other basket data problems, while seemingly similar, have requirements that the support-confidence framework does not support. For example, negative implications of the type: *"when people buy batteries, they do not usually also buy cat food."* While perhaps not so useful to the marketing staff of supermarkets, such implications can be helpful in many other settings. For example, fire code inspectors trying to mine useful fire prevention measures might like to know of any negative correlations between certain types of electrical wiring and the occurrence of fires.

The bigger problem is that the support-confidence framework does not work well when correlation is the appropriate measure.

EXAMPLE 4.9

Suppose we have market–basket data from a grocery store, consisting of *n* baskets. Let us focus on the purchase of tea and coffee. In the following tabe (Table 4.7), rows t and $\overline{t}$ correspond to baskets that do and do not, respectively, contain tea, ad similarly columns c and $\overline{c}$ correspond to coffee. The numbers represent the percentage of baskets.

Table 4.7

	c	$\overline{c}$
t	20	5
$\overline{t}$	70	5

Let us apply the support-confidence framework to the potential association rule, t ⇒ c. The support for this rule is 20%, which is fairly high. The confidence is defined to be the conditional probability that a customer buys coffee, given that she buys tea, i.e., 20/25 = 0.8 or 80%, which too is pretty high. At this point, we may conclude that the rule t ⇒ c is a valid rule.

However, consider now the fact that the a priori probability that a customer buys coffee is 90%. In other words, a customer who is known to buy tea is less likely to buy coffee (by 10%) than a customer about whom we have no information. Of course, it may still be interesting to know that such a large number of people who buy tea also buy coffee, but stating that rule by itself is at best incomplete information and at worst misleading. The truth here is that there is a negative correlation between buying tea and buying coffee; at least that information should be provided along with the association rule $t \Rightarrow c$. One way to deal with this situation is to identify the rules $\overline{c} \Rightarrow t$, $\overline{t} \Rightarrow c$ and $c \Rightarrow t$. Another way of measuring correlation is to compute $P[t \wedge c]/(P[t] \times P[c])$. The fact that this quantity is significantly less than 1 indicates a negative correlation, since the numerator is the actual likelihood of seeing a customer purchase both tea and coffee, and the denominator is what the likelihood would have been in the case when the two purchases are completely independent.

4.15 Association Rules with Item Constraints

In practice, the users are often interested only in a subset of associations, for instance, those containing at least one item from a user-defined subset of items. A straightforward way of doing this is to carry out a filtering as a post-processing step after any association rule mining algorithm is invoked. However, it would be desirable to incorporate these constraints within the steps of the association discovery algorithm.

Let B be a Boolean expression over the set of itemsets A. We assume, without loss of generality, that B is in disjunctive normal form (DNF). That is, B is of the form, $D_1 \vee D_2 \vee \ldots \vee D_m$, where each disjunct D_i is of the form $\alpha_{i1} \wedge \alpha_{i2} \ldots \wedge \alpha_{in}$. Each of the α refers either to the presence of an item, l_{ij} or to the absence of an item, $\neg l_{ij}$.

The problem of the mining association rule with item-constraint B is to discover all rules that satisfy B and have support and confidence greater than or equal to the user-specified minimum support and minimum confidence, respectively.

We can split the problem into three phases.

Phase 1

Find all frequent itemsets that satisfy the Boolean expression, B. Remember that there are two types of operations used for this problem: candidate-set generation and counting support. The techniques for counting support remains unchanged for the current problem. However, the earlier method of candidate-set generation may not assure that the frequent sets are those which satisfy the Boolean constraints.

This subproblem is tackled in the following way:

1. Generate a set of selected items S such that any itemset that satisfies B will contain at least one selected item.
2. Modify the candidate-generation procedure to generate only candidates that contain selected items.
3. Discard frequent itemsets that do not satisfy B.

Phase 2

To generate rules from these frequent itemsets, we need to find the support of all subsets of frequent itemsets that do not satisfy B. Recall that to generate a rule ABCD, we need the support of AB to find the confidence of the rule. However, AB may not satisfy B and hence may not have been counted in Phase 1. So we generate all subsets of the frequent itemsets found in Phase 1, then make an extra pass over the data set to count the support of those subsets that are not present in the output of Phase 1.

Phase 3

To generate rules from the frequent itemsets found in Phase 1, using the frequent itemsets found in phases 1 and 2 to compute confidence.

Generating Selected Items

We can generate S by choosing one element α_{ij} from each disjunct D_i in S and adding either l_{ij} or all the elements in $A—\{l_{ij}\}$ to S, based on whether α_{ij} is l_{ij} or $\neg l_{ij}$, respectively. We define an element $\alpha_{ij} = l_{ij}$ in B to be present in S if l_{ij} is in S, and element $\alpha_{ij} = \neg l_{ij}$ to be present if all the items in $A—\{l_{ij}\}$ are in S.

Multiple Concept Level ARM

In real life, for many applications, it is difficult to find strong association rules between data items at low or primitive levels of abstraction due to the sparsity of data in multidimensional space. While strong association rules generated at a higher concept level may be common sense to some users but it also can be novel to other users. Multiple level association rule mining tries to mine strong association rules among and within different levels of abstraction. For example, besides the association rules between *milk* and *ham*, it can generalise those rules to relation between *drink* and *meat*; at the same time it can also specify the relation between certain brands of *milk* and *ham*.

Association Rule Discovery with Constraints

Constraints-based association rule mining is finding all rules from a given data-set meeting all the user-specified constraints, such as knowledge-based constraints, data constraints, dimensional constraints, interestingness constraints or rule formation constraints. In a sense, we can view the minimal support and minimal confidence as some sort of constraint. In Ng et al 1998 and Srikant et al, 1997, the authors proposed some algorithms with faster association rule mining by incorporating item constraints on the process of generating frequent itemsets. Item constraints restrict the items and combination of items that are interesting according to users, association rules are generated from those frequent itemsets. Also, some work has been done on measuring association rules with the interestingness parameter [Klemettinen et al 1994] [Brin et al 1997] [Smythe and Goodman 1992]. While item constraints focus on pruning frequent itemsets, the interestingness parameter focuses on pruning the association rules to get more general or informative association rules.

4.16 Summary

In this chapter, an attempt is made to summarise all the major techniques of discovering associations rules for large databases. The chapter begins with establishing the foundational concepts on this subject and discusses algorithms like Apriori, Partition, Pincer-Search, Dynamic Itemset Counting, FP-tree Growth, Eclat and dEclat. It also addresses related problems like incremental computation of association rules. It summarises the techniques of generalised association rule discovery and algorithms for association rules with item-constraints.

FURTHER READING

In 2000, Zaki introduced six new algorithms combining several features (database format, the decomposition technique, and the search procedure). These are Eclat (Equivalence CLAss Transformation), MaxEclat, Clique, MaxClique, TopDown and AprClique. Eclat is a well known depth-first search algorithm using set intersection.

The details of FP-tree algorithm will be found in Han, Pei et al (2004). In Han et al (2007), we find a complete overview of the state-of-the art in frequent patten mining and it also identifies future research directions. In Bruzzese and Davino (2000), the authors construct several statistical tests to evaluate the significance of discovered associations. Tan, Kumar and Sriastav in 2004 compare the properties of 21 objective measures (of interest). The measures in general lack agreement with each other. However, the authors show that if support-based pruning or table standardisation (of the contingency tables) is used, the measures become highly correlated. In Hahsler and Hornik (2007), a simple probabilistic framework for transaction data which can be used to simulate transaction data when no associations are present can be found. The authors also introduce the new probabilistic measures, namely, hyper-lift and hyper-confidence.

EXERCISES

1. Define a frequent set. Define an association rule.
2. Define a border set. Show that every subset of any itemset must contain either a frequent set or a border set.
3. Discuss the importance of discovering association rules.
4. The discovery of the association rule can be formulated in terms of relational algebraic operations. Comment.
5. Discuss the concepts of frequent sets, confidence and support.
6. Describe the working of the pincer-search algorithm.
7. The pincer-search algorithm is a bi-directional search, whereas the level-wise algorithm is a unidirectional search. Comment.
8. The pincer-search algorithm finds only maximal frequent sets. Comment.
9. Describe the principle of pruning in level-wise algorithms. The set of all frequent sets can be generated even by ignoring the pruning step. Comment.
10. Describe the candidate-generating step of level-wise algorithms. What is its importance?
11. Describe the working dynamic itemset counting technique. When do you move itemsets from dashed structures to solid structures.
12. What is the incremental discovery of an association rule? What are the algorithms for incremental discovery? Discuss the important features of the algorithm.
13. What is the problem of association rule with item-constraints? Propose a method for this.
14. Define a FP-tree. Discuss the method of computing a FP-tree.
15. Describe the search stategy of the Eclot and dEclat algorithm

BIBLIOGRAPHY

Dario Bruzzese and Cristina Davino. Pruning of discovered association rules. *Computational Statistics*, 16:387–398, 2001.

Douglas Burdick, Manuel Calimlim, and Johannes Gehrke. MAFIA: A maximal frequent itemset algorithm for transactional databases. In *Proceedings of the 17th InternationalConference on Data Engineering*, IEEE Computer Society, pp. 443–452, Washington DC, 2001.

Edward R. Omiecinski. Alternative interest measures for mining associations in databases. *IEEE Transactions on Knowledge and Data Engineering*, 15(1):57–69, Jan/Feb 2003.

Feng Tao, Fionn Murtagh, and Mohsen Farid. Weighted association rule mining using weighted support and significance framework. In *Proceedings of The Ninth ACM SIGKDD International Conference on Knowledge Discovery and Data Mining (KDD-2003)*, ACM Press, Washington, DC, 2003.

Francesco Bonchi and Claudio Lucchese. On condensed representations of constrained frequent patterns. *Knowledge and Information Systems*, 9(2):180–201, 2006.

Hannu Toivonen. Sampling large databases for association rules. In *VLDB '96: Proceedings of the 22th International Conference on Very Large Data Bases*, Morgan Kaufmann Publishers Inc., pp. 134–145, San Francisco, CA, USA, 1996.

Heikki Mannila, Hannu Toivonen, and A. Inkeri Verkamo. Efficient algorithms for discovering association rules. In *AAAI Workshop on Knowledge Discovery in Databases (KDD-94)*, AAAI Press, pp. 181–192, Seattle, Washington, 1994.

J. Han, H. Cheng, D. Xin, and X. Yan. Frequent pattern mining: Current status and future directions. *Data Mining and Knowledge Discovery*, 14(1), 2007.

Jiawei Han, Jian Pei, Yiwen Yin, and Runying Mao. Mining frequent patterns without candidate generation. *Data Mining and Knowledge Discovery*, 8:53–87, 2004.

Karam Gouda and Mohammed J. Zaki. GenMax: An efficient algorithm for mining maximal frequent itemsets. *Data Mining and Knowledge Discovery*, 11:1–20, 2005.

Liqiang Geng and Howard J. Hamilton. Interestingness measures for data mining: A survey. *ACM Computing Surveys*, 38(3):9, 2006.

Masakazu Seno and George Karypis. Finding frequent itemsets using length-decreasing support constraint. *Data Mining and Knowledge Discovery*, 10:197–228, 2005.

Michael Hahsler and Kurt Hornik. New probabilistic interest measures for association rules. *Intelligent Data Analysis*, 11(5):437–455, 2007.

Mohammed Zaki and Ching-Jui Hsiao. Efficient algorithms for mining closed itemsets and their lattice structure. *IEEE Transactions on Knowledge and Data Engineering*, 17(4):462–478, 2005.

Mohammed Zaki. Mining non-redundant association rules. *Data Mining and Knowledge Discovery*, 9:223–248, 2004.

Mohammed J. Zaki and Ching-Jiu Hsiao. CHARM: An efficient algorithm for closed itemset mining. In *Proceedings of the Second SIAM International Conference on Data Mining*, SIAM, Arlington, VA, 2002.

Mohammed J. Zaki. Scalable algorithms for association mining. *IEEE Transactions on Knowledge and Data Engineering*, 12(3):372–390, May/June 2000.

Nicolas Pasquier, Yves Bastide, Rafik Taouil, and Lotfi Lakhal. Efficient mining of association rules using closed itemset lattices. *Information Systems*, 24(1):25–46, 1999.

Pang-Ning Tan, Vipin Kumar, and Jaideep Srivastava. Selecting the right objective measure for association analysis.*Information Systems*, 29(4):293–313, 2004.

Salvatore Orlando, Claudio Lucchese, Paolo Palmerini, Raffaele Perego, and Fabrizio Silvestri. kdci: a multi-strategy algorithm for mining frequent sets. In *FIMI'03: Proceedings of the IEEE ICDM Workshop on Frequent Itemset Mining Implementations*, November 2003.

Toon Calders, Christophe Rigotti, and Jean-Francois Boulicaut. A survey on condensed representations for frequent sets. In *Constraint-Based Mining and Inductive Databases: European Workshop on Inductive Databases and Constraint Based Mining,* Hinterzarten, Germany, March 11–13, 2004, Revised Selected Papers, 3848:64–80, February 2006.

5

CLUSTERING TECHNIQUES

5.1 INTRODUCTION

Clustering is a useful technique for the discovery of data distribution and patterns in the underlying data. The goal of clustering is to discover both the dense and the sparse regions in a data set. Data clustering has been studied in the statistics, machine learning and database communities with diverse emphases. The earlier approaches do not adequately consider the fact that the data set can be too large to fit in the main memory. In particular, they do not recognise that the problem must be viewed in terms of how to work with limited resources. The main emphasis has been to cluster with as high an accuracy as possible, while keeping the I/O costs low. Thus, it is not relevant to apply the classical clustering algorithms in the context of data mining and it is necessary to investigate the principle of clustering to devise efficient algorithms which meet the specific requirement of minimizing the I/O operations. It is also to be noted that the basic principle of clustering hinges on a concept of distance metric or similarity metric. Since the data are invariably real numbers for statistical applications and pattern recognition, a large class of metrics exists and one can define one's own metric depending on a specific requirement. But in databases, there exist objects which cannot be ordered, and their attributes can be categorical in nature. For example, consider a market–basket database. Typically, the number of items, and thus the number of attributes, in such a database is very large, while the size of an average transaction is much smaller. Furthermore, customers with similar buying patterns, who belong to a single cluster, may buy a small subset of items from a much larger set that defines the cluster. Thus, conventional clustering methods that handle only numeric data are not suitable for data mining purposes.

This chapter deals with different clustering techniques for data mining. In the last five years, there has been increasing interest in devising efficient clustering algorithms for data mining. In a short span of 2–3 years a very large number of new and interesting algorithms have been proposed. The aim of this chapter is to survey these algorithms and present them in a form which will be useful to the research community for future research. We shall first discuss different approaches of clustering of numerical data and then the recent algorithms of clustering categorical data. The clustering algorithms for numerical data are again categorised into two classes: partition and hierarchical.

In Section 5.2 we shall briefly outline different approaches to clustering. Section 5.3 discusses the underlying principles of partitioning algorithms. Three different partitioning algorithms, namely PAM, CLARA and CLARANS, are discussed in Sections 5.4, 5.5 and 5.6, respectively. Section 5.7 introduces the concepts of hierarchical clustering algorithms. In this category, we discuss DBSCAN in Section 5.8; CURE in Section 5.9; and BIRCH in Section 5.10. The conventional mining algorithms handle only numeric data, while clustering techniques for the purpose of data mining are expected to handle categorical data also. We shall discuss the principles of clustering of categorical data in Section 5.11. Three algorithms in this category discussed in detail: STIRR, ROCK and CACTUS in Sections 5.12–5.14.

5.2 Clustering Paradigms

There are two main approaches to clustering—*hierarchical clustering* and *partitioning clustering*. Besides, clustering algorithms differ among themselves in their ability to handle different types of attributes, numeric and categorical, in accuracy of clustering, and in their ability to handle disk-resident data.

Hierarchical vs. Partitioning

The partition clustering techniques partition the database into a predefined number of clusters. They attempt to determine k partitions that optimise a certain criterion function. The partition clustering algorithms are of two types: k-means algorithms and k-medoid algorithms. Another type of algorithm can be k-mode algorithms.

The hierarchical clustering techniques do a sequence of partitions, in which each partition is nested into the next partition in the sequence. They create a hierarchy of clusters from small to big or big to small. The hierarchical techniques are of two types—*agglomerative* and *divisive*. *Agglomerative clustering* techniques start with as many clusters as there are records, with each cluster having only one record. Then pairs of clusters are successively merged until the number of clusters reduces to k. At each stage, the pairs of the clusters merged are the ones that are nearest to each other. If the merging is continued, it terminates in a hierarchy of clusters which is built with just a single cluster containing all the records, at the top of the hierarchy. *Divisive clustering* techniques take the opposite approach from agglomerative techniques. This starts with all the records in one cluster, and then tries to split that cluster into small pieces.

NUMERIC VS. CATEGORICAL

Clustering can be performed on both numerical data and categorical data. For the clustering of numerical data, the inherent geometric properties can be used to define the distances between the points. But for clustering of categorical data, such a criterion does not exist and many data sets also consist of categorical attributes, on which distance functions are not naturally defined. Recently, the problem of clustering categorical data has attracted interest. As an example, consider the MUSHROOM data set in the popular UCI machine-learning repository. Each tuple in the data set describes a sample of gilled mushrooms using twenty-two categorical attributes. For instance, the cap colour attribute can take values from the domain {brown, buff, cinnamon, gray, green, pink, purple, red, white, yellow}. It is hard to reason that one colour is less than another in a way similar to real numbers. It is also hard to determine an ordering or to quantify the dissimilarity among such attributes.

5.3 PARTITIONING ALGORITHMS

Partitioning algorithms construct partitions of a database of N objects into a set of k clusters. The construction involves determining the optimal partition with respect to an objective function. There are approximately $kN/k!$ ways of partitioning a set of N data points into k subsets. An exhaustive enumeration method that can find the global optimal partition is practically infeasible except when N and k are very small. The partitioning clustering algorithm usually adopts the *Iterative Optimisation* paradigm. It starts with an initial partition and uses an iterative control strategy. It tries swapping data points to see if such swapping improves the quality of clustering. When swapping does not yield any improvements in clustering, it finds a locally optimal partition. This quality of clustering is very sensitive to the initially selected partition. There are the two main categories of partitioning algorithms. They are

(i) k-means algorithms, where each cluster is represented by the centre of gravity of the cluster.
(ii) k-medoid algorithms, where each cluster is represented by one of the objects of the cluster located near the centre.

Most special clustering algorithms designed for data mining are k-medoid algorithms.

5.4 *k*-MEDOID ALGORITHMS

PAM

PAM (**P**artition **A**round **M**edoids) uses a k-medoid method to identify the clusters. PAM selects k objects arbitrarily from the data as medoids. Each of these k objects are representatives of k classes. Other objects in the database are classified based on their distances to these k-medoids (we say that the database is partitioned with respect to the selected set of k-medoids). The algorithm starts with arbitrarily selected k-medoids and iteratively improves upon this selection. In each step, a swap between a selected object O_i and a non-selected object O_h is made, as long as such a swap results in an improvement in the quality of clustering. To calculate the effect of such a swap between O_i and O_h, a cost C_{ih} is computed, which is related to the quality of partitioning the non-selected objects to k clusters represented by the medoids. The algorithm has two important modules—the partitioning of the database for a given set of medoids and the iterative selection of medoids.

PARTITIONING

If O_j is a non-selected object and O_i is a medoid, we then say that O_j belongs to the cluster represented by O_i, if $d(O_i, O_j) = \text{Min}_{Oe}\, d(O_j, O_e)$, where the minimum is taken over all medoids O_e and $d(O_a, O_b)$ determines the distance, or dissimilarity, between objects O_a and O_b. The dissimilarity matrix is known prior to the commencement of PAM. The quality of clustering is measured by the average dissimilarity between an object and the medoid of the cluster to which the object belongs.

ITERATIVE SELECTION OF MEDOIDS

Let us assume that $O_1, O_2,..., O_k$ are k-medoids selected at any stage. We denote $C_1, C_2, ..., C_k$ as the respective clusters. From the foregoing discussion, for a non-selected object O_j, $j \neq 1, 2, ..., k$

if $O_j \in C_m$ then $\text{Min}_{(1 \leq i \leq k)}\, d(O_j, O_i) = d(O_j, O_m)$.

Let us now analyse the effect of swapping O_i and O_h. In other words, let us assume that an unselected object O_h becomes a medoid replacing an existing medoid O_i. Thus, the new set of k-medoids is $Kmed' = \{O_1, O_2,..., O_{i-1}, O_h, O_{i+1},..., O_k\}$, where O_h replaces O_i as one of the medoids from $Kmed = \{O_1, O_2,..., O_k\}$. We shall now compare the quality of clustering. Due to the change in the set of medoids, there will be three types of changes that can occur in the actual clustering. For convenience, let us denote C_h as the new clusters with O_h as the representative.

1. A non-selected object O_j, such that $O_j \in C_i$ before swapping and $O_j \in C_h$ after swapping. This case arises when the following conditions hold:
   $\text{Min}\, d(O_j, O_e) = d(O_j, O_i)$,

   minimum taken over O_e in *Kmed*.

$\text{Min}_{e \neq i}\ d(O_j, O_e) = d(O_j, O_h)$,

minimum taken for all O_e in *Kmed'*.

Let us define a cost for this change as

$C_{jih} = d(O_j, O_h) - d(O_j, O_i)$

2. A non-selected object $O_j \in C_i$ before swapping and $O_j \in C_g$, $g \neq h$, after swapping. This case arises when

   $\text{Min}\ d(O_j, O_e) = d(O_j, O_i)$,

   minimum taken over O_e in *Kmed.*

   and $\text{Min}\ d(O_j, O_e) = d(O_j, O_g)$, $g \neq h$.

   minimum taken over O_e in *Kmed'*.

   Define a cost as $C_{jih} = d(O_j, O_g) - d(O_j, O_i)$

3. A non-selected object $O_j \in C_g$ before swapping and $O_j \in C_h$ after swapping. This case arises when

   $\text{Min}\ d(O_j, O_e) = d(O_j, O_g)$,

   minimum taken over O_e in *Kmed.*

   and $\text{Min}\ d(O_j, O_e) = d(O_j, O_h)$,

   minimum taken over O_e in *Kmed'*.

   Define a cost for this case as,

   $C_{jih} = d(O_j, O_h) - d(O_j, O_g)$

Please note that for any non-selected object O_j, only one of these three cases can occur. The total cost of swapping two medoids is the sum of such costs for all non-selected objects.

The following figures (Figures 5.1 and 5.2) illustrate the working of the swapping in PAM.

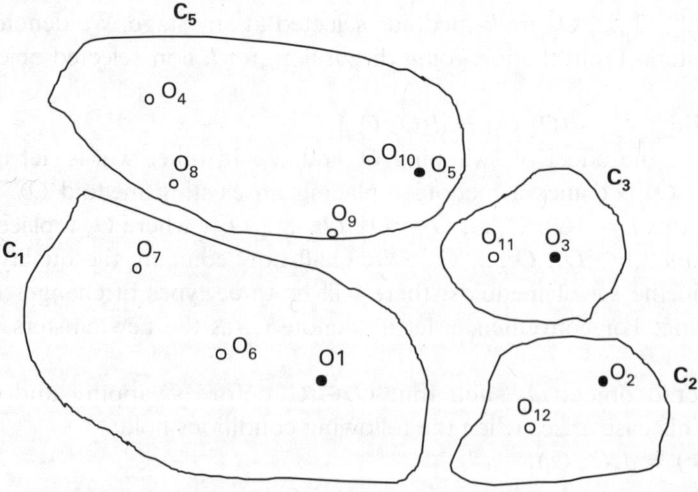

Figure 5.1 Partitioning before swapping

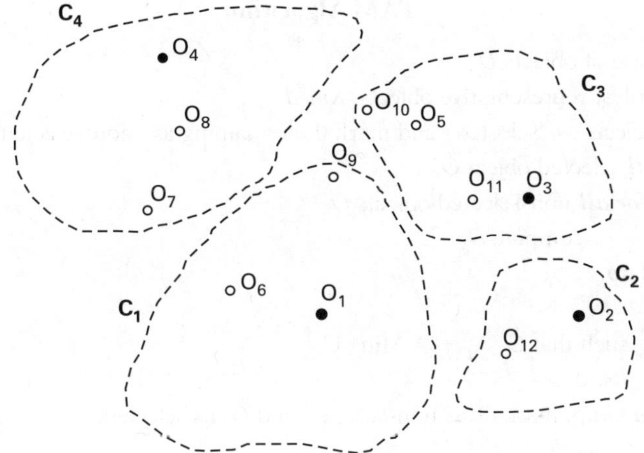

Figure 5.2 Clustering after swapping O_5 by O_4

There are 12 objects which are required to be classified into 4 clusters. Initially, the selected medoids are O_1, O_2, O_3 and O_5. Based on closest distance, the remaining objects are classified as shown in the figures. Let us assume that O_4 is introduced as a medoid in place of O_5. For convenience, we denote d_{ij} for $d(O_i, O_j)$ and the distance metric is symmetric. The three cases are illustrated below.

Case 1 The object O_8 which was in the cluster C_5 before swapping is now in the cluster C_4 after swapping.

Hence, the cost $C_{854} = d_{58} - d_{48}$.

Case 2 The object O_9 was in C_5 before swapping and is now in C_1 after swapping.

The cost for O_9 is $C_{954} = d_{19} - d_{59}$.

Case 3 The object O_7 was in the cluster C_1 before swapping and is in C_4 after swapping.

Thus, the cost is $C_{754} = d_{47} - d_{17}$.

Define the total cost of swapping O_i and O_h as

$$C_{ih} = \sum_j C_{jih},$$

where the sum is taken for all objects j.

In the above example, the sum is taken over all the 12 objects to compute C_{54}.

If C_{ih} is negative, then the quality of clustering is improved by making O_h a medoid in the place of O_i. PAM attempts to compute C_{ih} for all selected objects O_i and all non-selected objects O_h. The process is repeated until we cannot find a negative C_{ih}. If more than one pair of (i, h) with negative costs are found, then the pair corresponding to the most negative C_{ih} is chosen for swapping. The algorithm can be formally stated as follows:

PAM Algorithm

Input: Database of objects D.
select arbitrarily k representative objects, *Kmed*.
mark these objects as "selected" and mark the remaining as "non-selected".
    do for all selected object O_i
        do for all non-selected objects O_h
            compute C_{ih}
        end do.
    end do.
select i_{min}, h_{min} such that $C_{imin, hmin} = \text{Min}_{i,h} C_{ih}$
    if $C_{imin, hmin} < 0$
        then swap: mark O_i as non-selected and O_h as selected.
    repeat
find *clusters* $C_1, C_2, C_3, \ldots, C_k$.

PAM is very robust to the existence of outliers. The clusters found by this method do not depend on the order in which the objects are examined. However, it cannot handle very large volumes of data.

5.5 CLARA

It can be observed that the major computational efforts for PAM are to determine k-medoids through an iterative optimisation. Though CLARA follows the same principle, it attempts to reduce the computational effort. Instead of finding representative objects for the entire data set, CLARA draws a sample of the data set, and applies PAM on this sample to determine the optimal set of medoids from the sample. It then classifies the remaining objects using the partitioning principle. If the sample were drawn in a sufficiently random way, the medoids of the sample would approximate the medoids of the entire data set. The steps of CLARA are summarised below.

CLARA Algorithm

Input: Database of D objects.
repeat for m times
    draw a sample $S \subseteq D$ randomly from D.
    call PAM (S, k) to get k medoids.
    classify the entire data set D to $C_1, C_2 \ldots C_k$.
    calculate the quality of clustering as the average dissimilarity.
end.

5.6 CLARANS

CLARANS (**C**lustering **L**arge **A**pplications based on **Ran**domised **S**earch) is similar to PAM and CLARA, but it applies a randomised Iterative-Optimisation for the determination of medoids. It is easy to see that in PAM, at every iteration we examine $k(N\text{-}k)$ swaps to determine the pair corresponding to the minimum cost. On the other hand, CLARA tries to examine fewer elements by restricting its search to a smaller sample of the database. Thus, if the sample size is $S \leq N$, it examines at most $k(S\text{-}k)$ pairs at every iteration. Thus, in CLARA, an object can be a medoid only if it is in the randomly selected sample. But CLARANS does not restrict the search to any particular subset of objects. Neither does it search the entire data set. It begins with PAM and randomly selects few pairs (i, h), instead of examining all pairs, for swapping at the current state. CLARANS, like PAM, starts with a randomly selected set of k-medoids. It checks at most the "*maxneighbor*" number of pairs for swapping and, if a pair with negative cost is found, it updates the medoid set and continues. Otherwise, it records the current selection of medoids as a local optimum and restarts with a new randomly selected medoid set to search for another local optimum. CLARANS stops after the "*numlocal*" number of local optimal medoid sets are determined, and returns the best among these.

CLARANS Algorithm

```
Input (D, k, maxneighbor and numlocal)
select arbitrarily k representative objects.
mark these objects as "selected" and all other objects as "non-selected". Call it current.
set e = 1.
do while (e ≤ numlocal)
    set j = 1
    do while (m ≤ maxneighbor )
        select randomly a pair ( j, h) such that O_j is a selected object and O_h is a non-selected
        object.
        compute the cost C_jh.
        if C_jh is negative
            "update current"
            mark O_j non-selected, O_h selected and m = 1
        else
            increment m ← m + 1
    end do
    compare the cost of clustering with "mincost"
    if current_cost < mincost
        mincost ← current_cost
        best_node ← current
    increment e ← e + 1
end do
return "best node"
```

CLARANS is a medoid-based method, which is more efficient than the earlier medoid-based methods, but suffers from two major drawbacks: it assumes that all objects fit into the main memory, and the result is very sensitive to input order. In addition, it may not find a real local minimum due to the trimming of its searching, controlled by '*maxneighbor*'. Focussing techniques is a way to improve CLARANS's ability to deal with disk-resident data sets, by focussing only on relevant parts of the database using R* trees.

5.7 Hierarchical Clustering

Hierarchical algorithms create a hierarchical decomposition of the database. The algorithms iteratively split the database into smaller subsets, until some termination condition is satisfied. The hierarchical algorithms do not need k as an input parameter, which is an obvious advantage over partitioning algorithms. However, the disadvantage of the hierarchical algorithm is that the termination condition is to be specified. The hierarchical decomposition can be represented as a dendogram in two ways:

(i) Bottom-up (Agglomerative) approach, and
(ii) Top-down (Divisive) approach.

The basic agglomerative, hierarchical clustering algorithm works in the following way.

Initially, each object is placed in a unique cluster. For each pair of clusters, some value of dissimilarity or distance is computed. For instance, the distance may be the minimum distance of all pairs of points from the two clusters. At every step, the clusters with the minimum distances in the current clustering are merged, until the whole data set forms a single cluster. One can set the termination criteria by fixing the critical distance D_{min} between the clusters.

5.8 DBSCAN

DBSCAN (Density Based Spatial Clustering of Applications of Noise) uses a density-based notion of clusters to discover clusters of arbitrary shapes. The key idea of DBSCAN is that, for each object of a cluster, the neighbourhood of a given radius has to contain at least a minimum number of data objects. In other words, the density of the neighbourhood must exceed a threshold. The critical parameter here is the distance function for the data objects. The following concepts are introduced here in the context of DBSCAN.

Definition 5.1 ε-Neighbourhood of an Object

For a given non-negative value ε, the ε-*neighbourhood* of an object O_i, denoted by $N_\varepsilon(O_i)$, is defined by $N_\varepsilon(O_i) = \{O_j \in D \mid d(O_i, O_j) \leq \varepsilon\}$.

Definition 5.2 Core Object

An object is said to be a *Core Object* if $\mid N_\varepsilon(O) \mid \geq$ MinPts. A core object is one which has a neighbourhood of user-specified minimum density.

Definition 5.3 Directly-density-reachable

An object O_i is *directly-density-reachable* from an object O_j with respect to ε and MinPts if O_j is a core object and O_i is in its ε-neighbourhood.

1. $O_i \in N_\varepsilon(O_j)$
2. $|\ N_\varepsilon(O_j)\ | \geq$ MinPts. (In other words, O_j is a core object.)

Definition 5.4 Density-reachable

An object O_i is *density-reachable* from an object O_j with respect to ε and MinPts in D if there is a chain of objects $O_1, O_2, \ldots, O_n$, such that $O_1 = O_j$, $O_n = O_i$, such that $O_e \in D$ and O_{e+1} is directly-density-reachable from O_e with respect to ε and MinPts in D.

Generally, the density-reachability relation is transitive but not symmetric. If O_i is density-reachable from O_j, then O_j is a core object, but O_i need not be a core object. Thus, we cannot say that O_j is also density-reachable from O_i. The directly-density-reachable relation is a special case of the density-reachable relation.

Definition 5.5 Density-connected

An object O_i is *density-connected* to an object O_j with respect to ε and MinPts in D if there is another object $O \in D$, such that both O_i and O_j are density-reachable from O, with respect to ε and MinPts in D.

The density-connectivity relation is a symmetric one and within the set of density-reachable objects, the relation is reflexive too.

Definition 5.6 Cluster

A *Cluster* C with respect to ε and MinPts is a non-empty subset of D satisfying the following conditions:

- For all $O_i, O_j \in D$, if $O_i \in C$ and O_j is density-reachable from O_i with respect to ε and MinPts, then $O_j \in C$.
- For all $O_i, O_j \in C$, O_i is density-connected to O_j with respect to ε and MinPts.

Definition 5.7 Noise

Let $C_1, C_2, \ldots, C_k$ be the clusters of D with respect to ε and MinPts. Then, we define the noise as the set of objects in D which do not belong to any cluster C_i as *Noise* = $\{O \in D \mid \forall i, O \notin C_i\}$.

We identify two different kinds of objects in a DBSCAN—*core objects* and *non-core objects*. Non-core objects, in turn, are either border objects or noise objects. Two border objects are possibly not density-reachable from each other. However, a border object is always density-reachable from a core object. A noise object is a non-core object, which is not density-reachable from other core objects. DBSCAN's procedure for finding a cluster is based on the fact that a cluster is uniquely determined by any of its core objects. It can be seen that

1. Given an arbitrary object O_i for which the core object condition holds, the set $\{O \in D$: O is density reachable from $O_i\}$ forms a complete cluster C and $O_i \in C$.
2. Given a cluster C and an arbitrary core object $O_i \in C$, C in turn equals the set of all objects which are density-reachable from O_i in D.

The DBSCAN algorithm maintains the set of objects in three different categories. These are: classified, unclassified and noise. Each classified object has an associated cluster-id, indicating the cluster in which it is included. A noise object may also have an associated dummy cluster-id. For both classified and noise objects, the ε-neighbourhoods are already computed. The unclassified category of objects do not have any cluster-id and their neighbourhoods are not computed. The algorithm gradually converts an unclassified object into a classified or a noise object.

At every step, the algorithm starts with an unclassified object and a new cluster-id associated with it. We study its ε-neighbourhood to see if the neighbourhood is adequately dense or not. If its density does not exceed the threshold MinPts, then it is marked as a noise object. Otherwise, all the objects that are within its ε-neighbourhood are retrieved and put into a list of candidate objects. These objects may be either unclassified or noise. Note that the neighbourhood cannot contain a classified object. If the object is a noise object, the current cluster-id is assigned to it. If the object is unclassified, then the current cluster-id is assigned to it and it is included in the list of candidate objects for which the ε-neighbourhoods are to be obtained. The algorithm continues till the list of candidate objects is empty. Thus, one cluster with the given cluster-id is determined. The algorithm repeats this process for other unclassified objects and terminates when all the objects are marked as either classified or noise.

We present the algorithm below.

DBSCAN Algorithm

Algorithm DBSCAN (*D*, ε, MinPts)
Input: Database of objects *D*
do for all $O \in D$
    if *O* is unclassified
        call function **expand_cluster**(*O*, *D*, ε, MinPts)
end do.
Function expand_cluster (*O*, *D*, ε, MinPts):
get the ε-neighbourhood of *O* as $N_\varepsilon(O)$
    if $|N_\varepsilon(O)|$ < MinPts,
        mark *O* as noise
        return
    else
        select a new cluster_id and mark all objects of $N_\varepsilon(O)$ with this cluster-id and put them into candidate-objects.
        do while candidate-objects is not empty
            select an object from candidate-objects as current_object

```
            delete current-object from candidate-objects
            retrieve N_ε (current-object)
            if |N_ε (current-object) | ≥ MinPts
               select all objects in N_ε (current-object) not yet classified or marked as noise,
               mark all of the objects with cluster_id,
               nclude the unclassified objects into candidate-objects
         end do
   return.
```

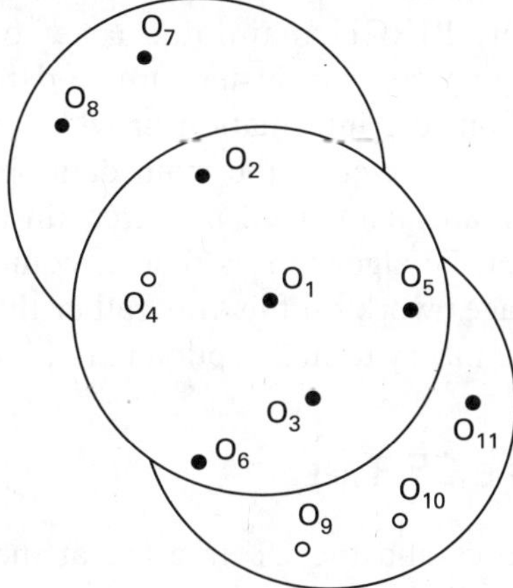

Figure 5.3 Illustration of DBSCAN algorithm. Starting from a candidate object O_1, the cluster expansion process of C_1 is shown here.

The critical component of the algorithm is the retrieval of its density-reachable neighbourhood. This can be accomplished by an R* tree structure or by an M tree. Thus, DBSCAN relies on the R* tree for speed and scalability in its nearest-neighbour search queries. An illustration of the expand-cluster phase of the algorithm is given below. In Figure 5.3, assume MinPts = 6 and we start with an unclassified object O_1. We find that there are 6 objects in the ε-neighbourhood of O_1. These are: O_1, O_2, O_3, O_4, O_5, and O_6. So, put all these points in the candidate-objects and associate them with cluster-id of O_1 (say, C_1). We shall select an object from the candidate-objects, say O_2. We find that $N_\varepsilon(O_2)$ does not contain an adequate number of points. Hence, we mark this as a noise object. The object O_4 is already marked as a noise (shaded), so there is no further action for this point. Let us select the object O_3 from the candidate-objects. $N_\varepsilon(O_3)$ contains 7 points, O_1, O_3, O_5, O_6, O_9, O_{10} and O_{11}. Among these, O_9, and O_{10} are already marked as noise objects, O_1 and O_3 are already classified, and the others are unclassified. All the seven objects are associated with new cluster-id, C_1. The unclassified objects are included in the candidate-objects for the next iteration.

5.9 BIRCH

BIRCH (**B**alanced **I**terative **R**educing and **C**lustering using **H**ierarchies) is a hierarchical-agglomerative clustering algorithm. It was proposed by Zhang, Ramakrishnan and Livny. It is designed to cluster large datasets of n-dimensional vectors using a limited amount of main memory. BIRCH proposes a special data structure, *CF Tree*, to condense information about subclusters of points. The key idea of the algorithm is as follows.

BIRCH is based on the principles of agglomerative clustering, that is, at any given stage there are smaller subclusters and the decision at the current stage is to merge subclusters based on some criteria. BIRCH handles this task in a novel manner. Instead of maintaining all the objects of a subcluster, BIRCH maintains a set of *Cluster Features*(CF) of the subcluster. The criteria for merging two subclusters are so defined that the decision to merge two subclusters can be taken from the information provided solely by the set of CFs of the respective subclusters. One need not refer to the main data objects for this task. The Cluster Features of different subclusters are maintained in a tree (in a B^+ tree fashion). This tree is called the *CF Tree*. The nicety of the algorithm is that it requires just one pass to construct a CF Tree, and the subsequent stages work on this tree rather than the actual database. The last stage, which the proposers of the theory term as optional, requires one more database pass.

Clustering Features and the CF Tree

The concept of clustering features and the CF tree are at the core of BIRCH. A clustering feature is a triple, summarizing the information about a cluster.

Definition 5.8 Vector

Let C be a cluster containing the data objects $O_1, O_2, \ldots, O_n$. Then, the clustering feature vector (CF) of C is defined as a triple: CF = (n, ls, ss); where n is the number of data objects in C, ls is the linear sum of the data objects, and ss is the square sum of the data objects in C. In other words,

$$|C| = n;$$

$$\sum_{i \in C} O_i = ls$$

$$\sum_{i \in C} O_i^2 = ss$$

Since the objects are multidimensional, the summations and exponentiation in the above expressions are dealt with component-wise. The dimensions of ls and ss are the same as that of the objects in C. For example, if $O_1(x_{11}, x_{12}, x_{13}), O_2(x_{21}, x_{22}, x_{23}), \ldots, O_n(x_{n1}, x_{n2}, x_{n3})$, then

$ls = (ls_{(1)}, ls_{(2)}, ls_{(3)})$, such that

$ls_{(1)} = x_{11} + x_{21} + \ldots + x_{n1}$,

$ls_{(2)} = x_{12} + x_{22} + \ldots + x_{n2}$ and

$ls_{(3)} = x_{13} + x_{23} + \ldots + x_{n3}$

$ss = (ss_{(1)}, ss_{(2)}, ss_{(3)})$ such that

$ss_{(1)} = x_{11}^2 + x_{21}^2 + \ldots + x_{n1}^2,$

$ss_{(2)} = x_{12}^2 + x_{22}^2 + \ldots + x_{n2}^2$ and

$ss_{(3)} = x_{13}^2 + x_{23}^2 + \ldots + x_{n3}^2.$

BIRCH assumes that the distance functions between clusters are so defined that they can be expressed in terms of the parameters encoded in the CF vectors. Thus, the algorithm necessarily assumes the database to be numeric in nature. Moreover, it cannot handle all kinds of distance (metric) functions or dissimilarity functions. However, there are many important distance functions that can be described in terms of the CF vectors.

Additive Properties of Cluster Features

Interestingly, the CF vector follows the additive properties. Assume that $\text{CF}_1 = (n_1, ls_1, ss_1)$ for cluster C_1 and $\text{CF}_2 = (n_2, ls_2, ss_2)$ for cluster C_2, such that $C_1 \cap C_2 = \varnothing$. Then, the CF vector of the cluster that is formed by merging the two disjoint clusters is $(n_1+n_2, ls_1+ls_2, ss_1+ss_2)$.

It is easy to see that given the CF vectors of a cluster, the following metric information can be calculated.

Definition 5.9 Centroid

For a cluster $C = \{O_1, O_2, \ldots, O_n\}$, the centroid is defined as an object given by

$$O_{\text{centroid}} = \frac{\sum_{i=1}^{n} O_i}{n} = \frac{ls}{n}$$

Definition 5.10 Radius

The radius R of a cluster $C = \{O_1, O_2, \ldots, O_n\}$, is defined as

$$R = \left[\frac{\sum_{i=1}^{n} (O_i - O_{\text{centroid}})^2}{n}\right]^{\frac{1}{2}} = \left[\frac{ss - \frac{2(ls)^2}{n} + \frac{(ls)^2}{n^2}}{n}\right]$$

Definition 5.11 Diameter

The diameter of a cluser $C = \{O_1, O_2, \ldots, O_n\}$, is defined as

$$D = \sqrt{\frac{\sum_{i=1}^{n}\sum_{j=1}^{n} (O_i - O_j)^2}{n(n-1)}}$$

Similarly, the following distance parameters between two clusters can also be computed using CF vectors. I leave this exercise to the readers—to express these distance measures in terms of vectors.

DEFINITION 5.12 EUCLIDEAN INTERCLUSTER DISTANCE D_0

For two clusters C_1 and C_2 with cluster centroids $O_{centroid,1}$ and $O_{centroid,2}$, respectively, the *Euclidean intercluster* distance between these clusters is defined as

$$D_0\,(C_1, C_2) = \text{The Euclidean distance between } O_{centroid,1} \text{ and } O_{centroid,2}.$$

Thus,

$$D_0(C_1, C_2) = \left[\sum_i (O^i_{centroid,\,1} - O^i_{centroid,\,2}\right]^{\frac{1}{2}}$$

where the superscript denotes the components of a vector.

DEFINITION 5.13 MANHATTAN INTERCLUSTER DISTANCE D_1

For two clusters C_1 and C_2 with cluster centroids $O_{centroid,1}$ and $O_{centroid,2}$, respectively, the *Manhattan intercluster* distance between these clusters is defined as

$$D_1\,(C_1, C_2) = \text{The Manhattan distance between } O_{centroid,1} \text{ and } O_{centroid,\,2}.$$

Thus,

$$D_1(C_1, C_2) = \left[\sum_i |O^i_{centroid,\,1} - O^i_{centroid,\,2}|\right].$$

DEFINITION 5.14 AVERAGE INTERCLUSTER DISTANCE D_2

For two clusters C_1 and C_2 with cluster centroids $O_{centroid,1}$ and $O_{centroid,2}$, respectively, the *average intercluster* distance between these clusters is defined as

$$D_2(C_1C_2) = \left[\frac{1}{n_1 n_2} \sum_{i \in C_1}^{n} \sum_{j \in C_2}^{n} (O_i - O_j)^2\right].$$

DEFINITION 5.15 AVERAGE INTRACLUSTER DISTANCE

For two clusters C_1 and C_2 with cluster centroids $O_{centroid,1}$ and $O_{centroid,2}$, respectively, the *average intracluster distance* between these clusters is defined as

$$D_3(C_1C_2) = \left[\frac{1}{(n_1+n_2)(n_1+n_2-1)} \sum_{i,\,j \in C_1 \cup C_2}^{n} (O_i - O_j)^2\right]$$

We shall now study the four phases of the BIRCH clustering process.

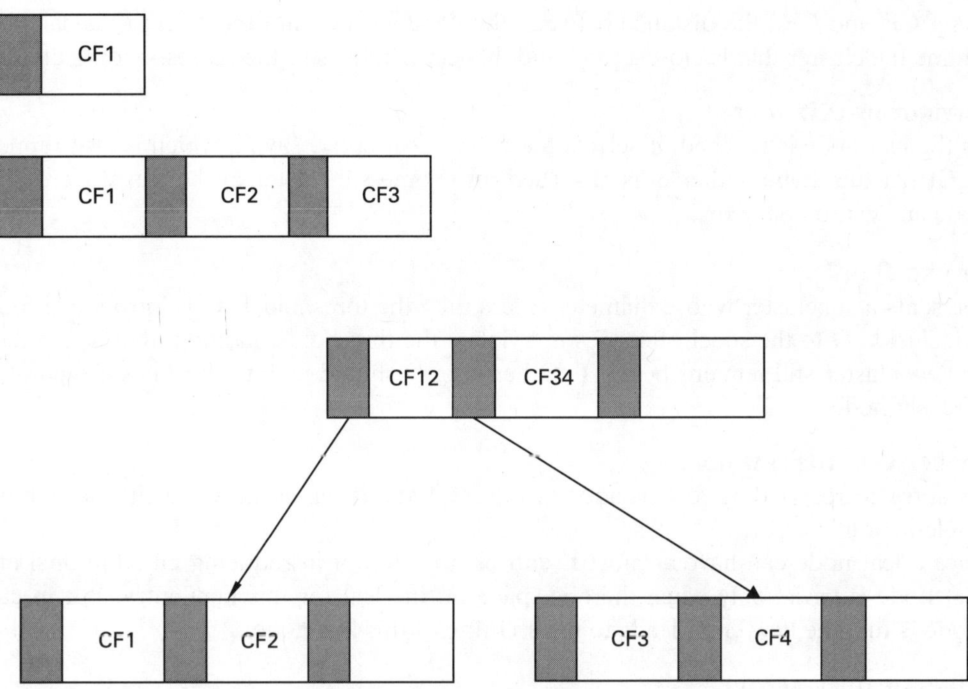

Figure 5.4 CF tree construction process. O_1, O_2, O_3 and O_4 are inserted.

Phase I Construction of a CF Tree

A CF Tree is a height-balanced tree with two parameters: (i) the branching factor **B**, and (ii) the threshold **T**. Each non-leaf node contains at most B entries of the form [CF_i, $child_i$], where $child_i$ is a pointer to its ith child node and CF_i is the of the subcluster represented by this child. So, a non-leaf node represents a cluster made up of all the subclusters represented by its child nodes. A leaf node contains at most **B** entries of the form [CF_i]. In addition, each leaf node can have two pointers; '*prev*' and '*next*', which can be used to chain all leaf nodes together for an efficient scan. A leaf node represents a cluster made up of all subclusters represented by its entries. All the entries in a leaf node must satisfy the threshold requirements with respect to the threshold value **T**, that is, *the diameter of the subcluster must be less than T*. A CF Tree is built dynamically and incrementally as new data objects are inserted.

It is necessary to understand the insertion process in a CF Tree. It is assumed that the readers are familiar with B Trees and B^+ Trees. Let us assume that a new object *O* is being inserted into the CF Tree. Let $CF_0=[1, O, O^2]$. The stages described below are involved in the insertion process.

Identifying the appropriate leaf

Starting from the root, *O* moves recursively downwards by selecting at every step the closest child node according to the chosen distance metric.

Using CF_i and CF_0, the distance between the ith subcluster and the object O is calculated to determine the cluster that is closest to O and, hence, O moves to the corresponding child node.

MODIFYING THE LEAF NODE

When the leaf node is reached, it selects the closest leaf entry, say L_i, which is also represented by its CF. At this stage, either O is absorbed into some subcluster in the leaf node or it has a separate entry into this node.

ABSORBING *O* IN *L*$_i$

L_i represents a subcluster whose diameter is less than the threshold **T**. O is introduced to L_i only if the inclusion O to the subcluster does not violate the threshold condition; that is, the diameter of the new cluster still remains below **T**. Otherwise, O should be introduced as a separate entry into the leaf node.

INTRODUCE O IN THE LEAF NODE

A new entry corresponding to O is added to the leaf and it represents a subcluster with just the single element O.

Since a leaf node can have at most **B** entries, the step of introducing an additional entry to the leaf node is trivial only when there is space on the leaf for this new entry. But in case the leaf node is full, the new entry leads to the splitting of this leaf node.

SPLITTING OF THE LEAF NODE

The leaf node is split to form two leaf nodes. The node splitting is done by choosing the farthest pair of entries as seeds in the leaf node, and redistributing the remaining entries based on the closest criteria.

MODIFYING THE PATH TO THE LEAF

- When O is absorbed in L_i, the CF vector of L_i is modified with a new value. This, in turn, will affect the cluster features of all the nodes from L_i to the root.
- Similarly, if O is added as a separate entry on L_i but without splitting L_i, then the CF vector of the parent node of L_i will be updated and all the other nodes in the path will reflect this change.
- If there is a node split, there is a new entry at the parent node of L_i and this entry consists of the CF vector together with a pointer to the new leaf node. This process may propagate upwards, in case the parent node of L_i does not have enough space to accommodate the new entry. It may be necessary to split the parent as well and so on, up to the root. If the root is split, the height of the tree increases by one.

MERGING REFINEMENT

Suppose that there is a leaf split and the propagation of this split stops at some non-leaf node, N_j. In other words, N_j can accommodate the additional entry resulting from the split. We now scan the node N_j to find the two closest entries. If they are not the pair corresponding to the split, we try to merge them and the corresponding two child nodes. If there are more entries in the two-child node to be accommodated in a merge, we split the merging again by redistributing. During such re-splitting, in case one seed attracts enough merged entries to fill a page, we just put the rest of the entries with the other seed.

EXAMPLE 5.1

The above process is illustrated in Figures 5.4–5.7 for 8 objects $O_1, O_2, \ldots, O_8$ in order. The branching factor **B** is taken to be 3.

For the first three objects O_1, O_2 and O_3 the insertion is trivial, with the CF tree consisting of just one node. When O_4 is inserted, the node is split to two leaf nodes corresponding to the farthest pairs of objects, O_1 and O_4. The other objects are allocated to the leaf nodes based on the closest distance condition. As the second object is closer to O_1, it is in the first leaf node. The root node maintains the details of the two subclusters corresponding to the leaf nodes. When O_5 is introduced, since it is at a distance beyond the threshold **T** from any of the subclusters, one more child node of the root node is created. The details at the root node and the new leaf node are updated. The object O_6 is allocated to the third leaf node according to the closest distance criterion. The objects O_7 and O_8 are allocated to the first leaf node. But since **B**=3, this node is now split into two leaf nodes. The necessary redistribution is illustrated in Figure 5.7.

Thus, Phase I works as follows. It scans the data set record by record to form a CF tree. If the tree cannot be accommodated in the main memory, the leaf nodes are reinserted to make the tree smaller. Ideally, with the proper choice of **B** and **T**, the method requires just one scan of the database and it returns a CF Tree.

PHASE II CONDENSATION OF THE CF TREE

The size of the CF Tree generated in Phase I is dependent on **B** and **T**. A smaller T generates a larger tree. One can easily see the geometric interpretation of the data objects represented by a CF Tree. At the leaf level, it represents a set of subclusters not exceeded in its diameter by **T**. The centroids of any two subclusters are separated by the distance **T**. At most, **B** number of the closest subclusters at one level are merged to represent a parent node at the next higher level. If **T** is too small, then there may be too many subclusters at the leaf level. As a result, for a large number of points, the resulting CF Tree may be too deep.

Phase II deals with processing the CF Tree by redefining the threshold, so that tree size becomes manageable. Phase II has yet another aim. It removes the isolated subclusters as outliers during the process of condensing. It scans the leaf entries in the initial CF Tree to rebuild a smaller CF Tree, while removing the outliers and grouping crowded subclusters into larger ones.

PHASE III HIERARCHICAL AGGLOMERATIVE CLUSTERING

Starting with the set of subclusters at the leaf nodes, any one of the conventional hierarchical clustering techniques (global or semi-global) is utilised to obtain the set of user-specified clusters. The target number of clusters is an input from the user for this phase. This phase employs the clustering technique directly to the subclusters which are represented by their CF vectors. It uses the distance metric, described above, which can be calculated from the CF vectors. One advantage of this method is that the user can either specify the desired number of clusters or the threshold diameter. Phase III also works on the CF Tree and does not require any database scan.

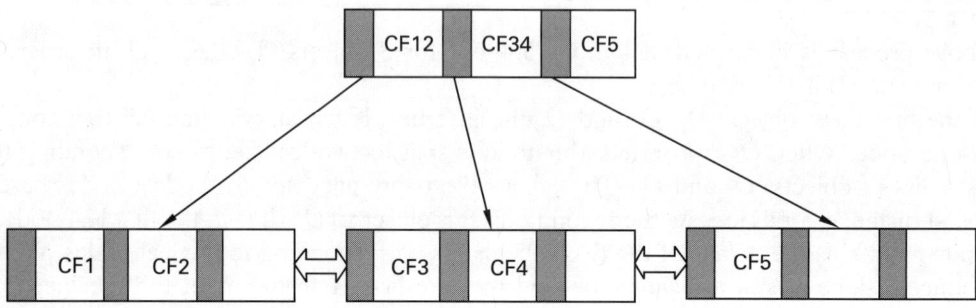

Figure 5.5 CF Tree after inserting O_5

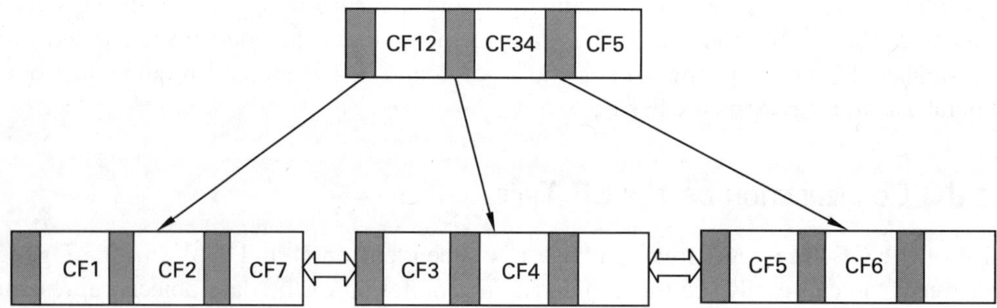

Figure 5.6 CF Tree after O_6, O_7 are inserted. The root node and left-most child node are full.

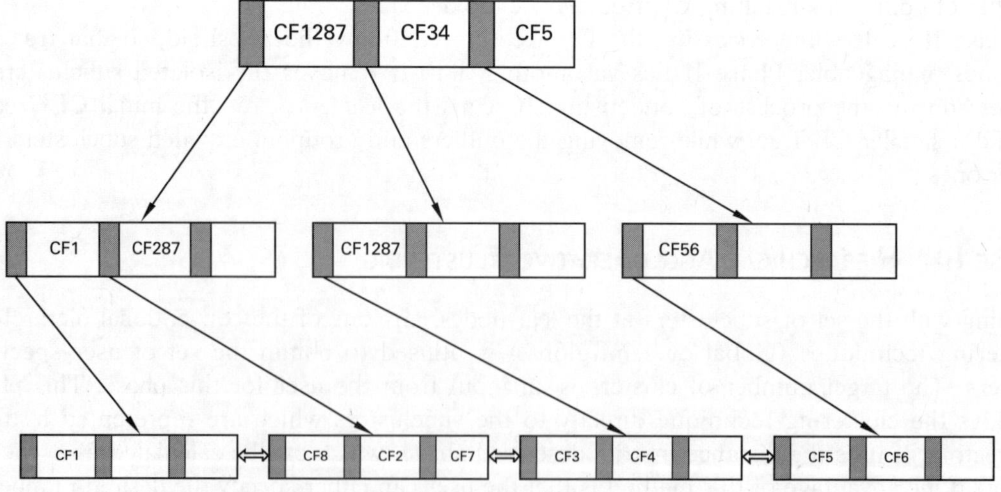

Figure 5.7 CF Tree after O_8 is inserted. Nodes split and the tree expands.

PHASE IV CLASSIFICATION

Phase IV uses the centroid of the clusters produced by Phase III as seeds and redistributes the data objects to I, the closest seed, to obtain a set of new clusters. This allows the objects to migrate from one cluster to the other, and it ensures that multiple copies of the same object are included in the same clusters. It may be noted that the CF tree-building algorithm depends on the order of presentation of the data objects, and it is likely that two copies of the same object presented at different instances of the sequence may land up at different nodes.

The CF Tree is one of the novel algorithms for data mining. The more efficient version uses a CF* Tree as the basic data structure.

5.10 CURE

CURE – **C**lustering **U**sing **Re**presentatives – is yet another interesting algorithm. It is also a hierarchical clustering technique, adopting an agglomerative scheme. CURE shares certain common motivations with BIRCH. As we have discussed in the previous section, BIRCH maintains CF vectors that are used for merging subclusters during the agglomerative process. The main argument in favour of this strategy is that it avoids the *all-points* (brute-force) method of maintaining all points of the subclusters. One does not have to examine all the data objects of two subclusters to decide whether or not to merge. BIRCH adopts a *centroid point*, in place of the *all-points* paradigm for merging using the distance from the centroid as the merging criterion. We can view all-points and the centroid point as two extreme strategies and there can be a host of other strategies that have a trade-off between accuracy and efficiency. Please note that the all-points strategy is an exact measure compared to the approximate measure of the centroid point. Similarly, the all-points strategy is computationally intensive and time consuming, whereas the centroid point is efficient. CURE attempts to strike a balance between these two extremes.

CURE maintains a set of representative points of each subcluster. The representative points are reasonably smaller in number to avoid the inefficiency of the all-points strategy. The representative points are well-scattered within the subcluster so as to properly represent the whole subcluster, rather than the notional single point representative as in the case of centroid. In the event, the subcluster being spherical in shape, the centroid is the best representative of the shape. But most real-life situations cannot guarantee the clusters as being spherical in shape. Maintaining a set of well-scattered representative objects of each subcluster is the single most important aspect of CURE.

The algorithm works as follows. As with any agglomerative algorithm, it begins with every single data object as a cluster and the object itself is the sole representative of the corresponding cluster.

At any given stage of the algorithm, we have a set of subclusters and, associated with each subcluster, we have a set of representative points. The distance between two subclusters is the smallest pair-wise distance between their representative points. For every subcluster, C, its nearest subcluster $C_{nearest}$ is computed at this stage. Define a measure

$$D_{closest}(C) = \text{Distance}(C, C_{nearest})$$

The subclusters are arranged in the increasing order of $D_{closest}(C)$. Hierarchical clustering works by merging the closest pair of subclusters. The subcluster C corresponding to the smallest value of $D_{closest}(C)$ is the candidate subcluster to be merged with its nearest subcluster $C_{nearest}$ for the next stage. Once the clusters are merged, a new set of representative points are computed for the merged cluster. The merging process continues till the prespecified number of clusters are obtained.

The problem now is to compute the set of representative points of the new subcluster. The set of representative points of individual subclusters may not represent the well-scattered set of points of the merged cluster. The method to recompute the representative points of the newly-formed cluster is as follows. It begins with the centroid of the new cluster and finds the farthest data object from the centroid. This is the first representative point. In subsequent iterations, a point in the subcluster is chosen, that is farthest from the previously chosen representative points. The points are then shrunk towards the centroid by a fraction α. The idea of shrinking these points towards the centroid is to get over the problem of the outlier object as a scattered representative.

CURE maintains a heap-data structure to determine the closest pair of subclusters at every stage. It also maintains a *k-d* tree for efficient implementation. While implementing the algorithm, one can think of many refinements and adjustments at each stage. For example, one can maintain the pair-wise distances between all the representative points of all subclusters for the efficient computation of the closest pair of subclusters.

CURE is a sampling-based, hierarchical clustering algorithm that is able to discover clusters of arbitrary shapes. However, it relies on vector operations and therefore cannot apparently cluster data in any distance space. The idea of maintaining representative points in this approach is very elegant.

5.11 CATEGORICAL CLUSTERING ALGORITHMS

Although algorithms like BIRCH, CURE and CLARANS are suitable for large data sets, these are designed primarily for numeric data. There have been a few proposals for clustering using a categorical data set. The important algorithms are STIRR, ROCK and CACTUS. One interesting common feature of these three algorithms is that they attempt to model the similarity of categorical attributes in more or less a similar manner. A and B are deemed to be similar if the sets of items with which they co-occur have a large overlap, even though these never co-occur together. ROCK tries to introduce a concept called neighbours and link. Two items have a link if they have a common neighbour. STIRR defines a weighted node and the weights of co-occurring items are propagated and, as a result, two items sharing common co-occurring items will exhibit a similar magnitude of weights. CACTUS also makes use of occurrences as the similarity measure. One can even go one step further to say that if A and B are similar and B and C are deemed similar, then we should be able to infer a weak type of similarity between A and C. In that way, similarity may uncover more distant co-relations. In the following three sections, we shall briefly outline these three algorithms.

5.12 STIRR

STIRR (**S**ieving **T**hrough **I**terated **R**elational **R**einforcement), proposed by Gibson, Kleinberg and Raghavan, is an iterative algorithm based on non-linear dynamical systems. The salient features of STIRR are the following.

The database is represented as a graph, where each distinct value in the domain of each attribute is represented by a weighted node. Thus, if there are N attributes and the domain size of the ith attribute is d_i, then the number of nodes in the graph is $\Sigma_i d_i$. For each tuple in the database, an *edge* represents a set of nodes which participate in that tuple. Thus, a tuple is represented as a collection of nodes, one from each attribute type. We assign a weight to each node. The set of weights of all the nodes define the configuration of this structure. The algorithm proceeds iteratively to update the weight of each node, based on the weights of other nodes to which it is connected. Thus, it moves from one configuration to the other till it reaches a stable point. The updating of the weights depends on a combiner function that combines the weights of the nodes participating in a given tuple. Their convergence is dependent on the combiner function.

INITIAL CONFIGURATION

The initial weights of nodes can be assigned uniformly, randomly or by a focussing technique. In uniform initialisation, all weights are set to 1. In random initialisation, each weight is an independently selected random value in the interval [0, 1]. We can focus a portion of the graph by initializing the portion to 1 and the remaining part of the graph to 0.

WEIGHT UPDATE

STIRR iteratively changes the configuration by updating the weight of any single node. The new weight of any node is calculated, based on a *combiner function*. Typically, a combiner function combines the weights of other nodes participating in any tuple with the given node for which the weight is to be updated. We illustrate this step for a specific combiner function in Figure 5.8. A combiner function can simply add all the weights, multiply all the weights, or combine them in some other way.

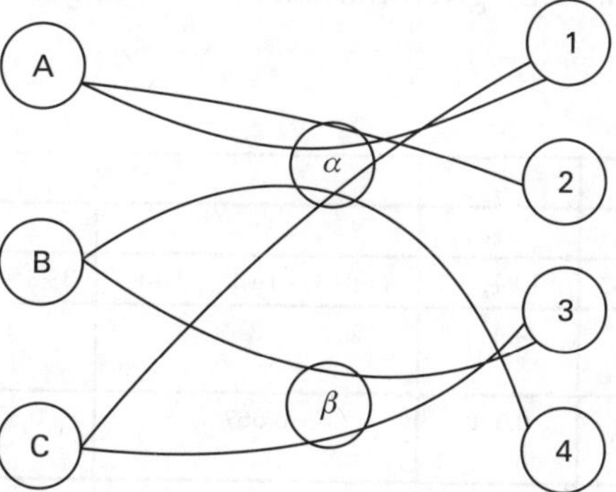

Figure 5.8 Graph for tuples in Table 5.1

EXAMPLE 5.2

The concept of weight-update is illustrated in the following diagram. We assume the database given in the following table (Table 5.1). The graph corresponding to this database is given in Figure 5.8.

Table 5.1

Attrib1	Attrib2	Attrib3
A	α	1
A	α	2
B	β	3
B	α	4
C	α	1
C	β	3

Let us assume that at any stage the weight of the node B is w_B and we are to update the weight of this node.

B participates in two tuples, tuple 3 and tuple 4. For tuple 3, the other nodes are 'α' and '4'. Thus, the weights w_α and w_4 are to be combined to get the *combine*(w_α, w_4) and similarly for the tuple 4, we get this expression as *combine*(w_β, w_3). Then, in order to get the weight of B, we add these to the combined weights.

If the combiner function is 'sum', then the new weight of B is

$$w_\alpha + w_4 + w_\beta + w_3.$$

If multiplication is taken as the combiner function, the new weight of B is

$$w_\alpha\, w_4 + w_\beta\, w_3.$$

The algorithm computes the new weights of all the nodes by the weight propagation scheme. Before beginning the next iteration, all the nodes are normalised. There can be two different types of normalisation. Global normalisation normalises the weights so that the squared sum of all weights is 1. Local normalisation rescales the weights so that the squared sum of all weights for each attribute is 1.

The following table (Table 5.2) gives the change in weight of each of the nodes for two iterations.

Table 5.2

	A	B	C	α	β	1	2	3
Initial wts	1	1	1	1	1	1	1	1
Combiners	α+2+α+1	α+4+β+3	α+1+β+3	A+B+C+1+1+2+4+A	B+3+C+3	A+α+C+α	A+α	B+β+C+β
Iteration 1 New wts	4	4	4	8	4	4	3	4
Normalised wts	0.333	0.338	0.338	0.667	0.338	0.338	0.169	0.338
Iteration 2 New wts	1.521	1.352	1.352	1.521	1.69	1.352	0.845	1.352

The algorithm proceeds in this manner till it converges to a fixed point. Analysing the stability is difficult for any arbitrary combiner function. However, for simple combiner functions like sum or multiplication, the system definitely converges to a fixed point. Even if we start from different initial weights, it is likely that the system converges to a fixed configuration. Such fixed-point configurations are called *basins*. It is easy to see that for categorical attributes, the values which are related through common tuples influence each other during weight modification. Thus, one does not really require any similarity metric to be defined for categorical attributes.

Interestingly, in order to cluster the set of tuples, STIRR maintains multiple copies of the weights. As a result, the configuration is no longer a one-dimensional vector of weights, but becomes a matrix of weights. For instance, if we maintain two copies of the graph of 10 nodes, we have a 10 × 2 matrix of weights. The weights of each node are updated independently. But normalisation is carried out by converting the matrix to an orthonormal form. This process induces negative weights. However, during the weight modification process, each row of this matrix is treated as a single configuration. The first row is termed the principal configuration.

Thus, STIRR maintains multiple copies b_1, ..., b_m, called basins, of this set of weighted vertices. The weights on any given vertex may differ across basins; b_1 is called the *principal basin*; b_2, ..., b_m are called *non-principal basins*. Starting with a set of weights on all vertices (in all basins), the system is "iterated" until a fixed point is reached. When the fixed point is reached, the weights in one or more of the basins b_2,..., b_m isolate two groups of attribute values on each attribute: the first with large positive weights and the second with large negative weights. The nodes with large positive weights and large negative weights are grouped to determine clusters.

The underlying idea of STIRR is unique, but it may be hard to analyse the stability of the system for any useful combiner function. It requires rigorous experimentation and fine-tuning of parameters to arrive at meaningful clustering.

5.13 ROCK

ROCK (**Ro**bust hierarchical **C**lustering with Lin**k**s) is an adaptation of an agglomerative hierarchical clustering algorithm. An agglomorative hierarchial clustering normally uses distance-based representatives (such as centroids) to determine the similarity between clusters. It is observed that such similarity functions tend to merge clusters which have a disjoint set of attributes. Moreover, it is not possible to extend the concept of centroid to categorical attributes. ROCK makes use of links for defining similarity. Informally, the number of links between two tuples is the number of common neighbours they have in the data set. Starting with each tuple in its own cluster, the two closest clusters are merged until the required number of clusters are obtained. ROCK, instead of working on the whole data set, clusters a sample randomly drawn from the data set, and then partitions the entire data set based on the clusters from the sample. Before stating the algorithm, we shall introduce some definitions.

DEFINITION 5.16 NEIGHBOURS

An object's neighbours are those objects that are considerably similar to it. Let $sim(O_i, O_j)$ be a similarity function that is normalised and captures the closeness between the pair of objects O_i and O_j. The similarity function *sim* assumes values between 0 and 1. Given a threshold θ (between 0 and 1), a pair of objects O_i and O_j are defined as *neighbours* if

$$sim(O_i, O_j) \geq \theta.$$

DEFINITION 5. 17 LINKS

The $link(O_i, O_j)$ between the objects is defined as the number of common neighbours between O_i and O_j. Intuitively, if the $link(O_i, O_j)$ is large, then it is more probable that O_i and O_j belong to the same cluster.

ROCK attempts to maximise the sum of $link(O_q, O_r)$ for pairs of objects O_q, O_r belonging to a single cluster and at the same time, to minimise the sum of the $link(O_q, O_r)$ for object pairs belonging to different cluster.

EXAMPLE 5.3

Let us consider the transaction database of Table 4.1. We assume each transaction as one object and define the similarity function as

$$sim\ (O_i, O_j) = \frac{|O_i \cap O_j|}{|O_i \cup O_j|}$$

Hence, $sim(O_1, O_2) = 1/6$ and $sim(O_2, O_6) = 1/2$.

If we set $\theta = 1/2$, then we say that the objects O_2 and O_6 are neighbours whereas for the given θ, O_1 and O_2 are not neighbours. Note that $sim(O_{10}, O_{11}) = 1$, which means that these two objects are identical. On the otherhand, $sim(O_1, O_4) = 0$, which means that there is nothing in common between the objects O_1 and O_4.

If we set $\theta = 1/6$, then the neighbours of O_1 are O_2, O_3, O_5, O_8, O_9, O_{10}, O_{11} and O_{12}. Similarly, the neighbours of O_6 are O_2, O_3, O_4, O_{10}, O_{11}, and O_{15}.

Thus, O_1 and O_6 have 5 common neighbours. Hence, $link(O_1, O_6) = 5$.

DEFINITION 5.18 LINK BETWEEN CLUSTERS

For two clusters, C_i, C_j, define $link[C_i, C_j]$ as follows

$$link\ [C_i, Cj] = \sum_{O_q \in C_i,\ O_r \in C_j} link\ (O_q, O_r)$$

The link-based approach adopts a global perspective of the clustering problem. It captures the global knowledge of neighbouring data points into the relationship between the individual pair of points.

After drawing a random sample from the database, a hierarchical clustering algorithm that employs links is applied to the sample objects. It follows the standard principle of hierarchical clustering. It starts with a singleton object as an individual class and progressively merges the clusters based on the goodness criteria, determined by the link structure. Finally, thė clusters involving only the sample objects are used to assign the remaining data objects on the disk to the appropriate clusters.

The goodness measure, $g(C_i, C_j$, for merging two clusters, C_i, C_j, is defined as

$$g(C_i, C_j) = \frac{link\ [C_i, C_j]}{(n_i + n_j)^{1+2f(\theta)} - n_i^{1+2f(\theta)} - n_f^{1+2f(\theta)}}$$

where $link[C_i, C_j]$ stores the number of cross links between clusters C_i and C_j, and the denominator expression gives the expected numer of cross-links between C_i and C_j. $|C_i|=n_i$, and $n_i^{1=2f(\theta)}$ is expected number of links in C_i; $f(\theta)$ is a funcion that is dependent on the data set; we define

$$f(\theta) = \frac{1-\theta}{1+\theta}, \theta < 1$$

The algorithm is described below.

ROCK Algorithm

Input: (*S*, *k*) where *S* is the set of *n* sampled objects to be clustered and *k* is the number of desired clusters.

Initially, the link for each pair of objects in *S* is computed.

for each s ∈ *S*, *q*[*s*] maintains a local heap structure of objects linked to s in decreasing order.

A ***global heap***, *Q*, is also maintained to indicate the number of clusters that are created so far out of *S*.

```
while (size(Q) > k)) do
    select a cluster u from Q and select the nearest element v from q[u]
    delete v from Q
    w = merge (u, v)
    for each x ∈ q[u] ∪ q[v] do
        link[x, w] = link[x, u] + link[x, v]
        delete u from q[x]
        delete v from q [x]
        insert w to q[x]  and compute g(x, w)
        insert x to q[w] and g(x, w)
        update (Q, x, q[x])
    end
    insert (Q, w, q[w])
end
Procedure for computing links
begin
    compute nbrlist[O_i] for every point i in S
    set link[O_i, O_j] to zero for all i, j
```

```
    for i = 1 to n do
    N = nbrlist[O_i]
    for j = 1 to |N| - 1 do
        for l = j + 1 to |N| do
        link[N[O_j],N[O_l]] = link[N[O_j], N[O_l]] +1
end
```

5.14 CACTUS

CACTUS – **C**lustering **C**ategorical Data **U**sing **S**ummaries – was devised by Ganti, Gehrke and Ramakrishnan. The nicety of CACTUS lies in its problem decomposition. Let us assume that the database D is a set of tuples each having k fields or attributes. The clustering techniques are essentially attempting to cluster the tuples by considering the tuple as an primitive object. CACTUS attempts to split the database vertically and tries to cluster the set of projections of these tuples to only a pair of attributes. The questions that arise are

a. how to find clusters for the tuples only on two attributes, and
b. how to effectively utilise this information for clustering on all the attributes.

Though CACTUS is designed for a categorical database, let us reinforce this concept by giving the following geometric interpretation.

Imagine a set of 3-dimensional vectors. These can be represented as a set of points in the 3-dimensional space. Now consider the projections of these points in two-dimensions, say on the first two dimensions. Consider the clusters formed by these projected points. It may look like Figure 5.9. There are three clusters: C1, C2 and C3. Their projections on the first dimension are

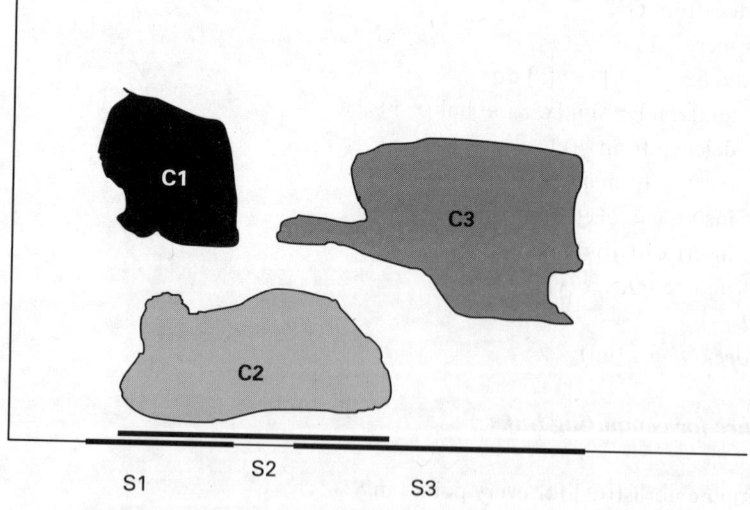

Figure 5.9 Clusters and their projections

S1, S2 and S3. We call these cluster projection sets in Dimension 1, with respect to Dimension 2. We can get another collection of sets Qs for Dimension 1 with respect to Dimension 3. Let us imagine a similar diagram for the Dimension 1 and Dimension 3 of the same set of points. We may get a different set of clusters. Consider their projections on Dimension 1 and let these projections be Q1 and Q2 (assuming that there are just two clusters for this pair of dimensions).

Knowing S1, S2, S3 and Q1 and Q2, we can derive information about the projections of clusters with all three dimensions on Dimension 1. If we consider intersections of the sets of Ss with the sets of Qs, we get the projections of the clusters when all the three dimensions are taken into account. The main principle is that a cluster on a set of attributes induces a cluster on a subset of the attributes. Thus, if we take the intersecting sets, we get the projections sets of the clusters. CACTUS extends this idea to the categorical attributes. It tries to find clusters for the subsets of attributes, and the clusters for the whole attribute set can be found by intersecting these clusters.

CACTUS has two more important characteristics. The algorithm assumes that categorical domains have a small number of attribute values (i.e., the domain sizes are small). The central idea of CACTUS is that the summary information constructed from the data set is sufficient for discovering well-defined clusters. The properties that the summary information typically fits into main memory and that it can be efficiently constructed in a single scan of the data set are the key ideas of the algorithm.

Based on the foregoing discussion, we shall now describe the algorithm in detail. However, in the beginning let us define some terms to facilitate the understanding of new concepts and to visualise the clusters in terms of individual attributes.

Let us consider two attribute values of two different attributes in the database. Say, a_i of attribute type A and a_j of attribute type B. There may be tuples where a_i and a_j co-occur. The support of these two values in the database is the proportion of tuples in which they appear together. If this support exceeds a prespecified value, we say that these values are strongly connected. D_A denotes domain of the attribute A; s denotes the support value.

DEFINITION 5.19 STRONGLY CONNECTED ATTRIBUTE VALUES

Let $a_i \in D_A$, $a_j \in D_B$, and $\alpha > 1$. The attribute values a_i and a_j are *strongly connected* with respect to domain D if

$$s_D(a_i, a_j) > \frac{\alpha|D|}{|D_A||D_B|}.$$

The function $\sigma^*_D(a_i, a_j)$ is defined as

$$\sigma_D{}^*(a_i, a_j) = \begin{cases} s_D(a_i, a_j) & \text{if } a_i \text{ and } a_j \text{ are strongly connected.} \\ 0 & \text{otherwise} \end{cases}$$

The above definition can be extended to define strongly connected value sets. Let a_i be an attribute value and S a set of attribute values of another attribute type. We say that a_i is strongly connected to S if it is strongly connected to each element of S. Similarly, two attribute value sets

S and R are said to be strongly connected if each value a in S is strongly connected to R, and each value b in R is strongly connected to S. We use this concept to define a cluster.

Definition 5.20 Cluster

Let C_i be the attribute value set of ith attribute; a subset of the domain D_i, such that $| C_i | > 1$. Then, $C = <C_1 ,...., C_n>$ is said to be a *cluster* over the database of n attributes if the following three conditions are satisfied:

1. For all $i, j \in \{1,.....,n\}$, $i \neq j$, C_i and C_j are strongly connected.
2. For all $i, j \in \{1,....,n\}$, $i \neq j$, there exists no $C_i' \supset C_i$ such that or all $j \neq i$, C_i' and C_j are strongly connected.
3. $s_D(C) \geq \dfrac{\alpha\, |D| \times |C_1| \times ... \times |C_n|}{|D_1| \times |D_2| \times ... \times |D_n|}$

Definition 5.21 K-Cluster

A cluster on k attributes is called a k-cluster. It is also known as a subspace cluster.

Definition 5.22 Cluster Projection

A cluster on a database that is a projection of the original database D is called a cluster projection, with respect to the attributes present in the projection operation. C_i above is called the cluster projection of C on attribute A_1.

Definition 5.23 Similarity Measure of Elements of One Attribute

We define a similarity measure between two values of an attribute, i.e., for a_1, $a_2 \in D_i$ with respect to another attribute A_j, as the number of elements of D_j that are strongly connected to both a_1, and a_2.

$$\gamma^j (a_1, a_2) = |\{x \in D_j : \sigma^*_D(a_1, x) > 0 \text{ and } \sigma^*_D(a_2, x) > 0|$$

Definition 5.24 Inter-Attribute Summary

Let $A_1 ,..., A_n$ be a set of categorical attributes with domains $D_1 ,..., D_n$, respectively, and let D be an aa set. The inter-attribute summary Σ_{IJ} is defined as

$$\Sigma_{IJ} = \{ \Sigma_{ij} | i,j \in \{l, ..., n\}, \text{ and } i \neq j\}$$

where $\Sigma_{ij} = \{a_i, a_j, \sigma^*_D(a_i, a_j) | a_i \in D_i, a_j \in D_j \text{ and } \sigma^*_D(a_i, a_j) > 0\}$.

Definition 5.25 Intra-Attribute Summary

The intra-attribute summary Σ_{II} is defined as

$$\Sigma_{II} = \{ \Sigma_{ii}^{j} | i, j \in \{l, ..., n\}, \text{and } i \neq j\}$$

where $\Sigma_{ij}^{j} = \{(a_i, a_j, \gamma^j(a_{i1}, a_{i2})) | a_{i1}, a_{i2} \in D_i, \text{ and } \gamma^j(a_{i1}, a_{j2}) > 0\}$.

CACTUS first identifies the cluster projections on an attribute for the two clusters involving this attribute. Then, it generates an intersecting set to represent the cluster projection on this attribute for the n-cluster (involving all the attributes). Once all the cluster projections on individual attributes are generated, these are synthesised to obtain the clusters of the database. Thus, the major steps of CACTUS are

1. Finding cluster projections $CP_i[i, j]$ on a given attribute A_i with respect to another attribute A_j in a 2-cluster involving these two attributes. This is done for all attributes A_i.
2. Intersecting these $CP_i[i, j]$ for a fixed A_i to get $CP_i[1, 2, ..., k]$; that is, a cluster projection of A_i with respect to all the attributes. It is also done for all A_i.
3. Synthesizing the set of $CP_i[1, 2, ..., k]$, for all i, to obtain the clusters.

We shall discuss each step separately. The most interesting aspect of these steps are that they can be computed using the inter-attribute and intra-attribute summary. It is not necessary to refer to the original database. Hence, we assume that these summaries are available as the outcome of preprocessing. Needless to say, these summaries can be computed by the level-wise algorithm discussed in Chapter 4.

Clustering Phase

The clustering phase is a two-step process. In the first step, each attribute's cluster projections are computed. In the second step, candidate clusters on sets of attributes from the cluster projections are computed. This method contains a set of modules. It first finds the set of distinguishing sets, then extends these distinguishing sets to determine the cluster projection of 2-clusters. Let us first understand the concept of a distinguishing set.

Definition 5.26 Distinguishing Set

A distinguishing set DS, on an attribute A_i, is a set of values having the following properties:

- All pairs of values in DS are strongly connected (refer to the similarity measure above).

To find a distinguishing set, the algorithm uses the principle of downward closure property (Chapter 4). It first finds the pair of values which are strongly connected. It then extends these pairs in a level-wise fashion to get k-sets of strongly connected elements, every time deleting the superset which has at least one proper subset that violates the desired property.

Distinguishing sets are extended further. Let $DS_i[j]$ be a distinguishing set of A_i with respect to A_j. Let us identify the values in A_j which are strongly connected to the values in $DS_i[j]$. For these attribute values in A_j, we refer to the ith attribute to determine other values of A_i which are strongly connected and add these values to $DS_i[j]$.

Intersection of Cluster Projections

Once we have computed the collection of all the distinguishing sets $DS_i[j]$ and their extensions, we intersect these collections over all j to determine the cluster projections $CP_i[1, 2, ..., k]$ for the attribute A_i. Thus, once the cluster projections on A_i of 2-clusters over attribute pairs (A_i, A_j) are found using the intersection operation on the sets, the set of cluster projections on A_i of clusters over $\{A_1, A_2,..., A_n\}$ can be found. Thus, the clusters so obtained are the candidate clusters. This can be carried out as a main memory operation.

We employ a level-wise principle for the synthesis of cluster projection. We start with cluster-projections on A_1 and then, extend them to clusters over (A_1, A_2), then to clusters over (A_1, A_2, A_3), and so on. Let C_i be the set of cluster projections on attribute A_i. Let C^k denote the set of candidate clusters over A_1, ..., A_k. Hence $C^1=C_1$. We successively generate C^{j+1} from C^j by checking the summarised information.

Validation Phase

This step scans through the database to compute the support for each of the candidate clusters.

CACTUS requires only two scans of the database and hence, it is fast and stable. The algorithm can find clusters in subsets of all attributes also, and thus can perform subspace clustering.

5.15 Conclusions

We have studied quite a few algorithms, each advocating a new idea.

Let us attempt to extract the general principles. The first one is sampling the database. When the database is very large, randomly sampling the data for clustering has proved to be an efficient approach. We have seen that CLARA, ROCK and CURE follow this approach. Another important feature is summarisation. It is worthwhile to extract some features from the database so that these extracted features carry sufficient information for clustering and hence, one does not have to refer to the original database. BIRCH, CACTUS, and CURE follow this approach. For categorical data, however, co-occurrence strength is uniformly taken as the similarity measure. One can perhaps think of some other measure. Another important aspect of the algorithms is the vertical partitioning of the database by projecting on a subset of attributes. CACTUS adopts this for categorical attributes.

Further Reading

Clustering is another well-studied subject and, indeed, a very vast one. k-means algorithms can be found in Pattern Recognition and Image Processing literature. One of the very recent k-means algorithm is given in Alsabti [1998]. A general study on clustering is very well dealt with in [Jain, 1988] and in Anderberg [1973]. PAM was proposed by Kaufman et al [1990].

CLARANS was introduced by Ng [1994]. DBSCAN was proposed by Ester et al [1995]. BIRCH was proposed by Zhang et al [1996]. Guha et al introduced the CURE algorithm in 1998 and the ROCK algorithm [1999]. CACTUS was designed by Ramakrishnan and his team [Ganti, 1999].

There are many other important algorithms like BUBBLE, MAFIA [Goil, 2000], WaveCluster [Sheikholeslami, 1998], ITERATES [Biswas, 1995], CHAMELON [Karyapis, 1997] etc. Wavecluster is for numeric, mutlidimensional data and it uses wavelet transforms for the purpose of clustering. BUBBLE is designed for arbitrary metric space and draws its foundation from BIRCH.

Exercises

1. What is clustering? What are the different clustering techniques?
2. Discuss the importance of similarity metric in clustering. Why it is difficult to handle categorical data for clustering?
3. Describe the working of the PAM algorithm. Compare its performance with CLARA and CLARANS.
4. How is CLARANS different from CLARA? Illustrate this using a small example.
5. Describe the working of the DBSCAN algorithm. Explain the concept of a cluster as used in DBSCAN.
6. Explain the concept of a cluster as used in ROCK. Compare this definition of cluster with that of the DBSCAN.
7. Define a core object. Define density reachability. Why is density reachability not a symmetric function? What is a noise object?
8. BIRCH is independent of any clustering algorithm. It is just a clustering paradigm. Comment.
9. How are CF Tree operations different from B^+ Tree operations. Describe the operations for the CF Tree.
10. Discuss the importance of cluster features. How do these help in clustering large databases. How are these different from the cluster representatives used in CURE?
11. What are the different phases of BIRCH? How are they important in clustering?
12. CURE is a sampling-based hierarchical clustering. Justify.
13. Describe the features of ROCK that are necessary for categorical attributes.
14. Define the following
    a. *k*-clusters
    b. strongly connected attributes
    c. inter-attribute summary
    d. intra-attribute summary
    e. cluster projection
15. Describe the underlying principle of the CACTUS algorithm.

16. List the different features that can be computed from the three cluster features. Which of them are additive function of CFs?
17. Describe the salient features of CURE clustering techniques.
18. For STIRR, complete the example given in the text to reach the fixed point.
19. In STIRR, suppose that the combiner function is the max function. Compute the fixed-point for the example in the text.
20. PAM requires prior specification of the number of clusters. True or false?
21. DBSCAN is a hierarchical divisive algorithm. True or false?
22. If C is a cluster in n-dimension, its projection in n–1 dimension may be a single cluster or more than one cluster. True or false?
23. If the medoid O_j and unselected object O_h swap roles, it is acceptable if the cost of swapping is negative. True or False?
24. The noise object is one that is not density reachable from any other object. True or false?
25. In a cluster as defined in DBSCAN, any two objects are density connected. True or false?
26. Express the average intra-cluster distance in terms of the cluster features.
27. Distinguish between global and local normalisation in STIRR.
28. Define a link and a neighbour as defined in ROCK.
29. What are the similarities among the three algorithms: ROCK, STIRR and CACTUS?

Bibliography

Agarwal Pankaj K., and Procopiuc Cecilia M. Exact and approximation algorithms for clustering. In *Proceedings of SODA*, 1998.

Aggarwal C., Procopiuc C., Wolf J.L., Yu P.S., and Park J.S. A framework for finding projected clusters in high dimensional spaces. In *Proceedings of ACM SIGMOD International Conferenceon Management of Data*, 1999.

Agrawal R., Gehrke J., Gunopulos D., and Raghavan P. Automatic subspace clustering of high dimensional data for data mining applications. In *Proceedings of ACM SIGMOD International Conference on Management of Data*, 1998.

Alsabti K., Ranka S., and Singh V. An efficient k-Means clustering algorithm. In *IPPS/SPDP Workshop on High Performance Data Mining*, Orlando, Florida, 1998.

Anderberg M.R. *Cluster Analysis for Applications*. Academic Press, NY, 1973.

Ankerst M., Breunig M., H.-P. Kriegel, and Sander J. OPTICS: Ordering points to identify the clustering structure. In *Proceedings ACM SIGMOD International Conference on Management of Data*, Philadelphia, PA, 1999.

Biswas G., Weinberg J., and Li C. ITERATE: A conceptual clustering method for knowledge discovery in databases. *Artificial Intelligence in the Petroleum Industry*, pp. 111–139, Paris, France, 1995.

Bradley P.S., Mangasarian O.L., and Street W.N. Clustering via concave minimization. *Advances in Neural Information Processing Systems,* MIT Press, 9:368–374, Cambridge, MA 1997.

Bradley P.S., and Mangasarian O.L. K-plane clustering. *Mathematical Programming Technical Report 98–08*, Department of Computer Science, University of Wisconsin, Madison, August1998.

Brinkhoff T., and H.-P. Kriegel. The impact of global clustering on spatial database systems.In *Proceedings of 20th International Conference on Very Large Databases*, pp. 168–179, Santiago, Chile, 1994.

Castro V.E. Convex group clustering of large geo-referenced data sets. In *11th Canadian Conference on Computational Geometry*, University of British Columbia, Vancouver, Canada, 1999.

Charikar M., Chekuri C., Feder T., and Motwani R. Incremental clustering and dynamic information retrieval. In *Proceedings of the 29th Annual ACM Symposium on Theory of Computing*, pp. 626–635, 1997.

Eldershaw C., and Hegland M. Cluster analysis using triangulation. In *Computational Techniques and Applications*, pp. 201–208, World Scientific, Singapore, 1997.

Ester M., H.-P. Kriegel, and Xu X. A database interface for clustering in large spatial databases. In *Proceedings of 1st International Conference on Knowledge Discovery & Data Mining*, pp. 94–99, Montreal, Canada, 1995.

Ester M., H.-P. Kriegel, Sander J., and Xu X. A density-based algorithm for discovering clusters in large spatial databases with noise. In *Proceedings 2nd International Conference on KnowledgeDiscovery and Data Mining* (KDD-96), pp. 226–231, Portland, OR, 1996.

Ester M., H.-P. Kriegel, Sander J., and Xu X. Clustering for mining in large spatial databases. Special Issue on Data Mining, *KI-Journal*, ScienTec Publishing, (1), 1998.

Ester M., H.-P. Kriegel, Sander J., Wimmer M., and Xu X. Incremental clustering for mining in a data warehousing environment. In *Proceedings 24th International Conference on Very Large Databases*, pp. 323–333, New York, 1998.

Fisher D. Iterative optimization and simplification of hierarchical clusterings. *Technical Report CS-95-01*, Department of Computer Science, Vanderbilt University, 1995.

Ganti V., Ramakrishnan R., Gehrke J., Powell A. and French J. Clustering large data sets in arbitrary metric spaces. In *Proceedings of the International Conference on Data Engineering*, 1999.

Ganti V., Gehrke J., and Ramakrishnan R. CACTUS: Clustering categorical data using summaries. In *Proceedings of ACM SIGKDD, International Conference on Knowledge Discovery & Data Mining*, San Diego, CA, USA, 1999.

Gibson D., Kleinberg J., and Raghavan P. Clustering categorical data: an approach based on dynamical systems. In *Proceedings of the 24th VLDB Conference*, New York, USA, 1998.

Gonzalez T.F. Clustering to minimize the maximum intercluster distance. *Theoretical Computer Science*, **38**:293–306, 1985.

Guha S., Rastogi R., and Shim K. CURE: An efficient algorithm for clustering large databases. In *Proceedings of ACM-SIGMOD 1998 International Conference on Management of Data*, Seattle, 1998.

Guha S., Rastogi R., and Shim K. ROCK: A robust clustering algorithm for categorical attributes. In *Proceedings of the IEEE International Conference on Data Engineering*, Sydney, March 1999.

Han Eui-Hong (Sam), Karypis George, Kumar Vipin and Mobasher B.. Clustering based on association rule hypergraphs. In *SIGMOD'97 Workshop on Research Issues on Data Mining and Knowledge Discovery*, 1997.

Han E.H., Karyapis G., Kumar V., and Mobasher B. Clustering in a high-dimensional space using hypergraph models. *Technical Report 97-019*, Department of Computer Science, University of Minnesota.

Han Eui-Hong, Karyapis George, Kumar Vipin and Mobasher B. Hypergraph based clustering in high-dimensional data sets: a summary of results. *Bulletin of the Technical Committee on Data Engineering*, **21**(1), March 1998.

Hinneburg A., and Keim D. Cluster discovery methods for large databases: From the past to the future, tutorial session. In *Proceedings of ACM SIGMOD International Conference on Management of Data*, 1999.

Huang Z. A fast clustering algorithm to cluster very large categorical data sets in data mining. In *Proceedings of SIGMOD Workshop on Research Issues on Data Mining and Knowledge Discovery*, 1997.

Jain A.K., and Dubes R.C. *Algorithms for Clustering Data*. Prentice-Hall, NJ, 1988.

Karyapis G., Han E.H., and Kumar V. CHAMELEON: A hierarchical clustering algorithm using dynamic modelling. In *IEEE Computer, Special Issue on Data Analysis and Mining*.

Ng R.T, and Han J. Efficient and effective clustering methods for spatial data mining. In *Proceedings of 1994 International Conference on Very Large DataBases (VLDB'94)*,pp. 144–155, Santiago, Chile, September 1994.

Ohta Y., Okahama S., and Yugami N. *Clustering Algorithm for Large-scale Databases*. Fujitsu Laboratories Ltd.

Procopiuc Cecilia M. *Clustering Problems and their Applications: A Survey*. Department of Computer Science, Duke University.

Ramkumar G.D., and Swami A. Clustering data without distance functions. *Bulletin of the IEEE Computer Society Technical Committee on Data Engineering*, 1998.

Sheikholeslami G., Chatterjee S., and Zhang A. WaveCluster: A multi-resolution clustering approach for very large spatial databases. In *24th International Conference on Very Large Databases*, New York City, August 24–27, 1998.

Xu X., Ester M., H.P. Kriegel, and Sander J., A distribution-based clustering algorithm for mining in large spatial databases. In *Proceedings 14th International Conference on Data Engineering (ICDE'98)*, pp. 209–218, Orlando, FL, 1998.

Yu D., Chatterjee S., and Sheikholeslami G.. Efficiently detecting arbitrary shaped clusters in very large data sets with high dimensions. Department of Computer Science and Engineering, SUNY Buffalo, *Technical Report*, November 1, 1998.

Zhang Tian, Ramakrishnan Raghu, and Livny Miron. BIRCH: An efficient data clustering method for very large databases. In *Proceedings of ACM SIGMOD International Conference on Management of Data, 1996.*

6

DECISION TREES

6.1 INTRODUCTION

The classification of large data sets is an important problem in data mining. The classification problem can be simply stated as follows. For a database with a number of records and for a set of classes such that each record belongs to one of the given classes, the problem of classification is to decide the class to which a given record belongs. But there is much more to this than just simply classifying. The classification problem is also concerned with generating a description or a model for each class from the given data set. Here, we are concerned with a type of classification called supervised classification. In supervised classification, we have a training data set of records and for each record of this set, the class to which it belongs is also known. Using the training set, the classification process attempts to generate descriptions of the classes, and these descriptions help classify the unknown records. In addition to the training set, we can also have a test data set which is used to determine the effectiveness of a classification.

There are several approaches to supervised classifications. *Decision trees* (essentially, *classification trees*) are especially attractive in the data-mining environment as they represent rules. Rules can readily be expressed in natural language and are easily comprehensible. Rules can also be easily mapped to a database access language, like SQL.

This chapter is concerned with decision trees as techniques for data mining. Though the decision-tree method is a well-known technique in statistics and machine learning, these algorithms are not suitable for data mining purposes. The specific requirements that should be taken into consideration while designing any decision tree construction algorithm for data mining are that

a. the method should be efficient in order to handle a very large-sized database, and
b. the method should be able to handle categorical attributes.

Recent developments in data mining research have led to some interesting decision tree algorithms. This chapter discusses most of the major algorithms on this topic. We shall begin with studying, in Section 6.2, the basic features of decision tree building. Section 6.3 discusses the generic algorithm of decision tree construction. Almost all the known algorithms follow the principles outlined in this section. We shall also outline three major design considerations that should be taken into account while studying a specific algorithm. We shall also study two important measures in Section 6.5, namely Entropy-based gain and the Gini Index. Section 6.6 deals with the method of determination of splitting points for both numerical and categorical attributes.

The specific algorithms are discussed from Section 6.8 onwards. In sections 6.8–6.10, we shall discuss three important and well-known algorithms, which provide the foundation for all subsequent algorithms. In fact, all other algorithms are only adaptions of these algorithms to suit different aspects of data mining. In Section 6.13, we shall discuss one of the recent and popular algorithms, namely SPRINT. In this section, we also study SLIQ, which is the initial version of SPRINT. These algorithms demonstrate a process that avoids repeated sorting—a major computational overhead in earlier algorithms. Historically, SLIQ was proposed first and SPRINT is an improvement on SLIQ. Both are based on a similar principle. The next section outlines the specific improvement that SPRINT exhibits over SLIQ.

Besides the exact methods, in order to efficiently handle large data sets, there are also approximate methods of construction of decision trees; we shall discuss these methods in Section 6.14. There are generally two approaches for devising approximate construction. They are sampling and discretisation. CLOUDS combines both these approaches. It carries out a kind of discretisation on a sample of the original training set. The construction process proceeds on this discretised version of the sample. But in order to get an accurate construction from a coarse construction, the algorithm employs a hill-climbing heuristic to estimate the gini indices of the coarse intervals. It exploits the features of the gini function and reduces the search space by eliminating certain intervals.

In Section 6.15, we shall discuss yet another approximate algorithm, with the acronym BOAT. BOAT adopts a bootstraping technique to determine a coarse decision tree. However, it subsequently searches only one confidence interval per attribute at each node.

In Section 6.18 , we shall study the well-known pruning strategy—MDL. The pruning process is generally a post-processing step and is employed after the complete construction of the decision tree.

A question that comes to mind is whether pruning can be integrated with the tree construction process. We have noted that CHAID follows this principle. However, SPRINT employs an MDL pruning step after the full decision tree is expanded. PUBLIC is one of the recent algorithms which attempts to integrate these two steps. Section 6.19 focusses on this method of decision tree building.

6.2 WHAT IS A DECISION TREE?

A decision tree is a classification scheme which generates a tree and a set of rules, representing the model of different classes, from a given data set. The set of records available for developing classification methods is generally divided into two disjoint subsets—a *training set* and a *test set*. The former is used to derive the classifier, while the latter is used to measure the accuracy of the classifier. The accuracy of the classifier is determined by the percentage of the test examples that are correctly classified.

We categorise the attributes of records into two different types. Attributes whose domain is numerical are called *numerical attributes,* and those whose domain is not numerical are called *categorical attributes*. There is one distinguished attribute called the *class label*. The goal of classification is to build a concise model that can be used to predict the class of the record whose class label is not known.

EXAMPLE 6.1

In order to have a clear idea of a decision tree, let us consider the following data sets—the training data set (see Table 6.1) and the test data set (see Table 6.2). The data set has five attributes. There is a special attribute: the attribute *class* is the class label. The attributes *temp* (temperature) and *humidity* are numerical attributes and the other attributes are categorical, that is, they cannot be ordered. Based on the training data set, we want to find a set of rules to know what values of *outlook, temperature, humidity* and *wind* determine whether or not to play golf. Figure 6.1 gives a sample decision tree for illustration.

In the tree (Figure 6.1), we have five leaf nodes. In a decision tree, each leaf node represents a rule. The following rules correspond to the tree given in Figure 6.1.

Table 6.1 Training data set

OUTLOOK	TEMP(F)	HUMIDITY(%)	WINDY	CLASS
sunny	79	90	true	no play
sunny	56	70	false	play
sunny	79	75	true	play
sunny	60	90	true	no play
overcast	88	88	false	no play
overcast	63	75	true	play
overcast	88	95	false	play
rain	78	60	false	play
rain	66	70	false	no play
rain	68	60	true	no play

RULE 1 *If it is sunny and the humidity is not above 75%, then play.*

RULE 2 *If it is sunny and the humidity is above 75%, then do not play.*

RULE 3 *If it is overcast, then play.*

RULE 4 *If it is rainy and not windy, then play.*

RULE 5 *If it is rainy and windy, then don't play.*

Please note that this may not be the best set of rules that can be derived from the given set of training data.

The classification of an unknown input vector is done by traversing the tree from the root node to a leaf node. A record enters the tree at the root node. At the root, a test is applied to determine which child node the record will encounter next. This process is repeated until the record arrives at a leaf node. All the records that end up at a given leaf of the tree are classified in the same way. There is a unique path from the root to each leaf. The path is a rule which is used to classify the records.

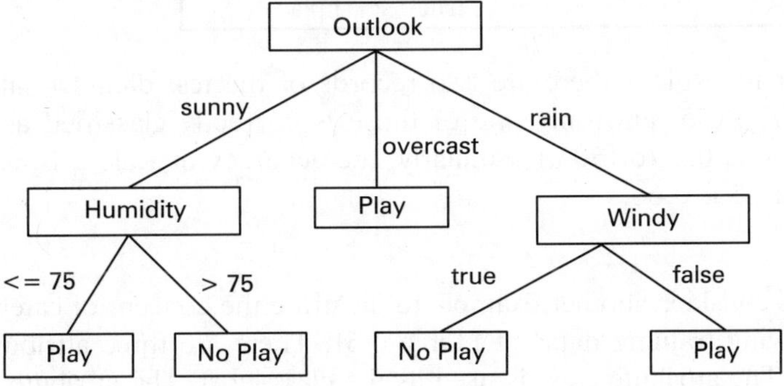

Figure 6.1 A decision tree

In the above tree, we can carry out the classification for an unknown record as follows. Let us assume, for the record, that we know the values of the first four attributes (but we do not know the value of the *class* attribute):

outlook= rain; temp = 70; humidity = 65; and windy= true

We start from the root node to check the value of the attribute associated at the root node. This attribute is the *splitting attribute* at this node. Please note that for a decision tree, at every node there is an attribute associated with the node called the *splitting attribute*. In our example, *outlook* is the splitting attribute at the root. Since for the given record, *outlook = rain*, we move to the right-most child node of the root. At this node, the splitting attribute is *windy* and we find that for the record we want to classify *windy = true*. Hence, we move to the left child node to conclude that the class label is "no play".

Note that every path from root node to leaf node represents a rule. It may be noted that many different leaves of the tree may refer to the same class label, but each leaf refers to a different rule.

The accuracy of the classifier is determined by the percentage of the test data set that is correctly classified. Consider the following test data set (Table 6.2).

Table 6.2 Test data set

OUTLOOK	TEMP(F)	HUMIDITY(%)	WINDY	CLASS
sunny	79	90	true	play
sunny	56	70	false	play
sunny	79	75	true	no play
sunny	60	90	true	no play
overcast	88	88	false	no play
overcast	63	75	true	play
overcast	88	95	false	play
rain	78	60	false	play
rain	66	70	false	no play
rain	68	60	true	play

We can see that for Rule 1 there are two records of the test data set satisfying *outlook= sunny* and *humidity* $\leq$ *75*, and only one of these is correctly classified as *play*. Thus, the accuracy of this rule is 0.5 (or 50%). Similarly, the accuracy of Rule 2 is also 0.5 (or 50%). The accuracy of Rule 3 is 0.66.

EXAMPLE 6.2

At this stage, let us consider another example to illustrate the concept of categorical attributes. Consider the following training data set (Table 6.3). There are three attributes, namely, *age, pincode* and *class*. The attribute *class* is used as the class label. The attribute *age* is a numeric attribute, whereas *pincode* is a categorical one. Though the domain of pincode is numeric, no ordering can be defined among pincode values. You cannot derive any useful information if one pincode is greater than another pincode. Figure 6.2 gives a decision tree for this training data. The splitting attribute at the root is *pincode* and the splitting criterion here is *pincode = 500 046*. Similarly, for the left child node, the splitting criterion is *age* ≤ *48* (the splitting attribute is *age*). Although the right child node has the same attribute as the splitting attribute, the splitting criterion is different.

Table 6.3 Example illustrating the concept of categorical attributes

ID	AGE	PINCODE	CLASS
1	30	5600046	C1
2	25	5600046	C1
3	21	5600023	C2
4	43	5600046	C1
5	18	5600023	C2
6	33	5600023	C1
7	29	5600023	C1
8	55	5600046	C2
9	48	5600046	C1

Most decision tree building algorithms begin by trying to find the test which does the best job of splitting the records among the desired categories. At each succeeding level of the tree, the subsets created by the preceding split are themselves split according to whatever rule works best for them. The tree continues to grow until it is no longer possible to find better ways to split incoming records, or when all the records are in one class. In Figure 6.2, we see that at the root level we have nine records. The associated *splitting criterion* is *pincode = 500046*. As a result, we split the records into two subsets, Records 1, 2, 4, 8 and 9 are assigned to the left child node and the remaining to the right node. This process is repeated at every node.

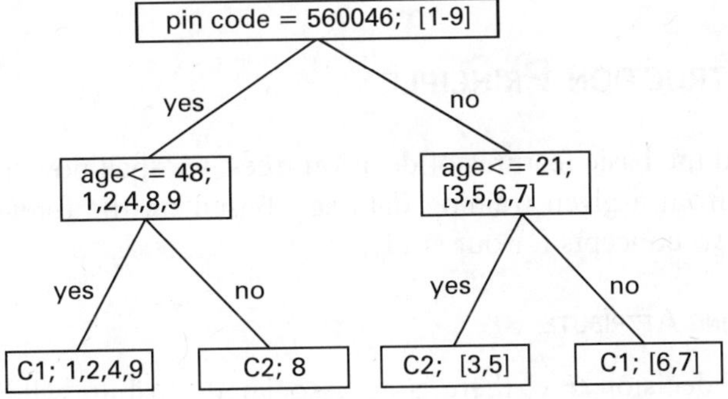

Figure 6.2 A decision tree

A decision tree construction process is concerned with identifying the splitting attributes and splitting criteria at every level of the tree. There are several alternatives and the main aim of the decision tree construction process is to generate simple, comprehensible rules with high accuracy.

Some rules are apparently better than others. In the above example, we see that Rule 3 is simpler than Rule 1. The measure of simplicity is the number of antecedents of the rule. It may happen that another decision tree may yield a rule such as: "if the temperature lies between 70° F and 80° F, and the humidity is between 75% and 90%, and it is not windy, and it is sunny, then play". Naturally, we would prefer a rule like Rule 1 to this rule. That is why simplicity is sought after.

Sometimes the classification efficiency of the tree can be improved by revising the tree through some processes like pruning and grafting. These processes are activated after the decision tree is built.

Advantages and Shortcomings of Decision Tree Classifications

The major strengths of the decision tree methods are as follows:

- decision trees can be used to generate understandable rules,
- they can handle both numerical and categorical attributes, and
- they provide a clear indication of which fields are most important for prediction or classification.

Some of the weaknesses of decision trees are:

- some decision trees can only deal with binary-valued target classes. Others can assign records to an arbitrary number of classes, but are error-prone when the number of training examples per class gets small. This can happen rather quickly in a tree with many levels and/or many branches per node.
- the process of growing a decision tree is computationally expensive. At each node, each candidate splitting field is examined before its best split can be found.

6.3 Tree Construction Principle

After having understood the basic features of decision trees, we shall now focus on the methods of building such trees from a given training data set. Based on the foregoing discussion, we shall formally define a few concepts for our study.

Definition 6.1 Splitting Attribute

With every node of the decision tree, there is an associated attribute whose values determine the partitioning of the data set when the node is expanded.

DEFINITION 6.2 SPLITTING CRITERION

The qualifying condition on the splitting attribute for data set splitting at a node is called the splitting criterion at that node. For a numeric attribute, the criterion can be an equation or an inequality. For a categorical attribute, it is a membership condition on a subset of values.

All the decision tree construction methods are based on the principle of recursively partitioning the data set till homogeneity is achieved. We shall study this common principle later and discuss in detail the features of different algorithms individually.

The construction of the decision tree involves the following three main phases:

- *Construction phase* The initial decision tree is constructed based on the entire training data set. It requires recursively partitioning the training set into two, or more, sub-partitions using a *splitting criteria,* until a stopping criteria is met.
- *Pruning phase* The tree constructed in the previous phase may not result in the best possible set of rules due to overfitting (explained below). The pruning phase removes some of the lower branches and nodes to improve its performance.
- *Processing the pruned tree* to improve understandability.

Though these three phases are common to most well-known algorithms, some of them attempt to integrate the first two phases into a single process.

THE GENERIC ALGORITHM

Most of the existing algorithms of the construction phase use *Hunt's method* as the basic principle in this phase. Let the training data set be T with class labels $\{C_1, C_2, \ldots, C_k\}$. The tree is built by repeatedly partitioning the training data, using some criterion like the goodness of the split. The process is continued till all the records in a partition belong to the same class.

- **T is homogeneous** T contains cases that all belong to a single class C_j. The decision tree for T is a leaf identifying class C_j.
- **T is not homogeneous** T contains cases that belong to a mixture of classes. A test is chosen, based on a single attribute, that has one or more mutually exclusive outcomes $\{O_1, O_2, \ldots, O_n\}$. T is partitioned into the subsets $T_1, T_2, T_3, \ldots, T_n$, where T_i contains those cases in T that have the outcome O_i of the chosen test. The decision tree for T consists of a decision node identifying the test, and one branch for each possible outcome. The same tree building method is applied recursively to each subset of training cases. Most often, n is chosen to be 2 and hence, the algorithm generates a binary decision tree.
- **T is trivial** T contains no cases. The decision tree T is a leaf, but the class to be associated with the leaf must be determined from information other than T.

The generic algorithm of decision tree construction outlines the common principle of all algorithms. Nevertheless, the following aspects should be taken into account while studying any specific algorithm. In one sense, the following are three major difficulties which arise when one uses a decision tree in a real-life situation.

Guillotine Cut

Most decision tree algorithms examine only a single attribute at a time. As mentioned in the earlier paragraph, normally the splitting is done for a single attribute at any stage and if the attribute is numeric, then the splitting test is an inequality. Geometrically, each splitting can be viewed as a plane parallel to one of the axes. Thus, splitting one single attribute leads to rectangular classification boxes that may not correspond too well with the actual distribution of records in the decision space. We call this the guillotine cut phenomenon. The test is of the form (X > z) or (X < z), which is called a *guillotine cut,* since it creates a guillotine cut subdivision of the Cartesian space of the ranges of attributes.

However, the guillotine cut approach has a serious problem if a pair of attributes are correlated. For example, let us consider two numeric attributes, height (in metres) and weight (in kilograms). Obviously, these attributes have a strong correlation. Thus, whenever there exists a correlation between variables, a decision tree with the splitting criteria on a single attribute is not accurate. Therefore, some researchers proposed an *oblique decision tree* that uses a splitting criteria involving more than one attribute.

Overfit

Decision trees are built from the available data. However, the training data set may not be a proper representative of the real-life situation and may also contain noise. In an attempt to build a tree from a noisy training data set, we may grow a decision tree just deep enough to perfectly classify the training data set.

Definition 6.3 Overfit

A decision tree T is said to overfit the training data if there exists some other tree T' which is a simplification of T, such that T has smaller error than T' over the training set but T' has smaller error than T over the entire distribution of instances.

Overfitting can lead to difficulties when there is noise in the training data, or when the number of training examples is too small. Specifically, if there is no conflicting instances in the training data set, the error of the fully built tree is zero, while the true error is likely to be bigger. There are many disadvantages of an overfitted decision tree:

a. Overfitted models are incorrect.
b. Overfitted decision trees require more space and more computational resources.
c. Overfitted models require the collection of unnecessary features.
d. They are more difficult to comprehend.

The pruning phase helps in handling the overfitting problem. The decision tree is pruned back by removing the subtree rooted at a node and replacing it by a leaf node, using some criterion. Several pruning algorithms are reported in literature. We shall discuss these algorithms in the latter part of this chapter.

Attribute Selection Error

Most of the decision tree algorithms exhibit a systematic, unwarranted preference for certain types of variables. Some decision tree algorithms are far more likely to construct models that use discrete variables with many values, than discrete variables with relatively few values. This behaviour occurs even though models that use the latter variables have a consistently higher score when tested on a new data set. For example, in a data set, between two attributes, say a state of domicile and gender, the former which has a larger number of distinct values is preferred over the latter. This behaviour of the algorithm is not desirable.

6.4 Best Split

We have noticed that there are several alternatives to choose from for the splitting attribute and the splitting criterion. But in order to build an optimal decision tree, it is necessary to select those corresponding to the best possible split. The main operations during the tree building are

1. evaluation of splits for each attribute and the selection of the best split; determination of the splitting attribute,
2. determination of the splitting condition on the selected splitting attribute, and
3. partitioning the data using the best split.

The complexity lies in determining the best split for each attribute. The splitting also depends on the domain of the attribute being numerical or categorical. The generic algorithm for the construction of decision trees assumes that the method to decide the splitting attribute at a node and the splitting criteria are known. The desirable feature of splitting is that it should do the best job of splitting at the given stage.

The first task is to decide which of the independent attributes makes the best splitter. The best split is defined as one that does the best job of separating the records into groups, where a single class predominates. To choose the best splitter at a node, we consider each independent attribute in turn.

Assuming that an attribute takes on multiple values, we sort it and then, using some evaluation function as the measure of goodness, evaluate each split. We compare the effectiveness of the split provided by the best splitter from each attribute. The winner is chosen as the splitter for the root node. How does one know which split is better than the other? We shall discuss below two different evaluation functions to determine the splitting attributes and the splitting criteria.

6.5 Splitting Indices

In this section, we shall study two different methods of determining the goodness of a split. One index is based on information theory, that is, information gain based on entropy. The other one is derived from economics as measure of diversity. This is called the gini index.

ENTROPY

Entropy provides an information-theoretic approach to measure the goodness of a split. Assume that there are n equally probable possible messages. The probability p of each is $1/n$ and hence, the information conveyed by a message is $-\log_2(p) = \log_2(n)$. If there are 16 messages, then since $\log(16) = 4$, we need 4 bits to identify each message. Henceforth, let us assume that all logarithms are in base 2.

DEFINITION 6.4 ENTROPY

If we are given a probability distribution $P = (p_1, p_2, ..., p_n)$, then the information conveyed by this distribution, also called the entropy of P, is

$$\textbf{Entropy}(\boldsymbol{P}) = -[p_1 \log(p_1) + p_2 \log(p_2) + \ldots + p_n \log(p_n)].$$

For example, if P is (0.5, 0.5), then Entropy(P) is 1; if P is (0.67, 0.33), then Entropy(P) is 0.92; if P is (1, 0), then Entropy(P) is 0. Note that the more uniform the probability distribution, the greater its information.

In the context of decision trees, if the outcome of a node is to classify the records into two classes, C_1 and C_2, the outcome can be viewed as a message that is being generated and entropy gives the measure of information for the message to be C_1 or C_2. If a set of records T is partitioned into a set of disjoint exhaustive classes $C_1, C_2, \ldots, C_n$ on the basis of the value of the class attribute, then the information needed to identify the class of an element of T is

$$\text{Info}(T) = \text{Entropy}(P),$$

where P is the probability distribution of the partition $C_1, C_2, \ldots, C_n$. P is computed based on their relative frequencies, ie.,

$$P = \left(\frac{|C_1|}{|T|}, \frac{|C_2|}{|T|}, \ldots, \frac{|C_n|}{|T|} \right).$$

Suppose a data set has three distinct classes: C_1, C_2 and C_3. In other words, the class attribute has a domain consisting of $\{C_1, C_2, C_3\}$ and each category has 40, 30, 30 data, respectively. We summarise this in Table 6.4.

Table 6.4

T	C1	C2	C3
100	40	30	30

The value of entropy of the whole data set is

$$Info(T) = -\frac{40}{100}\log\frac{40}{100} - \frac{30}{100}\log\frac{30}{100} - \frac{30}{100}\log\frac{30}{100} = 1.09$$

DEFINITION 6.5 INFORMATION FOR A PARTITION ON X

If T is partitioned based on the value of the non-class attribute X, into sets $T_1, T_2, \ldots, T_n$, then the information needed to identify the class of an element of T becomes the weighted average of the information to identify the class of the element of T_i, i.e:, the weighted average of $Info(T_i)$

$$Info\ (X, T) = \sum_{i=1}^{n} \frac{|T_1|}{|T|} Info\ (T_i).$$

Let us consider splitting the data set into two subsets, S_1 and S_2, with n_1 and n_2 data, respectively, where $n_1 + n_2 = n$. If we assume $n_1 = 60$ and $n_2 = 40$, the splitting is as follows (Table 6.5):

Table 6.5a

S2	C1	C2	C3
40	0	20	20

Table 6.5b

S1	C1	C2	C3
60	40	10	10

The entropy index value of the data set after the segmentation is

$$\frac{40}{100}\left(-\frac{20}{40}\log\frac{20}{40}-\frac{20}{40}\log\frac{20}{40}\right)+\frac{60}{100}\left(-\frac{40}{60}\log\frac{40}{60}-\frac{10}{60}\log\frac{10}{60}\log\frac{10}{60}\log\frac{10}{60}\right)=0.80$$

DEFINITION 6.6 GAIN

We define the information gain due to a split on attribute X as

$$Gain(X, T) = Info(T) - Info(X, T).$$

The information gain represents the difference between the information needed to identify an element of T and the information needed to identify an element of T after the value of attribute X is obtained. That is, the information gain due to attribute X.

In the above example, splitting decreases the value of entropy by 0.29. In other words, the gain is 0.29.

Let us consider another splitting as given in Table 6.6.

Table 6.6a

S1	C1	C2	C3
60	20	20	20

Table 6.6b

S2	C1	C2	C3
40	20	10	10

In this case, the value of the associated entropy is 1.075 and the gain is 0.015. Thus, we can use this notion of gain to rank attributes and to build decision trees where, at each node, the attribute with the greatest gain becomes the splitting attribute.

Example 6.3

In our earlier example on playing, we had

$$Info\ (T) = Entropy\left(\frac{9}{14}, \frac{5}{14}\right) = -\frac{9}{14}\log\frac{9}{14} - \frac{5}{14}\log\frac{5}{14} = 0.94$$

Consider the attribute *outlook*. It has three distinct values—sunny, overcast and rain, with 5, 4 and 5 records, respectively. Among the 5 records which have *outlook* = *sunny*, 2 records are in the *play* class and 3 are in the *no play* class. Thus, these five records have a distribution (3/5, 2/5). Similarly, the distributions for *overcast* and *rain* are (1, 0) and (3/5, 2/5), respectively.

$$\begin{aligned} Info\ (outlook, T) &= \sum_{i=1}^{3} \frac{|T_1|}{|T|}\ Info\ (T_1) \\ &= \frac{5}{14}\ Info\left(\frac{3}{5}, \frac{2}{5}\right) + \frac{4}{14} Info\ (1,0) + \frac{5}{14}\ Info\left(\frac{3}{5}, \frac{2}{5}\right) \\ &= \frac{5}{14}\left(-\frac{3}{5}\log\frac{3}{5} - \frac{2}{5}\log\frac{2}{5}\right) + \frac{5}{14}\left(-\frac{3}{5}\log\frac{3}{5} - \frac{2}{5}\log\frac{2}{5}\right) \\ &= 0.694 \end{aligned}$$

Thus,

$$\text{Gain (outlook, } T) = \text{Info}(T) - \text{Info(outlook, } T) = 0.94 - 0.694 = 0.246.$$

Let us consider the attribute *humidity*. If we take all the distinct numeric values of this attribute, there are nine values – 65, 70, 75, 78, 80, 85, 90, 95 and 96 – with frequencies 1, 3, 1, 1, 3, 1, 2, 1 and 1, respectively.

Thus

$$\begin{aligned} Info\ (humidity, T) = &\frac{3}{14}\left(-\frac{2}{3}\log\frac{2}{3} - \frac{1}{3}\log\frac{1}{3}\right) + \frac{3}{14}\left(-\frac{2}{3}\log\frac{2}{3} - \frac{1}{3}\log\frac{1}{3}\right) \\ &+ \frac{2}{14}\left(-\frac{1}{2}\log\frac{1}{2} - \frac{1}{2}\log\frac{1}{2}\right) = 0.5364. \end{aligned}$$

$$Gain\ (humidity, T) = Info\ (T) - Info\ (humidity, T) = 0.94 - 0.5364 = 0.4036.$$

So, the gain due to selecting *humidity* as the splitting attribute is high. But the number of branches are many—one branch for each distinct value; this is not practical (Note: this may lead to overfitting too). Let us assume that we categorise these values into two sets, *high* and *low*, such that the value exceeding 75 is said to be of high humidity or else, it is of low humidity. There are nine records with high humidity, of which four are in the *no play* class and five are in the *play* class. Similarly, out of the five records of low humidity, one is in the *no play* class and the remaining four are in the *play* class. In such a situation, the gain is calculated as folows:

$$Info\ (humidity, T) = \frac{9}{14}\left(-\frac{4}{9}\log\frac{4}{9} - \frac{5}{9}\log\frac{5}{9}\right) + \frac{5}{14}\left(-\frac{4}{5}\log\frac{4}{5} - \frac{1}{5}\log\frac{1}{5}\right) = 0.8435.$$

Hence, the gain is 0.0965.

For the attribute *windy*, we have the following expression

$$Info\ (windy,\ T) = \frac{6}{14}\left(-\frac{3}{6}\log\frac{3}{6}-\frac{3}{6}\log\frac{3}{6}\right)+\frac{8}{14}\left(-\frac{6}{8}\log\frac{6}{8}-\frac{2}{8}\log\frac{2}{8}\right) = 0.892.$$

Thus, the gain is 0.082.

For the attribute *temperature*, we have

$$Info\ (temp,\ T) = \frac{8}{14}\left(-\frac{5}{8}\log\frac{5}{8}-\frac{3}{8}\log\frac{3}{8}\right)+\frac{6}{14}\left(-\frac{4}{6}\log\frac{4}{6}-\frac{2}{6}\log\frac{2}{6}\right) = 0.939.$$

Thus, the gain is 0.001.

Splitting on *outlook* provides the maximum gain. The root node is expanded with three child nodes, one for each value of *outlook*. The data set is also partitioned into three subsets—one subset is associated with each child node. The algorithm proceeds recursively till the termination criterion is met.

Gain Ratio

The notion of gain, introduced earlier, tends to favour attributes that have a large number of values. For example, if we have an attribute X that has a distinct value for each record, then *Info*(X,T) is 0, thus *Gain*(X, T) is maximal. We noticed this for *humidity* above. To compensate for this, Quinlan suggests using the following gain ratio instead of gain.

Definition 6.6 Gain Ratio

$$Gain\_ratio\ (X,\ T) = \frac{Gain\ (X,\ T)}{Info\ (X,\ T)}$$

For example,

$$Gain\_ratio\ (outlook,\ T) = \frac{Gain(outlook,\ T)}{Info\ (outlook,\ T)} = \frac{0.246}{0.694} = 0.3544$$

Gini Index

One of the goodness measures can be related to the measure of diversity. There are several ways of calculating the index of diversity for a set of records. With all of them, a high index of diversity indicates that the set contains an even distribution of classes; while a low index means that members of a single class predominate. The best splitter is the one that decreases the diversity of the record sets by the greatest amount, in other words, we want to maximise diversity(before split) – (diversity(left child) + diversity(right child)).

The gini index is a diversity measure from economics. It can also be used to evaluate the goodness of a split.

DEFINITION 6.7 GINI INDEX

If a data set T contains n classes, then *gini(T)* is defned as

$$gini\ (T) = 1 - \Sigma\, p_i^2.$$

where p_j is the relative frequency of class j in T. If the split divides T into T_1 and T_2 , then the index of the divided data is given as

$$gini_{split}\ (T) = \frac{n_1}{n}\, gini\ (T_1) + \frac{n_2}{n} gini\ (T_2)$$

In the above example,

$$gini(T) = 1 - \left[\frac{9}{14}\right]^2 - \left[\frac{5}{14}\right]^2 = 0.46$$

Thus, the gini index due to splitting on *outook* is

$$gini_{outlook}(T) = \frac{5}{14}\left[1 - \left[\frac{3}{5}\right]^2 - \left[\frac{2}{5}\right]^2\right] + \frac{4}{14}\,[1-1] + \frac{5}{14}\left[1 - \left[\frac{3}{5}\right]^2 - \left[\frac{2}{5}\right]^2\right] = 0.343$$

The best splitter is determined as the attribute which has the smallest gini value.

6.6 SPLITTING CRITERIA

While determining the splitting attribute, we should keep in mind the splitting criterion too. For instance, some algorithms generate only binary decision trees. In other words, these algorithms carry out only binary splits. If the domain of the splitting attribute is binary this does not pose any problem, as the attribute itself takes two distinct values only. But, on the other hand, if the attribute that is selected for splitting takes more than two values, or takes continuous values, or is a categorical attribute, a binary split necessarily implies that we must determine the splitting criterion. Please note that the choice of the splitting criterion cannot be a different process from that of determining splitting attributes. It is a part of the latter, as the gain index is calculated after we know the resulting partition of the data set. For a non-binary split, most algorithms partition the data set for all distinct values. However, some algorithms (mostly the AID families of algorithms) have variable split size. We shall discuss below some strategies for binary splits for numerical and categorical attributes.

BINARY SPLITS FOR NUMERICAL ATTRIBUTES

The numerical attributes are split by the binary split of the form $A \leq v$, where v is a real number. All the numerical attributes are sorted on the values of the attribute being considered for splitting. Let $A_1, A_2, \ldots, A_n$ be the sorted values of a numerical attribute A. Since any value between A_i and A_{i+1} divides the data into two subsets, we need to examine only $n-1$ possible splits. The midpoint of A_i and A_{i+1} is taken as the split point. Thus, while computing the splitting index (gain or gini index), we take into account these candidate split points and determine the split points corresponding to the best split.

CLASS HISTOGRAM

We have noted in the foregoing discussion that in order to compute the splitting indices, whether it is entropy-based gain or gini index, we need the frequency distribution of class values for the attribute under consideration. This distribution is represented as a *class histogram*.

DEFINITION 6.8 CLASS HISTOGRAM

Let the training data set be T with class labels $\{C_1, C_2, \ldots, C_k\}$. If T is partitioned based on the value of the non-class attribute X into sets $T_1, T_2, \ldots, T_n$, then the class histogram for the partition is a table of k columns and n rows. The (i, j)-th entry indicates the number of records in the data set in the partition T_i and class C_j.

For a numerical attribute A, let us assume that we want to compute the splitting index for the possible split $A \leq v$. Then, the class histogram is a table of two rows and k columns, where k is the number of classes. The first row represents the frequency distribution of the set of records satisfying $A \leq v$. The second row represents the frequency distribution for each class, for those records which do not satisfy the condition.

EXAMPLE 6.3

Consider the following data (Table 6.7) and the class histogram (Table 6.8) for the attribute 'Salary', when the possible splitting criterion is Salary ≤ 70. We can see that out of four records satisfying this condition, there are two records in class '*B*' and two in class '*G*'. This is indicated in first row as 'left', denoting the left child node of the current node. Similarly, the right child node corresponds to the second row of the table.

Table 6.7 Training data set

	Age	Salary	Class
1	30	65	G
2	23	15	B
3	40	75	G
4	55	40	B
5	55	100	G
6	45	60	G

Table 6.8 Class histogram for *salary* with splitting criterion 'Salary ≤ 70'.

SALARY ≤ 70	B	G
left	2	2
right	0	2

Please note that the class histogram contains all the information for the computation of the splitting index. For the following generic histogram, the gini index is given below.

	C1	C2
L	$a1$	$a2$
R	$b1$	$b2$

$$gini = \frac{(a1 + a2)}{n}\left[1 - \left(\frac{a1}{a1+a2}\right)^2 - \left(\frac{a2}{a1+a2}\right)^2\right] + \frac{(b1 + b2)}{n}\left[1 - \left(\frac{b1}{b1+b2}\right)^2 - \left(\frac{b2}{b1+b2}\right)^2\right]$$

This concept can be generalised for cases where the split is non-binary. In such cases, the number of rows is equal to the number of partitions. Hence, one can also define a class histogram for a categorical attribute[1].

Binary Splits for Categorical Attributes

The splitting point for categorical attributes is different. Since we cannot have any ordering of the values of a categorical attribute, there cannot be a value n such that it splits the attribute into two. If $S(A)$ is the set of possible values of the categorical attribute A, then the split test is of the form $A \in S'$ where $S' \subset S$. For an attribute with n values, there are 2^n possible splits. If n is small, the split index value is found for all the possible combinations and the best split is taken. If n is large, then the split is made by some heuristics and the best split among them is found. The construction of an attribute list is similar to that of numerical attributes. But instead of having a class histogram, a count matrix is maintained for the categorical attribute.

Definition 6.9 Count Matrix

The count matrix has n rows (for n distinct values of the attribute) and k columns (for k classes). Each entry, say (i, j)-entry, represents the number of records in the data set having i^{th} value of the attribute and in the jth class.

Note that the count matrix is independent of any partition, whereas the class histogram is specific to a partition. Different splitting criteria result in different class histograms.

[1] When such a table is constructed for all distinct values of an attribute, it is called the Count Matrix. This is useful in the context of categorical attributes.

EXAMPLE 6.4

Table 6.10 illustrates the count matrix for the data given in Table 6.9.

Table 6.9 Attribute list for a categorical attribute

	Class	record_id
family	high	1
sports	high	2
sports	high	3
family	low	4
truck	low	5
family	high	6

Table 6.10 Count matrix

	H	L
family	2	1
sports	2	0
truck	0	1

The count matrix contains all the information necessary for determining the splitting index.

For example, if we select $S' = \{\text{family, truck}\}$ as the possible splitting subset, then the gini index is given by

$$gini_S\,(T) = \frac{4}{6}\left[1-\left(\frac{2}{4}\right)^2-\left(\frac{2}{4}\right)^2\right]+\frac{2}{6}\left[1-\left(\frac{2}{2}\right)^2-\left(\frac{0}{2}\right)^2\right]=\frac{1}{3}.$$

Such a calculation is to be carried out for each subset of {family, truck, car} to determine the splitting criteria.

6.7 DECISION TREE CONSTRUCTION ALGORITHMS

A number of algorithms for inducing decision trees have been proposed over the years. These algorithms more or less follow the principles discussed above. However, they differ among themselves in the methods employed for selecting splitting attributes and splitting conditions. In the following few sections, we shall study some of the major methods of decision tree construction. We categorise these algorithms into two types. The first type is classical algorithms which handle only memory-resident data. Efficiency and scalability arc thc fundamental issues concerning the classification of data. The second category of algorithms described below can handle these efficiency and scalability issues. But they are, in a sense, derivatives of the first category. These algorithms remove the memory restrictions and are fast and scalable. They also present a unifying framework for decision tree classifiers, that separate the scalability aspects of the algorithm for constructing a decision tree from the central features that determine the quality of the tree. In this category, we shall study two exact algorithms, namely, SPRINT and RainForest. We shall also study some approximate algorithms like BOAT and CLOUDS.

6.8 CART

CART (**C**lassification **A**nd **R**egression **T**ree) is one of the popular methods of building decision trees in the machine learning community. CART builds a binary decision tree by splitting the records at each node, according to a function of a single attribute. CART uses the gini index for determining the best split. CART follows the above principle of constructing the decision tree. We outline the method for the sake of completeness.

The initial split produces two nodes, each of which we now attempt to split in the same manner as the root node. Once again, we examine all the input fields to find the candidate splitters. If no split can be found that significantly decreases the diversity of a given node, we label it as a leaf node. Eventually, only leaf nodes remain and we have grown the full decision tree. The full tree may generally not be the tree that does the best job of classifying a new set of records, because of overfitting.

At the end of the tree-growing process, every record of the training set has been assigned to some leaf of the full decision tree. Each leaf can now be assigned a class and an error rate. The error rate of a leaf node is the percentage of incorrect classification at that node. The error rate of an entire decision tree is a weighted sum of the error rates of all the leaves. Each leaf's contribution to the total is the error rate at that leaf multiplied by the probability that a record will end up there.

6.9 ID3

Quinlan introduced ID3, **I**terative **D**ichotomiser 3, for constructing decision trees from data. In ID3, each node corresponds to a splitting attribute and each arc is a possible value of that attribute. At each node, the splitting attribute is selected to be the most informative among the attributes not yet considered in the path from the root. Entropy is used to measure how informative a node is. This algorithm uses the criterion of information gain to determine the goodness of a split. The attribute with the greatest information gain is taken as the splitting attribute, and the data set is split for all distinct values of the attribute.

6.10 C4.5

C4.5 is an extension of ID3 that accounts for unavailable values, continuous attribute value ranges, pruning of decision trees and rule derivation. In building a decision tree, we can deal with training sets that have records with unknown attribute values by evaluating the gain, or the gain ratio, for an attribute by considering only those records where those attribute values are available. We can classify records that have unknown attribute values by estimating the probability of the various possible results. Unlike CART, which generates a binary decision tree,

C4.5 produces trees with variable branches per node. When a discrete variable is chosen as the splitting attribute in C4.5, there will be one branch for each value of the attribute.

6.11 CHAID

CHAID, proposed by Kass in 1980, is a derivative of AID (**A**utomatic **I**nteraction **D**etection), proposed by Hartigan in 1975. CHAID attempts to stop growing the tree before overfitting occurs, whereas the above algorithms generate a fully grown tree and then carry out pruning as a post-processing step. In that sense, CHAID avoids the pruning phase.

In the standard manner, the decision tree is constructed by partitioning the data set into two or more subsets, based on the values of one of the non-class attributes. After the data set is partitioned according to the chosen attributes, each subset is considered for further partitioning using the same algorithm. Each subset is partitioned without regard to any other subset. This process is repeated for each subset until some stopping criterion is met. In CHAID, the number of subsets in a partition can range from two up to the number of distinct values of the splitting attribute. In this regard, CHAID differs from CART, which always forms binary splits, and from ID3 and C4.5, which form a branch for every distinct value.

The splitting attribute is chosen as the one that is most significantly associated with the dependent attributes according to a chi-squared test of independence in a contingency table (a cross-tabulation of the non-class and class attributes). The main stopping criterion used by such methods is the p-value from this chi-squared test. A small p-value indicates that the observed association between the splitting attribute and the dependent variable is unlikely to have occurred solely as the result of sampling variability.

If a splitting attribute has more than two possible values, then there may be a very large number of ways to partition the data set based on these values. A combinatorial search algorithm can be used to find a partition that has a small p-value for the chi-squared test. The p-values for each chi-squared test are adjusted for the multiplicity of partitions. Bonferroni adjustment is used for the p-values computed from the contingency tables, relating the predictors to the dependent variable. The adjustment is conditional on the number of branches (compound categories) in the partition, and thus does not take into account the fact that different numbers of branches are considered.

6.12 Summary

The above algorithms (mainly two) form the basis of all the decision tree constructions for data mining. We can use either entropy-based information gain or the gini index as the splitting index. We can use a binary split or a variable number of splits. The recent algorithms proposed specifically for data mining are based on the basic principles discussed above. However, the recent proposals are more suitable for very large databases. There are two different ways of handling large databases for the construction of decision trees.

One way is to construct the tree on a smaller subset of data. Quinlan proposed a 'windowing' technique. Others proposed sampling of the data set. We shall discuss this aspect later. The disadvantage of this process is that these approaches try to compromise on accuracy. The accuracy of the tree constructed from the whole training set is better than that of the tree constructed from a subset of the training set.

The second approach is to improve upon the construction method without any relaxation on the accuracy. It can seen that while determining the best split at every node, a major computational overhead is sorting. At every node, the values of each attribute are arranged in an order to determine the class histogram and the splitting index. For a large database, this is a very expensive method. The major question that comes to mind is: "Can we avoid this repeated sorting?". In the following section, we shall discuss a novel algorithm which avoids such repeated sorting.

6.13 Decision Tree Construction with Presorting

Researchers on the QUEST project at IBM (Rakesh Agrawal and team) proposed two algorithms: SLIQ (**S**upervised **L**earning **I**n **Q**uest) and SPRINT (**S**calable **P**arallelisable **I**nduction of Decision **T**ree**)** in sequel. The latter, SPRINT, is aimed at parallelizing the older one, SLIQ. However, SLIQ has very interesting and novel features. SLIQ imposes no restrictions on the amount of training data or the number of attributes in the examples. We shall now discuss the novel features proposed by SLIQ and SPRINT. The algorithm presented here is very close to SPRINT but is not exactly the same as the original proposal of SPRINT. The additional features of the original SPRINT that are different from the present algorithm are discussed in the next section.

SLIQ (and SPRINT) is a scalable algorithm, which uses a pre-sorting technique integrated with a breadth-first tree growing strategy for the classification of the disk-resident data. It builds a decision tree in a breadth-first manner and avoids repeated sorting at every step. The choice of the splitting criterion depends on the domain of the attribute being numeric or categorical.

Definition 6.10 Attribute List

Let the training data set be T with class labels $\{C_1, C_2, \ldots, C_k\}$, and let X be a non-class attribute of T. An attribute list of X with respect to T is a table with three columns. The columns corresponds to *attribute value, class label,* and *record_id (rid)* of the record of T from which these values are obtained. The number of rows in the attribute list is same as the number of tuples in T. If X is a numeric attribute, then the attribute list is sorted on the field *attribute value.*

Note that the attribute list is sorted by the attribute values only once, when it is first created. The attribute lists can be disk-resident, if necessary.

Definition 6.11 Record List

A record list is a table which has two columns: the first one contains the record id (*rid*), and the second one is the *node number* of the tree to which the record is currently allocated.

Recall that every node corresponds to a subset of the data set. In other words, the record list can at any time identify the partition to which a record belongs. Thus, during the construction, any record is allocated to a node—initially to the root. In this list, the rids appear in the same order as the records appear in the original data set. This structure is required to be randomly accessed and hence is memory-resident.

The concept is illustrated through the following examples.

EXAMPLE 6.5

Table 6.11 contains six records and three attributes. One extra column is introduced to show the record number. The attributes 'Age' and 'Salary' are non-class attributes. So, we have two attribute lists, one for each of these two attributes. Tables 6.12 show the attribute list corresponding to Age and Salary. Note that in an attribute list, the values are arranged in the sorted order of the values of the attribute. Table 6.13 shows the record list at the root.

Table 6.11 Another sample data set

rid	Age	Salary	Class
1	30	65	G
2	23	15	B
3	40	75	G
4	55	40	B
5	55	100	G
6	45	60	G

Table 6.12a Attribute list for age

Age	Class	rid
23	B	2
30	G	1
40	G	3
45	G	6
55	G	5
55	B	4

Table 6.12b Attribute list for salary

Salary	Class	rid
15	B	2
40	B	4
60	G	6
65	G	1
75	G	3
100	G	5

Table 6.13 Record list (at root)

rid	Leaf
1	N1
2	N1
3	N1
4	N1
5	N1
6	N1

The advantage of the attribute list structure is that it does not require repeated sorting. The initial lists created from the training data set are associated with the root node. As the tree grows, and the data sets are partitioned, the order of records in the attribute list is preserved. Thus, the new partitions at the child nodes do not require any further sorting. The major steps of determining the split are

- splitting index for each value of each attribute,
- determining the best split, and
- partitioning the data set of the current node and allocate to each child node.

Computation of Splitting Index

The gini index is used as the goodness measure. The attribute lists come in very handy to compute the class histogram. In fact, one needs to have just one pass over the attribute list for determining the splitting point of an attribute.

The splitting index of each value of a given attribute is computed by one pass over the attribute list. The attribute list is never partitioned at any stage as a result of the construction process, we have only one list per attribute to be scanned. The advantage is that we can make just one scan of an attribute list to evaluate the split index of this attribute throughout the tree (at each of the current leaf nodes of the tree). This is the motivation for expanding the tree in a breadth-first manner. The actual partitioning is recorded only in the record list which is memory resident. This record list is updated at every split.

For Numerical Attributes

For numeric attributes, the candidate split point is taken to be the midpoint of two consecutive distinct values. We read each tuple of the attribute list one by one. Initially, the class histogram has all the records in the second row, that is the 'right' row. All the entries in the 'left' row are 0. After reading each tuple, the histogram is updated for the new value of the attribute. Since the attribute list is sorted, the histogram for the next tuple can be updated using the previous values. Thus, the gini values for all the attribute lists can be computed in one pass and the best split point can be found. As the attribute list is not physically split, the process of computation of the gini index for intermediate nodes is only slightly different. This is because the root node corresponds to the whole data set, whereas the intermediate nodes represent only a subset of the data set. The tree is expanded in a breadth-first manner and hence, all the current-leaf nodes are processed at any stage. For each attribute, the corresponding attribute list is scanned once for the given level to evaluate the splitting indices for all the nodes at that level. We illustrate this process for our example given in Table 6.11.

At the Root Node

The histogram for 'Salary' is intialised as follows. This is before reading any tuple of the attribute list associated with 'Salary'. The gini index can also be calculated from this histogram.

Table 6.14

Salary <15	B	G
L	0	0
R	2	4

The histogram is updated after the first record of the attribute list is read. It is observed that the first record is in class 'B'. The splitting value is taken as 28, the midpoint of 15 and 40.

Table 6.15

Salary <28	B	G
L	1	0
R	1	4

The second tuple is read and it is also in class 'B' and thus, we get the updated histogram as follows. We give below the sequence of updates of the histogram.

Note that these tables carry adequate information to evaluate the splitting criteria for the salary attribute. This process is to be carried out for each of the attributes.

Table 6.16

a

Salary <50	B	G
L	2	0
R	0	4

b

Salary <63	B	G
L	2	1
R	0	3

c

Salary <70	B	G
L	2	2
R	0	2

d

Salary <88	B	G
L	2	3
R	0	1

At Any Intermediate Node

Let us assume that we are at the second level of the tree. The root node has been expanded with an initial split of *age* ≤ 35. Thus, the updated record list is as follows (Table 6.17). The records 1 and 2 are allocated to node N2 (left child node of the root node), and the remaining records are allocated to N3 (right child node).

In order to determine the splitting index for each value of the attribute 'Salary' for each of the nodes N2 and N3, we again make one more pass over the attribute list of 'Salary'. At this stage, we maintain two class histograms—one for each of the leaf nodes. Before reading the first tuple, the class histograms are initialised as follows (Table 6.18).

Table 6.17

rid	Leaf
1	N2
2	N2
3	N3
4	N3
5	N3
6	N3

Table 6.18 Class histograms for child nodes of N1 at the beginning

Salary < 15	B	G
L	0	0
R	1	1

Salary < 15	B	G
L	0	0
R	1	3

After reading the first tuple of the attribute list,

Table 6.19 Class histogram for child nodes of N1

Salary < 28	B	G
L	1	0
R	0	1

Salary < 28	B	G
L	0	0
R	1	3

After reading the second tuple of the attribute list,

Table 6.20

Salary < 50	B	G
L	1	0
R	0	1

Salary < 50	B	G
L	1	0
R	0	3

After reading the third record, we have

Table 6.21

Salary < 70	B	G
L	1	1
R	0	0

Salary < 70	B	G
L	1	1
R	0	2

When we read the fourth record, the new class histograms are

Table 6.22

Salary < 88	B	G
L	1	1
R	0	0

Salary < 88	B	G
L	1	2
R	0	1

After the fifth record, we have

Table 6.23

Salary < 88	B	G
L	1	1
R	0	0

Salary < 88	B	G
L	1	2
R	0	1

After reading the last tuple,

Table 6.24

Salary > 100	B	G
L	1	1
R	0	0

Salary > 100	B	G
L	1	3
R	0	0

For Categorical Attributes

The process of finding splitting criteria is different for categorical attributes. For numerical attributes, after every tuple of the attribute list is read, the histogram is updated. For categorical attributes, we make a complete scan through the attribute list collecting the counts in the histogram (it is called the *count matrix* for categorical attributes). Once we are finished with the scan, the count matrix is used to find the split points. If the number of distinct values is reasonably small, we consider all the subsets of attribute values as possible split points and compute the corresponding gini index. If there are n values, it amounts to checking 2^n possibilities. If n exceeds a threshold, a greedy algorithm can be used. In the greedy method, we start with an empty subset S' and add the element of S (domain of categorical attribute A) that gives the maximum decrease in the gini index. The process is repeated by adding one element at every step, until there is no reduction in the gini index.

Example 6.6

The example shown below (Table 6.25) indicates the histogram construction for the categorical attribute.

Table 6.25 Histogram for the categorical attribute

	Class	rid
family	high	1
sports	high	2
sports	high	3
family	low	4
truck	low	5
family	high	6

Table 6.26 Count matrix

	H	L
family	2	1
sports	2	0
truck	0	1

One way to calculate the splitting criteria is to check the gini index for all eight subsets of {family, sports, truck} and decide the splitting condition based on the minimum gini index. All the distinct values are taken with their class distributions. In the given example, all the possible combinations are [{family}, {sports,truck}], [{family, sports}, {truck}], [{family, truck}, {sports}]. If the set is very large, checking all subsets is not practical. In such a situation, we employ some sort of heuristics. One popular method is to use a greedy method for this purpose. We demonstrate the working of the greedy method for the above example.

Greedy Method to Determine the Splitting Point of Categorical Attributes

We begin with the empty subset, $S' = \emptyset$. Hence, the gini index is 2/3. We now check each element to see if adding any element to S' results in a decrease in the gini index and, if there are such elements, then to choose the element that decreases the index value to the maximum. Let us assume that $\text{gini}_{S'}(T)$ represents the gini index for the possible split with S'.

Thus, $\text{gini}_{\{\text{family}\}}(T) = 4/9$, $\text{gini}_{\{\text{sport}\}} = 1/3$ and $\text{gini}_{\{\text{truck}\}} = 4/15$. Thus, when S' is either {sport} or {truck}, the gini decreases. But the maximum decrease is due to {truck}. Thus, S' is updated as {truck}. In the next step, we compute $\text{gini}_{\{\text{truck, family}\}} = 1/3$ and $\text{gini}_{\{\text{truck, sport}\}} =$ 8/9. None of these results in a decrease in the gini index. Hence, the construction process stops here and the splitting criteria is based on $S' = \{\text{truck}\}$.

Updating the Record List

Once the best split is found, the next step is to partition the data, create the child nodes for each leaf node and update the record list. Recall that the record list depicts the allocations of records to nodes. Since at any split, nodes are expanded and data sets are partitioned, the records are allocated to newly-generated leaf nodes. This change should be incorporated in the record list. The algorithm for updating the class list is given below.

For each attribute A used in the split, traverse the attribute list of A. At each value n in the attribute list, using *rid* as the reference field, find the corresponding entry (node number) in the record list, (say e). Find the node number of a new child node, say f, to which n belongs, by applying the splitting test corresponding to node e. Update the record list, replacing e with f.

Example 6.5 (contd.)

Consider the example shown in Table 6.11. Let us suppose that the best split is found for *salary* ≤ 50. The salary attribute is traversed and the class list entries for the leaf, corresponding to the class list indexes for *salary* ≤ 50, are updated. Here, the class list indexes for *salary* ≤ 50 are 2 and 4 and so the leaf node of the record list corresponding to the entries 2 and 4 are updated to the new leaf node N2 and the other entries of the leaf are updated to N3. The above two steps of splitting the nodes and updating the leaf nodes are repeated until each leaf node contains records belonging to the same class and thus, no further splits are needed.

Table 6.27 Updating the class list

rid	Leaf
1	N3
2	N2
3	N3
4	N2
5	N3
6	N2

SPRINT

SPRINT is the updated version of SLIQ and is meant for parallel implementation. In SPRINT, the attribute list is partitioned at each split, whereas in SLIQ, a single attribute list is maintained for an attribute. Once the split point is found, the split is done by creating the child nodes and partitioning the attribute records between the child nodes. The attribute lists for all the attributes are split at each node among the child nodes. Splitting the winning attribute, i.e., the attribute list that has the split point, is straightforward. All the attribute records above the split point are moved to the left child node, while the other records are moved to the right child node. For the other attribute lists, we use the 'rid' field of the attribute list. While splitting the winning attribute, the record list is referred to note the child node to which the record is allocated. SPRINT, instead of maintaining a record list, keeps this information in a hash table.

Please remember that the basic principle of SLIQ and SPRINT is independent of the evaluation function. One can use the entropy-based method also. The basic idea of the above algorithm is to avoid repeated sorting, by maintaining an attribute list for each attribute. This principle works well, irrespective of which splitting index is used. We can replace the computation of the gini index by an entropy-based information gain. As long as the splitting index can be computed from the class histogram, the main steps of the algorithm remain unchanged.

6.14 RainForest

RainForest, like other algorithms, is a top-down decision tree induction scheme. It is similar to SPRINT, but instead of attribute lists it uses a different structure called the AVC-set. The attribute list has one tuple corresponding to each record of the training data set. But the AVC-set has one entry for each distinct value of an attribute. Thus, the size of the AVC-set for any attribute is much smaller.

Definition 6.12 AVC-set

The AVC *(Attribute **V**alue, **C**lass)*-set of a non-class attribute X at a node *n* is defined as a set of distinct values of X in the records allocated to the node *n* and the class label, whereby the individual class labels are aggregated.

The *AVC-group* of a node *n* is defined as the set of all AVC-sets for all attributes at node *n*.

The size of the AVC-set of an attribute depends only on the number of distinct attribute values of X and the number of class labels at node *n*. It is observed that for most real-life data sets, the whole AVC-group of the root node fits into the main memory. If not, at least the AVC-set of each attribute fits into main memory. The AVC-set contains the aggregated information that is sufficient for decision tree construction. The RainForest algorithm proceeds in the same way as SPRINT.

There are different versions of the RainForest algorithm. Depending on the amount of main memory available, three cases can be distinguished.

THE AVC-GROUP OF THE ROOT NODE FITS INTO MAIN MEMORY

This version of RainForest is called RF-Write. This algorithm assumes that the AVC-group of the root node fits into main memory. The database is scanned and the AVC-group of the root node is constructed. The standard classification algorithm is applied and the split point is found. The database is scanned and each tuple is written to one of the child nodes, based on the split point. The algorithm then recurses in turn on each of the partitions, till all the class labels in a partition belong to the same class. For each level of the tree, the entire database is read twice and written once.

THE AVC-SET FITS INTO MAIN MEMORY

Each individual AVC-set of the root node fits into main memory, but the AVC-group of the root node does not fit into main memory. It is called the *RF-Read* version. This algorithm reads the original database instead of writing the partitions for the child nodes. When the AVC-group of the child nodes does not fit into memory, the database is read many times to construct the AVC-groups for an unexamined subset of the new nodes in the tree.

THE INDIVIDUAL AVC-SETS ARE TOO LARGE

This method is called *RF-Hybrid.* The method proceeds like RF-Read, whenever a level of the tree L has all the AVC-groups fitting into main memory. At a particular level, when the main memory is not sufficient, it switches to RF-Write.

6.15 APPROXIMATE METHODS

Another way of handling a large database for the construction of a decision tree is to adopt an approximate method, contrary to the above methods which are exact methods. There are two different approaches for devising approximate constructions of decision trees. These are: (a) Discretisation and (b) Sampling. Discretisation reduces the size of the database by grouping the attribute values to a smaller set. Sampling selects a subset of the training data set and thus operates on a smaller data set. Since the original training data set is tampered with in any of these processes, accuracy is the most important measure of efficiency for these algorithms.

WINDOWING

The *windowing* technique is useful to construct decision trees on very large data sets. A subset of the training set, called *window*, is chosen at random and a decision tree is constructed using only this window. All other records in the training data set are subjected to classification using this tree. If the tree gives the correct classification for the entire training data set, the process terminates. If not, a selection of the incorrectly classified objects is added to the window, and the process continues.

ATTRIBUTE-ORIENTED INDUCTION

Attribute-oriented induction is another way of discretisation. The training data set is compressed with a *concept tree ascension* technique, which is similar to moving up in the dimension hierarchy (discussed in Chapter 2). By this technique, the individual attribute values are replaced by some generalised value provided in the higher level of the concept tree. For example, rather than having individual readings of humidity measures, we can have just high and low humidity. The concepts 'high' and 'low' are higher in the level in the concept tree than 75%, 35%, etc. In this process, the data set contains generalised tuples, and each generalised tuple has a count associated with it. The count corresponds to the number of tuples in the original data set that a generalised tuple represents. In addition to substantially reducing the size of the training set, attribute-oriented induction allows the rules to be comprehensible. The concept hierarchy is generally obtained from the individual application domain. For numerical attributes, such hierarchy can also be generated automatically from the data. It is worthwhile to work out the method of maintaining a class histogram in such cases.

ATTRIBUTE REMOVAL

Attribute-oriented induction can also be useful for removing some attributes from the set of candidate splitting attributes. If an attribute has a large number of distinct values and there is no higher concept for it, then the attribute can be ignored for decision tree construction.

Another technique of attribute removal can be based on *relevance analysis*. The information theoretic measure for relevance is the uncertainty coefficient. One can retain only the top *h* most relevant attribute or retain only those attributes whose relevance exceed a specified threshold. The uncertainty coefficient is defined as follows.

DEFINITION 6.13 UNCERTAINTY COEFFICIENT

The *uncertainty coefficient* for an attribute X is gven by

$$UC(X) = \frac{gain\ (X,T)}{Info\ (T)}$$

6.16 CLOUDS

CLOUDS (Classification of Large or Out-of-core Data Sets) is a kind of approximate version of the SPRINT method. It also uses a breadth-first strategy to build the decision tree. CLOUDS uses the gini index for evaluating the split index of the attributes. There are different criteria for splitting the categorical and numerical attributes. The method of finding the gini index for the categorical attributes is the same as that used in the SPRINT algorithm. Categorical attributes do not require any sorting, but they refer to the count matrix. We discuss the steps in which CLOUDS differs from the SPRINT method.

Coarse Splitting Points for Numeric Attributes

A random sample S of size s is drawn from the data set. This requires one read operation of the whole data set, only at the root level. The sample S is used to divide the values of any attribute into q intervals by regular sampling. This corresponds to q regularly-spaced quantiles of the set S. The range of ith interval is $[z_{i-1}, z_i)$; z_0 and z_q are the minimum and the maximum values of the attribute in S. We construct the class histogram for these intervals (note that it differs from the earlier method, where we store the class frequency with respect to each value of the attribute). In order to generate the class frequency for any attribute with respect to these intervals, we need to have an additional database pass. For each value of an attribute in class i, determine the corresponding interval using the binary search and update the class frequency of class i.

At this stage, the gini index is evaluated at each interval boundary and the minimum value of the gini index among all the intervals and across all the numeric attributes is found, which is given by $gini_{min}$. This is taken as a measure of the splitting criterion for numerical attributes. The split point with the $gini_{min}$ is used as the splitter.

The splitting criterion is applied to each record of S to determine its partition, i.e., left or right. For the node i at level l of the tree, set S is partitioned, using the splitting criteria, into two samples S_1 and S_2. The sample sets S_1 and S_2 are used for the left and right subtrees of node i, respectively. The class frequencies for the interval boundaries are updated while reading the data for splitting a given node. The frequency vectors corresponding to S_1 and S_2 are updated, which avoids a separate pass over the entire data to evaluate these frequencies.

Sampling the Splitting Points with Estimation

By an additional process, **S**ampling the **S**plitting **P**oints with **E**stimation (SSE), CLOUDS improves upon the above process and searches in certain selected intervals for the exact splitting point. In the above method, the split point is a coarse estimation in the sense that the splitter is necessarily one of interval boundaries and not one of the data points. The SSE phase proceeds further from this step and examines the individual data points within the intervals. Since the number of intervals can be many, it is not practical to search the details within every interval. The SSE attempts to eliminate some of the intervals, which may not contain the actual splitter and narrows its search to only some candidate intervals to determine the exact splitter. This is accomplished by estimating the gini value for an interval. It uses a heuristic for computing an estimate. It also makes use of some characteristics of the gini function.

- The value of the gini index along a given attribute generally increases or decreases slowly. The number of good local minima is small compared to the size of the entire data set. This is especially true for attributes along which the best splitting point is obtained.
- The minimum value of the gini index for the splitting point along the splitting attribute is significantly lower than most of the other points along the splitting attribute, as well as other attributes.

CLOUDS with SSE divides the range of the numeric attributes and finds the minimum gini value ($gini_{min}$) as described above. Further, it estimates a lower bound $gini^{est}$ of the gini value for each interval. All the intervals with $gini^{est} \geq gini_{min}$ are eliminated to derive a list of potential candidate intervals (*alive* intervals). An *alive interval* is an interval for which $gini^{est} < gini_{min}$. For an *alive* interval along each numeric attribute, the class frequencies for the intervals are computed and the gini index is evaluated at each point in the interval to find the splitter. This requires reading the entire data set corresponding to the internal node and storing the points that belong to *alive* intervals. If all the *alive* intervals do not fit into the memory, they are written onto the disk. Another pass is required to read these *alive* intervals one at a time. If the survival ratio is small, and all the alive intervals can fit into the memory, the extra pass is not required.

COMPUTATION OF ESTIMATE GINI^{EST}

We describe below the algorithm to compute the $gini^{est}$. The algorithm is a hill-climbing heuristic, and begins with an initial estimate of 1. For a given interval, it finds the gradient of the gini value with respect to each class. After determining the class corresponding to the minimum gradient, the set of data points that are within the interval are assumed to be shifted to the left of the interval and the gini index is computed for this change. This is repeated for each of the classes as long as the estimate monotonically decreases. The method stops at a step when the estimate is not reduced. In a similar manner, we can shift the data points to the right of the interval and get another estimate. The smaller of the two is taken as the final estimate. The algorithm is illustrated with the help of the above example.

The estimate computed for the given interval is $[z_{i-1}, z_i)$. Assume that if z_{i-1} is considered as the splitting point, it splits n data points into two groups n_1 (to the left) and n_2 (to the right of the point). From n_1 data elements there are $p_{(i-1)j}$ in class C_j, similarly, from n_2 data elements there are $q_{(i-1)j}$ in class C_j. To determine the gradient of the gini with respect to a given class and selecting the class corresponding to the smallest gradient, we compute

$$d_j = \frac{2}{n_1 n_2}\left[(p_{(i-1)j} + q_{(i-1)j})\right]\frac{n_1}{n} - p(i-1)j$$

The algorithm to compute the estimate is described below.

Estimate_Left_to_right Algorithm

C be the initial list of set of classes
set $gini^{est} = 1$;
do for every class j until C is empty
  Let C_j be the class with smallest value d_j.
  delete C_j from C.
  compute the gini index with z_{i-1} as the splitting point but replacing $p_{(i-1)j}$ by p_{ij}. (that is assuming that there are p_{ij} data elements of jth class to the left of the split.)
  If the new gini index is less than the $gini^{est}$
  then update the estimate.
end do.

Let us consider the attribute 'Age' for illustration; the intervals are [23, 39) and [39, 55); calculate the estimate at 39 (left to right). There are two classes, B and G

$$d_B = -1/12 \quad \text{and} \quad d_G = 1/12.$$

Though there is one point to the left of 39 of class B, we consider it as if there are two data elements to its left and compute the gini index. We get the gini index as 3/24. Since it is less than the initial value 1, the gini^{est} is updated as 3/24. The next class is G, but the new gini index is not less than the current estimate and hence the method returns 3/24 as the left-to-right estimate.

The performance of the SSE method depends on the quality of the estimated lower bound of the gini index and on the fraction of the elements in the *alive* intervals, that is, the survival ratio. Since the gini index is calculated for each of the splitting points in these intervals, the computational cost is proportional to the survival ratio.

6.17 BOAT

BOAT (**B**ootstrap **O**ptimistic **A**lgorithm for **T**ree Construction) is another approximate algorithm based on sampling. As the name suggests, it is based on a well-known statistical principle called *bootstrapping*.

We take a very large sample D from the training data set T, so that D fits into the main memory. Now, using the bootstrapping technique, we take many small samples with replacement of D as D_1, D_2, ..., D_k and construct, by any of the known methods, decision trees DT_1, DT_2, ..., DT_k, respectively, for each of these samples. From these trees, called *bootstrap trees*, we construct a single decision tree for the sample data set D. We call this the sample tree. The sample tree is a coarse decision tree in the sense that the splitting conditions at any node is not of the form $A \leq n$ but is specified in the form of a confidence interval $[z_L, z_R]$, and the exact split point n lies in this interval. After constructing the sample tree, there is a separate process, a clean-up process, when the exact value of n is determined within the confidence interval.

Construction of Sample Tree

We assume that by some standard construction method, k bootstrap trees DT_1, DT_2, ..., DT_k are constructed from the training samples D_1, D_2, ..., D_k, respectively. In order to construct the sample tree, we process these trees in a top-down manner. For each node n, we check whether the k bootstrap splitting attributes at n are identical. If the splitting attribute is not the same for all the k bootstrap trees, then we delet node n and its subtree in all bootstrap trees.

If we have the same splitting attribute for all bootstrap trees at node n, and if the attribute is a categorical one, then we check whether the splitting criteria is the same for all the bootstrap trees. If not, we delete node n and its subtree from all trees. We assume the splitting attribute for the sample tree to be the bootstrap splitting attribute, and the splitting criterion of the sample tree as the bootstrap splitting criterion.

If the bootstrap splitting attribute at node n is numerical, we consider all the k bootstrap splitting points to define a confidence interval $[z_L, z_R]$. This confidence interval becomes the coarse splitting criterion for the sample tree. The exact splitting point is assumed to lie within this confidence interval. The method of computing the exact splitting point is described below.

Computation of Exact Splitting Criteria

We assume that the sample tree is available with coarse splitting conditions for each of the numerical attributes. The algorithm is based on the assumption that the bootstrapping technique results in correct coarse splitting conditions. That is, the exact splitting point lies within the confidence interval so computed, with high probability. We make one scan over the database to determine the class histogram for the portion of the original training set that lies within the confidence intervals. Then, the splitting indices are computed at each distinct value of the attributes within the confidence interval. This process can be achieved in just one pass for the whole tree.

The confidence interval can be strengthened by constructing a larger number of bootstrap trees. For certain data sets, if the original sample D is not a proper representative, the sample tree may be very small. This is because we may be deleting the portions of the tree which are not in consensus with all bootstrap trees. It may happen that we delete a major portion of the bootstrap trees. In such cases, we should take one more sample D and start constructing afresh.

6.18 Pruning Technique

The decision tree built using the training set deals correctly with most of the records in the training set. This is inherent to the way it was built. Overfitting is one of unavoidable situations that may arise due to such construction. Moreover, if the tree becomes very deep, lopsided or bushy, the rules yielding from the trees become unmanageable and difficult to comprehend. Therefore, a pruning phase is invoked after the construction to arrive at a (sort of) optimal decision tree.

The pruning of the decision tree is done by replacing a subtree by a leaf node. The replacement takes place if a decision rule establishes that the expected error rate in the subtree is greater than in the single leaf.

There are two schools of thought in adopting pruning strategies. They are based on whether to use the same training data set that is used for building the tree for pruning, or to use a separate test data set for pruning. Both the training data set and test data set are pre-classified data, that is, the class labels of each tuple are known for this set. Most often, it is hard to have a large collection of such data to warrant both the test and training sets. One may think of using the complete set of data for training. In that case, pruning is carried out based on the training set. In case the known data is sufficiently large so as to keep aside a portion of it for testing, the second approach is preferable. CART uses the train-and-test approach for pruning. In the train-and-test approach, we train on one set and test on another—the *reduced error pruning* algorithm greedily prunes nodes that gain information on the test set. The error is measured based on test data classification. The *post-pruning approach* prunes after the rules are obtained from the tree. It removes the preconditions that improve estimated accuracy and filters out poor rules.

We concentrate on a pruning strategy, based on minimum description length.

The MDL (**M**inimum **D**escription **L**ength) principle states that the 'best' tree is the one that can be encoded using the fewest number of bits. Thus, the challenge for the pruning phase is to find the subtree that can be encoded with the least number of bits. So it is necessary to study the scheme for encoding the decision tree.

Cost of Encoding Tree

The cost of encoding the tree comprises three separate costs.

A. The Cost of Encoding the Structure of the Tree

The structure of the tree can be encoded by using a single bit, in order to specify whether a node of the tree is an internal node or a leaf node. A non-leaf node can be represented by 1 and a leaf node by 0.

B. The Cost of Encoding for Each Split

The cost of encoding each split involves specifying the attribute that is used to split the node and the value for the attribute. The splitting attribute can be encoded using *log a* bits, if the total number of attributes is a. The splitting point can be specified in a different way for categorical and numerical attributes. If the splitting attribute is numeric with v distinct values then, since there are $(v–1)$ possible splitting points, $\log(v–1)$ bits are needed to encode the split point. On the other hand, for a categorical attribute, there are 2^v different subsets of values, of which the empty set and the full set cannot be splitting sets. Thus, the cost of encoding the split is $\log(2^v–2)$. $C_{\text{split}}(n)$ denotes the cost of splitting the node n.

c. The Cost of Encoding the Classes of Data Records in Each Leaf of the Tree

For the cost of encoding the classes of data records T, the following equation an also be used.

$$C(T) = \sum_i n_i \log \frac{n}{n_i} + \frac{k-1}{2} \log \frac{n}{2} + \log \frac{\pi^{k/2}}{\Gamma\left(\frac{k}{2}\right)}$$

where k is the number of classes; n_i is the number records of T in class i and n is the total number of records in T.

In the above equation, the first term is simply n times the entropy of T. Also, since k never exceeds n, the sum of the last two terms is always non-negative.

Minimum Cost Subtree Rooted at a Node

Let S be the set of records associated with a node n. If n is a leaf node, then the minimum cost subtree rooted at n is simply n itself. The cost of the cheapest subtree rooted at n is given by

$$min\_cost(n) = C(S) + 1.$$

On the other hand, if n is an internal node in the tree with children $n1$ and $n2$, then the minimum cost subtree is either the node n itself or the node n along with the children n_1 and n_2 and the minimum cost subtrees rooted at n_1 and n_2. The cost of the cheapest subtree is given by

$$min\_cost(n) = MIN[C(S)+1,\ C_{split}\ (n)\ +\ 1+min\_cost(n_1)+min\_cost(n_2)],$$

where $C_{\text{split}}(n)$ is the cost of splitting node n and min_cost(n_i) is the minimum cost tree at n_i.

Pruning Algorithm

Now that we have formulated the cost of a tree, we next turn our attention to computing the minimum cost subtree of the tree constructed in the building phase. The main idea is that if minimum cost at a node is the cost of the node, then the splitting of the node would result in a higher cost and hence the subtree at this node is removed. In other words,

If $min\_cost(n) = C(S) + 1$, then prune the child nodes n_1 and n_2.

Example 6.7

Let us consider the example discussed earlier (Figure 6.2), presented here again for ready reference.

The cost of each leaf node can be computed as follows:

Since each leaf node represents a pure node, that is, all the records at this node are in one class, the first two terms of the cost vanish.

$$C(N4) = C(N5) = C(N6) = C(N7) = \log \frac{\pi^{1/2}}{\Gamma(1/2)} = 0$$

The cost of nodes at the intermediate level is given by

$$C(N2) = 4\log\frac{5}{4} + \log\frac{5}{1} + \frac{1}{2}\log\frac{5}{2} + \frac{\pi}{\Gamma(1)} = 5.92$$

$$C(N3) = 2\log 2 + 2\log 2 + \frac{1}{2}\log\frac{4}{2} + \log\frac{\pi}{\Gamma(1)} = 6.1522$$

$C_{\text{split}}\ (N2) = \log 4 = 2$ (Note that the splitting attribute a N2 is numerical)

$$min\_cost\ (N2) = Min[C(N2)+1,\ C_{split}\ (N2)\ +\ C(N4)\ +\ C(N5)\ +\ 1]$$

$$= Min[6.92, 3] = 3$$

So $N2$ need not be pruned.

$$min\_cost\ (N3) = Min[C(N3) + 1,\ C_{split}\ (N3)+1] = Min[7.1522,\ 2.58] = 2.58.$$

So the node $N3$ will not be pruned.

$$C(N1) = 6\log\frac{6}{9} + 3\log\frac{3}{9} + \frac{1}{2}\log\frac{9}{2} + \log\frac{\pi}{\Gamma(1)} = 17.003$$

$C_{spilt}\ (N1) = \log(2^2 - 2) = \log 2 = 1$ (The splitting attribue is categorical)

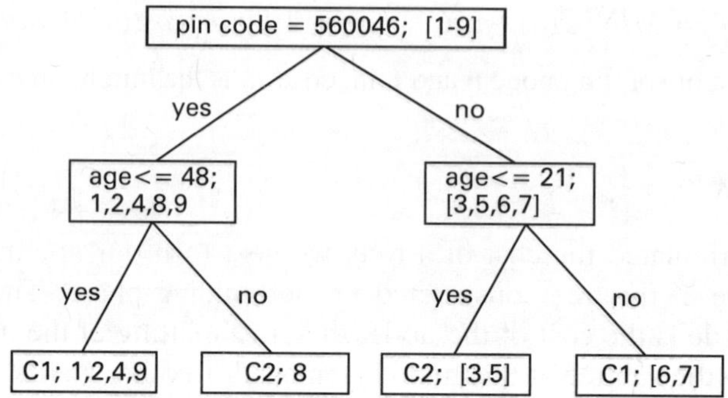

Figure 6.2

$$min\_cost\ (N1) = Min[C(N1)+1,\ C_{\text{split}}\ (N1) + min\_cost\ (N2) + min\_cost\ (N3) + 1]$$

$$= Min[18.003,\ 1+3+2.58+1].$$

Hence, the node $N1$ is also not pruned.

6.19 INTEGRATION OF PRUNING AND CONSTRUCTION

A natural question that arises is whether we can incorporate the pruning step within the construction process of the decision tree. In other words, instead of pruning being a post-processing step after the tree is fully built, whether it is possible to identify a node that need not be expanded right at the time of construction as it is likely to be pruned eventually. We have seen that CHAID attempts to accomplish this. Recently, Rastogi and Shim have proposed a new algorithm, PUBLIC, which also attempts to integrate the pruning step within the tree-building process.

PUBLIC

Recall that the pruning method identifies whether the minimum cost subtree at that node is due to the subtree, by splitting of the node or due to the node itself. During the construction process, before expanding the node, if we can check this condition, we can decide whether to expand the node or not. The critical part is that the *min_cost* is calculated recursively in a bottom-up approach. The cost of a min_cost of a node cannot be known unless the cost of its subtrees are known. This becomes the main reason to employ the pruning step after the tree is fully constructed. PUBLIC (**Pru**ning and **Buil**ding **I**ntegrated in **C**lassification) attempts to get over this limitation by estimating a lower bound of the *min_cost* of any node, before the node is expanded. It can easily be seen that if the pruning criterion is satisfied with the lower bound, then it is also satisfied with the actual value.

PUBLIC distinguishes among three types of current leaf nodes:

- The first kind of nodes are those that are yet to be expanded. For such nodes, the lower bound on cost is estimated, as the exact value cannot be computed.

- The second is a node which is a leaf node due to pruning its subtrees.
- The third is a node that cannot be expanded further in the construction phase. For the last two categories of nodes, the *min_cost* of the node can be accurately computed as $C(n)+1$.

Thus, the main part of the PUBLIC algorithm is to estimate the lower bound on the cost of the first kind of nodes. A simple estimate of the lower bound on the cost of a node is 1. We give below another algorithm to compute the lower bound.

Let us assume that for a node n, S is the set of records associated with this node and let k be the number of classes for the records in S. Let n_i be the number of records belonging to class i in S. Let us also assume, without any loss of generality, that the n_i values are arranged in decreasing order. The lower bound is estimated iteratively, with the initial estimate being set to 1.

Lower Bound Estimation

Initialize s = 1;

lower_bound = $3+\log a + \sum_{i=3}^{k}=3\ n_i$, where a is the total number of attributes

while $s + 1 < k$ and $n_{s+2} > 2 + \log a$

lower_bound=lower_bound + $2 + \log a - n_{s+2}$

increment s;

Note that if there are only two classes, the lower bound is directly estimated, without any iteration, as $3 + \log a$, where a is the total number of attributes.

Thus, the lower bound so computed is compared with the cost of the node and a decision is taken whether to stop expanding the node at this stage.

6.20 SUMMARY: AN IDEAL ALGORITHM

After studying different strategies for building a decision tree for a large database, let us try to build an ideal decision tree algorithm based on these principles.

We are given a training data set. First of all, we must discover the concept hierarchy of each of the attributes. This technique is essentially similar to dimension modelling, which we learned about in Chapter 2. This study helps in removing certain attributes from the database. As we move up this hierarchy, some of the numerical attributes may turn into categorical ones. We now identify the numerical and categorical attributes. Just having the numerical data type does not necessarily imply that the attribute is numerical (for example, *pincode*). We take a large sample of the training set so that the sample fits into the memory. Sampling involves *select* operations (tuple sampling) and *project* operations (attribute removal). Construct the attribute list for each attribute. Construct a generalised attribute list for each attribute, based on dimension hierarchy (how do you do this? Given as exercise). Construct a coarse decision tree. It is coarse because of many reasons: (a) generalised attribute list, (b) bootstrapping, and

(c) discretizing on the sample data. Search for the exact splitting point from the coarse splitting point. Prune the tree using the MDL scheme. The question is whether to first prune the coarse tree and then search for exact splitting point or whether the exact tree to be pruned can be investigated. Generate rules from the tree and simplify the rules if a test data set is available.

There are many other strategies proposed in the literature. For example, clustering techniques can be used for determining splitting attributes (for example, SPEC). Oblique trees can also be an useful strategy. Some researchers formulate the decision tree problem also as an optimisation problem.

6.21 OTHER TOPICS

We shall focus on some of the related topics here. Though these topics do not directly contribute to the study of the construction process, they are certainly helpful while applying the decision tree process for data mining.

PARALLEL ALGORITHMS

The decision tree construction algorithms have some natural characteristics that prompts for parallelisation. Once a node is generated, all of its children can be simultaneously expanded. Furthermore, the process of computing the splitting attributes and criteria can also be decomposed by performing data decomposition on the training data set. Nevertheless, parallelisation of the decision tree construction algorithm is a challenging problem for the reasons given below:

- The shape of the decision tree is very irregular and cannot be predicted beforehand.
- The amount of work associated with each node varies and is data-dependent. Hence, any static allocation scheme may not work well with regard to proper load balancing.
- There can be high-cost data movement. This is because the training set available at any node is to be partitioned and distributed over all its child nodes for concurrent processing.

The general approach of parallel algorithms for constructing a decision tree are

- node-based decomposition, and
- attribute-based decomposition.

SPRINT, and ScalParc are some parallel decision tree construction methods.

OBLIQUE TREES

It is not always possible to have data sets in real-life such that all the attributes are free of any correlations. If two attributes are highly correlated in any application, the decision tree with a single attribute-splitting criteria is not useful. In such cases, construct trees with a splitting criteria involving more than one attribute at any node.

INCREMENTAL COMPUTATION

Very often, we come across dynamic situations where the database is constantly incremented. It is necessary to devise a decision tree algorithm that can be updated with incremental training data sets. BOAT can support the incremental induction of a decision tree. However, not many researchers concentrate on such methods. One argument could be that in a supervised training environment, training may be an expensive process and should not be carried out very frequently. As the database is incremented, only the classification phase can be carried out to update the error of classification.

6.22 CONCLUSIONS

Classification is one of the important problems in data mining, and particularly classification using decision trees is currently one of the most active research areas in data mining research. We have tried to give a detailed account of this subject in this chapter. It will be of great help for a student to learn the techniques of constructing decision trees for possible application in data mining. It is envisaged that this chapter will also introduce researchers to state-of-the-art work on this topic.

FURTHER READING

Decision trees are a very well investigated area and a large number of results have been documented on diverse research areas. The foundations of Classification Tree and Decision Tree are dealt with in [Breimann, 1984], [Quinlan, 1986]. Quinlan proposed ID3 in [Quinlan, 1986] and C4.5 in [Quinlan, 1993]. Magidson proposed CHAID in 1993 [Magidson, 193]. SLIQ was introduced by [Mehta, 1996] and subsequent improvement as SPRINT was proposed by [Shafer, 1996]. Readers are referred to [Efron, 1993] for fundamentals of the bootstrap techniques. The BOAT algorithm was proposed by Gehrke, Ganti, Ramakrishnan and Loh in [Gehrke, 1999]. Rastogi et al described PUBLIC in [Rastogi, 1998]. The RainForest family of algorithms can be found in [Gehrke, 1998]. CLOUDS was introduced in [Alsabti, 1998]. ScalParC was given in [Joshi, 1998]. The MDL-based pruning method was given in [Mehta, 1995]. Oblique decision tree concepts are dealt in [Fukuda, 1996] and [Murthy, 1994]. The parallel implementation of the decision tree was proposed by Vipin Kumar and his team in [Srivastava, 1997]. Different pruning methods are compared in [Mingers, 1989].

EXERCISES

1. Describe the essential features in a decision tree. How is it useful to classify data?
2. What is a classification problem? What is supervised classification? How is a decision tree useful in classification?

3. What is a splitting attribute? What is a splitting criterion? Are the splitting criteria different for numeric attributes and categorical attributes?
4. What are the different methods of computing the best split? What is the gini index? What are entropy gain and gain ratio?
5. What are the disadvantages of the decision tree over other classification techniques?
6. What are advantages and disadvantages of the decision tree approach over other approaches of data mining?
7. Describe the ID3 algorithm of the decision tree construction. Why is it unsuitable for data mining applications?
8. Describe the class histogram, count matrix and AVC-sets. Are they similar in some respect?
9. Discuss the SLIQ and SPRINT algorithms. How do they differ from each other? Why are they suitable for data mining? Compare these algorithms with ID3 and CART.
10. What is windowing? When would you prefer to use this technique?
11. Describe the PUBLIC algorithm. How does it handle pruning while building the tree?
12. Describe the estimation of gini index for a node used in the PUBLIC algorithm.
13. Describe the CLOUD algorithm and discuss its advantages over SLIQ.
14. Describe the RainForest algorithm and compare its features with other algorithms.
15. Based on the algorithms described in the text, devise an ideal decision tree algorithm and give reasons for selecting the different strategies.
16. Let us assume that the training data set has attributes with three levels of dimension hierarchy. How would you maintain the count matrix for different levels of this hierarchy?
17. Describe different pruning strategies.
18. What is Attribute Induction? What is Relevance Analysis? In what context are these useful?
19. What are the three phases of construction of a decision tree? Describe the importance of each of the phases.
20. Describe the generic algorithm of the decision tree construction method.
21. Decision tree classification is a supervised classification because in addition to classifying the data set, it also generates the descriptions of the classes. True or False?
22. Overfitting is an inherent characteristics of decision tree and its occurrence depends on the construction process and not on the training data set. True or False?
23. Pruning is essentially to avoid overfitting. True or False?
24. The accuracy of the classification of a decision tree is calculated using the gini index. True or False?
25. Bootstrapping is carried out in the main memory. True or False?
26. The coarse numeric splitting criterion is a range of values, whereas there is nothing like a coarse splitting criterion for categorical attributes. True or False?
27. An oblique tree is relevant when
    a. The attributes are correlated
    b. The attributes are independent

c. There are only two attributes
d. All attributes are categorical

28. The ID3 generates a
a. Binary decision tree
b. A decision tree with as many branches as there are distinct values of the attribute
c. A tree with a variable number of branches, not related to the domain of the attributes
d. A tree with an exponential number of branches.

29. Gain ratio has an advantage over gain when an attribute is
a. Categorical with only two possible values
b. Numerical with two possible values
c. Categorical with a large number of distinct values
d. Numerical with a large number of distinct values

30. In order to select the attribute to split at a given node by taking the gini index, we select the attribute which has the
a. Maximum value of the gini index
b. Minimum value of the gini index

31. The importance of using an attribute list is
a. To avoid repeated sorting of the data set
b. To get a more accurate splitting criterion
c. To have an alternative method for the gini index and gain index
d. To approximate the data set to a smaller size.

32. Which of the following algorithms integrates the construction and the pruning phase?
a. CLOUD
b. RainForest
c. PUBLIC
d. CART

33. Which of the following is an approximate algorithm?
a. ID3
b. C4.5
c. SLIQ
d. CLOUD

34. The count matrix is used in
a. PUBLIC algorithm for categorical attributes
b. SPRINT/SLIQ algorithms for numeric attributes
c. CLOUD algorithm for numeric attributes

35. The following example represents the training database that gives information of whether or not to play golf, given a set of climatic conditions. Illustrate the working of PUBLIC, CLOUD and SPRINT using this example.

Outlook	Temp	Humidity	Windy	Class
sunny	75	70	true	play
sunny	80	90	true	no play
sunny	85	85	false	no play
sunny	72	95	false	no play
sunny	69	70	false	play
overcast	72	90	true	play
overcast	83	78	false	play
overcast	64	65	true	play
rainy	81	75	false	play
rainy	71	80	true	no play
rainy	65	70	true	no play
rainy	75	80	false	play
rainy	68	80	false	play

36. Consider the following examples.

MOTOR	WHEELS	DOORS	SIZE	TYPE	CLASS
NO	2	0	small	cycle	bicycle
NO	3	0	small	cycle	tricycle
YES	2	0	small	cycle	motorcycle
YES	4	2	small	automobile	Sports car
YES	4	3	medium	automobile	minivan
YES	4	4	medium	automobile	sedan
YES	4	4	large	autobobile	sumo

Use this example to illustrate the working of different algorithms.

Bibliography

Alsabti Khaled, Ranka Sanjay, and Singh Vineet. CLOUDS: A decision tree classifier for large datasets. In *Proceedings of the International Conference on Knowledge Discovery and Data Mining (KDD-98)*, New York City, August 1998.

Bioch Jan C., van der Meer Onno, and Potharst Rob. Invariate Decision Trees. In *Principles of Data Mining and Knowledge Discovery*, First European Symposium, PKDD'97, Springer LNAI 1263, pp. 232–242, Trondheim, Norway, 1997.

Breiman, Friedman, and Olshen. *Stone: Classification and Decision Trees.* Wadsworth, 1984.

Cohen W. Fast effective rule induction. In *Proceedings of the 12th International Conference on Machine Learning,* Lake Tahoe, California, 1995.

Corruble V., Brown D.E., and Pittard C.L. A comparison of decision classifiers with back propagation neural network for multimodal classification problems. *Pattern Recognition,* **26**: 953–961, 1993.

Efron B., and Tibshirani R.J. *An Introduction to the Bootstrap*. Chapman & Hall, 1993.

Fayyad U.M. *On the induction of decision trees for multiple concept learning*. PhD Thesis, University of Michigan, 1991.

Frank E., and Witten I.H. Generating accurate rule sets without global optimization. In *Proceedings of the International Conference on Machine Learning,* 1998.

Fukuda T., Morimoto Y., Morishita S., and Tokuyama T. Data mining using two-dimensional optimized association rule. *SIGMOD,*1996.

Frank E., Wang Y., Inglis S., Holmes, G., and Witten. I.H. Using model trees for classification. *Machine Learning* **32**(1):63–76, 1998.

Gehrke J.E., Ramakrishnan R., and Ganti V. RAINFOREST: A framework for fast decision tree construction of large data sets. In *Proceedings of the 24th International Conference on Very Large Databases,* New York, 1998.

Gehrke J.E., Ganti V., Ramakrishnan R., and Loh W.Y. BOAT—Optimistic decision tree construction. In *Proceedings of SIGMOD'99,* Philadelphia, 1999.

Joshi Mahesh V., Karypis George, and Kumar Vipin. ScalParC: A new scalable and efficient parallel classification algorithm for mining large datasets. In *Proceedings of the 12th International Parallel Processing Symposium (IPPS/SPDP),* Orlando, USA, April 1998.

Kamber M., Winstone L., Gong W., Cheng S., and Han J. Generalization and decision tree induction: efficient classification in data mining. *Technical Report,* Simon Fraser University.

Liu Bing, and Hsu Wynne. Post analysis of learned rules. In *Proceedings of the 13th National Conference on Artificial Intelligence (AAAI-96),* pp. 828-834, Portland, Oregon, USA, August 4-8, 1996.

Liu Bing, Hsu Wynne, and Chen Shu. Discovering conforming and unexpected classification rules. In *Workshop on Intelligent Data Analysis in Medicine and Pharmacology* (*IDAMAP-97*), *IJCAI-97,* Nagoya, Japan, August 23–29, 1997.

Liu Bing, Hsu Wynne, and Chen Shu. Using general impressions to analyze discovered classification rules. In *Proceedings of the 3rd International Conference on Knowledge Discovery and Data Mining(KDD-97),* pp. 31–36, Newport Beach, California, USA, August 14–17, 1997.

Liu Bing, Hsu Wynne, and Ma Yiming. Integrating classificationand association rule mining. In *Proceedings of the 4th International Conference on Knowledge Discovery and Data Mining (KDD-98)*, New York, USA, 1998.

Magidson J. The CHAID approach to segmentation modelling. In *Advanced Methods of Marketing Research, Blackwell Publishing*, Cambridge, MA., USA, 1995.

Mehta M. Rissanen J., and Agrawal R. MDL-based decision tree pruning. In *Proceedings of the 1st International Conference on Knowledge Discovery in Databases and Data Mining*, Montreal, Canada, August 1995.

Mehta M., Agrawal R., and Rissanen J. SLIQ: A fast scalable classifier for data mining. In *Proceedings of the 5th International Conference on Extending Database Technology,* Avignon, France, March 1996.

Mingers J. An empirical comparison of pruning methods for decision tree induction. *Machine Learning*, **4**(3):227–243, 1989.

Murthy S.K., Kasif S., Salzberg S., and Beigel R. OC1: Randomized induction of oblique decision trees. In *Proceedings of AAAI'93*, 1993.

Murthy S.K., Kasif S., and Salzberg S. A system for induction of oblique decision trees.*Journal of Artificial Intelligence Research,***2**:1–32, 1994.

Quinlan J.R. Induction of decision tree. *Machine Learning*, **1**:81–106, 1986.

Quinlan J.R. *C4.5: Programs for Machine Learning*. Morgan Kauffman, 1993.

Rachlin J., Kasif S., Salzberg S., and Aha D. Towards a better understanding of memory-based and Bayesian classifiers. In *Proceedings 1994 International Conference on Machine Learning*, pp. 242–250, New Brunswick, NJ, 1994.

Rastogi Rajeev and Shim Kyuseok. PUBLIC: A decision tree classifier that integrates building and pruning. In *Proceedings of the 24th International Conference on Very Large Databases(VLDB98)*, New York, 1998.

Shafer J.C., Agrawal R., and Mehta. M. SPRINT: A scalable parallel classifier for data mining. In *Proceedings of the 22nd International Conference on Very Large Databases*, Mumbai (Bombay), India, September 1996.

Srivastava A., Han E-. H., Kumar V. and Singh V. Parallel Formulation of Decision Tree classification algorithms. *Technical Report*, University of Minnesota, 1997.

Wang K., and Liu. B. Concurrent discretization of multiple attributes. *PRICAI 98*, Singapore, August 1998.

Zaki M.J., Ho C-T., and Agrawal R. Scalable parallel classification for data mining on shared memory multiprocessors. In *IEEE International Conference on Data Engineering*, March 1999.

7

ROUGH SET THEORY

7.1 INTRODUCTION

The *rough set theory* is a tool of sets and relations for studying imprecision, vagueness and uncertainty in data analysis. It is a relatively new mathematical and artificial intelligence technique. The rough set method was introduced by Z. Pawlak in early 1980 for discovering patterns in databases when the data are ambiguous or incomplete. After almost 25 years, the approach has now reached a certain degree of maturity, with the rough set theory becoming an alternative to usual classification methods. It is being increasingly applied to derive rules, provide reasoning and discover relationships in qualitative, incomplete or imprecise data. The recent years have witnessed a rapid growth of interest in rough set theory for data mining.

In rough set theory, the available information is represented as a decision table which is made up of the universe of the discourse, a family of equivalence relations over the universe and two kinds of attributes, *condition* and *decision*. We are concerned with assessing the contribution of condition attributes affecting the decision attributes. In more general terms, we study the influence of one attribute on another. The rough set is the approximation of a vague concept (set) by a pair of precise (or crisp) concepts, called the *lower* and *upper* approximations. The foundation of rough set theory is based on the assumption that for every object in the universe, however imprecise it is, there is some associated crisp concept or information that can approximate it. Objects characterised by the same set of information are indiscernible. The indiscernibility relation generated this way is the mathematical basis of rough set theory.

Interestingly, in contrast to other classification techniques, the rough set theory does not depend on data distribution. The rule discovery process in rough set analysis involves simplifying the decision tables with the elimination of superfluous attributes and their values and finding out simple rules relating the condition and decision attributes. Please note that the decision table in the present context is similar to the training set that we had discussed in the context of decision trees. The decision attribute is a class attribute while the condition attribute is a non-class attribute.

7.2 DEFINITIONS

The starting point of rough-set-based data analysis is a data set, called the *information system*. An information system is a table (or decision table) whose columns are attributes and rows, the objects of interest. We distinguish two disjoint classes of attributes, called *condition attributes* and *decision attributes*, respectively. Objects of the universe are classified based on the predefined class of the decision attributes.

DEFINITION 7.1 INFORMATION SYSTEMS

An *information system,* $\mathbf{S} = (U, C, D)$, where U, C and D are finite, non-empty sets called the *universe*, *condition attributes* and *decision attributes* respectively.

$Q = C \cup D$ is called attribute set, A is a subset of the attribute set Q. $X \subseteq U$ is the object set which we are interested in. We associate with every attribute $a \in A$ a set of values V_a, called the *domain* of a.

DEFINITION 7.2 INDISCERNIBILITY RELATION

Any A such that $A \subseteq Q$ determines a binary relation A^+ on U. This is called an *indiscernibility relation* and is defined as follows: $(x, y) \in A^+$ if and only if $x[a] = y[a]$ for every $a \in A$, where $x[a]$ denotes the value of attribute a for the object $x \in U$.

Clearly, A^+ is the equivalence relation defined by A, and U/A^+ is the partition of U on this equivalence relation. If $(x, y) \in A^+$, we say that x and y are *A-indiscernible* (*indiscernible with respect to attribute set A*). Equivalence classes of the relation A^+ are referred to as *A-elementary sets* or *A-granule.*

Every non-empty subset of Q defines an indiscernibility relation and hence, there can be $2^{|Q|-1}$ possible indiscernibility relations. Each indiscernibility relation induces a partition generating granules with respect to the corresponding set of attributes. For a partition U/A^+ induced by A, the possible number of granules can be $\Pi_{a \in A} |V_a|$.

Consider an information system represented by the decision table given by Table 7.1. This is a sample data from a study carried out to see whether a product should be introduced in the market based on other observations. In Table 7.1, seven cases are presented showing three condition attributes: *growth, financial and development,* and one decision attribute, *strategy*. The associated values and the meaning of the attributes are: demand growth rate (its domain being *high* or *low*); financial strength (*strong* or *weak*); cost of development (*high* or *low*) and entry strategy (*go* or *nogo*), respectively.

Table 7.1

Cases	Growth	Financial	Development	Entry
1	high	strong	low	go
2	high	strong	high	go
3	high	weak	low	go
4	high	weak	high	go
5	high	weak	high	nogo
6	low	strong	low	nogo
7	low	weak	high	nogo

Let us take an attribute set A = {*financial, development*}. We see that cases 1 and 6 (the first and the sixth rows) have the same values for attributes in A. These two cases are said to be indiscernible with respect to A. Similarly, cases 4 and 7 (the fourth and the seventh rows) are also indiscernible with respect to A. Can we think of partitions of the set of tuples in the decision table with respect to the relation A^+? The partitions are {1,6}, {4, 5, 7}, {2} and {3}. These are called granules with respect to A or *A-granules*. Let us take another attribute set, B = {*entry*}. We see that *B-granules* are {1,2,3,4} and {5, 6, 7}. We can thus find the set of granules for any choice of A. The concept is formed by the attributes, *financial* and *development*. The granules correspond to *strong financial-high development; strong financial-low development; weak financial-high development and weak financial-low development*.

We can view the granules as the atomic units of our concepts. In the present situation, we use some attributes to represent the concept. Different combination of values of these attributes define granules for the concept. Let us see the way in which any arbitrary set of objects in our universe respond to the said concept.

APPROXIMATION OF A SET BY *A*-GRANULES

Every finite union of granules is called a *composed set*. Given a set of objects X, we try to represent this set as the union of granules (say, *A-granules*). We desire that X should be a composed set and hence, X can be expressed as the union of A-granules. When the set X is not a composed set, we cannot represent X in terms of granules, and we then approximate X by two composed sets: one that is the maximal composed set contained in X, and the other the minimal composed set containing X. The upper approximation of X with respect to A is the least composed set of *A-granules* that contains X. The lower approximation of X with respect to A

is the greatest composed set of *A-granules* that is contained in X. For example, if we choose $X = \{1, 2, 3, 4\}$, then X is not a composed set with respect to A. In other words, it is not a union of granules of A. But we can find some granules that are totally contained in it. Thus, we are approximating X with respect to granules of A. We define below these approximations.

DEFINITION 7.3 LOWER APPROXIMATION AND UPPER APPROXIMATION

Lower approximation of X with respect to A: $A_*(X) = \cup\{Y \in U/A^+ : Y \subset X\}$

Upper approximation of X with respect to A: $A^*(X) = \cup\{Y \in U/A^+ : Y \cap X \neq \varnothing\}$

The boundary of X are the *A-granules* that overlap with X but not totally in X. Similarly, the negative area of X are the *A-granules* that do not overlap with X.

DEFINITION 7.4 BOUNDARY

Boundary of X with respect to A : $\quad BND_A(X) = A^*(X) - A_*(X)$

Negative area of X with respect to A: $\quad NEG_A(X) = \cup\{Y \in U/A^+ : Y \cap X = \varnothing\}$

DEFINITION 7.5 ROUGH SET

The rough set is a pair $(A_*(X), A^*(X))$. If the boundary region is the empty set, then the set X is called a *crisp set*. Alternatively, X is called a *rough set*. If X is a crisp set, then X is a composed set.

In Table 7.1, let us take $X= \{1,2,3,4\}$. We see that the *A-granules* $\{2\}$ and $\{3\}$ are the only granules that are totally contained in the set of objects $X= \{1,2,3,4\}$. Thus the composed set $\{2,3\}$ is the lower approximation of $\{1,2,3,4\}$ with respect to A. In this case the upper approximation with respect to A is the set of all objects, U. If A represents a concept and we want to express the set X in terms of this concept, then we observe that X cannot be *crisply* represented in terms of the granules induced by A. But X can be approximated roughly in terms of two composed sets, $\{2,3\}$ and U. Let us take another X, the other *B-granule*, $\{5,6,7\}$. We can see that the set of *A-granules* $\{1,6\}$ and $\{4,5,7\}$ have a non-empty intersection with the chosen X. Hence the composed set $\{1, 4, 5, 6, 7\}$ is the upper approximation of *B-granule* $\{5, 6, 7\}$. It is interesting to note that its lower approximation is the empty set. These are rough sets. We can think of a measure of roughness as follows.

$$\alpha_A(X) = \frac{|A_*(X)|}{|A^*(X)|}$$

The coefficient $\alpha_A(X)$ is known as the *accuracy of approximation*. Clearly, $0 \leq \alpha_A(X) \leq 1$, and for the crisp set this coefficient is 1.

When can we have $\alpha_A(X) = 0$? This is true if the lower approximation is empty. This happens when X does not contain any granule, when the granules are too big to be inside X or when X, though small, partially overlaps or is a disjoint of every granule.

In the above example, we note that when X is $\{5, 6, 7\}$, the lower approximation of X is empty, but when X is $\{1, 2, 3, 4\}$, it has a non-empty lower approximation. Thus, $\alpha_A(\{5,6,7\}) = 0$. Higher the value of α, the more precise is the representation.

We have the following properties of rough sets. It is easy to prove them.

i.	Contraction	$A_*(X) \subseteq X$
ii.	Extension	$X \subseteq A^*(X)$
iii.	Multiplication	$A_*(X \cap Y) = A_*(X) \cap A_*(Y)$
iv.	Addition	$A^*(X \cup Y) = A^*(X) \cup A^*(Y)$
v.	Lower-complement relation	$A_*(U - A_*(X)) = U - A_*(X)$
vi.	Upper-complement relation	$A^*(U - A^*(X)) = U - A^*(X)$

These are characteristics properties of lower and upper approximations and many other properties can be deduced from these set of properties. We give some of them as exercises.

Approximating *B*-Granules by *A*-Granules

We just studied the way in which a given set of objects X can be approximated in terms of the granules induced by a chosen A. We now extend this idea to examine the relationships between two sets of attributes. Thus, instead of a relationship between A (attribute set) and X (a set of objects), we now discuss the relationship between two sets of attributes, A and B. Though A and B can be any set of attributes, it is more relevant to discuss this when A is a set of condition attributes and B is a set of decision attributes.

Let $U/A^+ = \{X_1, X_2, \ldots, X_n\}$ and $U/B^+ = \{Y_1, Y_2, \ldots, Y_m\}$ denote the partitions on U induced by the equivalence relations with respect to A and B, respectively. To determine the extent that partition U/B^+ can be approximated by partition U/A^+ (in other words, approximate *B-granules* in terms of *A-granules*), we define the *positive region, boundary region* and *negative region* of U/B^+ as follows.

Definition 7.6

Positive region, negative region and *boundary region* of B with respect to A are defined as follows.

$$\text{POS\_REG}_A(B) = \cup_{Yj} A_*(Y_j)$$

$$\text{BND\_REG}_A(B) = \cup_{Yj} (A^*(Y_j) - A_*(Y_j))$$

$$\text{NEG\_REG}_A(B) = U - \cup_{Yj} A^*(Y_j)$$

For example, when A={financial, development} and B = {entry}, then $\text{POS\_REG}_A(\text{B})$ = $A_*(\{1, 2, 3, 4\}) \cup A_*(\{5, 6, 7\}) = \{1, 2, 3, 4, 5, 6, 7\} = U$. Similarly, $\text{BND\_REG}_A(\text{B}) = \{1, 4, 5, 6, 7\}$ and $\text{NEG\_REG}_A(\text{B}) = \varnothing$.

We can now define several quantitative measures to relate the two sets of attributes.

DEFINITION 7.7 DEPENDENCY MEASURE

The measure of dependency of B on A, denoted as $\gamma_A(B)$, is defined as

$$\gamma_A(B) = \frac{|\text{POS\_REG}_A(B)|}{|U|}.$$

Clearly, $0 \leq \gamma_A(B) \leq 1$.

When $\gamma_A(B) = 1$, B is said to be *totally dependent* on A.

When $\gamma_A(B) = 0$, B is said to be *totally independent* of A.

In other situations, B is said to be *roughly dependent* on A.

In the above example, we see that B is totally dependent on A. It is interesting to note that every subset of A is totally dependent on A. This is because every B-granule, $B \subseteq A$, is a composed set of union of A-granules. The *dependency measure* is 1 in such cases.

We can define another measure of dependency, the as *discriminant index*.

DEFINITION 7.8 DISCRIMINANT INDEX

The discriminant index, $\beta_A(B)$ of B with respect to A is defined as

$$\beta_A(B) = \frac{|\text{POS\_REG}_A(B) \cup \text{NEG\_REG}_A(B)|}{|U|}$$

$$= \frac{U - \text{BND\_REG}_A(B)|}{|U|}$$

For example, when A={financial, development} and B = {entry}, then $\beta_A(B)$ is 5/7. You can note that when the boundary region of B with respect to A is empty, the discriminant index is 1.

We can also define another measure of importance called *significance*. The significance of B on any single conditional attribute a is the difference between the dependency of B on the set of all condition attributes C and the dependency of B on the set of all condition attribute without a.

DEFINITION 7.9 SIGNIFICANCE

The significance of B on a specific attribute a, $\sigma_a(B)$ is defined as follows.

$$\sigma_a(B) = \gamma_C(B) - \gamma_{C-\{a\}}(B).$$

We can further extend the significance of a to a subset A also. Please note that the *dependency* and the *discriminant index* are direct measures focussing on the direct contribution of one or more condition attributes. On the other hand, the *significance* is a complementary measure that assesses the importance of the condition attributes for the given set of decision attributes. When there are few elements in the positive regions, it is not useful to have the dependency and discriminant indices. Under such circumstances, the significance measure becomes useful. We shall illustrate these concepts in the following section.

7.3 Example

Consider another example (Table 7.2) where there are four condition attributes, *a, b, c* and *d; e* is the decision attribute. All the tuples together constitute *U*.

Table 7.2

	a	*b*	*c*	*d*	*e*
1	1	2	2	1	1
2	1	2	3	2	1
3	1	2	2	2	1
4	2	2	2	1	1
5	2	3	2	2	2
6	1	3	2	1	1
7	1	2	3	1	2
8	2	3	1	2	1
9	1	2	2	2	1
10	1	1	3	2	1
11	2	1	2	2	2
12	1	1	2	3	1

Let us determine the equivalent classes for each of the individual condition attributes. The equivalence relation to condition attribute *a* is denoted by a^+. There are two distinct values of *a* in V_a. Hence *U* is partitioned into two classes by a^+. We denote these classes by identifying the corresponding attribute values, for example, by $a^+_{a=1}$, where we mean the equivalent class corresponding to the value 1. Thus we get the following different partitions.

For the attribute *a*, the different granules are the following.

$$a^+_{a=1} = \{1, 2, 3, 6, 7, 9, 10, 12\};$$

$$a^+_{a=2} = \{4, 5, 8, 11\}.$$

Similarly, for the attribute *b:*

$$b^+_{b=1} = \{10, 11, 12\};$$

$$b^+_{b=2} = \{1, 2, 3, 4, 7, 9\};$$

$$b^+_{b=3} = \{5, 6, 8\}.$$

For the attribute *c*:

$$c^+_{c=1} = \{8\};$$

$$c^+_{c=2} = \{1, 3, 4, 5, 6, 9, 11, 12\};$$

$c^+_{c=3} = \{2, 7, 10\}$.

For the attribute d:

$d^+_{d=1} = \{1, 4, 6, 7\}$;

$d^+_{d=2} = \{2, 5, 8, 9, 10, 11\}$;

$d^+_{d=3} = \{3, 12\}$.

For the set $X = \{1, 2, 3, 4, 6, 8, 9, 10, 12\}$, which is a granule for $e = 1$, the upper and lower approximation of X with respect to different attributes are as follows.

$a_*(X) = \varnothing$, $\quad a^*(X) = \{1, 2, 3, 4, 5, 6, 7, 8, 9, 10, 11, 12\}$;

$b_*(X) = \varnothing$, $\quad b^*(X) = \{1, 2, 3, 4, 5, 6, 7, 8, 9, 10, 11, 12\}$;

$c_*(X) = \{8\}$, $\quad c^*(X) = \{1, 2, 3, 4, 5, 6, 7, 8, 9, 10, 11, 12\}$;

$d_*(X) = \{3, 12\}$ $\quad d^*(X) = \{1, 2, 3, 4, 5, 6, 7, 8, 9, 10, 11, 12\}$.

Clearly, $\alpha_a(X) = 0$, $\alpha_b(X) = 0$, $\alpha_c(X) = 1/12$ and $\alpha_d(X) = 1/6$.

$$\text{NEG}_a(X) = \text{NEG}_b(X) = \text{NEG}_c(X) = \text{NEG}_d(X) = \varnothing,$$

Boundary of X with respect to a is given by

$$\text{BND}_a(X) = a^*(X) - a_*(X) = \{1, 2, 3, 4, 5, 6, 7, 8, 9, 10, 11, 12\}.$$

Similarly,

$$\text{BND}_b(X) = b^*(X) - b_*(X) = \{1, 2, 3, 4, 5, 6, 7, 8, 9, 10, 11, 12\}$$

$$\text{BND}_c(X) = c^*(X) - c_*(X) = \{1, 2, 3, 4, 5, 6, 7, 9, 10, 11, 12\}$$

$$\text{BND}_d(X) = d^*(X) - d_*(X) = \{1, 2, 4, 5, 6, 7, 8, 9, 10, 11\}$$

The other partition of U with respect to $e=2$ is the set $Y = \{5, 7, 11\}$

$a_*(Y) = \varnothing$, $\quad a^*(Y) = \{1, 2, 3, 4, 5, 6, 7, 8, 9, 10, 11, 12\}$;

$b_*(Y) = \varnothing$, $\quad b^*(Y) = \{1, 2, 3, 4, 5, 6, 7, 8, 9, 10, 11, 12\}$;

$c_*(Y) = \varnothing$, $\quad c^*(Y) = \{1, 2, 3, 4, 5, 6, 7, 9, 10, 11, 12\}$;

$d_*(Y) = \varnothing$, $\quad d^*(Y) = \{1, 2, 4, 5, 6, 7, 8, 9, 10, 11\}$.

Clearly, $\alpha_a(Y) = 0$, $\alpha_b(Y) = 0$, $\alpha_c(Y) = 0$ and $\alpha_d(Y) = 0$.

$$\text{NEG}_a(Y) = \text{NEG}_b(Y) = \varnothing, \ \text{NEG}_c(Y) = \{8\}, \ \text{NEG}_d(Y) = \{3, 12\}.$$

Boundary of Y with respect to a is given by

$$BND_a(Y) = a^*(Y) - a_*(Y) = \{1, 2, 3, 4, 5, 6, 7, 8, 9, 10, 11, 12\}.$$

Similarly,

$$BND_b(Y) = \{1, 2, 3, 4, 5, 6, 7, 8, 9, 10, 11, 12\},$$

$$BND_c(Y) = \{1, 2, 3, 4, 5, 6, 7, 9, 10, 11, 12\},$$

$$BND_d(Y) = \{1, 2, 4, 5, 6, 7, 8, 9, 10, 11\}.$$

$$POS\_REG_a(\{e\}) = a_*(X) \cup a_*(Y) = \varnothing.$$

$$BND\_REG_a(\{e\}) = BND_a(X) \cup BND_a(Y) = \{1, 2, 3, 4, 5, 6, 7, 8, 9, 10, 11, 12\}.$$

$$NEG\_REG_a(\{e\}) = \varnothing.$$

Please note that the dependency index and indiscriminant index both are 0. Thus the decision attribute e is totally independent of the condition attribute a.

Let us take $A = \{a, b\}$. We see that $POS\_REG_A(\{e\}) = \{4, 6, 10, 11, 12\}$. Thus the dependency measure $\gamma_A(B) = 5/12$ and hence $\{e\}$ is roughly dependent on $\{a,b\}$.

As an exercise, you can compute the dependency measure and significance for other conditional attributes. Interestingly, the indiscriminant index $\gamma_{\{a\}}(\{e\})$ is 0. In such cases, every object is a boundary element and hence, the discriminant factor is the least.

7.4 REDUCT

We observe that we have to search for combinations of attributes with which we can discern objects and object classes from each other. In this context, we introduce the concept of *reduct attributes* for identifying a set of condition attributes which are indispensable and not superfluous. The minimal set of attributes that forms such a combination is called a *reduct*. We can derive decision rules using reducts. Let us revisit the earlier definition of dependency measure. It may be recalled that when the dependency measure is 1, we say that a set of attributes is totally dependent on the other.

Let us consider the following example (Table 7.3).

Table 7.3

Object	Height	Hair	Eyes	Class
o_1	short	blond	blue	#
o_2	short	blond	brown	---
o_3	tall	red	blue	#
o_4	tall	dark	blue	---
o_5	tall	dark	blue	---
o_6	tall	blond	blue	#
o_7	tall	dark	brown	---
o_8	short	blond	brown	---

We obtain the following partitions with respect to subsets of the attributes.

{height}; $\{o_1, o_2, o_8\}, \{o_3, o_4, o_5, o_6, o_7\}$.

For sake of notational convenience, we have listed only the partitions. This is equivalent to our earlier notation:

$$\text{height}^{\#}_{\text{height=short}} = \{o_1, o_2, o_8\};$$

$$\text{height}^{\#}_{\text{height=tall}} = \{o_3, o_4, o_5, o_6, o_7\}.$$

The partitions with respect to other combinations of attributes are the following.

{hair}; $\{o_1, o_2, o_6, o_8\}, \{o_3\}, \{o_4, o_5, o_7\}$;

{eyes}; $\{o_1, o_3, o_4, o_5, o_6\}, \{o_2, o_7, o_8\}$;

{height; hair}; $\{o_1, o_2, o_8\}, \{o_3\}, \{o_4, o_5, o_7\}, \{o_6\}$;

{height; eyes}; $\{o_1\}, \{o_2, o_8\}, \{o_3, o_4, o_5, o_6\}, \{o_7\}$;

{hair; eyes}; $\{o_1, o_6\}, \{o_2, o_8\}, \{o_3\}, \{o_4, o_5\}, \{o_7\}$;

{height; hair; eyes}; $\{o_1\}, \{o_2, o_8\}, \{o_3\}, \{o_4, o_5\}, \{o_6\}, \{o_7\}$.

We can see that if we take A = {*hair, eyes*} and B = {*class*}, then every partition in U/A^+ is a union of of classes in U/B^{+}. Thus we can say that the attribute *class* is dependent on {*hair, eyes*}, i.e., {*class*} →{*hair, eyes*}. On the other hand, we cannot say that {*class*} is dependent on the attribute set {*height, hair*}. The attribute *class* is dependent on the attribute set {*height, hair, eyes*}. Thus the attribute *height* seems to be redundant as {*hair, eyes*} and {*height, hair, eyes*} induce the same decision classes. Can we now formalise this concept of redundant attribute?

DEFINITION 7.10 REDUCT

A set $A \subseteq B \subseteq Q$ is called a *reduct* of B if $U/A^+ = U/B^+$ and for each proper subset C of A we have $U/C^+ \neq U/A^+$.

In other words, $A \subseteq B$ is a reduct of B if A is minimal among all subsets of B, which generate the same classification as B. It is not hard to see that each $B \subseteq Q$ has a reduct and this is not necessarily unique. In the trivial case B itself is the reduct of B.

Let us consider B' = {*hair, eyes, height, class*} and A' = {*hair, eyes*}. We can check that A' is a reduct of B' whereas neither the attrbute set {*hair, height*}, nor the set {*height, eyes*}, is a reduct of B'. In fact, in this example {*hair, eyes*} is the unique reduct of this set. By definition, {*hair, eyes*} and {*hair, eyes, height, class*} yield the same partition of the information system. Thus, the attribute height is not significant in classifying the attribute *class* using {*hair, eyes, height*}.

Henceforth we shall concentrate only on the reducts of C, the set of condition attributes or, the reducts of Q, the set of all attributes. A *super-reduct* B is a set of attributes such that the granules induced by B is the granules induced by Q (or C). *Super-reducts* are sets of attributes that retain the characteristics of the data. We remove the attributes that are not necessary and keep only those that are required to distinguish two objects. If B is a super-reduct and no proper subset of B can induce the equivalence relation equal to that of Q (i.e., B is minimal), then B is a *reduct*.

The set of all reducts of B is denoted $red(B)$. There may be many such sets that are minimal, but of different sizes compared to one another. Reducts correspond to keys of a relational database and the problem of finding all reducts of an information system is, in general, NP-complete. Please note that it may not be hard to find a reduct, but it is computationally hard to find all the reducts.

Definition 7.11 Core

The intersection of all reducts of B is called core of B, written as $core(B)$ and the elements of the core are *indispensable* for B.

If an attribute $a \in B$ is not an element of any reduct, then a is *redundant* or superfluous. In the above example, the attribute *height* is redundant.

7. 5 Propositional Reasoning and PIAP to Compute Reducts

Let the letters a, b, c, ..., with or without subscripts, represent propositional variables. If a is a variable, $\hat{a}$ denotes the negation of a. Both a and $\hat{a}$ are referred to as literals. A *disjunctive clause* is a disjunction of literals. A disjunctive clause σ_i is said to subsume another clause σ_j if every literal in σ_i occurs in σ_j. A clause is called a *conjunctive clause* if it is a conjunction of literals. A propositional formula $\mathcal{F}$ is said to be in *conjunctive normal form* (CNF) if it is a conjunction of disjunctive clauses. A formula is in *disjunctive normal form* (DNF) if it is a disjunction of conjunctive clauses.

A conjunctive clause π is an *implicant* of a CNF formula $\mathcal{F}$ if and only if π implies $\mathcal{F}$. π is a prime implicant of $\mathcal{F}$ if π is an implicant and there is no other implicant π' of $\mathcal{F}$ such that π implies π'. The prime implicants of a formula exist and are finite in number.

Reduct and prime implicants

Definition 7.12 Discernibility matrix

Let $\boldsymbol{S}$ be an information system with n objects (see Table 7.4). An alternative way of representing discernibility is to cross-classify objects by assigning to each pair of objects the set of attributes where they differ. The *discernibility matrix* $\boldsymbol{C}$ of $\boldsymbol{S}$ is a symmetric $n \times n$ matrix with entries $\mathbf{c}_{ij}$ as given in Table 7.4. Each entry consists of the set of attributes upon which objects x_i and x_j differ.

$$\mathbf{c}_{ij} = \{a \in Q \mid x_i[a] \neq x_j[a]\} \text{ for } i, j = 1, \ldots, n.$$

The discernibility matrix for the information system (Table 7.4) is given in Table 7.5.

Table 7.4

Object	*Speed*	*Colour*	*Humidity*
Car1	medium	green	high
Car2	medium	yellow	low
Car3	high	blue	high

Table 7.5

	Car1	Car2	Car3
Car1		c,h	S,c
Car2	c,h		s,c,h
Car3	s,c	s,c,h	

Let the Boolean variables $a_1^*,\ldots, a_m^*$ correspond to the attributes $a_1,\ldots, a_m$. Let us associate a clause σ_{ij} with every c_{ij} as

$$\sigma_{ij} = \vee_{a_k \in c_{ij}} a_k^*.$$

Then we can also define a propositional formula (we call it here the *discernibility formula*) with respect to C as the CNF as $\wedge_{ij}\sigma_{ij}$.

In the above example, the discernibility formula is given by

$$(c\vee h) \wedge (s\vee c) \wedge (c\vee h)\wedge (s\vee c\vee h)\wedge(s\vee c)\wedge(s\vee c\vee h) = (c\vee h) \wedge (s\vee c).$$

This formula describes the constraints for preserving the discernibility between all pairs of discernible objects. It requires that we keep at least one attribute from each non-empty entry of the discernibility matrix, i.e., corresponding to any pair of discernible objects. Skowron and Rauszer have shown that the sets of all minimal sets of attributes preserving discernibility between objects are the set of all reducts. Thus the reduct set corresponds to the set of prime implicants of the discernibility formula.

Consider the information system shown in Table 7.6.

Table 7.6

	a	b	c	*d*
x_1	15	26	36	27
x_2	15	26	18	19
x_3	14	37	18	48
x_4	14	37	18	48

The discernibility matrix of the information system is given as Table 7.7.

Table 7.7

	x_1	x_2	x_3	x_4
x_1	ϕ	{c,d}	{a,b,c,d}	{a,b,c,d}
x_2	{c,d}	ϕ	{a,b,d}	{a,b,d}
x_3	{a,b,c,d}	{a,b,d}	ϕ	ϕ
x_4	{a,b,c,d}	{a,b,d}	ϕ	ϕ

Each entry in the matrix generates a clause. The following are the clauses:

$$\sigma_{12} = c^* \vee d^*$$

$$\sigma_{13} = a^* \vee b^* \vee c^* \vee d^*$$

$$\sigma_{14} = a^* \vee b^* \vee c^* \vee d^*$$

$$\sigma_{23} = a^* \vee b^* \vee d^*$$

$$\sigma_{24} = a^* \vee b^* \vee d^*$$

By simplifying, we get the propositional formula as $(c^* \vee d^*) \wedge (a^* \vee b^* \vee d^*)$. We can see that the prime implicants are d^*, $a^* \wedge c^*$ and $b^* \wedge c^*$.

PROPOSITION 7.1

If Q is a prime implicant of the CNF, then Q is a reduct.

Thus the reducts are $\{d\}$, $\{a,c\}$ and $\{b,c\}$. We introduce here an algorithm to compute the set of prime implicants and the set of reducts. The binary matrix representation of a CNF formula is introduced here. Any clause is considered as a binary vector. The occurrence of a literal in the clause is represented by 1, otherwise 0. In the matrix representation, the number of rows in the matrix is equal to the number of literals in the formula and the number of columns in the matrix is equal to the number of clauses in the formula. Though for general cases we have negative literals appearing in a clause, in the present context, when CNF is derived from a discernibility matrix, there is no negative literal.

$$M(x, i) = \begin{cases} 1, & \text{if } x \text{ occurs in } d \\ 0 & \text{otherwise} \end{cases}$$

A column j of $\mathcal{M}(\mathcal{F})$ is said to absorb another column k if $\mathcal{M}(y, j) \leq \mathcal{M}(y, k)\ \forall\, y$. Absorption of column in matrix representation is the same as subsumption of clauses. The jth column absorbs the ith column if and only if the jth clause subsumes the ith clause. A path in $\mathcal{M}$ is a set p of literals such that for every column i, there is an $x \in p$ such that $\mathcal{M}(x, i) = 1$. A path p subsumes another path q if and only if $p \subseteq q$. A path is a *prime path* if and only if for a path q, $q \subseteq p$ if and only if $q = p$.

For $R \subseteq C$, $T \subseteq L$, $M\,[R,T]$ is the submatrix of $\mathcal{M}(\mathcal{F})$ consisting of columns of R and ignoring the rows in T. $P\,[R, T]$ denotes the set of all prime paths of $M[R, T]$. We use a recursive algorithm for computing the set of all prime implicants of $M[R,T]$. Initially, R is C and T is empty.

INPUT: M[R,T]
OUTPUT: $P[R,T]$ all prime paths of $M\,[R,T\,]$
INTIALISE P_1, P_2, P_3, P_4 $P[R,T]$ as $\varnothing$.
    select a row $r \notin T$.
    compute $P[S - S_r, T \cup \{r\}]$ and $P[S_r, T \cup \{r\}]$
    for all $p \in P[S - S_r, T \cup \{r\}]$ **do**
if there is a path q in $P[S_r, T \cup \{r\}]$ such that $q \subseteq p$
    then do
    update $P_1 = P_1 \cup \{p\}$
    update $P[S - S_r, T \cup \{r\}\,] = P[S - S_r, T \cup \{r\}\,] - \{p\}$
    for all .....

There are many approaches to finding reducts based on discernibility matrix [Bazan, 2000].

7.6 Types of Reducts

The intersection of all reducts is the *core* and the core decides the essential set of attributes. As discussed above, it is hard to compute all reducts. Thus the set of all reducts are approximated by computing the set of all 'relevant' reducts. There are different approaches to restrict the set of all reducts to special kinds of reducts. Several techniques have been developed to select relevant reducts or their approximations. These are *decision-relative* reducts, *dynamic* reducts, *a*-reducts, etc.

k-Relative Reduct

A *k-relative reduct* is the minimal set of attributes that is needed to discern o_k (the kth object) from all other objects. To construct a k-relative reduct, we take the kth column of the discernibility matrix and construct a disjunction for each of the attributes in an entry. The conjunction of all these terms forms the *k-relative discernibility function*. Its prime implicant is the k-relative reduct.

Let us consider the sixth column of the above discernibility matrix to compute the 6-relative reducts. We get the following CNF for this example.

$$(d \vee e) \wedge (d \vee e \vee r) \wedge (d \vee e \vee r) \wedge (r) \wedge (e \vee r) \wedge (d \vee f \vee r) \wedge (d \vee e \vee f)$$

The prime implicants (and hence the 6-*relative reducts*) are $r \wedge d$ and $r \wedge e$.

Decision-Relative Reduct

Decision-relative reducts are in a sense a special case of the k-relative reducts. A decision-relative reduct is one that induces the same granules as that of the decision attribute. To discern objects of different decision classes, we need a decision-relative reduct.

In order to compute the decision-relative reducts, first we take all the entries of the decision column of the discernibility matrix and write the corresponding disjunctions. The prime implicants of this boolean formula give the set of all decision-relative reducts.

α-REDUCT

α-reduct is not a reduct but an approximation of a reduct with $\alpha \in [0,1]$. The set of attributes, $B \subseteq A$, is called an α-reduct if B has a non-empty intersection with at least $\alpha \times 100\%$ of non-empty sets $c_{i,j}$ of the discernibility matrix with respect to A.

DYNAMIC REDUCT

A *dynamic reduct* of the information system **S** is a reduct of **S** that is also a reduct for the subsystem **S′** of **S**. A subsystem of S is essentially a selection of rows of the decision table. In order to make the problem simpler and meaningful, we identify only a family of subsystems (not all subsystems) *F* of **S** and we say that *R* is a *dynamic reduct* of **S** if it is also a reduct for all the subsystems in *F*.

There are many heuristic algorithms proposed in literature to compute different types of reducts.

7.7 RULE EXTRACTION

Decision rules are expressions of the form "*if... then...*". Let **S** be an information system. For a set of attributes *B*, we construct propositional formula using attribute-value pairs (a,v), where $a \in B$ and $v \in V_a$ represent decision rules.

The general form of the decision rules is

$$\text{if } (a_1 = v_1) \wedge (a_2 = v_2) \wedge \ldots (a_n = v_n) \text{ then } (b = d_1 \vee b = d_2 \vee \ldots b = d_k)$$

where a_i's are condition attributes and b is a decision attribute.

When $k = 1$, the rule is said to be deterministic. For $k > 1$ the rule is non-deterministic. Various procedures are available for extracting decision rules from the decision table. These approaches aim at generating minimal number of rules that cover all objects in the information system. With reference to Table 7.6, we can write a few rules directly by inspection.

- if $(a=15)$ then $(d=27 \vee d=19)$
- if $(a=15) \wedge (b=26) \wedge (c=18)$ then $(d=19)$
- if $(c=18)$ then $(d=19 \vee d=48)$

In the above example, the first and third rules are non-deterministic whereas the second rule is deterministic. We can also categorise rules as *certain* or *possible* rules with respect to each lower or upper approximation of a decision class.

There are several methods of rule inductions. We discuss one such simple technique here. The rules are generated directly from the upper and lower approximations. Decision rules, which are logical implications, constitute the logical counterpart of approximations. Rules corresponding to the lower approximations are called *certain rules* whereas the uncertain rules corresponding to the boundary regions are called *possible rules*.

For every granules of the decision attribute, we find the lower and upper approximations with respect to the condition attributes. Let us assume that the granule under consideration is X. The lower approximation of X with respect to attributes set A is $A_*(X)$, for simplicity we call this X_L. The complement of X is X^C. For every pair of objects (i, j) such that $i \in X$ and for every $j \in X^C$, we select attributes $a \in A$ such that as the atomic rule $(a = v)$ is satisfied by the object i and not by the object j. We denote this atomic rule as M_{ij}. Then the rule for this granule can be written as

$$\vee_{i \in X_L} \wedge_{j \in X^C} (\vee M_{ij}).$$

We illustrate the method using the example given in Table 7.2. Let us consider one *e-granule* say, $X=\{1, 2, 3, 4, 6, 8, 9, 10, 12\}$. Let us take an attribute set $A=\{a, b\}$. The lower approximation of X with respect to $A = \{a, b\}$ is $X_L = \{4, 6, 10, 12\}$. The complement of X is $X^C = \{5, 7, 11\}$.

Let us take first $i = 4$ and $j=5$. For objects 4 and 5 with respect to attributes a and b, $b= 2$ makes object 4 to satisfy and object 5 to violate. Thus we take the atomic rule $b=2$. For $i = 4$, $j = 7$, the corresponding atomic rule is $a =2$. The other atomic rules for every pair (i, j) is given in Table 7.8.

Table 7.8

i	j	
4	5	$b=2$
4	7	$a=2$
4	11	$b=2$
6	5	$a=1$
6	7	$b=3$
6	11	$a=1, b=3$
10	5	$a=1, b=1$
10	7	$b=2$
10	11	$a=1$
12	5	$a=1, b=1$
12	7	$b=1$
12	11	$a=1$

Thus we generate the rule as

$$\text{If } (b=2 \wedge a=2 \wedge b=2) \vee (a=1 \wedge b=3 \wedge (a=1 \vee b=3)) \vee ((a=1 \vee b=1) \wedge b=2 \wedge a=1) \vee ((a=1 \vee b=1) \wedge b=1 \wedge a=1) \text{ then } e=1.$$

We can simplify this further. We do this for every decision granule to get the whole set of rules.

POSSIBLE RULES

To induce *possible* rules we follow the same procedure except that we replace X_L by the upper approximation X_U of X with repect to A and replace X^C by the complement of X_U.

The coverage of a rule is the set of objects in U that satisfy the antecedent part of the rule. The *certainty factor* and the *coverage factor* of rules are conditional probabilities which express how exact is our knowledge (data). From a logical point of view, the certainty factor can be interpreted as a degree of truth of the decision rule, i.e., how strongly the decision can be trusted in view of the data. On the contrary, the coverage factor can be viewed as to what degree the reasons for a decision can be trusted in view of the data.

Chevre et al showed that the rules generated by the rough set theory have very high classification accuracy for data sets that have high variability. They showed that for the given set of data, the rough set-based rules gives 91% classification accuracy whereas the decision tree gives 88% accuracy. Moreover, it is observed that the rough set-based classification rules are easier to interpret whereas the decision tree-based rules are more economical and complete. Mak and Munakata also carried out a comparative analysis of rough set theory-base rule extraction with other methods such a neural network and decision trees. They observed the following.

> *Overall, the rough set method offers much better explanatory capability than the neural network method and distills the data into a set of simple and usable rules. When the sample size is small or if the underlying distribution of the data deviates significantly from multivariate normal distribution, rough set may perform better since there is no assumption on the data size and distribution. Rough set may also perform better when the data are incomplete, imprecise, heterogenous or non-numeric.*

In case of neural network-based rule discovery, training time is long, comprising the computational time before the network stabilises or converges. Sometimes if the data are inconsistent or incomplete, neural networks may fail to converge. On the other hand, the training time for rough set is considerably shorter. It is also observed that when the data is numeric, neural network-based rule extraction performs better whereas for categorical data rough set analysis is better.

7.8 DECISION TREE

We can use rough set theory for constructing decision trees. Rough set theory identifies the importance of condition attributes with respect to the decision attributes and hence, it becomes much easier to determine splitting attributes. Several measures can be used to determine the splitting attributes. We can use the attribute that has the smallest boundary region as the splitting attribute. We can also use the attribute with largest discriminating index as another way of determining the splitting attribute.

DEPENDENCY INDEX FOR DETERMINING SPLITTING ATTRIBUTE

The degree of dependency of the decision attribute on the condition attribute can be used as a heuristic for selection of the splitting attribute that will best separate the samples into individual classes. The larger the degree of dependency of the decision attribute on a condition attribute is, the more certain information is included in it. Hence, the condition attribute with highest level of dependency can be chosen as the splitting attribute (this method is proposed in [Huang, 2007]). Readers can refer to Section 6.5 of Chapter 6 where several methods of computing the splitting index are discussed. The dependency index provides yet another way of computing splitting index.

In order to illustrate the procedure, let us take the decision table given in Table 7.3. The dependency indices of the decision attribute with respect to individual condition attribute are the following.

$$\gamma_{\{height\}}(\{class\}) = 0,\ \gamma_{\{hair\}}(\{class\}) = 3/8, \gamma_{\{eyes\}}(\{class\}) = 3/8.$$

We can choose *hair* or *eyes* as the splitting attributes. If we choose *hair*, then the splitting criteria are *hair* = "blond", *hair* = "black" and *hair* = "red". You will face difficulty in finding a splitting attribute if the dependency index for every condition attribute is 0. In that case, the dependency index can be regularised by redefining a dependency index with upper approximation.

There are several other ways of determining splitting attributes.

7.9 Rough Sets and Fuzzy Sets

Many researchers relate the fuzzy set theory to the rough set theory. How is rough set theory different from the fuzzy set theory? The rough set theory is certainly somewhat similar to that of fuzzy theory in term of the target objectives. But the two techniques differ in their approaches. One fundamental difference is that rough set theory can be considered as a machine learning technique whereas the fuzzy set theory does not have learning capability. The generic fuzzy set theory assumes fuzzy membership functions for the analysis. On the other hand, the rough set theory expresses vagueness not by means of membership, but by employing a boundary region for a set. Rough sets can be also defined employing rough membership function, which is more general than fuzzy membership function. The membership function is computed empirically from the data. In order to compare the concepts of rough sets and fuzzy sets, Pawlak defines the rough membership function as follows.

Definition 7.13 Rough membership function

Given an object x and a set X, we define the rough membership function of x in X with respect to an attribute set A as follows.

$$\mu_A^X : U \to [0,1] \text{ where } \mu_A^X(x) = \frac{|A(x) \cap X|}{|X|}.$$

$A(x)$ is the A-granule containing x.

The rough membership function has the following properties.

1. $\mu_A^X(x) = 0$ if and only if $x \in \text{NEG}_A(X)$.
2. $\mu_A^X(x)$ lies in (0, 1) if $x \in \text{BND}_A(X)$.

3. The rough membership of any x for $X \cup Y$ is at least the maximum of the rough membership of x for X and for Y. Hence,

$$\mu_A^{X \cap Y}(x) \geq \max(\mu_A^X(x)\ \mu_A^Y(x)).$$

4. The rough membership of any x for $X \cap Y$ is at most the minimum of the rough membership of x for X and for Y. Hence,

$$\mu_A^{X \cap Y}(x) \leq \min(\mu_A^X(x)\ \mu_A^Y(x))$$

Thus, though the fuzzy membership for union and intersection of sets can be computed from the membership for the constituent sets, we can only give a one side bound for these values for rough membership. Thus as Pawlak indicates, rough membership is more general than the fuzzy membership.

7.10 Granular Computing

We observe that one of the fundamental concepts of the rough set theory is the concept of *granules*. This approach led to the development of a new research topic, *Granular Computing* (GrC). The granular computing is a field of theories and techniques that makes use of granules for data analyses. Recently, a granular computing model for knowledge discovery and data mining was proposed by combining results from formal concept analysis and granular computing. Each granule is viewed as the extension of a certain concept and a description of the granule is an intension of the concept. The basic ingredients of granular computing are the subsets, classes and clusters of a universe. There are many fundamental issues in granular computing, such as granulation of the universe, description of granules, relationships between granules and computing with granules. Granulation of a universe involves the decomposition of the universe into parts, or the grouping of individual elements into classes, based on available information and knowledge. The concept of granular computing led to the extension of rough set theory to define granules in a variety of ways. We discuss below one such granularisation as an extension of the conventional rough sets.

Variable Precision Rough Set

This is one of the popular extension of the rough set theory where the lower and upper approximations are defined with a precision level β, with $0.5 < \beta \leq 1$. β-lower approximation and b-upper approximation are defined as follows.

β-Lower approximation of X with respect to A:

$$A_*^\beta(X) = \cup\left\{Y \in U / A^+ : \frac{|Y \cap X|}{|X|} \geq \beta\right\}$$

β-Upper approximation of X with respect to A:

$$A^{\beta*}(X) = \cup\left\{Y \in U / A+ : \frac{|Y \cap X|}{|X|} > 1-\beta\right\}$$

Variable precision rough set (VPRS) has become a major research area of rough set theory in recent years.

Covering-Based Rough Sets

As discussed above, granular computing addresses the approximation of any set of objects in terms of composed sets. However, the rough set theory defines the set of granules in terms of indiscernibility relations as an equivalence relation induced by a set of attributes. There can be several other ways of granularisation. *Covering-based rough sets* is a technique of granularisation that takes covering instead of partition into account for defining the granules.

Definition 7.13 Covering

Let C be a family of subsets of U. If none of the subsets in C is empty and if $\cup C = U$, C is called a *covering* of U.

It is clear that a partition of U is a covering of U and any covering is not necessarily a partition. The concept of covering is more general than the concept of partition. We can define the lower and upper approximation of a set of objects using coverings and thus, generalise the concept of the rough sets to covering-based rough sets.

Definition 7.14 Lower and Upper Approximation

For any set X, the lower and upper approximations respectively of X with respect to the covering C is given by

$$C_*(X) = \cup\{K \mid K \in C \text{ and } K \subseteq X\}.$$

$$C^*(X) = C_*(X) \cup \{\text{neighbour } (x) \mid x \in X - C_*(X)\}.$$

We can now use this pair of approximation as the rough sets and use the results of conventional rough sets.

Further Reading

The rough set approach to data mining has some advantage over other approaches in that it

* provides efficient algorithms
* finds minimal set of data (data reduction)
* evaluates significance of data
* generates a set of decision rules from the data

* offers straightforward interpretation of the result
* can be used for clustering, classification, etc.

RS theory has been applied in medical diagnosis, industrial control, marketing analysis, credit card application analysis, prediction of company acquisition, etc.

EXERCISES

1. Discuss the underlying principles of the rough set theory. Discuss the situations when this theory may be useful for data mining?
2. Show that
   a. $A^*(U) = U$.
   b. $A^*(\varnothing) = \varnothing$.
   c. $A^*(A^*(X)) = A^*(X)$.
   d. $X \subseteq Y$, then $A^*(X) \subseteq A^*(Y)$.
3. Prove the following.
   a. $A_*(X) \subseteq X$
   b. $X \subseteq A^*(X)$
   c. $A_*(X \cap Y) = A_*(X) \cap A_*(Y)$
   d. $A^*(X \cup Y) = A^*(X) \cup A^*(Y)$
   e. $A_*(U - A_*(X)) = U - A_*(X)$
   f. $A^*(U - A^*(X)) = U - A^*(X)$
4. How do you compare POS_REG_A (B) and POS_REG_B (A)? Construct an example when both are equal.
5. Answer the same question for BND_REG_A(B) and BND_REG_B(A).
6. When do you have β_A(B) = 0?
7. When is BND_REG_A(B) = U?
8. Consider the following information system.

	occupation	age	shoe size	credibility
o_1	thief	35	42	high
o_2	doctor	45	44	medium
o_3	thief	35	41	low
o_4	farmer	23	46	high
o_5	thief	53	45	high
o_6	thief	53	45	low
o_7	thief	37	42	medium
o_8	doctor	49	44	low
o_9	doctor	49	44	low

a. Find the upper and lower approximation of $\{o_1, o_2, o_6, o_7, o_8\}$ with respect to {age, shoe size}.
b. Find the $POS\_REG_{\{age\}}$ {credibility}, $BND\_REG_{\{shoe\ size\}}$ {credibility}.
c. Compute the discriminant index, dependency index of {credibility} with respect to {age, shoe size}.
d. Build a decision tree using dependency index.
e. Can you sudggest another method of building decision tree, say by using discrimant index?
f. Can you find a set of all reducts? What are the core attributes? Can you use core attributes to decide on splitting attributes?
g. Determine decision-relative reducts.

9. Consider the following information system.

Objects	c1	c2	c3	c4	c5	c6	d1
o1	1	1	1	1	1	1	M
o2	1	0	1	0	1	1	M
o3	0	0	1	1	0	0	M
o4	1	1	1	0	0	1	F
o5	1	0	1	0	1	1	F
o6	0	0	0	1	1	0	F
o7	1	0	1	0	1	1	F

a. Find the upper and lower approximation of the decision attribute with respect to the attribute set $\{c_1, c_3, c_5\}$.
b. What is boundary region of the set $X = \{o_1, o_2, o_7\}$.
c. Compute the set of all reducts of Q.

10. Given a transaction database, define some equivalence relations on the set of attributes or the set of tuples. Find the lower and upper approximation. Is it possible to discover some information from this?

BIBLIOGRAPHY

M. Banerjee and M. K. Chakraborty. Rough logics: A survey with further directions. In Incomplete information; Rough Sets Ananlysis, Physica-Verlag, Heidelberg, 1997.

J. Bazan, H. S. Nguyen, S. H. Nguen, P. Synak and J. Wroblewski. Rough set algorithms in classification problems. In Rough set Methods and Applications: Studies in Fuzziness and soft computing,Physica-Verlag, pp. 49–88, Heidelberg, 2000.

Z. Pawlak. Reasoning about Data – A rough set perspective, Adams, E.W.: The logic of Conditionals, An Application of Probability to Deductive Logic. D., Reidel Publishing Company, Dordrecht, Boston, 1975.

W. Bandler and L. Kohout. Fuzzy power sets and fuzzy implication operators. Fuzzy Sets and Systems 4, 1980.

N. Chevre, F. Gagne, P. Gagnon, C. Blaise. Application of rough set analyi to identify polluted aquatic sites based on a battery of biomarkers: a comparison with classical methods. Cmosphere 51:13 – 23, 2003.

S. Demri and E. Orlowska. Logical analysis of indiscernibility.ICS Research Report 11/96, Institute of computer science, Warsaw University of Technology.

W. Ziarkow and N. Shan. KDD-R; A comprehensive systems for knowledge discovery using rough sets.In Proceedings of the international Workshop on Rough Sets and Soft Computing (RSSC '94), 1994.

S. Greco, B. Matarazzo and R. Slowinski. A new Rough Set Approach to Multicriteria and Multiattribute Classification.

L. Huang, M. Huang, B. Guo, Z. Zhang. A new method for constructing decision tree based on rough set theory.IEEE International Conference on Granular Computing,pp. 241–245, 2007.

B. Mak, T. Munakata, Rule extraction from expert heuristic: A comparative study of rough set with neural networks and ID3. European Journal of Operational Research, 136:212–229, 2002.

S. Nguyen, S. Hoa and P. Synak. Rough sets in data mining: approximate description of decision classes.

S. K. M.Wong and W. Ziarkow.On learning and evaluation of decision rules in the context of rough sets.InProceedigns of the InterantionalSyposium on Methodologies for Intelligent systems, 1986.

W Zhu.Toploical approaches to covering rough sets.Information Sciences, 2006.

I. Düntsch and G. Gediga. Rough Set Data Analysis *–A Road to Non-invasive Knowledge Discovery*.Metodos Publisher, Bangor, Bissendorf, 2000.

J.D. Gunn and J.W. Grzyma a-Busse. Global temperature stability by rule induction: an interdisciplinary bridge. *Human Ecology,*22:59–81, 1994.

S.K. Pal and A. Skowron (Eds.). *Rough Fuzzy Hybridization*.Springer, Berlin, 1999.

Z. Pawlak. Rough Sets – Theoretical Aspects of Reasoning about Data.Kluwer Academic Publishers, Boston, London, Dordrecht, 1991.

Z. Pawlak. Decision rules, Bayes' rule and rough sets. In *New Direction in Rough Sets, Data Mining, and Granular-Soft Computing,*Springer, pp. 1–9, Berlin, 1999.

L. Polkowski and A. Skowron (Eds.).*Rough Sets and Current Trends in Computing Lecture Notes in Artificial Intelligence*.Springer1424, Berlin, 1998.

L. Polkowski and A. Skowron (Eds.).*Rough Sets in Knowledge Discovery* vols. 1–2.PhysicaVerlag, A Springer Company, Berlin, 1998.

L. Polkowski, S. Tsumoto, T.Y. Lin (Eds.).Rough Set Methods and Applications – New Developments in Knowledge Discovery in Information Systems. Springer, Berlin, 2000, to appear.

N. Zhong, A. Skowron and S. Ohsuga (Eds.).*New Direction in Rough Sets Data Mining and Granular-Soft Computing*.Springer, Berlin, 1999.

8

Genetic Algorithm

8.1 Introduction

Genetic algorithms (GAs), first proposed by Holland in 1975 (*Adaptation in Natural and Artificial Systems, 1975*), are computational models for finding a solution to a problem, mostly optimisation, modelled loosely on the principles of evolution via natural selection. They are useful when the search space for solutions is large and complex, and no mathematical analysis exists to narrow down the search space. In the natural selection process, a population of individuals undergo selection in the presence of variation-inducing operators such as recombination (crossover) and mutation to evolve to a population with a set of characteristics better suited to survive. Genetic algorithms, using the same analogy, consider that the genetic pool of a population potentially contains the solution to a given adaptive problem. However, this solution is not alive because the required genetic combination is split between several subjects. Only the association of different genes that occurs during reproduction and crossover will lead to its coming into being. Sometimes, the given solution may not be existing at all in a given genetic pool of the considered population, and it takes a process like mutation to make it emerge.

A genetic algorithm emulates biological evolution by first considering a set of individuals (the population, characterised by a set of chromosomes) in the current generation and a set of biologically-inspired operators that can change these individuals to a newer generation of population. Chromosome, which carry genetic information, is comprised of genes, each encoding a particular trait of an individual, for example the colour of eyes. The complete set of genetic material (all chromosomes) of a particular species is called its genome or the gene pool. An individual of a species is characterised by its own settings for genes; the particular set of genes distinguishing the induvidual is called its genotype. According to evolutionary theory, only the fittest of individuals are likely to survive and generate off-springs by transmitting their biological heredity to new generations. In computing terms, the chromosome is essentially a string of bits, and genetic algorithms (GAs) map these strings of bits to each potential solution. Each solution becomes an individual in the population, and each string becomes the representation of an individual. The genetic algorithm then manipulates the most promising strings in the set of strings, or the population, in its search for an improved set of solutions. It eliminates weak elements by favouring the retention of optimal individual, and recombines features of good individuals (through reproduction process) to perhaps generate better individuals. The algorithm performs in cycles of generations. In each generation, the GA creates a set of new solutions (or chromosomes) by different genetic operations that correlate to the processes of natural reproduction.

Genetic algorithms have been shown to be an effective tool in data mining. Essentially, when a problem in data mining is viewed as a search problem or an optimisation problem, there is a scope of applying GA. It has been shown to be successful in association rule mining, clustering and classification. To take an example, there are two different approaches to applying GA for classification—apply GA directly to find the decision boundary in an N-dimensional feature space or, use GA as an optimisation tool for resetting the parameters in other classifiers.

Let us first look at the essential steps of GA.

8.2 Basic Steps of GA

GA Cycle

A population of individuals, each representing a possible solution to a problem, is initially created at random. Then, pairs of individuals combine (crossover) to produce offsprings for the next generation. A mutation process is also used to randomly modify the genetic structure of some members of each new generation. The algorithm runs to generate solutions for successive generations. The probability of an individual reproducing is proportional to the goodness of the solution it represents. Hence, the quality of the solutions in successive generations improves. The process is terminated when an acceptable or optimum solution is found, or after some fixed time limit set has elapsed.

A GA begins its search with a random set of solutions; we call this set the *population* of a generation comprising individuals, each representing a possible solution to a problem. The solutions are represented by a string of symbols, analogous to *chromosomes*. Once a random population of solutions is created, each individual solution is evaluated in the context of the underlying objective and a *fitness* value is assigned to each solution. A termination condition is checked. If the termination criterion is not satisfied, the population is modified by the three genetic operators—selection, recombination and mutation—and a new and possibly better population is created as the next generation. The generation counter is incremented to indicate that one generation of the GA is completed. The algorithm operates through a simple cycle consisting of the following steps.

- Creation of a population of strings
- Evaluation of each string
- Selection of the best strings
- Genetic operation to create a new population of strings

Figure 8.1 gives the flow diagram of GA. Each cycle produces a new generation of possible solutions (individuals) for a given problem. In the first stage, a population of possible solutions is created as a start point. Each individual in this population is encoded into a string (chromosome) to suit manipulation by the genetic operators. In the next stage, the individuals

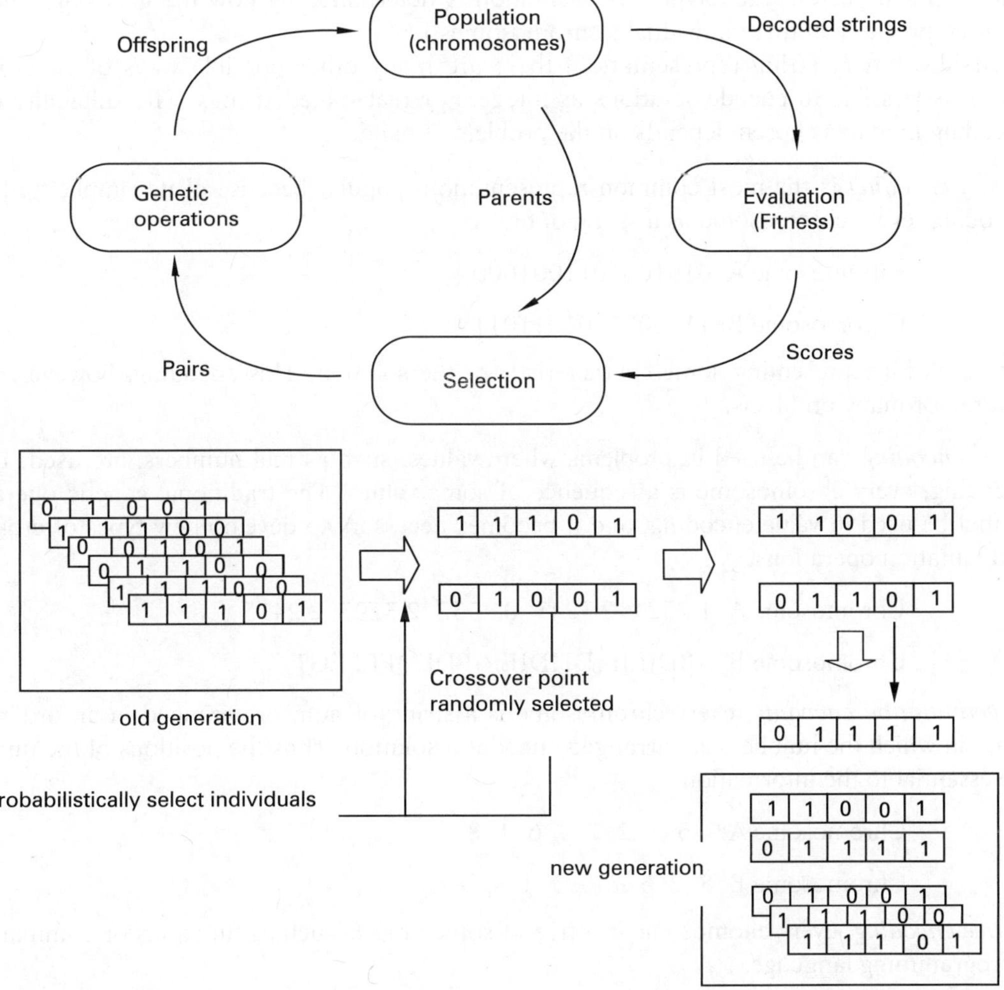

Figure 8.1 GA cycle

are evaluated based on a *fitness function*, which determines how fit an individual is in relation to the others in the population. Based on each individual's fitness, a selection mechanism chooses the fittest pairs of individuals for the genetic manipulation process. The selection policy assures the survival of the fittest individuals.

Representing a solution

Before a genetic algorithm can be put to work on any problem, it is necessary encode the potential solutions of the problem into a format on which the genetic operators can be applied. One common approach is to represent each solution as a binary string, i.e., a sequences of 1's and 0's, such that each position represents some aspect of the problem. This process of coding is intended to achieve a pseudochromosomal representation of a solution in the search space. Natural cromosomes are made of many genes, each of which can take one of many different values. (Each person's genotypic representation is determined by how the genes are encoded /written precisely in that induvidual's chromosomes.)

Besides binary string representation, there are many other possible ways of encoding in GA. It is possible to encode solutions as integers or real valued strings. The suitability of the encoding methods chosen depends on the problem at hand.

Binary encoding is the most common representation, popular because of its simplicity. In this encoding, every chromosome is a string of bits, e.g.,

Chromosome A: 0101001011001000

Chromosome B: 1100001101011011

with each bit representing some characteristic of the solution. This encoding, however, is not natural for many problems.

Value encoding can be used in problems where values, such as real numbers, are used. In this encoding, every chromosome is a sequence of some values. The traditional genetic operations cannot be used in value encoding, and it becomes necessary to develop new types of crossover and mutation operations.

Chromosome A 1.2324 2.3243 0.4532 2.3293 2.2435

Chromosome B ABDJEIFJDHDIERJFDLDFLFEGT

In *permutation encoding,* every chromosome is a string of numbers aranged in an order. The order in which the numbers are arranged encodes a solution. Thus the positions of the numbers are essential to the information.

Chromosome A 9 5 3 2 7 4 6 1 8

Chromosome B 8 2 6 7 5 3 1 4 9

In *tree encoding*, every chomosome is a tree of some objects such as functions or commands of a programming language.

FITNESS

In order to determine which chromosomes are good for retention and which are weak, it becomes necessary to ascertain the fitness of a choromosome. Thus, a fitness function that captures the desirability of a chromosome in the context at hand is defined, which assigns a value—an objective function—to each string (chromosome). It may be noted that GAs are normally employed in optimisation problems, and each problem will have a different objective function (fitness function).

The manipulation process applies genetic operators to the pairs chosen for reproduction to produce a new population of individuals (the *offsprings)* by manipulating the genetic information possessed by them (stored in the strings describing the individuals). Two operators are used: **crossover** and **mutation**. The offsprings generated by this process take the place of the older population and the cycle is repeated until a desired level of fitness in attained, or kill a determined number of cycles is reached.

The genetic operators are described next.

8. 3 SELECTION

The main objective of this step is to retain a good selection of solutions for subjecting to genetic operations and to eliminate those that are not fit enough. That is, selection is used to determine which individuals survive to the next generation by taking part in the process of reproduction. If the selection process is not judiciousely designed for the problem in hand, the algorithm may have some shortcomings and result in unsatisfactory outcomes. For instance, the population may become homogenous prematurely due to *selective pressure*. By homogenous, we mean that all solution converge to one solution, and by selective pressure we mean the prevailing conditions strongly favouring the selection of one type of string only. Variation is fundamental to evolution, and if no variation occurs the evolution of population does not take place. Thus, what a large selective pressure causes is a decrease in diversity from generation to generation, limiting the exploration possibility in the search space. Another factor to be noted is that we cannot increase the population size arbitrarily. While moving from one generation to the next, the population size must be kept almost constant.

Thus, the primay objective of the selection operator is to make duplicates of good solutions and eliminate bad solutions while keeping the population size constant. This is done in the following way.

- Identify good (above-average) solution in a population.
- Make multiple copies of the good solutions.
- Eliminate bad solutions from the population so that multiple copies of good solutions can be placed in the population.

GAs employ the following types of selection.

Random Selection

The selection operator randomly selects a string from the population for duplication.

Tournament Selection

This is a two-stage selection process. In the first stage a pool of competitiors are selected and a tournament is played between a pair of selected solutions. In the second stage, a copy of the winner solution is selected. If carried out systematically, each candidate can be made to participate in exactly two tournaments. The best solution will win both times resulting in two copies in the mating pool. Likewise, the worst solution will not be included in the mating pool. Any solution will have zero, one, or two copies in the new population. Tournament process is carried out by randomly choosing pairs of individuals from the population in such a way that every individual is selected twice.

Proportionate Selection

In the proportionate selection procedure, the number of copies of a candidate is proportional to its fitness value. If the average fitness of the population is *avg_fitness*, a solution with fitness f_i gets an expected number f_i / *avg_fitness* number of copies.

Roulette Wheel Selection

This is a type of proportionate selection method. In this method the first step is to calculate the cumulative fitness S of the whole population by summing of the fitnesses of all individuals. Individuals are then mapped one-to-one into contiguous segments in a roulette wheel of size S. The size of each individual interval corresponds to the fitness value of the associated individual. The circumference of the roulette wheel is the sum of all fitness values of the individuals. The fittest individual occupies the largest segment, whereas the lesser fit have correspondingly smaller segments within the roulette wheel. To select an individual, a random number is generated in the interval [0, S] and the individual whose segment spans the random number is selected. This process is repeated until the desired number of individuals has been selected. In this mode of selection, if the fitness of the ith chromosome in the population at time t is $f(x_i^t)$, then the probability of selecting this chromosome in the population at time $t+1$ is given by

$$P(x_i^{t+1}) = \frac{f(x_i^t)}{\Sigma_{i=1}^{n} f(x_i^t)}$$

where there are n number of choromosomes in the population in the tth generation.

Rank-based Selection

In the *rank-based selection* the solutions are first sorted according to their fitness, from the worst to the best. Each member in the sorted list is assigned a fitness equal to the rank of the solution in the list. Thereafter, the proportionate selection operator is applied with the ranked fitness values. Thus, individuals are selected based on their fitness rank rather than their absolute fitnesses.

Rank-based selection has lower selective pressure compared to fitness based selection. There are several variations of rank-based selection such as linear ranking, exponential ranking, etc. We describe here the linear ranking scheme.

We assign a value s, $1 \leq s \leq 2$, to the fittest chormosome and a value $(2 - s)$ to the weakest chromosome. The internediate chromosomes are assigned values by interpolation as follows.

$$f(i) = s - \frac{2(i-1)(s-1)}{(N-1)} \quad \text{for } 1 \leq i \leq N$$

The average value automatically happens to be 1. Hence this value directly translates to the expected number of offsprings. If s is set to 2, the weakest chromosome has 0 probability of selection. s can be increased beyond 2 to negative values for weak chromosomes.

Elitist Selection

In this scheme, the best individuals from the current population are allowed to survive without alteration directly into the next generation. A consequence is that the diversity of the next generation reduces if more individuals from the current population are carried over to the next generation; however, elitist selection improves the convergence of the genetic algorithm.

Replacement Selection

In this selection scheme, an offspring individual replaces one parent individual in the next generation.

8.4 Crossover

Crossover is one of the genetic operators used to recombine highly fit individuals in a population. This operator takes two chromosomes and swaps part of their genetic information to produce new chromosome. For this, two strings, called parents, are selected from the *mating pool* at random and some portions are exchanged between the strings to create two new strings, called offsprings. The *single-point crossover* (or one-point crossover) operator randomly chooses a crossover point along the string and an exchange of all bits on the right of the crossing site takes place to produce a pair of new offsprings(see Figure 8.2a). In *two-point crossover*, two points are selected and a part of the chromosome between these two points is swapped to generate two individuals of the new generation (see Figure 8.2b). We can also define an n-point crossover, where the portions of strings between n alternate points are swapped. For example, if it is a 5-point crossover, then the substrings between crossover points 1 and 2, 3 and 4 are swapped to get an individual and the substrings between 2 and 3, 4 and 5 are swapped to get another individual. In general, one can have a binary vector as a crossover

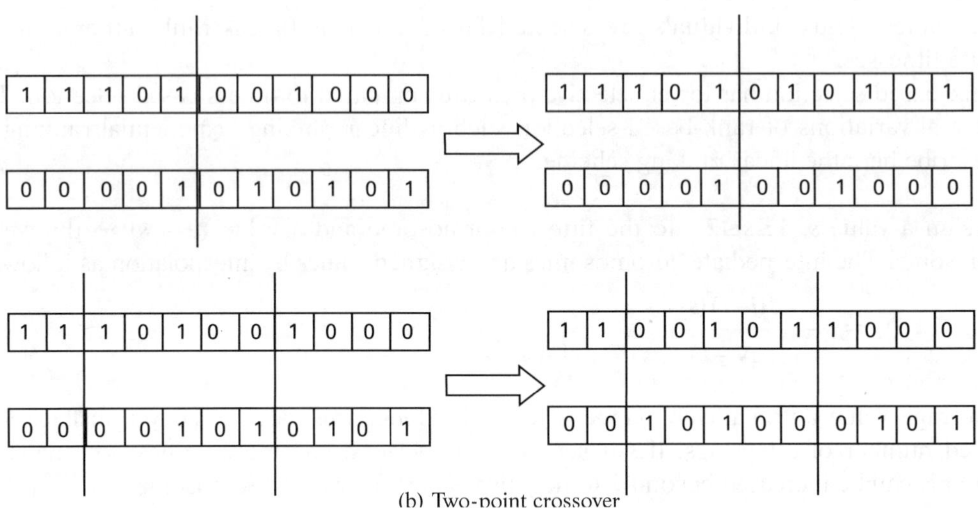

Figure 8.2 Crossover

template to determine which portions of both parents are going to be combined to get the offspring.

It is important to note that the crossover operator is expected to create better individuals in the next generation. But every crossover between any two parents from a population may not find an offspring better than both parents. However, the chances of generating fitter individuals are high. This is true because the parents are not any two arbitrary random strings. These strings have survived tournaments played with other solutions during the earlier reproduction phase. Thus, they possibly have some good bit combinations. Even when we get a worse solution resulting from a crossover, it gets eliminated in the next reproduction operation. On the other hand, a good solution is likely to get more copies in the next reproduction stage.

The *mating pool* need not consist of all the solutions in the current generation. We choose the mating pool based on the a crossover probability, *pc*. We select $pc \times 100\%$ of individuals from the population for crossover. The remaining $100\ (1 - pc\ )\ \%$ of individuals of the population are simply copied to the new population. If *pc* is set to 1, all choromosomes in the population will be included in the mating pool; if *pc* is 0.5, only half of the population will perform crossover and the other half will be included into the new population directly without change.

We can see that the mechanics of selection and crossover operations are surprisingly simple and involve only string copying and partial string exchanges. But these two operations give the GA the real power, a power obtained from the principle of evolution, where the fittests survive. Goldberg justifies this as follows.

"To see this, consider a population of n strings over some alphabet coded so that each is a complete idea or prescription for performing a particular task. Substring within each string contains various notions of what is important or relevant to the task. Viewed in this way, the population contains not just a sample of n ideas, rather it contains a multitude of notions and rankings of those notions for task performance. Genetic algorithms carefully exploit this wealth of information about important notions by

1. reproducing quality notions according to their performance and
2. crossing these notions with many other high performance notions from other strings.

Thus the act of crossover with previous reproduction speculates on new ideas constructed from the high performance building blocks of past trials."

In yet another crossover operation, the *tree crossover*, one crossover point is selected in both parents and parents are divided at that point and the parts below the crossover points are exchanged to produce a new offspring (Figure 8.3).

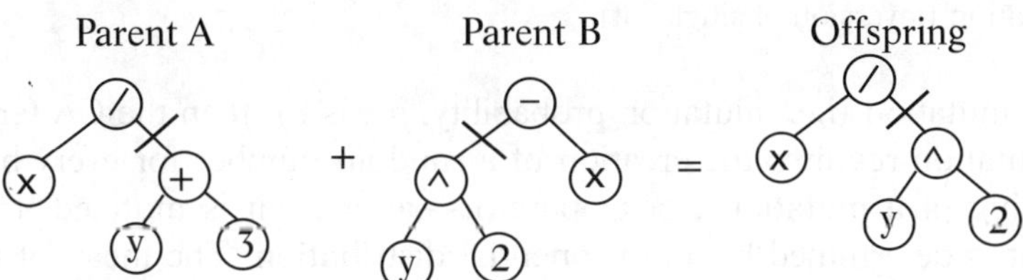

Figure 8.3 Tree crossover

8.5 MUTATION

The crossover attempts to generate fitter individual based on the genetic characteristics of the parents, i.e., the individuals in the current generation. Sometimes, if the population does not contain the requisite information to get to the solution, no amount of gene mixing will produce a satisfactory solution. It becomes necessary then to create new genetic structure. The mutation operator does this. It introduces new genetic structures in the population by randomly changing some of the string bits. In other words, mutation is implemented by occasionally altering a random bit in a chromosome. In evolutionary biology, random deformations of the genetic information of an individual occur due to the effect of radioactive radiation or other environmental influences, and the probability that a certain gene is mutated is almost equal for all genes. In computational perspective, since the modification is totally random and thus not related to any previous genetic structures present in the population, mutation creates different structures in a different region of the search space. The need for mutation is to retain diversity in the population.

The role of mutation operator in GA is also to prevent GA converging prematurely to suboptimal solutions. Moreover, some important regions of the search space may never be explored if this operator is not introduced. In order that the operator plays its role well, it should be applied by controlling the degree of goodness/fitness of the individuals.

The algorithm for mutation is given below.

for i := 1 to n ***do***
if random[0,1] <, p_m, ***then***
invert s[i];

It is recommended that the mutation probability, p_m, should be very low in order to avoid the GA behaving chaotically like a random search. Again, the choice of the appropriate mutation technique depends on the coding and the problem itself.

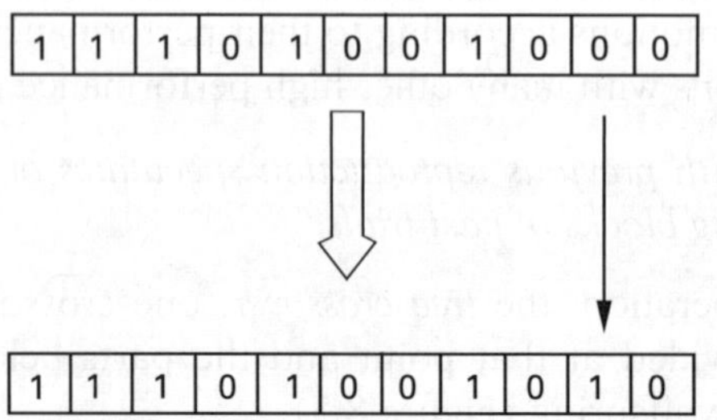

Figure 8.4 Mutation (inversion of single bit)

If there is no mutation (i.e., mutation probability, p_m, is 0), then the GA terminates very fast. The bit-wise mutation requires the creation of a random number for every bit. This is achieve by the functioning of a mutation clock operator—after a bit is mutated, the location of the next mutated bit is determined by an exponential distribution. The mean of the distribution is assumed to be $\mu = 1/p_m$.

Mutation can be detrimental too, as a fit candidate solution may mutate to produce undesirable solution. High mutation rate has an advantage that individuals may explore newer areas of the search space and may step into new solutions or step out of some solutions. On the other hand, low mutation rate may exploit and and refine a current position in the search space.

Mutation operation can be effected in the following ways.

Inversion of single bit: In this process one randomly chosen bit is negated with a probability p_m. Figure 8.4 shows the operator being applied to the tenth element of a chromosome.

Bitwise inversion: In this operation, the whole string is inverted, bit by bit, with probability p_m.

Random selection: In this operation, a string is replaced by a randomly chosen one with probability p_m.

Real mutation: This is a variant of the mutation operation for strings whose bits are group-coded for integer or real variables. Rather than applying bit-flip mutation, each subgroup, encoded as a real number, is subjected to a "real number" mutation with either a uniform or a Gaussian probability distribution. The new real number is then translated back to the corresponding sequence of bits and reinserted in the solution string [Whitley, 2000].

Adaptive mutation: The adaptive mutation operator or the intelligent mutation operator accomplishes the objective of effecting mutation by removing the bad design variables from an individual [Whitley, 2000]. The probability of the adaptive mutation operator is given by

$$p_m = \begin{cases} \dfrac{0.5(f_{\max} - f)}{f_{\max} - f'} & \text{if } f \geq f' \\ 0 & \text{otherwise} \end{cases}$$

where, f_{max} is the maximum fitness value in the population, f' the average fitness of the population, and f the fitness of an individual. When the fitness of an individual is smaller than the average fitness of the population, the probability of mutation, p_m, is equal to 1.0. If the value of f is the same with that of f', then p_m is equal to 0.5; p_m becomes zero if f comes close to f_{max}. It can be seen that an increment in the fitness of an individual decreases the probability of mutation.

Keenan in 1996 designed a wide set of mutation operators like Complement, Transpose, Jump, Invert, Rotate and Increment by 1, by 2, or by powers of 10. These operators could operate both at the string level and within a gene, at bit level. In either case they affect more than one locus at the same time. There are several other types of mutation operations like Uniform Mutation, Inorder Mutation, Gaussian Mutation, etc.

A number of other operators other than crossover and mutation have been introduced since the basic model was proposed. They are usually versions of the recombination and genetic alterations processes adapted to the constraints of a particular problem. Examples of other operators are inversion, dominance and genetic edge recombination.

ENCODING

The choice of the underlying encoding for the solution of the optimisation problem (the individuals on the population) is critical to the GA's performance. Traditionally, binary encodings have been used because they are easy to implement. The crossover and mutation operators described earlier are specific to binary encodings. When symbols other than 1 or 0 are used, the crossover and mutation operators must be tailored accordingly.

THE EVALUATION STEP

The evaluation step in the cycle, shown in Figure 8.1, is the one more closely related to the actual application the algorithm is trying to optimise. It takes the strings representing the individuals of the population and, from them creates the actual individuals to be tested. The way the individuals are coded in the strings will depend on what parameters one is trying to optimise and the actual structure of possible solutions (individuals). After the actual individuals have been created, they have to be tested and scored. These two tasks again are very closely related to the actual system being optimised. The testing depends on what characteristics should be optimised, and the scoring on the production of a single value representing the fitness of an individual. The latter depends on the relative importance of each different characteristic value obtained during testing.

Though we have described the basic steps of GA, in real implementation one has to take into account a number of problem-dependent parameters. For instance, whether the offspring produced by the genetic manipulation (the next population to be evaluated) replaces the whole population (generational approach), or just its less fitted members (steady-state approach). The problem constraints will dictate the best option. Other parameters to be adjusted are the population size, crossover and mutation rates, evaluation method, and convergence criteria. There are many variations of the basic model, and readers are referred to books on GA for more information. We will focus on the application of GA in data mining.

8.6 Data Mining Using GA

The application of genetic algorithm in the context of data mining is generally on tasks of *hypothesis testing* and *refinement*, where the user poses some hypothesis and the system first evaluates the hypothesis and then seeks to refine it. Hypothesis refinement is achieved by starting with some initial hypotheses and then allowing some or all parts of it to vary. One can use varieties of evaluation functions to determine the fitness of a candidate for refinement. The important aspect of GA application is in the encoding of the hypothesis and in the formulation of the evaluation function for fitness.

Another way to use GA for data mining is to design hybrid techniques by blending one of the known data mining techniques with GA. For example, it is possible to use genetic algorithm for optimal decision tree induction. As we learnt in Chapter 6, we can take samples of the training data set to build a decision tree. Thus, by randomly generating different samples we can build many decision trees using any of the traditional techniques. But we are not sure of the optimal tree. At this stage GA is very useful in deciding the optimal tree and the optimal splitting attributes. The genetic algorithm evolves a population of biases for the decision tree induction algorithm. We can use a two-tiered search strategy. The GA can be used to control the preference for one type of decision tree over another.

One can view predictive modelling as the determination of unknown or future values of the variables of interest using some set of known variables. The traditional weighted average or linear multiregression models of prediction require a basic assumption that there is no interaction among the attributes or variables. GA is able to handle attribute interaction in a better manner. One can think of an adaptive GA for learning the nonlinear multiregression from a set of training data.

We shall now discuss a specific data mining task, namely rule discovery, and the use of GA for this task.

8.7 GA for Rule Discovery

One of the data mining tasks is to discover classification rules from a given training set. We discuss in the section the method of using GA for rule discovery. Our goal here is to find a set of rules that collectively can have high predictive accuracy. Thus, high classification accuracy becomes our objective and this governs the definition of fitness function. It is possible that other measures like comprehensiveness or interestingness can become other objectives.

Michigan Approach and Pittsburgh Approach to Coding Rules

Rules are typically encoded in two ways, namely the Michigan approach and the Pittsburgh approach. In Michigan approach each individual encodes a single prediction rule, whereas in the Pittsburgh approach each individual encodes a set of prediction rules. The choice between these two approaches strongly depends on which kind of rule we want to discover, or equivalently, which kind of data mining task we are addressing. For example, for classification task we usually evaluate the quality of a rule set as a whole rather than the quality of an individual rule. In other words, the interaction among rules is important. Thus it is natural to adopt the Pittsburgh approach. If the data mining task is to discover a small set of high-quality prediction rules so that the quality of each rule is important, independent of other rules, then the Michigan approach is more appropriate. The Michigan approach has two main components. The credit assignment component evaluates the classification efficiency of individual rules and the discovery component acts on the rule level seeking for new promising rules that can improve the classification performance.

ENCODING THE ANTECEDENT

Consider a rule of the form

$$IF \quad cond_1 \quad \text{AND} \quad cond_2 \quad \text{AND} \quad cond_3 \quad \text{AND.... THEN} \quad class = c_i.$$

whcre, cach condition is of thc form $A \leq v$ or $A \in S$. Thc antcccdcnt is

$cond_1$ AND $cond_2$ AND $cond_3$ AND.... and the consequent is $class = c_i$.

The antecedent and consequent parts are encoded separately. A simple approach to encode the rule condition into an individual is to use a binary encoding. Suppose that a given attribute can take k discrete values. Then we can encode a condition on the value of this attribute by using k bits. We can use a bit for the logical operator in the condition too. Rules with several antecedents can be encoded by concatenating the respective bit strings. It may be noted that the antecedent encodes the disjunctions and the concatenation encodes the conjunctions. Note that if all k bits of a given attribute are "on", it means that the corresponding attribute is effectively ignored by the rule antecedent. To avoid generation of invalid chromosomes during crossover, some alignment is necessary in the position of different attribute values. Attributes appear in a fixed sequence in every rule. Otherwise, the crossover operation may not yield a valid rule.

When the attribute is continuous valued, the binary representation of the value can be used to encode the condition. One can also use the attribute oriented induction for this purpose. For example, consider the training set as given below.

G	F	L	K
High	Strong	Low	go
High	Strong	High	go
High	Weak	Low	go
High	Weak	High	nogo
High	Weak	High	nogo
Low	Strong	Low	nogo
Low	Weak	High	nogo

A rule can be *If* "G = HIGH" *AND* "L = LOW" *then* "go'.

This rule can be coded as 01 | 11 | 10 | 1.

Encoding the Consequent

There are three ways of representing the consequent. The first possibility is to encode the class in the binary representation of the rule. In such cases, the class parameter is also the subjected to the process of evolution. The second possibility is to associate all individual of a population with the same predicted class, which is never modified during the running of the algorithm. Hence, if we want to discover a set of classification rules predicting k classes, we would need to run the algorithm at least k times so that in the ith run the algorithm discovers only rules predicting the ith class. The third possibility is to choose the predicted class most suitable for a rule in a kind of deterministic way, as soon as the corresponding rule antecedent is formed. The chosen class can be the class that has more representatives in the training set.

Fitness function

Fitness of an individual is measured by computing the confidence factor.

We make use of the following fitness function.

$$f = \left[\frac{TP}{TP + FN}\right] \times \left[\frac{TN}{FP + TN}\right]$$

where, TP is true positive, FP is false positive, TN is true negative, and FN is false negative. In the above formula, the term $(TP/(TP + FN))$ is often called *sensitivity*, whereas the term $(TN/(FP + TN))$ is often called *specificity*. Several other fitness functions that take into account both predictive accuracy and comprehensibility of a rule are described in the literature. Another measure that is also considered is the interestingness of the rule.

8.8 GA and the Decision Tree

One can use the above rule discovery technique along with some other techniques of data mining. For example, we learnt in an earlier chapter how to find rules using decision trees. The drawback of decision-tree-building algorithms is the fragmentation problem, where the set of examples belonging to a tree node gets smaller and smaller as the depth of the tree is increased, making it difficult to induce reliable rules from deep levels of the tree. In such a situation one can use GA in conjunction with decision tree method to get over this difficulty.

Carvalho and Freitas have proposed such a hybrid technique. The basic idea is to use a well-known decision-tree algorithm to classify examples belonging to large disjuncts and use a genetic algorithm to discover rules classifying examples belonging to small disjuncts. This approach tries to combine the best of both worlds. Decision-tree algorithms have a bias towards generality that is well suited to large disjuncts, but not for small disjuncts.

In a decision tree, each path from the root to a leaf node corresponds to a rule predicting the class specified in the corresponding leaf node. Hence, a decision tree with d leaves is transformed into a rule set with d rules (or disjuncts). Carvalho and Freitas categorise each of these rules into either a small-disjunct or large (non-small) disjunct, depending on whether or not its coverage (the number of examples covered by the rule) is smaller than or equal to a given threshold. A large-disjunct rule is kept aside and the small-disjunct rules are passed to the GA, triggering the second training phase. This second phase comprise the use of GA to discover rules covering these small-disjunct examples.

The set of small-disjunct rules returned by the decision tree method forms the initial set of individuals. Thus, in GA formalism an individual represents antecedent of a small-disjunct rule. The consequent of the rule, which specifies the predicted class, is not represented in the genome. Rather, it is fixed for a given GA run so that all individuals have the same rule consequent during that entire run. The algorithm runs once for each class and in each run the best individual is selected to represent the rule for the corresponding class. Thus the GA runs *d.c* times, where *d* is the set of rules (small disjuncts) and *c* is the number of classes.

Each rule's condition is of the form $A_i\, Op_i\, V_{ij}$, where A_i is the *i*th attribute; V_{ij} is the *j*th value of the domain of A_i; and Op_i is a logical/relational operator compatible with attribute A_i. B_i represents an active bit which takes on the value 1 or 0 to indicate whether or not, respectively, the *i*th condition is present in the rule antecedent.

Figure 8.5 illustrates the format of representing a rule for GA application. Figure 8.6 depicts instances of rules in this format and application of crossover operation thereby.

$A_1OP_1V_{1j1}$	B_1	$A_2OP_2V_{1j2}$	B_2	....	$A_tOP_tV_{tjt}$	B_t

Figure 8.5

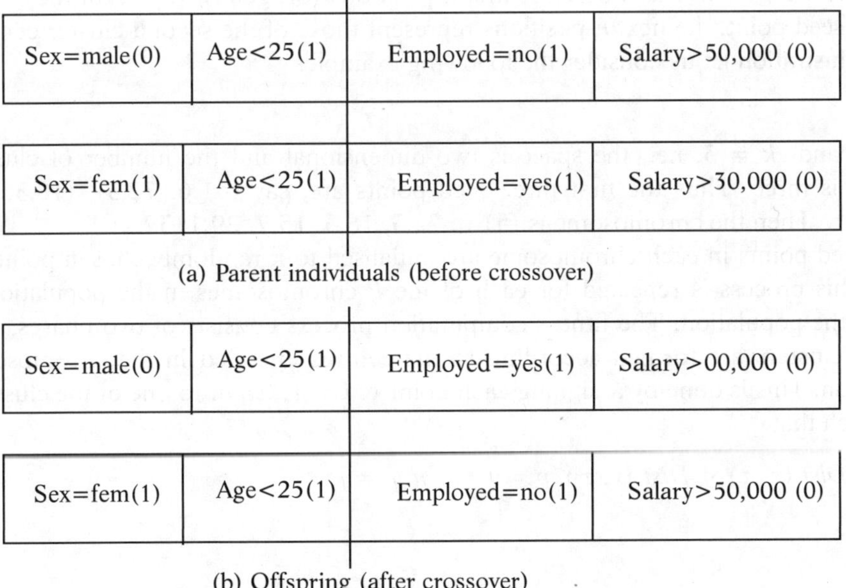

(a) Parent individuals (before crossover)

(b) Offspring (after crossover)

Figure 8.6 One-point crossover in a population (Carvalho and Freitas, 2002)

It is interesting to note here the variation of mutation operation. The mutation operator changes the V_{ij} randomly for the selected condition, A_i OP_i V_{ij}. Thus, once the mutation point is chosen, say at (Age < 25), the mutation operator selects a random value, say 30, and replaces the condition to (Age < 30). The fitness function is the same as the one discussed above.

8.9 Clustering Using GA

As we know, clustering algorithms like k-means are essentially optimisation problems. Thus at the first look it seems that one can directly use GA for clustering. It is, in a sense, true, provided one can work out the details of coding the problems in terms of chromosomes and by defining the genetic operators. Maulik and Bandopadhaya proposed a GA-based clustering algorithm which is essentially the use of GA for k-means clustering.

Recall that in k-means clustering we start with a set of seed points and classify other data points based on their distance to the seed points. We recomputed the seed points as the mean-point of each cluster and repeated this process till the algorithm stabilised by generating the same set of seed points in consecutive iterations.

The GA considers the initial set of seed points as its initial population. During the GA cycles the algorithm generates a new set of seed points based on genetic operations. An interesting deviation of this algorithm from the traditional one is that here the chromosomes are defined in terms of strings of real numbers and not by strings of bits. Hence there is a difference in the manner of defining the crossover and mutation operations.

Each chromosome represents a valid partition of the given data set. Each string is a sequence of real numbers representing the k-cluster centres. For an n-dimensional space, the length of a chromosome is $n \times k$ words, where the first n positions (or, genes) represent the n dimensions of the first seed point, the next n positions represent those of the second cluster centre, and so on. As an illustration let us consider the following example.

Example 1

Let $n = 2$ and $k = 3$, i.e., the space is two-dimensional and the number of clusters being considered is three. Thus the first three seed points are, say (51.6, 72.3), (18.3, 15.7) and (29.1, 32.2). Then the chromosome is (51.6, 72.3, 18.3, 15.7, 29.1, 32.2).

The k seed points in each chromosome are initialised to k randomly chosen points from the data set. This process is repeated for each of the P chromosomes in the population, P being the size of the population. The fitness computation process consists of two phases. In the first phase, the clusters are formed according to the centres encoded in the chromosome under consideration. This is done by assigning each point x_i, $i = 1, \ldots, n$, to one of the clusters C_j with centre z_j such that

$$Dist\ (x_i, z_j) < Dist\ (x_i, z_p),\ p = 1, \ldots, n,\ p \neq j.$$

Conclusions

Genetic algorithm approaches to data mining are increasingly becoming popular and there are several extensions of the basic GA for different applications. In addition, there are other population-based techniques such Ant Colony Algorithm and Particle Swarm techniques that are being developed, which share some foundational concepts with GA.

Excercises

1. Discuss the salient features of genetic algorithm.
2. How is population diversity ensured in genetic algorithms? Describe how the choice of mutation probability affects the outcome of the solution to a problem.
3. What are the methods generally adopted to encode potential solutions?
4. How can a data mining problem be an optimisation problem? How do you use GA in such cases?
5. Describe the use of GA in conjunction with decision tree algorithm to aid rule discovery process.

Further Reading

Readers may read Whitley's tutorial for a good exposure to GA. (There are many other good textbooks dealing with GA). Some of the selected list of papers from which the current text is compiled is given below. The use of GA for clustering by Maulik and Bandopadhyaya is recommended to all.

Bibliography

Carvalho Deborah R. and Freitas A. A. A genetic algorithm for discovering small-disjunct rules in data mining. *Applied Soft Computing*, vol 2, pp 75–88, 2002.

Coley, A.D. *An Introduction to Genetic Algorithms for Scientists and Engineers,* World Scientific, Singapore, 188p. 1999.

Fogel D.B. (Ed.). *Evolutionary Computation*, IEEE Press, New York, 1998.

Freitas A.A. *Data Mining and Knowledge Discovery with Evolutionary Algorithms*, Springer, Berlin, 2002, p. 956.

Goldberg D.E. *Genetic Algorithm in Search, Optimization and Machine Learning*. Addison-Wesley Publishing Company, 1989.

Holland J.H. *Adaptation in Natural and Artificial System* (2nd edition). Prentice Hall, 1992.

Keenan M. Novel and combined generation, selection, recombination and mutation operators for evolutionary computing. In *Proceedings of the Ninth International Conference on Computer Applications in Industry*. ISCA Publisher, 1996.

Marmelstein R., and Lamont G. Pattern Classification using a hybrid genetic program-decision tree approach. In *Proceedings of the 3rd Annual genetic Programming Conference*, pp. 223–231, 1998.

McCallum R. and Spackman K. Using genetic algorithms to learn disjunctive rules from examples. In *Proceedings of the 7th International Conference on Machine Learning*, pp. 149–152, 1990.

Maulik U. and Bandopadhyay S. Genetic Algorithm based clustering technique. *Pattern Recognition*, Vol 33, 1455-1465 (2000).

Michalewicz Z. *Genetic Algorithms + data Structures + Evolutionary Programs*, Springer Berlin, 1999.

Michalewicz Z., *Genetic algorithms + Data Structures = Evolution Programs*, 3rd ed. Springer, Berlin, 1996.

Noda E., Lopes H.S., Freitas A. A. Discovering interesting prediction rules with a genetic-algorithm. In *Proceedings of the Congress on Evolutionary Computation* (CEC-99), IEEE Press, pp.1322–1329,1999.

Ryan M.D. and Rayward Smith V.J. The evolution of decision trees. In *Proceedings of the Third Annual Genetic Programming Conference*, pp. 350–358, 1998.

Schmitt Lothar M. Fundamental study theory of genetic algorithms, *Theoretical Computer Science,* 259, pp 1–61, 2001.

Syswerda G. In *First Workshop on the Foundations of Genetic Algorithms and Classification Systems*, Morgan Kaufmann, 1990.

Whitley D. A genetic algorithm tutorial, *http://www.cs.colostate.edu/~genitor/MiscPubs/tutorial.pdf.*

Witten I.H., Frank E. *Data Mining: Practical Machine Learning Tools and Techniques with Java Implementations*. Morgan Kaufmann, Los Altos, CA, 2000.

9

OTHER TECHNIQUES

9.1 INTRODUCTION

In Chapters 4 to 8 we studied in detail the algorithms for discovering association rules for clustering and building decision trees. These, in fact, have been the main areas of research in data mining algorithms in recent years. Data mining is essentially a task of learning from data and hence, any known technique which attempts to learn from data can, in principle, be applied for data mining purposes. But it is crucial, as we have noticed in the earlier chapters, that these algorithms be suitably modified to handle the large data residing in the secondary memory. This problem is better illustrated by considering the case of propositional reasoning. Since the days of Boole to the current state in machine learning and propositional reasoning of AI, researchers have been proposing algorithms with increasing efficiency for computing prime implicates/implicants, converting a CNF to DNF, and so on. It is a trivial exercise to notice that these problems are directly related to finding frequent sets. Readers may refer to Heiki Mannila's pioneering work in this direction. But for theoretical importance, these algorithms are inefficient to handle disk-resident data and unless appropriately modified, they are unsuitable in practice for data mining applications. This is just a single case of a variety of known techniques in other disciplines which share the same theoretical foundation as the techniques required for data mining, but cannot be readily applied for practical data mining applications. We have noted the tricks of modifying decision trees and clustering algorithms in Chapters 5 and 6.

In general, data mining algorithms aim at minimising I/O operations of disk-resident data, whereas conventional algorithmics are more concerned about time and space complexities, accuracy and convergence. Besides the techniques discussed in the earlier chapters, a couple of other techniques hold promise of being suitable for data mining purposes. These are Neural Networks (NN) and Support Vector Machines (SVM). There are many books available on the these topics. The intention of this chapter is to briefly present the underlying concepts of these subjects and demonstrate their applicability to data mining.

In Section 9.2, we introduce the principles of neural computing and give an outline of MLP architecture and RBF architecture. Section 9.3 discusses the learning techniques of MLP and RBF. Section 9.4 deals with one of the most popular techniques namely, Kohonen's model of Self-organising Maps. We present a case study of data mining using NN techniques in Section 9.5.

Section 9.6 is concerned with Support Vector Machines (SVM). A few techniques of data mining using SVMs are proposed.

9.2 What is a Neural Network?

Neural networks are a different paradigm for computing that draws its inspiration from neuroscience. The human brain consists of a network of neurons, each of which is made up of a number of nerve fibres called *dendrites,* connected to the *cell body* where the *cell nucleus* is located. The *axon* is a long, single fibre that originates from the cell body and branches near its end into a number of *strands*. At the ends of these strands are the transmitting ends of the *synapses* that connect to other biological neurons through the receiving ends of the synapses found on the dendrites as well as the cell body of biological neurons. A single axon typically makes thousands of synapses with other neurons. The transmission process is a complex chemical one which effectively increases or decreases the electrical potential within the cell body of the receiving neuron. When this electrical potential reaches a threshold value (action potential), it enters its excitatory state and is said to *fire*. It is the connectivity of the neuron that give these simple 'devices' their real power.

Artificial neurons (or processing elements, PE) are highly simplified models of biological neurons. As in biological neurons, an artificial neuron too has a number of inputs, namely a cell body (most often consisting of the summing node and the transfer function), and an output which can be connected to a number of other artificial neurons. Artificial neural networks are densely interconnected networks of PEs, together with a rule (learning rule) to adjust the strength of the connections between the units in response to externally supplied data.

The evolution of neural networks as a new computational model originates from the pioneering work of McCulloch and Pitts in 1943. They suggested a simple model of a neuron that commuted the weighted sum of the inputs to the neuron and an output of 1 or 0, depending on whether the sum was over a threshold value or not. A 0 output would correspond

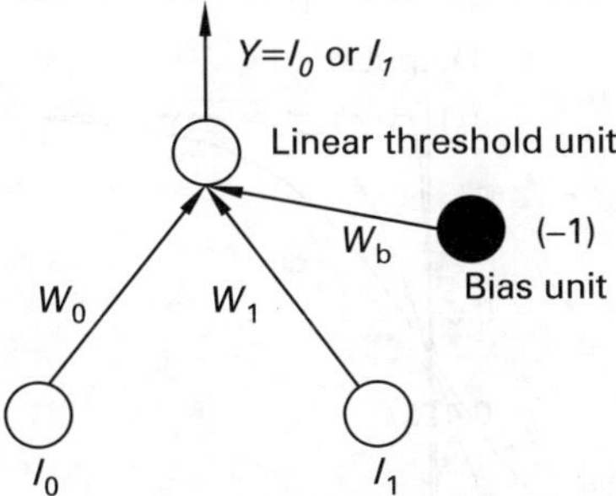

Figure 9.1 A simple perceptron

to the inhibitory state of the neuron, while a 1 output would correspond to the excitatory state of the neuron. Consider a simple example illustrated below.

The network has two binary inputs, I_0 and I_1, and one binary output Y. W_0 and W_1 are the connection strengths of input 1 and input 2, respectively. Thus, the total input received at the processing unit is given by

$$W_0 I_0 + W_1 I_1 - W_b,$$

where W_b is the threshold (in another notational convention, it is viewed as the bias). The output Y takes on the value 1, if $W_0 I_0 + W_1 I_1 - W_b > 0$, otherwise, it is 0 if $W_0 I_0 + W_1 I_1 - W_b \leq 0$.

But the model, known as perceptron, was far from a true model of a biological neuron as, for a start, the biological neuron's output is a continuous function rather than a step function. This model also has limited computational capability as it represents only a linear-separation. For two classes of inputs which are linearly separable, we can find the weights such that the network returns 1 as output for one class and 0 for another class.

There have been many improvements on this simple model and many architectures have been presented recently. As a first step, the threshold function or the step function is replaced by other more general, continuous functions called *activation functions*. Figure 9.2 illustrates the

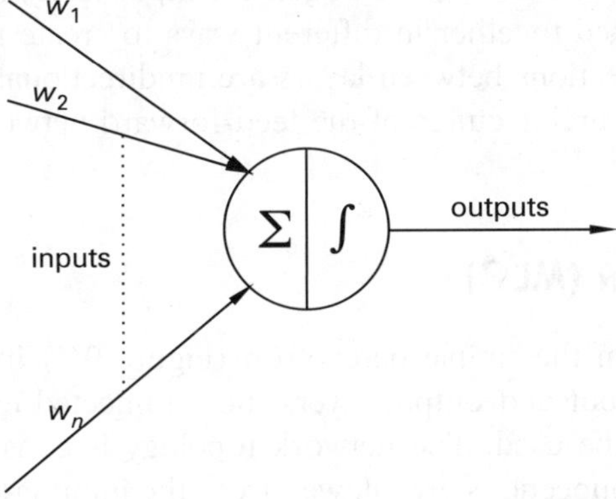

Figure 9.2 A typical artificial neuron with activation function

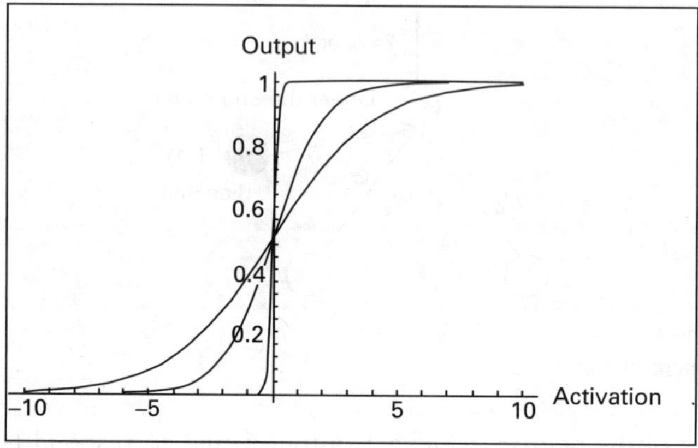

Figure 9.3 Sigmoid functions

structure of a node (PE) with an activation function. For this particular node, n weighted inputs (denoted W_i, $i = 1,\ldots, n$) are combined via a *combination function* that often consists of a simple summation. A *transfer function* then calculates a corresponding value, the result yielding a single output, usually between 0 and 1. Together, the combination function and the transfer function make up the *activation function* of the node.

Three common transfer functions are the sigmoid, linear and hyperbolic functions. The sigmoid function (also known as the logistic function) is very widely used and it produces values between 0 and 1 for any input from the combination function. The sigmoid function is given by (the subscript n identifis a PE):

$$Y = \frac{1}{1+ \exp\,(-\zeta(\sum_i W_{in} X_{in}))}$$

Note that the function is strictly positive and defined for all values of input. When plotted, the graph takes on a sigmoid shape, with an inflection point at (0, .5) in the Cartesian plane. The graph (Figure 9.3) plots the different values of ζ as the input varies from –10 to 10.

Individual nodes are linked together in different ways to create neural networks. In a feed-forward network, the connections between layers are unidirectional, from input to output. We discuss below two different architectures of the feed-forward network, Multi-Layer Perceptron and Radial Basis Function.

Multi-Layer Perceptron (MLP)

MLP is a development from the simple perceptron (Figure 9.4) in which extra *hidden layers* (layers additional to the input and output layers, not connected externally) are added. More than one hidden layer can be used. The network topology is constrained to be *feed-forward,* i.e., loop-free. Generally, connections are allowed from the input layer to the first (and possibly only) hidden layer; from the first hidden layer to the second, and so on, until the last hidden

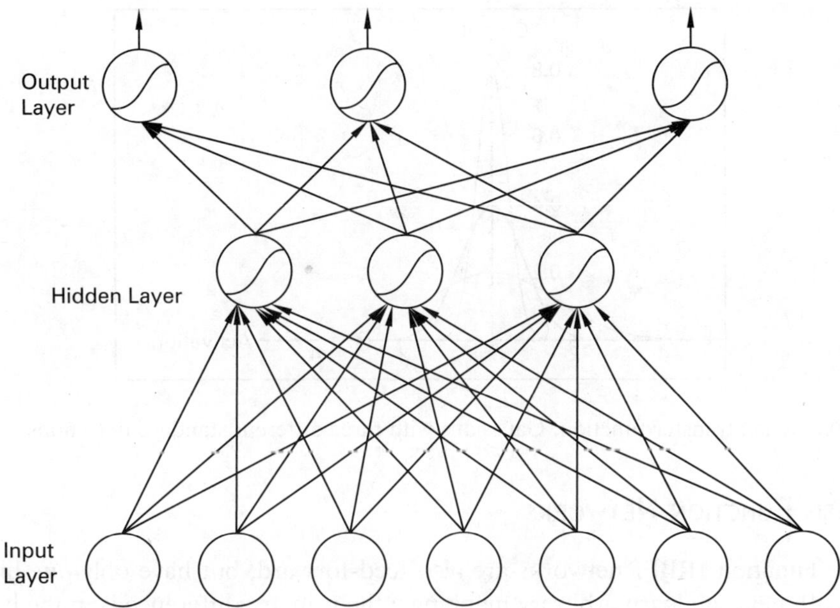

Figure 9.4 Multi-layer perceptron

layer to the output layer. The presence of these layers allows an ANN to approximate a variety of non-linear functions. The actual construction of a network, as well as the determination of the number of hidden layers and the determination of the overall number of units, is something of a trial-and-error process, determined by the nature of the problem at hand. The transfer function is generally a sigmoid function. The architecture is illustrated in Figure 9.5.

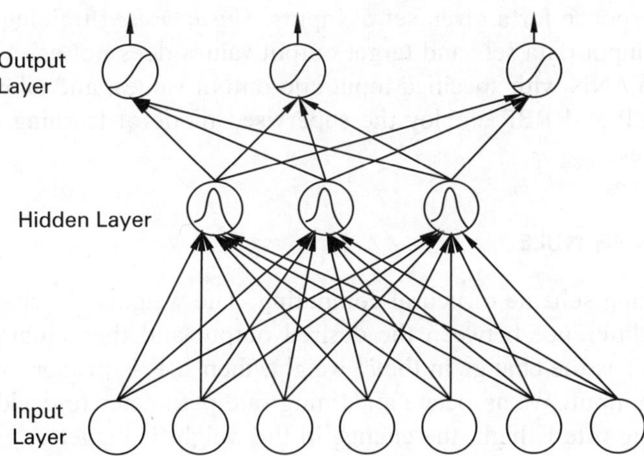

Figure 9.5 RBF arcitecture

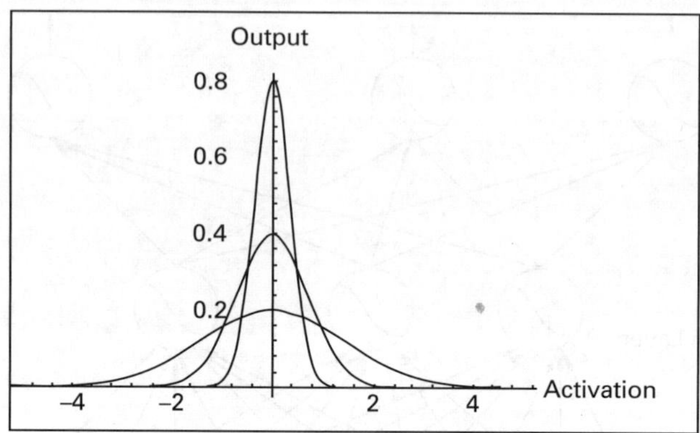

Figure 9.6 Gaussian transfer function. Gaussians with three different standard deviations.

Radial Basis Function Networks

Radial Basis Function (RBF) networks are also feed-forward, but have only *one* hidden layer. Like MLP, RBF nets can learn arbitrary mappings; the primary difference is in the hidden layer. RBF hidden layer units have a *receptive field* which has a *centre;* that is, a particular input value at which they have maximal output. Their output tails off as the input moves away from this point. Generally, the hidden units have a Gaussian transfer function. Figure 9.6 illustrates the Gaussian functions. In Figure 9.5 the architecture of RBF is shown.

9.3 Learning in NN

In order to fit a particular ANN to a particular problem, it must be *trained* (or *learned)* to generate a correct response for a given set of inputs. *Unsupervised* training may be used when a clear link between input data sets and target output values does not exist. *Supervised* training involves providing an ANN with specified input and output values, and allowing it to iteratively reach a solution. MLP and RBF employ the supervised mode of learning. We describe below these learning schemes.

Perceptron Learning Rule

This is the first learning scheme of neural computing. The weights are changed by an amount proportional to the difference between the desired output and the actual output. If W is the weight vector and ΔW_i is the change in the ith weight, then ΔW_i is proportional to a term which is the error times the input. We associate a learning rate parameter to decide the magnitude of change. If the learning rate is high, the change in the weight is bigger at every step. Formally, the rule is given by

$$\Delta W_i = \xi\,(D - Y).I_i,$$

where ξ is the learning rate, D is the desired output, and Y is the actual output. Single perceptrons are limited to learning the simple hyperplane decision surface. In other words, if the classes are visualised geometrically in n-dimensional space, then the perceptron generates descriptions of the classes in terms of a set of hyperplanes that separate these classes. When the classes are actually not linearly separable, then the perceptron is not effective in properly classifying such cases. This was one of the major disadvantages of the perceptron (single layer). The classical example is to compute XOR by a neural network, where the class corresponding to output 0 and the class corresponding to output 1 are not linearly separable. Hence, the perceptron cannot compute the XOR function.

Training in MLP

The multi-layer perceptron overcomes the above shortcoming of the single layer perceptron. But learning in MLP is not trivial. The idea is to carry out the computation layer-wise, moving in the forward direction. Similarly, the weight adjustment can be done layer-wise, by moving in backwards. For the nodes in the output layer, it is easy to compute the error as we know the actual outcome and the desired result. For the nodes in the hidden layers, since we do not know the desired result, we propagate the error computed in the last layer backward. This process gives the change in weight for the edges layer-wise. This standard method used in training MLPs is called the *back propagation* algorithm. Briefly, it involves using a gradient-descent approach to minimise the squared error between generated output values and target output values. Though there is a risk of being "trapped" in the local minima by employing such a method (convergence to a global minimum is *not* guaranteed), it has proved very efficient. The weight change rule is a development of the perceptron learning rule. The weights are changed by an amount proportional to (*the error at that unit*) times (*the output of the unit feeding into the weight*).

Formally, the learning steps consist of the following.

Forward pass

The outputs and error at the output units are calculated.

Backward pass

The output unit error is used to alter weights on the output units. Then, the error at the hidden nodes is calculated (by *back-propagating* the error at the output units through the weights), and the weights on the hidden nodes are altered using these values.

For each training data, a forward pass and backward pass is performed. This is repeated over and over again, until the error is at an acceptably low level (or we give up!).

Training RBF Networks

The RBF design involves deciding on their centres and the sharpness (standard deviation) of their Gaussians. Generally, the centres and SDs (standard deviations) are decided first by examining the vectors in the training data. RBF networks are trained in a similar way as MLP. The output layer weights are trained using the delta rule.

MLP is the most widely applied neural network technique. RBFs have the advantage that one can add extra units with their centres near parts of the input, which are difficult to classify.

9.4 Unsupervised Learning

Simple perceptrons MLP and RBF networks are supervised networks. In an unsupervised mode, the network adapts purely in response to its inputs. Such networks can learn to pick out structures in their input. One of the most popular models in the unsupervised framework is the *self-organizing map* (SOM).

Competitive Learning

Competitive learning or *winner-takes-all* may be regarded as the basis of a number of unsupervised learning strategies. A competitive learning consists of k units with weight vectors w_k, of equal dimension to the input data. During the learning process, the unit with its weight vector closest (in some metric) to the input vector x is adapted in such a way that the weight vector becomes closer to the input vector after the adaptation. The unit with the closest weight vector is termed the winner of the selection process. This learning strategy is generally implemented by gradually reducing the difference between the weight vector and input vector. The actual amount of reduction at each learning step may be guided by means of the so-called *learning rate,* ζ. During the learning process, the weight vectors converge towards the mean of the set of input data.

Kohonen's SOM

The self-organising map (SOM) was a neural network model developed by Teuvo Kohonen during 1979–82. SOM is one of the most widely used unsupervised NN models and employs competitive learning steps. It consists of a layer of input units, each of which is fully connected to a set of output units. These output units are arranged in some topology (the most common choice is a two-dimensional grid; see Figure 9.7). The input units, after receiving the input patterns X, propagate them as they are onto the output units. Each of the output units k is

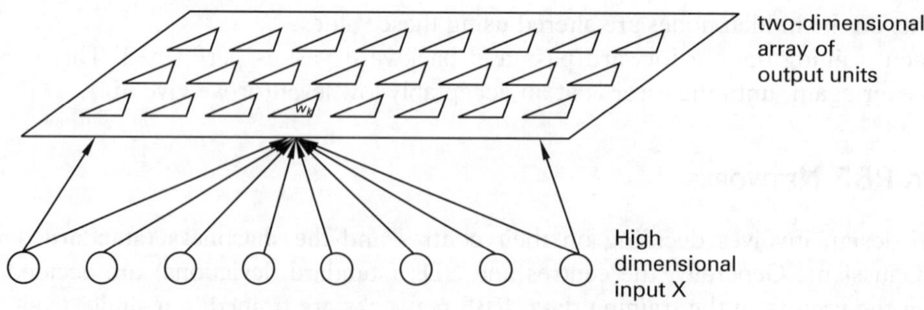

Figure 9.7 SOM architecture

assigned a weight vector w_k. During the learning step, the unit c corresponding to the highest activity level with respect to a randomly-selected input pattern X, is adapted in a such a way that it exhibits an even higher activity level at a future presentation of X. This is accomplished by the competitive learning described above. Usually, the similarity metric is chosen to be the Euclidean distance.

During the learning steps of SOM, a set of units around the winner is tuned towards the currently presented input pattern, enabling spatial arrangement of the input patterns, such that similar inputs are mapped onto regions close to each other in the grid of output units. Thus, the training process of SOM results in a topological organisation of the input patterns. It is, in some sense, related to k-means clustering. Thus, SOM takes a high-dimensional input and clusters it, but still retains some topological ordering of the output. After training, an input will cause some of the output units in some area to become active. Such clustering (and dimensionality reduction) is very useful as a preprocessing stage, whether for further neural network data processing or for more traditional techniques.

Applications of Neural Networks

These days, neural networks are used in a very large number of applications. We list here some of those relevant to our study. Neural networks are being used in

- investment analysis:
  to predict the movement of stocks, currencies etc., from previous data. There, they are replacing earlier simpler linear models.
- monitoring:
  networks have been used to monitor the state of aircraft engines. By monitoring vibration levels and sound, an early warning of engine problems can be given.
- marketing:
  neural networks have been used to improve marketing mailshots. One technique is to run a test mailshot, and look at the pattern of returns from this. The idea is to find a predictive mapping from the data known about the clients to how they have responded. This mapping is then used to direct further mailshots.

9.5 Data Mining Using NN: A Case Study

In this section, we outline a case study to illustrate the potential application of NN for data mining. This case study is taken from Shalvi [1996].

Knowledge Extraction through Data Mining

Kohonen self-organising maps (SOMs) are used to cluster a specific medical data set containing information about the patients' drugs, topographies (body locations) and morphologies (physiological abnormalities); these categories can be identified as the three

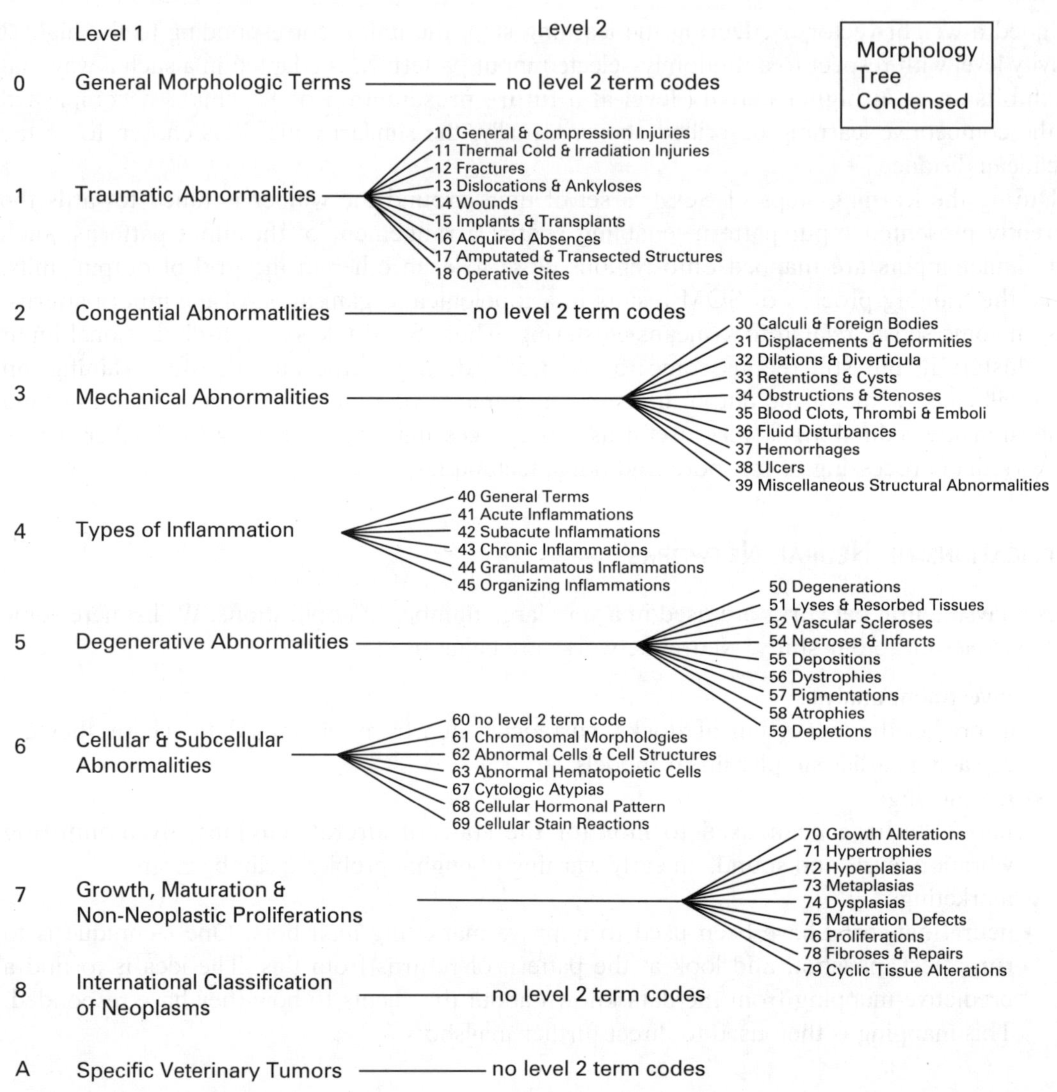

Figure 9.8 Morphology tree

input subspaces. Data mining techniques are used to collapse the subspaces into a form suitable for network classification. The goal is to acquire medical knowledge which may lead to tool formation, automation and to assist medical decisions regarding population. The data is organised as three hierarchical trees, identified as Drugs, Topography and Morphology. The most significant portion of the morphology tree is displayed in Figure 9.8. Before presenting the data to the neural network, certain preprocessing should be done. Standard techniques can be employed to clean erroneous and redundant data.

The data is processed at the root level of each tree—fourteen root level drugs, sixteen root level topographies and ten root level morphologies. By constraining all the data to the root level, the degree of differentiation has been greatly reduced from thousands to just 40. Each tuple is converted into a bipolar format. Thus, each tuple is a 40-dimensional bipolar array—a value of either 1 or –1 depending on whether any data existed for the leaves of that root node.

The Kohonen self-organising map (SOM) was chosen to organise the data in order to make use of a spatially ordered, two-dimensional map of arbitrary granularity. An $n \times n$ SOM was implemented for several values of n. We describe below only the case with $n=10$. The input layer consists of 40 input nodes; the training set consists of 2081 tuples; and the training period was of 30 epochs. The learning coefficient ζ is initialised to 0.06. After approximately 7½ epochs, ζ is halved to 0.03. After another 7½ epochs, it is halved again to 0.015. For the final set of 7½ epochs, it is halved again to become 0.0075.

After the network is trained, it is used for one final pass through the input data set, in which the weights are not adjusted. This provides the final classification of each input data tuple into a single node in the 10 × 10 grid. The output is taken from the coordinate layer as an (x, y) pair. The output of the SOM is a population distribution of tuples with spatial significance (Figure 9.9). This grid displays the number of tuples that were classified into each Kohonen layer node (square) during testing; for example, square (1,1) contains 180 tuples.

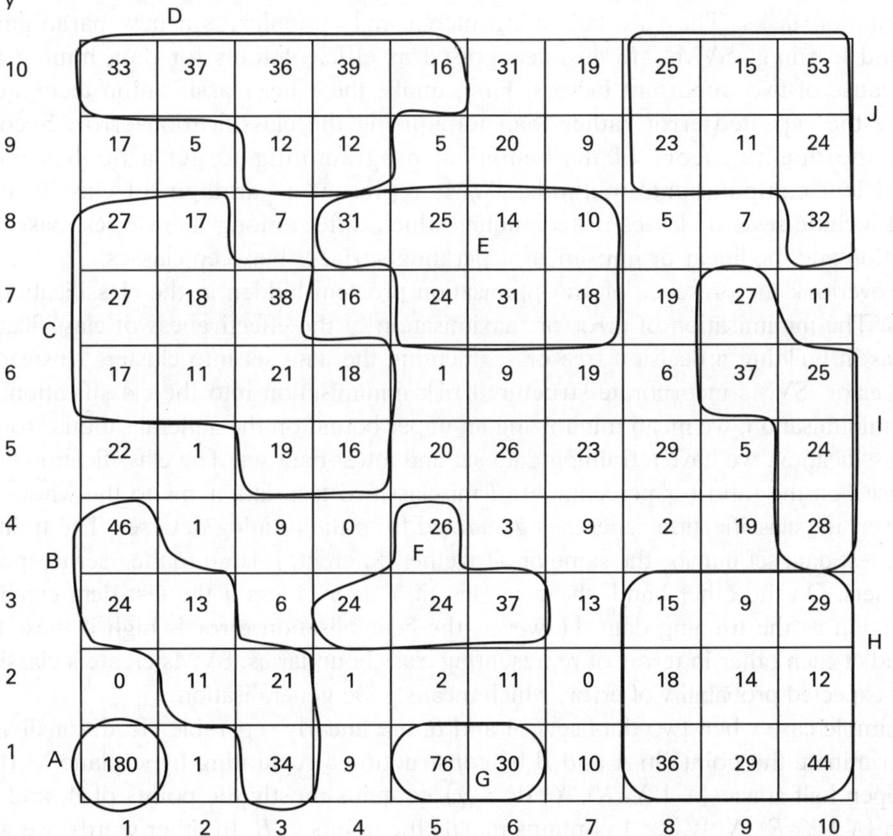

y \ x	1	2	3	4	5	6	7	8	9	10
10	33	37	36	39	16	31	19	25	15	53
9	17	5	12	12	5	20	9	23	11	24
8	27	17	7	31	25	14	10	5	7	32
7	27	18	38	16	24	31	18	19	27	11
6	17	11	21	18	1	9	19	6	37	25
5	22	1	19	16	20	26	23	29	5	24
4	46	1	9	0	26	3	9	2	19	28
3	24	13	6	24	24	37	13	15	9	29
2	0	11	21	1	2	11	0	18	14	12
1	180	1	34	9	76	30	10	36	29	44

Figure 9.9 Population clusters

Upon examination of the raw data within these clusters, one finds similarities between the tuples which are indicative of medical relationships or dependencies. Numerous hypotheses can be made regarding these relationships, many of which were not known a priori. *The* SOM groups together tuples in each square according to their similarity. The only level at which the SOM can detect similarities between tuples is at the root level of each of the three subspace trees, since this is the level of differentiation presented to the SOM's input. For example, every one of the tuples in square (1,1) contains root level data only for Drug 6, Topography 6 and Morphology 5. The tuple at square (2,1) contains these three root level nodes as well as Drug 7, a difference slight enough for the network to distinguish the tuple by classifying it one square away from (1,1). All 34 tuples in square (3,1) contain Drug 6, Topography D and Morphology 5; but only 29 of the 34 tuples contain Topography 6. Clearly, the difference between square (3,1) and square (1,1) is greater than the difference between square (2,1) and square (1,1).

9.6 SUPPORT VECTOR MACHINES

Support vector machines are learning machines that can perform binary classification and regression estimation tasks. They are becoming increasingly popular as a new paradigm of classification and learning. SVMs are also recognised as efficient tools for data mining and are popular because of two important factors. First, unlike the other classification techniques, SVMs minimise the expected error rather than minimizing the classification error. Second, SVMs employ the duality theory of mathematical programming to get a dual problem that admits efficient computational methods. SVMs represent a paradigm of classification techniques and include several classes of techniques which differ among themselves, based on the kernel function and the linear or non-linear separating surfaces between classes.

One cannot overlook the presence of an optimisation problem hidden in the classification or clustering tasks. The minimisation of error or maximisation of the effectiveness of classification are the key ideas in building a decision tree or segmenting the data set into clusters. Instead of minimising the error, SVMs incorporate structured risk minimisation into the classification. By structured risk minimisation, we mean minimizing an upper bound on the generalisation error. In a supervised classification, we have a training data set and a test data set. The classification error is calculated based on the ratio (or percentage) of misclassified test data items to the whole test data set. However, the classification scheme is generated from the training data set. The training data set and the test data set may be the same or altogether different. It is up to the user to specify these two data sets. On the other hand, the generalisation error is less if the test data exhibit a similar classification as the training data. However, the generalisation error is high if these two data sets contradict each other in terms of representing class boundaries. SVMs create a classifier with minimised expected probability of error, which means good generalisation.

Consider a simple case when two data sets, A and B, are linearly separable. Traditionally, we attempt to discriminate the points in A and B by constructing a separating hyperplane $X^t W = \gamma$, so that the open half space $\{X \mid X \in R^n, X^t W > \gamma\}$ contains mostly the points of A, and the open half space $\{X \mid X \in R^n, X^t W < \gamma\}$ contains mostly the points of B. In other words, we wish to determine W and γ such that the following two inequalities are satisfied.

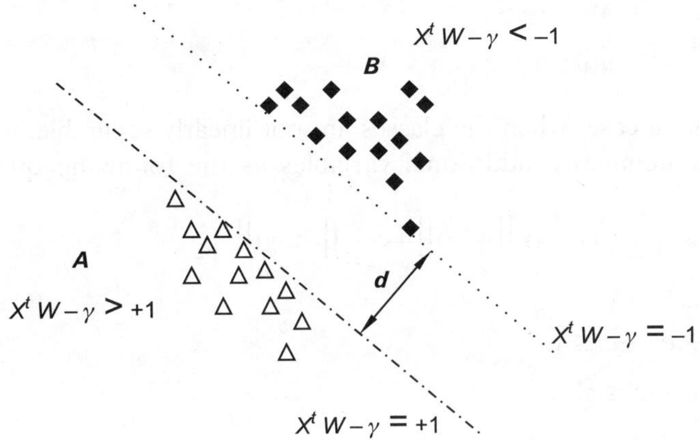

Figure 9.10 Parallel hyperplanes separating two classes. The distance between the two planes is $d = 2/||(W, \gamma)||_2$

$$\boldsymbol{A}W > e\gamma \quad \text{and} \quad \boldsymbol{B}W < e\gamma,$$

where $\boldsymbol{A}$ denotes the matrix corresponding to all X in class A; $\boldsymbol{B}$ denotes a matrix for data in B; and e is the vector of all 1s.

One can see that there can be an infinite number of planes satisfying these conditions. Neural networks attempt to determine the hyperplane satisfying these conditions such that the error is minimised. On the other hand, SVMs attempt to determine, among the infinite number of planes, the one that will have smallest generalisation error.

We can write the normalised version of the above pair of inequalities as

$$\boldsymbol{A}W \geq e\gamma + e \quad \text{and} \quad \boldsymbol{B}W \leq e\gamma - e.$$

This means that for every X in class A, we have $X^t W - \gamma < +1$, and for every X in class B, we have $X^t W - \gamma < -1$ (Figure 9.10). This represents a pair of parallel hyperplanes separating the two classes. The SVM focuses on determining two maximally apart parallel hyperplanes. Thus, SVMs choose the planes that maximise the margin separating two classes. The key idea is that the classifier must reduce the expected classification error and the confidence interval to ensure good generalisation. Geometrically, this corresponds to widening the gap between two parallel planes, one supporting class A and the other supporting class B. The wider the gap, the smaller the generalisation error.

We say that the hyperplane determined by (W, γ) supports the set A, when every element X of A satisfies $XW \geq \gamma$ (or, $XW \leq \gamma$) and there is at least one element that satisfies this as equality. In order to get two maximally apart parallel hyperplanes, it is necessary that these planes are the supporting surfaces of the respective classes.

In order to determine the hyperplane whose two parallel planes support A and B, so that the gap between these parallel planes is the widest, we formulate the following optimisation problem:

$$\text{Maximise}_{W,\gamma} \ \frac{2}{\|(W, \gamma)\|}$$

$$\text{Subject to} \begin{cases} AW - e\gamma \geq e \\ -BW + e\gamma \geq e. \end{cases}$$

For the more general case, when the classes are not linearly separable, we formulate the same problem by introducing two additional variables as the following quadratic programming problem:

$$\text{Minimise}_{w,\gamma,y,z}\ (1-\lambda)\ \|(y, z)\| + \frac{\lambda}{2}\ \|(W, \gamma)\|$$

such that

$$-AW + e\gamma + e \leq y,$$

$$BW - e\gamma + e \leq z,$$

$$y \geq 0,\ z \geq 0.$$

This is a convex quadratic programming problem. We can consider different norms to construct a different linear SVM. A simple case can be written as follows:

$$\text{Minimise}_{w,\gamma,y,z}\ (1-\lambda)(y'y + z'z) + \frac{\lambda}{2}(W'W + \gamma^2)$$

such that

$$-AW + e\gamma + e \leq y,$$

$$BW - e\gamma + e \leq z,$$

$$y \geq 0,\ z \geq 0.$$

Clearly, for the above quadratic problem, the following condition is satisfied at the optimal point

$$y = (-AW + e\gamma + e)_+,$$

$$z = (BW - e\gamma + e)_+,$$

where $(x)_+$ denotes $\text{Max}(x, 0)$.

Thus, the quadratic programming problem can be written as the unconstrained convex quadratic optimisation problem, by substituting these values for y and z. The dual of this problem is simple to solve even for high input dimensions and carries very simple constraints. Readers are referred to literature on convex programming problems for deriving the dual of the problem and for the solution techniques. Often, one can even determine a close form solution for the dual. This makes the computation task very simple. It is interesting to study the iterative scheme proposed by Mangasarian [2000].

The SVMs differ among themselves in using different norms and kernel functions while formulating the optimisation problem. SVMs are very useful for knowledge discovery, classification and regression analysis. Bennett et al proposed a method of using SVMs for decision tree constructions.

Let use consider the data set depicted in Figure 9.11 to demonstrate the use of SVM for the construction of a decision tree. We can employ one SVM to partition the data sets into two

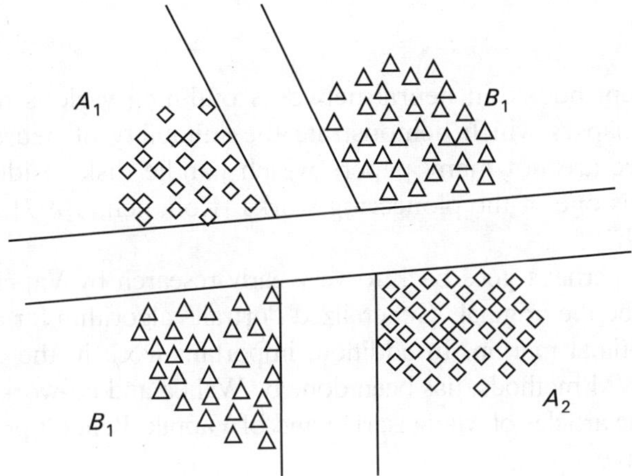

Figure 9.11 Oblique decision tree using SVMs

subsets: one consisting of $A_1 \cup B_1$, and the other of $A_2 \cup B_2$. This constitutes the first level splitting of the decision tree. For each of the subsets, we can use one more SVM to split and classify the two classes, *A* and *B*. Bennett et al showed that all the three SVMs can be equivalently formulated as a single optimisation problem whose dual is simple to solve. It is also easy to find the primal solution from the dual. Thus, SVM can be utilised to construct a generalised decision tree more efficiently.

Joachims demonstrated the applications of SVMs to text categorisation, to achieve error rates significantly below those achievable by other known classification techniques. SVMs provide a significant improvement in accuracy, but at the cost of simplicity and time efficiency.

Intuitively, SVMs map non-linearly their n-dimensional input space into a high-dimensional feature space. In this high dimensional feature space, a linear classifier is constructed. Two results make this approach successful:

- The generalisation ability of this learning machine depends on the VC dimension of the set of functions that the machine implements, rather than on the dimensionality of the space. A function that describes the data well and belongs to a set with low VC dimension will generalise well, regardless of the dimensionality of the space.
- The construction of the classifier only needs to evaluate an inner product between two vectors of the training data. An explicit mapping into the high-dimensional feature space is not necessary. In a Hilbert space, inner products have simple kernel representations and, therefore, can be easily evaluated.

9.7 Conclusion

In this chapter we discussed the techniques of neural networks and support vector machines. They are undoubtedly important and efficient techniques for data mining applications. In this chapter we have not focused on the algorithmic aspects of SVMs, but have only outlined the basic principles.

FURTHER READING

There are many excellent books on neural networks outlining various models. There are also many recent research papers which demonstrate the suitability of neural computing for data mining. However, there are not many papers which handle disk-resident training data sets. Kohonen's WEBSOM is one of the pioneering works [Kohonen, 1997]. The case study in the text is taken from [Shalvi].

The origin of SVMs perhaps goes back to very early research by Vapnik [1974] and [1979]. These two books describe the original "Generalized Portrait" algorithm for constructing separating hyperplanes with an optimal margin. In addition, important work in the context of reproducing kernels, related to the SVM methods, has been done by Wahba and co-workers. An introduction to SVM can be found in the articles of Mangasarian and of Vapnik. Bennett proposes the use of SVM for an oblique decision tree.

EXERCISES

1. Describe the principle of neural computing and discuss its suitability to data mining.
2. How is SVM different from MLP-based classification?
3. Propose a method of implementing MLP with error back-propagation learning, such that the system can learn and classify based on disk-resident data. Discuss the possibility of minimizing the I/O operation during learning.
4. Is it possible to use the perceptron for building decision trees? Please recall that a decision tree also defines a hyperplane for splitting. Distinguish between these methods.

BIBLIOGRAPHY

Fausett L. *Fundamentals of Neural Networks*. Prentice-Hall, 1994.

Gurney K. *An Introduction to Neural Networks*.UCL Press, 1997.

Hassoun M.H. *Fundamentals of Artificial Neural Networks*. MIT Press, Cambridge, MA, 1995.

Hertz J., Krogh A., and Palmer R.G. *Introduction to the Theory of Neural Computation*. Addison-Wesley, Redwood City, California, 1991.

Kohonen Tuevo. The self-organizing map. In *Proceedings of the IEEE*, **78(9)**:1464–1480, Sept. 1990.

McCulloch W.S., and Pitts W. A Logical Calculus of the Ideas Imminent in Nervous Activity. *Bulletin of Mathematical Biophysics*, 5:115–133, 1943.

Merkl D., Text data mining. In *A Handbook of NLP: Techniques and applications for the processing of language as text,* Marcel Dekker, 1998.

Mitchell. *Machine Learning*. WCB/McGraw Hill, Boston, 1997.

Shalvi D., and DeClaris N. An Unsupervised Neural Network Approach to Medical Data Mining Techniques. www.eng.umd.edu/medlab/papers/dcsThShort/thpaper1.htm, 1996.

Bennett K.P., and Blue J.A. A support vector machine approach to decision tree. In *IJCNN'98*, 1998.

Bradley P.S., Fayyad U.M., and Mangasarian O.L. Mathematical programming for data mining: Formulations and challenges. *Microsoft Research Tech Report*, MSR-TR-98-04, 1998.

Bradley P.S., and Mangasarian O.L. Massive data discrimination via linear support vector machines. *Tech Report 98-05*, University of Wisconsin, 1998.

Burges C.J.C. A tutorial on support vector machines for pattern recognition .*Data Mining and Knowledge Discovery*, pp. 121–167, 1998.

Cortes C., and Vapnik V.N. Support vector networks. *Machine Learning*, **20**:273–297, 1995.

Joachims T. Text categorization with support vector machines, learning with many relevant features. In *Proceedings of ECML-98, 1998*.

Kimeldorf G.S., and Wahba G. Some results on Tchebycheffian spline functions. *J. Math. Anal. Applic.*,**33**(1):82–95, 1971.

Mangasarian O.L. A generalized support vector machine.ftp://ftp.cs.wisc.edu/math-prog/tech-reports/98.14.ps., 1998.

Mangasarian O.L., and Musicant D.R. Lagrangian.Support Vector Machines. ftp://ftp.cs.wisc.edu/math-prog/tech-reports, 2000.

Nashed Z., and Wahba G. Generalized inverses in reproducing kernel spaces: An approach to regularization of linear operator equations. *SIAM J. Math.Anal.*5(6):974–987, 1974

Vapnik V., and Chervonenkis V. *A Theory of Pattern Recognition* [*in Russian*]. Nauka, Moscow,1974. (German Translation: W. Wapnik, and A. Tscherwonenkis. *Theorie der Zeichenerkennung*. Akademie-Verlag, Berlin, 1979.)

Vapnik V. *Estimation of Dependences Based on Empirical Data [in Russian]*. Nauka, Moscow, 1979. (English translation: Springer Verlag, New York, 1982)

Vapnik V., Golowich S.E., and Smola A. Support vector method for function approximation, regression estimation and signal processing. In *Advances in Neural Information Processing Systems,* MIT Press,**9**, 1997.

10

Performance Evaluation – ROC Curve

10.1 Introduction

In the previous chapters we studied many classification algorithms such as decision trees, rough set theory and SVM. When there are so many classification techniques at disposal, it becomes necessary to understand which classifier performs better in a given situation. A simple way to evaluate the performance of a classifier is to measure its predictive accuracy: the number of test instances that are predicted correctly by the classifier. However, accuracy may not be a suitable measure always. Current research in data mining has shifted away from simply presenting accuracy results when empirically evaluating the performance of a classification algorithm. There other ways of evaluating the performance of a classifier, such as precision–recall graph, ROC curve and cost curves. This chapter introduces the ROC (*receiver operating characteristic*) curve that is being used increasingly in the recent years to evaluate the performance of classification algorithms.

We learn many interesting and new concepts in this chapter. We first study the notion of false positive, true negative and the ROC space. In Section 10.3 we learn different types of classifiers such as perfect classifiers and random classifiers. Section 10.4 introduces the distinction between discrete classifier and probabilistic classifiers. We shall see that though discrete classifiers correspond to a single point in the ROC space, probabilistic classifiers generate a curve which is called ROC curve. Based on the relative structure of the ROC curve, we can infer one classifier as better or worse than another. We learn about a single-pass algorithm for generating ROC curve from a given dataset. Concavities in an ROC curve and the repair of such concavities is discussed while analysing convex hull of the ROC curve. Three different methods of finding the optimal threshold point in an ROC curve are discussed. We shall also learn about AUC, i.e., area under the ROC curve, and the method for computing AUC and about its uses. When a classifier is applied to several data sets or several samples of a dataset (like bootstrapping), we get many ROC curves, one for each sample. The averaging of multiple ROC curves is discussed in such situations and also the use of the same in computing confidence intervals. We shall also learn about the difference between ROC curve and other popular curves. Though ROC analysis is essentially used in two-class problems, its extension to multiclass problems is also touched upon.

10.2 Classification Accuracy

Let us begin with a two-class classification problem which aims at classifying each data-instance x to one element of the set {*pos, neg*} of positive and negative class labels. Assume that when the classifier classifies any instance, it labels the outcome as either Y (if the classifier considers the instance is in pos) or N (if otherwise). There are four possible outcomes arising from whether an instance is actually in *pos* class or *neg* class and the classifier labelling it as Y or N. We define each of these four cases below.

True Positive

If the instance is positive, i.e., $x \in pos$ and it is classified as positive (the output is Y), the classification outcome is *true positive*.

False Negative

If an instance $x \in pos$ but the output of the classifier is N, we call the outcome as *false negative*.

True Negative

If the instance is negative, i.e., $x \in neg$ and it is classified by the classifier as N, it is considered as a *true negative*.

False Positive

If the instance is *neg*, and if it is classified as Y, it is counted as a *false positive*.

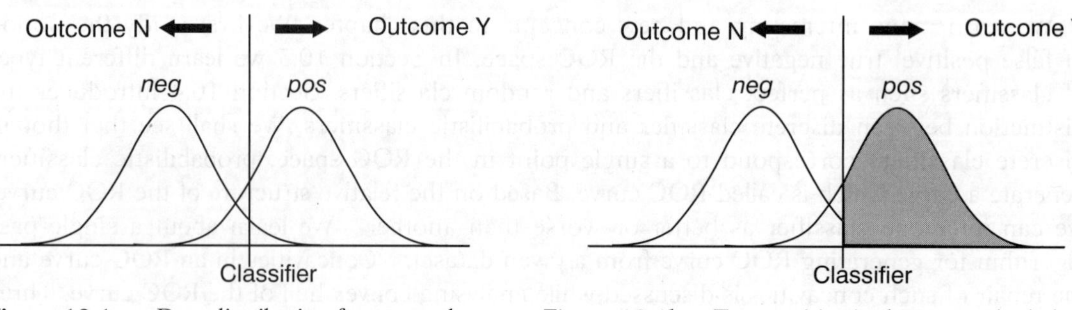

Figure 10.1a Data distribution for pos and neg classes

Figure 10.1b True positive is shown as shaded region

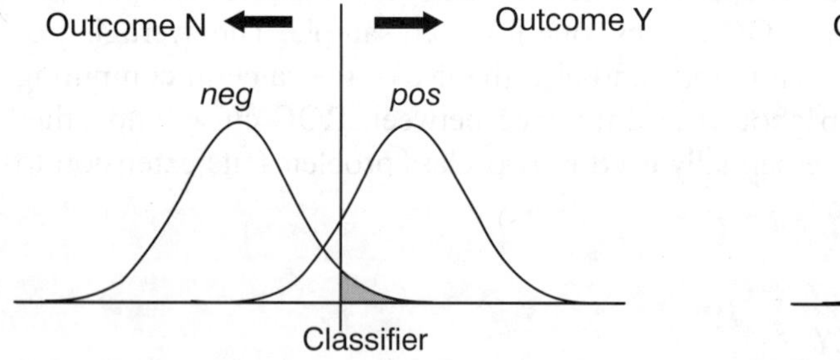

Figure 10.1c False positive region

Figure 10.1d True negative

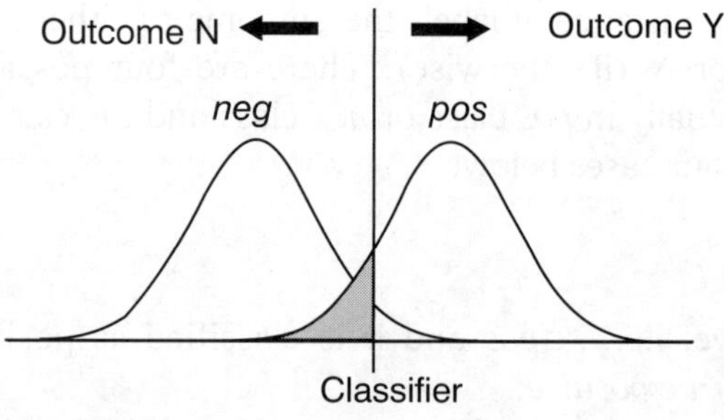

Figure 10.1e False negative

These concepts can be visualized graphically by plotting the probability density functions f_{pos} and f_{neg} of *pos* and *neg* classes (Figures 10.1a–e). Figure 10.1a depicts two classes as two normal distribution regions. The vertical line represents a classifier such that the points lying to the right of the line are recognized by the classifier as Y and those lying to the left are recognized as *N*. Figures 10.1b, 10.1c, 10.1d and 10.1e depict the regions of data points representing true positives, false positives, true negatives and false negatives respectively. For instance, the area below f_{neg} to the left of vertical line (Figure 10.1d) comprises instances of *neg* class classified as *N*; hence true negative.

Confusion Matrix

Given a classifier and a set of instances (the test set), the above four quantities can be arranged in a two-by-two array called the *confusion matrix,* also called the *contingency table*. This matrix forms the basis for many common metrics. The columns represent the categories of true status and the rows represent the outcomes of a classifier. The numbers along the major diagonal represent the correct decisions made, and the numbers off this diagonal represent the errors, i.e., the confusion amongst the various classes.

Table 10.1 Confusion matrix

	Total *pos* instances (*pos*)	**Total *neg* instances (*neg*)**
Y	Number of true positive instances TP	Number of false positive instances FP
N	Number of false negative instances FN	Number of true negative instances TN

We can derive several parameters from this table.

True Positive Rate (tp rate) or Recall

The true positive rate (also called *hit rate* and *recall*) of a classifier is the ratio of positively correctly classified instances to the total number of positive instances.

False Positive Rate (fp rate)

Similarly, false positive rate (*fp rate*) is the ratio of number of false positive instances to the total negative instances.

These two parameters can be formally defined as follows. Note that the values of *fp rate* and *tp rate* are in the range [0, 1].

$$tp\ rate = \frac{TP}{pos}, \quad fp\ rate = \frac{FP}{neg}$$

Precision

Precision is a well-known measure for classifiers. It is the ratio of correctly classified positive instances to all instances classified as *Y* (all positively classified instances). It is defined as follows.

$$Precision = \frac{TP}{TP+FP}$$

Accuracy

Accuracy is the ratio of correctly classified instances to total number of instances.

$$\text{Accuracy} = \frac{TP + TN}{pos + neg}$$

F-MEASURE

$$\text{F-measure} = \frac{2}{\frac{1}{\text{precision}} + \frac{1}{\text{recall}}}$$

SENSITIVITY

The *sensitivity* measure is defined as the ratio of number true positive instances to total number *pos* instances. It is same as the *tp rate*.

$$\text{Sensitivity} = \frac{TP}{TP+FN}$$

SPECIFICITY

Similarly, *specificity* is defined as follows. It is the same as *true negative rate*.

$$\text{Specificity} = \frac{TN}{TN+FP}$$

EXAMPLE 10.1

Let us consider an example for illustration. Table 10.2 represents the outcome of classification of 20 instances by a classifier, C. We see that instance 1 is an example of *true positive* because its given label is *pos* and is classified as *Y* by the classifier. Instance 2 is an example of *false negative* as a *pos* instance is classified as *N*; instance 14 is a case of *true negative* and instance 3 is a case of *false positive*.

Table 10.2 Classifier C

Instance	Actual class	Predicted class			
1	*pos*	Y	11	*pos*	N
2	*pos*	N	12	*neg*	Y
3	*neg*	Y	13	*pos*	N
4	*pos*	N	14	*neg*	N
5	*pos*	Y	15	*neg*	Y
6	*pos*	N	16	*neg*	Y
7	*neg*	Y	17	*pos*	Y
8	*neg*	Y	18	*neg*	N
9	*pos*	Y	19	*pos*	Y
10	*neg*	Y	20	*neg*	N

The confusion matrix for this example is the following.

	10	10
12	5	7
8	5	3

The *fp rate* and *tp rate* for classifier C in this example are 0.7 and 0.5 respectively. Other parameters can be calculated such as *precision* = 5/(5+7) = 5/12= 0.417; *recall* = 0.5; *accuracy* = 8/20 = 0.4; *F-measure* = 10/22; and *specificity* = 0.3.

Class Distribution

The proportion of positive to negative instances is called *class distribution*. In Example 10.1, the class distribution is 1:1.

10.3 ROC Space

The *ROC space* is a two-dimensional space with abscissa as *fp rate* and *tp rate* as ordinate. As these values are in the range of [0, 1], the ROC space is essentially a unit square.

At this stage, let us understand briefly the notions of discrete and probabilistic classifiers. A *discrete classifier* (also known as *crisp* classifier) is a classifier that outputs only one class label for a given instance, say, *Y* or *N*. A *probabilistic classifier* (also termed *soft* classifier) on the other hand, is one that outputs an estimate of probability of the instance being either in *Y* or in *N*. For a given test dataset, a *discrete classifier* produces a (*fp rate, tp rate*) pair, and this corresponds to a single point in the ROC space. Thus, the ROC space is the two-dimensional unit square where a point corresponds to the performance of a discrete classifier with respect to a data set. We will see that a probabilistic classifier produces a curve in the ROC space. Such an ROC graph is a sort of cost-benefit analysis and depicts the relative trade-offs between benefits (true positives) and costs (false positives).

Let us continue our earlier example with additional set of classifiers. The classifier C in Table 10.2 will be referred to as Classifier 1. Table 10.3 gives classification results of 6 more discrete classifiers, Classifier 2, Classifier 3, ..., Classifier 7. Figure 10.2 depicts the ROC space, where the points from the last row of Table 10.3 corresponding to these seven discrete classifiers plotted. We consider the 20 given instances as the representative dataset to measure the performance of different classifiers.

We see that each classifier is represented by a point in ROC space, based on its *fp rate* and *tp rate*. One classifier is said to be better than another one if its ROC point is to the northwest of the ROC point of the classifier against which it is being compared. In our example, Classifier 6 has better performance than those of Classifier 1, Classifier 2 and Classifier 3. A point lying northwest with respect to another implies that the *tp rate* is higher, the *fp rate* is lower, or both. Classifier 5 exhibits the best performance among all the classifiers in terms of the ROC space. Let us study some more characteristics of the classifiers based on ROC points.

EXAMPLE 10.1 (CONTD.)

Table 10.3

Instance	Class	Classifier 2	Classifier 3	Classifier 4	Classifier 5	Classifier 6	Classifier 7
1	*pos*	Y	Y	Y	Y	Y	N
2	*pos*	N	Y	Y	Y	Y	Y
3	*neg*	Y	Y	Y	N	Y	N
4	*pos*	N	Y	Y	Y	Y	Y
5	*pos*	Y	Y	Y	Y	Y	N
6	*pos*	N	N	Y	Y	Y	Y
7	*neg*	Y	Y	Y	N	Y	N
8	*neg*	N	N	Y	N	N	N
9	*pos*	Y	Y	Y	Y	Y	Y
10	*neg*	Y	Y	Y	N	N	N
11	*pos*	N	N	Y	Y	Y	Y
12	*neg*	Y	Y	Y	N	Y	N
13	*pos*	N	N	Y	Y	N	Y
14	*neg*	N	N	Y	N	N	N
15	*neg*	Y	Y	Y	N	N	N
16	*neg*	N	Y	Y	N	Y	N
17	*pos*	Y	Y	Y	Y	Y	N
18	*neg*	N	N	Y	N	N	N
19	*pos*	Y	Y	Y	Y	N	N
20	*neg*	N	Y	Y	N	N	Y
ROC point		(0.5, 0.5)	(0.7, 0.7)	(1, 1)	(0, 1)	(0.4, 0.8)	(0.2, 0.6)

PERFECT CLASSIFIER

The lower left point, (0, 0) of the ROC space represents the case when the *tp rate* is zero and the *fp rate* is zero. It means that the classifier maps all the instances to label *N*. Similarly, the other extreme is (1, 1), where the classifier predicts every instance as a Y instance (see Classifier 4 of the example).

Point (0, 1) represents the situation when there is no false positive and the *tp rate* is the highest. Such a classifier is a *perfect* classifier. One can see that Classifier 5 is a perfect classifier and perfectly classifies every instance of the test set.

CONSERVATIVE AND LIBERAL CLASSIFIERS

Some classifiers make few false positive errors, but they often have low true positive rates as well. This is a case where the classifier is willing to misclassify positive instances but certainly

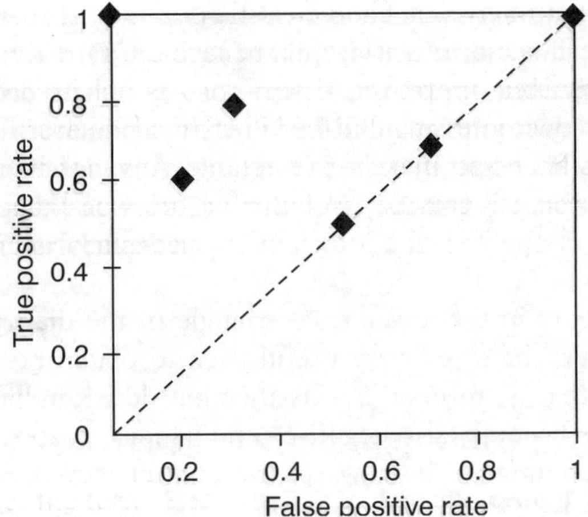

Figure 10.2 Basic ROC graph showing different classifiers

does not wish to misclassify any negative instances. These classifiers are thought of as *conservative* classifiers.

Some classifiers, on the other hand, make positive classifications with weak evidence so that they classify nearly all positives correctly, but they often have high false positive rates. This is the case where the classifier is more for accurately classifying all positive instances, no matter if some negative instances are misclassified in the process. Such a classifier can be thought of as a *liberal* classifier. In our example, Classifier 7 is more conservative than Classifier 6.

Which kind of classifiers is preferable, conservative or liberal, depends on the application. In medical diagnosis, for instance, missing a cancer diagnosis has serious consequences and the patient could lose his/her life because of a delay in treatment. If the positive cases are normal cases, then any classification in the present context should aim at correctly classifying the negative instances correctly even if some positive instances are wrongly classified. On the other hand, in the context of intrusion detection, we are interested in correctly identifying an intrusive behaviour without offending the normal users of a network. Thus, we aim at reducing false positive so that normal users are not identified as intruders even if we miss some true positives in the process.

Random Classifier

A point on the diagonal line connecting (0, 0) and (1, 1) represents the strategy of randomly guessing a class. Given an instance, if a classifier randomly guesses the *Y* class half the time, then irrespective of whether the instance is in class *pos* or in *neg*, it predicts the instance as *Y* half of the time. Its *fp rate* is 0.5 and its *tp rate* is also 0.5. Thus, this yields the point (0.5, 0.5) in the ROC space. Similarly, if a classifier guesses for any instance the positive class (*Y*) for 90% of the time, it can be expected to get 90% of the positives correct but its false positive rate will increase to 90% as well, yielding (0.9, 0.9) in the ROC space. Thus a *random classifier* will produce an ROC point on the diagonal line. Classifier 2 and Classifier 3 are random classifiers. One can note that the typical characteristic of a random classifier is that no matter if an instance is a positive instance or otherwise, its behaviour is the same. Thus, the information encoded in the specific instance—positive or negative—is not used by a random classifier. It only predicts based on its own guesses. On the other hand, a classifier is expected to use the information of the test instance and make a prediction. Any classifier on the diagonal may be said to have no information about the class. A classifier below the diagonal may be said to have useful information, but it is applying the information incorrectly or not using the information about the given instances.

Any classifier that appears in the lower right triangle of the diagonal performs worse than random guessing. However, there is a very useful trick to obtain better than random models. If we negate a classifier, that is, reverse its classification decisions on every instance, then its true positive classifications become false negatives and its false positives become true negatives. This corresponds to exchanging of the rows in the contingency table, leading to a new true positive rate of $FN/pos = 1 - TP/pos$, i.e., one minus the original true positive rate. Similarly, we obtain a new false positive rate of $TN/neg = 1 - FP/neg$. Geometrically, this corresponds to mirroring the original ROC point through the midpoint on the ascending diagonal. Therefore, any classifier that produces a point in the lower right triangle can be negated to produce a point in the upper left triangle.

We call this trick as *repair*. The above repair procedure can be generalised to line segments connecting arbitrary classifiers. For instance, consider Figure 10.3 depicting ROC points of three classifiers, C_1, C_2 and C_3. Denote the sets of true and false positives of classifier C_i by TP_i and FP_i. Let us assume that these classifiers satisfy the following monotonic conditions:

$$TP_1 \subseteq TP_3 \subseteq TP_2 \text{ and}$$

$$FP_1 \subseteq FP_3 \subseteq FP_2.$$

We can construct classifier C_4 by repairing C_3. In particular, these inclusion constraints are satisfied if C_1, C_2 and C_3 are obtained by setting thresholds on the same probabilistic model. We build a new classifier C_4 from C_1, C_2 and C_3 with following classification rules.

* If both C_1 and C_2 predict *N*, then C_4 to predict *N*
* If both C_1 and C_2 predict *Y*, then C_4 to predict *Y*
* If C_1 predicts *N* and C_2 predicts *Y*, then C_4 to predict the opposite of what C_3 predicts
* Otherwise, C_4 to predict what C_3 predicts

10.4 ROC Curves

Discrete Classifier vs. Probabilistic Classifier

We have briefly touched upon discrete classifier earlier. Many classifiers, such as decision trees and perceptron are designed to produce only a class decision, i.e., a *Y* or *N* for each instance. When such a *discrete classifier* is applied to a test set, it yields a single confusion matrix, which in turn corresponds to one ROC point, as seen in the previous section. Some classifiers like

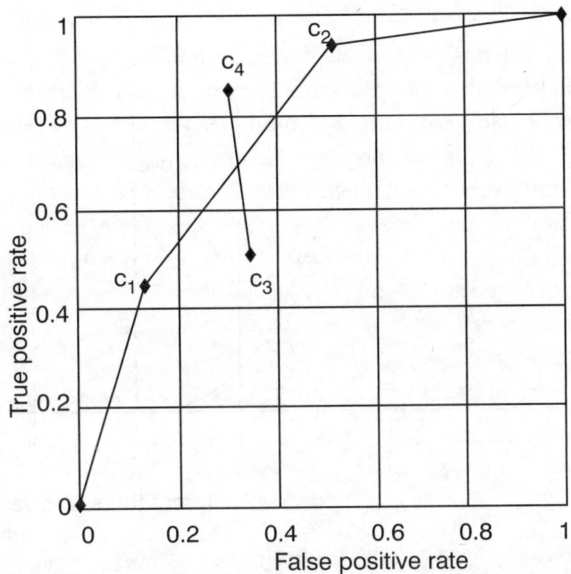

Figure 10.3 Classifier C_3 is negated with the help of classifiers C_1 and C_2

Bayes classifier produce a continuous output as an estimate of the probability of an instance's class membership. These yield an instance probability or a *score*, which is a numeric value that represents the degree to which an instance is a member of any of the classes (the reference class is mostly taken as *pos*). The probability estimate can be strict probabilities, or they can be some numeric scores (or confidence measure), in which case the only property that holds is that a higher score indicates a higher probability. We denote such classifiers as *probabilistic classifiers*, even when the output may not be a proper probability.

THRESHOLDING

In principle, almost all classification methods can produce probability estimates on instances (both training and test instances). Without loss of generality, let us assume that a classifier provides for each sample a value x in the range [0, 1], which is a confidence degree (or score) that the instance belongs to the *pos* class. The sample is consequently assigned to the class N if $x \rightarrow 0$ and to the class Y if $x \rightarrow 1$. A confidence threshold t is usually chosen so as to attribute the sample to the class N if $x < t$ and to the class Y if $x \geq t$. In other words, *thresholding* simply finds the best probability from the training instances as the threshold and uses it to predict the class label of test instances. A test example with predicted probability above or equal to this threshold is predicted as Y; otherwise it is predicted as N. A probabilistic or soft classifier is equivalent to a discrete or crisp classifier if the threshold is fixed. A classifier's ability can be studied in a better manner by varying the value of the threshold. For a given threshold value t, we can determine two appropriate performance quantities namely the *tp rate*(t) and the *fp rate*(t). The pair (*fp rate*(t), *tp rate*(t)) is sufficient to completely characterize the performance

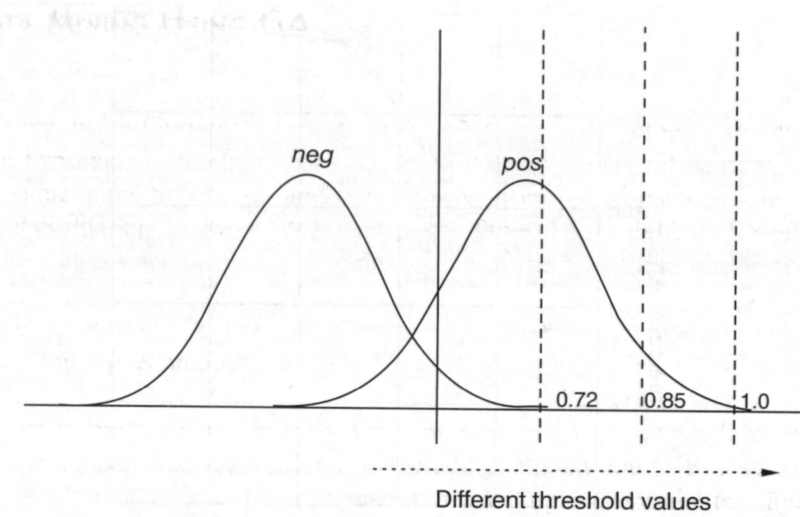

Figure 10.4 Probabilistic classifier with different threshold values to indicate different ROC points

of the classifier when the decision threshold is set to t, since such values provide an estimate of the accuracy obtained by the classifier on each class.

With reference to the example shown in Figure 10.1a, a probabilistic classifier with different values of t can be visualized as a vertical line at different positions, say 0.72, 0.85, and 1.0 (Figure 10.4). Each value of t generates one point in the ROC space.

ROC Curve

We have seen that the discrete classifier produces only a single point in ROC space. In case of a probabilistic classifier, each threshold value produces a point in ROC space. Thus, a ROC curve is a two-dimensional curve in which the *tp_rate* is plotted against the *fp rate* for different values of threshold. Conceptually, we may imagine varying t from $-\infty$ to $+\infty$ and tracing a curve for (*fp rate*(t), *tp rate*(t)) through the ROC space. This is called the *ROC curve*. In practice, we vary t only within a range that is relevant to the ROC space. The ROC curve starts in the bottom left corner of the ROC space, representing a threshold at which all cases are classified as negative, and ends up in the upper right corner, representing a threshold at which all cases are classified as positive. A *parametric ROC* curve typically assumes that a pair of normal distributions underlies the data and increases monotonically with the *fp rate*. An *empirical ROC* curve may be obtained by connecting the observed set of ordered pairs (*fp rate*(t), *tp rate*(t)), and therefore, it makes minimal assumptions. ROC curves hold special appeal because they allow classification models to be compared independent of the threshold used in an application. Given two ROC points, a and b in the ROC space, a is defined as *superior* to b if $fp\ rate_a \leq fp\ rate_b$ and $tp\ rate_a \geq tp\ rate_b$. If one ROC curve has all its points superior to those of another curve, it dominates the latter. When the curve of one model is superior to another model, it is clear that the model will perform better regardless of what threshold is used. But if two curves cross, the determination of which classifier is better again depends on what threshold will be used. If a ROC curve has $tp\ rate_x \geq fp\ rate_x$ for all its points x, then it is a *proper* ROC curve. The ROC curve gives an estimate of the classifier performance that is independent from the chosen decision criterion and prior probabilities of the two classes. Informally, it may be stated that the nearer a curve is to the upper left corner of the diagram, the better is its performance (higher *tp rate* and/or lower *fp rate*).

EXAMPLE 10.2

Let us consider a probabilistic classifier for 20 instances as shown in Table 10.4. The numeric estimate (or confidence measure) and the actual class for each instance are given in the table. For example, for instance 1 which belongs to class *pos*, the classifier labels a confidence measure 0.9; it means that the confidence of labelling this as Y is 0.9 and labelling it as N in 0.1. We can get exact classification by deciding a threshold t on the confidence measure.

Table 10.4 A probabilistic classifier with confidence measure or score. Instances are ordered in decreasing order of scores (Source: Fawcett, 2006, with permission)

Instance	Class	Score
1	*pos*	.9
2	*pos*	.8
3	*neg*	.7
4	*pos*	.6
5	*pos*	.55
6	*pos*	.54
7	*neg*	.53
8	*neg*	.52
9	*pos*	.51
10	*neg*	.505
11	*pos*	.4
12	*neg*	.39
13	*pos*	.38
14	*neg*	.37
15	*neg*	.36
16	*neg*	.35
17	*pos*	.34
18	*neg*	.33
19	*pos*	.30
20	*neg*	.1

Suppose that the threshold is 0.8. The classification with threshold 0.8 is given in Table 10.5. Please note that when the threshold is 0.8, the *tp rate* is 0.2 and the *fp rate* is 0.

Table 10.5 Actual classification with a threshold of 0.8

Instance	Class	Estimate
1	*pos*	Y
2	*pos*	Y
3	*neg*	N
4	*pos*	N
5	*pos*	N
6	*pos*	N
7	*neg*	N
8	*neg*	N
9	*pos*	N
10	*neg*	N
11	*pos*	N
12	*neg*	N
13	*pos*	N
14	*neg*	N
15	*neg*	N
16	*neg*	N
17	*pos*	N
18	*neg*	N
19	*pos*	N
20	*neg*	N

As the threshold decreases from 0.8 to 0.7, the *tp rate* and *fp rate* remain unchanged in threshold range (0.7, 0.8], but the *fp rate* increases by 0.1 (from the old value of 0) when the threshold is 0.7. As *t* varies from 0.9 to 0.1, we get different ROC points, and by joining these ROC points the ROC curve is obtained. It is left as an exercise to readers to compute ROC points for different values of *t*. We can thus find the ROC curve by varying the threshold. In this case, the ROC curve is a discrete set of points corresponding to different values of the threshold in the ROC space. If we have a very large set of test points, it is possible to get a curve as the *tp rate* and *fp rate* can be depicted for every value of the threshold. Any ROC curve generated from a finite set of instances is actually a step function, which approaches a true curve as the number of instances approaches infinity. The ROC point at (0.1, 0.5) produces the highest accuracy (70%). Note that the best accuracy occurs at a threshold of 0.54, as there is no point in the curve which yields better accuracy.

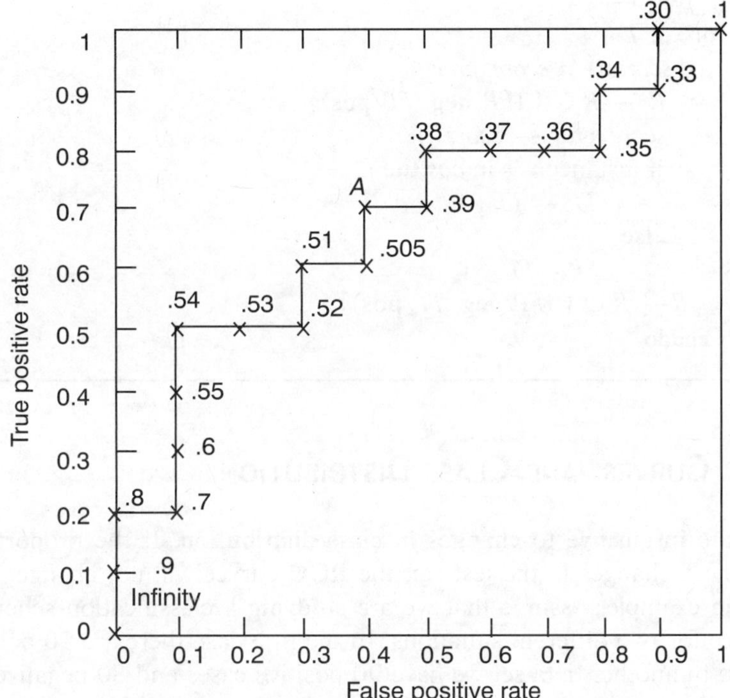

Figure 10.5 ROC Curve generated by varying threshold value (Reproduced with permission from Fawcett, 2006)

Algorithm to Compute Roc Curve

The ROC curve can be computed by a single scan of the test data if we sort the instances in decreasing order of score. There some interesting observations that can be immediately made. A probabilistic classifier exhibits a monotonicity property as follows.

Monotonicity property: Any instance that is classified positive with respect to a given threshold will be classified positive for all lower thresholds as well.

Due to this monotonicity property, an ROC graph can be constructed from a single scan of the data. We can sort the instances decreasing by their scores and move down the list, processing one instance at a time. We can thus identify incrementally the values of threshold where the ROC point changes. When the scan is complete, all ROC points are generated.

Algorithm: Generate ROC Curve

L: list of instances sorted in decreasing order of score; instance x has *score*(i)
R: list of ROC points
  FP ← 0
  TP ← 0
  R ← ∅

```
score_prev ←−∞
do for x ∈ L
    if score(i) ≠ score_prev
        R ← R ∪ { (FP/neg, TP/pos)}
        score_prev ← score(i)
        if instance x is in pos then
            TP ← TP+1
        else
            FP ←FP +1
    R← R ∪ { (FP/neg, TP/pos)}
enddo
```

10.5 ROC CURVES AND CLASS DISTRIBUTION

ROC curves are insensitive to changes in class distribution. If the proportion of positive to negative instances changes in the test set, the ROC curves will not change. To see why this is so, consider an example. Assume that we are studying a classification scheme and evaluating its performance for two different situations. In the first case there are 90 positive cases and 10 negative cases. In another data set we have 90 positive cases and 80 negative cases. Confusion matrices for both cases are given in Table 10.6 (a, b).

Table 10.6a

	90	10
52	45	7
48	45	3

Table 10.6b

	90	80
101	45	56
69	45	24

One can see that in both the cases we get the same point in the ROC space. Interestingly, if we take accuracy as the performance measure, then both behave differently. The accuracy for the first case is 0.48, whereas the accuracy for the second case is 0.406. Thus we observe that even when the classifiers have similar basic characteristics, the accuracy changes based on class distribution but the ROC does not change.

Note that the class distribution, i.e., the proportion of *pos* to *neg* instances, is the relationship of the left column to the right column. Any performance metric that uses values from both columns will be inherently sensitive to class skews. ROC graphs are based on *tp rate* and *fp rate*, in which each dimension is a strict columnar ratio, and so does not depend on class distributions. Even if the class distributions are different for both the cases, the fundamental predictive ability of the classifier remains for both the situations, i.e., the classifier guesses 50% times correctly for a positive instance and 30% times correctly for negative instances.

Other measures such as *precision, recall* and *F-score* are sensitive to class distribution. As class distribution changes, these measures change as well even if the fundamental classifier performance does not change.

This is an important observation because in many applications we come across changes in class distribution. For example, in medical decision making, epidemics may cause the incidence of a disease to increase over time. In fraud detection, proportions of fraud vary significantly from month to month and place to place. Changes in manufacturing practices may cause the proportion of defective units to increase or decrease. Such fluctuations will affect the accuracy measure but not the ROC parameters.

10.6 ROC CONVEX HULL (ROCCH)

Given that the underlying distributions are generally considered fixed, an ROC curve will always be proper and convex. As mentioned earlier, in practice the empirical ROC plot is a step-like function which approaches a true curve as the number of samples (number of threshold values) approaches infinity. An empirical ROC curve is therefore not necessarily convex as illustrated in Fig. 10.5. Concavities indicate local performance that is worse than random behaviour. Concavities occur due to unequal variances between classes with large skew in the data, or when the classifier is unable to capture the modality of the data (e.g., classifying multimodal data with a linear classifier). Let us first learn more about the convex hull in the ROC space.

The ROC convex hull (ROCCH) of a single crisp classifier connects its resulting point to the (0, 0) and (1, 1) points (Figure 10.6a).

The ROCCH of an empirical ROC is the piece-wise outer envelope connecting only the superior points of the ROC with straight lines (Figure 10.6b). Generating the ROCCH of a single classifier can be viewed as finding an isotonic transformation of the scores that maximizes the area under the ROC curve (AUC).

The ROCCH is also applicable to multiple classifiers which may be crisp or soft. If one classifier has a dominant ROC curve over *fp rate* values, its convex hull constitutes the overall ROCCH. When there is no clear dominance among multiple classifiers across different regions of the ROC space, the ROCCH corresponds to the envelope connecting the superior points in each region (Figure 10.6c).

The initial purpose of the ROCCH was to facilitate the selection of the classifier that is optimal for given misclassification cost, and the elimination of classifiers that are never optimal, regardless of the misclassification costs. Figure 10.7 shows both the ROC curve for a probabilistic model evaluated on a small test set and its convex hull. Four points of the ROC curve (*a, b, c* and *d*) are located on the convex hull. Each of these points corresponds to a threshold, and thus each segment of the convex hull corresponds to a threshold interval. For instance, the convex hull in the figure has three segments corresponding to three disjoint intervals. They delineate concave regions of the ROC curve, indicated as A, B and C. Area A is delineated by line *ab* and the ROC curve between point *a* and point *b*. In general, a concave area means that the ranking obtained from the probabilistic model in this threshold interval is worse than random. There is a need to repair such concavities.

REPAIRING CONCAVITIES

Consider area C in Figure 10.7, which has the largest concavity. The simplest way to repair this concavity is by ignoring the score calculated by the probabilistic model in this interval and

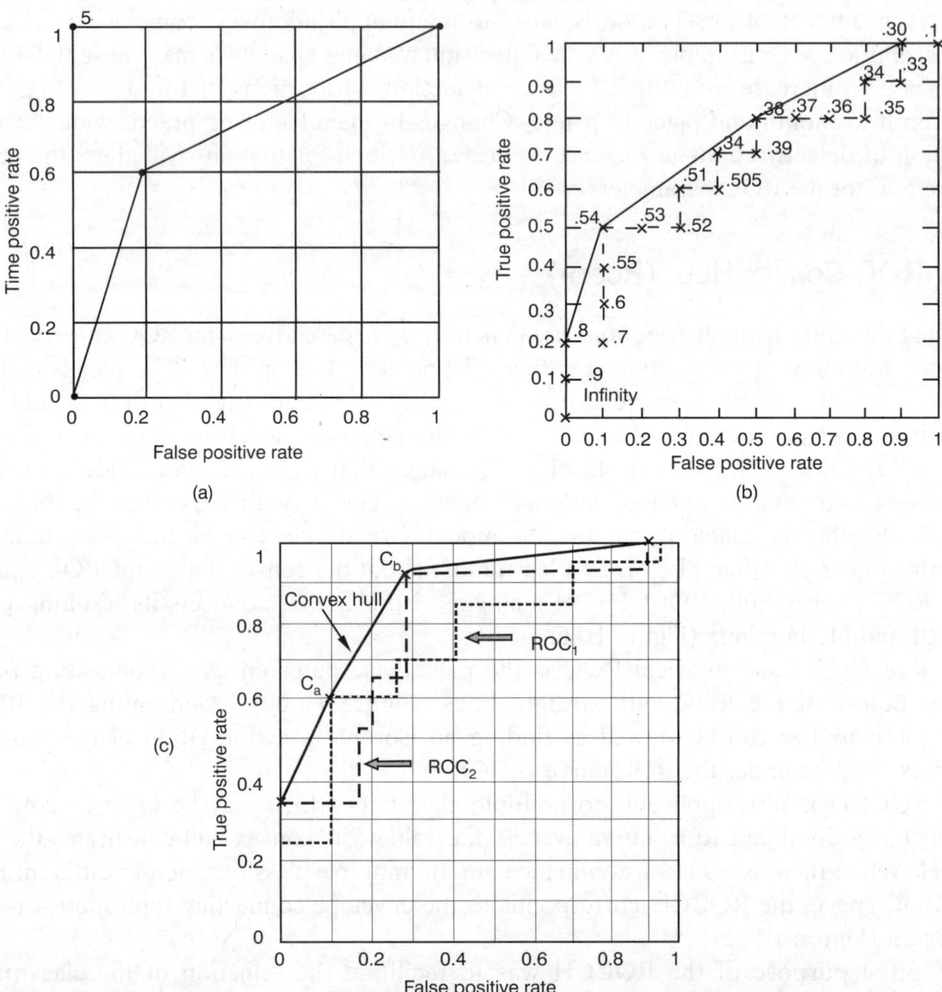

Figure 10.6 ROC convex hull of: (a) a single discrete classifier, (b) an ROC curve, (c) two ROC curves

output a constant score, e.g., the mid-point of the interval. This will replace the concave region of the ROC curve with line segment *cd* (ties are broken randomly). It is interesting to note that if this procedure is followed for all concavities, it corresponds to constructing the convex hull by discretizing the probability scores.

A better way of repairing concavities is by adapting our earlier repairing algorithm of negating a classifier. For instance, by applying this algorithm to the classifier corresponding to threshold C_2, this point would be point-mirrored through the midpoint on line segment *cd* to the other side of the convex hull. The same can be done for the other thresholds. The resulting ROC curve is shown in Figure 10.8. We can note that the area C under the curve has been replaced by an equally large area C' above the curve. The AUC of the repaired curve is therefore larger than both the AUC of the original curve and the AUC of its convex hull.

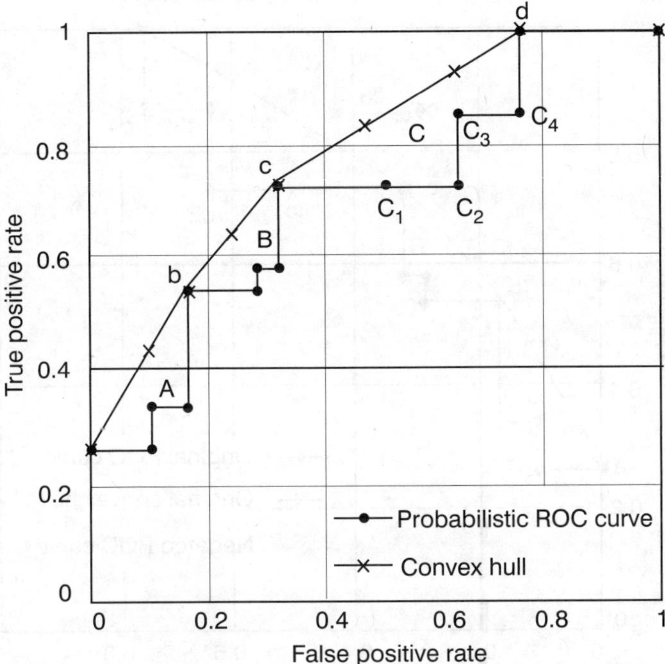

Figure 10.7 An ROC curve and its convex hull

10.7 METHOD TO FIND THE 'OPTIMAL' THRESHOLD POINT

We observe that an ROC curve is obtained empirically by varying the value of threshold t; it is expected to be convex and proper and it may have some concavities. We also know that it is possible to repair concavities to obtain a better classifier. These analyses provide insights into the behaviour of a classifier. However, for a specific classification in hand, it is necessary to have a good scheme of classification, or in other words, the means to decide a good choice of the threshold value. Optimal threshold is the point that gives maximum correct classification. Three criteria are generally used to find optimal threshold point from an ROC curve. The first two give equal weight to sensitivity and specificity and the third criterion considers costs, which mainly comprises the cost for correct and false diagnosis.

POINT ON CURVE CLOSEST TO (0, 1)

By this method the optimal value of the threshold is obtained by minimizing the distance between point (0, 1) and any point on the ROC curve. To obtain the optimal threshold to discriminate the instances, this distance is calculated for each observed threshold value, and the point where the distance is minimum is located.

Consider the ROC curve of Figure 10.5. The nearest ROC point to (0,1) is the point corresponding to threshold 0.54. Thus the optimal value of the threshold, t^*, is 0.54.

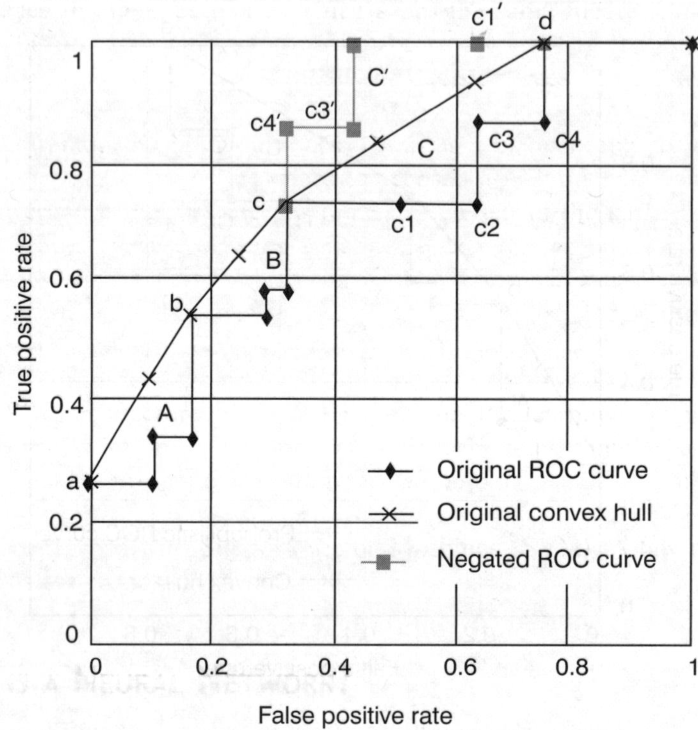

Figure 10.8 Negating a concave part of the ROC curve

YOUDEN INDEX

The second is *Youden index* that maximizes the vertical distance from line of equality to the points on ROC curve as shown in Fig 10.9. In other words, *Youden index J* is the point on the ROC curve which is farthest from the diagonal line representing random classifiers. The main aim of Youden index is to maximize the difference between *tp rate* and *fp rate*. Maximizing this index allows one to find, from the ROC curve, an optimal cut-off point independently from the prevalence. The value of *J* for continuous test can be located by doing a search of plausible values where sum of *sensitivity* and *specificity* can be maximum. Youden index is a more commonly used criterion because it reflects the intension to maximize the correct classification rate; it is also easy to calculate.

If $F(x)$ is the function describing the ROC curve, with x = *tp rate* = 1 – *specificity*, we may write $J(x) = F(x) - x$. When J is maximal, $J'(x) = 0$, where J' is the derivative of J. Hence, $J'(x) = F'(x) - 1$, where F' is the derivative of F. Hence, when J is maximal, $F'(x) = 1$, meaning that the tangent to the ROC curve is parallel to the line with slope = 1. It implies that around this point a gain (or a loss) in specificity results in a loss (or a gain) of the same amplitude in sensitivity (Figure 10.9).

J can be determined graphically by plotting the probability density functions f_{pos} and f_{neg} of *pos* and *neg* (Figure 10.10). J is the difference of the area under f_{pos} and f_{neg} to the right of the cut–point, with it being negative area when $f_{pos} < f_{neg}$. The optimal cut–point, the value

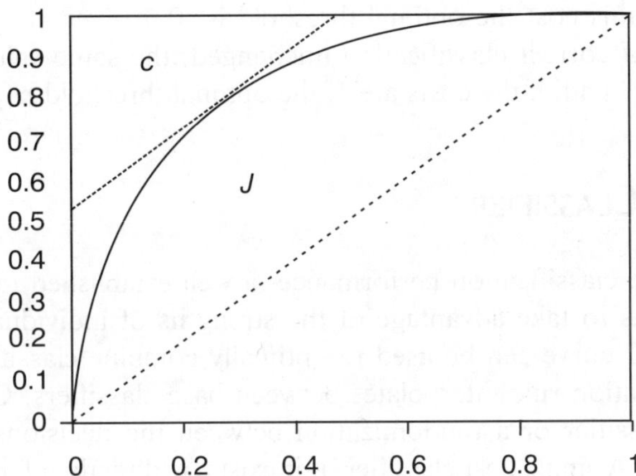

Figure 10.9 ROC curve depicting Youden index and optimal cut-point

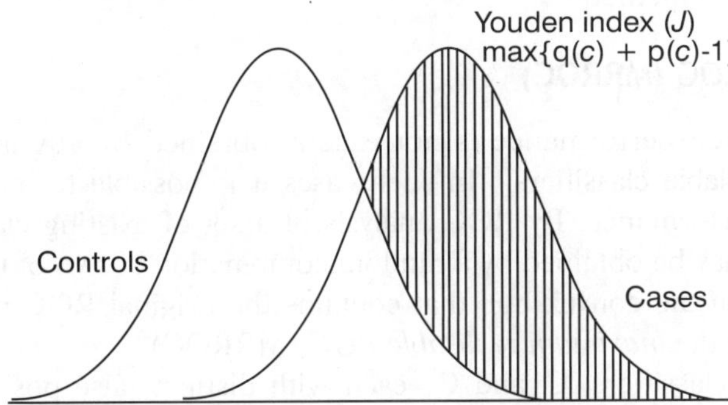

Figure 10.10 Graphical representation of the Youden index and the optimal cut-point (c) under nomality and equal variance assumptions

used to separate these groups, and *J* occur at an intersection between the probability density functions of *pos* and *neg*. The number of intersections is a function of the variances of *pos* and *neg*. When there are more than one intersections, *J* occurs at one of the intersection points.

Cost Method

Consider a probabilistic classifier C_h that outputs confidences in its predictions. By ranking all examples $x \in X$ by their confidences $h(x)$ from the largest to the smallest (denoted by $X = \{x_1, \ldots, x_n\}$), one achieves a set of $n + 1$ binary classifiers by setting thresholds $\{\theta_i = (h(x_i)+h(x_{i+1}))/2,\ 1 \le i < n\} \cup \{h(x_1) - \lambda,\ h(x_n)+\lambda\}$ for some constant $\lambda > 0$. Given a relative cost *c* of true positive error to false positive error and a validation set *X* of labelled examples, one can find the optimal threshold θ based on *X* and *c*. To do so, simply rank the examples in *X*, try every threshold θ_i as described above and select the θ_i that minimizes the total cost of all errors on *X*.

Let us take the same example given in Figure 10.5. Assume that the cost of correctly classifying a positive class is taken as 1; there is a penalty of 0.25 for false positive instances.

One can see that with this cost the optimal threshold is 0.3. Even for a cost of 0.5 for false positive with the cost of correct classification unchanged, the same value remains the optimal threshold. On the other hand, if the costs are 1, the optimal threshold happens to be 0.54.

10.8 Combining Classifiers

In order to improve the classification performance, a well established technique is to combine multiple classifiers so as to take advantage of the strengths of individual classifiers and avoid their weaknesses. ROC curve can be used to optimally combine classifiers. The ROC convex hull (ROCCH) combination rule interpolates between base classifiers, C_1, C_2, ..., C_n, selecting either a single best classifier or a randomization between the decisions of two classifiers for every false positive rate. A single best classifier, if it exists, is directly inferred from ROCCH. We describe below two methods combining classifiers for a given *fp rate*, namely MRROC method and logical combination method.

Maximum Realisable ROC (MRROC)

Sometimes, the desired performance is not exactly obtained by any available classifier but lies between two available classifiers. In such cases it is possible to interpolate classifiers to obtain the desired performance. By ROC analysis of a set of existing classifiers, a set of new realisable classifiers may be obtained by a random combination of two of the existing classifiers. These classifiers lie on the convex hull that contains the original ROC points for the existing classifiers. This hull is the *maximum realisable ROC* (MRROC).

Take two discrete classifiers, C_1 and C_2, each with distinct false positive and true positive rates. These two classifiers correspond to two ROC points and are the end points of a straight line in ROC space, L_{12}. The line L_{12} defines a set of classifiers. Each point $(tpr_x, fpr_x) \in L_{12}$ represents the classifier C_x that would produce true positive rates tpr_x and false positive rates fpr_x. Given only C_1 and C_2, one may realise the output of classifier C_x by randomly choosing between the output of C_1 and C_2. The probability of choosing the output of C_1 over that of C_2 is determined by the distance along L_{12} between C_x and C_1.

Example 10.3

Consider the following example. There is a set of 4000 clients to whom a new insurance policy is to be marketed. The budget dictates that only 800 of them can be attended to, and so the problem is to select the 800 who are most likely to respond to the offer. The expectation of responders is 6%, so that within the population of 4000 we can expect to have 240 responders (positives) and 3760 non-responders (negatives). Let us consider two classifiers, C_1 and C_2, which score clients by the probability of their buying the policy. Let us assume also that the ROC space of C_1 is (0.1, 0.2) and that of C_2 is at (0.25, 0.6). We want to market to exactly 800 people. The line joining these two ROC points represents a set of classifiers with different values of false positive rates. We can find the appropriate classifier corresponding to our desired false positive rate, i.e., 800.

This can be expressed as the following constraint:

fp rate × 3760 + *tp rate* × 240 = c (number candidates to market).

c = 800

For the classifier C_1 we have

0.1 × 3760 + 0.2 × 240 = 424 candidates.

For the classifier C_2, we have

0.25 × 3760 + 0.6 × 240 = 1084 candidates.

Clearly, we want a classifier between C_1 and C_2 and we can achieve it using linear interpolation of C_1 and C_2.

If we take the linear combination of C_1 and C_2 with weights x_1 and $(1-x_1)$ such that $x_1 \times 424 + (1-x_1)1084 = 800$, then x_1 is 0.43. This combination corresponds to one ROC point.

LOGICAL COMBINATION RULES FOR DISCRETE CLASSIFIERS

Let us investigate the consequences of combining two or more discrete classifiers into an enhanced test. We subsequently extend this idea to probabilistic classifiers. We will look at combining two classifiers by disjunction and conjunction to get new classifiers – one with resulting error rates better than that of the stronger of the two, and the other with error rate worse than that of the weaker of the classifiers.

Let us revisit the concepts of *tp rate* and *fp rate* to recall that *tp rate* of a classifier *C* is the probability of classifying an instance in *pos* class as *Y*. We denote this as P(C =1| 1). Suppose there are two classifiers, C_1 and C_2. Let $P_{11|1}$ denote the probability of both C_1 and C_2 detecting instances in *pos* class as *Y*. We can define, similarly, other probabilities; $P_{11|1}$, $P_{10|1}$, $P_{01|1}$, $P_{00|1}$, $P_{11|0}$, $P_{10|0}$, $P_{01|0}$, and $P_{00|0}$. This is represented in Table 10.7, similar to the contingency table discussed earlier (Table 10.1)

Table 10.7

C_1	C_2	Total *pos* instances (*pos*)	Total *neg* instances (*neg*)
Y	Y	$P_{11\|1}$	$P_{11\|0}$
Y	N	$P_{10\|1}$	$P_{10\|0}$
N	Y	$P_{01\|1}$	$P_{01\|0}$
N	N	$P_{00\|1}$	$P_{00\|0}$

CONDITIONAL INDEPENDENCE ASSUMPTION

If we assume that the classifiers are conditionally independent, then we can conclude that $P_{11|1} = P(C_1 = 1|\ 1) \times P(C_2 = 1|\ 1) = tp\ rate_1\ tp\ rate_2 = tpr_1\ tpr_2$ (notation *tpr* and *fpr* are adopted for convenience).

Table 10.8

C_1	C_2	**Total *pos* instances (*pos*)**	**Total *neg* instances (*neg*)**
Y	Y	$tpr_1\, tpr_2$	$fpr_1\, fpr_2$
Y	N	$(1-tpr_1)\, tpr_2$	$(1-fpr_1)\, fpr_2$
N	Y	$tpr_1\, (1-tpr_2)$	$fpr_1\, (1-fpr_2)$
N	N	$(1-tpr_1)\, (1-tpr_2)$	$(1-fpr_1)\, (1-fpr_2)$

DISJUNCTION RULE ('OR' RULE)

A new classifier C_3 as disjunction of two discrete classifiers C_1 and C_2, denoted as $C_1 \vee C_2$, responds as *Y* if either C_1 or C_2 or both C_1 and C_2 recognize an instance as *Y*. Assume that fpr_i and tpr_i are false positive rate and true positive rate respectively of classifier C_i.

If we assume conditional independence of classifiers, then fpr_3, the false positive rate of C_3 is given by

$$fpr_3 = 1-[(1-fpr_1) \times (1-fpr_2)] = fpr_1 + fpr_2 - fpr_1\, fpr_2.$$

Similarly, the true positive of C_3 is given by

$$tpr_3 = 1-[(1-tpr_1) \times (1-tpr_2)] = tpr_1 + tpr_2 - tpr_1\, tpr_2.$$

CONJUNCTION RULE ('AND' RULE)

A new classifier C_4 as conjunction of two discrete classifiers C_1 and C_2, denoted as $C_1 \wedge C_2$ responds as *Y* if either C_1 and C_2 (or both) recognizes the instance *x* as *Y*. Assume that fpr_i and tpr_i are false positive rate and true positive rate respectively of classifier C_i.

Under conditional independence assumption, the true positive rate of C_4 is given by

$$tpr_4 = tpr_1 \times tpr_2$$

and the false positive rate of C_4 is

$$fpr_4 = fpr_1 \times fpr_2.$$

EXAMPLE 10.4

Consider the following example for purpose of illustration. Given in Table 10.9 are two classes C_1 and C_2. New classifiers are generated as disjunction and conjunction of these two classifiers. We see that both result in superior classifiers than the input classifiers.

Conditional independence assumption is violated in most real-world applications. When conditional independence is not satisfied by the classifiers, the confusion matrix is given Table 10.10.

When two discrete classifiers C_1 and C_2 are combined by disjunction as $C_3 = C_1 \vee C_2$ and C_1 and C_2 are not known to be conditionally independent, we have following relationship to get the *fp rate* and *tp rate* of C_3.

Table 10.9 Illustration of disjunction and conjunction of discrete classifiers

Instance	class	C_1	C_2	$C_1 \vee C_2$	$C_1 \wedge C_2$
1	*pos*	Y	N	Y	N
2	*pos*	Y	Y	Y	Y
3	*neg*	Y	N	Y	N
4	*pos*	Y	Y	Y	Y
5	*pos*	Y	N	Y	N
6	*pos*	Y	Y	Y	Y
7	*neg*	Y	N	Y	N
8	*neg*	N	N	N	N
9	*pos*	Y	Y	Y	Y
10	*neg*	N	N	N	N
11	*pos*	Y	Y	Y	Y
12	*neg*	Y	N	Y	N
13	*pos*	N	Y	Y	N
14	*neg*	N	N	N	N
15	*neg*	N	N	N	N
16	*neg*	Y	N	Y	N
17	*pos*	Y	N	Y	N
18	*neg*	N	Y	Y	N
19	*pos*	N	N	N	N
20	*neg*	N	Y	Y	N
ROC point		(0.4, 0.8)	(0.1, 0.6)	(0.6, 0.9)	(0, 0.5)

Table 10.10

C_1	C_2	Total *pos* instances *pos*	Total *neg* instances *neg*
Y	Y	$tpr_1\, tpr_2 < P_{11\|1} <$ min $(tpr1,\, tpr_2)$	$fpr_1 + fpr_2 - 1 + P_{00\|0}$
Y	N	$tpr_1 - P_{11\|1}$	$(1 - fpr_2) - P_{00\|0}$
N	Y	$tpr_2 - P_{11\|1}$	$(1 - fpr_1) - P_{00\|0}$
N	N	$1 - tpr_1 - tpr_2 + P_{11\|1}$	$(1 - fpr_1)(1 - fpr_2) < P_{00\|0} <$ min$((1 - fpr_1),\, (1 - fpr_2))$

$$[(1-fpr_1) \times (1-fpr_2)] \leq 1-fpr_3 \leq \min((1-fpr_1),\, (1-fpr_2))$$

$$[(1-tpr_1) \times (1-tpr_2)] \leq 1-tpr_3 \leq \min((1-tpr_1),\, (1-tpr_2))$$

For $C_4 = C_1 \wedge C_2$, in the absence of conditional independence assumption, we have the following rules.

$tpr_1 \times tpr_2 " tpr_4 \leq \min(tpr_1, tpr_2)$

$fpr_1 \times fpr_2 " fpr_4 \leq \min(fpr_1, fpr_2)$

Rules for Combining Probabilistic Classifiers

We have learnt about disjunction and conjunction of two discrete classifiers. A discrete classifier corresponds to one ROC point or one pair of (*tpr*, *fpr*). Probabilistic classifiers, on the other hand, have a series of such pairs, one for each value of the threshold. For probabilistic classifiers, a resulting fused classifier may not yield a better classifier due to concavities in ROC curves.

We outline here a technique of combination proposed by Kherich et al [2019] for probabilistic classifiers, which is an extension of combination rules of discrete classifiers. We know that for a single value of the threshold, a probabilistic classifier is represented by a single ROC point and hence can be treated as a discrete classifier. For combination, the combination rule of discrete classifiers is applied to each threshold on the first ROC curve with respect to each threshold of the second curve. If there are *m* distinct values of threshold of first curve and *n* distinct values of threshold for the second, then the combination rule is applied *mn* times. Each combination yields one ROC point. We ignore the resulting ROC points which are not superior to points in the convex hull of the given ROC curves.

The technique, called BC_{ALL}, inputs a pair of ROC curves defined by a series of thresholds, T_1 and T_2. Interestingly, BC_{ALL} is not limited only by disjunction and conjunction; it uses all possible Boolean operators. BC_{ALL} fuses the response of each threshold from the first curve with the responses of each threshold from the second curve. Each of the fused responses is used to compute the fused *fpr* and *tpr*, and thereby an ROC point is determined. Any ROC point that is inferior to (lies below) the ROCCH of original pair of ROC curves are ignored; only the superior ROC points are taken. With the help of these superior points, the original ROCCH is updated to get a new ROCCH. The outputs are the vertices of the final ROCCH, where each ROC point is the results of two thresholds from the ROC curves fused with the corresponding Boolean function. These thresholds and Boolean functions are applied for classification of unknown instances. The BC_{ALL} algorithm is given on the next page.

10.9 Area Under the ROC Curve (AUC)

An ROC curve is a two-dimensional depiction of a classifier's performance, and the geometrical properties of the curve is used for optimizing the performance of the classifier with reference to various metrics. However, often, since there is no clear predominance of some ROC curve above others, it is difficult to compare two classifiers by looking at the respective curves. Hence it is preferable to employ a single value measure which summarizes the performance of the classifier. A common method for ding so is to calculate the area under the ROC curve, abbreviated as AUC. Since the AUC is a portion of the area of the unit square under the ROC curve, its value will always be between 0 and 1. However, because random guessing produces the diagonal line between (0, 0) and (1, 1) with an area of 0.5, no realistic classifier should have an AUC less than 0.5. Maximum AUC = 1, and and AUC of 1implies that the classifier is perfect in differentiating *pos* and *neg* instances. This also implies that both sensitivity and specificity are one and false positive and false negative are zero. This is extremely unlikely to happen in practice; an AUC close to 1 is indicative of a better performance classifier. Just as AUC =1 represents a perfectly accurate classifier, likewise, a perfectly inaccurate classifier yields AUC=0, again an unlikely happen.

Algorithm 1. BC_{ALL}(Ta,Tb,labels) Boolean combination of two ROC curves.

Input : Thresholds of two ROC curves, T_a and T_b and *labels* (of validation set)
Output: ROCCH and fused responses (*Rab*) of combined curves, where each point is the result of two fused thresholds along with the corresponding Boolean function (*bf*)

let $m \leftarrow$ number of distinct thresholds in T_a
let $n \leftarrow$ number of distinct thresholds in T_b
Allocate F an array $[2, m \times n]$ `//holds temporary results of fusions`
$BooleanFunctions \leftarrow \{a \wedge b, \neg a \wedge b, a \wedge \neg b, \neg(a \wedge b), a \vee b, \neg a \vee b, a \vee \neg b, \neg(a \vee b), a \oplus b, a \equiv b\}$
Compute $ROCCH_{old}$ of the original curves
foreach $bf \in BooleanFunctions$ **do**
  for $i \leftarrow 1$ to m **do**
  $R_a \leftarrow (T_a \geq T_{ai})$ `// converting threshold of 1st ROC to responses`
  for j = **1** to n **do**
    $R_b \leftarrow (T_b \geq T_{bj})$ `// converting threshold of 2nd ROC to responses`
    $R_c \leftarrow bf\,(R_a, R_b)$ `// combined responses with bf`
    Compute (*tpr, f pr*) using R_c and *labels*
    Push (*tpr, fpr*) onto *F*
  Compute $ROCCH_{new}$ of *F*
  Store **thresholds** and corresponding **Boolean** functions that exceeded $ROCCH_{old}$
$S^{+}_{global} \leftarrow (T_{ax}, T_{by}, bf)$ `// to be used during operations`
Store the responses of these emerging points into R `//to be used with` BCM_{ALL} `and` IBC_{ALL}
$ROCCH_{new} \leftarrow ROCCH_{old}$ `// Update ROCCH`
Return $ROCCH_{new}$, R, S^{+}_{global}

AUC is often used when a general measure of predictiveness is desired; it is a better criterion for the predictive performance of dichotomizers or binary classifiers. However, classifiers that aim at minimizing error rate may not lead to the best possible AUC values. The total area under ROC curve is a *single index* for measuring the performance a classifier. Two common interpretations of area under the ROC curve are: (i) the average value of sensitivity for all possible values of specificity, and (ii) the average value of specificity for all possible values of sensitivity. The larger the AUC, the better is the overall performance of a classifier for correctly picking up the positive and negative instances. Equal AUCs of two classifiers represents similar overall performance, but this does not necessarily mean that both the curves are identical. They may cross each other. It is possible that a high-AUC classifier performs worse in a specific region of ROC space than a low-AUC classifier.

10.10 Methods to Compute AUC

Trapezoidal Rule

This is a non-parametric method as it does not require any distribution pattern of instances and the resulting area under the ROC curve is empirical. It calculates the area by just joining consecutive points on the ROC curve corresponding to intervals of threshold values, and from each point in the curve it draws a straight vertical line joining the *x*-axis. This forms several trapezoids whose areas can be easily calculated and summed. The area calculated by this method gives the exact value of AUC if the ROC curve is an empirical one. But if the ROC curve is a parametric one, then the curve is first approximated as a piecewise linear curve by a selecting a limited number of points on the curve. The trapezoidal rule gives an underestimation of the area.

Example 10.5

Consider the ROC curve given in Figure 10.5. We use trapezoidal rule by dropping vertical lines from selected points on the curve. This gives us a set of trapeziums whose areas can be easily calculated as seen in Table 10.11. Summing up the areas of all trapeziums gives the value of AUC.

Table 10.11

Trapezium	Area
R_1	0.02
R_2	0.10
R_3	0.06
R_4	0.07
R_5	0.24
R_6	0.09
R_7	0.10
AUC	0.68

With reference to Figure10.1a, we can give another interpretation of AUC. The AUC is the probability that a randomly chosen member of *pos* will be to the right of a randomly chosen member of *neg* with respect to a given classifier. This is known as a two-alternative forced-choice (2AFC) test. The AUC is equivalent to the probability of correctly distinguishing an event from a non-event in a 2AFC test. The AUC can be calculated by repeated sampling of the event and non-event cases and tallying the frequency with which the event received a higher detection probability than the non-event. The 2AFC test is not described in further detail here as it is beyond the scope of this book. Instead, we will use directly the following formula to find AUC.

Let a classifier C assign a score h to every instance x_i, a real value $h(x_i)$, such that $h(x_i)$ is the numerical score to indicate the confidence that x_i belongs to the *pos* class. Then AUC can be calculated as:

$$\text{AUC} = \frac{\sum_{x_i \in pos} \sum_{x_j \in neg \wedge x_j > x_i}}{pos \times neg}$$

where $s(x_i, x_j)$ is defined as

$$S(x_i, x_j) = \begin{cases} 1, & \text{if } h(x_i) > h(x_j) \\ 0.5, & \text{if } h(x_i) = h(x_j) \\ 0, & \text{if } h(x_i) < h(x_j) \end{cases}$$

EXAMPLE 10.6

Consider the same example as above taken in a different form (Table 10.4). The non-zero values of $s(x_i, x_j)$ can be calculated as follows.

$s(x_1, x_3) = s(x_1, x_7) = s(x_1, x_8) = s(x_1, x_{10}) = s(x_1, x_{12}) = s(x_1, x_{14}) = s(x_1, x_{15})$
$= s(x_1, x_{16}) = s(x_1, x_{18}) = s(x_1, x_{20}) = 1$

$s(x_2, x_3) = s(x_2, x_7) = s(x_2, x_8) = s(x_2, x_{10}) = s(x_2, x_{12}) = s(x_2, x_{14}) = s(x_2, x_{15})$
$= s(x_2, x_{16}) = s(x_2, x_{18}) = s(x_2, x_{20}) = 1$

$s(x_4, x_7) = s(x_4, x_8) = s(x_4, x_{10}) = s(x_4, x_{12}) = s(x_4, x_{14}) = s(x_4, x_{15}) = s(x_4, x_{16})$
$= s(x_4, x_{18}) = s(x_4, x_{20}) = 1$

$s(x_5, x_7) = s(x_5, x_8) = s(x_5, x_{10}) = s(x_5, x_{12}) = s(x_5, x_{14}) = s(x_5, x_{15}) = s(x_5, x_{16})$
$= s(x_5, x_{18}) = s(x_5, x_{20}) = 1$

$s(x_6, x_7) = s(x_6, x_8) = s(x_6, x_{10}) = s(x_6, x_{12}) = s(x_6, x_{14}) = s(x_6, x_{15}) = s(x_6, x_{16})$
$= s(x_6, x_{18}) = s(x_6, x_{20}) = 1$

$s(x_9, x_{10}) = s(x_9, x_{12}) = s(x_9, x_{14}) = s(x_9, x_{15}) = s(x_9, x_{16}) = s(x_9, x_{18}) = s(x_9, x_{20}) = 1$

and so on. Finally, when all non-zero values are added we get the area as 0.68.

Note that while this method will produce the same AUC as the previous method, it cannot be used to generate a ROC curve.

AUC can be viewed as the summary measure of the separability of the pair of distributions that corresponds to the two classes and can be interpreted as the average sensitivity over all possible specificity values. AUC is also the probability that the decision score (t_1) of a randomly chosen positive case is larger than that of a randomly chosen negative case (t_0) plus half of the probability that two such cases have the same score (tie), assuming without loss of generality that the score of the positive class is larger than that of the negative class on an average.

$$AUC = Pr(t_0 < t_1) + \tfrac{1}{2}\, Pr(t_0 = t_1)$$

Here, *Pr* denotes probability.

Parametric Methods

When the outcomes for each class follows normal distribution, parametric approach is used for estimating AUC. Binormal distribution is commonly used for this purpose. If the data is actually binormal or a transformation such as log, or square makes the data binormal, then the relevant parameters can be easily estimated by the values of means and variances. If, however, the distribution of raw data from a quantitative test is far from Gaussian, the AUC and the corresponding standard error (SE) derived from a directly fitted binormal model is most likely to be seriously distorted. So when the data is continuous and appear to be non-Gaussian, the nonparametric approach to estimating the AUC is more appealing than the binormal model.

AUC for Feature Selection

ROC analysis can be used for feature selection, a critical procedure for high-dimensional data classification. The commonly used techniques for feature selection are filter approach, wrapper approach, and embedded approach. The wrapper approach evaluates features by performing internal classification with a given inductive algorithm and is attractive for many reasons despite being computation-intensive. A common practice in all approaches is to first create as many potential features as possible and then select an optimal subset from them. To determine this optimal subset, a feature selection process is used which begins with an empty set of features and repeatedly adds or removes features until no change produces a better subset. This feature selection process requires a metric for comparing the quality of potential feature subsets; accuracy is commonly used for the purpose. However, it is well known that overall accuracy as a metric is biased when the class distribution is imbalanced in the data. A more reliable way to compute the fitness of a feature set in such a case is to use the area under the ROC curve (AUC) because AUC measures performance at all thresholds.

10.11 Averaging ROC Curves

We have seen that for one test dataset we get one ROC curve by varying the threshold values. There are many testing methods such as bootstrap method or cross-validation method where it is necessary to carry out the performance evaluation for a collection of test dataset, in which case for one single classifier we have more than one test set. One approach is to gather all the *(fp rate, tp rate)* pairs generated from all the test sets for all values of threshold and trace one single curve to study the predictive performance of the classifier. However, the primary reason for using multiple test sets is to derive a measure of variance. This purpose is defeated if one merges all the points of ROC space corresponding to all test sets. *Averaging* is a strategy to combine multiple ROC curve obtained from various test sets. However, ROC space is two-dimensional and any average is necessarily one-dimensional. There are two known methods for averaging ROC curves: *vertical averaging* and *threshold averaging.* In vertical averaging, for a fixed value of *fp rate*, the *tp rate* of ROC curves are averaged. Threshold averaging is to take average of *(fp rate, tp rate)* for fixed a value of threshold. In vertical averaging there is only one single dependent variable, *tp rate*, for the independent variable *fp rate*. However, one cannot always control the values of independent variable. Since averaging is required to find some sort of variance, confidence intervals of the averaged curve can be used in various ways to compute these parameters.

Figure 10.11 shows 5 different ROC curves for a classifier with 5 different samples of test data, while Figure 10.12 depicts the average ROC curve with *vertical averaging* and the confidence intervals for *tp rate* for a given *fp rate*. Figure 10.13 illustrates the technique of *threshold averaging.* One can see that we have confidence bands for *fp rate* as well as for *tp rate*.

In vertical averaging approach, by freezing the *fp rate*, it is possible to generate a (parametric) confidence interval for the *tp rate* based on the mean and variance; multiple curves are generated using cross-validation or other sampling techniques. A potential weakness of this method is the practical lack of independent control over a model's false-positive rates.

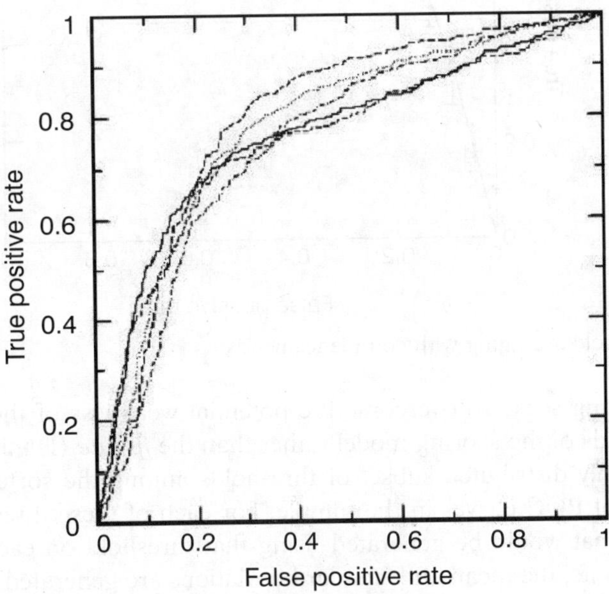

Figure 10.11 ROC Curves for 5 different sampling of test data

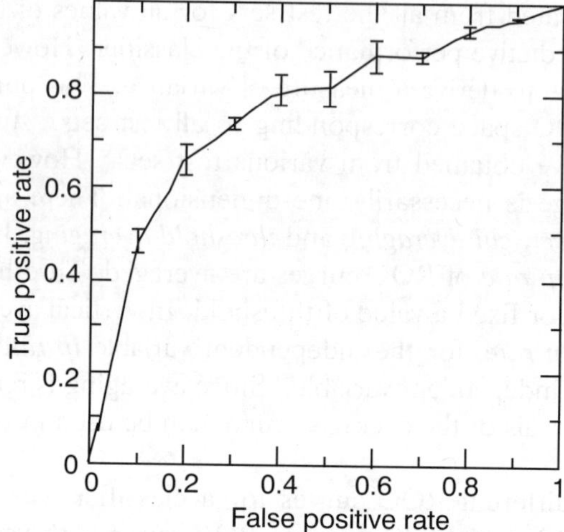

Figure 10.12 Vertical averaging and confidence band for ROC curves of Figure 10.11

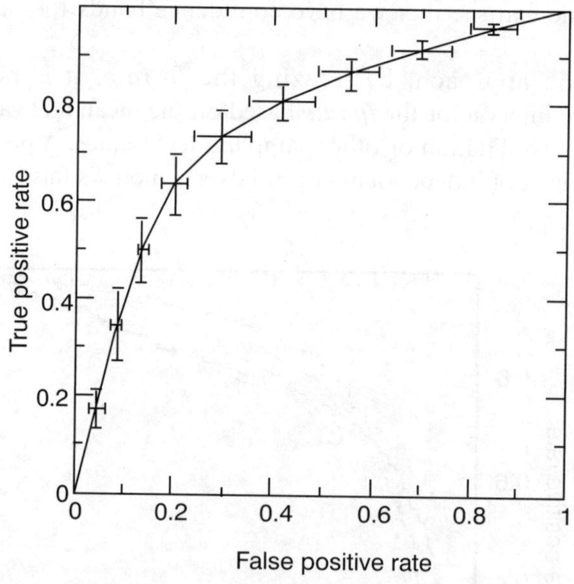

Figure 10.13 Threshold averaging with confidence bands

Threshold averaging seeks to overcome the potential weakness of the vertical averaging by freezing the thresholds of the scoring model rather than the *fp rate* (Hanley and McNeil, 1982). It chooses a uniformly distributed subset of thresholds among the sorted set of all thresholds seen across the set of ROC curves in the sample. For each of these thresholds, it identifies the set of ROC points that would be generated using that threshold on each of the ROC curves. From these ROC points, the mean and standard deviations are generated for the *fp* and *tp rates*, giving the mean ROC point as well as vertical and horizontal confidence intervals.

10.12 ROC FOR MULTI-CLASS CLASSIFIERS

The success of binary ROC analysis gives hope that it may be possible to extend similar ideas to multi-class problems. This , however, is not a trivial task. One key aspect to binary ROC analysis is that it is highly efficient for representing trade-offs of misclassifying one class into the other via binary ROC curves. In addition, the AUC nicely characterizes the classifier's ability to produce correct rankings without committing to any particular operating point.

Let us attempt to generalise ROC analysis to multi-class problem by first considering a case of three-class situation. The contingency table is 3×3 matrix shown in Table 10.12.

Table 10.12 Contingency table for 3-class classifier

	Total instances of class 1	**Total instances of class 2**	**Total instances of class 3**
Detection as class 1	TP_1	FD_{12}	FD_{13}
Detection as class 2	FD_{21}	TP_2	FD_{23}
Detection as class 3	FD_{31}	FD_{32}	TP_3

For the two-class problem, knowing one element from each column in contingency table was sufficient, but for the three-class problem, two elements are needed to fully determine the column. Thus, whereas the two-class problem spans two dimensions, the three-class spans not three but six dimensions. It becomes hard to visualize six-dimensional surfaces. To overcome this difficulty, we adopt some approximation scheme. Note that ROC curve can also be equivalently visualised if we plot true positive rate (ordinate) against false negative rate instead of false positive rate. These two quantities are diagonal elements of normalized contingency table. The columns of the table are normalized. Thus, to avoid a six-dimensional ROC space for 3-class problem, we can only consider the diagonal elements of column-normalized 3×3 contingency table as tp_rate_1, tp_rate_2 and tp_rate_3 and we get 3-dimensional ROC point.

For the three-class problem, let us assume that there are two threshold quantities and that we have following decision criteria:

If confidence is less than t_1 then decide class 1, else

if for confidence value is between t_1 and t_2, then decide class 2, else

if confidence greater than t_2, then decide class 3.

Varying the two decision thresholds, t_1 and t_2, then results in a three-dimensional ROC surface (Fig. 10.15). The AUC in multi-class problems is generalized to VUS (volume under surface).

A perfect ordering of the three classes results in a volume under the sphere, VUS = 1, while random forecasts, i.e., the three identical distributions $p1$, $p2$, and $p3$ give a VUS = 1/6. This is the area beneath a plane intersecting the unit cube at the vertices (1, 0, 0), (0, 1, 0), and (0, 0, 1). Intuitively, assuming again that the three distributions are identical, there is a 1/3 chance that the class 3 sample will have a higher score than both the class 1 and class 2 samples; there is a 1/2 chance that the class 2 sample will have a higher score than the class 1 sample. In other

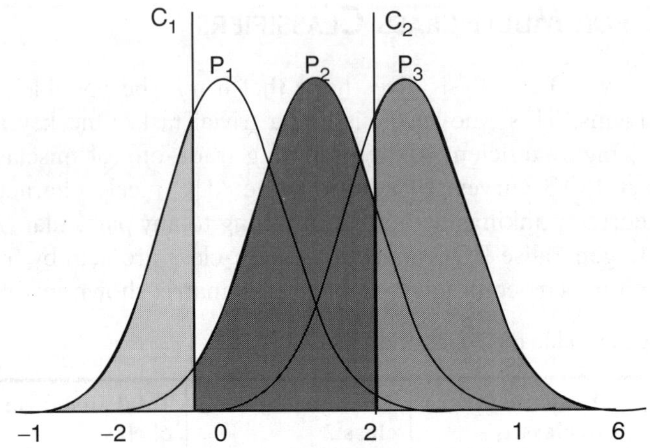

Figure 10.14 Hypothetical distributions of instances for a three-class problem. The vertical lines represent the decision thresholds, t_1 and t_2. The light-, medium- and dark-shaded regions represent tp_1, tp_2, and tp_3 respectively.

words, there are six possible orderings of the three samples, giving an overall probability of 1/6. While the computation and visualization of the three-class problem are greatly simplified through this approach, this simplification comes at the cost of lost information—specifically, all information about misclassification errors, i.e., due to the off-diagonal elements of the 3×3 contingency table being disregarded.

More generally, n classes result in an $(n^2 - n)$-dimensional problem and the ROC curve is generalized to an $(n^2 - n)$-dimensional ROC surface. The AUC is generalized to VUS. Though many properties of two-dimensional ROC analysis can be extended to higher dimensional ROC surfaces, many of the properties are either hard to visualize or are ambiguous.

Pareto Front

Fieldsend and Everson in 2010 extended the concept of the ROC convex hull (ROCCH) to multi-class classifiers using the idea of *Pareto front*. Consider the following formulation: let $R_{j,k}(h)$ be the misclassification rate of predicting examples from class j as class k by classifier C_h. The goal is to find h that minimizes $R_{j,k}(h)$ for all j, k with $j \leq k$. Consider two classifiers C_h and $C_{h'}$. We say C_h strictly dominates $C_{h'}$ if all misclassification rates for C_h are no worse than $C_{h'}$ and at least one rate is strictly better. The set of all feasible classifiers such that no one is dominated by the other forms the *Pareto front*.

A simple extension of the AUC that can be used in multi-class problems was proposed in by Hand and Till (2001). For a multi-class classification problem containing c classes, a classifier assigns c scores to every instance. Each score corresponds to one of the c classes and indicates the confidence that the instance belongs to this class. Hence, the scores for all the n instances can be represented by an $n \times c$ matrix, the columns and rows of which correspond to classes and instances respectively. Let A_{ij} (A_{ji}) be the AUC calculated according to the ith (jth) column

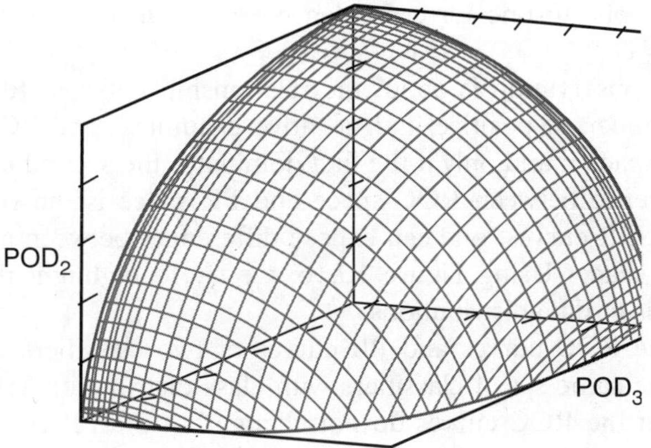

Figure 10.15 The three-dimensional ROC surface resulting from varying the decision thresholds t_1 and t_2 in Fig. 10.14

of the matrix with respect to the instances from class *i* and class *j*. Multi-class AUC (MAUC) is defined as follows:

$$\text{MAUC} = \frac{2}{c(c-1)} \sum_{i=1}^{c} \sum_{j=i+1}^{c} \frac{A_{ij} + A_{ji}}{2}$$

We can see that the MAUC value of a classification system is actually the average AUC value over all $c(c-1)/2$ one-versus-one binary sub-problems. In other words, this means that maximizing the AUC value of each binary sub-problem is of equal importance in calculating a classification system's MAUC.

10.13 Precision-Recall Graph

Precision–Recall (PR) curves are another approach to study the performance of classifiers. Precision–Recall (PR) curves have been considered as an alternative to ROC curves for tasks with a large skew in the class distribution. Like ROC space, PR space is a two-dimensional space with abscissa as *recall* value and ordinate as *precision*. For a given discrete classifier, we get a point in precision–recall space as the ordered pair (precision, recall), and for a probabilistic classifier we get a PR curve when we vary the threshold.

There exists a deep relationship between ROC and PR spaces. A point in ROC space corresponds to a unique confusion matrix when the dataset is fixed. It may be noted that in PR space, false negative (FN) does not have any role, and hence, each point may correspond to multiple confusion matrices. However, with a fixed number of positive and negative examples, given the other three entries in a matrix, FN is uniquely determined. Of course, if Recall = 0, we cannot recover FP (false positive). Thus, for a given dataset of positive and negative examples, there exists a one-to-one correspondence between a curve in ROC space and a curve in PR space if Recall ≠ 0.

Another interesting observation is about the relationship between ROC space and the PR space. For a fixed number of positive and negative examples, one ROC curve dominates a second curve in ROC space if and only if the first dominates the second in the PR space.

An important difference between ROC space and PR space is the visual representation of the curves. Looking at PR curves, one can expose differences between algorithms that are not apparent in the ROC space. Using Figure 10.16, we try to highlight the advantage of ROC curve for different types of data distributions.

In Figure 10.16, the ROC curves and PR curves of two classifiers are plotted for a class distribution of 1:1. The same set of classifiers with class distribution 1:10 are given in Figure 10.17. We can see that the ROC curves do not change but the PR curves change drastically, implying that the PR curve is sensitive to class distribution whereas ROC is not.

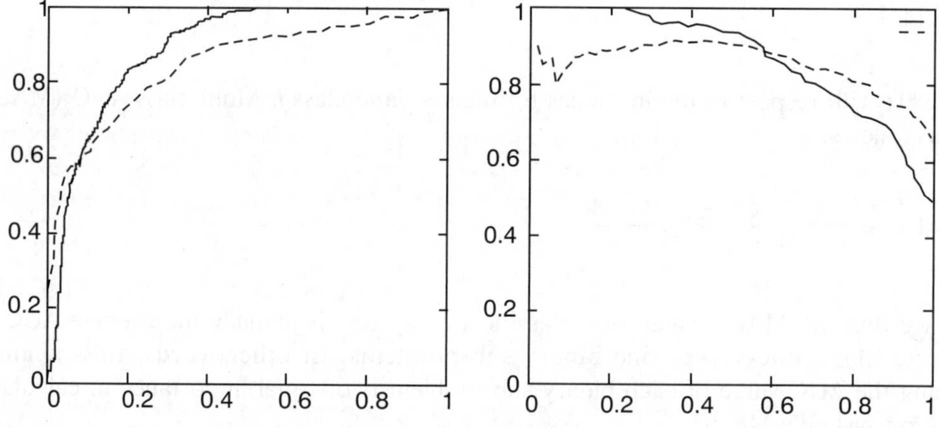

Figure10.16 ROC curve and PR curve for class distributions 1:1 (Fawcett, 2006)

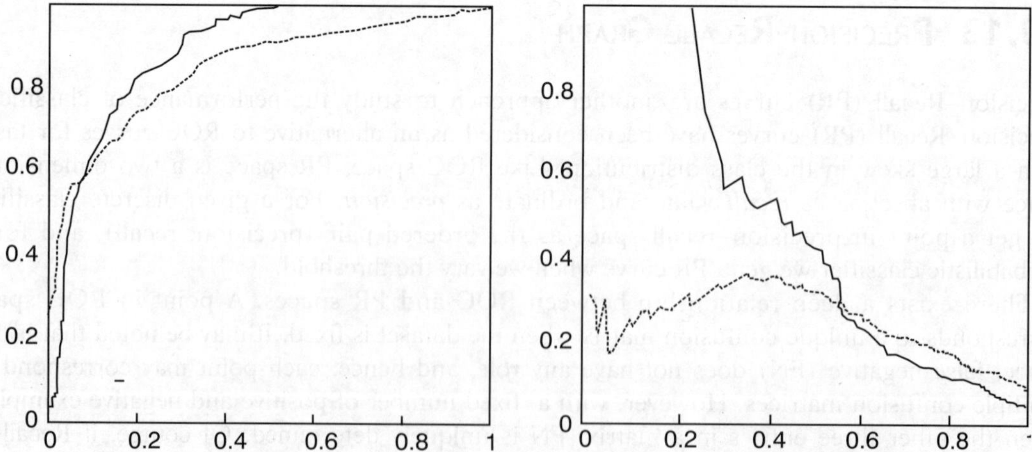

Figure 10.17 ROC curve and PR curve for class distributions 1:10 (Fawcett, 2006)

10.14 DET Curves

In certain situations, detection tasks are viewed as involving a trade-off between two error types: false positive and false negative. When there is a trade-off of error types, a single performance number is inadequate to represent the capabilities of a system. Such a system is best represented by a performance curve. DET (detection error trade-off) curve is essentially a curve that represents the trade-off between the error types. DET graphs plot false positive in the ordinate and false negative in the abscissa. In that sense DET graph treats both the errors uniformly. If the resulting curves are straight lines, then the underlying likelihood distributions from the system are normal; the diagonal $y = -x$ on the normal deviate scale represents random performance. For well-performing classifiers with low false positive rates and/or low false negative rates, the DET curve tend to be bunched up in the lower left portion of the graph. In order to give a spread-out representation, the DET curve is normally log-scaled, which gives this region greater surface area and allows the classifiers to be compared more easily.

10.15 Cost Curves

Drummond and Holte (2000; 2002) point out that reading slope angles from an ROC curve may be difficult to do. Determining the regions of superiority, and the amount by which one classifier is superior to another, is challenging when the comparison lines are curve tangents rather than simple vertical lines. Drummond and Holte reason that if the primary use of a curve is to compare relative costs, the graphs should represent these costs explicitly. They propose cost curves as an alternative to ROC curves. On a cost curve, the x-axis ranges from 0 to 1 and measures the proportion of positives in the distribution; the y-axis, also from 0 to 1, is the relative expected misclassification cost. A perfect classifier is a horizontal line from (0, 0) to (0, 1).

Cost curves are a point-line dual of the ROC curves. A point (i.e., a discrete classifier) in ROC space is represented by a line in cost space, with the line designating the relative expected cost of the classifier. For any X point, the corresponding Y points represent the expected costs of the classifiers. Thus, while in ROC space the convex hull contains the set of lowest-cost classifiers, in cost space the lower envelope represents this set.

Example-Specific Costs

In some domains all errors are not equally costly, and the cost of a particular kind of error is not constant throughout the population but varies by example. (For example, the cost of prescribing a medicine to an allergic patient can be much higher than the cost of not prescribing the medicine to a non-allergic patient when alternative form of treatment is available.) Consider the simple credit card transaction domain used by Elkan (2001) in which the task is to decide whether to approve or refuse a given transaction. Elkan describes a benefit matrix for the task, shown in Figure 10.18. This cost matrix is justified with the following explanation. A refused fraudulent transaction has a benefit of \$20 because it may prevent future fraud. Refusing a legitimate transaction has a negative benefit because it annoys the customer. Approving a fraudulent transaction has a negative benefit proportional to the transaction amount (x).

Approving a legitimate transaction generates a small amount of income proportional to the transaction amount ($0.02x$).

	Fraudulent	**Legitimate**
Refuse	\$20	–\$20
Approve	$-x$	$0.02x$

Figure 10.18 Benefit matrix from Elkan C, 2001

ROC graphs have been criticized because of their inability to handle example-specific costs as they are based on simple counts of TP and FP examples, which is in turn based on the assumption that all true positives are equivalent and all false positives are equivalent. However, with a straightforward transformation we can show how ROC graphs may be used with example-specific costs. For this, let us assume for the credit card example above that a Y decision corresponds to approving a transaction and N means denying it. To use the matrix for an ROC graph, we transform it into a cost–benefit matrix where the costs are relative only to Y (approve) decisions. First, we subtract the first row from both rows in the matrix. Conceptually this matrix now corresponds to a baseline situation where all transactions are refused, so all fraud is denied and all legitimate customers are annoyed. We then negate the approved fraudulent cell to turn it into a cost. This yields the cost–benefit matrix which forms the definition of the cost function $c(Y, p, x)$ and $c(Y, n, x)$.

A Note of Historical Interest

You may be wondering where the name *Receiver Operating Characteristic* came from. ROC analysis is part of a field called *Signal Detection Theory* developed during World War II for the analysis of radar images. Radar operators had to decide whether a blip on the screen represented an enemy target, a friendly ship, or just noise. Signal detection theory measures the ability of radar receiver operators to make these important distinctions. Their ability to do so was called the Receiver Operating Characteristics. It was not until the 1970s that signal detection theory was recognized as useful for interpreting classification ability.

Further Reading

The paper by Fawcett(2006) is very informative and readers can get more detailed information on the concepts touched upon in this chapter. The content of this chapter is mostly the compilation of results of the papers presented in the bibliography below.

Exercises

1. For Table 10.6a and Table 10.6b, compute F-measure, precision and recall.
2. Consider the data in Table 10.4 and assume $t = 0.45$. Find the actual classification of each instance.
3. For the same table, find the classification with $t = 0.2$.
4. Use algorithm to compute ROC curve for the dataset in Table 10.4.

5. Consider the example given in Table 10.3 and rename Classifier 6 as C_1, Classifier 7 as C_2 and Classifier 2 as C_3. There is no subset inclusion relationship between TP_1 and TP_2. Even if the required condition is not satisfied, build another classifier C_4 from the given three classifiers by the process of repair.
6. For C_1 and C_2 above, compute $C_1 \wedge C_2$, $C_1 \vee C_2$, and $C_3 \vee \neg C_2$.
7. The data from http://www.medicalbiostatistics.com/roccurve.pdf is to be considered for instances with pre-labor rupture of membrane to find if the duration since rupture can help in predicting the caesarean delivery. The following table gives the sensitivity and specificity for different durations of rupture.

Duration (hr) greater than or equal to	**Sensitivity**	**1 – Specificity**
.00	1.0	1.0
.63	1.0	0.976
5.13	0.971	0.583
5.38	0.971	0.575
5.75	0.971	0.551
6.25	0.914	0.378
6.75	0.914	0.346
7.13	0.857	0.291
7.38	0.857	0.283
7.75	0.857	0.276
8.25	0.800	0.1892
8.75	0.800	0.181
9.25	0.743	0.110
9.75	0.743	0.102
10.25	0.543	0.039
10.75	0.543	0.31
11.50	0.457	0.024
12.5	0.400	0.008
13.5	0.343	0.00
14.5	0.286	0.00
15.5	0.257	0.00
16.5	0.200	0.00
17.5	0.171	0.00
18.5	0.143	0.00
19.5	0.114	0.00
20.25	0.057	0.00
21.5	0.000	0.00

a. Draw ROC curve for the data.
b. Draw PR curve for this data.
c. Find the optimal threshold value using minimum distance from (0, 1).
d. Find Youden index *J* for this data.
e. Find AUC using the trapezium rule.

BIBLIOGRAPHY

Bradley, A. P. The use of the area under the ROC curve in the evaluation of machine learning algorithms. *Pattern Recognition* 30(7), 1145–1159, 1997.

Drummond, C. and R. C. Holte. Explicitly representing expected cost: An alternative to ROC representation. In R. Ramakrishnan and S. Stolfo (eds.): *Proceedings of the Sixth ACM SIGKDD International Conference on Knowledge Discovery and Data Mining*, pp. 198–207, ACM Press, 2000.

Drummond, C. and R. C. Holte. Classifier cost curves: Making performance evaluation easier and more informative. Unpublished manuscript available from the authors, 2002.

Egan, J. P. *Signal Detection Theory and ROC Analysis*, Series in Cognition and Perception. New York: Academic Press, 1975.

Elkan, C. The foundations of cost-sensitive learning. In *Proceedings of the IJCAI*-01, pp. 973–978, 2001.

Fawcett T. An introduction to ROC analysis. In *Pattern Recognition Letters*, 27(8): 861–874, 2006.

Flach, P. and S. Wu. Repairing concavities in ROC curves. In *Proc. 2003 UK Workshop on Computational Intelligence*, pp. 38–44, 2003.

Fieldsend, J. E. and Everson, R. E. Formulation and comparison of multi-class ROC surfaces, *2nd ROCML Workshop, part of the 22nd International Conference on Machine Learning (ICML)*, Bonn, Germany, 2005.

Hand, D. J. and R. J. Till. A simple generalization of the area under the ROC curve to multiple class classification problems. *Machine Learning*, 45(2), 171–186, 2001.

Hanley, J. A. and B. J. McNeil. The meaning and use of the area under a receiver operating characteristic (ROC) Curve. In *Radiology* 143, 29–36, 1982.

Kheric W, Granger E, Miri A, and Sabourin R. Iterative Boolean combination of classifiers in the ROC space: An application to anomaly detection with HMMs. In *Pattern Recognition*, 43(2010) 2732–2752, 2010.

Lane, T. Extensions of ROC Analysis to multi-class domains. In T. Dietterich, D. Margineantu, F. Provost, and P. Turney (eds.): *ICML-2000 Workshop on Cost-Sensitive Learning*, 2000.

Macskassy, S. A. and F. Provost. Confidence bands for ROC curves. In *ICML-2004* (Submitted to), 2004.

Martin, A., G. Doddington, T. Kamm, M. Ordowski, and M. Przybocki. The DET curve in assessment of detection task performance. In *Proc. Eurospeech '97*. Rhodes, Greece, pp. 1895–1898, 1997.

Provost, F. and P. Domingos. Well-trained PETs: Improving probability estimation trees. *CeDER Working Paper* #IS–00–04, Stern School of Business, New York University, NY, 2001.

Srinivasan, A. Note on the location of optimal classifiers in n-dimensional ROC space. *Technical Report PRG-TR-2-99*, Oxford University Computing Laboratory, Oxford, England, 1999.

Zou, K. H. Receiver operating characteristic (ROC) literature research. Online bibliography at http://splweb.bwh.harvard.edu:8000/pages/ ppl/zou/roc.html

11

WEB MINING

11.1 INTRODUCTION

In recent years we have witnessed an ever-increasing flood of written information, culminating in the advent of massive digital libraries. The world wide web has become a very popular medium of publishing. Though the web is rich in information, gathering and making sense of this data is difficult because publication on the web is largely unorganised. Having studied the data mining techniques, a question that naturally comes to our minds is whether we can extract implicit, previously unknown information from the massive collection of documents available in the web. And, if so, do we have to design new techniques or we can make use of the standard data mining techniques available? In this chapter the essential features of web mining are identified. We also discuss the subproblems, where these standard techniques can be employed. It will be shown here that text mining research is the most important aspect of web mining.

The objective of this chapter is to present a brief overview of web mining techniques. Readers may notice that, unlike the earlier chapters, details of the techniques are not discussed here, only the fundamental principles are covered here. We shall, however, provide sufficient information for a researcher to initiate a research programme in web mining.

11.2 Web Mining

We make use of the web in several ways. As Kosala et al put it, we interact with the web for the following purposes.

Finding Relevant Information

We either browse or use the search service when we want to find specific information on the web. We usually specify a simple keyword query and the response from a web-search engine is a list of pages, ranked by their similarity to the query. However, today's search tools have the following problems:

- *Low precision*: This is due to the irrelevance of many of the search results. We may get many pages of information which are not really relevant to our query.
- *Low recall*: This is due to the inability to index all the information available on the web. Because some of the relevant pages are not properly indexed, we may not get those pages through any of the search engines.

Discovering New Knowledge from the Web

We can term the above problem as a query-triggered process (retrieval oriented). On the other hand, we can have a data-triggered process that presumes that we already have a collection of web data and want to extract potentially useful knowledge out of it (data mining-oriented).

Personalised Web Page Synthesis

We may wish to synthesise a web page for different individuals from the available set of web pages. Individuals have their own preferences for the style of the content and presentation while interacting with the web. The information providers like to create a system which responds to user queries by potentially aggregating information from several sources, in a manner which is dependent on the user.

Learning about Individual Users

This is about knowing what the customers do and want. Within this problem are subproblems, such as mass customizing the information to the intended consumers or even personalizing it to individual users, problems related to effective web site design and management, problems related to marketing, etc.

Web mining techniques provide a set of techniques that can be used to solve these problems. Sometimes, web mining techniques provide direct solutions to these problems. On the other hand, they can be used as a part of a bigger application that addresses these problems. However, web mining techniques are not the only tools available to handle these problems. Other related techniques from different research areas, such as database (DB), information retrieval (IR) and natural language processing (NLP), can also be used.

Web mining, when looked upon in data mining terms, can be said to have three operations of interests—clustering (e.g., finding natural groupings of users, pages, etc.), associations (e.g., which URLs tend to be requested together) and sequential analysis (e.g., the order in which URLs tend to be accessed). As in most real-world problems, the clusters and associations in web mining do not have clear-cut boundaries and often overlap considerably.

Mining techniques in the web can be categorised into three areas of interest (Figure 11.1), based on which part of the web is to be mined [Madria, 1998]. They are

- Web content mining,
- Web structure mining, and
- Web usage mining.

11.3 Web Content Mining

Web content mining describes the discovery of useful information from web content. However, what comprises web content could encompass a very broad range of data.

The web contains many kinds of data. We see that more and more government information are gradually being placed on the web in recent years. We also know the existence of digital libraries accessible from the web. Many commercial institutions are transforming their businesses and services electronically. We cannot ignore another type of web content—the existence of web applications, which users could access through web interfaces. Many applications and systems are being migrated to the web and many types of applications are emerging in the web environment itself. Some of the web content data are hidden data, and some are generated dynamically as a result of queries and reside in the DBMSs. These data are generally not indexed.

Basically, the web content consists of several types of data such as text, image, audio, video, metadata, as well as hyperlinks. Recent research on mining multi-types of data is termed

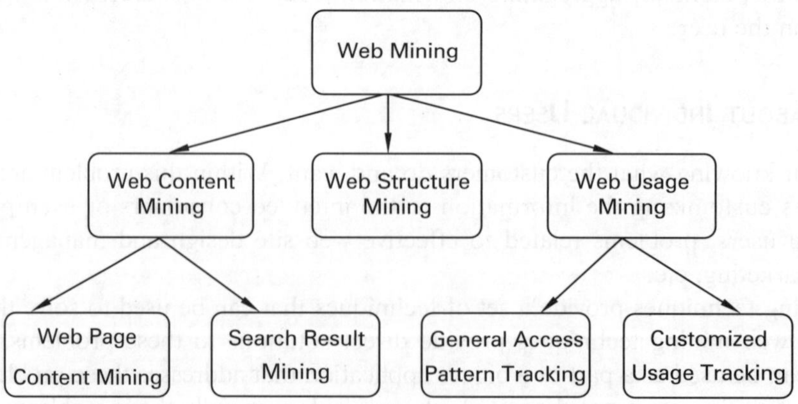

Figure 11.1 Web mining tasks

multimedia data mining. This line of research is yet to receive proper attention and most of the efforts on web content mining are concentrated on the text or hypertext contents. The textual parts of web content data consist of unstructured data such as free texts, semi-structured data such as HTML documents, and more structured data such as data in the tables or database-generated HTML pages. Undoubtedly, much of the web content data is unstructured, free text data. As a result, the techniques of text mining can be directly employed for web content mining in such cases. We shall study text mining techniques later in this chapter.

11.4 Web Structure Mining

Web structure mining is concerned with discovering the model underlying the link structures of the web. It is used to study the topology of hyperlinks with or without their description. This model can be used to categorise web pages and is used to generate information such as the similarity and relationship between different web sites. Web structure mining can be used to discover authority and overview (or hub) sites for the subjects that point to many authorities. It may be noted that while web content mining attempts to explore the structure within a document (intra-document structure), web structure mining studies the structures of documents within the web itself (inter-document structure).

We can view any collection, V, of hyperlinked pages as a directed graph $G = (V, E)$: the nodes correspond to the pages, and a directed edge $(p, q) \in E$ indicates the presence of a link from p to q. We say that the outdegree of a node p is the number of nodes to which it has links, and the indegree of p is the number of nodes that have links to it. If $W \subseteq V$ is a subset of the pages, we use $G[W]$ to denote the graph induced on W—its nodes are the pages in W, and its edges correspond to all the links between the pages in W.

Some algorithms have been proposed to model web topology such as HITS, PageRank, CLEVER; these models are mainly applied as a method to calculate the quality rank or relevancey of each web page. We shall outline below some of the techniques that are useful in modelling web topology.

PageRank

The motivation is from academic citation literature, where the importance of a document is measured by counting citations or backlinks to a given document. This gives some approximation of a document's importance or quality. This concept is extended to web pages. The intuitive justification is that a page can have a high PageRank if there are many pages that point to it, or if there are some pages that point to it which have a high PageRank. Intuitively, pages that are well cited from many places around the web are worth looking at. Also, pages that have perhaps only one citation from something like the Yahoo! homepage are also generally worth looking at. PageRank handles both these cases and everything in between, by recursively propagating weights through the link structure of the web.

PageRank is defined as follows:

We assume page *A* has pages T_1, ..., T_n, which point to it (i.e., are citations). The parameter *d* is a damping factor which can be set between 0 and 1 and is usually set to 0.85. *out_deg*(A) denotes the number of links going out of page A (outdegree of A).

DEFINITION 11.1 PAGERANK

The PageRank of a page A is given as follows:

$$PR(A) = (1 - d) + d\left(\sum_{i=1}^{n} \frac{PR(T_i)}{out\_deg(T_i)}\right)$$

PageRank or *PR*(*A*) can be calculated using a simple iterative algorithm, and corresponds to the principal eigenvector of the normalised link matrix of the web. Let *n* be the number of documents we have. We define the link matrix *M*, where the M_{ij} entry is $1/n_j$ if there is a link from document *j* to document *i*, otherwise M_{ij} is 0. n_j is the number of the forward link of document *j* (out degree of *j*). Then we can compute the PageRank on the graph which is the dominant eigenvector of the matrix *A*.

Note that the PageRanks form a sort of a probability distribution over the web pages. PageRank also provides models of user behaviour. Consider a surfer starting from a web page at random, who keeps clicking on links, never hitting "back", but eventually gets bored and switches to another random page. The probability that the surfer visits a page is its PageRank. The damping factor *d* is to model the probability that at each page the surfer would get bored and request another random page.

SOCIAL NETWORK

Social network analysis is yet another way of studying the web link structure. It uses an exponentially varying damping factor. Web structure mining utilises the hyperlinks structure of the web to apply social network analysis, to model the underlying links structure of the web itself. The social network studies ways to measure the relative *standing* or importance of individuals in a network. The same process can be mapped to study the link structures of the web pages. The basic premise here is that if a web page points a link to another web page, then the former is, in some sense, endorsing the importance of the latter. Links, in this network, may have different weights, corresponding to the strength of endorsement.

Kautz et al in a pioneering work on web structure mining, *The Hidden Web*, proposed a measure of *standing* of a node based on path counting. They carry out social network analysis to model the network of AI researchers. The standing of a node(page) can be defined as follows.

DEFINITION 11.2 STANDING OF A NODE

For nodes *p* and *q*, let $P_{pq}^{(r)}$ denote the number of paths of length exactly *r* from *p* to *q*. Let $b < 1$ be a constant, chosen to be small enough so that $Q_{pq} = \Sigma_r\, b^r P_{pq}^{(r)}$ converges. One can view b^r as the damping factor. Please note that the damping factor varies with the length of the path.

The *standing* of the node *q*, σ_q is defined as $\Sigma_p\, Q_{pq}$.

TRANSVERSE AND INTRINSIC LINKS

Kleinberg discusses a heuristic method of giving weightage to links. A link is said to be a *transverse link* if it is between pages with different domain names, and an *intrinsic link* if it is between pages with the same domain name. Here, by "domain name", we mean the first level in the URL string associated with a page. Since intrinsic links very often exist purely to navigate the infrastructure of a site, they convey much less information than transverse links about the importance of the pages to which they point. Thus, while computing the PageRank or standing of a page, the intrinsic links need not be taken into account. Kleinberg proposes to delete all intrinsic links from the graph, keeping only the edges corresponding to transverse links. This is a very simple but effective heuristic

REFERENCE NODES AND INDEX NODES

Botafogo et al propose another way of ranking pages. They define the notion of index nodes and reference nodes.

DEFINITION 10.3 INDEX NODE

An index node is one whose outdegree is significantly larger than the average outdegree of the graph.

DEFINITION 10.4 REFERENCE NODE

A reference node is a node whose indegree is significantly larger than the average indegree of the graph.

CLUSTERING AND DETERMINING SIMILAR PAGES

For determining the collection of similar pages, we need to define the similarity measure between the pages. There can be two basic similarity functions.

DEFINITION 10.5 BIBLIOGRAPHIC COUPLING

For a pair of nodes, p and q, the bibliographic coupling is equal to the number of nodes that have links from both p and q.

DEFINITION 10.6 CO-CITATION

For a pair of nodes, p and q, the co-citation is the number of nodes that point to both p and q.

We give a simple graph of clustering techniques for clustering the web documents based on the web structure.

We first identify the *influential* pages that are referred by substantially large number of pages. The next step is to create a soft cluster around each of the influential pages based on citation count. The pages are assigned to the soft cluster if they are co-cited along with the influential page. After creating those soft clusters, the similarity between the soft clusters are calculated and based on the values of the similarity measure, certain soft clusters are merged in the hierarchical agglomorative clustering principle.

In order to determine the set of influential pages, it is necessary to define a threshold λ and identify the nodes whose degree exceeds the value λ. There are different variations to this approach. One can only count the outdegree or indegree and count either the transverse or intrinsic degrees. In order to build a soft cluster around an influential node v, we identify all other nodes x, such that there is at least one node y that cites both x and v. In some cases we can take into account both *bibliographic* and *co-citation couplings*. The similarity measure between two sub-clusters S_x an S_y is computed as

$$\frac{|S_x \cap S_y|}{|S_x \cup S_y|}$$

EXAMPLE 11.1

Let us understand the working of the algorithm based on the set of URLs taken from www.cora.jprc.com (see Addendum at the end of this chapter). In the subsequent discussion we shall refer to these URLs by their respective serial numbers. There are 101 URLs. We assume λ to be 8. Based on the adjacency list of the graph, Figure 11.2, the set of influential nodes are identified as nodes 1, 2, 3 and 5. The soft clusters are computed by co-citation links, as shown in Figure 11.3. Figure 11.4 shows the merging of clusters based on similarity function.

11.5 WEB USAGE MINING

Web usage mining deals with studying the data generated by the web surfer's sessions or behaviours. Note that the web content and structure mining utilise the real or primary data on the web. On the contrary, web usage mining mines the secondary data derived from the interactions of the users with the web. The secondary data includes the data from the web server access logs, proxy server logs, browser logs, user profiles, registration data, user sessions or transactions, cookies, user queries, bookmark data, mouse clicks and scrolls, and any other data which are the results of these interactions.

This data can be accumulated by the web server. Analyses of the web access logs of different web sites can facilitate an understanding of user behaviour and the web structure, thereby improving the design of this colossal collection of information. There are two main approaches in web usage mining driven by the applications of the discoveries.

GENERAL ACCESS PATTERN TRACKING

This is to learn user navigation patterns (impersonalised). General access pattern tracking analyses the web logs to understand access patterns and trends. These analyses can shed better light on the structure and grouping of resource providers.

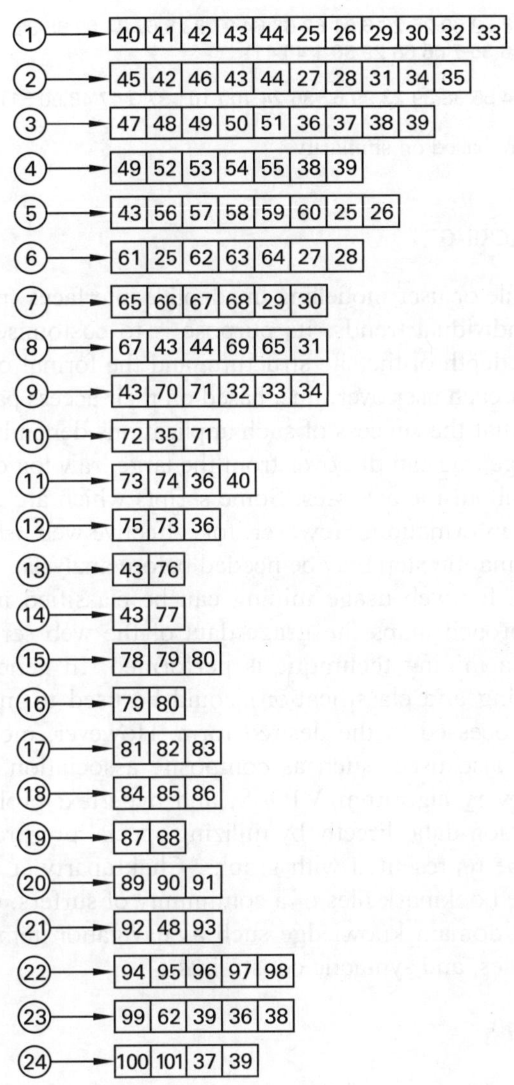

Figure 11.2 Adjacency list of the graph formed by the URLs

Soft Cluster 1: {7 65 66 67 68 29 30 8 43 44 69 31 9 70 71 32 33 34 **1** 40 41 42 25 26}

Soft Cluster 2: {6 61 25 62 63 64 27 28 8 67 43 44 69 65 31 9 70 71 32 33 34 **2** 45 42 46 35}

Soft Cluster 3: {4 49 52 53 54 55 38 39 23 99 62 36 24 100 101 37 **3** 47 48 50 51}

Soft Cluster 4: {**5** 43 56 57 58 59 60 25 26}

Figure 11.3 The set of soft clusters. Number in boldface indicates the influential nodes.

{5 43 56 57 58 59 60 25 26 6 61 62 63 64 27 28 8 67 44 69 65 31 9 70 71 32 33 34 2 45 42 46 35 7 66 68 29 30 1 40 41}

{4 49 52 53 54 55 38 39 23 99 62 36 24 100 101 37 3 47 48 50 51}

Figure 11.4 Merged clusters based on similarity

Customised Usage Tracking

This is to learn a user profile or user modelling in adaptive interfaces (personalised). Customised usage tracking analyses individual trends. Its purpose is to customise web sites to users. The information displayed, the depth of the site structure, and the format of the resources can all be dynamically customised for each user over time, based on their access patterns.

It is important to note that the success of such applications depends on what and how much valid and reliable knowledge one can discover from the large, raw log data. Current web servers store limited information about the accesses. Some scripts which are custom-tailored for some sites, may store additional information. However, for effective web usage mining, an important cleaning and data transformation step may be needed before analysis.

The mining techniques for web usage mining can be classified into two commonly used approaches. The first approach maps the usage data of the web server into relational tables before a (traditional) data mining technique is performed. In general, typical data mining methods (such as clustering and classification) could be used to mine the usage data after the data have been pre-processed to the desired form. However, modifications of the typical data mining methods are also used, such as composite association rules, an extension of a traditional sequence discovery algorithm MIDAS, and hypertext probabilistic grammars. The second approach uses the log data directly by utilizing special pre-processing techniques. The web usage data can also be represented with graphs. Chakrabarty et al proposed a method of extracting themes from the bookmark files of a community of surfers. Often, web usage mining uses some background or domain knowledge such as navigation templates, web content, site topology, concept hierarchies, and syntactic constraints.

11.6 Text Mining

Due to the continuous growth of the volumes of text data, automated extraction of implicit, previously unknown, and potentially useful information becomes more necessary to properly utilise this vast source of knowledge. Text mining, therefore, corresponds to the extension of the data mining approach to textual data and is concerned with various tasks, such as extraction of information implicitly contained in the collection of documents, or similarity-based structuring.

Text collection, in general, lacks the imposed structure of a traditional database. The text expresses a vast range of information, but encodes the information in a form that is difficult to decipher automatically. The data mining techniques that have been discussed in the earlier chapters are essentially designed to operate on structured databases. When the data is structured, it is easy to define the set of items and hence, it becomes easy to employ the traditional mining techniques. Identifying individual items or terms is not so obvious in a textual database. Thus, unstructured data, particularly free-running text, places a new demand on data mining methodology. Specific techniques, called text mining techniques, have to be developed to process the unstructured textual data to aid in knowledge discovery.

The inherent nature of textual data, namely unstructured characteristics, motivates the development of separate text mining techniques. One way is to impose a structure on the textual database and use any of the known data mining techniques meant for structured databases. The other approach would be to develop a very specific technique for mining that exploits the inherent characteristics of textual databases. Irrespective of the approach chosen for text mining, one cannot ignore the close interactions of other related subjects, such as computational linguistics, natural language processing, and information retrieval. In this chapter we shall briefly discuss the relationships among these fields of research. A detailed discussion on these topics is beyond the scope of this book.

Other Related Areas

It is important to study the relationship between areas like information retrieval (IR), information extraction (IE) and computational linguistics with text data mining. We are just beginning to see the emergence of a text-based knowledge discovery system, while the information retrieval community has been tackling the querying issues for over 30 years.

Information Retrieval

IR is concerned with finding and ranking documents that match the users' information needs. The way of dealing with textual information by the IR community is a keyword-based document representation. A body of text is analysed by its constituent words, and various techniques are used to build the core words for a document. The goals are

- To find documents that are similar, based on some specification of the user.
- To find the right index terms in a collection, so that querying will return the appropriate document.

What is still missing are tools providing assistance for an explorative search and pattern finding. It may be noted that the IR problem is not so much that the desired information coexists with many other valid pieces of information; the problem is one of homing in on what is currently of interest to the user. It is rarely the process of pattern finding or of exploration.

Actually, IR is the automatic retrieval of all relevant documents while at the same time retrieving as few of the non-relevant ones as possible. IR has the primary goals of indexing the text and searching for useful documents in a collection. However, recent trends in IR research include modelling, document classification and categorisation, user interfaces, data visualisation, filtering, etc. The task that can be considered to be an instance of text mining is document classification or categorisation, which could be used for indexing. Viewed in this respect, text mining is part of the IR process. However, we should note that not all of the indexing tasks use data mining techniques.

Information Extraction

IE has the goal of transforming a collection of documents, usually with the help of an IR system, into information that is more readily digested and analysed. IE extracts relevant facts from the documents, while IR selects relevant documents. Thus, in general, IE works at a finer granularity level than IR does on the documents. Most IE systems use machine learning or data mining techniques to learn the extraction patterns or rules for documents semi-automatically or automatically. Within this view, text mining is part of the IE process.

The results of the IE process could be in the form of a structured database, or a compression or summary of the original text or documents. For the former, IE is a kind of pre-processing stage in the text mining process, which is the step after the IR process and before data mining techniques are performed. In a similar view, IE can also be used to improve the indexing process, which is part of the IR process. From another viewpoint, IE is an instance of text mining, since the summary or compressed form of a document is a form of information that did not exist before.

Computational Linguistics

Corpus-based computational linguistics computes statistics over large text collections in order to discover useful patterns. These patterns are used to inform algorithms for various subproblems within natural language processing, such as part-of-speech tagging, word-sense disambiguation, etc. The aims of text data mining are also rather similar to this. However, within the computational linguistics framework, patterns are discovered to aid other problems within the same domain, whereas text data mining is aimed at discovering unknown information for different applications.

11.7 Unstructured Text

Unstructured documents are free texts, such as news stories. Traditionally, most of research uses bags of words to represent unstructured documents and extract different features from it.

Features

For an unstructured document, features are extracted to convert it to a structured form. Some of the important features are listed below.

Word Occurrences

The bag of words or vector representation takes single words found in the training corpus as features ignoring the sequence in which the words occur. This representation is based on the statistic about single words in isolation. Such a feature is said to be Boolean, if we consider whether a word either occurs or does not occur in a document. The feature is said to be frequency based if the frequency of the word in a document is taken into consideration.

Stop-words

The feature selection includes removing the case, punctuation, infrequent words, and stop words. A good site for the set of stop-words for the English language is www.dcs.gla.ac.uk/idom/ir_resources/linguistic_util/stop_words

Latent Semantic Indexing

Latent Semantic Indexing (LSI) transforms the original document vectors to a lower dimensional space by analysing the correlational structure of terms in the document collection, such that similar documents that do not share terms are placed in the same topic.

Stemming

Stemming is a process which reduces words to their morphological roots. For example, the words "informing", "information", "informer", and "informed" would be stemmed to their common root "inform", and only the latter word is used as the feature instead of the former four.

n-gram

Other feature representations are also possible, such as using information about word positions in the document, or using n-grams representation (word sequences of length up to n) (In WEBSOM).

Part-of-speech (POS)

One important feature is the POS. There can be 25 possible values for POS tags. Most common tags are noun, verb, adjective and adverb. Thus, we can assign a number 1, 2, 3, 4 or 5, depending on whether the word is a noun, verb, adjective, adverb or any other, respectively.

Positional Collocations

The values of this type of feature are the words that occur one or two position to the right or left of the given word.

Higher Order Features

Other features include phrases, document concept categories, terms, hypernyms, named entities, dates, email addresses, locations, organisations, or URLs. These features could be reduced further by applying some other feature selection techniques, such as information gain, mutual information, cross entropy, or odds ratio.

Once the features are extracted, the text is represented as structured data, and traditional data mining techniques can be used. The techniques include discovering frequent sets, frequent sequences and episode rules. We describe below the preprocessing stage to fund frequent episodes.

11.8 EPISODE RULE DISCOVERY FOR TEXTS

Ahonen et al proposed to apply sequence mining techniques for text data. (We shall discuss in detail the techniques of sequence mining later on.) They consider text as sequential data which consists of a sequence of pairs (feature vector, index), where the feature vector is an ordered set of features and the index contains information about the position of the word in the sequence. A feature can be any of the textual features described above.

Define a text episode as a pair $\alpha = (V, \leq)$, where V is a collection of feature vectors and $\leq$ is a partial order on V. Given a text sequence S, a text episode $\alpha = (V, \leq)$ occurs within S if there is a way of satisfying the feature vectors in V, using the feature vectors in S so that the partial order $\leq$ is respected. In other words, the feature vectors of V can be found within S in an order that satisfies $\leq$.

For example, the text *Pathfinder photographs Mars* can be represented as

((*pathfinder*_noun_singular, 1), (*photographs*_verb_singular, 2), (*Mars*_noun_singular, 3))

Similarly, the text *knowledge discovery in databases* can be represented as the sequence

((*knowledge*_noun_singular, 1), (*discovery*_noun_singular, 2), (*in*_preposition, 3), (*databases*_noun_plural, 4))

Instead of considering all occurrences of the episode, a restriction is set that the episode must occur within a prespecified window of size, w. Thus, we examine the substrings S' of S such that the difference of the indices in S' is at most w.

For $w = 2$, the subsequence (*knowledge*_noun_singular, *discovery*_noun_singular) is an episode contained in the window, but the subsequence (*knowledge*_noun_singular, *databases*_noun_plural) is not contained within the window.

The support of α in S is defined as the number of minimal occurrences of α in S. With this formalism, the episode discovery technique of sequence mining can be used to discover frequent episodes in a text. Ahonen et al [1998, 1999] also proposed a technique of discovering maximal frequent subsequences in the text.

11.9 HIERARCHY OF CATEGORIES

When a user enters a query into a search engine, the system often brings back many different pages. It is then necessary to organise the documents into meaningful groups. There are many different ways in which we can show how a set of documents are related to one another. One way is to group together all documents written by the same author, or all documents written in the same year, or published by the same publisher. We can group them according to subject matter as well. Libraries organise some of their information this way, using classification systems like the Dewey Decimal.

A problem with assigning documents to single categories within a hierarchy (as seen in, for example, Yahoo), is that most documents discuss several different topics simultaneously.

A better solution is to describe documents by a set of categories as well as attributes (such as source, date, genre, and author), and provide good interfaces for manipulating these labels.

For this purpose, Feldman et al proposed an elegant data structure of concept hierarchy. Concept hierarchy is a directed acyclic graph of concepts, where each of the concepts is identified by a unique name. An arc from concept *a* to *b* denotes that *a* is a more general concept than *b*. We can tag the text with concepts. Each text document is tagged by a set of concepts that correspond to its content.

Tagging a document with a concept implicitly entails its tagging with all the ancestors of the concept hierarchy. It is, therefore, desired that a document should be tagged with the lowest concepts possible. The method to automatically tag the document to the hierarchy is a top-down approach. An evaluation function determines whether a document currently tagged to a node can also be tagged to any of its child nodes. If so, then the tag moves down the hierarchy till it cannot be moved any further.

The outcome of this process is a hierarchy of documents and, at each node, there is a set of documents having a common concept associated with the node. The hierarchy of documents resulting from the tagging process is useful for many text mining processes. It is assumed that the hierarchy of concepts is known a *priori*. We can even have such a hierarchy of documents without a concept hierarchy, by using any hierarchical clustering algorithm which results in such a hierarchy.

Popescul et al posed a related problem of tagging key words to the set of documents arranged in a hierarchy. The method is a two-phase principle. It starts with a bag of key words at the leaf level and moves up the hierarchy. The set of key words for a non-leaf node is obtained by combining all the key words to all its child nodes. After finding the set of key words for the root node, the process starts with a top-down approach. If a key word at any node is also equally probable for all of its child nodes, then the key word is associated with the current (parent) node and not with any of the child nodes. Otherwise, if the key word is more probable for a child node, it is moved down to the most probable set of child nodes.

11.10 Text Clustering

Text clustering is another important task of text mining. Once the features of an unstructured text are identified or the structured data of the text is available, text clustering can be done by employing any of the clustering techniques discussed in Chapter 5. One popular text clustering algorithm is Ward's Minimum Variance method. It is an agglomerative hierarchical clustering technique and it tends to generate very compact clusters. We shall discuss the essential features of this method.

We can take either the Euclidean metric or Hamming distance as the measure of dissimilarities between feature vectors. The clustering method begins with *n* clusters, one for each text. At any stage, two clusters are merged to generate a new cluster. The clusters, C_k and C_l, are merged to gt a new cluster C_{kl}, based on the following criterion:

$$V_{kl} = \text{MIN}_{i,j} V_{ij}$$

$$V_{ij} = \frac{\| x_i - x_j \|^2}{\frac{1}{n_1} + \frac{1}{n_2}}$$

where x_i is the mean value of the dissimilarity for the cluster C_i, and n_i is the number of elements in this cluster.

Scatter/Gather

It is a method of grouping the documents using clustering. The scatter/gather interface uses text clustering as a way to group documents, according to the overall similarities in their content. Scatter/gather is so named because it allows the user to scatter documents into clusters, or groups, then gather a subset of these groups and re-scatter them to form new groups. Each cluster in scatter/gather is represented by a list of topical terms, that is, a list of words that attempt to give the user a gist of what the documents in the cluster are about. The user can also look at the titles of the documents in each group. The documents in the cluster can have other representations as well, such as summaries. If a cluster still has too many documents, the user can re-cluster the documents in the cluster; that is, re-group that subset of documents into still smaller groups. This re-grouping process tends to change the kinds of themes of the clusters, because the documents in a subcollection discuss a different set of topics from all the documents in the larger collection.

11.11 Conclusions

In this chapter we have outlined three different modes of web mining, namely web content mining, web structure mining and web usage mining. Needless to say, these three approaches cannot be independent, and any efficient mining of the web would require a judicious combination of information from all the three sources. Clustering of hyperlinked documents can rely on a combination of textual and link-based information. Similarly, information about the web structure would greatly enhance the capability of web usage mining. We have noted that web content mining mostly concentrates on text mining, and textual content in the web can be in an unstructured, semi-structured or structured form. For an unstructured text, features are extracted to view the document in a structured form. Similarly, for unstructured text such as XML, features can be extracted for mining purposes. Recently, Garofalakis et al proposed a sequence mining–based method to extract a document-type description for a set of XML pages. We give below an extensive bibliography for the readers. Merkl proposed a neural network-based text for data mining. Kohonen and his group's pioneering work resulted in WEBSOM; a self-organizing map model for document mining.

FURTHER READING

Soumen Chakrabarti's [2000] work on mining hypertext makes excellent reading. PageRanking and web search information can be got from Brin [1998]. Readers are referred to Botafogo [Botafogo, 1993] for text clustering techniques. The first proposal of text mining is due to Feldman [1995]. Marti Hearst's [1999] work on text mining is also important. This gives a clear understanding of how text mining is not just any other data mining. Kosala's survey on web mining is yet another interesting source of information [2000]. Brin and Page[1998] give a good discussion on PageRank. A landmark paper by Kautz, "The Hidden Web" introduces the application of social networks. Cooley's paper [2000] is yet another source of information about web usage mining. Example 8.1 is the part of the work of my student, M. Prabhavathamma.

EXERCISES

1. What are the different types of web mining?
2. How is web usage mining different from web structure mining and web content mining?
3. What is the underlying principle of *The Hidden Web*?
4. How is text mining related to web mining? What are the techniques of text mining?
5. Discuss the relationship between text mining and information retrieval and information extraction.
6. What is PageRank? How is it computed?
7. What is concept hierarchy? How is it related to web mining?
8. Discuss the principles underlying text clustering.
9. How do you extract structures from unstructured text data? What features are extracted in this process?
10. Based on the details given in Chapter 5, discuss the suitability of some of the clustering algorithms for text clustering.
11. Which frequent itemset mining is suitable for text mining?
12. What are the differences between the mining techniques of structured data, semi-structured data and unstructured data?

BIBLIOGRAPHY

Ahonen H., Heinonen O., Klemettinen M., and Verkamo A. Applying data mining techniques for descriptive phrase extraction in digital document collections. In *Advances in Digital Libraries (ADL'98)*, Santa Barbara, California, USA, April 1998.

Ahonen H., Heinonen O., Klemettinen M., and Verkamo A. Applying data mining techniques in text analysis. http://www.cs.helsinki,fi/~hahonen.

Baeza-Yates R., and BerthierRibeiro-Neto E. *Modern Information Retrieval*. Addison-Wesley Longman Publishing Company, 1999.

Borges J., and Levene M. Mining association rules in hypertext databases. In *Proceedings of the 4th International Conference on Knowledge Discovery and Data Mining (KDD-98)*, New YorkCity, New York, USA, August 27–31, 1998.

Borges J., and Levene M. Data mining of user navigation patterns. In *Proceedings of the WEBKDD'99 Workshop on Web Usage Analysis and User Profiling*, pp. 31–36, San Diego, CA, USA, August 15, 1999.

Botafogo R.A. Cluster analysis for hypertext systems.*ACM-SIGIR*, 1993.

Brin S., and Page L. The anatomy of a large-scale hypertextual web search engine. In *7th International World Wide Web Conference*, Brisbane, Australia, 1998.

Buchner A., Baumgarten M., Anand S., Mulvenna M., and Hughes J. Navigation pattern discovery from internet data. In *Proceedings of the WEBKDD'99 Workshop on Web Usage Analysis and User Profiling*, San Diego, CA, USA, August 15, 1999.

Chakrabarti S., Dom B., and Indyk P. Enhanced hypertext categorization using hyperlinks.In *Proceedings ACM SIGMOD International Conference on Management of Data,* ACM Press,pp. 307–318, Seattle, Washington, USA, June 2–4, 1998.

Chakrabarti S., Dom B., Gibson D., Kleinberg J., Kumar S., Raghavan P., Rajagopalan S., and Tomkins A. Mining the link structure of the world wide web. *IEEE Computer*, **32**(8):60–67, 1999.

Chakrabarti S. Data mining for hypertext: A tutorial survey. *ACM SIGKDD Explorations*, **1**(2):111, 2000.

Chakrabarti S., and Batterywala Y. Mining themes from bookmarks. In *ACM SIGKDD 200 Workshop on Text mining*, 2000.

Cooley R., Mobasher B., and Srivastava J. Web mining: Information and pattern discovery on the world wide web. In *Proceedings of the 9th IEEE International Conference on Tools with Artificial Intelligence (ICTAI'97), 1997.*

Cooley R., Mobasher B., and Srivastava J. Data preparation for mining world wide web browsing patterns. *Knowledge and Information Systems*, **1**(1), 1999.

Cooley R.W. Web usage mining: Discovery and application of interesting patterns from web data. *PhD Thesis*, Dept. of Computer Science, University of Minnesota, May 2000.

Cutting D.R., Karger D., Pederson J., and Tukey J.W. Scatter/Gather: A cluster-based approach to browsing large document collections.In *Proceedings of 15th Annual International ACM/SIGI Conference*, pp. 318–329, Copenhagen, Denmark, June 1992.

Deerwester S., Dumais S., Furnas G., Landauer T., and Harshman R. Indexing by latent semantic analysis. *Journal of the American Society for Information Science*, **41**(6):391–407, 1990.

Feldman R. and Dagan I. Knowledge discovery in textual databases (KDT). In *Proceedings of the 1st International Conference on Knowledge Discovery and Data Mining (KDD-95)*, pp. 112–117, Montreal, Canada, 1995.

Feldman R., Fresko M., Kinar Y., Lindell Y., Liphstat O., Rajman M., Schler Y., and Zamir O. Text mining at the term level. In *Principles of Data Mining and Knowledge Discovery, 2nd European Symposium, PKDD '98*, **1510** of Lecture Notes in Computer Science, Springer, pp. 56–64, 1998.

Garofalakis M.N., Rastogi R., Seshadri S., and Shim K. Data mining and the web: Past, present and future. In *Workshop on Web Information and Data Management*, pp. 43–47, 1999.

Garofalakis M.N., Rastogi R., Seshadri S., and Shim K. XTRACT: A system for extracting document type descriptors from XML documents. *SIGMOD 2000*, 2000.

Hearst M.A. Untangling text data mining. In *Proceedings of ACL'99: the 37th Annual Meeting ofthe Association for Computational Linguistics*, 1999.

Honkela T., Kaski S., Lagus K., and Kohonen T. WEBSOM—self-organizing maps of document collections. In *Proceedings of the Workshop on Self-Organizing Maps 1997 (WSOM'97)*, pp. 310–315, 1997.

Kautz H., Selman B., and Shah M. The hidden web. *AI magazine*, **18**(2):27–36, 1997.

Kleinberg J.M. Authoritative sources in a hyperlinked environment. In *Proceedings of ACMSIAM Symposium on Discrete Algorithms*, pp. 668–677, 1998.

KoasalaR., and Blockeel H. Web mining research: A survey. *ACM SIGKDD*, **2**(1):1–15, 2000.

Lent B., Agrawal R., and Srikant R. Discovering trends in text databases. In *Proceedings of the 3rd International Conference On Knowledge Discovery and Data Mining (KDD 1997)*, pp. 227–230, 1997.

Madria S.K., Bhowmick S.S., Ng W.K., and Lim E.-P. Research issues in web data mining. In *Proceedings of Data Warehousing and Knowledge Discovery, 1st International Conference, DaWaK '99*, pp. 303–312, 1999.

Mladenic D. and Grobelnik M. Feature selection for unbalanced class distribution and naive Bayes distribution. In *Proceedings of the 16th International Conference on Machine Learning ICML-99*, pp. 258–267, 1999.

Masand B. and Spiliopoulou M. Webkdd-99: Workshop on web usage analysis and user profiling. *SIGKDD Explorations*, **1**(2), 2000.

Merkl D. Text data mining. In A *Handbook of Natural Language Processing: Techniques and Applications for the Processing of Language as Text*, Marcel Dekker, New York, 1998.

Paliouras G., Papatheodorou C., Karkaletsis V., Tzitziras P., and Spyropoulos C. D. Large scale mining of usage data on web sites. In *AAAI 2000 Spring Symposium on Adaptive User Interfaces*, 2000.

Peleato R.A., Chappelier J-.C., and Rajman M. Using information extraction to classify newspaper advertisements. *IADT2000*, 2000.

Rajman M., and Besancon R. Text mining—knowledge extraction from unstructured textual data. In *6th Conference of International Federation of Classification Societies, IFCS'98*, pp. 473–480, 1998.

Spiliopoulou M. Data mining for the web. In Principles of Data Mining and Knowledge Discovery*, 2nd European Symposium, PKDD '99*, pp. 588–589, 1999.

Srivastava J., Cooley R., Deshpande M., and Tan P.-N. Web usage mining: Discovery and applications of usage patterns from web data. *SIGKDD Explorations*, 1–2, 2000.

Tan A.-H. Text mining: The state of the art and the challenges. In *Proceedings of the Pacific Asia Conference on Knowledge Discovery and Data Mining, PAKDD'99*, Workshop on Knowledge Discovery from Advanced Databases, pp. 65–70, 1999.

Vaithyanathan S. Introduction: Data mining on the internet. *Artificial Intelligence Review*, **13** (5/6):343–344, 1999.

Yang Y. An evaluation of statistical approach to text categorization. *Information Retrieval Journal*, 1999.

Zaiane O.R., Han J., Li Z.-N., Chee S.H., and Chiang J. Multimedia miner: A system prototype for multimedia data mining. In *Proceedings ACM SIGMOD International Conference on Management of Data*, pp. 581–583, 1998.

ADDENDUM

1. www.cs.washington.edu/research/jair/home.html
2. www.cs.cmu.edu/afs/cs.cmu.edu/project/ai-epository/ai/html/air.html
3. www.dcs.gla.ac.uk/Keith/Preface.html
4. ai.bpa.arizona.edu/papers/mlir93/mlir93.html
5. mevard.www.media.mit.edu/groups/agents/
6. www.cs.bham.ac.uk/~amw/agents/
7. www.research.microsoft.com/research/datamine/
8. www.cs.bham.ac.uk/~anp/TheDataMine.html
9. www.ghgcorp.com/clips/CLIPS.html
10. www.nal.usda.gov/wqic/Bibliographies/eb9608.html
11. www.chesslab.com/PositionSearch.html
12. www.pricingcentral.com/fun/videogames.htm
13. www.ics.uci.edu/~mlearn/Machine-Learning.html
14. www.cs.cmu.edu/~tom/mlbook.html
15. www.cs.cmu.edu/afs/cs.cmu.edu/project/ai-repository/ai/html/faqs/ai/nlp/top.html
16. www.ai.univie.ac.at/oefai/nlu/
17. www.ifla.org/II/metadata.htm
18. www.math.utah.edu/~beebe/digital-libraries.html
19. www.nla.gov.au/nla/staffpaper/cathro4.html
20. www.public-domain.org/database/database.html
21. www.mri.mq.edu.au/~einat/web_ir/
22. www.sciam.com/0397issue/0397resnick.html
23. www.glue.umd.edu/enee/medlab/filter/filter.html
24. www.w3.org/DesignIssues/Filtering.html
25. ai.iit.nrc.ca/subjects/Agents.html
26. www.spectrum.ieee.org/webwatch/web07-31-00.html
27. www-cia.mty.itesm.mx/~lgarrido/Repositories/IA/agents.html
28. www.isis.vt.edu/~fanjun/text/ail.html
29. www-ai.cs.uni-dortmund.de/EVENTS/ICAI99/
30. www.mli.gmu.edu/michalski/teaching/inft910S99.html
31. www.kdnuggets.com/news/97/n04.html
32. www.cslab.ece.ntua.gr/~kblekas/expert.html
33. www.yahoo.com/Science/Computer_Science/Artificial_Intelligence/Expert_Systems/
34. www.gslis.utexas.edu/~palmquis/courses/ai96.html
35. www.rware.demon.co.uk/ail.html
36. citeseer.nj.nec.com/InformationRetrieval/
37. www.cs.colorado.edu/~summer/cs3202/final-reports/brendan.html
38. www.cs.umbc.edu/~jliu/ir.shtml
39. www.slis.indiana.edu/Research/ir.html
40. www.eurekalert.org/links/Journals_public.html
41. www.digitalcentury.com/encyclo/update/comp_hd.html
42. www.cs.reading.ac.uk/people/dwc/ai.html
43. www.cs.berkeley.edu/~russell/ai.html
44. www.yahoo.com/Science/Computer_Science/Artificial_Intelligence/
45. www.kantrowitz.com/kantrowitz/mark.html
46. www.sil.org/linguistics/computing.html
47. www.sims.berkeley.edu/research/overview.html
48. www.searchtools.com/related/info-retrieval.html
49. www-cse.ucsd.edu/users/rik/MLIA.html
50. www.library.ucsb.edu/untangle/larger.html
51. www.cs.princeton.edu/~aslp/www_resources.html
52. www.cs.mu.oz.au/~leon/agentlinks.html
53. www.cs.rice.edu/~siruguri/gen_pages/docs/bookmarks.html
54. www-ils.unc.edu/iris/sbookmark.html
55. www.cs.umbc.edu/abir/bibliography.shtml
56. www.research.microsoft.com/research/ui/persona/related.html
57. www-isl.stanford.edu/~gray/iii.html
58. www.webreference.com/internet/software/agents.html
59. lieber.www.media.mit.edu/people/lieber/
60. www.cs.cmu.edu/afs/cs.cmu.edu/project/oz/web/related-work.html
61. www.yahoo.com/Science/Computer_Science/Human_Computer_Interaction_HCI_/
62. lieber.www.media.mit.edu/people/lieber/Hotlist.html
63. info.webcrawler.com/mailing-lists/robots/0569.html
64. www.research.microsoft.com/research/ui/persona/isbister.html
65. www.ai.univie.ac.at/oefai/ml/ml-resources.html
66. www.almaden.ibm.com/cs/quest/PUBS.html
67. industry.ebi.ac.uk/~brazma/dm.html
68. www.digimine.com/usama/datamine/specials.html
69. www.cs.bham.ac.uk/~amw/local.html
70. www.ai.univie.ac.at/imkai/lv/winf-ai/lv-ws.html
71. www.princeton.edu/~stengel/MAE345.html
72. www.aaai.org/Pathfinder/html/agri.html
73. www.clark.net/pub/pribut/chess.html
74. www.ai.uniview.ac.at/~juffi/links.html
75. akala.terrashare.com/pricingcentral.html
76. www.aic.nrl.navy.mil/~aha/research/machine-learning.html
77. www.cs.wisc.edu/~shavlik/cs760.html
78. www.yahoo.com/Science/Computer_Science/Artificial_Intelligence/Natural_Language_Processing/
79. www.abacom.com/innomagi/online/computing/ai.html
80. webopedia.internet.com/TERM/n/natural_language.html
81. www.canis.uiuc.edu/~bgross/dl/
82. hul.harvard.edu/ldi/html/metadata.html
83. www.nla.gov.au/padi/format/org.html
84. www.oasis-open.org/cover/gen-apps.html
85. www.sics.se/~lalle/bookmarks.html
86. www.dcc.ufmg.br/~loureiro/pesquisa.html
87. www.doi.org/handbook_2000/bibliography.html
88. web.simmons.edu/~schwartz/mydigital2.html
89. www.codata.org/codata/data_access/wiporefs.html
90. www.cerias.purdue.edu/coast/hotlist/law/
91. lists.essential.org/1996/info-policy-notes/msg00048.html
92. www.dlib.org/dlib/january99/01clips.html
93. www.dmoz.org/Computers/Software/Information_Retrieval/
94. www.w3.org/PICS/
95. www.telnet.edu/jumpstart/parents.html
96. www.ifla.org/II/metadata.html
97. www.research.att.com/projects/tech4kids/t4k.html
98. www.sciam.com/0397issue/0397intro.html
99. www.tispa.org.au/kinnaman/filtering.html
100. www.efa.org.au/News/issue4_1.html
101. www.ukoln.ac.uk/web-focus/w3c/briefings/brief-feb-1998.html

12

TEMPORAL AND SPATIAL DATA MINING

12.1 INTRODUCTION

Many applications maintain temporal and spatial features in their databases; these features cannot be treated like other attributes and need special attention. To put it in another way, so far we have been asking ourselves 'what' knowledge is being mined, but finding 'when' and 'where' knowledge is also equally important, and these cannot be trivially handled by the methods discussed thus far. In this chapter we shall study the mining techniques of temporal and spatial data. The widespread use of GIS by local and federal governments and other institutions, necessitates the development of adequate mining tools for geo-referenced data.

Perhaps, the second generation of data mining techniques would contribute in a major way to spatial and temporal data mining.

The first part of this chapter deals with temporal mining techniques. Here, we begin with the basic concepts of temporal mining and why special-purpose techniques are needed for this problem. Then, we proceed to discuss some of the major techniques. It may be mentioned here that we discuss the mining of *sequence data* and *time-series data* in this chapter. Though these topics are relevant in the context of temporal data, they are also important in other applications such as DNA sequencing. The second part of this chapter deals with spatial data mining. The motivation for special-purpose algorithms for spatial data mining is almost the same as that of temporal mining. Some of the techniques of temporal mining can be trivially extended to spatial data. There are also certain similar mining tasks in these approaches. To avoid repetition, we concentrate only on the techniques specific to spatial data in the second part of this chapter.

In Section 12.2 we shall outline different types of temporal data and inferences. Section 12.3 briefly discusses the features of temporal association rules. In Section 12.4, we give an account of sequence mining techniques. GSP algorithms for sequence mining are discussed in Section 12.5. Other algorithms for sequence mining are outlined in Section 12.6. One of the major temporal data mining techniques is episode mining; Section 12.7 deals with this problem. The event prediction problem, which is a different approach to that of sequence mining and episode mining, is discussed in Section 12.8. Section 12.9 is concerned with time-series analysis for data mining applications. Another related data mining problem is spatial data mining. We discuss the techniques of SDM in the remaining sections of this chapter.

12.2 WHAT IS TEMPORAL DATA MINING?

By taking into account the time aspect of data in mining techniques, we gain some insight into the temporal arrangement of events and thus an ability to discover cause and effect. *Temporal Data Mining* is an important extension of data mining and it can be defined as the non-trivial extraction of implicit, potentially useful and previously unrecorded information with an implicit or explicit temporal content, from large quantities of data. It has the capability to infer causal and temporal proximity relationships, and this is something that non-temporal data mining cannot do. It may be noted that data mining from temporal data is not temporal data mining, if the temporal component is either ignored or treated as a simple numerical attribute. Also note that temporal rules cannot be mined from a database which is free of temporal components by traditional (non-temporal) data mining techniques. Thus, the underlying database must be a temporal one and specific temporal data mining techniques are also necessary.

Consider, for example, an association rule —"Any person who buys a car also buys a steering lock". But if we take the temporal aspect into consideration, this rule would be—"Any person who buys a car also buys a steering lock *after* that". Another temporal rule could be—"Flooding in the east coast occurs only *during* the monsoon". A static association rule algorithm would be able to induce that "East-coast flooding occurs only with the monsoon". The concepts of *during* and *after* are explicitly temporal. Take another example: "Data Mining is becoming increasingly popular". It shows another technique of mining from previously mined rules, to find trends in rule sets. Some other examples of temporal knowledge discovery are—"A drop in atmospheric pressure precedes rainfall in 60% of the cases"; "The sequence {semester examination, grading, result processing} occurs every semester"; "Some patients tend to develop reactions after two months with this combination of drugs".

Thus, temporal data mining aims at mining new and hitherto unknown knowledge, which takes into account the temporal aspects of the data. Let us first concentrate on the different temporal aspects of the data.

TYPES OF TEMPORAL DATA

When do we say that data contains temporal features? There can be four different levels of temporality.

STATIC

Static data are free of any temporal reference and the inferences that can be derived from this data are also free of any temporality.

SEQUENCES (ORDERED SEQUENCES OF EVENTS)

In this category of data, though there may not be any explicit reference to time, there exists a sort of qualitative temporal relationship between data items. The market–basket transaction is a good example of this category. The entry-sequence of transactions automatically incorporates a sort of temporality. If a transaction appears in the database before another transaction, it implies that the former transaction has occurred before the latter. There may not be any reference to quantitative temporal relationships. While most collections are often limited to the sequence relationships *before* and *after*, this category also includes the richer relationships, such as *during*, *meet*, *overlap*, etc. Such relationships are called qualitative relationships between time events. Sequence mining is one of the major activities in temporal data mining.

TIMESTAMPED

In this category, the temporal information is explicit. Note that the relationship can be quantitative, in the sense that we can not only say that one transaction occurred before another, but also the exact temporal distance between the data elements. Some examples include census data, land-use data and satellite meteorological data. The inference made here can be temporal or non-temporal. Time series data are a special case of this category, with the events being uniformly spaced on the time scale. Time series data mining is another topic that we shall be discussing in this chapter.

FULLY TEMPORAL

In this category, the validity of the data element is time-dependent. The inferences are necessarily temporal in such cases.

Temporal Data Mining Tasks

Some of the conventional mining tasks can be extended with some additional temporal information as described below.

Temporal Association

The association rule discovery can be extended to temporal association. In static association rule discovery tasks, we were trying to find static associations between two non-temporal itemsets. In temporal association discovery, we attempt to discover temporal associations between non-temporal itemsets. We can say that: "70% of the readers who buy a DBMS book also buy a Data Mining book *after* a semester".

Temporal Classification

We can cluster the data items along temporal dimensions. For example, we can identify a set of people who go for a walk in the evening and a set of people who go for a walk in the morning. We can categorise sets of patients based on their visit sequence to different medical experts. We can also categorise sets of net surfers based on the mouse-click sequence.

Temporal Characterisation

An interesting experiment would be to extend the concept of decision tree construction on temporal attributes. For example, a rule could be: "The first case of filaria is normally reported after the first pre-monsoon rain and during the months of May–August".

Trend Analysis

The analysis of one or more time series of continuous data may show similar trends, i.e., similar shapes across the time axis. For example, "The deployment of the Data Mining system is increasingly becoming popular in the banking industry". This type of analyses are of a higher level than the earlier ones. Here, we are trying to find the relationships of change in one or more static attributes, with respect to changes in the temporal attributes.

Sequence Analysis

Events occurring at different points in time may be related by causal relationships, in that an earlier event may appear to cause a later one. To discover such relationships, sequences of events must be analysed to discover common patterns. This category includes the discovery of frequent events and also the problem of event prediction. It may be noted that frequent sequence mining finds the frequent subsequences; while event prediction predicts the occurrences of events which are rare.

In the following sections, we shall elaborate upon some of the techniques for the tasks discussed above.

12.3 Temporal Association Rules

Association rules identify whether a particular subset of items is supported by an adequate number of transactions. They are normally static in character. As we have mentioned earlier, a static association rule discovers the association between any two events—for instance, the purchase of aerated soft drinks and stomach upsets. However, the association may not indicate any causal relationship, unless the temporality in the association is brought out. One can extend the association rule discovery to incorporate temporal aspects too. It should be noted that the presence of a temporal association rule may suggest a number of interpretations, such as

- The earlier event plays some role in causing the later event.
- There is a third set of reasons that causes both events.
- The confluence of events is coincidental.

Temporal association rules are sometimes viewed in the literature as *causal rules*. Causal rules describe relationships, where changes in one event cause subsequent changes in other parts of the domain. They are common targets of scientific investigation within the medical domain, where the search for factors that may cause or aggravate a particular disease is important. The static properties, such as gender, and the temporal properties, such as medical treatments, are taken into account during mining.

While the concept of association rule discovery is the same for temporal and non-temporal rules, algorithms designed for conventional rules cannot be directly applied to extract temporal rules. The reason is that classical association rules have no notion of order, whilst time implies an ordering.

12.4 Sequence Mining

An efficient approach to mining causal relations is sequence mining. As observed earlier, sequence mining is a topic in its own right and many application domains such as DNA sequence, signal processing and speech analysis require mining of sequence data, even though there is no explicit temporality in the data. Discovering sequential patterns from a large database of sequences has been recognised as an important problem in the field of knowledge discovery and data mining. To put it briefly, given a set of data sequences, the problem is to discover subsequences that are frequent, in the sense that the percentage of data sequences containing them exceeds a user-specified minimum support.

Mining frequent sequential patterns has found a host of potential application domains, including retailing (i.e., market–basket data), telecommunications and, more recently, the World Wide Web (www). In market–basket databases, each data sequence corresponds to items bought by an individual customer over time, and frequent patterns can be useful for predicting future customer behaviour. In telecommunications, frequent sequences of alarms output by network switches capture important relationships between alarm signals that can then be employed for online prediction, analysis and correction of network faults. In the context of the WWW, server sites typically generate huge volumes of daily log data capturing the sequences of page accesses for thousands or millions of users. Let us begin with formally defining the sequence mining problem.

SEQUENCE MINING PROBLEM

The most general form of the sequence mining problem [Zaki, 1998] can be stated as follows:
Let $\Sigma = \{i_1, i_2, \ldots, i_m\}$ be a set of m distinct items comprising the alphabet.

An event is a non-empty, disordered collection of items. Without any loss of generality, we write the items in an event in some predefined order. An event is denoted as $(i_1, i_2, \ldots, i_k)$, where i_j is an item in Σ. Often, we drop the ',' and parentheses for notational convenience.

Any event that is given as input will also be called a transaction. Thus, transactions and events have the same structure, except that a transaction is known to us prior to the process and an event is generated during the algorithm. We use both terms interchangeably if there is no ambiguity.

DEFINITION 12.1 SEQUENCE

A *sequence* is an ordered list of events. A sequence, α, is denoted as $(\alpha_1 \to \alpha_2 \to \ldots \to \alpha_q)$, where α_i is an event. A sequence is called a k-sequence if the sum of the cardinalities of α_i is k.

A subsequence is a sequence within a sequence, preserving the order. In other words, its items need not be adjacent in time but their ordering in a sequence should not violate the time ordering of the supporting events. A subsequence can be obtained from a sequence by deleting some items and/or events. A formal definition of a subsequence is given below.

DEFINITION 12.2 SUBSEQUENCE

The sequence $s = (\alpha_1 \to \alpha_2 \to \ldots \to \alpha_q)$ is said to be a subsequence of $s^1 = (\beta_1 \to \beta_2 \to \ldots \to \beta_r)$ if there exist indices $t1 < t2 < \ldots < tq$ of s^1 such that $\alpha_1 \subseteq \beta_{t1}, \alpha_2 \subseteq \beta_{t2}, \ldots, \alpha_q \subseteq \beta_{tq}$.

A sequence s^1 is said to *support* another sequence s if s is a subsequence of s^1. A sequence is a set of temporally-ordered transactions.

DEFINITION 12.3 FREQUENCY

The frequency of a sequence s, with respect to this database **D**, is the total number of input sequences in **D** that support it.

DEFINITION 12.4 FREQUENT SEQUENCE

A frequent sequence is a sequence whose frequency exceeds some user-specified threshold. A frequent set is *maximal* if it is not a subsequence of another frequent sequence.

The rationale behind frequent sequences lies in detecting precedence and causal relationships that make them statistically remarkable.

EXAMPLE 12.1

Let us consider the following transaction database (Table 12.1). There are six items, that is,

$\Sigma=\{A, B, C, D, E, F\}$, and the database depicts the purchases made by four customers during a certain period of time. The transactions are ordered chronologically. Table 12.2 extracts one sequence.

Table 12.1 A sample of sequence data

Customer	A	B	C	D	E	F
C1	1	1	0	1	1	1
C2	0	0	1	1	0	1
C1	0	1	1	0	1	1
C3	0	0	0	1	1	1
C2	1	1	1	1	0	1
C1	0	1	0	0	1	0
C3	1	0	1	1	1	0
C2	0	1	0	0	1	0
C4	1	1	1	1	1	1
C1	0	0	1	1	1	1
C4	0	1	0	0	0	1
C3	1	0	1	1	1	1
C2	0	1	1	0	0	0
C4	1	0	1	1	1	1
C2	0	1	0	0	0	0

Table 12.2 One sequence from the sequence data of Table 12.1

Customer	A	B	C	D	E	F
C1	1	1	0	1	1	1
C1	0	1	1	0	1	1
C1	0	1	0	0	1	0
C1	0	0	1	1	1	1

We write the transaction sequences of all customers in the following form, thereby indicating the items a transaction contains.

Sequence 1: (A, B, D, E, F) → (B, C, E, F) → (B, E) → (C, D, E, F)
Sequence 2: (C, D, F) → (A, B, C, D, F) → (B, E) → (B, C) → (B)
Sequence 3: (D, E, F) → (A, C, D, E) → (A, C, D, E, F)
Sequence 4: (A, B, C, D, E, F) → (B, F) → (A, C, D, E, F)

Thus, the database of sequences **D** consists of four sequences.

Please note that AC (it is, in fact, an abbreviation of (A, C)) is not a subsequence of Sequence 1, but a subsequence of Sequence 3 and also of Sequence 4. But the sequence A → C is a subsequence of Sequence 1, whereas it is not a subsequence of Sequence 3. By AC, we mean that there should be a transaction containing both A and C. By A $\rightarrow$ C, we mean that there is a transaction containing C which appears after – not necessarily, immediately after – another (different) transaction containing A.

The frequency of AC in **D** is 3. Note that we do not count multiple occurrences of AC in the same sequence. The total number of sequences that support AC is only three, namely Sequence 2, Sequence 3 and Sequence 4. Similarly, the frequency of B $\rightarrow$ D is 2. The sequences supporting B $\rightarrow$ D are Sequence 1 and Sequence 4.

Note that B $\rightarrow$ BE is not supported by Sequence 4, which supports BE $\rightarrow$ B. The subsequence B $\rightarrow$ BE indicates that a transaction containing B and E follows (sometime later) another transaction containing B. On the other hand, BE $\rightarrow$ B represents a subsequence of transactions, in which a transaction containing B and E occurs before a transaction containing B. Both are 3-sequences.

Normally, a simple sequence mining problem is concerned with the temporal order of the events within a sequence of transactions. A more general problem is when we also focus on the temporal distance between the events. That is, A $\rightarrow$ C should indicate the temporal gap between the transaction containing A and the transaction containing C. It is relevant when the correlation between the two events ceases to be effective after some period of time. For example, when we are trying to find out the causal relationship between consuming a beverage and having a stomach upset, it will be irrelevant to correlate two such events occurring within a gap of one year of each other. Thus, we can specify the time distance in terms of a distance threshold, **d**. So, B $\rightarrow_{\mathbf{d}}$ BE denotes that the event containing B and E occurs in not more than **d** transactions after the transaction containing B.

For example, there is no sequence which supports ABD $\rightarrow_1$ D, whereas ABD $\rightarrow_2$ D is supported by Sequence 4. When $\mathbf{d} = 1$, we say that the problem is a *contiguous sequence mining problem*.

A simple sequence mining problem is the sequence mining problem where each transaction contains a single item. There are many applications in which simple sequence mining is relevant.

12.5 The GSP Algorithm

The algorithms for solving sequence mining problems are mostly based on the *a priori* (level-wise) algorithm. One way to use the level-wise paradigm is to first discover all the frequent items in a level-wise fashion. It simply means counting the occurrences of all singleton elements in the database. Then, the transactions are filtered by removing the non-frequent items. At the end of this step, each transaction is a modified transaction consisting of only the frequent elements it contains. We use this modified database as an input to the GSP algorithm. This process requires one pass over the whole database.

GSP makes multiple passes over the database. In the first pass, all single items (1-sequences) are counted. From the frequent items, a set of candidate 2-sequences are formed, and another pass is made to gather their support. The frequent 2-sequences are used to generate the candidate 3-sequences, and this process is repeated until no more frequent sequences are found. There are two main steps in the algorithm.

Candidate Generation

Given the set of frequent (k–1)-frequent sequences $F_{(k-1)}$, the candidates for the next pass are generated by joining $F_{(k-1)}$ with itself. A pruning phase eliminates any sequence, at least one of whose subsequences is not frequent.

Support Counting

Normally, a hash tree–based search is employed for efficient support counting. Finally non-maximal frequent sequences are removed.

GSP Algorithm

F_1 = the set of frequent 1-sequence
k = 2,
do while $F_{k-1} \neq \varnothing$;
  generate candidate sets C_k (Set of candidate k-sequences);
  for all input sequence s in the database ***D do***
  increment count of all a in C_k if s supports a
  $F_k = \{a \in C_k$ such that its frequency exceeds the threshold$\}$
$k = k + 1$
set of all frequent sequences is the union of all F_ks
  end do.

The above algorithm looks like the apriori algorithm. One main difference is, however, the generation of candidate sets. Let us assume that A → B and A → C are two frequent 2-sequences. The items involved in these sequences are (A, B) and (A, C), respectively. The candidate generation in the usual apriori style would give (A, B, C) as a 3-itemset, but in the present context, we get the following 3-sequences as a result of joining the above 2-sequences

$$A \rightarrow B \rightarrow C,\ A \rightarrow C \rightarrow B, \text{ and } A \rightarrow BC.$$

The candidate-generation phase takes this into account.

The GSP algorithm discovers frequent sequences, allowing for time constraints such as maximum gap and minimum gap, among the sequence elements. Moreover, it supports the notion of a sliding window, i.e., of a time interval within which items are observed as belonging to the same event, even if they originate from different events.

12.6 SPADE

SPADE is another algorithm based on the level-wise paradigm. In the year 2000, Zaki proposed **SPADE** (**S**equential **PA**ttern **D**iscovery using **E**quivalence classes) for discovering the set of all frequent sequences. SPADE draws its motivation from the level-wise algorithm (GSP too) and vertical mining. Initially, SPADE uses a vertically structured database (recall

VIPER and FP-Tree in Chapter 4). In this structure, a list is associated with each item. This list include the *sequence-id* and the *transaction-id* containing the item. Using this structure, all frequent sequences can be enumerated via simple temporal joins (or intersections) on id-lists. The vertical structure for the sequence database is illustrated below. For every item, we have a list containing the sequence-id and the transaction id containing the item.

EXAMPLE 12.2

For Example 12.1, the vertical structure can be written as follows

A:
(Seq1, Trans1), (Seq2, Trans2), (Seq3, Trans2), (Seq3, Trans3), (Seq4, Trans1), (Seq4, Trans3).

B:
(Seq1, Trans1), (Seq1, Trans2), (Seq1, Trans3), (Seq2, Trans2), (Seq2, Trans3), (Seq2, Trans4), (Seq2, Trans5), (Seq4, Trans1), (Seq4, Trans2).

C:
(Seq1, Trans2), (Seq1, Trans4), (Seq2, Trans1), (Seq2, Trans2), (Seq2, Trans4), (Seq3, Trans2), (Seq3, Trans3), (Seq4, Trans1), (Seq4, Trans3).

D:
(Seq1, Trans1), (Seq1, Trans4), (Seq2, Trans1), (Seq2, Trans2), (Seq3, Trans1), (Seq3, Trans2), (Seq3, Trans3), (Seq4, Trans1), (Seq4, Trans3).

E:
(Seq1, Trans1), (Seq1, Trans2), (Seq1, Trans3), (Seq1, Trans4), (Seq2, Trans3), (Seq3, Trans1), (Seq3, Trans2), (Seq3, Trans3), (Seq4, Trans1), (Seq4, Trans3).

F:
(Seq1, Trans1), (Seq1, Trans2), (Seq1, Trans4), (Seq2, Trans1), (Seq2, Trans2), (Seq3, Trans1), (Seq3, Trans3), (Seq4, Trans1), (Seq4, Trans2), (Seq4, Trans3).

It is not important to have exactly the same list as shown above to represent the vertical structure. The main idea is to store for each item the set of pairs—(*sequence-id, transaction-id*). The actual implementation of this structure can be different. The vertical structure is very useful to generate candidate sets in a level-wise fashion. For example, we can generate a similar structure for A → B, by checking the transaction ids of occurrences of A and B. The corresponding structure is as follows:

A → B
(Seq1, Trans1) → (Seq1, Trans2), (Seq1, Trans3),
(Seq2, Trans2) → (Seq2, Trans3), (Seq2, Trans4), (Seq2, Trans5),
(Seq4, Trans1) → (Seq4, Trans2).

The core of SPADE is to employ a level-wise paradigm (similar to GSP) with the vertical structure and the temporal join, using the vertical structure. However, it is space-consuming to carry the vertical structure along the levels for the candidate sets. Note that though GSP requires to store only the frequency of A → B as 3, SPADE maintains the structure shown above for this 2-sequence. SPADE surmounts this difficulty by decomposing the problem into smaller subproblems.

SPADE exploits the lattice structure of the set of all subsequences to decompose the problem into smaller subproblems. We have discussed the lattice structure of itemsets in the context of the association rule discovery in Chapter 4. The nicety of the lattice structure is not preserved when we consider the set of sequences in place of the set of items. The main difficulty is that there is no unique k-sequence resulting from the join of two (k–1)-sequences (on the other hand, we can get a unique k-itemset as a result of the join of two (k–1)-itemsets). We have noticed this phenomenon above. By relaxing the uniqueness of the join and allowing multiple candidates as the result of the join of two subsequences, we can get a *hyper-lattice* structure of the set of sequences. In principle, the hyper-lattice is unbounded at the top. The item A can generate an infinite sequence A→A→.... A→... But when the transactions are of finite length and the set of transactions in a sequence is bounded from above, the hyper-lattice structure is also bounded.

Thus, SPADE starts from the bottom-most (the least element) of the lattice and gradually works in a bottom-up way to generate all frequent sequences. It maintains the vertical structure as it proceeds from the least element to the maximal elements.

In order to optimise memory requirement and efficiency, SPADE decomposes the original search space (lattice) into smaller subspaces (sublattices), which can be processed independently in the main memory. The key idea of decomposition is a prefix-based equivalence relation. Consider a sequence D → BF → A and sequence D → BF → E. Note that although the sequences are distinct they share the same prefix, namely D → BF. DB → F → E and DBFC also share the same prefix. Similarly, the sequence D → BF → A and D → CE → A also share the prefix D. However, the length of common prefixes in the above two cases are different. It is easy to see that for a fixed value of the length, say k, an equivalence relation can be defined as q_k and two sequences are said to be equivalent with respect to this relation, if they share a common prefix of length k. The equivalence relation q_k induces a partition on the set of sequences (having a lattice structure) and each equivalent class is a sublattice in this structure. Each of these sublattices can be handled separately for the join operation. However, the pruning stage requires interaction among the sublattices.

In the above example, different equivalent classes of the equivalent relation q_1 are [A], [B], [C], [D], [E], and [F], where [X] denotes all the frequent sequences which have X as the first prefix. We can first independently solve the sequence mining subproblems [A], ..., [F] separately and by examining the interactions between the equivalent classes in the hyper-lattice, we can generate all the frequent sequences. The algorithm proceeds recursively. In order to solve [A], we may have to solve [AB], [A → B], etc. In practice, one need not go beyond two to three levels deep in the recursion process. In most cases, the size of the subproblem rapidly decreases and it becomes small enough to be handled in the main memory. SPADE begins from the bottom (least, $k = 0$) elements of this lattice and moves upwards either in a breadth-first manner or a depth-first manner. This bottom-up movement is carried out by incrementing k by 1 at every step (level-wise philosophy), and at every iteration pruning takes place. SPADE normally requires three database scans, one scan with some preprocessed information. SPADE appears to be an efficient method for frequent sequence mining.

12.7 SPIRIT

Garofarakasi, Rajeev Rastogi and K Shim, in 1999, observed that most of the earlier algorithms lacked user-controlled focus. The algorithms can be considered an 'unfocused' method. Typically, the user can only specify the support and confidence bounds and the system returns a very large number of sequential patterns. Most of the frequent patterns, so discovered, are hardly of any interest to the user. The *constrained sequence mining problem* allows the user to specify a set of constraints, so that only the set of frequent sequences that satisfy the constraints are returned. The question now is whether the user can specify his interest in some form. SPIRIT (Sequential Pattern Mining with Regular Expression Constraints) is an sequence mining algorithm that allows the user to specify the constraints in the form of regular expressions.

Constrained sequence mining problem is used to discover frequent sequences from **D**, such that each of these frequent subsequences satisfy the user-specified constraint set **C**. Such a problem requires two additional tools: 1) The user should be provided with a reasonably expressive language to express his constraint set **C**, and 2) The constraint set **C** should be properly blended within the frequent sequence discovery process. It becomes trivial and uninteresting to first discover all the frequent sequences and then check which of these satisfy the user-specified constraints **C**, so as to return only the required frequent patterns. Therefore, it is desirable that any constrained sequence mining algorithm must push the constraint-checking stage inside the candidate-generation step. But this is not easy. The level-wise paradigm cannot be trivially extended, as the downward closure (anti-monotone) property may be affected.

Let us assume that **C** possesses the downward-closure property. This means that for any subsequence that satisfies **C**, all its subsequences also satisfy **C**. In that case, we generate candidate sequences at level k from the subsequences of F_{k-1} and prune the k-sequences that do not satisfy **C**. In the pruning phase, we must also make sure that no subsequence of the candidate k-sequence is infrequent. Thus, the constraint checking can be done at the candidate-generation phase.

However, if **C** does not possess the downward-closure (or, anti-monotone) property, then the method of embedding constraint checking within the candidate generation process will not work. To see this, let us assume that **C** is so defined that $A \to B \to C$ satisfies **C**, but none of the frequent 2-sequences $A \to B$ and $A \to C$ satisfies **C**. In that case, F_{k-1} does not contain the frequent 2-sequences that can generate the 3-sequence $A \to B \to C$. In such cases, the brute force method would be inevitable to generate all unconstrained frequent sequences using GSP or SPADE and then retain only those frequent sequences which satisfy the constraint. There can also be a middle way. We can relax the constraint **C** to an even weaker constraint **C**$'$, such that **C**$'$ exhibits the downward-closure property. Then, we can embed **C**$'$ within the algorithm. In this process, the number of candidates would be much less, because we will be generating only those candidates which satisfy the weaker constraints. We will still have to check at the end, the original constraint **C**. Depending upon the closeness of **C**$'$ to **C**, the candidate-generation step can be optimised.

SPIRIT is an algorithm (a family of algorithms, to be precise) used to solve constrained sequence mining problems with simple sequences. In other words, SPIRIT focuses on sets of transactions having only single items. SPIRIT adopts regular expressions as the language to express **C** and attempts to embed these constraints within the mining process, to gain efficiency in mining. The major advantages of regular expressions as constraints are that they are sufficiently expressive in the context of sequence mining and it is equivalent to a deterministic finite automaton. In one sense, SPIRIT is a family of algorithms which differ among themselves in what extent the regular expression constraints are pushed into the mining process—how weak is the constraint relaxation. In fact, different levels of relaxation give rise to different types of algorithms within the SPIRIT family. The equivalence of the regular expression and the finite automata comes in handy here in the relaxation process. Since **C** is in the form of the regular expression, we can construct a finite automaton that accepts only those sequences that satisfy **C**. Acceptance by a finite automaton means that the items in the sequence admit a sequence of state transitions leading to any of the final (accept) states from the start state. The relaxation of **C** can be done in two ways:

- We can allow the sequences which admit a sequence of state transitions leading to a final state from any state (not necessarily from the start state).
- We can allow the sequences which admit state transition from any one state to any other state.

Note that these relaxations exhibit the downward-closure property to some extent. Hence, such relaxed constraints can be embedded within the candidate set generation stage. However, after completion of the level-wise algorithm, we have a final step of checking the original constraint to see which of the frequent sequences generated using relaxed constraints satisfy the original set of constraints. The main advantage of pushing relaxed constraints within the algorithm is that we have an optimal set of candidate sequences at every level for the frequency count.

12.8 WUM

WUM (**W**eb **U**tilisation **M**iner) is yet another constrained-sequence miner. It makes use of a language, MINT, for the user to specify the appropriate constraints for the application. Its primary purpose is to analyse the navigational behaviour of users on the web, but it is appropriate for sequential pattern discovery in any type of log. In MINT, frequent sequence discovery corresponds to the specification of a lowerbound support threshold. In exactly the same way, the user can specify an upperbound support threshold to restrict the search space to that of rare sequences. The main idea is to apply mining on disk-resident condensed data instead of the original log of events, but on a condensed disk-resident tree. This tree is built incrementally by a backend service that extracts sequences from the original log and adds them onto the tree, merging common sequence prefixes (recall the Prefix Tree in Chapter 4). The number of merged prefixes corresponding to each tree node is retained in the node's statistics and is used to compute support values during mining. The miner generates candidate sequences while traversing the tree, using heuristics to reject subsequences as soon as possible. By processing a relatively small preaggregated data structure, the execution overhead is reduced without large space tradeoffs.

12.9 Episode Discovery

Another important temporal data mining problem is the discovery of episodes that occur frequently within sequences. Heiki Mannila and his team formulated and devised algorithms for the discovery of frequent episodes. Zaki's formulation of sequence mining, given above, is general enough to have episode mining problem as its special case. Keeping the above definition in mind, we shall now formulate the episode discovery problem. Episode discovery is similar to sequence mining, but for the following special assumptions:

- The input sequence is a single long input sequence, unlike in the case of sequence mining where we have a set of data sequences.
- The events (in this context, referring to a transaction as an event is more appropriate) are typically single item events.
- An episode is a subsequence.

The frequent episode discovery problem is to find all episodes that occur frequently in the event sequence within a time window. Let us define some basic concepts that are necessary in the present context.

Definition 12.5 Event

An event is a pair $\{A, t\}$, where A is an single item event, and t is an integer timestamp of the occurrence of A.

Definition 12.6 Event Sequence

An event sequence *Ev_Seq* is a triplet (*Seq, T_start, T_end*), with *T_start* and *T_end* denoting the start and end time of the sequence; and $Seq = (\{A_1, t_1\},\{A_2, t_2\},\ldots\{A_k, t_k\})$ is an ordered sequence of events.

Definition 12.7 Time Window

A time window W for *Ev_Seq*(*Seq, T_start, T_end*), is an event sequence (W, t_s, t_e), where $t_s \geq$ *T_start* and $t_e \leq$ *T_end* and $(t_e - t_s)$ is said to be width of the window.

We shall represent the data in the form of a graph, where each event corresponds to a node. The precedence relationships among nodes represent the temporal precedence among events. Given a set of nodes and a set of events, it is necessary to specify the mapping to identify the correspondence between nodes and events.

Definition 12.8 Episode

An episode a is a triple $(V, \leq, g)$, where V is a set of nodes, $\leq$ is a partial order on V, and $g: V \rightarrow I$ is a mapping associating each node with an event satisfying the partial order.

DEFINITION 12.9 PARALLEL AND SERIAL EPISODES

If the partial order ≤ is a trivial partial order, the episode is called a *parallel episode*. If the partial order is a total ordering, then the episode is called *serial episode*.

An episode $A \rightarrow B \rightarrow C$ is a serial episode. A serial episode occurs in a given sequence only if *A*, *B* and *C* occur in this order relatively close. There can be other events occurring between these three. In a parallel episode, there is no constraints on the relative order of the events. In general, we can have an episode which has some partial constraints on order too.

DEFINITION 12.10 SUBEPISODE

An episode is to be a subepisode if it is obtained by deleting some events from an episode.

DEFINITION 12.11 OCCURRENCE OF AN EPISODE IN AN EVENT SEQUENCE

An episode is said to be occurring in a sequence if the events corresponding to the nodes of the episode appear in the sequencing, preserving the partial order of the episode.

DEFINITION 12.12 FREQUENCY OF AN EPISODE

The frequency of an episode, with respect to a given window width in a sequence, is the fraction of all the windows in the sequence of the specified width in which the episode occurs. Let us assume that $W(\omega)$ is the set of total number of time windows of width ω in the given sequence, and $W(\omega, \alpha)$ is the set of windows in $W(\omega)$ in which the episode α occurs. Then, the frequency is the ratio of $W(\omega, \alpha)$ to $W(\omega)$.

A frequent episode is the episode that has a frequency above a user-specified threshold.

The episode discovery problem can be stated as follows. Given a sequence *Ev_seq*, a class *C* of episodes, a window width ω, and a frequency threshold σ, it is to find all frequent episodes with respect to ω and σ in *Ev_seq*.

EXAMPLE 12.3

Consider the following sequence (Figure 12.1) on a time interval (0, 50).

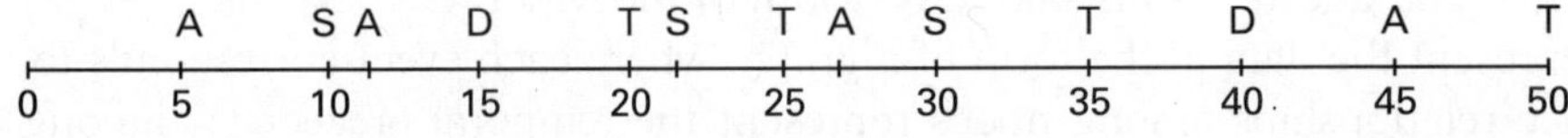

Figure 12.1 An example of a sequence

We define *Evt_Seq* as (*Seq*, 0, 50) and it consists of

(*A*, 5), (*S*, 10), (*A*, 12), (*D*, 15), (*T*, 20), (*S*, 22), ...

The following episodes are occurring in the sequence.

If we take the window width $\omega = 10$, then $A \rightarrow D$ occurs in only two windows of width 10 in the given sequence.

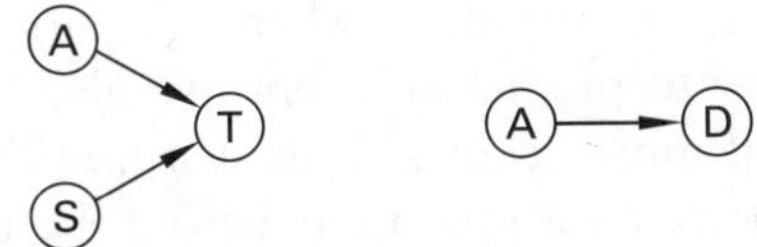

Figure 12.2 Serial and parallel episodes

Episode Discovery Process

Like many other mining problems, the discovery of a frequent episode is also influenced by the level-wise algorithm. The algorithm makes multiple passes and the candidate sets of $(k+1)$-episodes are generated from frequent k-episodes. This is done by finding the pair of frequent k-episodes having a common prefix of size $k-1$ and preserving the partial ordering.

It makes a database pass to count the frequency. Mannila and Toivonen distinguished between serial and parallel episodes, as well as between simple episodes (those containing no binary predicates) and non-simple episodes. They proposed an algorithm based on the iterative construction of simple frequent episodes from simple frequent subepisodes. They further extended their framework to discover generalised episodes, which allow one to express arbitrary unary conditions on individual sequence events, or binary conditions on event pairs. In order to count the frequency of occurrences of an episode, it is necessary to recognise an episode within a given window. Two adjacent windows $W_1 = (W_1, t_s, t_e)$ and $W_1 = (W_1, t_{s+1}, t_{e+1})$ are typically very similar to each other. Thus after determining the set of episodes present in W_1, we can make incremental updates to achieve the *slide* of the window.

12.10 Event Prediction Problem

The discovery of frequent sequences is inappropriate for many applications where sequence pattern discovery is relevant. Consider, for instance, error discovery which is an important application domain. Since errors are rare events, the statistical support of such a sequence is low. Hence, if we restrict the search space to frequent sequences, it will be hard to find rare events. On the other hand, if we reduce the threshold above which a sequence is considered frequent, it will be practically impossible to inspect the result and distinguish interesting patterns from any trivial sequence. The problem of predicting failure (or any other event) differs from sequence prediction problems in that the data (i.e., events) are timestamped, and differs from time-series prediction problems in that the data consists mainly of categorical, non-numerical transactions.

Event Prediction Problem

The event prediction problem is to predict a type of future event, the *target* event, based on past events. More specifically, the problem is to find a prediction rule that successfully predicts future target events by taking the input as timestamped records with categorical items. This problem is particularly interesting in situations where the target event occurs infrequently in the event sequence. When we try to predict an event, we also keep in mind the target event's *prediction period*, which means it must occur at least *warning time* time units before the target event and no more than *monitoring time* time units before the target event. It is interesting to note that in event prediction problems a target event is said to be correctly predicted if at least one prediction is made within its prediction period, regardless of any subsequent negative predictions. Thus, the reliability of a positive prediction is not affected by the presence of negative predictions.

Every event is represented by a tuple consisting of a timestamp field and a number of features. We introduce a wildcard in the event as '?'. Each feature in an event is permitted to take on any of a predefined list of valid feature values, as well as the wildcard ("?") value, which matches any feature value. For example, if the events in a domain are described by three features, then the event <?, ?, *b*> would match any event in which the third feature has the value "*b*".

We shall briefly outline the underlying principles of two major algorithms for prediction problems.

PlanMine

The PlanMine algorithm proposed by Zaki, Lesh and Ogihara deals with the prediction problem in the context of plan failure prediction. PlanMine attempts to identify frequent events that cause plan failure, by filtering out frequent but uninteresting events. When frequent and uninteresting events are removed, the remaining events become more dominant in the data set. The algorithm works as follows.

PlanMine applies the SPADE algorithm which produces an initial set of sequence rules. Then, pruning is applied in the following multiple phases:

- In the first phase, the data set of plans is split into good and failed plans. The 'good' events are separated and 'failed' events are retained. The 'good' events though are not used for prediction, they act as reference in the subsequent pruning stages.
- The next pruning phase removes patterns which correspond to sequences that are frequent in the data set of bad plans and have high support in the data set of good plans.
- The next pruning phase removes the redundant patterns. A sequence is redundant if it contains a subsequence having the same support value as itself for both data sets of good and bad plans.
- Finally, dominated patterns are removed. A pattern is dominated if it contains a subsequence with lower support in good plans and higher support in bad plans as the pattern itself.

Timeweaver

Weiss and Hirsh proposed a supervised learning technique to predict rare events in sequences. Their system Timeweaver, based on the genetic algorithm, is designed to predict hardware failure. It solves by generating prediction patterns that forecast the target events (in this case, the failures).

A prediction pattern is a sequence of events subject to ordering and temporal constraints. The GA algorithm is used to generate a population of prediction patterns. Each individual in GA is a prediction pattern. Let us formalise the concept of a prediction pattern.

A *prediction pattern* is a sequence of events in which consecutive events are connected by an ordering primitive. The following are the ordering primitives and these are used to define ordering constraints between these events:

- the *wildcard* "*". If we say A*D, then any number of events between A and D may be possible. So the prediction pattern A*D matches ABCD .
- the *next* "." This primitive indicates that no events occur in between. So the prediction pattern A.B.C only matches ABC.
- the *parallel* "|". This primitive allows events to occur in any order and is commutative so that the prediction pattern A|B|C will match, amongst others, CBA.

While expressing an ordering constraint, we can combine the set of primitives. The "|" primitive has highest precedence. For example, the pattern "A.B*C|D|E" matches an A, followed immediately by a B, followed sometime later by a C, D and E, in any order. Some of the matched patterns are

ABXXCED
ABAAEDC
ABBCDFGREDCAAA.

The basic steps in our steady state GA are shown below.

Genetic Algorithm

Initialize population
while do stopping criteria not met
    select two individuals from the population
    apply the crossover operator with probability P_C
    and mutation operator with probability P_M
    evaluate the two newly formed individuals
    replace two existing individuals with the new ones
end do

The population is initialised by generating prediction patterns which contain only a single event, where the feature values in this event are set 50% of the time to the wildcard value and the remaining time to a randomly-selected valid feature value.

Another crucial component of GA is the fitness measure. The fitness function must take an individual pattern and return a value indicating how good the pattern is at predicting target events. Conventional quality measures based on accuracy are not appropriate for this notion of event prediction. Two measures are defined, *recall* and *precision*. *Recall* is the percentage of events correctly predicted. *Precision* is the percentage of precisions that are correct. This latter measure is refined in several ways that differ in the treatment of false predictions.

Timeweaver, in order to prevent premature convergence and encourage diversity in the population, uses *shared fitness* as the basis of the crossover and selection operators. This measure depends on the precision and recall of the population member and on its phenotype distance from other members of the population. After generating a satisfactory initial group of patterns, a set of prediction rules are created in a second pass by selecting those patterns that improve the collective recall of the set without sacrificing precision. Timeweaver has proved to be very efficient.

A prediction pattern matches a sequence of events within an event sequence if:

1. The events within the prediction pattern match events within the event sequence,
2. The ordering constraints are satisfied, and
3. The matched events in the event sequence occur within a period not exceeding the pattern duration.

Once a match succeeds, a target event is predicted.

12.11 TIME-SERIES ANALYSIS

Time series are an important class of complex data objects; they arise in many applications. For example, stock price indices, volume of product sales, telecommunication data, onedimensional medical signals, audio data, and environmental measurement sequences are all time-series databases. Time-series data are sequences of real numbers representing measurements at uniformly-spaced temporal instances. Time-series analysis, like all other forms of data analysis, is used to characterise or explain the reasons for the behaviour of a system and/or to predict its future behaviour.

Time-series analysis is a well-studied subject in statistics and signal processing. We shall focus on the basic time-series analyses in the context of data mining. Note that the most important aspects of time-series data is that these are sequence data but uniformly spaced on the temporal attribute. Analysis tasks of time series include feature extraction of time-series data; computation of similarity measure among time series data set; segmentation of data set; matching two time series data; clustering and classifying time-series data. We shall introduce the related concepts first.

DEFINITION 12.13 *N*-SERIES

An n-series X is a sequence $\{x_1, x_2, \ldots, x_n\}$ of real numbers. Each n-series X has an average $\alpha(X)$ and a deviation $\sigma(X)$:

$$\alpha(X) = \frac{1}{n} \sum_{i=1}^{n} x_i \quad \text{and} \quad \sigma(X) = \left[\frac{1}{n} \sum_{i=1}^{n} (x_i - \alpha(X))^2\right]^{\frac{1}{2}}$$

Similarity Function

While mining a time-series database we need an essential primitive operation, called the *similarity function*. It is often necessary to search within a series database for those series that are similar to a given query series. This primitive is needed, for example, for prediction and clustering purposes. For instance, we may be interested in finding the months in five years having similar sales patterns; or in classifying companies based on similar stock price fluctuations. While the statistical literature on timeseries is vast, it has not studied similarity notions that would be appropriate for data mining applications. Typically, the task is to define a function Sim(X; Y), where X and Y are two time-series, and the function value represents how "similar" they are to each other.

A simple approach would be to define the similarity functions of X and Y in terms of their Lpdistance as points of R^n. The presence of outliers, which is common in time-series data, makes such schemes unsuitable. Outliers are values that are measurement errors and should be omitted when comparing the sequence against others. A grossly outlying value can cause two otherwise identical series to have a large distance. This similarity measure is not suitable to determine similarity for series in different scales and different shifts.

Scale-free Similarity: Assume that two companies have identical stock price fluctuations, but one's stock is worth twice as much as the others' at all times. Thus, though the fluctuation patterns are similar, the series containing numerical values are not similar. For a company, the sales pattern may be similar throughout the year but the sales volume may be different for different months. It is important to identify such similar time-series objects in data mining applications.

Shift-free Similarity: The temperature on two different days may start at different values, but then go up and down in an exactly similar way. Thus, we have the same series with two different baselines.

For example, consider a time series z = (20, 20, 21, 21, 20, 20, 23, 23) and the series z'= (43, 43, 45, 45, 43, 43, 49, 49). Note that these two series are similar, except that the latter has a different starting point and its fluctuations are nearly twice that of the former.

Similarly, z'' = (20, 21, 20, 23) is also similar to z.

When do we say that two time-series data are similar?

Definition 12.14 Similarity

We say that two time-series X and Y are similar, if there exist $a > 0$ and b, such that $y_i = ax_i + b$, for all i.

Distance Metric

Distance metric plays a major role in the measurement of similarity. We say that X and Y are approximately similar with respect to a distance metric d, if $d(X, Y) \leq \varepsilon$ for some tolerance ε. The distance metric can be defined such a way that the scale and shift invariances are taken care of within d. We study this aspect below.

The similarity defined above induces an equivalence relation in the time-series database and hence, the database can be partitioned into equivalent classes. The equivalent class X^* contains all the objects which are similar to X. We can define a unique representation for this class.

DEFINITION 12.15 NORMAL SERIES

An n-series X is normal if the average $\alpha(X) = 0$, and the deviation $\sigma(X) = 1$.

There exists a unique normal series for X^* and hence the normal form representation of all elements of X^*, is said to be the corresponding normal denoted by $n(X)$. The normal form can play an important role in determining similarity. Two objects are similar with regard to scale and shift, if their corresponding normal forms are similar.

Thus, we can determine similarity between two objects based on the distance between the corresponding normal forms. But computing similarity distance requires $O(n)$ operations. Since the similarity-based query will be required a number of times in a data mining process, it is better to look for an efficient method for computing the similarity value.

DEFINITION 12.16 DISCRETE FOURIER TRANSFORM (DFT)

The Discrete Fourier Transform of a n-sequence X is defined to be a sequence of n complex numbers $\text{DFT}_m(X)$, $m = 0, \ldots, (n-1)$, given by

$$\text{DFT}_m(X) = \frac{1}{\sqrt{n}} \sum_{j=1}^{n} x_i e^{\frac{-j(2\pi i)m}{n}}$$

where i is the imaginary unit, $\sqrt{(-1)}$. Note that $\text{DFT}_m(X)$ is a complex number.

DEFINITION 12.17 FINGERPRINT

A fingerprint F(X) of an n-series X is the sequence of first few DFT coefficients of X. In other words,

$$F(X) = (\text{DFT}_1(X), \text{DFT}_2(X), \ldots, \text{DFT}_k(X)),$$

where k assumes a very low value, between 3 and 5.

One interesting property of DFT, as a consequence of Parseval's Theorem, is that for two similar sequence in terms of the Euclidean distance metric, the corresponding fingerprints are also closer within the specified tolerance.

Thus, the computation of similarity can be restricted to only a few coefficients of DFT.

LONGEST COMMON SEQUENCE

A more reasonable similarity notion is based on the longest common subsequence concept, where intuitively X and Y are considered similar if they exhibit similar behaviour for a large part of their length. A similarity definition based on the concept of well-separated geometric sets has been introduced by Bollobas et al, and deterministic and randomised algorithms for computing this similarity measure also have been proposed. Traditionally, the least common subsequence problem can be solved by a dynamic programming problem.

Feature Extraction from Time Series

We can extract k features from every sequence and every sequence is then represented as a unique point in k-dimensional space. Then we can use a multidimensional index to store and search these points. Different multidimensional indexing methods that are currently popular are R^*-tress, k-d Trees, Linear Quad-trees etc. The major problems with these features extraction techniques are:

(a) Completeness of feature extraction: Completeness ensures that similarity between two objects are preserved in the feature space. That is, if two objects are similar in some distance metric, their corresponding maps in k-dimensional feature space should not be grossly dissimilar.
(b) Dimensionality Curse: Most multidimensional indexing scale up for high dimensionality. Such spatial indices do not work well for very high dimensional data.

There are many other distance-preserving orthonormal transformations. These can be categorised into two classes: (a) Data dependent transforms which need all the data to determine the transform, for example, Karhunen-Loeve, SVD, (b) Data-independent transforms, where the transform matrix is determined *a priori*, for example, DFT, DCT, Haar wavelet. DFT does a good job of concentrating energy in the first few coefficients. As we have mentioned earlier, if we keep only the first few coefficients in DFT, we can compute the lower bounds on the actual distance.

The time series segmentation technique partitions a time series into piece-wise linear segments. Each segment has a weight, representing its importance. Weights can be learnt from a training set, in case of supervised learning or else there can be a semiautomatic, user-specified weight adjustment.

Other Methods of Analysing Time Series

The original approach to time series analysis was the establishment of a mathematical model describing the observed system. While linear models were the dominant paradigm for several decades, non-linear models emerged later to deal with systems, showing properties for which linear models are less appropriate. Since the eighties, time-series analysis research has looked towards the exploitation of machine learning algorithms. Those algorithms analyse an unfamiliar time series by learning, that is, by emulating its structure.

Neural networks belong to the domain of supervised learning algorithms and they have been used for the prediction. A known test set can be used to tune the prediction model, so that it can predict the behaviour of an unknown time series in the future.

12.12 Spatial Mining

The immense explosion in geographically referenced data occasioned by developments in IT, digital mapping, remote sensing, and the global diffusion of GIS, emphasises the importance of developing data mining approaches to geographical analysis and modelling to aid the processes of scientific discovery. Indeed a number of data mining tools are being developed to assist the process of exploring large amounts of data in search of recurrent patterns and relationships.

Spatial data mining is the branch of data mining that deals with spatial (location, or geo-referenced) data. Consider a map of the city of Hyderabad containing various natural and man-made geographic features, and clusters of points (where each point marks the location of a particular house). The houses might be noteworthy because of their size, historical interest, or their current market value. Clustering algorithms exist to assign each point to exactly one cluster, with the number of clusters being defined by the user. We can mine varieties of information by identifying likely relationships. For example, "the land-value of the cluster of residential area to the east of 'Cyber-Tower' is high" or, "70% the Banjara migrants settle in the city around the market area". Such information could be of value to realtors, investors, or prospective home buyers, and also to other domains such as satellite images, photographs, oil and gas explorations. This problem is not trivial—there may be a large number of features to consider. We need to be able to detect relationships among large numbers of geo-referenced objects without incurring significant overheads.

As in the case of temporal data mining, conventional data mining techniques cannot fully exploit the spatial characteristics of data. It is necessary to devise algorithms that take this aspect into consideration.

12.13 Spatial Mining Tasks

The knowledge discovery tasks involving spatial data include finding characteristic rules, discriminant rules, association rules, or deviation and evolution rules, etc. A *spatial characteristic rule* is a general description of spatial data. For example, a rule describing the general price range of houses in various geographic regions in a city is a spatial characteristic rule. A *spatial discriminant rule* is a general description of the features discriminating or contrasting a class of spatial data from other class(es), like the comparison of price ranges of houses in different geographical regions. We shall identify some of the tasks in this section. The following sections deal with other tasks which need detailed study.

Spatial Association Rules

Spatial association rules describe the association between objects, based on spatial neighbourhood relations. We can associate spatial attributes with spatial attributes, or spatial attributes with non-spatial attributes. For example, rules like "The monthly rental of houses around the Cyber-Tower are mostly Rs 500 per sq mt." associates a spatial attribute with a non-spatial attribute. Similarly, a rule like "Uncontrolled tapping of borewell water in the Jubilee Hills area may most likely cause tremors in the neighbouring areas" associates two spatial features.

Attribute-Oriented Induction

Please recall the need of concept hierarchy for attribute-oriented induction. Similarly, the concept hierarchies of spatial and non-spatial attributes can be used to determine relationships between different attributes. This is more relevant in spatial databases. One may be interested in a particular category of land-use patterns. But the classification of land-use types are often hierarchical. A built-up area may be a recreational facility or a residential complex. Similarly, a recreational facility may be a cinema or a restaurant. A water body can be classified into many different categories such as a lake, or a stream. One has to be very specific regarding the level of details to which one wants to discover spatial knowledge.

Aggregate Proximity Relationships

One spatial data mining task is the problem of determining aggregate proximity relationships. This problem is concerned with relationships between spatial clusters based on spatial and non-spatial attributes. Given *n* input clusters, we want to associate the clusters with classes of features (e.g., educational institutions which, in turn, may be comprised of secondary schools and junior colleges or higher institutions). The problem is to find classes of features that are in close proximity to most (or all) of the spatial clusters. For example, if two of three spatial clusters are close to a girls' private schools, and the other cluster is close to a boys' private school, then it can be generalised to the fact that all three clusters are close to some private school. Another example would be—"A large banyan tree is normally present within the high-court premises."

Boundary Shape Matching

Another interesting problem can be that of partial boundary shape matching. Specifically, a cluster of points is compared to a large number of natural or man-made features to detect partial or total matches of the facing boundaries of the cluster and features.

The following sections deals with other major mining tasks.

12.14 Spatial Clustering

Different types of spatial clustering algorithms have been proposed. Many of the clustering algorithms discussed in Chapter 5 are directly applicable to spatial data, while some of them may require slight modification in order to be applied to spatial data. For example, GDBSCAN (recall DBSCAN in Chapter 5) relies on a density-based notion of clusters. The key idea of a density-based cluster is that for each point of a cluster, its epsilon neighbourhood has to contain at least a minimum number of points. We can generalise this concept in two different ways in the present context. First, any other symmetric and reflexive neighbourhood relationship can be used instead of an epsilon neighbourhood. While a distance-based neighbourhood is a natural notion of a neighbourhood for point objects, it may be more appropriate to use topological relations such as intersects, meets or above/below to cluster spatially extended objects such as a set of polygons. Second, instead of simply counting the objects in a neighbourhood of an object, other measures to define the "cardinality" of that neighbourhood can be used as well. With these modifications, the DBSCAN algorithm can be used for spatial clustering.

Spatial Characterisation

The task of characterisation is to find a compact description for a selected subset (the target set) of the database. A spatial characterisation is a description of the spatial and non-spatial properties, which are typical for the target objects but not for the whole database. The relative frequencies of the non-spatial attribute values and the relative frequencies of the different object types are used as the interesting properties. For instance, different object types in a geographic database are mountains, lakes, highways, railroads, etc. To obtain a spatial characterisation, not only the properties of the target objects, but also the properties of their neighbours (up to a given maximum number of edges in the relevant neighbourhood graph) are considered. A spatial characterisation rule of the form – "Apartments in Sainikpuri have a high occupany rate of retired army officers" – is an example.

12.15 Spatial Trends

A spatial trend is as a regular change of one or more nonspatial attributes, when moving away from a given spatially-referenced object. For instance, "When we move away eastwards from the Cyber-Tower, the rentals of residential houses decrease approximately at the rate of 5% per kilometer". One can also depict the spatial trends pictorially by overlaying the direction of trend on a map. The process is to identify a neighbourhood path starting from a location *O* and a regression analysis is performed on the respective attribute values for the objects of a neighbourhood path to describe the regularity of change. For the regression, the distance from *O* is the independent variable and the difference of the attribute values are the dependent variable(s) for the regression. The correlation of the observed attribute values with the values predicted by the regression function, yields a measure of confidence for the discovered trend. The general definition of trend detection for spatial databases is given below.

Definition 12.18 Spatial Trend Detection

Let *g* be a neighbourhood graph depicting the set of neighbouring points for any given point. Assume that *O* is an object (node) in *g* and let *a* be some subset of non-spatial attributes. We are interested in detecting the changing pattern in *a* while we move away from *O* in the neighbourhood graph. Let *t* be a type of function used for the regression and let *filter* be one of the filters for neighbourhood paths. A filter indicates the subsets of neighbour to be taken into consideration. For example, we may move only in the east to north direction. Let *minconf* be a real number and let *minlength* as well as *maxlength* be natural numbers. The task of spatial trend detection is to discover the set of all neighbourhood paths in *g* starting from *O* and having a trend of type *t* in attributes *a*, with a correlation of at least *minconf*. The paths have to satisfy the *filter* and their length must be between *minlength* and *maxlength*.

Ester et al. proposed two algorithms to determine the global trend and local trends.

Algorithm global-trends detects global trends around a start object, O. The existence of a global trend for a start object, O, indicates that if considering all objects on all paths starting from O, the values for the specified attribute(s) in general tend to increase (decrease) with increasing distance.

Spatial Trend Algorithm

```
global-trend(g, O, a, t, min-conf, min-length, max-length, f)
initialize P to be list of all paths in g from O of min-length with filter f;
initialize an empty set of observations;
initialize the last-correlation and last-paths as empty;
initialize first pos to 1;
initialize last pos to min length;
while P ≠ ∅ do
for each p ∈ P do
for every object O1 from first pos of p to last pos of p do
    calculate diff as a(O1) – a(O) and calculate dist as dist(O1, O);
    insert the tuple (diff, dist) into the set of observations;
    perform a regression of type t on the set of observations;
    if abs(correlation) of the resulting regression function ≥ min conf
    then
        set last correlation to correlation and last paths to P;
        if the length of the P < maxlength
        then
            replace the P by the paths of length 1;
            increment last pos by 1;
            set first pos to last pos;
        else set P to the empty list;
    else return last correlation and last paths;
return the last correlation and last paths;
```

Local-trends technique detects single paths starting from an object O and having a certain trend. The paths starting from O may show different pattern of change; for example, some trends may be positive while the others may be negative.

12.16 Conclusions

In this chapter we have outlined the current trends in temporal data mining and spatial data mining. We observe that conventional mining techniques are not suitable for temporal and spatial data. Episode discovery, time-series analysis and sequence mining are the most important tasks of temporal mining. Trend analysis, clustering and spatial characterisation are the tasks of spatial data mining. There are, in addition, many other areas of temporal and spatial data mining which could not be dealt with in this text.

Further Reading

Roddick's article gives an excellent survey of the techniques on temporal data mining. Allen [83], Pujari [1999] and Vijaya Kumari [1999] give different qualitative temporal constraints. Temporal association rules are in Chen [1998]. Sequence mining was first introduced by Rakesh Agrawal and his team in [1995] and GSP is proposed in Srikant [1996]. However, a general formulation is given by Zaki [1998] in the context of PLANMINE and SPADE. The other sequence mining algorithm, SPIRIT, was originally proposed by Garofarakasi [1999]. WUM was proposed by Weiss in 1998. Episode discovery problem was first posed and formulated by Heiki Mannila and his group at the University of Helsinki [1995]. The MEDD and MSDD algorithms [Oates, 1997] discover patterns in multiple event sequences; they explore the rule space directly instead of the sequence space. The similarity of time series is very elegantly presented by Gautam Das and others [Bollobas, 1998]. Sander [1998] gives GDBSCAN for clustering. Ester, in 1998, formulated important spatial data mining problems. Spatial association rules are discussed in Koperskim [1995].

Exercises

1. Describe the essential features of temporal data and temporal inferences.
2. Formulate the sequence mining problem.
3. Discuss the major algorithms of the sequence mining problem.
4. Discuss the essential features of the GSP algorithm.
5. What is the event-prediction problem? Propose one algorithm to solve this problem.
6. What are different tasks of time-series mining?
7. Describe different similarity measures of time-series data.
8. Discuss the major features of the timeweaver algorithm.
9. Describe the working of the SPADE algorithm.
10. Relate the two problems "Association rules with item constraint" and the "Problem class handled by the SPIRIT algorithm".
11. How do you distinguish spatial mining from temporal mining?
12. Is it possible to use BIRCH for spatial clustering? If so, devise a method for spatial clustering using BIRCH.
13. How do you handle spatial and non-spatial data, while carrying out any mining task?
14. Propose different neighbourhood relationships that can be used for density-based clustering of spatial data.

15. Why is concept hierarchy important for spatial data? Identify certain cases of occurrences of such hierarchies in spatial data.
16. How do you handle spatial or temporal data for decision tree construction?

Bibliography

Aho A.V. Algorithms for finding patterns in strings. In *Handbook of Theoretical Computer Science*, Volume A: Algorithms and Complexity, Elsevier, pp. 255–400, 1990.

Al-Naemi S. A theoretical framework for temporal knowledge discover. In *Proceedings of the International Workshop on Spatio-temporal Databases*, pp. 23–33, 1994.

Allen J.F. Maintaining knowledge about temporal intervals. *Commun. ACM*, **26**(11):832–843, 1983.

Brockwell P.J., and Davis R. *Introduction to Time Series and Forecasting*. Springer Verlag, 1996.

Brendt D.J., and Clifford J. Finding patterns in time-series: A Dynamic programming approach. In *Advances in Knowledge Discovery and Data Mining*, AAAI Press, 1995.

Chen M. S., Park J.S., and Yu P.S. Efficient data mining for path traversal patterns. *IEEE Transactions on Knowledge and Data Engineering*, **10**(2):209–221, March 1998.

Chen X., and Petrounias I. A framework for temporal data mining. In *Proceedings of DEXA'98, LNCS-1460*, Springer-Verlag, 1998.

Davison B., and Hirsh H. Probabilistic online action prediction. In *Proceedings of the AAAI Spring Symposium on Intelligent Environments*, 1998.

DietterichT., and Michalski R. Discovering patterns in sequences of events. *Artificial Intelligence*, **25**:187–232, 1985.

Ester M., Frommelt A., Kriegel H-P, and Sander J. Algorithm for characterization and trend detection in spatial databases. *Fourth KDD Conference*, 1998.

Ester M., Kriegel H.P., and Sander J. Knowledge discovery in spatial databases. In *Proceedings of 23rd German Conference on AI(KI'99)*, Bonn, Germany, 1999.

Faloutos C., Ranganathan M., and Manolopoulos Y. Fast subsequence matching in time series databases. In *SIGMOD'94*, 1994.

Garofalakis M.N., Rastogi R., and Shim K. SPIRIT: Sequential pattern mining with regular expression constraints. *Bell Labs Tech. Memorandum* BL0112370 990223 03TM, February 1999.

Giordana A., Saitta L., and Zini F. Learning disjunctive concepts by means of genetic algorithms. In *Proceedings of the 11th International Conference on Machine Learning*, pp. 96–104, 1994.

Goldin D.Q., and Kanellakis P.C. On similarity queries for timeseries data: constraint specification and implementation.

Jagadish H.V., Mendelzon A.O., and Milo T. Similarity based queries. In *Proceedings of the 14th Symposium on Principles of Database Systems (PODS'95)*, pp. 36–45, 1995.

Koperski K., and Han J. Discovering spatial association rules in geographic information databases. In *Proceedings of the 4th International Synposis on Large Spatial Databases*, pp. 47–66, 1995.

Mannila H., Toivonen H., and Verkamo A.I. Discovering frequent episodes in sequences. In *Proceedings of the 1st International Conference on Knowledge Discovery and Data Mining*, August 1995.

Ng R.T. Spatial data mining: Discovering knowledge of clusters of maps. In *Proceedings SIGMOD Workshop*, 1996.

Ng R.T., Lakshmanan L.V.S., Han J., and Pang A. Exploratory mining and pruning optimizations of constrained association rules. In *Proceedings of the 1998 ACM SIGMOD International Conference on Management of Data*, June 1998.

Openshaw S. Two exploratory space-time attribute pattern analyzers relevant to GIS. *GIS and Spatial Analysis*, Taylor and Francis, London,pp. 83–104, 1994.

Openshaw S. Developing automated and smart spatial pattern exploration tools for geographical information systems applications. *The Statistician,* 44:3–16, 1995.

Openshaw S. Building automated geographical analysis and exploration machines. In *Geocomputation: A Primer*, Wiley Chichester, pp. 95–115, 1998.

Pujari A.K., and Sattar A. A new framework of reasoning about points, interval and durations. In *Proceedings of IJCAI'99*, pp. 1259–1265, Sweden, 1999.

Roddick J.F., and Spiliopoulou M. *Temporal Data Mining: Survey and Issues*.

Sander J., Ester M., Kriegel H.-P., and Xu X. Density based clustering in spatial databases. A new algorithm and its applications, *Data Mining and Knowledge Discovery, an International Journal*, **2(2)**, 1998.

Sasisekharan R., Seshadri V., and Weiss S. Data mining and forecasting in large scale telecommunication networks. *IEEE Expert*, **11**(1):37–43,1996.

Shatkay H., and Zdonik S. Approximate queries and representations for large data sequences. In *ICDE'96*, 1996.

Spiliopoulou M., and Faulstich L.C. WUM-A tool for web utilization analysis. In *EDBT Workshop WebDB'98, LLNCS-1590*, Springer-Verlag, 1999.

Srikant R., and Agrawal R. Mining sequential patterns: Generalizations and performance improvements. In *Proceedings of the 5th International Conference on Extending Database Technology (EDBT'96)*, March 1996.

Srikant R., Vu Q., and Agrawal R. Mining association rules with item constraints. In *Proceedings of the 3rd International Conference on Knowledge Discovery and Data Mining*, August 1997.

Vijaya K., Pujari A.K., and Sattar A. INDU-Interval and duration network. In *Proceedings of Australian AI Conference*, Sydney, Australia, 1999.

Wang J.T.L., Chirn G. W., Marr T.G., Shapiro B., Shasha D., and Zhang K. Combinatorial pattern discovery for scientific data: Some Preliminary Results. In *Proceedings of the 1994 ACM SIGMOD International Conference on Management of Data*, May 1994.

Weiss G.M., and Hirsh H. Learning to predict rare events in event sequences. In *Proceedings of the 4th International Conference on Knowledge Discovery and Data Mining*, AAAI Press, pp. 359–363, 1998.

White D.A., and Jain R. Algorithms and strategies for similarity retrieval. *Technical Report VCL 96 101*, Visual Computing Laboratory, UC Davis, 1996.

Yazdani N., and Ozsoyoglu Z.M. Sequence matching of images. In *Proceedings of the 8th International Conference on Scientific and Statistical Database Management*, pp. 53–62, 1996.

Zaki N.J., Lesh N., and Ogihara M. PLANMINE: *Sequence mining for plan failures.* In *KDD'98*, 1998.

INDEX